Game Coding Complete

Mike McShaffry

Game Coding Complete

Limits of Liability and Disclaimer of Warranty

Trademarks

Paraglyph Press, Inc.
4015 N. 78th Street, #115
Scottsdale, Arizona 85251
Phone: 602-749-8787
www.paraglyphpress.com

Paraglyph Press ISBN: 1-932111-75-1

Printed in the United States of America
10 9 8 7 6 5 4 3 2

President
Keith Weiskamp

Editor-at-Large
Jeff Duntemann

Vice President, Sales, Marketing, and Distribution
Steve Sayre

Vice President, International Sales and Marketing
Cynthia Caldwell

Production Manager
Kim Eoff

Cover Designer
Kris Sotelo

Cover Art
Paul Steed

The Paraglyph Mission

This book you've purchased is a collaborative creation involving the work of many hands, from authors to editors to designers and to technical reviewers. At Paraglyph Press, we like to think that everything we create, develop, and publish is the result of one form creating another. And as this cycle continues on, we believe that your suggestions, ideas, feedback, and comments on how you've used our books is an important part of the process for us and our authors.

We've created Paraglyph Press with the sole mission of producing and publishing books that make a difference. The last thing we all need is yet another tech book on the same tired, old topic. So we ask our authors and all of the many creative hands who touch our publications to do a little extra, dig a little deeper, think a little harder, and create a better book. The founders of Paraglyph are dedicated to finding the best authors, developing the best books, and helping you find the solutions you need.

As you use this book, please take a moment to drop us a line at **feedback@paraglyphpress.com** and let us know how we are doing - and how we can keep producing and publishing the kinds of books that you can't live without.

Sincerely,

Keith Weiskamp & Jeff Duntemann
Paraglyph Press Founders
4015 N. 78th Street, #115
Scottsdale, Arizona 85251
email: **feedback@paraglyphpress.com**
Web: **www.paraglyphpress.com**
Phone: 602-749-8787

Look for these related books fromParaglyph Press:

Monster Gaming
By Ben Sawyer

Recently Published by Paraglyph Press:

Jeff Duntemann's Drive-By Wi-Fi Guide
By Jeff Duntemann

Mac OS X v. 10.2 Jaguar Little Black Book
By Gene Steinberg

Visual Basic .NET Black Book
By Steven Holzner

C++ Black Book
By Steven Holzner

C# Core Language Little Black Book
By Bill Wagner

The SQL Server 2000 Book
By Anthony Sequeira
and Brian Alderman

About the Author

Mike McShaffry, Author

Mike McShaffry, a.k.a. "Mr. Mike," started programming games as soon as he could tap a keyboard—in fact he somehow skipped 7th grade math entirely in favor of writing games in BASIC on an ancient Commodore Pet. In his single-minded pursuit of programming knowledge, he signed up for an extended stay at the University of Houston. To the surprise of himself and the Dean of Mathematics, he was actually graduated five and one-half years later. Shortly after graduation he entered the boot camp of the computer game industry: Origin Systems. He worked for Warren Spector and Richard Garriott, a.k.a. "Lord British," on *Martian Dreams*, *Ultima VII: The Black Gate*, *Ultima VIII: Pagan*, *Ultima IX: Ascension*, and *Ultima Online*. Exactly seven years from the day he was hired, Mike arranged his escape and in 1997 formed his first company, Tornado Alley.

Tornado Alley was a garage start-up whose goal was to create *No Grownups Allowed,* a massively multiplayer world for children—something that was sure to land Mike and anyone else at Tornado Alley front and center of a Congressional hearing. While *No Grownups* never left the tarmac, a kid's activity program called *Magnadoodle* by Mattel Media did, and in record development time. The entrepreneurial bug, a ravenous and insatiable beast, finally devoured enough of Mike's remaining EA stock to motivate him to take a steady gig at Glass Eye Entertainment, working for Monty Kerr, where he produced *Microsoft Casino.* Ten short months later, Monty asked Mike and his newly assembled team to start their own company called Compulsive Development, which would work exclusively with Microsoft on casual casino and card games.

Mike served as the primary coffee brew master and Head of Studio, and together with the rest of the Compulsive folks, twenty great people in all, produced three more casual titles for Microsoft until August 2002. Compulsive was acquired by Glass Eye Entertainment to continue work on Glass Eye's growing online casual games business.

Mike is currently the Head of Software Development for Glass Eye Entertainment. Mike is never too far away from technology development and research. He still writes code when he can, but he's also doing business development and project management as well. If Mike's fingers aren't tapping away at a keyboard, he's probably either "downhilling" on his mountain bike or enjoying a tasty beverage with his friends in Austin, Texas.

Paul Steed, Cover Artist

Paul Steed has been making art for computer games since 1991. He is a regular speaker at the Game Developers Conference in San Jose, CA. Best known for his work on id Software's Quake series, he is the author of *Modeling a Character in 3ds Max* (Wordware Publishing) and *Animating Real-time Game Characters* (Charles River Media). He can be contacted via email at st33d@nak3d.com.

Acknowledgments

Mom and Grandma Hawker

Thanks for never saying I'd never amount to anything, playing games all the time; you believed in me and it paid off.

Dad and Lynn

Thanks for showing me I should never be afraid of hard work.

Warren Spector and Richard Garriott

Thanks for believing a geeky college kid could help make the games I loved to play.

Monty Kerr

Thanks for giving me the best job I ever had, and for supporting my efforts in writing this book.

The Good Folks of Compulsive Development

I never worked with a better group of people, or learned so much—here's hoping we're all lucky enough to see those days again.

Ben Sawyer and Keith Weiskamp

Thanks for believing in a first time author.

Book Beta Testers

Kain In Shin, James Clarendon, Dennis Clark, Donavon Keithley, Ted Jump, Matthew Lamari, Jon-Eric Simmons, Will McBurnett, Keith Chenoweth, Mark Peskin, Jackie Woodall

Thanks for helping me write this book—I couldn't have done it without you.

And Especially

My Wife and My Best Friend, Robin

Thanks for letting me play for a living—
I promise I'll do some dishes before writing another book.

Contents at a Glance

Contents

Foreword

By Warren Spector

Let me start by admitting a couple of things. First, I've never written a foreword for a book before. I've written books but never a foreword. Honestly, I usually skip right over these things when I'm reading a book so, odds are, no one is ever going to read what I'm writing here anyway. That makes it safe for me to move on to admission number two: I'm not a programmer. Never have been and, I fear, never will be, despite some valiant efforts on my part (if I do say so myself).

I've done okay despite not knowing a blessed thing about programming. I'm not looking for sympathy or anything but I am here to tell you that a day doesn't go by when I don't think, "Damn, if only I knew my z-buffers from my BSP trees!" If you're already a programmer, you've got a huge leg up on me, when I tried to get into the electronic game biz! (And if you're not a programmer, do as I say and not as I do—learn to program ASAP. Mike has some advice about how to do that in the pages that follow. Pay attention.)

Okay, so with those two confessions out of the way, I figure there's a fair chance any credibility I might have had is pretty well shot. Luckily for you folks, the guy who wrote this book has credibility to burn. Mike McShaffry (or "Mr. Mike" as he's known to most everyone in the game biz) is the real deal. Mike is a genuine survivor. He is a guy who can talk the talk because, Lord knows, he's walked the walk enough times to earn some talking time.

Mike's experience of game development runs the gamut in a pretty remarkable way. He was there when teams were a dozen folks and he's been around in the era of twenty, thirty, and fifty person teams. He's done the start-up thing, worked for the biggest publishers in the business, worked on "traditional" games and decidedly untraditional ones—everything from Ultima to Blackjack, singleplayer, multiplayer, online and off and just about everything else you can imagine. When it comes to PC games, he speaks with the authority of someone who's worn just about every hat it's possible to wear—programmer, designer, project leader, director of development, studio head...

And I've had the privilege of watching him learn and grow with each new project and each new role. I was there when Mike got his first game job. I was one of the folks at Origin who interviewed him back in the Bone Ages, back in the 20th century, way back in 1990, when he applied for a programming job at Origin. (Seems like forever ago doesn't it, Mike? Whew!)

He started out as "just" a programmer on Martian Dreams, a game I produced for Origin, but by the end of the project he was the engine that drove that game to the finish line. The game wouldn't have happened without Mike. His drive, dedication, love of games, knack for on-the-fly design, natural leadership skills, ability to combine right brain and left brain (to say nothing of his willingness to work crazy hours), drove all of us to work that much harder and ensured that the game ended up something special (at least to those of us who worked on it together—it sure didn't sell many copies!).

I honestly don't even remember if I ever gave Mike the title "Lead Programmer," officially, on Martian Dreams, but he sure deserved it. The guy was a machine, working longer hours than most people I've worked with (and that's saying something, in the game business). He also managed to do more and better work in those hours than any human being should be allowed to. It just ain't fair to the rest of us mere mortals. When Mike was on, there was no touching him. And he was almost always on—after Martian Dreams, Mike did it again and again, on Ultima VII, VIII, IX and a bunch of others. Scary really.

In retrospect, all those hours and all the hard work that seemed so necessary, back in the day, when we were all younger and more foolish than we are now, was probably an indication that Mike, like the rest of us, didn't have a clue about software development or game design or much anything else. (Okay, we had a pretty good handle on the effects of sugar and caffeine on the human body, but that's about it.) We had to work so long and so hard just to have a chance in hell of ending up with something worthwhile.

Reading this book, I couldn't help but marvel at how much Mike's learned over the years and wonder how much more Mike—and the rest of us—would have gotten done, how much better our games might have been, if we'd had the benefit of the kind of information in the pages that follow. There just wasn't anyone around back then who knew enough about games, programming practices, and software development. We were making it up as we went along.

Today, there are plenty of books out there that can teach you the typing part of programming. There are even some books that go a bit further and teach you what makes game coding different from coding a word processing program or a billing system for your local health care providers (or, as we used to call 'em, "doctors"). But even now there just aren't many books that combine hardcore game programming advice with equally hardcore development process, scheduling, debugging and team-building information.

Development process? Team-building? Who cares about all that? You just want to write code, right? If you're like a lot of programmers I know that's just what you're thinking. And, man, are you wrong. There might have been a time when coders could just close their doors and type, not caring about how their work fit into the big picture of a game's development. *Maybe* that was true ten years ago or more (probably not, but maybe…). Well, it sure isn't true anymore. With teams getting bigger all the time, with timelines stretching and budgets bloating, process and team issues are everyone's concern nowadays.

Mike gets that, something that becomes clear in the very first chapter, when he says, "Being the best developer you can be requires that you have intimate knowledge about the real demands of the industry." Amen, brother. That, in a nutshell, is what makes this book special. Most people think enthusiasm and talent are enough to get them into the game business and to ensure success once they land that all-important first gig. "I play games all the time," they say, "and I'm a kickass coder, so what more is there to know. Sign me up!"

Well, I'm here to tell you that there's plenty more to know and that's probably the single most valuable lesson this book has to offer. Games are insanely complex, and their creation involves a unique combination of art and science (some call it "magic" and they're not far wrong). Game development is demanding in a way that can only be appreciated after a stint in the trenches. At least, I used to think that was the case but that's where Mike comes in. Having been in the trenches, he can save you the trouble and pain and scars and relationship breakups and company failures that all too often go along with game development. No matter what you may think, it isn't all glory, fame, wealth and intense personal satisfaction (though there is a better than fair share of that last item…).

There's a ton of great stuff in Mike's book. Even if you're a non-programmer, you'll get something out of the introductory chapters and the section about "Professional Game Production." And I love all the insider bits found in Mike's tales from the "pixel mines."

Of course, there's plenty of nuts-and-bolts stuff for folks who are already programmers but want to know what makes game programming so special (and believe me, it is). But even programmers will benefit from the other ton of stuff that often gets short shrift in the typical programming book—all that Big Picture stuff that doesn't involve code samples.

What's a game team look like? How do you structure development? How do you cost out your part of a project and schedule it? What can you do as an individual to make it more likely that your team will make its milestones? And Mike does a really nice job of outlining the ways in which projects, project needs, team structures, and schedules change at various points in a project.

These are critical to being the most effective developer you can be, whether you're a programmer or not. This is all stuff you can't get just anywhere. You have to have lived through the process (and the pain!) a bunch of times. Or you have to find a mentor and spend years sucking his or her brain dry. Or you can stop reading this foreword and start reading this book.

What are you waiting for?

Warren Spector
April 2003

Introduction

Who Is Mr. Mike and Why Should I Care?

Since I was in high school I had been playing the Ultima series of games by Richard Garriott, and was a die-hard fan. Every game he published I played all the way through, from Ultima I on the Apple][to Ultima V on the IBM PC. Ultima VI came out right as I graduated from college, and I noticed that the contact information for Origin Systems was in Austin, Texas. I was living in Houston at the time, and my wife and I were ready for a change. On a whim, I sent my resume and a letter to Richard Garriott.

Weeks went by. I heard nothing.

I finally called Origin and asked the receptionist about it. When she found out that I'd sent my resume to Richard she laughed and said that was the last thing I should have done. She gave me the name of Dallas Snell, Origin's Vice President of Product Development. I sent him my resume via Federal Express and hoped for the best. I got a call two days later, and Dallas asked me how soon I could get to Austin for an interview. I asked him if tomorrow was too soon! He told me he'd see me for the interview at 2 p.m. I was terrified. I wore a tie but my wife smartly told me to take it off before I entered the building. It was a good thing because Dallas was dressed in shorts, flip-flops, and a Hawaiian shirt.

I didn't have a shred of game programming experience, and during my interview I was asked by a panel of Origin upper crust how I knew I could cut it at Origin. I looked around the table and saw the likes of Richard Garriott, a.k.a. Lord British, Warren Spector, Chris Roberts of Wing Commander fame, and six other folks. I tried not to panic. After all, I couldn't know if I could cut it, could I? If I've never actually programmed a real game before, I couldn't stand before industry luminaries and just be arrogant.

Instead, I came right out and told them that I didn't know if I could cut it. I told them that programming games was a dream I had since I could reach up and tap a keyboard. I promised them that if they hired me, and I sucked, that I'd leave Origin and not return until I earned my place there. I wanted to be a game programmer, and I'd do anything to make that dream come true. I guess they liked my answer because I got a job offer the following Monday.

I was at Origin for seven years exactly, and I worked on Martian Dreams, Ultima VII: The Black Gate, Ultima VIII: Pagan, Ultima IX: Ascension, and Ultima Online. I spent most of my time programming, but I was asked to play a management role as well on the later projects. After Origin I started a little game company called Tornado Alley. Our idea was to create a massively multiplayer game for children. We had a lot of fun and learned a lot but we couldn't convince companies like Mattel and Hasbro to spend $5 million on a game—oh well!

After Tornado Alley I hooked up with a bunch of people that eventually formed Compulsive Development. We did casual games for Microsoft, one of which was Bicycle Casino featuring the MGM/Mirage Resorts in Las Vegas. The game wasn't a hardcore 3D shooter, but the all-expenses paid trips to Las Vegas were awesome. Compulsive Development taught me more about game production, and how computer game companies work, than any other job. We worked on four titles for Microsoft in two and one-half years, each one shipped exactly on schedule and on-budget. Compulsive Development was acquired by Glass Eye Entertainment in Austin, headed up by my friend Monty Kerr. I'm his Director of Product Development, and I now spend my time equally in technology, management, and business development.

If you are looking for a book written by someone who's actually been working in the games industry, you've come to the right place. While I'm a programmer at heart, I'm never too far from production either. I've worked on ten games in my career, eight of which made it to market. The games include hardcore fantasy role playing games like the Ultima series, a few massively multiplayer titles including Ultima Online, a kids game from Mattel called Magnadoodle, and Microsoft's casual games including Bicycle Casino.

The schedules for these games ranged from five weeks to as many years, and audiences from little kids to people my Mom's age. There's a lot to learn working on each kind of title, and I'll try my best to teach you as much as I can.

What You Should Know Before You Knock on My Door

This book is written for programmers. Non-programmers could probably get something from the book too, but if you flip through the pages you'll see how much C++ code is included—you'll find plenty. The code is written in C++, so if you are a die-hard C programmer you'll have to at least be able to read C++ to get the most out of this book. If you don't know either language, you'll probably struggle a little with the code samples, but I'll bet you can get enough from the comments and the explanations to feel you got your money's worth.

All of the code in this book works under Visual Studio.NET, or at least it did when I copied it into Microsoft Word, which is how I wrote the book. I apologize ahead of time for making no attempt whatsoever to make sure the code worked in other compilers like CodeWarrior or GNU C++. I hope you'll forgive me. I figured my time would be better spent by covering as much technical ground as possible, instead of working on multi-compiler compatible code.

The code in this book also has a heavy Win32 bias. I'm a Win32 programmer, and I was a DOS programmer before that. I've had some brief forays into Unix on the Ultima Online server code, but I'm hardly an expert. Much of the code in this book assumes Win32, and I didn't change the code to support cross compiling into other operating systems for much the same reason as I chose a single compiler. It was simply better for me to cover lots of technical issues than for me to check my code under Linux.

As far as graphics APIs are concerned, I assume you'll use DirectX 7 for 2D graphics and DirectX 9 for 3D. As to the reasons for this, you'll read about that later because it's something of a long story. I don't have anything against OpenGL, of course, I'm just not an expert in the nuances. Basically, if you have a good working knowledge in C++, Win32, and DirectX you'll be fine. You don't have to be godlike in your skill, but you should be pretty comfortable coding in these areas.

If you are a complete newbie, and perhaps only know a little C++, don't feel dejected and don't return this book! I have a plan for you. Throughout this book I'll refer to other tomes of knowledge that helped me learn how to program. They can help you too, and use them in conjunction with the humble collection of knowledge you hold in your hands. With a little concentration you can boot strap yourself into programming prowess. I learned more about programming in C++,

DirectX, and Win32 by looking at working code, of which there is plenty included in these pages for you to enjoy. Other than that, there are a few other things that you should be familiar with:

- Pixel pushers like Photoshop or Microsoft Paint
- The Standard Template Library (STL)

Pixel Pushers

Good programmers should be able to make their own art, which requires a working knowledge of bitmap tools like Adobe Photoshop or Microsoft Paint. Some of the code examples will require you to "res up" a bitmap for a texture or some other thing, and if you don't know how to do that you won't be able to run the example. Microsoft Paint is perfectly fine for this book, but if you want to get serious you'll want to get something like Photoshop.

In a real game company, it's also good to have some remedial skill with modeling tools like Maya or 3D Studio Max, but you won't need that for anything in this book. Luckily, DirectX has supplied some basic modeling tools, and we'll be using those in the 3D chapters.

The Standard Template Library (STL)

This book uses STL for common data structures. If you don't know anything about STL you'll see some good examples in this book, and I'm sure you'll be able to follow the code. I'm not attempting to teach you STL—something that is beyond the scope of this book. Instead, go read *The C++ Standard Library: A Tutorial and Reference* by Nicolai M. Josuttis. After you get your bearings, go read Scott Meyer's books on STL because they're fantastic.

STL is a body of code that is extremely well tested, has a widely understood API, and is available on almost every development platform. If you haven't seen it yet, stop reading right now and do a little research. You'll never have to write code for common data structures like linked lists, resizable arrays, and trees ever again. I've saved hours of grief using <list>, <vector>, and <map>.

Whatever happens, don't get caught writing your own linked list class or tree when STL would have worked. All implementations are extremely well tested. Every bug or implementation oddity has already been exposed and discussed on the Internet. Your own code, on the other hand, is not.

Source Code and Coding Standards

I despise technical books that include source code that doesn't compile. I cursed the name of every author and editor that created these books, filled with errors and broken code. I'm now doomed to join their ranks.

Microsoft Word just doesn't handle C++ source code very well, and the code highlighting has to be turned off, since this book is printed in black and white. I understand, now, why so many programming books are crawling with errors. I apologize to every author and editor I maligned. Until I wrote this book I had no idea how difficult it was. Enough groveling! I will make a valiant effort to check and recheck the source code in this book, and I'll do what I can to set anything right if I find it broken.

Now that my conscience is at ease, you should know something about how to read the source code in this book.

Where the Code Comes From

Every line of source code has its beginning in an actual game. Of course, the code is not 100% verbatim. My front door would be knocked down by a wave of lawyers from Microsoft, Electronic Arts, Mattel, and who knows else. Instead, the code has been sufficiently tweaked to protect the intellectual property of myself and for everyone who was crazy enough to employ me. The original code is much harder to read anyway. It usually contained optimizations and external references that I couldn't easily include in any form. Since they came from nearly twelve years of coding experience, you can imagine the wide variety of style and structure.

If you want to make your own game the source code in this book should give you a head start. You'll find some great skeletal work on which you can hang your own code. I'm even hoping that some of the code in here will save you some headaches so you can concentrate on your game.

The code in this book was written and tested on the Win32 platform under Visual Studio.NET. Console programming is a different beast, and where it makes sense I'll pull some advice from experts regarding a particular solution. If you're looking to use this code on a Win32 box but want to know how programming the same thing on the Xbox or PS2 is different, you're holding the right book.

You can freely use my code any way you see fit. If you happen to make millions, buy me a beer. Most likely you'll look at the code, get an idea to make it better, and write your own. That's the way it should be.

Coding Standards and Style

Source code standards are important. I'm not necessarily a standards dictator. I can find room for other opinions on code style and I'm happy to adopt reasonable standards when and where I must. I look at it like trying to learn a bit of the local language if you travel abroad. The locals will appreciate it and you might even learn something.

Origin Systems didn't have company wide coding standards. I was part of no less than three standards committees while I was there, to no avail. Every time we attempted to discuss C++ bracing style the meeting simply broke down into a screaming match. There were many programmers at Origin that simply wouldn't adapt to anyone else's style. It got so bad that somebody wrote a little utility that would parse a source file and change the bracing style from one to the other. Madness!

Your coding standards and style exist solely to communicate useful information to other programmers, and sometimes a future version of yourself.

I use a coding style in this book extremely similar to what I use professionally. The only departures are those that make the code simpler to read. For example, the source code in the book frequently eliminates obvious error detection and handling. If I used every line of source code exactly as it appeared in real projects this book would have to be twice as long. It was a tough tradeoff, but it's better to have more examples and leave the obvious stuff out of the book.

At Origin Systems, a particular programmer on Martian Dreams used goto at a frequency you'd find unpleasantly surprising. The new version of the Borland compiler was on everyone's desks, fresh from the presses. He'd just finished installing it, and went to lunch. I went to his machine and edited the compiler executable. I changed the keyword goto to goat. When he came back from lunch, three or four of us were pouring over the Borland docs in my office. We told him that Borland's software engineers decided to eliminate goto from their implementation of C. We were astonished, but he didn't believe us until he compiled a small test program in his newly installed compiler and received a "unexpected identifier or keyword: goto" message for his trouble. We told him the truth before he reached someone at Borland's customer service department.

Using Prefixes

Use one prefix letter per identifier, and don't under any circumstance worry about using prefixes for type, like Win32 APIs use. Modern IDEs like Visual

Studio.NET expose the type of an identifier with a tooltip, so programmers don't have to clutter the prefix with redundant information.

g	Use with global variables –	`g_Counter`
m	Use with member variables –	`m_Counter`
V	Use with virtual functions –	`VDraw()`
I	Use with Interface classes –	`class IDrawable`

I've seen some crazy use of prefixes that attach three or more characters to the front of any identifier. It must be hard to program in Hungary. The problem with this style is that every identifier that has the same prefix looks exactly alike. That's why the prefix should be as small as possible, and separated from the identifier with an underscore: it conveys useful information without overpowering the identity of the variable name. In your own code, feel free to add more prefixes to this list as you find good use for them. Just don't go overboard!

Prefixing variables for scope is an excellent use for prefixes. Programmers who change the value of something with global scope need to be slapped in the face so they can take proper precautions. Class member variables have a different scope than local variables. The 'm' prefix is a clean way to differentiate locals and members when they are used in the same method.

Virtual functions are powerful, and therefore dangerous when used to evil ends. A prefix on virtual functions reminds programmers that they should call the parent's overloaded virtual function, and that the cost of calling the function is higher.

I find it useful to apply a prefix to interface classes, ones that only define pure virtual functions and no data members, so programmers feel safe multiply inheriting from them. I avoid multiple inheritance of non-interface classes, and I advise you to do the same. The resulting code can be very confusing and hard to maintain.

Capitalization

I use capitalization to distinguish different classes of identifiers and make identifiers easier to read.

- **Variables and Parameters:** Always start with lower case, use a capital letter for each compound word—`g_BufferLength, m_BufferLength, returnValue`
- **Classes, Functions, Typedefs and Methods:** Always start with upper case, capitalize each compound word—`SoundResource, MemoryFile`

- **Macros:** All capitals, separate compound words with underscores – `SAFE_DELETE, MAX_PATH`

The first two capitalization styles help programmers distinguish between definitions of class and instances of those classes:

```
SoundResource soundResource;
MemoryFile memoryFile;
```

Macros, a source of frequent pain and suffering, should boldly state their existence in all capitals. If you want to find the definition of a macro it's easy to search for the `#define MACRO_NAME`. This sets them apart from functions or methods.

Const Correct Code

I try my best to make code const correct, and the code in this book is no exception. I'm sure some of you hardcore const correct programmers will be able to throw a few thousand consts in where I've forgotten them.

Const correctness is a pain in the ass, but it's important. Adding const to member variables, function returns, pointers, and references communicates important information to other programmers.

Strings and Localization

If you make your game for English speakers only, you're slashing your sales. Europe and Asia, especially mainland China, are hungry for quality games. Most players will put up with English but they'd rather get their hands on a good translation in their native language. Good localization technique deserves an entire book and a masters degree in foreign cultures. Since the book as a decidedly Win32 bias, I'm going to use `TCHAR` as the basic character data type. It can compile with or without `_UNICODE` defined. You'll notice that `CHAR` and `unsigned CHAR` is still used in code that needs eight bit values, specifically when dealing with graphics or sound data.

While I don't do this in the book, it's a good idea to use a good string class to hide the data type of the string. Most string classes depend on #defines or compile macros to set them into single or double byte strings, and the code that uses them doesn't have to care.

In the code samples I put literal strings in for clarity. In a real project every string that could possibly be seen by anyone playing the game is declared in a string table. The string class that I mentioned above is a great place to stick a constructor that uses the resource constant; and you have a simple way to grab strings from the resource table:

```
RString unknownErrorMessage(STRING_UNKNOWN_ERROR);
```

Regarding the resource constant, I don't attempt to encode the exact text of the string in the macro. It takes too long to type and muddles the code. I usually find a good abbreviation.

One final note about strings in real game code: debug strings or names for objects are fine as literals. You can declare them at will:

```
if (impossibleError == true)
{
   OutputDebugString(_T("Someone enabled the impossible error flag!"));
}
```

Commenting

Really good code comments itself, and I'm hoping the code in this book does exactly that. Good variable names and logic should obviate the need for wordy explanations. In the book, I'll sprinkle comments in the code where I think they do some good, but you'll usually find some meaty explanation immediately after the code sample.

In a real game, the meaty explanation should be inserted into the code, perhaps at the beginning of the file, so that other programmers can figure out what's going on. What seems obvious the moment you type the code degrades linearly with time to a confusing mess. For me, total confusion sets in approximately three months after I write the code—how could I possibly expect anyone else to understand it if I'm completely lost in something I wrote myself?

I always start projects with the intention of putting good comments in my code. I always end projects disappointed in other programmers and myself—we just didn't have enough time. That happens. Projects under pressure will see comments disappear because the programmers are spending 100% of their time coding like mad. The best policy is to start off with a lean, light commenting policy and keep it up as long as you can. If there comes a point in the project where comments are dwindling, try to make a good effort to go back in the code base after the project releases to document the code. A good friend of mine at Microsoft told me that shipping the product was a good feature. I agree.

Namespaces

The only namespace I use in the book is one that distinguishes code that I want you to write yourself. It is usually pretty simple stuff like line drawing or code that exists on the Internet. Here's how to recognize it:

```
yourcode::LineDraw(0,0,10,25);
```

Error Handling

There is very little error handling code in this book, so little that when I look at it I cringe. The fact is that robust error code gets a little wordy, and I wanted to spend time on the lines of code that will teach you about making games. You can use any form of error checking you want, and I talk about some different options in the chapter on debugging.

Every hard exit in your game should have an error message that is presented to the player:

"Bummer – your game is hosed because of some bug in objectdata.cpp, line 6502". Use `__FILE__` and `__LINE__` to identify the offending code. Unique error codes are a hassle to maintain. This data can be invaluable for the development team and customer service after the game ships. Many a patch or workaround traces their roots to a few hundred telephone calls and emails that finger a particular error code.

Where Is the Code? Must I Actually Type?

There's no CD in this book, as you've noticed. When we planned this book, the publisher convinced me to create a web site where you can download all of the code examples. This has two distinct advantages. First, the book is much cheaper to print, and therefore cheaper for you to buy. Second, it's much easier to fix problems on a web site that it is to fix them on thousands of CDs. Find the website here: **http://www.paraglyphpress.com**.

How This Book Is Organized

The book is organized into four parts:

- **Part One—Game Programming Fundamentals**: Exposes some stuff that you'll want in your game programming toolbox, like a good random number generator. It also introduces the major components of games and how they interact.

- **Part Two—Get Your Game Running:** You'll find your first meaty game code examples, including user interface code, 2D graphics code, and your main loop.
- **Part Three—Building Out Your Game:** The tougher code examples are in this section, such as 3D code, special code for Windows games, and some great debugging tools.
- **Part Four—Professional Game Production:** This section shows what it's like to actually work on games, from scheduling to testing and finally getting your game out the door and into the hands of your players.

Throughout the book you'll see a few insets that are identified by the following icons:

Gotcha: When you see this icon you'll read about a common mistake that I'm hoping you can avoid. Mostly likely, I didn't, and suffered the consequences.

Best Practice: This inset is something I do by habit, and it helps me avoid programming trouble. Usually, I learned these tips from someone else who taught me, and I'm passing on the good word.

A Tale from the Pixel Mines: Working in the Pixel Mines is slang for working on computer games. Since I've worked in the industry since 1990, and I'm a creature of observation, I couldn't help but bring a few tall tales to the book from my game industry experiences. Some tales are taller than others, but believe it or not they all actually happened.

Chapter 1

Game Programming Is Wacky Because...

Most people that want jobs in the computer game industry have some interesting and completely wrong opinions about what it's like working on games. When I started at Origin Systems in 1990 I really had no idea what to expect. What I got was a strange concentrated form of a regular life. In seven years I had as much fun, learning, and suffering as normal people get in twenty years. I'm glad I was young; the hours would have killed me if I had to sign up for a starting career as a game programmer now.

Programming games isn't like other kinds of programming. It's not better or worse, just different. Most of the good aspects of game programming have to do with the Hollywood side of things. Games are cool and everybody loves them. The bad side of professional game programming has to deal with the complexities of the task—game development is far from easy. The sweaty underbelly of this industry can be blamed mostly on insane deadlines and work hours, ever-changing SDKs and operating systems, and intense competition. In this chapter I'm going to walk you through the good, the bad, and the ugly aspects of game development. Being the best developer you can be requires that you have intimate knowledge about the real demands of the industry.

In case you were wondering, it's all worth it. Either that or I'm just the type to enjoy repeated blows to the head.

The Good

When I accepted my first job in the computer game industry, my second choice was a job with American General Life Insurance. They wore ties. Their employees took drug tests. For that I would have the distinct privilege of working on a Beta version of Microsoft's C++ compiler, programming little sales tools for insurance agents. Did I make the right decision or what?

Face it; there aren't many exciting programming jobs out there. The cool jobs fall into a few categories: jobs you can't talk about, ultra high budget simulations and control software, and games. Everything else falls quickly into the "Did you put a cover sheet on your TPS report?" category.

The Job

Here's my bottom line: It's cool to work on games. Games are as much art as they are science. I think that blending both halves of your brain on the job is immensely satisfying. Let's assume you are working on a difficult path finding algorithm. Path finding is well researched, but your implementation of it requires analytical thinking to apply the published solution with the particulars of your game. Once you get it working you may discover that it isn't aesthetically pleasing. Your algorithm might be technically correct but simply "look" wrong. It's up to you to tweak it, like an artist tweaks a background that is a little too dark.

It's great to take a game design discussion with you to lunch. You can have a heated debate on whether the master zombie characters come from outer space or originated here on earth—the result of some tragic experiment. You get the weirdest looks, as someone screams, "Damn it, everyone knows that it's better for the zombies to come from space!" I have the most fun coding, especially when things are going well. Game code is usually pretty difficult stuff, and you frequently have to break some new ground here and there. This is especially true when you are playing with new hardware like the latest video cards. It's also true when you figure out how to implement a customized version of a classic algorithm, so that it runs fast enough to be in a game instead of a textbook.

Probably the best part of game coding is starting from scratch and allowing everything in your libraries to be refreshed and rewritten if necessary. At the end of a project you can't make drastic changes, and you are forced to live with some annoying hacks and hastily designed objects. When the project is done and you are starting the next one, there's nothing better than throwing off those shackles. Re-factoring, reorganizing, and rewriting an older system so that it really shines is extremely rewarding. Games probably offer more freedom than other types of programming projects because game code doesn't usually last longer than about two years. The state of the art moves pretty fast, and as a game developer you'll be pedaling as fast as you can.

The People

If you work in the games industry people want to know about your company and your projects. They talk to you about your job because it's high profile. They want to know when they can play your game. Every now and then you find someone that played a game you worked on, and enjoyed it. It's great when fans get a buzz going about a game that's still in the design phase, or they start talking about the next version before you're back from vacation. They set up websites devoted to your game and argue endlessly about stuff that even the development team finds minor.

Never wear development team tee-shirts to places where nutty fans will hang out. I happened to be wearing an Ultima VII "Development Team" shirt when I walked into CompUSA to pick up a game. As I was browsing, a little nerdy guy walked up to me and started talking to me about gritty details of the game design. I'm pretty patient about this kind of thing, so I tried my best to steer the conversation to a close, where any normal human being would simply say, "Well, gee it was nice to meet you! Thanks!" and walk away. Fifteen minutes later I felt as if I wanted to chew my own arm off and give it to him, in the hopes I could make my escape! This person is a good example of why it's good to take a break from games and go outside, find a girlfriend, or even read a book.

Another category of people you come into contact with is the hopeful would-be game programmer. I enjoy these folks and I do everything I can for anyone who has talent and is willing to increase his or her skills. With today's mod scene and increasingly savvy hobbyists there is also an increase in amateur developers. These developers are taking things a step beyond the more casual hobbyist level to create things that are intensely interesting. Some even graduate to cult status, or better yet to the professional ranks. The best revenge is being able to tell your parents that playing all those games actually did you some good.

One of the best programmers I ever worked with started out as a dedicated amateur. This guy was so dedicated that he rewrote a large portion of Ultima VII on his own time and actually made a fantastic graphics engine that had Z-sprites before I even knew what they were. He showed us a demo that had the Avatar sink convincingly into a solid castle wall. We hired him.

The best people are those closest to you—the development team. By the end of a project they're like your family. Certainly you've seen them more than your family, and I've even seen teammates become family. Programmers, artists, designers, audio engineers, composers, and testers make an odd mix of people. You wouldn't think that these people could all hang out and get along. Somehow they figure out how to work together in varying degrees of success.

Most of your interactions in game programming are with other programmers. One big difference between the game industry and more boring jobs are that there's a significant portion of programmers that are self-taught in the game industry. That's not to say these folks are slackers by any shake of the stick. Instead, they tend to be absolutely brilliant. One difference between the self-taught hackers and the programmer with Bachelor's degrees is the hackers tends to design and code things before they realize that someone has already solved the problem and posted the code on the Internet somewhere. Sometimes you'll catch them describing a cool data structure they just came up with and you'll realize they are talking about a B+ tree. Their strength comes from their amazing ability to see right to the heart of a problem, without worrying about how hard it is. One of the most brilliant programmers I ever met never graduated high school.

I wish I were a better artist. This is a skill that I admire to the point of wide-eyed wonder. Even better than admiring the raw skills, the creative insight that artists conjure up makes working with them so fantastic. Don't get me wrong; many of them are completely insane, opinionated, temperamental, and ultra-perfectionists. Come to think of it that sounds exactly like most of the programmers I know. Probably the weirdest thing about working with artists on computer games is that you realize that artists and programmers are the same kind of people working on different sides of their brain.

The Tools—Software Development Kits (SDKs)

The most widely used SDK is DirectX from Microsoft. It provides APIs useful for creating game software. There are many more: SDKs for physics, SDKs for rendering 3D graphics, SDKs for audio, and SDKs for networking. One of these days there'll be an SDK for fantasy role-playing games or flight sims. You can't make a professional game without SDKs. You don't need all of them, but most certainly you'll use one or two. They boost your development schedule and give you some confidence that your graphics or audio system has been well tested.

When I first started writing this section it was in my "The Ugly" section at the end of this chapter. I felt a little guilty about giving SDKs such a bad rap. After all, if they were really useless why do I use them on every project? The truth is that SDKs give you a huge leg up. They can also be a huge pain in the ass. SDKs are widely used, so they can't appeal to the odd needs of every developer. Some of the expensive ones come with source code, but any customizations you perform might be invalidated by their next version. Most of the time you have to be satisfied with begging and pleading. Perhaps the SDK engineers will take pity upon you and consider your request.

What I like most about dealing with SDKs is having to spend a week tweaking a game when the new SDK doesn't support the same APIs as the old SDK. To give them credit, DirectX's use of COM does alleviate this pressure. I think COM is ugly as sin, but it does function well in an SDK that changes as fast as DirectX has changed for the last few years.

The Hardware

Games run on cool hardware. Well, most games do. I can't say that the Bicycle Casino project I developed for Microsoft exactly blew the doors off the hardware requirements, but the Ultima games I worked on sure as hell did. Many of the big budget PC titles are created on hardware that has yet to reach any serious market penetration, which means that the hardware manufacturers are constantly sending you the latest greatest stuff and even a tee-shirt every now and then. I used to return from a trade show with a whole other suitcase of hardware: video cards, audio boards, controllers, joysticks, and even virtual reality goggles. I think those days are over, but an established developer can still call any hardware company out there and get on their developer program. You don't exactly get truckloads of free hardware, but you do get a few boards to split amongst the programmers and the test group. That can save your ass if you find that your game crashes on the hottest video card—you can't fix the bug just by hoping it goes away.

The developer programs offered by hardware manufacturers are a great resource. Most of them have special developer websites and prerelease hardware programs. They also have dedicated engineers that can help you with a specific problem. An engineer at ATI verified a particular bug on one of the Microsoft projects I worked on. They had a new driver ready in a few days. Of course, I was happy to have the big gorilla named Microsoft standing behind us, but most hardware companies are really responsive when it comes to diagnosing driver problems.

The Platforms

There are a wide variety of gaming platforms, and they never stop growing. For many years we only had to deal with consoles and desktops. Since 2001, games have popped up on handheld devices like the Game Boy Advance, Palm systems, and even cellphones. Even weirder, your digital cable set top box (STB) has the equivalent power of older desktop computers. I've heard that folks in Germany can play networked Doom over their TVs. A group in England just released an entirely new (albeit retro) Tomb Raider game over a STB.

At the time of this writing, the big consoles on the market are Sony's Playstation 2, Nintendo's GameCube, and Microsoft's Xbox. Right now this battle is being won by PS2 which dwarfs the units sold of GameCube and Xbox. My analyst friends tell me, however, that the other systems are doing well-enough on their own so we'll likely see another round of new hardware before someone blinks. In the end it will probably be the company that puts out the best games and the that can hang financially. For best games, Sony and Nintendo take the Xbox easily. Microsoft isn't going out without a fight—and everyone knows that they have huge cash reserves. It's truly exciting to be part of such a slugfest. Imagine the Rumble in the Jungle with Foreman, Ali, and Fraiser in the ring at the same time!

Sony is making a big deal lately of adopting Linux as the development environment for the PS2 and future Sony game consoles. This is fantastic because I like stable, dependable, and standard development environments. Linux is exactly that, and will serve Sony well in the future. Developing software for the Xbox is almost exactly like developing for the PC. It's almost like developing under a cleaned up Win32 and DirectX 8, something desktop PC developers wish for every day. The best part of developing on the Xbox, or any other console, is the fact that you'll never have to worry about supporting a hellish grid of operating system and hardware configurations that are guaranteed to change at least twice during your development cycle.

Table 1.1 lists the various platforms that are leading the pack today. When you look at the hardware comparison, it seems pretty obvious that programmers will have the most fun on the Xbox. Not only is this platform the most familiar, but there is plenty of headroom

Table 1.1 Comparing the Top Platforms for Game Developers.

Platform	Xbox	PS2	GameCube
CPU	733 MHz	294.9 MHz	485 MHz
Graphics Processor	250 MHz	147.5 MHz	162MHz
Maximum Resolution	1920x1080	1280x1024	Up to HDTV
Memory	64MB RAM	40MB RAM	43MB RAM
Controller Ports	4	2 (4 optional)	4
Media	4x DVD-ROM (3.2-6.4Gb)	5x DVD-ROM (3.2-6.4Gb)	3 in DVD-ROM (1.5Gb)
3D Audio Support	Dolby 5.1	DTS in gameplay, Dolby 5.1 for DVDs	Dolby Pro Logic II
Audio Channels	64	48	64
Hard disk	Yes – 8Gb	Addon	No
Internet	10/100 Ethernet Port	Optional modem /broadband	Optional modem/ broadband
DVD Movies	Yes	Yes	No

in the CPU speed and system RAM. The graphics and audio chips support a wide variety of hardware accelerated features, and the stock hard drive and Ethernet ports are nice additions.

Console development in general is pretty specialized. Developers that get approval to make projects for these platforms must either jump thorough some amazing hoops or they must have standout intellectual property. If you happen to have a favorite uncle on the board of directors of Electronic Arts, you'll be in a great position.

Handheld devices include the Game Boy Advance, cellphones, Palm, PocketPC, and a few others. With these devices, game programming is returning to its roots: clever game designs and efficient implementation. Back in the mid 1980s, classic Williams games like Robotron, Joust, and Defender were technological marvels and the game designs were a blast. The handheld devices today actually have more processing and graphics power than those old stand up machines, and programmers and designers are making games that return to these classic designs.

Screen sizes vary significantly. The GBA supports a palletized 240x160 display, Palm devices are 160x160, and cellphone screens are all over the road. CPU speed and hardware capabilities are also extremely variable. These limitations force you to return to the basics. Far from having a huge development team and server farm for pre-rendering action shots, if you work on these platforms you'll be able to fit your whole development studio in a minivan. It does have a certain appeal, doesn't it?

Desktop development gives you the very best hardware. After all, you can't find CPUs topping 2Ghz in the console world, and you won't find any TV sets that can support a 1600x1200 display at 80Hz. Desktops are always ahead of consoles for raw processing and graphics power. The console programmers will try to tell you that this stuff makes you lazy. They'll say you don't have to be efficient when you have a few gigabytes of virtual memory, and you don't have to be careful if you can publish a patch over the Internet. They'll look down at you and at the same time quietly wish like hell they had all that power.

This awesome capability doesn't come without a cost. The dizzying array of hardware and operating system combinations makes compatibility a serious problem. You'll spend a serious amount of time chasing down some crazy bug that only happens on some version of Windows, like Windows ME, and a particular video card that hasn't been sold in three years, like the 3DFx VooDoo 2. What a hassle!

You also have to find ways to support old legacy hardware while you make your game look good on the bleeding edge gear. The CPU delta can be nearly 10:1, and the graphics delta is worse. It's pretty impossible to emulate a pixel shader on an old Matrox

Millenium card. That means your games need tons of configurable options so that players with crappy computers can turn off everything to get some decent frame-rate. Let the flamethrowers turn on multichannel MP3 decompression, full dynamic lighting and shadows, ultra-high texture and model density, stereo 1600x1200x32 displays, and quasi-telepathic AI. Each of these options deserves separate testing paths, on all the hardware configurations.

It makes you glad you can send patches over the Internet.

The Show

The game industry throws awesome tradeshows and parties. Find out for yourself and register for the Electronic Entertainment Expo (E3), usually held in Los Angeles in May. You have to be part of the industry to get registered, so if you don't have a game job launch a game review website and call yourself press. Everybody else does. The second most important thing to do at E3 is play the latest games and dork around with the latest console gear. E3 is a show for the retail buyers—the folks that decide what ends up on the game shelves at Wal-Mart and other retailers. Most of the games at E3 will be on the shelves for the Christmas season, but not all will make it. The show floor is where the game companies pull out all the stops to attract attention. You've got to go see for yourself. It's unbelievable.

Throughout this book, I'll be including a number of "best practice" tips from my years of experience as a developer. I couldn't resist including this one for your first "best practice" dose. The most important thing is to scam party invitations from the in-crowd, and talk your way into the "by invitation only" areas. A friend of mine that worked for Dell was able to get into virtually every private area of the show just by showing up, flashing his Dell credentials, and talking like he was someone important. Almost everyone bought it. It's all good fun.

If you want to learn about game development, go to the Game Developer's Conference in San Jose, held in March. It's brutally expensive, but you'll find the cream of the game development crop telling willing crowds some of their secrets. Before you sign up for any of the workshops, roundtables, or sessions, it's a good idea to do a Google search on the speakers and get an idea of what they've worked on recently. Choose the sessions that have speakers with the most game industry experience, and subject matter you're ready to hear—some of them are fairly advanced.

The Bad

Every job has its good parts and bad parts. Game programming is no different. First of all, game programming is hard. I could easily argue that programming games is the most challenging form of programming there is. Bad things are a matter of perspective; some people find these things challenging while others find them burdensome. You'll have to judge for yourself.

Game Programming Is Freaking Hard

It's not uncommon for a game programmer to do something completely new without losing any time on the development schedule. I'm not talking about a modification of a data structure to fit a certain problem; I'm talking about applying experimental and theoretical designs to a production system that meets deadlines. On Ultima VII one programmer wrote a 32-bit memory management system that was based on a little known Intel 486 processor flag and hand coded assembly, since there were no 32-bit compilers. On Ultima VIII one of the low-level engineers wrote a multithreaded real time multitasker two years before Win32 went beta. On Ultima IX the graphics programmer figured out how to make a software rasterizer appear to pump 32,000 textured polygons per second on a first generation Pentium. Everyone knows what Ultima Online did. I can't even begin to talk about the innovation that had to happen there just to get this system to work.

It would be one thing if this stuff were all research, where results come when they may and the pressure is bearable. A game project is different because the schedule is relentless. For all the media press about how late games are, I'm surprised that you see some of them at all given the level of difficulty.

Technology isn't the only thing that makes game programming hard. Game designers will push you farther than you ever thought you could go. I remember very well a conversation the senior staff at Origin had with Richard Garriott about the world design for Ultima IX. The team was pushing for a simple design that was reminiscent of the old Ultima games—the outdoor map was separate from the city maps. This was a simple design because each map could be loaded at once and no complicated map streaming would be required. Richard didn't go for it. He wanted a seamless map like Ultima VII. This was a much harder problem. We knew going into the meeting that if we couldn't convince Richard to use a simpler world design we'd have a hard time making our deadlines. We steeled ourselves with resolve, and armed with our charts and graphs and grim schedule predictions, we entered the conference room. Two hours later we all walked out of the room completely convinced that Richard was right, a seamless map was the way to go. I wish I knew how he does that!

Bits and Pieces

Games are built from more than code. Go find any PC game you bought recently and take a look at the directory where you installed it. You'll find the expected EXE and DLL files, with a few INIs or TXT files too. You'll also find gigabytes of other stuff with file extensions that don't necessarily map to any program you've ever seen. These other files hold packages of art, models, levels, sounds, music, and game data. This data didn't just fall out of the ether. Every texture was once a BMP or TIF file. Every sound was once a WAV, probably converted to MP3. Each model and game level had its own file too, perhaps stored in a 3D Studio MAX file. Even a small game will collect hundreds, if not thousands, of these bits and pieces, all of which need to be cataloged and organized into a manageable database of sorts.

No other software project has this problem. The only thing that comes close is a web site, and there just aren't that many assets. After all, they have to get sent over the Internet so there can't be that many. Certainly, not enough to fill up a DVD, and a compressed one at that.

Logistically these things can be a nightmare to manage. I've worked on projects where an artist wiped every file he'd worked on without even knowing it. Art files would get changed on the network but wouldn't get copied into the build, or even worse the artist would change the name of a file and it would get lost forever. When you have thousands of files to look though it's sometimes easier to just repaint it. Luckily there are some tools out there to help manage this problem. The situation is certainly better than when I started, where I think our best management scheme was a text file.

That's Not a Bug—That's a Feature

Actual Bug: I was walking along and the trees turned into shovels and the Avatar turned into a pair of boots and then the game crashed. You certainly won't see a bug report like that working on a database application. Seriously, some of these reports convince you beyond any shadow of doubt that the testers have their very own meth lab. As hard as I looked, I never found it.

You might wonder why I put something so amusing in the "bad" section of working on games. There are plenty of funny bugs; stuff goes wrong in a game and has a bizarre result. Luckily Quality Assurance (QA) should find it because it will be funnier for you as a developer than it will be for a player whose crashed game just lost a few hard hours of play.

Beyond the funny bugs, there's a dark side.

One bad thing is just the sheer volume of bugs. Games tend to be rushed into testing and the QA department obliges the producer by writing up every little thing they see. That is, after all, their job. I think they hope that eventually the producers will get the point and stop sending proto-ware into the test department. They hope in vain because the pressure to call the game "testable" is usually too much for the project management to bear. It's too bad that there tends to be no solid definition of "testable" unless you work in QA. From that point of view, it's pretty obvious.

The heavy bug volume weighs on everyone, developers and testers alike. They end up creating a logistical nightmare. The graphical reports that get spit out by the bug database are watched like the stock market; where a steep upward curve tends to have a negative effect on team morale. The worst part by far is what happens when the team can't quite keep the bug count under control, which is most of the time. The project leadership gathers together in a locked office and "fixes" bugs without ever touching the project. The bug simply becomes a feature, maybe a weird screwed up annoying feature, but a feature all the same.

There's nothing like having the rug pulled out from underneath you because of a bug that you intended to fix simply disappears. You might even have the code fixed on your machine, ready to check in for the next build. Instead, you get to undo the change. The final straw is when some critic on the Internet bashes the programmers for writing buggy code, and even points out the very bug that you intended to fix. Most programmers I know are perfectionists and take a lot of pride in their work, and because of that they lose sleep over bugs. The evil truth is that some bugs can't be fixed, even if they seem simple or benign.

The Tools

Richard Garriott, aka Lord British and creator of the Ultima RPG series, once said that the computer game industry was a lot like the movie industry. He also said that at the beginning of every game project we start by inventing new cameras, film and processing techniques, and projectors. He said that ten years ago, and while there is some middleware out there for sound and graphics, most game projects end up writing their own development tools.

Almost every game development team will end up writing tools to pack their graphics and audio data into resource files of some kind. WAD files are a good example of this. These files act like efficient databases for all media assets and game data, and are usually pre-converted to optimize loading speed or memory space. These files don't just manage themselves, and no one that I know uses Microsoft's CAB files. You'll have to write a custom tool to build and manage these proprietary files.

Most games have level or mission editors. When we developed the Ultima games we spent the first year or so of development writing the game editor—a tool that could import graphics, sounds, and models from all the

third-party packages like Photoshop, Lightwave, 3D Studio Max, and others. Ultima IX's level editor was fully networked and used TCP/IP to communicate peer/peer to all the designers and programmers running it. They could even edit the same map at the same time, since smaller portions of the map could be locked out for changes. The editor could launch into game mode at the press of a button, so the designer could test their work. Ultima Online's editor was much more like the game than Ultima IX. UO already had a client/server system up and running and it used a special god client to change the map levels and add new assets to the game.

Other games use a simpler strategy, a wise choice if you don't need twenty people building seamless maps and levels. The basic game level is assembled in a modeling tool like 3D Studio Max. A special editing tool usually loads that level and drops in special actions, dynamic object generators, and characters, almost as if you were playing the game. There's no need to have a complicated, multi-person aware tool if the levels are discrete entities as they are in most video games.

The first comprehensive level editors are starting to appear in middleware, most notably Criterion's Renderware Studio. Could the days of creating custom level and mission editors be over? I doubt it. These tools may give you a huge leg up, but you should expect quite a bit of customization in your schedule.

The Ugly

There are plenty of factors that make game coding a fluid and unpredictable task. The design of the game frequently changes drastically during development, motivated by many factors inside and outside the development team. Mounting schedule slippage and production pressure leads to the legendary "crunch mode" so prevalent on many game projects. Dependant software tools like DirectX change constantly, challenging software teams to keep up. Unlike many software projects, games frequently must support a wide variety of operating systems, graphics APIs, and platforms.

Hitting a Moving Target

Most industry software projects are carefully designed and planned. Systems analysts study customer requirements, case studies of previous versions of the software, and prospective architectures for months before the first line of code is ever written. Ultima VIII's architecture was planned by seven programmers in a single afternoon on a whiteboard.

1

Architecture notwithstanding, you can't design "fun." Fun is a "tweakable" thing, not something that exists in a design document. You hope like hell that the original design will result in a fun game, but the first playable version frequently leaves you with the distinct impression that the game needs some more chili powder and a little more time on the stove.

Ultima VIII's map design had a hub and spoke model. The hub was an underground dungeon that connected every other map. We released the game to QA and word came back that it was completely boring. The culprit was a sparse central map that wasn't much more than an underground maze with a few bad guys hanging out here and there. It wasn't good enough. Two designers worked day and night to rework the central map. Puzzles, traps, monsters, and other trickery finally added a little spice. The central map ended up being one of the best parts of the whole game.

Sometimes, the entire design is reworked. Ultima IX's architecture and game design changed no less than three times in development. I was there for two of them, and didn't stick around for the third. When a game is in development for multiple years, it's easy for new hardware technology to blaze past you. In Ultima IX's case, 3D accelerated video cards were just coming into their own as we were putting the finishing touches on what had to be the finest software rasterizer anyone ever wrote. It never saw the light of day.

Crunch Mode (and Crunch Meals)

Every now and then you end up at a technological dead end and have to start completely over. I was brought into the late stages of a Mattel project that was supposed to be in the test phase in about two weeks. I took one look at the code and realized, to my horror, that the entire graphics engine was using Windows GDI. Unless someone out there knows something I don't, the GDI can't texture map polygons. In less than five weeks the entire project was rebuilt from scratch.

Those five weeks were really more like fifteen weeks. The tiny development team worked late into each night and dragged themselves back each morning. There were no weekends. There were no days off. I'd estimate that we worked 90 hour workweeks on that project. You might think that unreasonable, and that nobody should have to work like that. That project was only five weeks. It was nothing compared to the pixel mines of Origin Systems circa 1992. Back then Origin had something called the "100 Club." The price of entry was working 100 hours in a single work week. The last time I counted there were only 168 hours in seven days, so the folks in the 100 Club were either working or sleeping.

To facilitate a grueling schedule the teams built bunk beds in the kitchen. Company kitchens are no place for bedding. My office was unfortunately located right across the hall, and I observed the kitchen/bedroom was getting higher occupancy than the homeless shelter in downtown Austin. After about a week I began to detect an odor emanating from across the hall. It seemed that the brilliant organizers of Hotel Origin never hired a maid service, and that an unplanned biology experiment was reporting its initial results via colorless but odorous gasses. Origin management soon liquidated the experiment.

It's not uncommon for companies insisting on long hours from salaried employees to provide meals. These "crunch meals" were usually ordered out and delivered to the team. Origin was able to get a local deli to bill them instead of requiring a credit card, so they began to order from them almost every night. Months went by, and everyone on the development team knew every item on the menu by heart, and knew exactly which bits of food were most likely to survive delivery intact. Ten years later I can still tell you what's on the menu at Jason's Deli, and even though the food is good, I rarely eat there.

Bah Humbug

Computer games are a seasonal business. They sell like crap in the summer, and profits soar at Christmas time. Of course, they only soar for your project if you're not still working on it. This puts a significant amount of pressure on development teams. Sometimes the pressure begins before the team begins working. Every game contract I signed stipulated specific schedule dates simply to make sure the boxes would have enough lead time to get built, shipped, and on store shelves.

This lead time varies from publisher to publisher. A big company like Microsoft has a huge manufacturing pipeline that includes everything from Bicycle Casino to Windows XP. Bicycle Casino was one of mine. I'll bet that if you were standing on the assembly line you'd be hard pressed to notice the brief flash of dark green as 50,000 boxes of the casino game whizzed by. You shouldn't be surprised to see a publisher like Microsoft requires you to finish your title by mid-summer in order to make the shelves by the holiday season.

Other publishers are more nimble, and they might be more accommodating if you've got a AAA title coming in hot and steep as late as November. You won't get the best sales if you release after Thanksgiving, but even getting out the week before Christmas is better than missing the season altogether. It's always best to have everything in the can before October if you want to see your game under Christmas trees.

Basically, Christmas is only merry if you're game is done.

Operating System Hell

Microsoft Excel doesn't need to support full-screen modes and it certainly doesn't need to worry about whether the installed video card has hardware-accelerated transform and lighting (also known as hardware T&L). That's one of the reasons that games get some special dispensations from Microsoft to qualify for logo compliance. Logo compliance means that your game exposes certain features and passes quality assurance tests from Microsoft. When your game passes muster you are allowed to display the Windows logo on the box—something that is good for any game but especially important for mass-market games.

The Microsoft projects we developed had to pass QA testing for Windows 98, Windows ME, Windows 2000, and all versions of Windows XP. By 2002 Microsoft wasn't supporting Windows 95 anymore, which was a good thing. It was hard enough building an old box for our Windows 98 test machine. The OS that required the most tweaking was Windows XP, mostly because of the new requirement that the "Program Files" directory was essentially read/only for non-administrator accounts. Most games store their dynamic data files close to the executable, which will fail under Windows XP Home.

There are so many of these annoying changes and differences from one operating system to the next that I've included a whole chapter in this book about that. The hell doesn't even stop there—some games choose to write graphics engines that work under DirectX and OpenGL. Some graphics middleware supports this natively, so you don't have to worry about it. Why would you bother? Performance.

Most video cards have DirectX and OpenGL drivers, but it's not guaranteed that you'll achieve equal performance or graphics quality under both. The performance differences are directly proportional to the effort put into the drivers, and there are cases where the OpenGL driver beats DirectX soundly. Of course, there are mirror cases as well, where DirectX is the way to go. Even better, the quality of the drivers change from operating system to operating system. The result of all this is a huge increase in effort on your side. Even if you choose one particular graphics API you still have to support a wide array of operating systems. This increase in effort simply widens the market for your game. It doesn't make your game fun or provide a deeper experience. It just keeps it from misbehaving on someone's computer.

I almost forgot, what about Linux? What about Mac? They are still tiny slivers of the gaming market. Linux is growing quickly and there are people out there with Mac computers. The question about writing a cross platform game for these operating systems is more logistical and financial than technological. Most game projects can be ported to similar platforms with a tolerable dose of programming hell.

Moving games to very dissimilar platforms can be nigh impossible, such as a direct port of a PC game to a console. The lack of a keyboard, lower screen resolution, and tiny secondary storage preclude some games from ever appearing on the console. That doesn't even begin to address the inherent design concerns that differ sharply from consoles to desktops.

Fluid Nature of Employment

The game industry, for all its size and billions of dollars of annual revenue, is not the most stable employment opportunity out there. You can almost guarantee that if you get a job in the industry you'll be working with a completely different set of people every two years or so, and perhaps even more often than that.

Every year at the Origin Christmas party, employees were asked to stand up as a group. Everyone who had worked there less than a year was asked to sit down, followed by second and third year employees. This process was repeated until only a handful of people were left. This was usually by the fourth or fifth year. In my sixth year, I became the twelfth most senior person in the company by time of service, and Origin had hundreds of employees. This is fairly common throughout the industry.

The stresses of incredibly short schedules and cancelled projects have chased many of my friends out of the industry altogether. Whole studios, including two of my own, take root for a while and then evaporate or get bought. Your boss today will not be your boss tomorrow, especially if your boss attempts to do something crazy, like start their own game studio!

It's All Worth It, Right?

There's something odd about human psychology. After a particularly scary or painful experience, some of us will say to ourselves, "Hey, that wasn't so bad. Let's do it again!" People that make games do this all the time. The job is incredibly difficult and can drive you completely mad. Your tools and supported operating systems change more often than you'd like, but less so than the game design. It seems that you delete more code than you write.

Taking three steps forward and five steps back is a good recipe for long hours, and you'll get an "all you can eat" buffet of overtime. It will get so bad that you'll feel guilty when you leave work before 7 p.m. on a Sunday night. When crunch mode is over, and you get back to a normal 60 hour work week, you'll wonder what to do with all the extra time on your hands.

Why bother? Looking at this description of the computer game industry is making that boring job at American General Life Insurance look pretty good. There are plenty of good things, but there's one that beats them all: After all the work, lost weekends, and screaming matches with producers and testers, your game finally appears on the retail shelves somewhere. A few weeks after it ships, you start looking. You make excuses to go to Wal-Mart, Circuit City, and Best Buy and wander the software section. Eventually you see it. Your game. In a box. On the shelf. Shrink-wrapped!

There's nothing like it. As you hold it in your hands someone walks up to you and says, "Hey, I was thinking of buying that game. Is it any good?" You smile and hand him the box, "Yeah, it's damn good."

Chapter 2

What's in a Game?

The first thing most programmers think of when they start coding a game is the graphics system. They'll start with a DirectX sample, import some of their own miserable programmer art, put an environment map or a bump map on everything in sight, and shout "Eureka! The graphics system is finished! We'll be shipping our game by next weekend!"

By the time the next weekend rolls around, the same newbie game programmers will have a long laundry list of things that need to be done, and there are a number of subtle things that they will have completely missed. These hidden systems are usually the heart of every game, and you're never aware of them when you play games because you're not supposed to be aware of them. By the end of this chapter, you'll have a brief overview of the main components of game code and how they fit together. The rest of this book digs into the details of these systems and how they are built.

Display Technologies: A Quick Overview of the Issues

Display decisions include bit depth and resolution and the core graphics technology that pushes pixels: 2D, 3D, or a hybrid of the two. The Playstation and Gamecube coders out there can skip the resolution and bit depth section because those are chosen for you. Xbox and desktop coders are still in the discussion because you have some choices about what resolutions your game will support. Only the desktop coders need worry about bit depth. Everyone should worry about the core graphics technology.

Resolution and Bit Depth

It might seem crazy to support a 640x480 8-bit palettized mode in the 21st century. I can promise you it's equally crazy to assume that everyone buying computer games has flame-thrower CPU/video card rigs that can push 1280x1024x32 at 75 fps. There's really one major question that you need to answer before finalizing on a minimum acceptable resolution/bit depth: What will sell the most games?

The Microsoft Casino/Card projects I worked on at Compulsive Development were clearly marketed at the casual gamer—people like my parents. They have computers that are three to four years old and therefore look ancient to most programmers. The VRAM is 1/8 of what most developers use, 1/4 of the CPU speed, and 1/8 of the system RAM. Face it, these computers are better used as boat anchors than game platforms! Still, there are plenty of those boxes out there if you are going for the Wal-Mart crowd, a lucrative market indeed.

On the complete opposite side of the spectrum, if you are working on the latest and greatest graphics game specifically for the hard core shooter market, you'd be nuts to code your game to the same pathetic standard. Instead, go for a bit depth and resolution that can make the newest and best game rig eek out a solid 60fps. You'll be pretty sure that the early adopters will have the best rig to make your game look completely fantastic at its highest resolution.

For the longest time, Ultima fans had to upgrade their computer every time the new version was released. Look at these minimum specs: Ultima I-IV: Apple][, Ultima V: IBM PC/CGA, Ultima VI: IBM PC/EGA or Hercules, Ultima VII: Intel 386/VGA, Ultima VIII: Intel 486/VGA, Ultima IX: Intel Pentium 233Mhz/VooDoo 3Dfx. Having worked on many of these games I realized that the programmers would always get the latest and greatest hardware at the beginning of the project and write the game to work well with that technology. The problem was that after 18 months of development, the code was already slow enough that the programmers were already screaming for hardware upgrades; after all those compile times were going to cut the company's productivity in half! It seemed that every Ultima was shipped requiring hardware that was considered bleeding edge only six to twelve months before. If you have a game that has a wide hardware requirement, make sure that at least one programmer has a second machine on his desk that matches the "dirtbag" minimum spec machine.

By the way, I think it is crazy to support 8-bit palettized displays in any game. This includes kids games or casual games. You can make a safe assumption that if a piece of hardware was bleeding edge five years ago, you'll find it in wide use in any casual gamer's hardware profile. Since the release of Windows 95, 16-bit displays were common, so I think it's a safe bet you don't have to support 8-bit displays. It's a good thing, too, because it's a real hassle to support 8-bit modes in a Windows compatible game.

Leaving 640x480 in the dust is a slightly harder decision if you are going for the low-end market. The two things that will limit you here are the ability to push pixels from system RAM to video memory (VRAM), and how much VRAM you have to play with. You'll find that low end machines with a 2Mb video card simply can't draw 800x600x16 screens with anything more than 35% overdraw before the frame rate will drop to the dismal teens.

Set every display related technology decision to meet your minimum frame rate goals. Consoles will require a minimum frame rate of 60fps, which is extremely difficult. Desktops can get away with much lower, but try to hit a minimum frame rate of 30fps.

To find your maximum theoretical frame rate, you first have to know how your game draws pixels: 2D, 3D, or a combination of the two. A sprite game generally copies memory from system RAM to VRAM, or from VRAM to VRAM, sometimes accomplishing some interesting blending tricks on the way. 3D games use software or hardware to fill a series of triangular areas of the screen with shaded color or texture data. Just in case it isn't completely obvious, these two methods are completely different and you have to use different methods of calculating your maximum theoretical frame rate.

A 2D sprite engine is easier to estimate. You can calculate your maximum theoretical frame rate by knowing something about your hardware and how you'll fill up the VRAM and system RAM. First look at the video hardware and find out the maximum transfer rate from system RAM to VRAM. There can be some tricky caveats to that, too, since some video cards transfer memory over different bus architectures (PCI, AGP, and so on), so be sure you have the proper transfer rate. Take a look at the transfer rate both directions, since you'll use a VRAM to system RAM copy to perform some of that interesting blending.

Once you have the transfer rates, take a look at your screen designs and try to estimate how much of the screen is going to be drawn every frame. You might discover that this figure exceeds 100% of the pixels. For example, if you have a multi-layered side scrolling fighting game, you'll be redrawing the background every frame as well as anything on top, such as the characters or special effects.

Take special note of anything that will use alpha blending or chroma-key. A completely opaque sprite, a rectangular shape that has no transparent or semi-transparent pixels, is essentially copied from memory to VRAM, an extremely fast operation. A sprite that has some completely transparent pixels must check the source sprite for a particular color value or chroma key before copying each pixel value. This is much slower, as pixel-per-pixel operations/comparisons use more CPU horsepower. The worst case, of course, is any sprite that uses semi-transparent pixels. This case requires both the source and destination pixels to have a blending calculation or lookup, which is much slower than a simple comparison and branch.

Clearly if your game design requires multiple layers of semi transparent sprites with an average of 180% pixels drawn per 800x600 frame, you won't accomplish this on an old Pentium 133Mhz and 2Mb video card. In fact, you'll find that 130% screen overdraw with simple chroma keyed sprites will still kill the frame rate of this old beast. If you are unlucky enough to be in the middle of this problem, you only have one reasonable solution: find a way to draw fewer pixels per frame. A good suggestion here is to attempt a dirty rectangle solution, where you draw only those parts of the screen that actually change.

Figuring your maximum frame rate on 3D games is a much trickier business, since there are many variables to consider. I'll start by making the assumption that your game is using VRAM intelligently for texturing and you are not thrashing textures into and out of VRAM. I'll also make the assumption that your rendering engine has a nice tricky way of skipping all hidden polygons, minimizing pixel overdraw. The big variables then become your polygon fill rate and your vertex transform rate. The fill rate is a measure of how fast your rasterizer can fill a polygonal area with the proper pixel values using lighting and texturing sources. The transform rate is how fast the rendering engine can message 3D world data and camera position into a list of 2D screen polygons with appropriate lighting data. Finally, many renderers put a reasonable cost on switching rendering states, such as loading new textures.

The thing that makes estimating these two variables and how they will affect your frame rate difficult is that most games don't have a scene that can be considered a standard benchmark. Good game and art designers will recognize that different scenes need varying levels of geometry and texture density. So what do you do?

If you are using an off the shelf renderer like Renderware or Intrinsic Alchemy, you've got excellent reference material in the games that have already shipped with the most recent version. Every middleware company out there will constantly improve their technology, and you can also count on getting some one-on-one help to get you over a frame rate hump. If set your game technology to target the upper end of the resolution and scene density of the top end of current games on the market, you'll be in good position to hit that target. If you happen to have someone like John Carmack on your team, of course, you can go a lot farther than that! The bottom line is you must take your team strength into consideration when choosing how far you want to push your maximum resolution.

Core Display Technology: 2D or 3D

Almost any game design can be executed in a 2D or 3D graphics engine. After all, PacMan™ was just a first generation shooter, wasn't it? I think it's a mistake to think that you have to choose a hot 3D graphics engine in order to sell more games. Instead, I'd like to believe that an excellent 2D game can set the world on fire simply due to a unique and focused game design. If you disagree with me you've probably never played Bedazzled or Tetris. The truth is that 2D and 3D graphics engines bring unique visualization possibilities to the table.

Before you read one more sentence make sure you understand an important point: *camera perspective has very little to do with the display engine.* This brash statement deserves repeating: Any game design requiring a particular perspective (first person, third person, and so on) can work in a 2D or 3D graphics engine if you are willing to make some concessions. The differences you'll find are primarily in five areas:

- Camera movement
- Game world design
- Art and animation
- Special effects
- Player expectation
- Cost and difficulty of production

Camera Movement

Camera movement is a primary constraint in a 2D engine. A 2D sprite engine can certainly depict a beautiful 3D world as was done in Myst or Riven, but it will never be able to move through that world like the player viewpoint in Unreal Tournament.

In Riven, the camera viewpoint didn't change in a continuous manner as you played the game (see Figure 2.1). The camera position and orientation were locked down and the player would interact with items they could see directly in front of the camera. The immense detail of the scene was simply too expensive to draw in real time. Pre-rendered backgrounds and environments are a great compromise to get a fantastic look at the expense of freedom of movement; so adventure games or puzzle games can make great use of this technique.

Diablo II was a fast-paced fantasy adventure game and the camera followed the movements of the player as shown in Figure 2.2. Because the camera never changed orientation, it was possible to draw the world with an enormous set of prebuilt pieces. Ultima games from Ultima I all the way to Ultima VIII were done in the same way.

Figure 2.1
Screenshots from Riven by Cyan.

It's important to note here that games like Ultima may have been drawn with sprites, but the game world had three dimensions. After all, how could the Avatar walk up a flight of stairs or climb on top of a roof if the world didn't have any depth?

Of course, lots more games use a simple sprite engine. This is quite common in kids games, trivia games, and other casual entertainment (see Figure 2.3).

Games that use 3D engines, on the other hand, have little or no constraints on their camera movement. The only thing you have to do is make sure that if the camera can look straight up and see the sky, that you put one there worth looking at!

Working on Ultima games was a dream come true for me, since I've played every single one of them, although I never finished Ultima VI for

Figure 2.2
Screenshots of Diablo II by Blizzard.

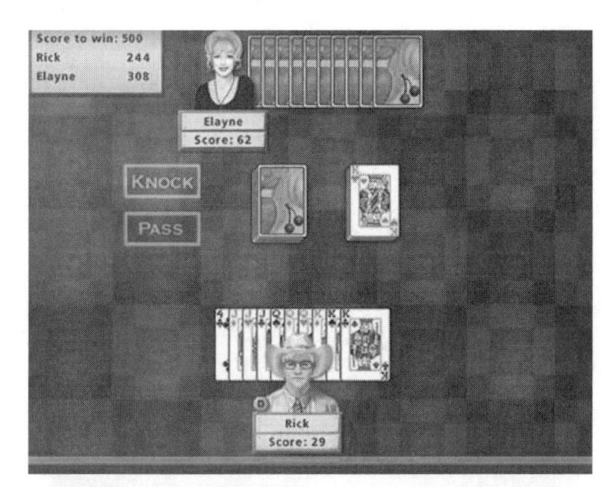

Figure 2.3
Screenshot of Hoyle Cards by Sierra and Marvel vs. Capcom 2 by Marvel/Capcom.

some reason. Richard wanted to move Ultima to a 3D engine for Ultima IX: Ascension and it was a real nightmare. Ultima games have always pushed a little too far with scene complexity and Ultima IX was no exception. The original design was going to use a third person camera in the same vein as classic Ultima games, but this time the camera was going to be able to swing around and show you the north and east sides of all the buildings! Richard really wanted to have a point of view camera, so the team obliged and put the camera right on the Avatar's shoulders. For the first time since Richard had been making Ultima games, some 18 years, he was able to walk right up to Lord British's castle gates and look up at the tower. It was nice to have a castle taller than 64 pixels.

Game World Design

The constraint you'll find in 3D engines is on your game world design. Perhaps that's an unfair statement. 3D engines will draw all the polygons you stuff into the graphics processing unit (GPU) even if it takes them forever. Forever, by the way, is defined as anything more than 50ms. The real problem a 3D engine has is choosing which polygons to draw to make the most compelling scene.

Consider the problem of a fight simulator like Microsoft Flight Simulator. When the plane is on the ground, the display looks a lot like every other 3D game out there. You see a few buildings, a few other planes, and a runway. You might also see some scenery in the distance like a mountain range or a city skyline (see Figure 2.4).

Once the plane is up in the air you have a different story altogether. You've increased the viewable surface by a few orders of magnitude, and therefore the potential viewable set of polygons. Anyone who attempts a naïve approach of simply drawing all the polygons will quickly learn that they can't get their plane more than 150 feet off the ground. The frame rate will fall in inverse geometric proportion to the altitude of the plane, because that's how many more polygons you have to draw to achieve a realistic look.

The actual approach to this problem uses different levels of detail to draw areas of terrain and objects depending on their distance from the viewer. On some flight simulators you can catch this happening. Simply begin a slow descent and watch as the terrain suddenly becomes better looking; the green patches will increase in detail and eventually become individual trees until you crash into them. One of the trickier parts of most 3D engines is getting the levels of detail to transition smoothly, avoiding the "popping" effect.

Another problem is avoiding overdraw. If your game is in a complex interior environment you'll achieve the fastest frame rate if you only draw the polygons that you

Figure 2.4
Screenshots of Microsoft Flight Simulator 2002 by Microsoft.

can see. Again the naîve approach is to simply draw all of the polygons in the view frustum, omitting any that are facing away from the camera. This solution will most likely result in extremely choppy frame rates in certain areas but not others, even if the camera is pointed straight at an interior wall. When the game is bogging down like this it is drawing an enormous number of polygons behind the wall, only to be covered up by the bigger polygons close to the camera. What a waste!

You'll need some advanced tools to help you analyze your level and calculate what areas can be seen given a particular viewing location. Renderware™ has a pretty good tool to do this. This analysis takes a long time, but the increase in performance is critical. Competitive games are all pushing the envelope for the illusion of extremely complicated worlds. The trick is to create these worlds such that the lines of sight are very short in areas of dense geometry and very long in areas of sparse geometry. Add to that mix of technology some nice levels of detail, and you can get a game that looks as good as Grand Theft Auto: Vice City, as shown in Figure 2.5.

Since 3D engines are only capable of drawing so much scenery per frame, an amazing amount of effort must go into creating the right level design. Any environment that is too dense must be fixed, or the frame rate will suffer and so will your reviews.

The most common mistake made on 3D games is not communicating with the artists about what the graphics engine can and can't do. Remember that the world environment is just a backdrop, and you'll still need to add interactive objects, characters, special effects, and a little bit of user interface before you can call it a day. All these things,

Figure 2.5
Screenshots of Grand Theft Auto: Vice City by Rockstar.

especially the characters, will drag your performance into the ground if the background art was too aggressive. Try to establish CPU budgets for drawing the background, objects, characters, and special effects early on and hold your artists and level designers to it like glue. Measure the CPU time spent preparing and rendering these objects and display it for all to see.

Art and Animation

A clear difference between 2D and 3D display technologies is the creation and presentation of art assets. While 2D sprites and 3D textures are quite similar, nothing in a 2D engine resembles animating or morphing 3D meshes. As you might expect, a 3D engine can use any 2D sprite trickery in its textures, making you think at first glance that a 3D engine will always be superior to a 2D engine.

A closer look at the visual results of a well directed 2D effort will cause you to think twice. Perhaps you'll come to believe that there is a place for 2D engines even in today's market. Now that I've confused you into second guessing your decision to go with the latest 3D engine, let's study the issues a bit and try to bring some focus to the problem. Technology aside, your decision to use 2D versus 3D will have interesting side effects:

- Storage requirements of dynamic objects, such as characters
- The "look and feel" of your game

Let's compare two games from Origin Systems: Ultima Online and Ultima IX. Ultima Online's technology was sprite based, while Ultima IX was a custom 3D engine. Both games are shown in Figure 2.6.

What's interesting and somewhat unexpected is that the art for both games was created by 3D Studio Max. Given the same camera angle, both characters look very similar. When you watch them move, however, you can begin to understand what concessions you have to make if you choose 2D.

Ultima Online characters were pre-rendered, which means that every conceivable position of their bodies had to be saved in a huge set of sprites that would be animated in the right sequence to make them move. The only difference between that manner of animation and how Tex Avery brought Bugs Bunny to life was the fact that Tex used pen and ink instead of 3D Studio Max.

What made matters worse for the Ultima Online artists is that they had to pre-render all possible animations in each direction any character or monster could walk: sixteen points of the compass in all. Table 2.1 shows the ramifications of this.

Figure 2.6
Screenshots of Ultima IX: Ascension and Ultima Online by Origin Systems.

Table 2.1 Storage Required for Different Activities.

Activity	Storage
Total animations (walk, run, stand, idle, kick, jump, crouch, ...)	24
Average frames of animation (2 seconds at 15 frames per second)	30
Total directions of the compass (N, NNW, NW, WNW, W, ...)	16
Total frames of animation (24 * 30 * 16)	11,520
Uncompressed size of one frame of animation assuming 50x50 pixels, 8 bit art (50 * 50)	2.44Kb
Total uncompressed animation size (11,520 * 2.44Kb)	27.41Mb

This seems completely unreasonable, doesn't it? How can so many games fit so much animation data on the CD-ROM? A little compression and some cheating will cut that number down to size. Most compression techniques will give you at least a 3:1 compression ratio on sprites, especially since a good portion of those sprites are made up of the background color. You'll want a compression algorithm that has a blazing decompression solution or you'll notice some nasty slowdowns in your game. You'll also want to be smart about decompressing sprites only when you need to; preferably when a level is loading. Compressing the animation sprites brings our storage of the main character down to 9.13Mb:

```
Uncompressed animations @ 27.41 Mb compressed at 3:1      = 9.13 Mb
```

The next little trick requires a bit of concession on your part to make your characters ambidextrous. Take a look at the two characters shown in Figure 2.7.

It's subtle, but notice that the same creature holds his weapon differently depending on what direction he's facing. Since the character is ventrally symmetrical it makes little difference if you draw a mirror image instead of an actual image. The only hang up is the handedness of the character. When the mirror image is drawn, a weapon that sits in the right hand will suddenly appear in the left hand. At first you might think this will detract from the game. When you consider this technique can store nearly twice the number of animations in the same space you'll come to the conclusion that gamers want those animations and could care less about whether they are beating you up left handed.

It turns out that all the eastward or westward sprites can be flipped, so our sixteen directions can drop to nine. This takes the total amount of storage space down to a much more reasonable number:

Figure 2.7
Ambidextrous Creatures from Ultima Online.

```
Dropping to 9 directions from the original 16                 = 5.13Mb
```

Assuming that the main character has four or perhaps five times the number of animations as every other character in your game, you'll be happy to find that even 50Mb will give you plenty of room to store people, animals, monsters, and anything else you'd like to dream up. 3D games store their art very differently, as you would expect. The original dataset for a dynamic object in a 3D game contains, at a minimum, the following things:

- *Mesh*: A definition of the geometry of the character given by lists of vertices, triangles, and bones.
- *Textures*: A set of textures that will be applied to the mesh.
- *Animation Data*: Lists of positions, orientations, and timing that can be applied to some or all parts of the character mesh.

For comparison purposes let's construct a character similar to the sprite based one we just studied. This character should have similar animation characteristics.

A character rendered offline in 3D Studio Max can have tens of thousands of polygons. If you recall the number of actual pixels in the entire 2D sprite, 2,500, you'll quickly realize that there's no use in creating a model of that complexity for real-time display. In fact, you'll probably be satisfied with no more than 300 or 400 polygons if the character is only taking up 1/10th of the screen height. I think the first rendering of the Avatar in Ultima XI was down to below 200 polygons, but it was pretty obvious in the joints and he was wearing a full-face helmet. The polygon count per character is purely a judgment call and there's no hard and fast rule except for *get it as small as you can*.

A 3D character of similar complexity to our 2D one would have very different storage characteristics as shown in Table 2.2.

It doesn't take a moron to notice the staggering difference in the space savings if you go for a 3D representation of your characters. You don't get any of this for free; the amount of CPU horsepower it takes to draw one horizontal line of pixels on a textured and lit polygon on a hierarchical 3D character running around a 3D world is a hell of a lot more than a *mov* instruction.

That extra CPU budget buys you plenty of things you simply can't get with a sprite engine. One of the best examples is mixing animations. Since animation data is stored as positions and orientations of the bones they affect from keyframe to keyframe it is a simple matter to mix two animations even if they affect the same bones. If the main character had a limping animation it could be mixed with the walk animation in varying

Table 2.2 Storage Characteristics for a 3D Character.

Activity	Storage
Total animations (walk, run, stand, idle, kick, jump, crouch, ...)	24
Average keyframes per animation (1 keyframe every 100ms, average animation is 2 seconds long)	20
Total directions of the compass	1
Total animation keyframes (24 * 20 * 1)	480
Uncompressed size of animation keyframe (25 bones with position and orientation data, 28 bytes each)	700 bytes
Total uncompressed animation size (240 * 700 bytes)	~328 Kb
Uncompressed size of the character mesh (400 polys @ ~20 bytes each)	8,000 bytes
Uncompressed size of the character texture (64x64, 16 bit)	8,192 bytes
Total uncompressed size of the character:	**~344 Kb**

degrees as the main character took damage. The effect is a subtle and continuous degradation of the character's walk. A sprite engine would simply use one animation or the other depending on the level of damage. Clearly the 3D engine provides a better solution.

Sprite games like Ultima Online: The Second Age put amazing effort into the ability for characters to wear different kinds of clothing or carry different weapons. Since it is a sprite game, each piece of clothing and each weapon must be pre-rendered in place for each possible animation. Imagine that the number of frames for every item in your game world had as many frames of animation as each main character. Ultima Online has tens of thousands of individual sprites to achieve this look.

A 3D game on the other hand can simply attach a weapon like a sword or a gun to an attachment point at the end of the main character's arm, essentially creating one more bone of animation data. This adds only about 13Kb to the animation data, and it works the same way for all weapons of that type.

Mixing 2D and 3D Technologies

I always preach that you should use the right tool for the right job. 2D is great if you want to control every last pixel on the screen but falls far short of being as flexible as a 3D engine. There are plenty of games out there that take advantage of both technologies. They generally do this by using 3D Studio Max or even hand painted art to draw static backgrounds and use 3D to draw dynamic objects and characters.

Figure 2.8
Screenshots of Grim Fandango by Lucas Arts.

Grim Fandango

This is one of my all time favorite games. The use of mixing 2D and 3D display technology is only shadowed by the brilliant design, especially the dialogue. If you haven't played it you should add it to your to do list.

Look at Figure 2.8 and you can tell immediately that the sets were created and pre-rendered in something like Max or perhaps Softimage. This game came out in 1998, when it was impossible to render these environments in real time with such accurate lighting effects. The characters achieved a very interesting look with very few polygons, which enabled Grim Fandango to run on computers without hardware acceleration.

The 3D characters could walk behind objects in the 3D sets, which could be achieved as easily as layered sprites but with today's hardware a pre-rendered depth buffer would be a better choice. Modern art tools like 3D Studio Max give artists the option of rendering the depth buffer along with the RGB channels, so generating this data is a piece of cake.

The characters reacted to things in their environment. The main character, Manny Calavera, would turn his head to look at interesting objects and he would stop walking when he ran into a solid object. Lucas Arts probably created a custom tool to create and maintain this data, but if they were going to do the same thing today they could simply use 3D Studio Max. Dummy objects and user data can go a long way to providing everything your game needs to make Manny take a longing glance at his would-be girlfriend, Mercedes Colomar.

Video Driver and Performance Issues

Hybrid 2D and 3D technologies can cause quite a bit of trouble for video drivers. Most drivers are written with the assumption that graphics applications will be all 2D or all 3D and nothing in between. Mixing 2D and 3D calls will cause the card to flush any pending operation such as drawing a set of polygons. This causes performance to drop significantly.

Graphics performance is optimized if the CPU and the GPU are working full speed 100% of the time. You can imagine two railroad workers hammering in a spike, each striking the spike in opposite rhythm from each other. If their timing is perfect they can cut the time it takes to perform their task in half. If their timing is exactly wrong, their work will come to a complete halt, since they'll constantly hit each other instead of their target. The same is true for optimizing your graphics performance.

An excellent graphics programmer can write the graphics pipeline to minimize any stalling. The CPU and GPU work at nearly 100% efficiency each on their own tasks. As soon as the GPU finishes drawing something the CPU has already provided it with the next set and it never skips a beat. This beautiful scenario is utterly destroyed if you mix 2D and 3D graphics calls. You'll need to do this if you have 2D and 3D objects sorting on top of each other in the same screen. Some graphics hardware and video drivers misbehave badly if you attempt to use hardware acceleration. You could see corrupt graphics, terrible performance, and even the dreaded blue screen of death.

There are a few solutions to this problem, given a few assumptions in your game design.

- *Draw everything in 3D*: 2D sprites are just a degenerate case of an arbitrary 3D polygon that happens to lie in parallel with the screen and doesn't use perspective transformations.
- *Draw 2D and 3D in different passes*: Draw all your 2D sprites at once, then your 3D polygons, and blend the two buffers.

The only problem moving to a completely 3D engine is that your game will require a 3D video card. This might be fine if you are making the latest iteration of Unreal Tournament, but probably not such a good idea if you are making Microsoft Casino.

Microsoft clearly didn't understand this concept when they proposed the API for DirectX 8, which dropped the DirectDraw API completely in favor of a "unified" graphics API. When I used DirectX 8 for the first time and saw the error message in my compiler: "Warning: Undefined symbol BltFast," I thought that they must have renamed it. I searched for the method in the DirectX help. Imagine my horror when I found that not only was BltFast missing, so was the entire DirectDraw interface! I sent an email to a friend of mine on the DirectX team asking about the missing API. The conversation went something like this:

Mr.Mike: So, let me make sure I understand this completely. You nuked DirectDraw from DX8?

DirectX Buddy: Yeah! Isn't it great?

Mr.Mike: How do I draw my game backgrounds?

DirectX Buddy: Oh that's easy. Just draw them as 3D polygons.

Mr.Mike: Won't that be terribly slow?

DirectX Buddy: Not at all. Hardware acceleration makes drawing polygons really fast.

Mr.Mike: Yeah...if I make the min spec require a 3D video card.

DirectX Buddy: Everyone loves 3D video cards! They're everywhere! No one uses 2D only video cards anymore.

Mr.Mike: Oh yeah? Did you happen to notice that four of the top ten PC games last Christmas were all 2D games like Hoyle Casino, Who Wants to be a Millionaire, and the Sims?

DirectX Buddy: Well..., uh......

...and the coups de grace...

Mr.Mike: Did you realize that the game I'm currently working on, Microsoft Casino, has a min spec that doesn't include 3D hardware?

DirectX Buddy: I'll get back to you.

It turned out that DirectDraw was miraculously back in DirectX 9. Go figure.

Drawing 2D and 3D in different passes actually works quite well. If your polygons sort in one layer with the 2D sprites you can render all your 3D polygons to an off-screen buffer, and blit the entire thing as one sprite. If you need to intersort 2D sprites and 3D polygons use a depth buffer. Create the depth buffer by associating a depth measurement with each layer of 2D sprites; when each 2D sprite is drawn make the associated entries into the depth buffer. Use this depth buffer when you send the 3D polygons into the GPU, and the polygons will sort correctly with the 2D sprites just as if they had been drawn as polygons.

Do I Have to Use DirectX?

If your game is on any console, even the Xbox, you already know the answer to this question. Skip ahead a bit and let the PC programmers worry about this section. The rest of you PC programmers have to consider whether to use DirectX in your game or try an alternative API for graphics, sound, input, or network communications.

Just to be perfectly clear, this section has nothing to do with how to draw a shaded polygon under Direct3D. This section is going to enlighten you about why you would choose something like OpenGL over Direct3D, or straight TCP/IP over DirectPlay. Believe it or not, the choice isn't clear-cut no matter what your religious beliefs.

It's not possible for me to be more tired of the religious nature of the OpenGL/DirectX debate. Any good programmer should understand what's under the hood of every API if you have to make a choice between them. Disregarding DirectX simply because Microsoft made it is asinine.

Design Philosophy of DirectX

DirectX was designed to sit between the application and the hardware. If the hardware was capable of performing an action itself DirectX would call the driver and be done with it. If the hardware wasn't there, such as an older video card not having a hardware transform and lighting pipeline, DirectX would emulate the call in software. Clearly that would be much slower.

One thing that was gained by this design philosophy was a single API for every hardware combination that supported DirectX. Back in the old days (that would be the early 1990s), programmers weren't so lucky. A great example was all the work that needed to be done for sound systems. Origin supported Adlib, Roland, and SoundBlaster with separate bits of code. Graphics were similar; the old EGA graphics standard was completely different than Hercules. What a pain!

Of course, DirectX isn't the simplest API to learn. COM is a weird thing to look at if you aren't used to it. It also seems weird to have fifty lines of code to initialize a 3D rendering surface when OpenGL does it so much easier. Herein lies the root of the religious argument: old time C versus newfangled COM. Get over it long enough to understand it.

DirectX exposes a lot more about what the hardware is capable of doing. Those CAPS bits can tell you if your video card can support hardware transform and lighting (T&L) for example, and perhaps that means you'll load up denser geometry or simply bring up a dialog box telling some loser that he needs a better video card. Your customer service people will thank you if you decide to leave the word "loser" out of the error message.

Direct3D or OpenGL

I'm not going to preach to you about why DirectX sucks and why OpenGL is God's gift. Instead, I hope to give you enough knowledge about how and why you would judge one against the other with the goal of making the best choice for your game, your team, and the good people that will throw money at you to play your latest game. I'm sure to get lovely emails about this section. Bring it on. I'm going to take a weirder tack on this argument anyway. Both APIs will get you a nice looking game. There are plenty of middleware rendering engines that support both. What does that tell you? It tells me that while there may be interesting bits and pieces here and there that are unique, the basic job of pushing triangles to the video card is essentially equivalent.

You don't have control over the quality of the driver. I'm sure we could find OpenGL drivers that suck, and we can certainly find Direct3D drivers that never should have seen the light of day. Given that unfortunate reality, you'd like to choose the API that has the best drivers for all the people who will play your game.

If you have a hard core title like Unreal Tournament you're pretty safe in choosing OpenGL, since the drivers for high end cards tend to have a high quality. Of course, the Direct3D drivers for these same cards are going to be equally good, since they're high-end cards after all. Your choice gets murkier if your game has a wider appeal and perhaps runs on older machines. It's a safe bet that there are more video cards out there that have Direct3D drivers than OpenGL drivers, and that on the low end cards the Direct3D drivers are going to be better.

Why is this true? The video card companies making low end cards had to make a choice too, and allocate resources to write drivers. They generally chose Direct3D first and got that driver out the door and on the install disk. The OpenGL driver might come later on the website, if they had time and resources to do it. Again, this points to the fact that a hard core audience will likely have OpenGL drivers on a rocking video card, because they sought it out.

The mass market went where they were told: Direct3D. I guess that's where you should go too, if you are doing a game with mass market appeal. Hard core games can make whatever choice they like.

DirectSound or Miles Sound by RAD Game Tools

For sound and video, I don't look any farther than RAD Game Tools, Inc. The Miles Sound System includes full source code, has a flat license fee, and works on Win32 and Macintosh. The Bink Video tools are cross platform and support Xbox, Gamecube, Win32, and Macintosh. Check out the latest at www.radgametools.com. It doesn't hurt that RAD has been in business since 1988 and has licensed their technology for thousands of games. They are probably the most used middleware company in the industry.

Miles can use DirectSound as a lower layer. This is quite convenient if you want to do some odd thing that Miles can't. The real nail in the coffin for DirectSound is that it doesn't include the ability to decode MP3 files. Part of your license fee for Miles pays for a license to decode MP3s, which are a fantastic alternative to storing bloated WAV files or weird sounding MIDIs. Bottom line, do yourself a favor and get Miles for your game.

DirectInput or Roll Your Own

DirectInput encapsulates the translation of hardware generated messages to something your game can use directly. This mapping isn't exactly rocket science, and most programmers can code the most used portions of DirectInput with their eyes closed. The weirder input devices, like the force feedback joysticks that look like an implement of torture, plug right into DirectInput. DirectInput also abstracts the device so that you can write one body of code for your game, whether or not your players have the weirdest joystick on the block.

DirectPlay, TCP, or UDP

This decision used to be easy. Action games were UDP. Most other Internet games were TCP. Nothing used DirectPlay. Since DirectX 8 was released, this decision isn't quite so clear cut, and it has to do with the way DirectPlay has changed in the last few years. When DirectPlay was first released its major breakthrough, if that's not going to far, was to provide a standard API by which you could communicate through any connection: modem, serial cable, IPX, or IP. Almost every multiplayer game out at the time used IPX for LAN games or the Internet protocols: TCP and UDP. I never actually played a game modem to modem and I never wanted to.

Client/server games under earlier versions of DirectPlay had horrible performance. I'm not talking about ten or fifteen players here, I'm talking about thousands like on Ultima Online. The login system was the only Windows based server and we used TCP with good old WINSOCK2. Its performance wasn't fantastic either, but it was light-years ahead of DirectPlay.

It turned out that the implementation of some critical Winsock statements, namely `select()`, had increasingly bad performance under a high number of connected clients. It turned out that there was a better way under Windows NT, and it used an interesting method called *I/O completion ports*. Without dragging you into too many details, suffice it to say that this method didn't degrade linearly with the number of connected clients. It easily handled thousands of simultaneous connections per server. It actually performed better under similar circumstances than Berkley sockets under Linux.

By the time DirectX 8 was going through its API review, it was obvious to the DirectPlay engineers at Microsoft that something had to be done. The entire module was rewritten from the ground up, incorporating optimizations such as I/O completion ports if they were available and made excellent progress towards an API that was actually more useful than straight TCP or UDP.

This is especially true for those programmers unfamiliar with Internet programming. Getting a socket set up between two computers is a piece of cake. Anyone could do it. What's not so simple is what to do when the connection is dropped. If it was unintentional you'll need to keep the socket session alive to reestablish it when the client reattaches. An intentional drop will have to be recognized eventually and cleaned up. There are plenty of special cases that must be covered even under simple TCP, and they will drive the beginner completely crazy. Don't go without a license.

It's important to know that DirectPlay is a UDP based system that has the ability to send guaranteed messages a'la TCP, without all the overhead of TCP. That won't convince the UDP hard liners out there but I hope it entices them to take a look at it.

DirectShow versus Bink

Someone out there is going to think someone at RAD Game Tools paid me off to constantly squawk about the virtue of using their wares in your game. I'd happily accept a couple of Bink licenses for the effort because it simply is the easiest way to get a big fat movie squashed into something that can make a nice intro. DirectShow is a streaming multimedia API designed to play back video files using codecs that are already installed in the machine. This is not going to help you when you're tight for space.

Bink is a decompression and playback API that comes with its own compression tool. The compression is gamer friendly, too. Unlike other codecs, it allows you to do nutty things like skip every other horizontal line of video. Sure, it looks a little darker but it compresses to half of the original size. Use Bink and save yourself some grief.

DirectMusic versus Rolling Your Own

DirectMusic was designed in the hopes that the CPU could choose the right music to play given certain input parameters. When I heard about this API for the first time I thought that the DirectX engineers had too much time on their hands. There might have been something of a use for it at one time, when computer music was mixed on the fly from bits and pieces just a few measures long.

Most music is digitally recorded, and plays for quite some time before changing to another piece. Usually transition measures exist if you have to pick up the pace and fly into a hard banging combat tune from something quieter. That might make you want to look into DirectMusic to see if it will help. Resist the urge.

Music can give players a huge emotional charge. You can give them a clue that something wicked this way comes. A good composer is going to know how he wants the various pieces to transition and he'll throttle you if you give this control away. If you don't believe me, play the DirectMusic samples yourself. If they're good enough for you, more power to you.

User Interface Code

A game without a user interface isn't much more than a screen saver. User interface code for games is quite a bit different than the user interface for other software, for two different reasons. First, Microsoft Word doesn't need a joystick, and it probably never will. Games have an amazing variety of user input devices: joysticks, steering wheels, and even fishing poles. The fishing pole has always amazed me. I just can't imagine fishing on my computer, but hey there are tens of thousands of computer fishing enthusiasts that will disagree with me.

Second, the user interface for a game doesn't look like the standard Windows GDI. They have a creative flair, and they should. This means that the user interface code needs to be baked fresh, especially since most operating systems don't have a standard user interface control for a health meter.

The irony of this is that games still need things like a text control, so players can easily enter strings of text for their name or the names of save game files. These controls aren't hard to write, but if you're like me you hate rewriting something that already exists and is well understood by both coders and players. Even so, it is difficult to get a game to hook into things like the Windows GDI because Windows doesn't understand complicated graphics systems that commonly exist in games. Bottom line: You'll probably roll your own, and hopefully keep that code around from game to game so you won't have to rewrite it ever again.

Resource Caching

This is one of those hidden systems I told you about. A game like Grand Theft Auto: Vice City has gigabytes of art and sound, and the CPU only has a fraction of the memory, perhaps less than one hundred megabytes. Imagine the problem of getting a crowd of people out of a burning building. Left to their own devices, the crowd will panic, attempt to force themselves through every available exit, and only a small fraction of the people will escape alive.

Now imagine another scenario, where the evacuation was completely organized. The crowd would divide themselves into single file lines, each line going out the nearest exit. If the lines didn't cross, people could almost run. It would be very likely that even a large building could be completely evacuated.

This analogy works well for game resources. The burning building is your optical media, and the doors are the limited bandwidth you have for streaming this media. The bits on the disk represent the crowd. Your job is to figure out a way to get as many of the bits from the optical media into memory in the shortest possible time. That's not the entire problem, though. A resource cache is exactly what the name implies—commonly used assets like the graphic for a mouse pointer are always in memory, and rarely used assets like the cinematic endgame are only in memory while it's playing, and most likely only a piece of it at that.

The resource cache manages assets like these in a way that fools the game into thinking that they are always in memory. If everything works well the game will never have to wait for anything, since the resource cache should be smart enough to predict which assets will be used and load them before they are needed.

Every now and then the cache might miscalculate and suffer a cache miss. Depending on the resource, the game might be able to continue without it until it has been loaded, such as the graphics for an object in the far distance. In that case the graphic can fade in once it is safely in memory. In other cases, the game isn't so lucky, such as a missing audio file for a character's lines. Since they are synched to the facial animations, the game has to wait until the audio is loaded before the character can begin speaking.

So, it's not enough to write a little cache that knows whether resources exist in memory at the moment they are needed. It has to be clever, predicting the future to some extent and even providing the game with a backup in case the cache suffers a miss.

The Main Loop

Most Windows software waits for the user to do something before they run any code. If the mouse isn't moving and the keyboard isn't being hammered, the application is completely idle. This is good for things like Microsoft Word and other applications because you can have a bunch of them up and running without a large CPU overhead. Games are completely different. Games are simulations that have a life of their own. Without player input, they'll happily send some horrific creature over to start pounding on your character's skull. That will probably motivate a few key presses.

The system that controls this ongoing activity is the main loop, and it has three major components: grabbing and translating player input, simulating the game world, and rendering the screen.

Player input is mapping changes in input devices like the mouse, a joystick, or the keyboard into game events. An example of this might be something like a keyboard event, such as pressing the "W" key, translated into a game event such as "add one meter per second to the player's forward speed." Notice that the event wasn't "move forward"—that implies that the game state is changed from within the user interface code, which would be a big mistake. The reasons for this are discussed in more detail in Chapter 5.

A body of code that simulates the world is usually broken down into discrete bits of very simple code, such as a bit of code to move an object along a linear path or rotate it at a given angular velocity. These bits of code can be combined to act on a single game object, which will have the effect of combining these movements. These bits of code are usually organized into classes, and can be instantiated for any game object. These classes can even have dependencies on each other, where one will wait for another to complete before starting. A good example of this is something you might use for a Molotov cocktail: one class tracks the parabolic movement of any game object until it collides with something, and another class creates a fireball explosion. Your game can string these classes together to create some amazingly cool effects.

The game renderer's job is drawing the screen as fast as it possibly can. It is decoupled from both the user interface and the game simulation code so that it will scale appropriately on different computers with a wide range of CPU power and under different game conditions. Generally, lower-end CPUs will cut expensive features to run at the best frame rate they can, but you'll always have a varying frame rate. Different game conditions will also place varying loads on even the best CPUs, and decoupling the renderer from the rest of the game code is the best way to manage this problem.

Other Bits and Pieces

There are tons of other bits and pieces to coding games, many of which you'll discover in the next chapter. These things defy classification, but they are every bit as important to games as a good random number generator.

Beyond that you'll find some things important to game coding such as how to convince Microsoft Windows to become a good platform for your game—a more difficult task than you'd think. Microsoft makes almost all of its income from the sales of business software like Microsoft Office, and the operating system reflects that. Sure, DirectX is supposed to be the hardcore interface for game coders, but you'll find that it's something of a black sheep even within Microsoft. Don't get me wrong, it works and works surprisingly well, but you can't ever forget that you are forcing a primarily business software platform to become a game platform, and sometimes you'll run into dead-ends.

Debugging and testing games is much more difficult than other software, mostly because there's a lot going on in real time and there are gigabytes of data files that can harbor nasty bugs. Combine that with the menagerie of game hardware like video cards, audio cards, user input devices, and even operating systems, it's a wonder that games work as well as they do. It's no secret that games are considered to be the most unstable software on the market, and it reflects the difficulty of the problem.

There are also a number of software development practices that work extremely well in game development—stuff that you'll think belongs in a government coding gulag for the DoD. Most game programmers shun this stuff—things like code reviews and build scripts and even source control, because if they wanted to work that way they would have applied to places like Computer Sciences Corporation or NASA. It turns out that these practices exist in these houses because of the risk of failure. A bug in a navigation system or flight control can kill people. Games don't share that problem, thankfully. Game code is extremely complicated and if you don't have some measure of discipline in your work, you'll spend more time chasing bugs than making your game fun. Remember that game code is still programming, just like everywhere else, and the application of process and discipline will result in a superior product. That's a software engineering way of saying you'll make a kick-ass game that's a blast to play, and hopefully a blast to make.

Chapter 3

"Dumb Stuff" All Game Programmers Should Know

The art of developing great game code involves knowing which mistakes and pitfalls to avoid and which coding techniques really work over time. The one important thing that I've learned over the years is that the distance between exuberance and experience is paved with mistakes, which makes older programmers a little less likely to embrace new things.

My goal in this chapter is to set the foundation for the coding techniques that we'll use throughout this book. I call this material the "dumb stuff" that you should know not because of its lack of importance but because it is the kind of techniques and advice that will make you feel really stupid if you don't use them properly.

We'll start by looking at design practices that you should always consider when writing a game and then we'll move on and look at specific programming techniques such as working with pointers, memory management, how to avoid memory leaks, working with scripting languages, and many other goodies. In the last part of the chapter I'll provide you with a few coding tools taken from my own personal toolbox that I usually employ to develop games for companies such as Microsoft and Origin.

Design Practices You Shouldn't Live Without

Isaac Asimov's Foundation series invented an interesting discipline called psycho-history, a social science that could predict societal trends and macro events with great certainty. Each historian in the story was required to contribute new formulas and extend the science. As a programmer, your job is similar. Every new module or class that you create gives you the opportunity to extend the abilities and usefulness of the code base. But to do this effectively, you must learn how to think ahead and design code with the goal of keeping it in use for many projects and many years.

Designing good code in an object-oriented language is actually much more difficult than in a procedural language like C or PASCAL. Why? The power and flexibility of the object-oriented language allows you to create extremely complicated systems that look quite simple. This is both good and bad. In other words, it's easy to get yourself into trouble without realizing it.

If you design your software properly your work can be extremely efficient. With a few keystrokes you can create interesting adaptations of existing systems. There's nothing like having such command and control over a body of code. It makes you more artist than programmer.

A different programmer might view your masterpiece entirely differently, however. For example, intricate relationships inside a class hierarchy could be difficult or impossible to understand without your personal guidance. Documentation, usually written in haste, is almost always inadequate or even misleading.

To help you avoid some of the common design practice pitfalls I'm going to spend some time in this chapter up-front discussing how you can:

- Avoid hidden code that performs nontrivial operations
- Keep your class hierarchies clear and simple
- Be aware of the difference between inheritance and containment
- Avoid abusing virtual functions
- Use interface classes and factories
- Separate user interface code from game logic
- Use stream constructors

Avoiding Hidden Code and Nontrivial Operations

Copy constructors, operator overloads, and destructors are all party to the "nasty" hidden code problem which plague game developers. This kind of code is terrible unless it is completely obvious. You should avoid copy constructors and operator overloads that perform non-trivial operations. If something looks simple, it should be simple and not something deceptive. For example, most programmers would assume that if they encountered some code that contained a simple equals sign or multiplication symbol that the it would not invoke some kind of near-infinite Taylor series. They would assume that the code under the hood would be as straightforward as it looked—a basic calculation between two `floats` or at worst two `doubles`.

Game programmers love playing with neat technology, and sometimes their sense of elegance drives them to push non-trivial algorithms and calculations into C++ constructs such as copy constructors or overloaded operators. They like it because the high level code performs complicated actions in a few lines of code, and on the surface it seems like the right design choice. It isn't.

Any operation with some meat to it should be called explicitly. This might annoy your sense of cleanliness if you are the kind of programmer that likes to use C++ constructs at each and every opportunity. Get over it. Of course there are exceptions. One is when every operation on a particular class is comparatively expensive, such as a 4x4 matrix class. Overloaded operators are perfectly fine for classes like this because the clarity of the resulting code is especially important and useful.

A recurring theme I'll present throughout this book is that you should avoid surprises. Programmers don't like surprises because most of them are incredibly bad surprises. Don't add to the problem by tucking some crazy piece of code away in a destructor or similar mechanism.

Class Hierarchies: Keep Them Simple

One of the biggest mistakes game programmers make is that they either over-design or under-design their classes and class hierarchies. Getting your class structure just right takes some real practice. Unfortunately, most of my experience came the hard way through trial and error. But you can learn from some of my mistakes and unique techniques that I've picked up along the way.

My first project at Origin developed with C++ was Ultima VII. This project turned out to be a poster child for insane C++. I was so impressed by the power of constructors, virtual functions, inheritance, and everything else that once I got the basics down I went nuts and made sure to use at least three C++ constructs on every line of code. What a horrible mistake! Some Ultima VII classes were seven or eight levels of inheritance deep. Some classes added only one data member to the parent—our impotent attempt at extending base classes.

We created so many classes in Ultima VII that we ran out of good names to use. The compiler was so taxed by the end of the project that we couldn't add any more variables to the namespace. We used global variables to store more than one piece of data by encoding it in the high and low words rather than creating two new variables. By the end of the project I was terrified of adding any new code, because the compiler would fail to build the project having hit some crazy limitation.

On the opposite end of the spectrum a common problem found in C++ programs is the "kitchen sink" class—the one that has everything (including the kitchen sink). Ultima VII actually had a C++ file named ksink.cpp, and sure enough it had a little bit of everything. I'll admit to creating such a class on one of the Microsoft Casino projects that I worked on that would have made intelligent programmers sick to their stomachs. My class was supposed to encapsulate the data and methods of a screen, but it ended up looking a little like MFC's `CWnd` class. It was huge, unwieldy, and simply threw everything into one gigantic bucket of semi colons and braces.

Don't make the same mistake. Good class architecture is not like a Swiss Army Knife; it should be more like a well balanced throwing knife.

Inheritance vs. Containment

Game programmers love to debate the topics of inheritance and containment. Inheritance is used when an object is evolved from another object, or when a child object *is* a version of the parent object. Containment is used when an object is composed of multiple discrete components, or when an aggregate object *has* a version of the contained object.

A good example of this relationship is found in user interface code. A screen class might have the methods and data to contain multiple controls such as buttons or check boxes. The classes that implement buttons and check boxes probably inherit from a base control class.

When you make a choice about inheritance or containment your goal is to communicate the right message to other programmers. The resulting assembly code is almost exactly the same, barring the oddities of virtual function tables. This means the CPU doesn't give a damn if you inherit or contain. Your fellow programmers will care, so be careful and clear.

Virtual Functions Gone Bad

Virtual functions are powerful creatures that are abused by most programmers. I've found that programmers create virtual functions when they don't need them or they create long chains of overloaded virtual functions that make it difficult to maintain base classes.

Take a look at MFC's class hierarchy. Most of the classes in the hierarchy contain virtual functions which are overloaded by inherited classes, or by new classes created by application programmers. Imagine for a moment the massive effort involved if some assumptions at the top of the hierarchy were changed. This isn't a problem for MFC because it's a stable code base, but your game code isn't a stable code base. Not yet.

An insidious bug is often one that is created innocently by a programmer mucking around in a base class. A seemingly benign change to a virtual function can have unexpected results. Some programmers might count on the oddities of the behavior of the base class that, if they were fixed, will actually break any child classes. Maybe one of these days someone will write an IDE that graphically shows the code that will be affected by any change to a virtual function. Without this aid, any programmer changing a base class must learn (the hard way) for themselves what hell they are about to unleash.

PRACTICE BEST

If you ever change the nature of anything that is currently in wide use, virtual functions included, I suggest you actually change its name. The compiler will find each and every use of the code and you'll be forced to look at how the original was put to use. It's up to you if you want to keep the new name. I suggest you do, even if it means changing every source file.

From one point of view, a programmer overloads a virtual function because the child class has more processing to accomplish in the same "chain of thought." This concept is incredibly useful and I've used it for nearly ten years. It's funny that I never thought how wrong it can be.

An overloaded virtual function changes the behavior of an object, and gains control over whether to invoke the original behavior. If the new object doesn't invoke the original function at all, the object is essentially different from the original. What makes this problem even worse it that everything about the object screams to programmers that it is just an extension of the original. If you have a different object, make a different object. Consider containing the original class instead of inheriting from it. It's much clearer in the code when you explicitly refer to a method attached to a contained object rather than calling a virtual function.

What happens to code reuse? Yes, have some. I hate duplicating code; I'm a lazy typist and I'm very unlucky when it comes to cutting and pasting code. It also offends me.

Try to look at classes and their relationships like appliances and electrical cords. Always seek to minimize the length of the extension cords, minimize the appliances that plug into one another, and don't make a nasty tangle that you have to figure out every time you want to turn something on.

Use Interface Classes

Interface classes are those that contain nothing but pure virtual functions. Here's an example:

```
class IAnimation
{
public:
   virtual void VAdvance(const int deltaMilliseconds) = 0;
   virtual bool const VAtEnd() const = 0;
   virtual int const VGetPosition() const = 0;
};
```

This sample interface class defines simple behavior common for a timed animation. We could add other methods such as one to tell how long the animation will run or whether the animation loops; that's purely up to you. The point is that any system that contains a list of objects inheriting and implementing the IAnimation interface can animate them with a few lines of code:

```
for(AnimationList::iterator itr = animList.begin(); itr != animList.end(); ++itr)
{
   (*itr).VAdvance( delta );
}
```

Interface classes are a great way to enforce design standards. A programmer writing engine code can create systems that expect a certain interface. Any programmer creating objects that inherit from and implement the interface can be confidant that object will work with the engine code.

Consider Using Factories

Games tend to build screens and other complex objects constructing groups of objects, such as controls or sprites, and storing them in lists or other collections. A common way to do this is to have the constructor of one object, say a certain implementation of a screen class, "new up" all the sprites and controls. In many cases, many types of screens are used in a game, all having different objects inheriting from the same parents.

In the book, *Design Patterns: Elements of Reusable Object-Oriented Software* by Erich Gamma et. al., one of the object creation patterns is called a *factory*. An abstract factory can define the interface for creating objects. Different implementations of the abstract factory carry out the concrete tasks of constructing objects.

Imagine an abstract factory that builds screens. The fictional game engine in this example could define screens as components that have screen elements, a background, and a logic class that accepts control messages. Here's an example:

```
class SaveGameScreenFactory : public IScreenFactory
{
public:
   SaveGameScreenFactory();

   virtual IScreenElements * const BuildScreenElements() const;
   virtual ScreenBackgroundSprite * const BuildScreenBackgroundSprite() const;
   virtual IScreenLogic * const BuildScreenLogic() const;
};
```

The code that builds screens will call the methods of the IScreenFactory interface, each one returning discrete portions of the screen. As all interface classes tend to enforce design standards, factories tend to enforce orderly construction of complicated objects. Factories are great for screens, animations, AI, or any nontrivial game object.

Separate Your User Interface from the Game Logic

Those programmers "lucky" enough to program in MFC noticed the Document/View architecture. The document is a model for data; the view is a model for the user interface. The view class doesn't have direct access to the raw bits of data in the document. Instead, the view class makes requests to change the data in the document by calling the methods in the document class's definition. This approach of separating "church and state" is actually an excellent design paradigm.

Before you slam this book closed and see if it makes pretty colors in your microwave, let me give you a good reason why you should consider using an approach like this. Let's assume you correctly separate your user interface from your game logic. You can then easily define proxy classes that can send your requests to modify data that actually exists on a server instead of the local machine. You can define AI classes that conform to the user interface API and you'll notice that the AI classes can't "cheat" because they only see information they are supposed to see. Even better, you get the ability to freely swap AI players and human players in your game.

An even greater benefit of this approach is that it can separate your very portable game logic from not so portable user interface and display code. If you ever had to write a game to work on a desktop PC and a handheld PDA you'll appreciate the separation.

Implement Stream Constructors

Any persistent object in your game should implement an overloaded constructor that takes a stream object as a parameter. If the game is loaded from a file, objects can use the stream as a source of parameters. Here's an example to consider:

```
class AnimationPath
{
public:
   //Build a path from a set of path points...
   AnimationPath(std::vector<AnimationPathPoint> const & srcPath);

   //... or construct it from a stream.
   AnimationPath(InputStream & stream);

   //Of course, lots more code follows.
};
```

The first constructor accepts a vector of `AnimationPathPoint` objects, and the second constructor accepts a stream, which probably includes data that can be used to create the same path objects in the first constructor. Both constructors accomplish the same task, the construction of an `AnimationPath`. The stream constructor can be used to create the object from a save game file, or even a network communications stream.

Test your stream constructors by loading and saving your game automatically in the DEBUG build at regular intervals. It will have the added side effect of making sure programmers keep the load/save code pretty fast.

Smart Pointers and Naked Pointers

Clearly, all smart pointers wear clothing.

If you declare a pointer to another object, you've just used a naked pointer. Pointers are used to refer to another object, but they don't convey enough information. Anything declared on the heap must be referenced by at least one other object or it can never be freed, causing a memory leak. It is common for an object on the heap to be referred multiple times by other objects in the code. A good example of this is a game object like a clock. A pointer to the clock will exist in the game object cache, the collision system, the animation system, and even the sound system.

If you use naked pointers you must remember which objects implicitly own other objects. An object that owns other objects controls their existence. Imagine a ship object that owns everything on the ship. When the ship sinks, everything else is destroyed along with it. If you use naked pointers to create these relationships you have to remember who owns who. This can be a confusing or even impossible task. You'll find that using naked pointers will quickly paint you into a corner.

Smart pointers, on the other hand, hold extra information along with the address of the distant object. This information can count references, record permanent or temporary ownership, or perform other useful tasks. In a sense an object controlled by a smart pointer "knows" about every reference to itself. The horrible nest of naked pointers evaporates, leaving a simple and foolproof mechanism for handling your dynamic objects.

Reference Counting

Reference counting stores an integer value that counts how many other objects are currently referring to the object in question. Reference counting is a common mechanism in memory management. DirectX objects implement the COM based `IUnknown` interface, which uses reference counting Two methods that are central to this task are `AddRef()` and `Release()`. The following code shows how this works:

```
MySound *sound = new MySound;
sound->AddRef();                    // reference count is now 1
```

After you construct a reference counted object, you call the AddRef() method to increase the integer reference counter by one. When the pointer variable goes out of scope, by normal scoping rules or by the destruction of the container class, you must call Release(). Release() will decrement the reference counter and destroy the object if the counter drops to zero. A shared object can have multiple references safely without fear of the object being destroyed, leaving bad pointers all over the place.

Good reference counting mechanisms automatically delete the object when the reference count becomes zero. If the API leaves the explicit destruction of the object to you, it's easy to create memory leaks—all you have to do is forget to call Release(). You can also cause problems if you forget to call AddRef() when you create the object. It's likely that the object will get destroyed unexpectedly, not having enough reference counts.

Anytime you assign a pointer variable to the address of the reference counted object you'll do the same thing. This includes any calls inside a local loop:

```
for (int i=0; i<m_howMany; ++i)
{
   MySound *s = GoGrabASoundPointer(i);
   s->AddRef();

   DangerousFunction();

   if (s->IsPlaying())
   {
      DoSomethingElse();
   }

   s->Release();
}
```

This kind of code exists all over the place in every game I've ever worked on. The call to DangerousFunction() goes deep and performs some game logic that might attempt to destroy the instance of the MySound object. Don't forget that in a release build that the deallocated memory retains the same values until it is reused. It's quite possible that the loop will work just fine even though the MySound pointer is pointing to unallocated memory. What's more likely to occur is a terrible corruption of memory.

Reference counting keeps the sound object around until Release() is called at the bottom of the loop. If there was only one reference to the sound before the loop started, the call to AddRef() will add one to the sound's reference count, making two references.

`DangerousFunction()` does something that destroys the sound, but through a call to `Release()`. As far as `DangrousFunction()` is concerned, the sound is gone forever. It still exists because one more reference to it, through `MySound *s`, kept the reference count from dropping to zero inside the loop. The final call to `Release()` causes the destruction of the sound.

SmartPtr

If you think calling `AddRef()` and `Release()` all over the place might be a serious pain in the ass, you're right. It's really easy to forget an `AddRef()` or a `Release()` call, and your memory leak will be almost impossible to find. It turns out that there are plenty of C++ templates out there that implement reference counting in a way that handles the counter manipulation automatically. Here's an example:

```
#ifndef SMARTPTR_H
#define SMARTPTR_H
/////////////////////////////////////////////////////////
//
//  Code modified from the original, to conform with
//  coding standards in the book.
//
//  Original Code by Sandu Turcan
//  Posted on the Code Project: http://www.codeproject.com/

template <class T> class SmartPtr;

///////////////////////////////////////////
// IRefCount
// is an interface for reference counting
// Classes can implement it themselves,
// or SmartPtr will provide its internal implementation of IRefCount

template <class T> class IRefCount {
    friend class SmartPtr<T>;
    protected:
    virtual void AddRef() = 0;
    virtual void Release() = 0;
    virtual T * GetPtr() const = 0;
};

//=================================================
///////////////////////////////////////////
// IRefCountImpl
// is a standart implementation of IRefCount
```

```
// To use it just derive your class from it:
// class CMyObject : public IRefCountImpl<CMyObject> { ... };
// Reminder: implementing IRefCount is optional but it would reduce
// memory fragmentation.

template <class T> class IRefCountImpl
  : public IRefCount<T>
{
private:
    int m_Count;

protected:
    virtual void AddRef() { m_Count++; }
    virtual void Release()
    {
   assert(m_Count>=0);
        m_Count—;
        if(m_Count<=0)
        {
            Destroy();
        }
    }
    virtual T * GetPtr() const { return ((T *)this); }
    virtual void Destroy() { if(GetPtr()!=NULL) delete GetPtr(); }

    IRefCountImpl() { m_Count = 0; }
};

//=======================================================

/////////////////////////////////////////
// SmartPtr

template <class T> class SmartPtr
{
private:
    IRefCount<T> *m_RefCount;

    /////////////////////////////////////////
    // RefCounter
    // An internal implementation of IRefCount
    // for classes that don't implement it
    // SmartPtr will automatically choose between its internal and
    // class' implementation of IRefCount
    class RefCounter : public IRefCountImpl<T> {
        private:
```

```
        T *m_Ptr;

        protected:
        virtual T * GetPtr() const { return m_Ptr; }
        virtual void Destroy()     { delete this; }

        public:
        RefCounter(T *ptr)  { m_Ptr = ptr; }
        virtual ~RefCounter()      { IRefCountImpl<T>::Destroy(); }
    };

    // this method is called if T does not implement IRefCount
    void Assign(void *ptr)
    {
        if(ptr==NULL)
            Assign((IRefCount<T> *)NULL);
        else
        {
            Assign(new RefCounter(static_cast<T *>(ptr)));
        }
    }

    // this method is picked over Assign(void *ptr)
    // if T implements IRefCount.
    // This allows some memory usage optimization
    void Assign(IRefCount<T> *refcount)
    {
        if( refcount!=NULL )
           refcount->AddRef();
        IRefCount<T> *oldref = m_RefCount;
        m_RefCount = refcount;
        if ( oldref!=NULL )
           oldref->Release();
    }

public:
    SmartPtr()                      { m_RefCount = NULL; }
    SmartPtr(T * ptr)               { m_RefCount = NULL; Assign(ptr); }
    SmartPtr(const SmartPtr &sp)    { m_RefCount = NULL; Assign(sp.m_RefCount); }
    virtual ~SmartPtr()             { Assign((IRefCount<T> *)NULL); }

    T *GetPtr() const { return (m_RefCount==NULL) ? NULL : m_RefCount->GetPtr(); }

    // assignment operators
    SmartPtr& operator = (const SmartPtr &sp) { Assign(sp.m_RefCount); return *this;
}
```

```
    SmartPtr& operator = (T * ptr)    { Assign(ptr); return *this; }

    // T access and const conversion
    T * operator ->()          { assert(GetPtr()!=NULL); return GetPtr(); }
    operator T* () const       { return GetPtr(); }

    // utilities
    bool operator !()                   { return GetPtr()==NULL; }
    bool operator ==(const SmartPtr &sp)  { return GetPtr()==sp.GetPtr(); }
    bool operator !=(const SmartPtr &sp)  { return GetPtr()!=sp.GetPtr(); }
};
#endif
```

Here's an example on how to use this template:

```
/////////////////////////////////////////
// SmartPtr.cpp
//
// Examples on how the SmartPtr template classes are used.
//

#include "stdafx.h"
#include "assert.h"
#include "smartptr.h"

class CMyObject
{
   char *name;
public:
   CMyObject(char *aname)    { name = aname; printf("create %s\n",name); }
   virtual ~CMyObject()      { printf("delete %s\n",name); }
   void print()              { printf("print %s\n",name); }
};

SmartPtr<CMyObject> f1(char *name)
{
   return SmartPtr<CMyObject>(new CMyObject(name));
}

void f2(CMyObject *o)
{
   printf("(print from a function) ");
   o->print();
}
```

3

```
int main(void)
{
   SmartPtr<CMyObject> ptr1(new CMyObject("1"));   // create object 1
   SmartPtr<CMyObject> ptr2 = new CMyObject("2"); // create object 2

   ptr1 = ptr2;              // destroy object 1
   ptr2 = f1("3");           // used as a return value
   ptr2 = NULL;              // destroy object 3
   f2(ptr1);

   // BAD USEAGE EXAMPLES....
   //
   // CMyObject o1;
   // ptr1 = &o1;         // DON'T ! It's on the stack....
   //
   // CMyObject *o2 = new CMyObject;
   // ptr1 = o2;
   // ptr2 = o2;          // DON'T ! unless CMyObject implements IRefCount
   //                     // try to use ptr1 = ptr2 instead, it's always safe;

   // You can even use SmartPtrs on ints!

   SmartPtr<int> a(new int);
   SmartPtr<int> b(new int);

   *a = 5;
   *b = 6;


   // No leaks!!!! Isn't that cool...
   return 0;
}
```

The template classes use overloaded assignment operators to handle the calls to `AddRef()` and `Release()`. As long as the `SmartPtr` object is in scope and you behave yourself by avoiding the bad usage cases you won't leak memory and you won't have to worry about objects getting destroyed while you are still referencing them from somewhere else.

This smart pointer will not work in every circumstance. One limitation is that it will not work in a multithreaded environment. There are two reasons. First, the `IRefCountImpl` class would have to be changed to lock access to `m_Count`, which is used to count references. If two threads attempted to increase or decrease the reference count at exactly the same time you'll end up with a reference count with the wrong value. Secondly, there is no safe access to the memory block in a multithreaded executable. Multiple threads can stomp through the bits at their leisure.

Don't ignore multithreaded access to shared memory blocks. You might think that the chances of two threads accessing the shared data are exceedingly low, and convince yourself that you don't need to go to the trouble of adding multithreaded protection. You'd be wrong, every time.

It is a good idea to have a separate template for multithreaded smart pointers since they run slower. Use the single threaded version in as many places as you can because it's more efficient. Save the multiple threaded version only for the cases you need it. I'll leave the happy task of making the SmartPtr template multithread-aware to you.

When you design your own smart pointer system, you should create many classes that perform limited scope tasks instead of one monolithic class that attempts to fill every role.

Using Memory Correctly

Did you ever hear the joke about the programmer trying to beat the Devil in a coding contest? Part of his solution involved overcoming a memory limitation by storing a few bytes in a chain of soundwaves between the microphone and the speaker. That's an interesting idea, and I'll bet we would have tried that one on Ultima VII had someone on our team thought of it.

Memory comes in very different shapes, sizes, and speeds. If you know what you're doing you can write programs that make efficient use of these different memory blocks. If you believe that it doesn't matter how you use memory, you're in for a real shock. This includes assuming that the standard memory manager for your operating system is efficient; it usually isn't and you'll have to think about writing your own.

Understanding the Different Kinds of Memory

The system RAM is the main warehouse for storage as long as the lights are on. Video RAM or VRAM is much smaller and is specifically used for storing objects that will be used by the video card. On top of it all, virtual memory hides a hard disk behind your lightning fast system RAM, and if you're not careful a simple `memcpy()` could cause the hard drive to seek. You might as well pack up and go to lunch if this happens.

System RAM

Your system RAM is a series of memory sticks that are installed on the mother board. Memory is actually stored in nine bits per byte, with the extra bit used to catch memory parity errors. Depending on the OS, you get to play with a certain addressable range of memory. The operating system keeps some to itself. Of the parts you get to play with, it is divided into three parts when your application loads:

- *Global memory*: This memory never changes size. It is allocated when your program loads and stores global variables, text strings, and virtual function tables.
- *Stack*: This memory grows as your code calls deeper into core code and it shrinks as the code returns. The stack is used for parameters in function calls and local variables.
- *Heap*: This memory grows and shrinks with dynamic memory allocation. It is used for persistent objects and dynamic data structures.

Old timers used to call global memory the DATA segment, harkening back to the days when there used to be near memory and far memory. It was called that because programmers used different pointers to get to it. What a disgusting practice! How I miss 16-bit segmented memory architectures. Not! Everything is much cleaner these days because every pointer is a full 32 bits. (Don't worry, I'm not going to bore you with the "When I went to school I used to load programs from a linear access tape cassette" story.)

Your compiler and linker will attempt to optimize the location of anything you put into the global memory space based on the type of variable. This includes constant text strings. Many compilers, including Visual Studio, will attempt to store text strings only once to save space:

```
const char *error1 = "Error";
const char *error2 = "Error";

int main()
{
   printf ("%x\n", (int)error1);
   // How quaint. A printf.
   printf ("%x\n", (int)error2);
   return 0;
}
```

This code yields interesting results. You'll notice that under Visual C++, the two pointers point to the same text string in the global address space. Even better than that, the text string is one that was already global and stuck in the CRT libraries. It's as if we wasted our time typing "Error." This trick only works for constant text strings, since the compiler knows they can never change. Everything else gets its own space. If you want the compiler to consolidate equivalent text strings, they must be constant text strings.

Don't make the mistake of counting on some kind of rational order to the global addresses. You can't count on anything the compiler or linker will do, especially if you are considering crossing platforms.

On most operating systems, the stack starts at high addresses and grows towards lower addresses. C and C++ parameters get pushed onto the stack from right to left—the last parameter is the first to get pushed onto the stack in a function call. Local parameters get pushed onto the stack in their order of appearance:


```
void testStack(int x, int y)
{
   int a = 1;
   int b = 2;

   printf("&x= %-10x &y= %-10x\n", &x, &y);
   printf("&a= %-10x &b= %-10x\n", &a, &b);
}
```

This code produces the following output:

```
&x= 12fdf0     &y= 12fdf4
&a= 12fde0     &b= 12fdd4
```

Stack addresses grow downward to smaller memory addresses. Thus it should be clear that the order in which the parameters and local variables were pushed was: y, x, a, and b. The next time you're debugging some assembler code you'll be glad to understand this, especially if you are setting your instruction pointer by hand.

C++ allows a high degree of control over the local scope. Every time you enclose code in a set of braces you open a local scope with its own local variables:

```
int main()
{
   int a = 0;

   {                          // start a local scope here...
      int a = 1;
      printf("%d\n", a);
   }

   printf("%d\n", a);
}
```

This code compiles and runs just fine. The two integer variables are completely separate entities. I've written this example to make a clear point, but I'd never actually write code like this. Opening up a local scope just to reuse a variable name is something they shoot programmers for down here in Texas. The real usefulness of this kind of code is for use with C++ objects that perform useful tasks when they are destroyed—you can control the exact moment a destructor is called by closing a local scope.

A singleton manager or global variable manager is a good example. Global variables are a pain in the butt, but are sometimes necessary evils. If you've ever programmed a game using a state based 3D renderer you use global variables every time to change the render state. The code tends to keep temporary variables around to store the old state of the global variables. After you are finished with the global variables, you'll use the value of the temporary variables to set them back to their old state. This kind of programming practice is rampant in Windows GDI code. Lucky for you there's a better way, using C++ destructors to cleanly set and reset globals:

```
//---------------------------
// singleton template manages setting/resettting global variables.
//---------------------------

template <class T>
class singleton
{
   T m_OldValue;
   T* m_pGlobalValue;

public:
   singleton(T newValue, T* globalValue)
   {
      m_pGlobalValue = globalValue;
      m_OldValue = *globalValue;
      *m_pGlobalValue = newValue;
   }

   ~singleton() { *m_pGlobalValue = m_OldValue; }
};
```

Instead of setting the global variable directly, use this template class. The constructor sets the value of the global after it saves the old value in a member variable. The destructor puts the global back to the original value.

Here's an example:

```
void main()
{
   extern bool g_FavorVRAMSurfaces;

   // We'll use the default favored VRAM
   MakeSomeTextures();

   {
      // Now put the textures in system memory
      singleton<bool> useSystemRAM(false, &g_FavorVRAMSurfaces);
      MakeSomeTextures();
   }
}
```


The example shows how the `singleton` template can be used in conjunction with the scoping rules of C++ to keep track of a global variable. The global, `g_FavorVRAMSurfaces`, is set to true whenever the fictional texture manager should favor allocating VRAM instead of system RAM. The code inside the main function shows how each call to `MakeSomeTextures()` can use the default value of the global or a specific value.

Video Memory (VRAM)

Video RAM is the memory installed on your video card, unless we're talking about an Xbox. Xbox hardware has unified memory architecture or UMI, so there's no difference between system RAM and VRAM. It would be nice if the rest of the world worked that way. Other hardware such as the Intel architectures must send any data between VRAM and system RAM over a bus. The PS2 has even more different kinds of memory. There are quite a few bus architectures and speeds out there and it is wise to understand how reading and writing data across the bus affects your game's speed.

As long as the CPU doesn't have to read from VRAM everything clicks along pretty fast. If you need to grab a piece of VRAM for something the bits have to be sent across the bus to system RAM. Depending on your architecture, your CPU and GPU must argue for a moment about timing, stream the bits, and go their separate ways. While this painful process is occurring, your game has come to a complete halt.

The hard disk can't write straight to VRAM, so every time a new texture is needed you'll need to stop the presses, so to speak. The smart approach is to load up as many new textures as you can, hopefully limiting any communication needed between the CPU and the video card.

Never perform per pixel operations on data stored in VRAM. If you can, keep a scratch copy in system RAM. If you must do something weird to VRAM, copy the whole thing into system RAM and perform the operation there. When you're done, copy it back to VRAM in one shot, hopefully using an asynchronous copy if your graphics library supports it. Under DirectX, the `NO_WAIT` flag is the ticket for an asynchronous `Blt()`. The exception to this rule: If your game can require the latest video cards, most per pixel operations can be programmed in pixel shaders.

If you've been paying attention you'll realize that the GPU in your video card is simply painting the screen using the components in VRAM. If it ever has to stop and ask system RAM for something, your game won't run as fast as it could. Of course, if the CPU never sent anything different for the video card to draw, your game would be pretty boring, unless you like watching images that never change.

The first texture manager I ever wrote was for Ultima IX. That was before the game was called Ultima: Ascension. I wrote the texture manager for 3DFx's Glide API, and I had all of an hour to do it. We wanted to show some Origin execs what Ultima looked like running under hardware acceleration. Not being the programmer extraordinare, my algorithm had to be pretty simple. I chose a variant of LRU, but since I didn't have time to write the code to sort and organize the textures, I simply threw out every texture in VRAM the moment there wasn't any additional space. I think this code got some nomination for the dumbest texture manager ever written, but it actually worked. The Avatar would walk around for ninety seconds or so before the hard disk lit up and everything came to a halt for two seconds. I'm pretty sure someone rewrote it before U9 shipped. At least, I hope someone rewrote it!

Optimizing Memory Access

Every access to system RAM uses a CPU cache. If the desired memory location is already in the cache, the contents of the memory location are presented to the CPU extremely quickly. If, on the other hand, the memory is not in the cache, a new block of system RAM must be fetched into the cache. This takes a lot longer than you'd think.

A good testbed for this problem uses multidimensional arrays. C++ defines its arrays in row major order. This ordering puts the members of the right most index next to each other in memory.

`TestData[0][0][0]` and `TestData[0][0][1]` are stored in adjacent memory locations.

Not every language defines arrays in row order. Some versions of PASCAL define arrays in column order. Don't make assumptions unless you like writing slow code.

If you access an array in the wrong order, it will create a worst case CPU cache scenario. Here's an example of two functions that access the same array, and do the same task. One will run much faster than the other:

```
const int g_n = 250;
float TestData[g_n][g_n][g_n];

inline void column_ordered()
{
   for (int k=0; k<g_n; k++)
      for (int j=0; j<g_n; j++)
         for (int i=0; i<g_n; i++)
            TestData[i][j][k] = 0.0f;
}

inline void row_ordered()
{
   for (int i=0; i<g_n; i++)
      for (int j=0; j<g_n; j++)
         for (int k=0; k<g_n; k++)
            TestData[i][j][k] = 0.0f;
}
```

The timed output of running both functions on my test machine showed that accessing the array in row order was nearly nine times faster:

```
Column Ordered=2817 ms   Row Ordered=298 ms    Delta=2519 ms
```

Any code that accesses any largish data structure can benefit from this technique. If you had a multistep process that affected a large data set, try to arrange your code to perform as much work in smaller memory blocks. You'll optimize the use of the L2 cache and make a much faster piece of code.

Memory Alignment

The CPU reads and writes memory-aligned data much faster than other data. Any N-byte data type is memory aligned if the starting address is evenly divisible by N. For example, a 32-bit integer is memory aligned if the starting address is 0x04000000. The same 32-bit integer is unaligned if the starting address is 0x04000002, since the memory address is not evenly divisible by 4 bytes.

You can perform a little experiment in memory alignment and how it affects access time by using example code like this:

```
#pragma pack(push, 1)
struct ReallySlowStruct
{
   char c : 6;
   __int64 d : 64;
   int b : 32;
   char a : 8;
};

struct SlowStruct
{
   char c;
   __int64 d;
   int b;
   char a;
};

struct FastStruct
{
   __int64 d;
   int b;
   char a;
   char c;
   char unused[2];
};

#pragma pack(pop)
```

I wrote a piece of code to perform some operations on the member variables in each structure. The difference in times is as follows:

```
Really slow=417 ms
Slow=222 ms
Fast=192 ms
```

Your penalty for using the `SlowStruct` over `FastStruct` is about 14% on my test machine. The penalty for using `ReallySlowStruct` is code that runs twice as slow.

The first structure isn't even aligned properly on bit boundaries, hence the name `ReallySlowStruct`. The definition of the 6-bit `char` variable throws the entire structure out of alignment. The second structure, `SlowStruct`, is also out of alignment but at least the byte boundaries are aligned. The last structure, `FastStruct`, is completely aligned for each member. The last member, unused, ensures that the structure fills out to an eight-byte boundary in case someone declares an array of `FastStruct`.

Notice the `#pragma pack(push, 1)` at the top of the source example? It's accompanied by a `#pragma pack(pop)` at the bottom. Without them, the compiler, depending on your project settings, will choose to spread out the member variables and place each one on an optimal byte boundary. When the member variables are spread out like that the CPU can access each member quickly, but all that unused space can add up. If the compiler were left to optimize `SlowStruct` by adding unused bytes each structure would be 24 bytes instead of just 14. Seven extra bytes are padded after the first `char` variable, and the remaining bytes are added at the end. This ensures the entire structure always starts on an eight byte boundary. That's about 40% wasted space, all due to a careless ordering of member variables.

Don't let the compiler waste precious memory space. Put some of your brain cells to work and align your own member variables. You don't get many opportunities to save memory and optimize CPU at the same time.

Virtual Memory

Virtual memory increases the addressable memory space by caching unused memory blocks to the hard disk. The scheme depends on the fact that even though you might have a 500Mb data structure, you aren't going to be playing with the whole thing at the same time. The unused bits are saved off to your hard disk, until you need them again. You should be cheering and wincing at the same time. Cheering because every programmer likes having a big memory playground, and wincing because anything involving the hard disk wastes a lot of time and, last time I checked, PS2s and GameCubes didn't sport harddrives out of the box.

Just to see how bad it can get, I took the code from the array access example and modified it to iterate through a three dimensional array 500 elements cubed. The total size of the array would be 476Mb, much bigger than the installed memory on the test machine. A data structure bigger than available memory is sometimes called *out-of-core*. I ran the `column_ordered()` function and went to lunch. When I got back about 30 minutes later the test program was still chugging away. The hard drive was seeking like mad, and I began to wonder whether my hard disk would give out. I became impatient and re-ran the example and timed just one iteration of the inner loop. It took 379.75 seconds to run the inner loop. The entire thing would have taken over 50 hours to run. I'm glad I didn't wait.

Remember that the original array, 250 elements cubed, ran the test code in 298 ms when the fast `row_ordered()` function was used. The large array is only 8 times bigger, giving an expectation that the same code should have run in 2384 ms, or just under two and a half seconds.

Compare 2384 ms with 50 hours and you'll see how virtual memory can work against you if your code accesses virtual memory incorrectly.

Any time a cache is used inefficiently you can degrade the overall performance of your game by many orders of magnitude. This is commonly called "thrashing the cache" and is your worst nightmare. The solution to this problem might be as simple as reordering a few lines of code. It might also be as heinous as reducing your data set.

Using Memory Mapped Files

A memory mapped file maps a virtual addressable memory space onto a file. The entire contents of the file can be read and written as easy as if it were entirely in memory. Win32 and Linux both support memory mapped files. Instead of writing your own low level memory cache, use memory mapped files to load any resources or data into your game. Since Windows uses memory mapping to load .EXE and .DLL files, it's a fair bet that the algorithm is fairly efficient. These files are especially useful for larger data sets that come in groups of 512Kb. Don't use these files for anything smaller. Check your system for the default size of a virtual memory page—that is the smallest chunk of memory a memory mapped file manipulates.

Under Win32, you can open a read-only memory mapped file with this code:

```
//
// Open a memory mapped file
//
// Please forgive the lack of error checking code,
// you should always check return values.

HANDLE fileHandle = CreateFile(
   fileName,
   GENERIC_READ,
   FILE_SHARE_READ,
   NULL,
   OPEN_EXISTING,                     // the file must already exist
   0,
   NULL);

//
// Create a mapping object from the file
//

HANDLE fileMapping = CreateFileMapping(
   fileHandle,
   NULL,
```

```
    PAGE_READONLY,
    0, 0,
    NULL);

//
// Map the file to memory pointer
//

char *fileBase = (char *) MapViewOfFile(
    fileMapping,
    FILE_MAP_READ,
    0, 0,
    0);
```

Once you have a valid memory map, you can read from the file by accessing the variable, fileBase, as shown here.

```
// Read the first 50 bytes and copy them to dest.
memcpy(dest, fileBase, 50);
```

The operating system doesn't copy the entire contents of the file into memory. Instead, it uses the same code used to manage virtual memory. The only thing that is different is the name of the file on secondary storage.

Don't memory-map a file if it exists on CD-ROM. If the CD is ejected, your memory map will become invalid. If the CD is ejected while data is being read, your application will suffer a crash. Sadly, the crash will happen before Windows has a chance to send the WM_DEVICECHANGE message, which is always sent when the CD is ejected.

An alternative to `MapViewOfFile`, `MapViewOfFileEx`, has an additional parameter that allows a programmer to specify the exact base address of the memory map. Ultima IX's original resource cache made use of this parameter, but in a very bad way. I know because I wrote it. Each resource file assumed that it would exist at a specific base address. This allowed me to code data structures, including pointers, directly as data in the memory mapped file. This seemed like a great idea until I realized Ultima IX would no longer run on Windows NT. It turns out that the allowable base address range was completely different from Windows 95. I knew when I coded the thing that it was a dream too good to be true. I eliminated the base address specific assumptions from the code and data files and it worked just fine.

Writing Your Own Memory Manager

Most games extend the provided memory management system. The biggest reasons to do this are performance, efficiency, and improved debugging. Default memory managers in the C runtime are designed to run fairly well in a wide range of memory allocation scenarios. They tend to break down under the load of computer games, where allocations and deallocations of relatively tiny memory blocks can be fast and furious.

You shouldn't purposely design your game to create a worst case scenario for the memory manager in the C runtime. I've known a few programmers who find it a fun and challenging task to write their own memory manager. I'm not one of them, and you should also resist the urge. The memory manager in the C runtime doesn't suck completely, and it has gone through more programming time and debugging than you'll have even if your game is in development for a number of years. Instead, you'll want to write a system that is either much simpler in design and features, or you will choose to simply extend the memory manager that is already there.

Ultima VII: The Black Gate had a legendary memory manager: The VooDoo Memory Management System. It was written by a programmer that used to work on guided missile systems for the Department of Defense, a brilliant and dedicated engineer. U7 ran in good old DOS back in the days when protected mode was the neat new thing. VooDoo was a true 32-bit memory system for a 16-bit operating system, and the only problem with it was you had to read and write to the memory locations with assembly code, since the Borland compiler didn't understand 32-bit pointers. It was done this way because U7 couldn't really exist in a 16-bit memory space—there were atomic data structures larger than 64Kb. For all its hoopla VooDoo was actually pretty simple, and it only provided the most basic memory management features. The fact that it was actually called VooDoo was a testament to the fact that it actually worked; it wasn't exactly supported by the operating system or the Borland compilers.

VooDoo MM for Ultima VII is a great example of writing a simple memory manager to solve a specific problem. It didn't support multithreading, it assumed that memory blocks were large, and finally it wasn't written to support a high number or frequency of allocations.

A standard memory manager, like the one in the C runtime, must support multithreading. Each time the memory manager's data structures are accessed or changed they must be protected with critical sections, allowing only one thread to allocate or deallocate memory at a time. All this extra code is time consuming, especially if you malloc and free very frequently. Most games are multithreaded to support sound systems, but don't necessarily need a multithreaded memory manager for every part of the game. A single threaded memory manager that you write yourself might be a good solution.

Simple memory managers can use a doubly linked list as the basis for keeping track of allocated and free memory blocks. The C runtime uses a more complicated system to reduce the algorithmic complexity of searching through the allocated and free blocks that could be as small as a single byte. Your memory blocks might be either more regularly shaped, fewer in number, or both. This creates an opportunity to design a simpler, more efficient system.

Default memory managers must assume that deallocations happen approximately as often as allocations, and they might happen in any order and at any time. Their data structures have to keep track of a large number of blocks of available and used memory. Any time a piece of memory changes state from used to available the data structures must be quickly traversed. When blocks become available again, the memory manager must detect adjacent available blocks and merge them to make a larger block. Finding free memory of an appropriate size to minimize wasted space can be extremely tricky. Since default memory managers solve these problems to a large extent, their performance isn't as high as another memory manager that can make more assumptions about how and when memory allocations occur.

If your game can allocate and deallocate most of its dynamic memory space at once, you can write a memory manager based on a data structure no more complicated than a singly linked list. You'd never use something this simple in a more general case, of course, because a singly linked list has O(n) algorithmic complexity. That would cripple any memory management system used in the general case.

A good reason to extend a memory manager is to add some debugging features. Two features that are common include adding additional bytes before and after the allocation to track memory corruption, or to track memory leaks. The C runtime adds only one byte before and after an allocated block, which might be fine to catch those pesky x+1 and x-1 errors but doesn't help for much else. If the memory corruption seems pretty random, and most of them sure seem that way, you can increase your odds of catching the culprit by writing a custom manager that adds more bytes to the beginning and ending of each block. In practice the extra space is set to a small number, even one byte, in the release build.

Anything you do differently from the debug and release builds can change the behavior of bugs from one build target to another. Murphy's Law dictates that the bug will only appear in the build target that is hardest, or even impossible, to debug.

Another common extension to memory managers is leak detection. MFC redefines the new operator to add __FILE__ and __LINE__ information to each allocated memory block in debug mode. When the memory manager is shut down all the unfreed blocks are printed out in the output window in the debugger. This should give you a good place to start when you need to track down a memory leak.

If you decide to write your own memory manager keep the following points in mind:

- *Data structures*: Choose the data structure that matches your memory allocation scenario. If you traverse a large number of free and available blocks very frequently, choose a hash table or tree based structure. If you hardly ever traverse it to find free blocks you could get away with a list. Store the data structure separately from the memory pool; any corruption will keep your memory manager's data structure in tact.
- *Single/multithreaded access*: Don't forget to add appropriate code to protect your memory manager from multithreaded access if you need it. Eliminate the protections if you are sure access to the memory manager will only happen from a single thread and you'll gain some performance.
- *Debug and testing*: Allocate a little additional memory before and after the block to detect memory corruption. Add caller information to the debug memory blocks; at a minimum you should use __FILE__ and __LINE__ to track where the allocation occurred.

Small Memory Allocations

One of the best reasons to extend the C runtime memory manager is to write a better system to manage small memory blocks. The memory managers supplied in the C runtime or MFC library are not meant for tiny allocations. You can prove it to yourself by allocating two integers and subtracting their memory addresses as shown here:

```
int *a = new int;
int *b = new int;

int delta1 = ((int)b - (int)a) - sizeof(int);
```

The wasted space for the C runtime library was 28 bytes for a release build and 60 bytes for the debug build under Visual Studio.NET. Even with the release build, an integer takes eight times as much memory space as it would if it weren't dynamically allocated.

Most games overload the new operator to allocate small blocks of memory from a reserved pool set aside for small allocations. Memory allocations that are larger than a set number of bytes can still use the C runtime. I recommend that you start with 128 bytes as the largest block your small allocator will handle, and tweak the size until you are happy with the performance.

Game Scripting Languages

You might be surprised to learn that C++ isn't the end-all, be-all language for developing games. C++ is great for implementing flexible and elegant technology. It's also good for speed. But as with any language, C++ has its downsides that can really bug game developers. I continually find that C++ is lacking features that I need to make games. Ultimas of every flavor used game scripts to cache huge amounts of localized text and script events—a cumbersome task in C++. Another feature lacking in C++ is reentrant code—a game script for something like an explosion effect might be played over a long period of time, and it's crazy to launch a thread to perform this simple task.

Game designers and level builders don't necessarily want a C++ compiler on their development machine. A game script exposes only those features that they need to build triggers, spawning points, and cut scenes. Even better, if the scripting language is interpreted rather than compiled, it's easy to get into a development zone. They can play it, hate it, tweak it, and replay it until they've got it the way they want it.

There are other languages besides C++, some of them with features like reentrancy, object oriented programming, and more. If a scripting language doesn't exist with exactly the features you want, you can write your own. The game scripts can be thought of as procedural game data, and can describe anything: mission parameters, screen layouts, or character AI.

Using Scripts to Handle Text

Because scripting languages can vary and they are a little tricky to describe, let's look at an example. My first experience with using game scripting languages was with Martian Dreams, a game based on the Ultima VI technology. This game had a simple scripting language to handle conversations, a central task in role playing games. Role playing games tend to lead the player through a tree-shaped set of choices in conversation. Ultima VI used typed keywords for user input. If a character in the game said something like, "Go into the western mountains to find the magic key," you might expect to find out more by typing the word "mountain" or "key." The Ultima VI scripting language used a flag-based system to manage conversations:

```
Character Gwenno
{
   "Key":
      if (GetFlag(ToldAboutKey))
      {
         Say("Don't you remember? ");
      }
      Say("The key will open the door to the hidden room in the King's Armory.
```

```
            There you will find enchanted armor and weapons you can use to
            defeat the drunken mountain troll.");
        SetFlag(ToldAboutKey);
        PopKeyword("Key");
        PushKeywords("troll", "armor", "weapons", "enchanted");

    "Enchanted":
        Say("The spell was cast on the armor long ago…");
}
```

You can see from this sample that Gwenno can tell you about a magic key and the spell that was placed on the King's armor and weapons. She can even remember that she told you about it. The flag, `ToldAboutKey`, was set the first time you asked Gwenno about the key. If you asked about it again later the conversation reflected the new game state.

This system was pretty easy to manage, but it was a little too simple. All the active keywords had the same priority, so Gwenno couldn't talk about more than one key. The flags were available to the C code and could be used to affect the game by unlocking passages and such, but more complex interactions between the script and the game engine were impossible. The system created fairly believable interactions with non-player characters, as simple as it was.

One feature that was added to the language by Ultima VIII was a natural support for localization. The different languages were coded in line with the English text, and comments were used to mark any English changes to the localization team. It was accomplished with a `#define` mechanism, which had the downside that the game scripts had to be compiled once for each language.

Another feature that was added by Ultima VIII was a tight integration with C++ code. The language compiler could read the MAP file output by the linker to figure out where and how to call free functions or even members of C++ classes. Of course, it was very compiler specific.

Event Scripting

Creating scripts to handle text processing can really be useful for certain types of games but what about events? After all, most games are based on the processing of numerous, and often complex, events. When I worked on Ultima VIII, all of the programmers wanted a better way to script complicated events. In the previous conversation with Gwenno, imagine that after she told you about the key that she actually walked over to you and cast a spell that gave you additional protection on your quest for the key. We thought that the team of game designers could use the additional features in the game scripting language to create highly interesting and theatrical performances on the part of the non-player characters.

Since Ultima VIII was based on a real-time multitasker we realized that each action of an NPC could be one of those processes, and the master process of the NPC could be the conversation process. The conversation process could slave off some animations and pick up where it left off after the animations were complete. Let's look at an example:


```
Character Gwenno
{
  "Key":
    if (GetFlag(ToldAboutKey))
    {
      Say("Don't you remember? ");
    }
    Say("The key will open the door to the hidden room in the King's Armory.
        There you will find enchanted armor and weapons you can use to
        defeat the drunken mountain troll.");
    Say("Let me help you by casting this protection spell. This won't hurt
        a bit, just hold still for a minute.");
    Avatar.SetInactive();

    Pathfind(Avatar, WALK);
    CastSpell(SPELL_Protection, Avatar);

    Say("All done! The protection spell only lasts a few hours, so hurry on.");
    SetFlag(ToldAboutKey);
    PopKeyword("Key");
    PushKeywords("troll", "armor", "weapons", "enchanted");

  "Enchanted":
    Say("The spell was cast on the armor long ago....");
}
```

This implies something you might have suspected about game scripts, especially scripts that define "stage direction," for lack of a better term. They execute at the whim of user input and the processes they launch. In my example the call to `Pathfind()` doesn't return until the Gwenno character successfully walks to the Avatar's location. Any of these processes might fail. I'm sure of this because a very similar piece of code was flummoxed by Origin QA, who built a small wall of wooden boxes in between Gwenno and the Avatar. Gwenno cast the protection spell anyway and managed to protect the wall of wooden boxes instead of the Avatar.

Your scripting language must be able to detect these problems and handle them in some meaningful way. In my example `Pathfind()` could return a boolean signaling success for failure. If the `Pathfind()` process failed we had Gwenno say something appropriate like, "I should really clean this place up first. Would you help?"

Interpretation versus Compilation

Compiling and linking large C++ programs can test the patience of any programmer, especially if you're the kind of programmer who needs to get away from your machine now and then to to play a game of Robotron. It would be nice if fast, new computers were issued the moment compile times averaged longer than 15 minutes. Like you, I too keep dreaming.

Interpreted game scripts take longer to load and they run a lot slower. That's not necessarily a bad thing depending on what your game scripts do. If they mostly control NPC conversations or launch other C++ processes, it's doubtful that your players will notice any performance problems in your interpreter. You'll also get a side benefit from interpretation. Since the script is loaded at run time you should be able to engineer the interpreter to reload the script without restarting the game. A game designer could change the script and rerun it for ultra fast development. If your system can do this, you'll save a lot of time and get a better game as a result.

Compiling and linking game scripts might sound a little alien. It seems that if a game script is going to be compiled and linked why not use C++ and be done with it. Just because a game script is compiled and linked doesn't mean that it doesn't support extra features that aren't included in C++, depending on your language syntax. Compiling is a translation process. The text file that represents your code and algorithms is compiled to pre-create the token stream of operators and operands, data structures, and symbol tables used in complicated languages. Linking takes the results of multiple compiled modules and assigns concrete addresses to external variables declared from module to module.

Strictly speaking, a language interpreter performs this sequence of actions on a line-by-line basis. If only a small number of lines of code are executed within a large module, interpretation will perform better than compilation. If the same lines are executed multiple times, compilation will begin to outperform interpretation. Compilation and linking will also be able to support language features like external variable references.

Ultima VIII and the original Ultima IX supported a compiled and linked language.

Rolling Your Own with Lex and Yacc

Assuming your language syntax is nontrivial, you'll want to use some tools to help you define your lexicon and your grammar. There are two classic and excellent tools to help you perform this task:

- *Lex:* A utility that generates C programs to be used in simple lexical analysis of text, or in plain language it matches input streams with a series of regular expressions.
- *Yacc:* An acronym for Yet Another Compiler Compiler. This tool takes as its input a context free grammar and a stream of tokens and is able to break down the input stream into a hierarchical data structure. Each node of the hierarchy corresponds to a statement in the language defined by the grammar. Each statement is processed by a custom piece of code that translates the original token stream into your target language, usually a series of simple statements composed of operators and operands.

Both Lex and Yacc require you to associate a regular expression or grammar fragment with an action written in C. You are still responsible for writing the C code to output something that you can use to interpret the source script into a series of executable or interpretable commands and parameters.

Lex and Yacc are old tools, but they withstand the test of time. You can find numerous good resources on the web—simply search for "Lex Yacc" and you'll find all you need. You can also find an O'Reilly book on the subject: *Lex and Yacc* by John R. Levine, Tony Mason, and Doug Brown.

Regular Expressions

If you are rusty on regular expressions, now is a good time to bone up. Regular expressions are shorthand strings that stand for longer series of strings. Here are some examples:

```
Hello[0123]  matches Hello0, Hello1, Hello2, Hello3 and nothing else
```

```
Hello[A-Z] matches any string from HelloA to HelloZ.
```

```
Hello[^0-9]  matches any string starting with 'Hello' and not ending in a number.
```

```
Hello$  matches any input line that ends with 'Hello'
```

```
[o]+    matches any string containing one or more instances of the letter 'o'
```

```
[o]*    matches any string containing zero or more instances of the letter 'o'
```

There is much more to regular expressions than these simple examples. Go take a look at *Mastering Regular Expressions* by Jeffrey E. F. Freidl (published by O'Reilly & Associates, Inc.).

Lex Example

Lex takes as input a series of regular expressions and C code fragments. Lex takes that input and creates a C source file, `lex.yy.c`, that will analyze any input file and perform the actions each time it finds a string that conforms with one of the regular expressions. Here is a sample input file for Lex:

```
%%
[A-Z]    putchar(yytext[0]+'a'-'A');
[ ]+$
[ ]+     putchar(' ');
```

This example has three regular expressions and their associated actions. The first regular expression matches any upper case character from A to Z. The action converts the character to lower case. The second expression matches any series of blanks appearing at the end of an input line. Since there is no action associated with it, the blanks are stripped and don't appear in the output file. The last regular expression matches any series of multiple blanks. The action replaces the multiple blanks with a single blank.

You can define regular expressions for your scripting language, and convert them to tokens. Take a look at a small portion of the Lex file for parsing ANSI C++:

```
D        [0-9]
L        [a-zA-Z_]
H        [a-fA-F0-9]
E        [Ee][+-]?{D}+
FS       (f|F|l|L)
IS       (u|U|l|L)*

%{
#include <stdio.h>

# define AUTO 286
# define BREAK 314
# define CASE 304
# define CHAR 288
# define CONST 296
# define CONTINUE 313
# define CONSTANT 258
# define STRING_LITERAL 259
```

```
# define RIGHT_ASSIGN 278
# define LEFT_ASSIGN 277
# define ADD_ASSIGN 275
# define SUB_ASSIGN 276
# define MUL_ASSIGN 272
# define DIV_ASSIGN 273
# define MOD_ASSIGN 274

void count();
%}

%%
"/*"        { comment(); }

"auto"        { count(); return(AUTO); }
"break"       { count(); return(BREAK); }
"case"        { count(); return(CASE); }
"char"        { count(); return(CHAR); }
"const"       { count(); return(CONST); }
"continue"    { count(); return(CONTINUE); }

0[xX]{H}+{IS}?        { count(); return(CONSTANT); }
0[xX]{H}+{IS}?        { count(); return(CONSTANT); }
0{D}+{IS}?            { count(); return(CONSTANT); }
\"(\\.|[^\\"])*\"     { count(); return(STRING_LITERAL); }

">>="       { count(); return(RIGHT_ASSIGN); }
"<<="       { count(); return(LEFT_ASSIGN); }
"+="        { count(); return(ADD_ASSIGN); }
"-="        { count(); return(SUB_ASSIGN); }
"*="        { count(); return(MUL_ASSIGN); }
"/="        { count(); return(DIV_ASSIGN); }
"%="        { count(); return(MOD_ASSIGN); }
.           { /* ignore bad characters */ }

%%


comment()
{
   char c, c1;

loop:
   while ((c = input()) != '*' && c != 0)
      putchar(c);
```

3

```
        if ((c1 = input()) != '/' && c != 0)
        {
            unput(c1);
            goto loop;
        }

        if (c != 0)
            putchar(c1);
}

void count()
{
        int i;

        for (i = 0; yytext[i] != '\0'; i++)
            if (yytext[i] == '\n')
                column = 0;
            else if (yytext[i] == '\t')
                column += 8 - (column % 8);
            else
                column++;

        ECHO;
}
```

Each regular expression associates a text string with a token. A token is an atomic and meaningful component of a language. All keywords, operators, constants, and identifiers are tokens. Notice the two functions `comment()` and `count()`. They are included verbatim in the Lex output, and handle more complicated parsing of the input stream into tokens. The `comment()` function simply finds the end of the comment so that it can be ignored. The `count()` function keeps track of the position of the parser in the input stream so that errors can be reported.

Yacc Example

The stream of tokens is sent on to Yacc, which will analyze the stream and match token sequences with a context free grammar. The grammar defines the structure of the scripting language.

Grammar construction is very tricky. The best reference is the "Dragon Book," *Compilers: Principles, Techniques, and Tools* by the team of Alfred V. Aho, Ravi Sethi, and Jeffrey D. Ullman. Blockade yourself from any outside distractions while you soak this in; it's difficult material. Unless your language script is fairly simple or you can steal a grammar from a well-known language like C++ I suggest you find someone who has done this before.

Constructing a proper LR(1) grammar is as hard as those annoying blacksmith puzzles that seem to require movement into the fourth dimension. If you don't have any idea what an LR(1) grammar is, I rest my case. Go get the Dragon Book and start reading, because I'd be a horrible replacement trying to teach any of that here.

This is a small portion of the Yacc grammar definition file for ANSI C++:


```
%token IDENTIFIER CONSTANT STRING_LITERAL SIZEOF
%token PTR_OP INC_OP DEC_OP LEFT_OP RIGHT_OP LE_OP GE_OP EQ_OP NE_OP
%token AND_OP OR_OP MUL_ASSIGN DIV_ASSIGN MOD_ASSIGN ADD_ASSIGN
%token SUB_ASSIGN LEFT_ASSIGN RIGHT_ASSIGN AND_ASSIGN
%token XOR_ASSIGN OR_ASSIGN TYPE_NAME

%token TYPEDEF EXTERN STATIC AUTO REGISTER
%token CHAR SHORT INT LONG SIGNED UNSIGNED FLOAT DOUBLE CONST VOLATILE VOID
%token STRUCT UNION ENUM ELIPSIS RANGE

%token CASE DEFAULT IF ELSE SWITCH WHILE DO FOR GOTO CONTINUE BREAK RETURN

%start file
%%


statement
    : labeled_statement
    | compound_statement
    | expression_statement
    | selection_statement
    | iteration_statement
    | jump_statement
    ;

labeled_statement
    : identifier ':' statement
    | CASE constant_expr ':' statement
    | DEFAULT ':' statement
    ;

compound_statement
    : '{' '}'
    | '{' statement_list '}'
    | '{' declaration_list '}'
    | '{' declaration_list statement_list '}'
    ;
```

```
declaration_list
    : declaration
    | declaration_list declaration
    ;

statement_list
    : statement
    | statement_list statement
    ;

expression_statement
    : ';'
    | expr ';'
    ;

selection_statement
    : IF '(' expr ')' statement
    | IF '(' expr ')' statement ELSE statement
    | SWITCH '(' expr ')' statement
    ;
```

Needless to say the real grammar is much larger, but not as large as you'd think. The example I found is only 433 lines of text. This grammar doesn't do anything useful until you add code for each line that creates semantic actions as shown here:

```
primary_expr
    : identifier                    { $$ = findIdent($1); }
    | CONSTANT                      { $$ = $1; }
    | STRING_LITERAL                { $$ = findString($1); }
    | '(' expr ')'                  { $$ = $2; }
    ;
```

Each grammar statement gets a semantic action, which can be any arbitrary C statement. In the example above, there are two custom functions: `findIdent()` and `findString()`. It's your responsibility to write the code for these functions and place them in the Yacc input file. The functions access a custom symbol table that you have to construct yourself. Depending on your language you might require the variables to be declared before they are used just like C++, and if they weren't you'd have to invoke some kind of error mechanism.

Putting It Together

Lex and Yacc are dinosaurs that refuse to die mainly because they are extremely powerful and they work. Even better, the grammars and other input files for every common language in existence is available on the internet for your use. If you wanted a scripting language that looks a lot like PHP but works under your custom semantic actions, it can be yours with a little elbow grease, Lex, and Yacc.

Ultima VIII and Ultima IX's language was defined in this way, and had an extremely complicated grammar. It was fully integrated with C++ classes, debuggable, had support for multiple languages, supported multi-process synchronization, and in many ways had all the features of Java, C++, and concurrent PASCAL. (So now you're probably thinking, "Where can I score a copy? I'm sure EA has it somewhere.")

You might believe that programming a game script is easier than C++, and junior programmers or even newbie level builders will be able to increase their productivity using game scripts. This is a trap. What tends to happen is the game scripting system becomes more powerful and complicated as new features are added during development. By the end of the project their complexity approaches or even exceeds that of C++. The development tools for the game script will fall far short of the compilers and debuggers for common languages. This makes the game scripting job really challenging. If your game depends on complicated game scripts make sure the development tools are up to the task.

Getting a working compiler or interpreter up and running is not the problem. You can have this in a few days. The accompanying support systems and development tools are a mountain of work. Ultima VIII incorporated pre-compilation into the compiler to minimize compile times. It also had a symbolic debugger that could pop up in the game so a game designer could see what was wrong with the script he just wrote. Recovering from semantic errors in compilation is also a difficult and time-consuming proposition for an experienced programmer. If you don't do that, your script compiler will give cryptic and misleading errors, which will waste everyone's time.

The bottom line: Don't underestimate the task of creating your own language for game scripts. Don't do it half-assed, either, or the good people forced to use your lame scripting language will likely have your head on a pike before the game ships—if it ships!

Python and Lua

A somewhat recent addition to scripting languages in computer games has been Python. Python is the scripting language of choice for many computer games. Python is basically an interpreted C++. One of the coolest features in Python is called a generator. A generator is a function that can return control to the calling code and resume where it left off the next time it is called, preserving the value of local variables. This is incredibly useful for scripting events and stage direction in games.

Python is extendable and integratable with other programming languages like C++. Go up to **www.python.org** to learn more. Some of my colleagues prefer Lua to Python, another scripting language that is much leaner than Python. Learn more about Lua at **www.lua.org**.

Mike's Grab Bag of Useful Stuff

Before we leave this chapter I wanted to arm you with some lifesaving snippets of code. Some code defies classification. It gets thrown into a toolbox with all the other interesting things that simply won't die. I try to dust them off and use them on every project and I'm never disappointed. I'll start with a great random number generator, show you a template class you can't live without, and end with a neat algorithm to traverse any set in random order without visiting the same member twice.

An Excellent Random Number Generator

There are as many good algorithms for generating random numbers as there are pages in this book. Most programmers will soon discover that the ANSI `rand()` function is completely inadequate because it can only generate a single stream of random numbers. In any game I've ever created multiple discrete streams of random numbers were required.

Unless your game comes with a little piece of hardware that uses the radioactive decay of cesium to generate random numbers, your random number generator is only pseudo-random. A pseudo-random number sequence can certainly appear random, achieving a relatively flat distribution curve over the generation of billions of numbers mapped to a small domain. Given the same starting assumption, commonly called a *seed*, the sequence will be exactly the same. A truly random sequence could never repeat like that.

This might seem bad because you might feel that a hacker could manipulate the seed to effect the outcome of the game. In practice, all you have to do is regenerate the seed every now and then using some random element that would be difficult or impossible to duplicate. In truth, a completely predictable random number generator is something you will give your left leg for when writing test tools or a game replay system.

Every Ultima from Ultima I to Ultima VIII used the same random number generator, originally written in 6502 assembler. In 1997 this generator was the oldest piece of continually used code at Origin Systems. Finally this RNG showed its age and had to be replaced. Kudos to Richard Garriott (aka Lord British) for making the longest-lived piece of code Origin ever used.

Here's a cool little class to keep track of your random numbers. You'll want to make sure you save this code and stuff it into your own toolbox. The RNG core is called a Mersenne Twister pseudorandom number generator and it was originally developed by Takuji Nishimura and Makoto Matsumoto:

```
/* Period parameters */
#define CMATH_N 624
#define CMATH_M 397
#define CMATH_MATRIX_A 0x9908b0df   /* constant vector a */
#define CMATH_UPPER_MASK 0x80000000 /* most significant w-r bits */
#define CMATH_LOWER_MASK 0x7fffffff /* least significant r bits */

/* Tempering parameters */
#define CMATH_TEMPERING_MASK_B 0x9d2c5680
#define CMATH_TEMPERING_MASK_C 0xefc60000
#define CMATH_TEMPERING_SHIFT_U(y)  (y >> 11)
#define CMATH_TEMPERING_SHIFT_S(y)  (y << 7)
#define CMATH_TEMPERING_SHIFT_T(y)  (y << 15)
#define CMATH_TEMPERING_SHIFT_L(y)  (y >> 18)

class CRandom
{
   // DATA
   unsigned int             rseed;
   unsigned long mt[CMATH_N];      /* the array for the state vector  */
   int mti;                 /* mti==N+1 means mt[N] is not initialized */


   // FUNCTIONS
public:
   CRandom(void);

   unsigned int     Random( unsigned int n );
   void   SetRandomSeed(unsigned int n);
   unsigned int     GetRandomSeed(void);
   void   Randomize(void);
};

CRandom::CRandom(void)
{
   rseed = 1;
   mti=CMATH_N+1;
}

// Returns a number from 0 to n (excluding n)
unsigned int CRandom::Random( unsigned int n )
{
    unsigned long y;
    static unsigned long mag01[2]={0x0, CMATH_MATRIX_A};

   if(n==0)
```

```
      return(0);

    /* mag01[x] = x * MATRIX_A  for x=0,1 */

    if (mti >= CMATH_N) { /* generate N words at one time */
        int kk;

        if (mti == CMATH_N+1)   /* if sgenrand() has not been called, */
            SetRandomSeed(4357); /* a default initial seed is used   */

        for (kk=0;kk<CMATH_N-CMATH_M;kk++) {
            y = (mt[kk]&CMATH_UPPER_MASK)|(mt[kk+1]&CMATH_LOWER_MASK);
            mt[kk] = mt[kk+CMATH_M] ^ (y >> 1) ^ mag01[y & 0x1];
        }
        for (;kk<CMATH_N-1;kk++) {
            y = (mt[kk]&CMATH_UPPER_MASK)|(mt[kk+1]&CMATH_LOWER_MASK);
            mt[kk] = mt[kk+(CMATH_M-CMATH_N)] ^ (y >> 1) ^ mag01[y & 0x1];
        }
        y = (mt[CMATH_N-1]&CMATH_UPPER_MASK)|(mt[0]&CMATH_LOWER_MASK);
        mt[CMATH_N-1] = mt[CMATH_M-1] ^ (y >> 1) ^ mag01[y & 0x1];

        mti = 0;
    }

    y = mt[mti++];
    y ^= CMATH_TEMPERING_SHIFT_U(y);
    y ^= CMATH_TEMPERING_SHIFT_S(y) & CMATH_TEMPERING_MASK_B;
    y ^= CMATH_TEMPERING_SHIFT_T(y) & CMATH_TEMPERING_MASK_C;
    y ^= CMATH_TEMPERING_SHIFT_L(y);

    return (y%n);

}

void CRandom::SetRandomSeed(unsigned int n)
{
   /* setting initial seeds to mt[N] using         */
   /* the generator Line 25 of Table 1 in          */
   /* [KNUTH 1981, The Art of Computer Programming */
   /*    Vol. 2 (2nd Ed.), pp102]                  */
   mt[0]= n & 0xffffffff;
   for (mti=1; mti<CMATH_N; mti++)
     mt[mti] = (69069 * mt[mti-1]) & 0xffffffff;

   rseed = n;
}
```

```
unsigned int CRandom::GetRandomSeed(void)
{
   return(rseed);
}

void CRandom::Randomize(void)
{
   SetRandomSeed(time(NULL));
}
```


The original code has been modified to include a few useful bits, one of which was to allow this class to save and reload its random number seed, which can be used to replay random number sequences by simply storing the seed. Here's an example of how to you can use the class:

```
CRandom r;
r.Randomize();
unsigned int num = r.Random(100);   // returns a number from 0-99, inclusive
```

You should use a few instantiations of this class in your game, each one generating random numbers for a different part of your game. Here's why: Let's say you want to generate some random taunts from AI characters. If you use a different random number sequence from the sequence that generates the contents of treasure chests, you can be sure that if the player turns off character audio the same RNG sequence will result for the treasure chests, which nicely compartmentalizes your game. In other words, your game becomes predictable, and testable.

I was working on an automation system for some Microsoft games, and the thing would just not work right. The goal of the system was to be able to record game sessions and play them back. The system was great for testers and programmers alike. It's hard to play a few million hands of blackjack. Every day. Our programming team realized that since the same RNG was being called for every system of the game, small aberrations would begin to result as calls to the RNG would begin to go out of sync. This was especially true for random character audio, since the timing of character audio was completely dependant on another thread, which was impossible to synchronize. When we used one CRandom class for each subsystem of the game, the problem disappeared.

Supporting Optional Variables with Optional<T>

A really favorite template of mine is one that encapsulates optional variables. Every variable stores values, but they don't store whether the current value is valid. Optional variables store this information to indicate if the variable is valid or initialized. Think about it, how many times have you had to use a special return value to signify some kind of error case?

Take a look at this code, and you'll see what I'm talking about:

```
bool DumbCalculate1(int &spline)
{
   // imagine some code here....
   //
   // The return value is the error, and the value of spline is invalid return
   false;
}

#define ERROR_IN_DUMBCALCULATE (-8675309)
int DumbCalculate2()
{
   // imagine some code here....
   //
   // The return value is a "special" value, we hope could never be actually
   // calculated
   return ERROR_IN_DUMBCALCULATE;
}

int _tmain(void)
{
   ////////////////////////////////////////////////////////////////////////////////
   // Dumb way #1 - use a return error code, and a reference to get to your data.
   //
   int dumbAnswer1;
   if (DumbCalculate1(dumbAnswer1))
   {
      // do my business...
   }

   ////////////////////////////////////////////////////////////////////////////////
   // Dumb way #2 - use a "special" return value to signify an error
   int dumbAnswer2 = DumbCalculate2();
   if (dumbAnswer2 != ERROR_IN_DUMBCALCULATE)
   {
```

```
        // do my business...
    }

}
```

There are two evil practices in this code. The first practice, "Dumb Way #1" requires that you use a separate return value for success or failure. This causes problems because you can't use the return value `DumbCalculate1()` function as the parameter to another function because the return value is an error code:

3

```
    AnotherFunction(DumbCalculate1());                // whoops. Can't do this!
```

The second practice I've seen that drives me up the wall is using a "special" return value to signify an error. This is illustrated in the `DumbCalculate2()` call. In many cases, the value chosen for the error case is a legal value, although it may be one that will "almost never" happen. If those chances are one in a million and your game sells a million copies, how many times per day do you think someone is going to get on the phone and call your friendly customer service people? Too many.

Here's the code for `optional<T>`, a template class that solves this problem.

```
#pragma once

//////////////////////////////////////////////////////////////////////////////
// optional.h
//
// An isolation point for optionality, provides a way to define
// objects having to provide a special "null" state.
//
// In short:
//
// struct optional<T>
// {
//       bool m_bValid;
//
//      T m_data;
// };
//
//

#include <new>
#include <assert.h>
```

```
class optional_empty { };

template <unsigned long size>
class optional_base
{
public:
    // Default - invalid.

    optional_base() : m_bValid(false) { }

    optional_base & operator = (optional_base const & t)
    {
      m_bValid = t.m_bValid;
      return * this;
    }

   //Copy constructor
    optional_base(optional_base const & other)
      : m_bValid(other.m_bValid)  { }

   //utility functions
   bool const valid() const         { return m_bValid; }
   bool const invalid() const       { return !m_bValid; }

protected:
    bool m_bValid;
    char m_data[size];  // storage space for T
};

template <class T>
class optional : public optional_base<sizeof(T)>
{
public:
    // Default - invalid.

    optional()          {    }
    optional(T const & t)  { construct(t); m_bValid = (true);  }
    optional(optional_empty const &) {      }

    optional & operator = (T const & t)
    {
        if (m_bValid)
        {
            * GetT() = t;
        }
        else
```

```
        {
            construct(t);
            m_bValid = true;        // order important for exception safety.
        }

        return * this;
    }

    //Copy constructor
     optional(optional const & other)
    {
      if (other.m_bValid)
      {
        construct(* other);
        m_bValid = true;    // order important for exception safety.
      }
     }

     optional & operator = (optional const & other)
     {
      assert(! (this == & other));  // don't copy over self!
      if (m_bValid)
      {              // first, have to destroy our original.
        m_bValid = false;   // for exception safety if destroy() throws.
                     // (big trouble if destroy() throws, though)
        destroy();
      }

      if (other.m_bValid)
      {
        construct(* other);
        m_bValid = true;    // order vital.

      }
      return * this;
     }

    bool const operator == (optional const & other) const
    {
      if ((! valid()) && (! other.valid())) { return true; }
      if (valid() ^ other.valid()) { return false; }
      return ((* * this) == (* other));
    }

    bool const operator < (optional const & other) const
    {
```

3

```
        // equally invalid - not smaller.
        if ((! valid()) && (! other.valid()))   { return false; }

        // I'm not valid, other must be, smaller.
        if (! valid()) { return true; }

        // I'm valid, other is not valid, I'm larger
        if (! other.valid()) { return false; }

        return ((* * this) < (* other));
    }

     ~optional() { if (m_bValid) destroy(); }

    // Accessors.

    T const & operator * () const     { assert(m_bValid); return * GetT(); }
    T & operator * ()                 { assert(m_bValid); return * GetT(); }
    T const * const operator -> () const  { assert(m_bValid); return GetT(); }
    T    * const operator -> ()     { assert(m_bValid); return GetT(); }

    //This clears the value of this optional variable and makes it invalid once
    // again.
    void clear()
    {
        if (m_bValid)
        {
            m_bValid = false;
            destroy();
        }
    }

    //utility functions
    bool const valid() const          { return m_bValid; }
    bool const invalid() const        { return !m_bValid; }

private:


     T const * const GetT() const { return reinterpret_cast<T const *
const>(m_data); }
     T * const GetT()
            { return reinterpret_cast<T * const>(m_data);}
     void construct(T const & t)  { new (GetT()) T(t); }
     void destroy() { GetT()->~T(); }
};
```

As you can see, it's not as simple as storing a Boolean value along with your data. The extra work in this class handles comparing optional objects with each other and getting to the data the object represents.

Here's an example of how to use `optional<T>`:


```
////////////////////////////////////////////////////////////////////////////////
// Optional.cpp : Defines the entry point for the console application.
//

#include "stdafx.h"
#include "optional.h"

optional<int> Calculate()
{
   optional<int> spline;
   spline = 10;                    // you assign values to optionals like this...
   spline = optional_empty();      // or you could give them the empty value
   spline.clear();                // or you could clear them to make them invalid

   return spline;
}

int main(void)
{
   ////////////////////////////////////////////////////////////////////////////////
   // Using optional<T>
       //
   optional<int> answer = Calculate();
   if (answer.valid())
   {
     // do my business...
   }
   return 0;
}
```

I personally don't see why so many programmers have it out for the value (-1). Everyone seems to use that to stand for some error case. I think (-1) is a fine upstanding number and I refuse to abuse it. Use `optional<T>`, and join me in saving (-1) from further abuse.

Pseudo-Random Traversal of a Set

Have you ever wondered how the "random" button on your CD player worked? It will play every song on your CD at random without playing the same song twice. That's a really useful solution for making sure players in your games see the widest variety of features like objects, effects, or characters before they have the chance of seeing the same ones over again.

The following code uses a mathematical feature of prime numbers and quadratic equations. The algorithm requires a prime number larger than the ordinal value of the set you wish to traverse. If your set had ten members, your prime number would be eleven. Of course, the algorithm doesn't generate prime numbers; instead it just keeps a select set of prime numbers around in a lookup table. If you need bigger primes, there's a convenient web site for you to check out.

Here's how it works: A skip value is calculated by choosing three random values greater than zero. These values become the coefficients of the quadratic, and the domain value (x) is set to the ordinal value of the set:

```
Skip = RandomA * (members * members) + RandomB * members + RandomC
```

Armed with this skip value, you can use this piece of code to traverse the entire set exactly once, in a pseudo random order:

```
nextMember += skip;
nextMember %= prime;
```

The value of skip is so much larger than the number of members of your set that the chosen value seems to skip around at random. Of course, this code is inside a while loop to catch the case where the value chosen is larger than your set but still smaller than the prime number. Here's the source code:

```
/******************************************************************
PrimeSearch.h

This class enables you to visit each and every member of an array
exactly once in an apparently random order.

NOTE: If you want the search to start over at the beginning again -
you must call the Restart() method, OR call GetNext(true).

*******************************************************************/

class PrimeSearch
{
   static int prime_array[];

   int skip;
```

```
   int currentPosition;
   int maxElements;
   int *currentPrime;
   int searches;

   CRandom r;

public:
   PrimeSearch(int elements);
   int GetNext(bool restart=false);
   bool Done() { return (searches==*currentPrime); }
   void Restart() { currentPosition=0; searches=0; }
};

/*********************************************************************
PrimeSearch.cpp
*********************************************************************/

int PrimeSearch::prime_array[] =
{
   // choose the prime numbers to closely match the expected members
   // of the sets.

   2, 3, 5, 7,
   11, 13, 17, 19, 23, 29, 31, 37, 41, 43, 47,
   53, 59, 61, 67, 71, 73, 79, 83, 89, 97,
   101, 103, 107, 109, 113, 127, 131, 137, 139, 149,
   151, 157, 163, 167, 173, 179, 181, 191, 193, 197, 199,
   211, 223, 227, 229, 233, 239, 241,

   // begin to skip even more primes

   5003, 5101, 5209, 5303, 5407, 5501, 5623, 5701, 5801, 5903,
   6007, 6101, 6211, 6301, 6421, 6521, 6607, 6701, 6803, 6907,
   7001, 7103, 7207, 7307, 7411, 7507, 7603, 7703, 7817, 7901,
   8009, 8101, 8209, 8311, 8419, 8501, 8609, 8707, 8803, 8923,
   9001, 9103, 9203, 9311, 9403, 9511, 9601, 9719, 9803, 9901,

   // and even more
   10007, 10501, 11003, 11503, 12007, 12503, 13001, 13513, 14009, 14503,
   15013, 15511, 16033, 16519, 17011, 17509, 18013, 18503, 19001, 19501,
   20011, 20507, 21001, 21503, 22003, 22501, 23003, 23509, 24001, 24509

   // if you need more primes - go get them yourself!!!!

   // Create a bigger array of prime numbers by using this web site:
```

```
   // http://www.rsok.com/~jrm/printprimes.html
};


PrimeSearch::PrimeSearch(int elements)
{
   assert(elements>0 && "You can't do a this if you have 0 elements to search
         through, buddy-boy");

   maxElements = elements;

   int a = (rand()%13)+1;
   int b = (rand()%7)+1;
   int c = (rand()%5)+1;

   skip = (a * maxElements * maxElements) + (b * maxElements) + c;
   skip &= ~0xc0000000;            // this keeps skip from becoming too
                                  // large....

   Restart();

   currentPrime = prime_array;
   int s = sizeof(prime_array)/sizeof(prime_array[0]);

   // if this assert gets hit you didn't have enough prime numbers in your set.
   // Go back to the web site.
   assert(prime_array[s-1]>maxElements);

   while (*currentPrime < maxElements)
   {
      currentPrime++;
   }

   int test = skip % *currentPrime;
   if (!test)
      skip++;
}

int PrimeSearch::GetNext(bool restart)
{
   if (restart)
      Restart();

   if (Done())
      return -1;

   bool done = false;
```

```
    int nextMember = currentPosition;

    while (!done)
    {
        nextMember = nextMember + skip;
        nextMember %= *currentPrime;
        searches++;

        if (nextMember < maxElements)
        {
            currentPosition = nextMember;
            done = true;
        }
    }

    return currentPosition;
}
```

I'll show you a trivial example to make a point.

```
void FadeToBlack(Screen *screen)
{
    int w = screen.GetWidth();
    int h = screen.GetHeight();

    int pixels = w * h;

    PrimeSearch search(pixels);

    int p;

    while((p=search.GetNext())!=-1)
    {
        int x = p % w;
        int y = h / p;

        screen.SetPixel(x, y, BLACK);

        // of course, you wouldn't blit every pixel change.
        screen.Blit();
    }
```

The example sets random pixels to black until the entire screen is erased. I should warn you now that this code is completely stupid, for two reasons. First, you wouldn't set one pixel at a time. Second, you would likely use a pixel shader to do this. I told you the example was trivial: use `PrimeSearch` for other cool things like spawning creatures, weapons, and other random stuff.

Well, That Wasn't So Dumb

I guess the stuff in this chapter wasn't so dumb after all, in fact some of it might have been downright intelligent. I wish I had more pages because there are tons of programming gems and even game programming gems out there. Most of it you'll beg or borrow from your colleagues. Some of it you'll create yourself after you solve a challenging problem.

However you find them, don't forget to share.

Chapter 4

Building Your Game

Do you ever freeze up just before starting a new project? I do. I get hung up thinking about the perfect directory structure, where the art and sound data should be stored, how the build process should work, and mostly how I will keep my new game from becoming a horrible mess. By the end of a project, it usually turns out to be a mess anyway! So, I'm always thankful I plan out a directory structure, employ good version control tools, and incorporate automation scripts that all keep entropy just low enough for a human like me to be able to keep track of what I'm doing.

In this chapter I'm going to tell you everything you need to know to get your game projects organized from the start, and how to use project files and version control tools effectively. This is an area where many game developers try to cut corners so my advice is to pay close attention and invest your time and money wisely to ensure that your projects go together smoothly.

As you read through this chapter you might feel that you are getting an education in software engineering. Try not to feel overwhelmed. These techniques are very critical to the process of successfully developing games and they are used by real game developers.

A Little Motivation

Games are much more than source code. A typical game includes processed art and sound data, map levels, event scripts, test tools, and more. The raw art and sound files are usually stored on a network or a secondary storage area because they are huge. Don't forget the project documentation—both the docs that ship with your project, such as the user guide, and the internal documents, such as the functional specs and test plans.

There are two essential problems that all these files create. First, the sheer number of game files for art, sound, music, and other assets need to have some rational organization—there can be thousands of these files. Word has it that games like Age of Empires have hundreds of thousands of asset files in production. With this many files it can be really easy to lose track of one, or a few hundred. The second problem is the difficulty of ensuring that sensitive debug builds and other internal files are kept separate from the stuff that will be burned onto the optical media. The best setup lets you burn a single directory tree to a test CD/DVD without worrying about deleting anything.

Over the last few years I've settled on a project organization that solves these two problems. But wait, there's more. The process of building a project should be as automatic as possible. You should be able to automatically build your game every night so that you can check your latest work. A game that can't build every day is in big trouble. Even dumb producers know this so if you want an easy way to get a project snuffed, just make it impossible to fulfill a build request at a moment's notice.

The directory structure, project settings, and development scripts you use should make building, publishing, and rebuilding a published build a snap. If you're lucky you'll have a nice source code repository like Perforce or CVS, and you can use branches to separate milestone builds from code under heavy development. It's a pain to stop coding just because everyone's paycheck is dependent on a milestone build!

Everyone does things differently but the project organization, build scripts and build process you'll learn in this chapter are hard to beat. I figure that if they're good enough for Microsoft, and they got our projects out the door on time, I'll keep them.

Creating a Project

This might sound a little hokey but every project I work on has its own code word. I picked this up from Microsoft and I love it. You should let your project team choose the code word, but try to make sure that the name chosen is somewhat cryptic. It's actually really convenient if you end up at the bar with a bunch of software developers from other companies. You can talk all day about finishing a build for "Slickrock" or that "Rainman" needs another programmer. Cloak and dagger aside, there's a real utilitarian reason to use short code words for projects.

The code word becomes the name for your top level directory. This is where all of your project files should be stored. Other files such as special build files or Visual Studio.NET SLN files should also be named using the code word. If you follow this standard, you can write one build script for your whole project, even if you have multiple projects taking place simultaneously.

Beyond that, a code word for a project has one other use: If you end up making multiple versions of the same product, you can use different code words to refer to them instead of version numbers. You are ready to start your project: choose a code word and create your top level directory. May whatever Gods you believe in have mercy on your soul:

```
mkdir <codeword>.
```

Creating a Bullet-Proof Directory Structure

Over the years of developing complex projects, I've experimented with different directory structures trying to find the ideal structure that will work with most projects. I've learned that it is important to have a good working directory structure from the start. It will help you work your way through all of the stages of developing a project—from writing your first lines of source code to testing and debugging your project. You also need to keep in mind that you'll likely need to share aspects of your project with others during the development process even if you are the only one writing all of the source code. For example, you might need to hire an independent testing team to work over your game. If you organize your project well, you'll be able to share files when you need to.

Keeping all of this in mind, here's my recommended directory structure where you should store each project you develop, including your game engine:

- Docs
- Source
- Obj
- Bin
- Test

The *Docs* directory is a reference for the development team. It should have an organized hierarchy to store both design documents and technical specifications. I always put a copy of the contract exhibits and milestone acceptance criteria for my team, since these documents specify our obligations to the publisher. (You don't want to ever forget who is paying the bills!) While I'm developing a project, it's not unusual to find detailed character scripts, initial user interface designs, and other works in progress in the Docs directory.

The source code lives in the *Source* directory. It should be organized by the programmers in whatever manner they see fit. The project's solution file or makefile should also reside in the Source directory, and be named according to the code word for the project. The rest of the source code should be organized into other directories below Source.

When a project is being built, each build target will place temporary files into the *Obj* directory. On most projects you'll have at least a *Debug* directory to hold the debug build and a *Release* directory to hold the release build. You may have other build targets, and if you do, put them in their own directory.

Visual Studio.NET does a really bad thing by assuming that software engineers want their build targets to clutter up the Source directory. I find this annoying, since I don't want a single byte of the Source directory to change when I build my project. Why, you ask? First, I like to be able to copy the entire Source directory for publishing or backup without worrying about large temporary files. Secondly, I can compare two different Source directories from version to version to see only the deltas in the source code, instead of wading through hundreds of useless OBJ, SBR, and other files. Thirdly, I know I can always delete the Obj directory to force a new build of the entire project. I also know that I never have to backup or publish the Obj directory.

The *Bin* directory should hold the release build and every game data file that is used to create your project. You should be able to send the contents of the Bin directory to a separate testing group or to someone in the press, and they'd have everything they would need to run and test the game. You also want to ensure that they don't get anything you want to keep to yourself, such as confidential project documentation or your crown jewels - the source code. If you take the time to set up a directory that stores the files that you may be providing to others from time to time, you'll likely avoid sending out your source code or internal project design documents.

The *Test* directory should hold the debug target of the game, and special files only for the test team. It usually contains test scripts, files that unlock cheats, and test utilities. Most importantly, it should contain the release notes for the latest build. The release notes are a list of features that work, or don't work in the latest build. They also contain quick instructions about anything the test team needs to know, such as how to expose a certain feature or a part of your game that needs special attention. As you are developing your project, I strongly encourage you to keep the release notes up to date. If you hand your game over to a testing team they won't have to pull out their hair trying to figure out how to get your project to work.

You'll discover that Visual Studio.NET doesn't like this directory structure very much, and it's a pain to create projects under this standard. VS.NET assumes that everything in the project lives underneath the directory that stores the solution file. It may be a pain to get VS.NET to conform to this structure but trust me it is worth it.

The directory structure is useful because it caters to all the different people and groups that need access to your game development files. The development team gets access to the whole thing. Executives and press looking for the odd demo can copy the Bin directory whenever they want. The test group grabs Bin and Test and they have everything they need. The Docs directory grows quickly, so separating it from Bin, Test, and Source helps you manage the size of your builds if you must FTP them to someone like Microsoft.

If you store the build targets in the Source directory, like Visual Studio.NET wants you to, you'll have to write complicated batch files to extract the build target, clean temporary files, and match game data with executables. Those batch files are a pain to maintain, and are a frequent source of bad builds. If you pound VS.NET for a little while to get a better directory structure started, you won't have to worry about a nasty batch file during the life of your product.

The files stored in the top level are helper batch files or scripts for the automatic build software. One of these helper files copies the right directories depending on who needs them, a batch file called *updaterelease.bat*.


```
@echo off
:: UpdateRelease.bat
:: ================================================

if '%1'=='' goto usage
if '%2'=='' goto usage

echo Updating %1

:: Remove and recreate the desintation directory
rd /s /q "%1"
md "%1"

:: Call parallel batch file for the game engine
cd ..\Engine
call updaterelease %1 %2

:: Set project by the code word
set PROJECT=Jokerz
cd ..\%PROJECT%

if '%2'=='test' goto test
if '%2'=='bin' goto bin
goto usage

:test
:: -------------------------
:: This copies all the files needed for testing:
::   Source tree - all the source code
::   Obj tree - symbol files and map files
::   Test tree - testing scripts, debug exes, etc.
::
echo d | xcopy Source "%1\%PROJECT%\Source" /s/e
echo d | xcopy Obj "%1\%PROJECT%\Obj" /s/e
echo d | xcopy Test "%1\%PROJECT%\Test" /s/e
```

```
rem NOTE THERE IS NO GOTO - IT FALLS THROUGH TO THE :bin label
rem
rem NOTE We don't copy the Docs directory - it's way too big!!!

:bin
:: -------------------------
:: This copies the Bin directory
::
echo d | xcopy Bin "%1\%PROJECT%\Bin" /s/e

:nuke
:: -------------------------
:: This deletes intermediate or temporary files,
:: if they were copied
::
del /s/q %1\*.scc %1\*.obj %1\*.sbr %1\*.ilk %1\*.pch

:: -------------------------
:: Make a file inventory
dir %1 /s  > %1\FileList.txt

echo Done updating %1.
SET PROJECT=
set errorlevel=0
goto exit

:usage
rem ─────────────────────
echo ======================================================
echo Usage - updaterelease [target directory] { test  bin }
echo    test:  copies Source, Obj, Test, Bin, Engine
echo    bin:   copies Bin
echo    All commands will remove SCC, OBJ, SBR, ILK, and PCH files.
echo ======================================================
set errorlevel=1

:exit
```

Our nightly builds for the Jokerz project were stored in S:\Nightly\Jokerz, a spot on our network. When the nightly build is completed the automatic scripts call the batch file and the files are copied:

```
updaterelease S:\Nightly\Jokerz test
```

Where to Put Your Game Engine

In case it wasn't clear, your game engine should get its own directory, with the same directory structure in parallel with your game. It should get its own `updaterelease.bat` file. On one project I worked on, our game engine had a terrible code name: **Engine**. It was stored in an Engine directory with Source, Docs, Obj, and Lib instead of Bin. There was some debate about separating the include files into an `Inc` directory at the top level. That's a winner of an idea because it allows the game engine to be published with only the include files and the library. The source code would remain safely in our hands.

Setting Visual Studio Build Options

I mentioned that you have to coax Visual Studio.NET to move its intermediate and output files outside the directory that stores the solution file. In the project settings dialog (or project properties in .NET) you set the output directory and intermediate directory to `..\Obj\Debug` for the debug build and `..\Obj\Release` for the release build. Plenty of temporary files are stored in the output directory—the precompiled header file, browser files, and other garbage. Put these files in the `Obj` directory tree to keep the `Bin` and `Test` directories free of these files. The executable is placed in the right spot by setting the output file of the linker.

Under the linker settings, you set the output file name to `..\Test\MyGamed.exe` for the debug build and `..\Bin\MyGame.exe` for the release build.

You can distinguish the debug and release files by adding a 'd' to the end of any final build target. If for any reason the files need to coexist in the same directory you don't have to worry about copying them or creating temporary names. Both executables can still find source code in `..\Source`, and debug symbols in `..\Obj\Debug` or `..\Obj\Release`.

With the target directories set right, Visual Studio.NET has some macros you can use in your project settings.

- $(IntDir): The path to intermediate files
- $(OutDir): The path to the output directory (`..\Bin\` or `..\Test\`)
- $(TargetDir): The path to the primary output file
- $(TargetName): The name of the primary output file of the build without the extension
- $(TargetPath): The fully qualified path and filename for the output file

Use these macros for the following settings:

- Debugging / Debugging Command: $(TargetPath) will call the right executable for each build target
- Debugging / Working Directory: Should always be ..`\Bin`. It works with all build targets
- C/C++ / Precompiled Headers / Precompiled Header File: $(IntDir)$(TargetName).pch
- C/C++ / Output Files: $(IntDir) for the ASM list location, object file name, and program database file name
- C/C++ / Browse Information / Browse Files: $(IntDir)
- Linker / Debug Settings / Generate Program Database File: $(IntDir)$(TargetName).pdb
- Linker / Debug Settings / Map File: $(IntDir)$(TargetName).map

There are plenty of third-party tools that work with Visual Studio. Most of them make the same assumptions about project default directories that Visual Studio does. They'll still work with my suggested directory structure but you'll have to tweak the search directories for source code and symbol files.

The macros also help to keep the differences between the build targets to a minimum. For example, $(IntDir) can stand for `..\Obj\Debug or ..\Obj\Release` because they are the same in all build targets and they don't disappear when you choose "All Configurations" in the project settings dialog.

Building Configurations

Every project should have two build targets at a minimum: debug and release. The release build will enable optimizations and remove symbols and other debug information. You could create another release build target, one that enables debugging symbols, but I'd advise against it. It's relatively rare to have to debug into a release build and it's easy enough to enable debugging a release build on someone's development machine and recompile. A separate build target bloats the build process.

Try to keep all your build targets alive and working every day. If you ignore any build configuration, especially the release build, it could take a very long time to figure out why it's not working properly.

Source Code Repositories and Version Control

In comparing game development with other kinds of software development projects what really stands out is the sheer number of parts that are required. Typically, hundreds of source code files of every description are used. Every sound effect comes from a source

WAV or MP3. Every texture has a source PSD or TGA and a companion JPG or BMP after it's been compressed. Every model has a MAX file (if you use 3D Studio) and has multiple source textures. You might also have HTML files for online help or strategy guides. The list goes on and on. Even small games have hundreds, if not thousands, of individual files that all have to be created, checked, fixed, rechecked, tracked, and installed into the game.

Back in the old days the source files for a big project were typically spread all over the place. Some files were stored on a network (if you knew where to look) but most were scattered in various places on different local desktop computers, never to be seen again after the project finished. Unfortunately, these files were frequently lost or destroyed while the project was in production. The artist or programmer would have to grudgingly recreate their work, a hateful task at best.

When I first arrived at Origin Systems I noticed some odd labels taped to people's monitors. One said, "The Flame of the Map" and another "The Flame of Conversation." I thought these phrases were Origin's version of Employee of the Month but I was wrong. This was source control in the days of SneakerNet, when Origin didn't have a LAN. If someone wanted to work on something, they physically walked to the machine that was the "Flame of Such and Such" and copied the relevant files onto a floppy disk, stole the flame label, and went back to their machine. Then they became the "Flame." When a build was assembled for QA, everyone carried their floppy disks to the build computer and copied all the flames to one place. Believe it or not, this system worked just fine.

Source control management is a common process used by programmers throughout the game industry. Team programming is simply too hard and too risky to manage without it. Source control can also track media assets such as sound and art, but non-programmers find source control systems unwieldy and will bitterly complain for a better solution.

Most companies choose to track these bits and pieces with the help of a database. The tool you use doesn't have to be anything more than an Excel spreadsheet to keep a list of each file, who touched it last, what's in the file, and why it is important to your game. If you're really cool you might even write a little PHP/MySQL portal site and put a complete content management intranet up on your local network to track files.

To help you put your own version control process in place, I'll introduce you to some of the more popular version control tools that professional game developers use in their practice. I'll also tell you which ones to avoid. Of course, keep in mind that there is no perfect, one-size-fits-all tool or solution. The important thing is that you put some type of process together and that you do it at the beginning of any project.

AlienBrain from NXN

For those of you with really serious asset tracking problems and a good budget to blow, there's a pretty good solution out there that will track your source code and other assets: AlienBrain from NXN. NXN has a client list with over sixty companies that looks like a who's who of the PC and console computer game industry. Their software integrates with nearly every programming and artist tool out there: CodeWarrior, Visual C++, 3DStudio Max, Maya, Photoshop, and many others. An example of AlienBrain is shown in Figure 4.1.

The downside to AlienBrain is that it's expensive; however, the company, to its credit, has been bringing the price down. The way I view the cost issue is that if a tool like this saves each person on your team ten hours or more of work by keeping good assets from getting wiped out, it will easily pay for itself.

Programmers and "build gurus" will like the fact that AlienBrain has sophisticated branching and pinning mechanisms just like the more advanced source code repositories on the market. (I'll discuss the importance of branching a little later in this chapter.) Artists and other contributors will actually use this product, unlike others that are mainly designed to integrate well with Visual Studio and not creative applications such as Photoshop and 3D Studio Max. One of the big drawbacks to other products is their rather naïve treatment of non-text files. AlienBrain was written with these files in mind.

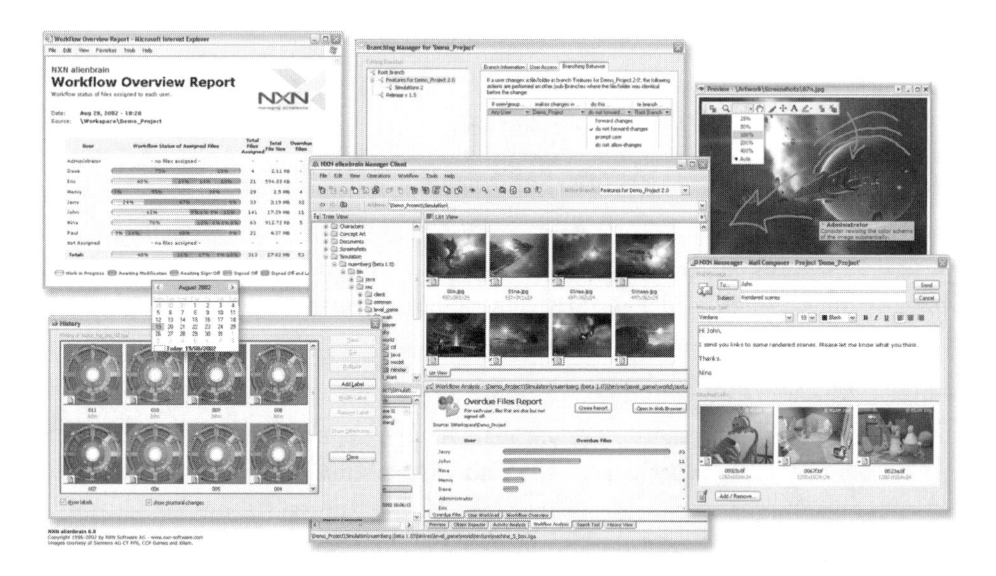

Figure 4.1
AlienBrain from NXN.

Visual SourceSafe from Microsoft

Visual SourceSafe is the source repository distributed with Microsoft's Visual Studio and it is an excellent example of, "You get what you pay for." What attracts most people to this product is a easy to use GUI interface and an extremely simple setup. You can be up and running on SourceSafe in ten minutes if you don't type slowly.

The biggest problem with SourceSafe is how it stores the source repository. If you dig a bit into the shared files where the repository is stored you'll find a **data** directory with a huge tree of files with odd names like **AAAAAAAB.AAA** and **AAACCCAA.AAB**. The contents of these files are clear text, or nearly, so this wacky naming scheme couldn't have been for security reasons. If anyone out there knows why they did it this way drop me an email; I'm completely stumped.

Each file stores a reverse delta of previous revisions of a file in the repository. Every revision of a file will create a new SourceSafe file with one of those wacky names. For those of you paying attention you'll remember that many of these files will be pretty small, given that some source changes could be as simple as a single character change. The amount of network drive space taken up by SourceSafe is pretty unacceptable in my humble opinion.

There's also a serious problem with speed. Even small projects get to be a few hundred files in size, and large projects can be tens, or even hundreds of thousands of files. Because SourceSafe uses the network directory structure to store its data, access time for opening and closing all these files is quite long and programmers can wait forever while simply checking to see if they have the most recent files. SourceSafe doesn't support branching (see my discussion on branching a little later), unless you make a complete copy of the entire tree you are branching.

Forget attempting to access SourceSafe remotely. Searching thousands of files over a pokey internet connection is murder. Don't even try it. Finally, SourceSafe's file index database can break down, and even the little analyzer utility will throw up its hands and tell you to start over. I've finished projects under a corrupted database before, it just happened that the corruption was affecting a previous version of a file that I didn't need. I was lucky.

If I haven't convinced you to try something other than SourceSafe, let me just say it: *Don't use SourceSafe*. I've heard rumors that Microsoft doesn't use it either. I guess they don't eat their own dogfood, huh?

The Free Ones: CVS, RCS, ...

Those hard core folks in the Linux community will be happy to know I fully support the use of RCS, CVS, and the other free source code repositories out there. These tools are command line repositories, although the industrious web surfer can find GUI utilities and integration utilities for those of us who have forgotten what a command line looks like.

The great thing about these applications is that they have hundreds of thousands of users and an enormous following. If you have any problems using these tools or getting them set up (which is usually the most difficult part), you'll find lots of help quickly. Probably the most important thing about using these tools is that they are free. You can't argue with that.

Perforce by Perforce Software

If AlienBrain is just out of reach for you financially, you should get Perforce. I've used this product for years and it's never let me down. For any of you lucky enough to move from SourceSafe to Perforce, the first thing you'll notice is its speed. It's damn fast.

Perforce uses a client/server architecture and a Btrieve-based database for storing the repository. That architecture simply blows the pants off anything that uses the network directory hierarchy. More than storing the current status of each version of each file, it even stores the status of each file for everyone who has a client connection. That's why most SourceSafe slaves freak out when they use Perforce the first time; it's so fast they don't believe its actually doing anything. Of course, this makes remote access as fast as it can possibly be.

Since Perforce "knows" the status of any file on your system, you have to be careful to inform it if you do anything to a file outside of the Perforce utilities, such as changing a file you don't have checked out or opened for edit. Perforce will assume you know what you are doing and happily ignore the change. SourceSafe actually does local data/time comparisons, so it will tell you that the local file is different than the network copy. This comes at a horrible degradation in speed.

Perforce has a nice GUI for anyone who doesn't want to use the command line. The GUI will perform about 95% of the tasks you ever need to perform, so you can leave the command line to someone who knows what they're doing.

The branching mechanisms are extremely efficient. If you make a branch from your main line of development to a test line, Perforce only keeps the deltas from branch to branch. Network space is saved, and reemerging branches is also very fast.

You'll find almost as many third party tools that work with Perforce as with some of the free repositories. Free downloads are available including tools that perform graphical merges, C++ APIs, conversion tools from other products like SourceSafe and PVCS, and tons of others.

The Really Expensive Tools: StarTeam and ClearCase

You know these products are expensive when they don't even list the cost per seat on their web site. Instead, you have to send your contact information to a salesman, who is bound to call you more than once.

Starbase's StarTeam and Rational's ClearCase are used at "serious" software companies that have equally serious budgets. These tools have some fantastic features that make all the programmers raise their eyebrows and go, "ohhhhh…" One in particular I found was a branch merge utility that graphically depicted the changes from one branch to another. Nice.

The reality of it is that if you can afford these packages you can afford AlienBrain, which is used by all the serious game studios. If you've really got that much money to burn, buy AlienBrain for everyone on your team and take the rest of the money and give everyone bigger bonuses.

Using Source Control Branches

I freely admit that just until last year I didn't use branching. I also admit that I didn't really know what it was for, but it also wasn't my fault. I blame Microsoft. Their Visual Source Safe tool is distributed with Visual Studio and many engineers use it without question. Microsoft engineers don't use it, and for good reason. Microsoft Office has hundreds of thousands of source files and many hundreds of engineers. SourceSafe was never designed to handle repositories of that size, and it doesn't have some critical features, especially branching.

Branching is a process where an entire source code repository is copied so that parallel development can proceed unhindered on both copies simultaneously. Sometimes the copies are merged back into one tree. It is equally possible that after being branched, the branched versions diverge entirely and are never merged. Why is branching so important? Branches of any code imply a fundamental difference in the lifecycle of that code. You might branch source code to create a new game. You might also branch source code to perform some heavy research. Sometimes a fundamental change, such as swapping out one rendering engine for another or coding a new object culling mechanism is too dangerous to attempt in the main line of code. If you make a new branch, you'll wall off your main line and get the benefits of source control.

SourceSafe's branching mechanism makes a complete copy of the entire source tree. That's slow and fat. Most decent repositories keep track of only the deltas from branch to branch. This approach is much faster and it doesn't penalize you for branching the code.

Here are the branches I use and why:

- *Main*: Normal development branch
- *Research*: A "playground" branch where anything goes, including trashing it entirely
- *Publish*: The branch submitted for milestone approval

The Research and Publish branches originate from the main branch. They may or may not be merged with the main branch, depending on what happens to the code. The Main branch supports the main development effort; most of the files in your project are changed in the main branch.

The Research branch supports experimental efforts. It's a great place to make some core API changes, swap in new middleware, or make any other crazy change without damaging the main line. The Publish branch is for milestone submissions or important demos. Programmers can code fast and furious in the main line while minor tweaks and bug fixes needed for milestone approval are tucked into the Publish branch.

Perhaps the best evidence for branching code can be found in how a team works under research and release scenarios. Consider a programming team about to reach a major milestone. The milestone is attached to a big chunk of cash, which is only paid out if the milestone is approved. The team is old fashioned and doesn't know anything about branching. Just before the build, the lead programmer runs around and makes everyone on the team promise not to check in any code while the build is compiling. Everyone promises to keep their work to themselves, but since the build takes a long time everyone continues to work on their own machines.

The build doesn't even compile the first time. One of the programmers forgets to check in a few files. They already started working on other things, but it was easier to revert the changes and fix the compile errors than attempt to finish their work. The programmer loses an hour of work for that—a big penalty. Another programmer considers making a big change to the AI code, but stops short. The AI code might have a few bugs that might halt the milestone, and it's too risky to make major changes. The programmer heads home for the weekend; a little annoyed that the build blocked productive work.

The completed build is FTP'd to the publisher's test department. Just for fun let's assume they upload the build late on Friday night. The test team downloads the new build on Monday morning and finds some heinous problem and can't even begin to run through the milestone acceptance checklist. They get on the phone and call the team; they need a new build pronto.

The problem is tracked to the sound system. The programmer working on the sound system came in over the weekend and ripped out the kitchen because he knew it was buggy, but he's halfway through and it will take two or three days to finish it. The only way a new build can happen fast is by making a band-aid change to the source code that existed on Friday, and launching a new build. Without a branch, the programmer grabs the build code by grabbing the version by date and time, or perhaps with a label if they were smart enough to set one. He hacks together a build and hopes it works. He can't check in the change, so the build has to happen on his machine or by hand copying code to the build machine, with the version control disabled. After the build is approved, all the changes have to be merged back into the latest code without losing anything or even worse, losing everything.

If you don't think this is that bad, you are probably working without branches and have trained yourself to enjoy this little hellish scenario. You never lose any code because you are careful, and so is everyone on your team. I used to think that way too, and I thought branches were too much trouble until I tried them myself.

From experiences like this, I've learned that there is a much better way to manage and build projects. Here's a much better way to do builds:

The lead programmer walks around and makes sure the team has all the milestone changes checked in. She goes to the build machine and launches a milestone build by double clicking on an icon. The build finishes with the same failure as the first team. Instead of reversing their latest work, the compile error is fixed on the build machine in the publish branch, leaving the main branch to be fixed later. No one loses any work. The AI programmer and sound programmer continue working, blissfully in the zone, and get loads of excellent code in the main branch.

The finished build is checked and sent to the publisher via the same FTP site on Friday night. When the phone call comes in Monday morning, the build is hosed, but the simple tweak is made in the publish branch. Every change is in the code repository but in two different branches. The milestone is approved and the lead programmer launches another build script to merge the changes in the publish branch back to the main line. The close script detects a merge conflict in the sound code and they fix it. All the code is back in the main line.

Every change, both the tweaks to fix the build and the ongoing development, is in the source repository. No one loses a single minute of time or line of code. Now, which approach do you like better?

Building the Game: A Black Art?

You can't build a testable version of your game by simply grabbing the latest source code and launching the compiler. Most games have multiple gigabytes of data, install programs, multiple languages, special tools, and all manner of components that have nothing at all to do with the executable. All of these components come together in one way or another during the build. Every shred of code and data must make it onto the install image on one or more CDs or on the network for the test team. Frequently, these components don't come together without a fight. Building the game is something of a black art, assigned to the most senior code shamans.

Ultima VIII had a build process that was truly insane. It went something like this:

1. Grab the latest source code: editor, game, and game scripts.
2. Build the game editor.
3. Run the game editor and execute a special command that nuked the local game data files and grab the latest ones from the shared network drive.
4. Build the game.
5. Run the UNK compiler (Ultima's game scripting language) to compile and link the game scripts for English. Don't ask me what UNK stands for…
6. Run the UNK compiler twice more, and compile the French and German game scripts.
7. Run the game and test it. Watch it break and loop back to Step 1, until the game finally works.
8. Copy the game and all the game data into a temp directory.
9. Compress the game data files.
10. Build the install program.
11. Copy the English, French, and German install images to 24 floppy disks.

12. Copy the CD-ROM image to the network. (The only CD burner was on the first floor.)
13. Go to the first floor media lab and make three copies of each install: 72 floppy disks and three CDs. Then, hope like hell there are enough floppy disks.

Before you ask, I'll just tell you that the fact that the build process for Ultima VIII had thirteen steps never sat very well with me. Each step generally failed at least twice for some dumb reason, which made building Ultima VIII no less than a four hour process—on a good day.

The build was actually fairly automated with batch files. The game editor even accepted command line parameters to perform the task of grabbing the latest map and other game data. Even so, building Ultima VIII was so difficult and fraught with error that I was the only person that ever successfully built a testable version of the game. That wasn't an accomplishment; it was a failure.

On one of my trips to Microsoft I learned something about how they build Office. The build process is completely automatic. The build lab for Office has a fleet of servers that build every version of Office in every language, and they never stop. The moment a build is complete they start again, constantly looking for compile errors introduced by someone in the last few minutes. Office is a huge piece of software. If Microsoft can automate a build as big and complex as this, surely you can automate yours.

Automate Your Builds

My experience has taught me that every project can and should have an automatic build. No exceptions. It's far easier (and safer) to maintain build scripts that automate the process instead of relying on a witchdoctor. My suggestion is that you should try to create Microsoft's build lab in miniature on your own project. Here is what's needed:

- Create a build machine.
- Find good tools for automatic building.
- Invest time up front creating automation scripts (and make sure you maintain them as your project progresses).

The Build Machine

Don't try to save a buck and use a programmer's development box as your build machine. Programmers are always downloading funky software, making operating system patches, and installing third-party development tools that suit their needs and style. A build machine should be a pristine environment that has known versions and updates for each piece of software: the operating system, compiler, internal tools, install program, and anything else used to build the game.

A complete backup of the build machine is good insurance. If you need to build an old project, the backup of the build machine will have the right versions of the compiler, operating system, and other tools. New versions and patches come out often, and even a project just twelve months old can be impossible to build, even if the source code is readily available in the source code repository. Just try to build something ten or twelve years old and you'll see what I mean. If anyone out there has a good copy of Turbo Pascal and IBM DOS 3.3, let me know!

The build machine should be extremely fast, have loads of RAM, and have a nice hard disk—preferably multiple hard disks. Compiling is RAM and hard disk intensive, so try to get the penny pinchers to buy a nice system. If you ever used the argument about how much money your company could save by buying fast computers for the programmers, imagine how easy it will be to buy a nice build machine. The entire test team might have to wait on a build; how much is that worth?

Automated Build Scripts

Automated builds have been around as long as there have been makefiles and command line compilers. I admit that I've never been good at the cryptic syntax of makefiles, which is one reason I've put off automating builds. If you use Visual Studio, you might consider using the pre-build or post-build settings to run some custom batch files or makefiles. I wouldn't, and here's why: You'll force every programmer to run the build scripts every time they build. That's probably wasteful at best, completely incorrect at worst.

Pre-build and post-build steps should run batch files, makefiles, or other utilities that are required every time the project is built. Build scripts tend to extract and prepare game executables and data for the test team. As an example, the build script will always grab the latest code from the source repository and rebuild the entire project from scratch. If you forced every programmer to do that for every compile, they'd lynch you.

Batch files and makefiles are perfectly fine solutions for any build script you need. There are some better tools for those like myself who like GUIs, such as Visual Build Pro from Kinook Software (see Figure 4.2).

This tool is better than batch files or makefiles because you can understand a complicated build process with failure steps and macros in a snap. The build script is hierarchical, each group possibly taking different steps if a component of the build fails. Visual Build also integrates cleanly with a wide variety of development tools and source code repositories.

Whatever scripting tool you use, make sure they can run from the command line. If you create internal tools to edit or analyze map data, run a proprietary compression

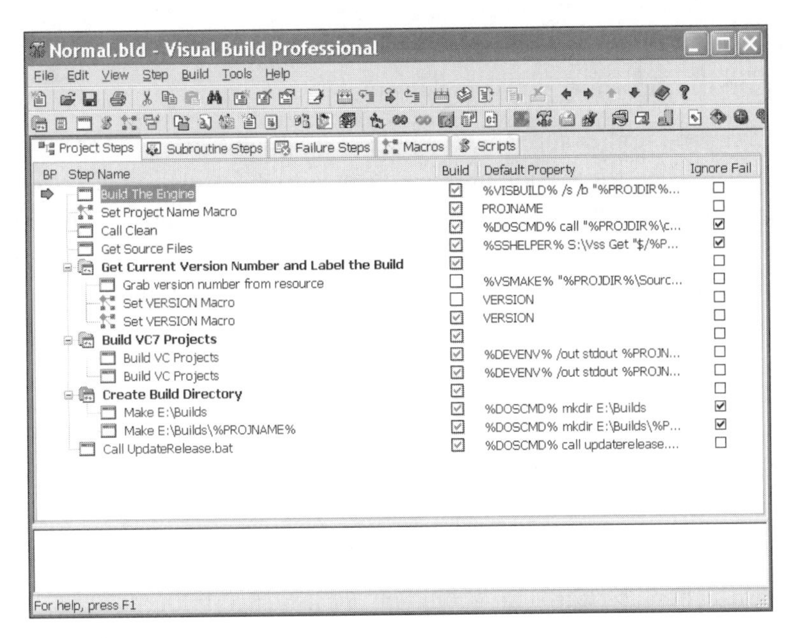

Figure 4.2
Visual Build Pro from Kinook Software.

technology, or a related task, your tool must be able to take input from the command line, or you won't be able to automate your build process.

Creating Build Scripts

You'll want to create a few build scripts for your project. Most builds will simply grab the latest code, build it, and copy the results somewhere on the network. The milestone build is a little more complicated and involves branching and merging the source code repository.

Normal Build

The normal build script builds a clean version of the game and copies the results somewhere useful. It is run as a part of the milestone build process, but it can also run automatically at regular intervals. I suggest you run a normal build at least once per day, preferably in the wee hours of the morning to check the code on the network for any errors. The normal build script is also useful for building ad-hoc versions of the game for the test team.

The normal build script performs the following steps:

1. Clean the build machine. If you use the directory structure I suggest at the beginning of this chapter, you can run a command to delete everything.

2. Get the latest source code. Since the whole project will be cleaned in the previous step, everything in the repository will come down.
3. Grab the latest version number and label the build. Optionally, change the version number each night. When the version number changes, the destination directory of the build changes too. This is a really handy technique to keep old versions of a game around without copying them by hand. Visual Build Pro has a utility to grab or even change the version number of Visual Studio resource files, but it's pretty easy to write one yourself.
4. Compile and link the debug and release versions of the project. The project settings will make sure everything goes into the right place.
5. Run automatic test scripts. If you have automated testing, have the build machine run the test scripts to see if the build is a good one. This is more reliable than a bleary eyed programmer attempting to test the game at 4 a.m.
6. Process and copy the build results. This should be encapsulated in the `updaterelease.bat` file. The destination directory should use the code name of the project and the version number to distinguish it from other projects or other versions of the same project. For example, version 2.0.8.25 of the Rainman project would go into `E:\Builds\Rainman\2.0.8.25`. The nightly build of the same project would always go into `E:\Builds\Rainman\Nightly`.

If you're paying attention you'll realize that the build scripts themselves should be checked to make sure they haven't changed. If the build script is running, how can it clean itself off the build machine and get itself from the source code repository? It can't, at least not easily. If you standardize your projects with a single directory structure it's better to create a master build script that works for any project. Project specific build commands are put into a special build script that lives in the same directory as the project files. The master build script should only change when the build process for every project is changed—something that should be extremely rare.

Milestone Build

Milestone builds are entirely different creatures since they involve branching the code. They also involve an approval process that takes days or weeks instead of minutes. A milestone build takes this extra work because it keeps the team from hitting a moving target.

At Origin Systems we didn't do anything special for milestone builds on the Ultima projects. Some unlucky programmer, usually me, launched the build on their desktop machine and after plenty of cussing and a few hours the new version was ready to test. The other programmers kept

adding features and bugs as fast as the test team could sign off old features. New code and features would break existing code—stuff the test team approved. The bugs would pile up and it was difficult to figure out if the project was making any progress.

The Microsoft projects I worked on were entirely different, mostly due to ditching SourceSafe. Our source code repository, Perforce, had excellent branching and merging capabilities. The programming team resisted at first, but quickly saw that milestone builds were linked directly to their paychecks. A few milestones later everyone wondered how we ever developed projects without branching.

Every project should have a Main branch and a Publish branch. Every source code repository does this a little differently. When a milestone build is launched, the first thing that happens is the Publish branch gets a fresh copy of the Main branch. The branches are synchronized without merging. When a build begins the two branches should be identical. The build machine runs the build scripts from the Publish branch to make the milestone build. This implies that the Main and Publish branch can exist on the same machine at the same time. This is true. Generally different branches are stored in different directory trees.

Most source code repositories allow a great degree of freedom for each client to configure how they view the contents of the repository. It's pretty easy to configure the client to put all the Main branches of every project into a D:\Projects\Main directory and all the Publish branches into D:\Projects\Publish. The build scripts can use a branch macro to figure out which branch needs building.

Once the milestone build is assembled it should be packaged and sent to testing. In our case, this meant Zip'ing up the entire build and putting it on our FTP site so Microsoft test could grab it.

If you have to FTP builds to another group, it's a good idea to zip or tar the files into one monolithic file. The FTP protocol can spend a lot of time opening and closing files and if your game has hundreds of components you'll find that one big file FTP is much faster. One more thing: big companies like Microsoft have internal and secure FTP sites for developers that are usually accessed via FTP internally. FTPing the file twice takes much longer, usually. Set up your own FTP site, secure it, and have the test team pull the build from your FTP site. That's much faster.

I almost never submit milestone builds that were approved on the first shot. Most of the time I make a few minor fixes. Every now and then I have to do something major. Either way, the fixes get made to the Publish branch and the milestone build is resubmitted.

This process continues, sometimes for almost a week, until the test team is satisfied. The Publish branch is then merged to the Main branch. This is usually an automatic process, but sometimes merge conflicts force a programmer to stare at the code and fix them.

Here are the build scripts that were used on the Microsoft projects to open and close milestone builds. These scripts are designed to be used with Perforce, but most source code repositories have similar commands or features:

Open Publish Phase:

```
rem Get the Latest Main
p4 sync %PROJECTSDIR%\Main\...

rem Unlock the target branch and revert any unlocked files
p4 unlock %PROJECTSDIR%\%BRANCHNAME%\...
p4 revert %PROJECTSDIR%\%BRANCHNAME%\...

rem Force Integrate from Main to target branch, resolve, and submit
p4 integrate -b %BRANCHNAME%
p4 resolve -at %PROJECTSDIR%\%BRANCHNAME%\...
p4 submit %PROJECTSDIR%\%BRANCHNAME%\...
```

Close Publish Phase:

```
rem Get the Latest from the target branch
p4 sync %PROJECTSDIR%\%BRANCHNAME%\...

rem Integrate from target branch to Main - resolve changes and sumbit
p4 integrate -r -b %BRANCHNAME%
p4 resolve -am %PROJECTSDIR%\Main\...
p4 submit %PROJECTSDIR%\Main\...


rem Lock the target branch so noone changes anything
p4 edit %PROJECTSDIR%\%BRANCHNAME%\...
p4 lock %PROJECTSDIR%\%BRANCHNAME%\...
```

The integration commands are expected, but if you look at the last two lines of the close publish phase you'll see that the target branch, usually Publish, is checked out to the build machine and locked so that no one can change it. The open publish phase unlocks the files and reverts any changes. Why bother? This makes absolutely sure that the Publish branch, or any other branch that is keeping pace with the Main branch, is only open for changes during milestone approval. If no milestone build is in test, there should be no reason to change the Publish branch.

This has an added side effect: Anyone who wants the latest approved milestone build can simply grab the code in the Publish branch and build the game. This is especially useful if the odd executive or representative of the press wants to see a demo of some kind. Even if the last build is missing from the network, you can always recreate it by building the Publish branch.

Multiple Projects and Shared Code

It's difficult to share code between multiple projects if the shared code is still under rapid development. Two different teams will eventually be in different stages of development because it is unlikely they both will have the same project schedule. Eventually, one team will need to make a change to the shared code that no one else wants.

There are a couple of different cases you should consider:

- One team needs to put a "hack" in the shared code to make a milestone quickly, and the other team wants to code the "real" solution.
- One team is close to shipping and has started a total code lockdown. No one can change anything. The other team needs to make modifications to the shared code to continue development.

How do you deal with this sticky problem? Branching, of course.

In the case of the scenario where two project teams need to share a common game engine, the game engine has three branches:

- *Main*: The normal development branch
- *Publish_Project_A*: The Publish branch for the first project
- *Publish_Project_B*: The Publish branch for the second project

The branching scripts for opening and closing the publish phases for the shared code work because the target branch is a macro: %BRANCHNAME%.

While both projects are in normal development, they both make changes to the shared engine code in the Main branch. If either project goes into a milestone approval phase, they fix milestone blockers in the Publish branch for their project. This allows both projects to be in a milestone acceptance phase at exactly the same time. After their milestone has been approved, the changes get merged back into the main line. When either project hits code lockdown, meaning that only a few high priority changes are being made to the code, the project stays in the Publish branch until it ships.

All this work assumes the two teams are motivated to share the game engine, and continually contribute to its improvement. There might be a case for one project permanently branching the shared code, in which case it should get its own code line apart from the Main branch of the original shared code. It's trivial to merge any two arbitrary code lines as long as they originated from an original source.

Some Parting Advice

This chapter has likely shown you that there is a lot of drudgery on any software project and games are no exception. Back in the dark ages I built game projects by typing in commands at the command prompt and checking boxes on a sheet of paper. Since most of this work happened way after midnight I made tons of mistakes. Some of these mistakes wasted time in copious amounts—mostly because the test team had a broken build on their hands, courtesy of a under caffeinated Mike McShaffry.

Without using branching techniques, all the programmers had to tiptoe around their code during a build. Everyone knew that moving targets are impossible to hit. Programmers take a long time to get in a good zone. If you break their concentration by halting progress to do a build you lose valuable time.

My parting advice is to always automate the monkey work, give the test team a good build every time, never ever get in the way of a programmer in the zone, and find a way to share your code. Sounds like heaven to me.

Chapter 5

User Interface Programming and Input Devices

Any game programmer who wants to remain being a game programmer for very long quickly needs to master the art of developing great user interfaces so that players can better interact with their games. The trick to building successful interfaces is to make sure that the interface really matches the format and complexity (or simplicity) of the game you are building. For example, an interactive movie-style game such as Wing Commander III can get away with a simple interface that basically operates (and looks like) Windows Media Player. After all, for this game you only need to play, pause, rewind, and whatnot. If all games could be that simple we'd have it made in the shade!

The game that you're developing might need nothing more than a gamepad, or it might require something more complicated, such as user selectable mouse and joystick controls with keyboard hotkeys. In any case, you need to have a clue how to grab the input from these devices and how to map these events to bits of code that change the state of your game.

Because processing user input is such an important component of user interfaces (especially with interactive games), I'm going to spend a bit of time up front in this chapter covering input devices. My personal feeling is that if you have a mastery of input devices you'll be about 80% closer to being able to build good interfaces. After exploring input devices we'll move up a level and discuss the components that are required to create functional interfaces for games.

Getting the Device State

No matter what type of device you use—keyboard, mouse, joystick, and so on—you'll need to understand the techniques and subtleties of getting and controlling the state of your input devices. We'll start by working at the lowest level and then we'll work our way up the input device food chain. The interfaces to input devices are completely dependant on the platforms you use, and to some extent any middleware you might be using. Many 3D graphics engines also provide APIs to all the input hardware. Regardless of the API used or devices they control, there are two schemes for processing user input:

- *Polling*: This method is a little old fashioned and requires an application to query each device for every trip around the main loop. When the device status changes, you call the appropriate handler. You might see this approach at work with handheld devices or non-Win32 platforms.
- *Callbacks or Messages*: This method is much more common. Here you'll intercept calls or messages from the operating system and write handler functions.

If your game is developed for Win32, you either intercept messages like `WM_MOUSEMOVE` or you might consider using DirectX's DirectInput API. I'll discuss this API a little later in this chapter.

Some other platforms use a callback method. In this case your game registers a callback function for each device. Each time the status of the device changes, your function is called. Renderware, the 3D engine from Criterion, uses the callback approach as this simple example illustrates:

```
// Attach input devices is called during game initialization
RwBool AttachInputDevices(void)
{
   // These functions are Renderware APIs that register device callbacks…
   RsInputDeviceAttach(rsKEYBOARD, KeyboardHandler);
   RsInputDeviceAttach(rsMOUSE, MouseHandler);
   return TRUE;
}
```

The two functions, `KeyboardHandler` and `MouseHandler` parse the input parameters and translate them into actions that change the game state. Here's an example of the `MouseHandler` function:

```
// NOTE: Don't bother searching MSDN for RsEventStatus or anything else in here.
// This code is pulled straight from a 3D action/adventure game demo that used
// Renderware from Criterion. Just look it over, and get a feel for the
// structure.
//
// You'll be seeing this kind of thing in every mouse handler, regardless of
// the platform.

RsEventStatus MouseHandler(RsEvent event, void *param)
{
   RsMouseStatus *mouseStatus = (RsMouseStatus *)param;

   switch( event )
   {
```

```
        case rsLEFTBUTTONDOWN:
        {
            LeftButtonDown(mouseStatus);
            return rsEVENTPROCESSED;
        }

        case rsLEFTBUTTONUP:
        {
            LeftButtonUp(mouseStatus);
            return rsEVENTPROCESSED;
        }

        case rsRIGHTBUTTONDOWN:
        {
            RightButtonDown(mouseStatus);
            return rsEVENTPROCESSED;
        }

        case rsRIGHTBUTTONUP:
        {
            RightButtonUp(mouseStatus);
            return rsEVENTPROCESSED;
        }

        case rsMOUSEMOVE:
        {
            MouseMove(mouseStatus);
            return rsEVENTPROCESSED;
        }

        default:
        {
            return rsEVENTNOTPROCESSED;
        }
    }
}
```

Of course, every platform operates a little differently, but the code looks very similar; mouse buttons still go up and down and the entire device moves on a two dimensional plane. It's not crazy to assume that most device-handling code reflects the nature of the specific device:

- *Buttons*: They will have up and down states. The down state might have an analog component. Most game controllers support button pressure as an 8-bit value.

- *One axis controllers*: They will have a single analog state, with zero representing the unpressed state. Game controllers usually have analog triggers, for use in features such as accelerators in driving games.
- *Two axis controllers*: A mouse and joystick are 2D controllers. Their status can be represented as integers or floating-point numbers. When using these devices, you shouldn't assume anything about their coordinate space: The coordinate (0,0) might represent the upper left-hand corner of the screen or it might reprsent the device center.

Game controllers, even complicated ones, are built from assemblies of these three component types. The tricked-out joysticks that the flight simulator fans go for are simply buttons and triggers attached to a 2D controller. To support such a device, you'll need to write a custom handler function for each component. Depending on the way your handler functions get the device status, you might have to factor the device status for each component out of a larger data structure. Eventually, you'll call your handler functions and change the game state.

Using DirectInput

DirectInput is the DirectX API for input devices such as the mouse, keyboard, joystick, game controllers, and force feedback devices. You might notice that this module of DirectX is a little different than most of the other APIs. There's no HAL, and that means there's nothing to hardware accelerate. DirectInput simply provides a way to interface with input devices.

Windows can certainly grab user input with DirectInput. Mouse and keyboard messages are well understood by a Win32 programmer the moment they create their first Win32 application. You might not be aware that the Win32 Multimedia: Platform SDK has everything you need to accept messages from your joystick. You don't even need DirectInput for that, so why bother? Straight Win32 code might not expose every feature of the weirder varieties of joysticks or PC game controller pads. That's where DirectInput will have to help you out. This is certainly true if you want an easy way to use the force-feedback devices.

Beyond this, another feature of DirectInput that's pretty useful is called *action mapping*. This is a concept that binds actions to virtual controls. Instead of looking at the X-axis of the joystick to find the direction of a car's steering wheel, DirectInput can map the action of steering the car to a virtual control. The actual controls can be mapped to the virtual controls at the whim of the player, and are the basis for providing a completely configurable control system. Hardcore gamers really love this. If you are making a hardcore game, you'll need configurable controls. DirectInput isn't the only way to make that work, however, but it does buy you a few other things like a standard way to tweak the force-feedback system.

Mass market games that don't use any advanced features of joysticks or don't have insanely configurable controls can work just fine with Windows messages and the Windows Multimedia Platform SDK. You don't have to learn to use DirectInput to make games, and Windows messages are easy and familiar. There are plenty of DirectInput samples in the DirectX SDK for you to look at, so I'm not going to waste your time or any trees on the subject. What I want to work on is the fact that there's plenty to talk about in terms of user interface code, regardless of the API you use.

Working with the Mouse (and Joystick)

I'm not going to talk about basic topics like grabbing `WM_MOUSEMOVE` and pulling screen coordinates out of the `LPARAM`. Many books have been written to cover these programming techniques. If you need a primer on Win32 and GDI, I suggest you read Charles Petzold's book: *Programming Windows: The Definitive Guide to the Win32 API.* Besides, if you don't know how to read mouse input you're probably in the wrong class. The prerequisite for this class is "Beginning Windows Programming" down the hall. But don't forget to come back when you're done.

Instead, I'll focus on giving you some good advice about using mouse input in games, and show you a few of my special tricks. First, here is the advice you should follow when using the mouse.

1. *Stay with well known conventions.* There are plenty of standard conventions for using the mouse control, from Microsoft Windows to Quake. When you sit down to write your interface code, don't be tempted to be a cowboy programmer and break out into new directions with the interface. You'll likely end up with a lot of arrows in your back—ouch! After all, before the shooter-style game was popular, how many games used the mouse as a model for a human neck? This idea worked well in a case like this for two reasons: It solved a new problem and the solution was intuitive.

If you're solving an interface problem that has a standard solution and you choose a radically different approach, you take a risk of annoying players. If you think their annoyance will transition into wonder and words of praise as they discover (and figure out) your novel solution, then by all means give it a try. Make sure you test your idea first with some colleagues you can trust. They'll tell you if your idea belongs on the garbage heap. Be careful with interfaces, however. A friend of mine once judged the many entrants into the Indie Games Festival (**www.indiegames.com**) and he said the biggest mistake he saw that killed promising entrants was poor interface controls. He was amazed to see entries with incredible 3D graphics not make the cut because they were simply too hard to control. In short, don't be afraid to use a good idea just because it's already been done.

2. *Avoid context sensitive controls.* Context sensitivity in controls can be tough to deal with as a player. It's easy to make the mistake of loading too much control onto too little a device. The Ultima games generally went a little too far, I think, in how they used the mouse. A design goal for the games was to have every conceivable action be possible from the mouse, so every click and double click was used for something. In fact, the same command would do different things if you clicked on a person, a door, or a monster. I'm sometimes surprised that we never implemented a special action for the "shave and a haircut, two bits" click.

3. *Use the cursor for user feedback.* One thing I think the Ultima games did well was how they used the pointer or cursor. The cursor would change shape to give the player feedback on what things were and whether they could be activated by a mouse command. This is especially useful when your screens are very densely populated. When the mouse pointer changes shape to signify that the player can perform an action, players immediately understand that they can use the pointer to explore the screen.

4. *Avoid pixel perfect accuracy.* It's a serious mistake to assume that players of all ages can target a screen area with pixel perfect accuracy. An example of this might be a small click target on a draggable item or a small drop point on the screen. Anything that will change as a result of a mouse click should have a little buffer zone, widening the available target area. If the area is already pretty large, like the menu bar of a window, you can get away without using the buffer zone.

   Anyone who has attempted to cast spells in the original version of Ultima VIII will agree. The reagents that made some of the spells work had to be placed exactly. This requirement made spell casting frustrating and arbitrary. Both the mouse and the joystick are moved with bigger muscles in the arm and wrist, which are less accurate than the index finger.

The Ultima VII mouse code detected objects on the screen by performing pixel collision testing with the mouse (x,y) position and the sprites that made up the objects in the world. Most of these sprites were chroma-keyed, and therefore had spots of the transparent color all through them. This was especially true of things like jail cell bars and fences. Ultima VII's pixel collision code ignored the transparent color, allowing players to click through fences and jail cell bars to examine objects on the other side. That was a good feature, and it was used in many places to advance the story. The problem it created, however, was that sometimes the transparent colored pixels actually made it harder for players to click on an object. For example, double clicking the door of the jail cell was difficult. If you use an approach like this, take some care in designing which objects are active, and which are simply scenery and make sure you make this clear to your players.

This is an extremely important issue with casual games or kids games. Very young players or older gamers enjoy games that include buffer zones in the interface because they are easier to play.

With Ultima VIII, the left mouse button serves as the "walk/run" button. As long as you hold it down, the Avatar character will run in the direction of the mouse pointer. Ultima games require a lot of running; your character will run across an entire continent only to discover that the thingamajig that will open the gate of whosiz is back in the city you just left, so you go running off again. By the time I'd played through the game the umpteenth time, my index finger was so tired of running I started using tape to hold the mouse button down. One thing people do in a lot of FPS games when playing online is set them to "always run" mode. I wish we'd had done that with Ultima VIII.

Capturing the Mouse

I'm always surprised that Win32 documentation doesn't make inside jokes about capturing the mouse. At least we can still laugh at it. If you've never programmed a user interface before, you probably don't know what capturing the mouse means or why any programmer in his right mind would want to do this. Catching a mouse isn't probably something that's high on your list.

To see what you've been missing, go to a Windows machine right now and bring up a dialog box. Move the mouse over a button, hopefully not one that will erase your hard drive, and click the left mouse button and hold it down. You should see the button graphic depress. Move the mouse pointer away from the button and you'll notice the button graphic pop back up again. Until you release the left mouse button, you can move the mouse all you want, but only the button on the dialog will get the messages. If you don't believe me, open up Microsoft Spy++ and see for yourself. Microsoft Spy++ is a tool that you use to figure out what Windows messages are going to which window, and it's a great debugging tool if you are coding a GUI application. Here's a quick tutorial:

1. In Visual Studio, select Spy++ from the Tools menu.
2. Close the open default window, and select "Find Window" from the main menu or hit Ctrl-F.
3. You'll then see a little dialog box that looks like the one shown in Figure 5.1.
4. Click and drag the little finder tool to the window or button you are interested in, and then click the "Messages" radio button at the bottom of the dialog. You'll get a new window in Spy++ that shows you every message sent to the object.

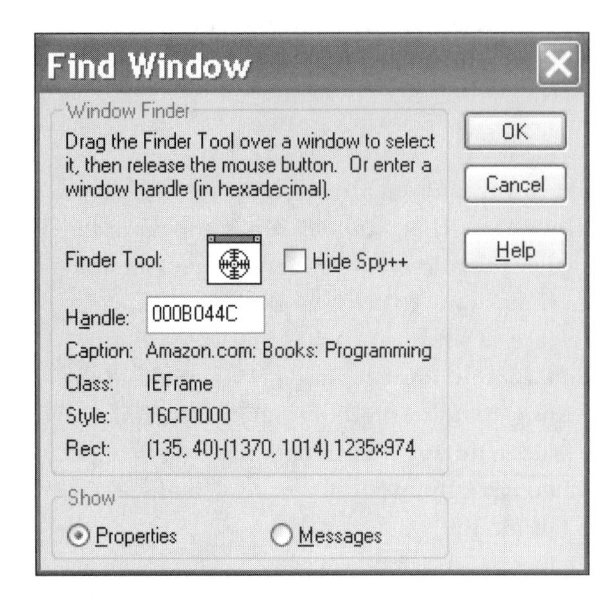

Figure 5.1
The Find Window with Spy++.

Perform the previous experiment again, but this time use Spy++ to monitor the Windows messages sent to the button. You'll find that as soon as you click on the button, every mouse action will be displayed even if the pointer is far away from the button in question. That might be interesting, but why is it important? If a user interface uses the boundaries of an object like a button to determine whether it should receive mouse events, capturing the mouse is critical. Imagine a scenario where you can't capture mouse events:

1. The mouse button goes down over an active button.
2. The button receives the event and draws itself in the down position.
3. The mouse moves away from the button, outside its border.
4. The button stops receiving any events from the mouse since the mouse isn't directly over the button.
5. The mouse button is released.

The result is that the button will still be drawn in the down position, awaiting a button release event that will never happen. If the mouse events are captured, the button will continue to receive mouse events until the button is released.

To better understand this, take a look at a code snippet that shows some code you can use to capture the mouse and draw lines:

```
LRESULT APIENTRY MainWndProc(HWND hwndMain, UINT uMsg, WPARAM wParam,
                             LPARAM lParam)
{
   static POINTS ptsBegin;        // beginning point

   switch (uMsg)
   {
      case WM_LBUTTONDOWN:

          // Capture mouse input.

          SetCapture(hwndMain);
          ptsBegin = MAKEPOINTS(lParam);
          return 0;

      case WM_MOUSEMOVE:

          // When moving the mouse, the user must hold down
          // the left mouse button to draw lines.

          if (wParam & MK_LBUTTON)
          {
              // imaginary code - you write this function
              yourcode::ErasePreviousLine();

              // Convert the current cursor coordinates to a
              // POINTS structure, and then draw a new line.

              ptsEnd = MAKEPOINTS(lParam);

              // also imaginary
              yourcode::DrawLine(ptsEnd.x, ptsEnd.y);
          }
          break;

      case WM_LBUTTONUP:

        // The user has finished drawing the line. Reset the
        // previous line flag, release the mouse cursor, and
        // release the mouse capture.

        fPrevLine = FALSE;
        ReleaseCapture();
        break;

   }
   return 0;
}
```

If you were to write functions for erasing and drawing lines, you'd have a nice rubber band line drawing mechanism, which you can thank mouse capturing for. By using it, your lines would stop following the mouse if you ever left the window's client area.

Making a Mouse Drag Work

You might wonder why a mouse drag is so important. Drags are important because they are prerequisites to much user interface code in a lot of games. When you select a group of combatants in Command and Conquer, for example, you drag out a rectangle. When you play Freecell in Windows, you use the mouse to drag cards around. In Sims Online, you drag objects around to arrange the furniture in your house or give objects to other players. Most assuredly, your game will use drags too.

Dragging the mouse adds a little complexity to the process of capturing it. Most user interface code distinguishes a single click, double click, and drag as three separate actions, and therefore will call different game code. Dragging also relates to the notion of legality; it's not always possible that anything in your game can be dragged to anywhere. If a drag fails, you'll need a way to set things back to the way they were. This issue might seem moot when you consider that dragging usually affects the look of the game—the dragged object needs to appear like it is really moving around, and it shouldn't leave a copy of itself in it's original location. That might confuse the player big time.

The code to support dragging requires three phases:

- Detect and initiate a drag event
- Handle the mouse movement and draw objects accordingly
- Detect the release and finalize the drag

The actions that define a drag are typically a mouse press (button down) followed by a mouse movement, but life in the mouse drag game is not always that simple. Also, during a double click event, a slight amount of mouse movement might occur, perhaps only a single pixel coordinate. Your code must interpret these different cases.

In Windows, a drag event is only allowed on objects that are already selected, which is why drags usually follow on the second "click and hold" of the mouse button. The first click of the left mouse button always selects objects. Many games differ from that standard, but it's one of the easier actions to code since only selected objects are draggable.

Back to the task at hand—detecting a drag event. Since a drag event involves multiple trips around the main loop, you must assume that every mouse button down event could be the beginning of a drag event. I guess an event is assumed draggable until proven innocent. In your mouse button down handler you need to look at the mouse coordinates and determine if they are over a draggable object. If the object is draggable, you must create a temporary reference to it that you can find a few game loops later. Since this is the first button down event, you can't tell if it's a bona fide drag event just yet.

The only thing that will make the drag event real is the movement of the mouse, but only movement outside of a tiny buffer zone. On an 800x600 screen, a good choice is five pixels in either the x or y coordinate. This is large enough to indicate that the drag was real, but small enough that small shakes in the mouse during a double click won't unintentionally initiate a drag. Here's the code that performs this dirty work:

```
// Place this code at the top of your mouse movement handler
if (m_aboutToDrag)
{
      CPoint offset = currentPoint - dragStartingPoint;
   if (abs(offset.x) > DRAG_THRESHOLD || abs(offset.y) > DRAG_THRESHOLD)
   {
      // We have a real drag event!
      bool dragOK = yourcode::InitiateDrag(draggedObject, dragStartingPoint);
      SetCapture( GetWindow()->m_hWnd );
      m_dragging = TRUE;
   }
}
```

The call to `yourcode::InitiateDrag` is something you write yourself. Its job is to set the game state to remove the original object from the display and draw the dragged object in some obvious form, such as a transparent sprite. The call to `SetCapture` is the same Win32 function I showed you in the previous section.

Until the mouse button is released, the mouse movement handler will continue to get mouse movement commands, even those that are outside the client area of your window! Make sure your draw routines don't freak out when they see these odd coordinates.

What must go down, must finally come up again. When the mouse button is released, your drag is complete, but it might not be legal:

```
// Place this code at the top of your mouse button up handler
if ( m_dragging )
{
   ReleaseCapture();
   m_bDragging = false;

   if (!yourcode::FinishDrag(point))
   {
      yourcode::AbortDrag(dragStartingPoint);
   }
}
```

5

This bit of code would exist in your handler for a mouse button up event. The call to `ReleaseCapture()` makes sure mouse events get sent to all their normal places again. `yourcode::FinishDrag()` is a function you'd write yourself. It should detect if the destination of the drag was legal, and perform the right game state manipulations to make it so. If the drag is illegal, the object has to snap back to its previous location as if the drag never occurred. This function can be trickier to write than you'd think, since you can't necessarily use game state information to send the object back to where it came from.

In Ultima VII and Ultima VIII, we created a complicated system to keep track of object movement, specifically whether or not an object could legally move from one place to another. It was possible for a game designer to use the all powerful game editor to force objects into any location, whether it was legal or not. If these objects were dragged to another illegal location by the player, the object had to be forced back into place. Otherwise the object would exist in limbo. What we learned is that the drag code could access the game state at a low enough level to run the abort code.

Working with the Keyboard

There are a many ways to grab keyboard input from Win32. They each have their good and bad points, and to make the right choice you need to know how deep you need to pry into keyboard input data. Before we discuss these various approaches, let's get a few vocabulary words out of the way so that we're talking the same language:

- *Character code*: Describes the ASCII or UNICODE character that is the return value of the C function, `getchar()`.
- *Virtual scan code*: Macros defined in Winuser.h that describe the components of data sent in the wParam value of `WM_CHAR`, `WM_KEYDOWN`, and `WM_KEYUP` messages.
- *OEM scan code*: The scan codes provided by OEMs. They are useless unless you care about coding something specific for a particular keyboard manufacturer.

Those definitions will even resonate more once you've seen some data, so let's pry open the keyboard and do a little snooping.

Mike's Keyboard Snooper

I wrote a small program to break out all of the different values for Windows keyboard messages, and as you'll see shortly, this tool really uncovers some weird things that take place with Windows. Taken with the definitions we just discussed, however, you'll soon see that the different values will make a little more sense. Each line in the tables below contains the values of wParam and lParam for Windows keyboard messages. I typed the following sequence of keys, 1 2 3 a b c, to produce the first table. Look closely at the different values that are produced for the different Windows messages such as WM_KEYDOWN, WM_CHAR, WM_KEYUP, and so on:

```
WM_KEYDOWN  Code: 49 '1'  Repeat:1  Oem:  2  Ext'd:0  IsAlt:0  WasDown:0  Rel'd:0
WM_CHAR     Code: 49 '1'  Repeat:1  Oem:  2  Ext'd:0  IsAlt:0  WasDown:0  Rel'd:0
WM_KEYUP    Code: 49 '1'  Repeat:1  Oem:  2  Ext'd:0  IsAlt:0  WasDown:0  Rel'd:1
WM_KEYDOWN  Code: 50 '2'  Repeat:1  Oem:  3  Ext'd:0  IsAlt:0  WasDown:0  Rel'd:0
WM_CHAR     Code: 50 '2'  Repeat:1  Oem:  3  Ext'd:0  IsAlt:0  WasDown:0  Rel'd:0
WM_KEYUP    Code: 50 '2'  Repeat:1  Oem:  3  Ext'd:0  IsAlt:0  WasDown:0  Rel'd:1
WM_KEYDOWN  Code: 51 '3'  Repeat:1  Oem:  4  Ext'd:0  IsAlt:0  WasDown:0  Rel'd:0
WM_CHAR     Code: 51 '3'  Repeat:1  Oem:  4  Ext'd:0  IsAlt:0  WasDown:0  Rel'd:0
WM_KEYUP    Code: 51 '3'  Repeat:1  Oem:  4  Ext'd:0  IsAlt:0  WasDown:0  Rel'd:1
WM_KEYDOWN  Code: 65 'A'  Repeat:1  Oem: 30  Ext'd:0  IsAlt:0  WasDown:0  Rel'd:0
WM_CHAR     Code: 97 'a'  Repeat:1  Oem: 30  Ext'd:0  IsAlt:0  WasDown:0  Rel'd:0
WM_KEYUP    Code: 65 'A'  Repeat:1  Oem: 30  Ext'd:0  IsAlt:0  WasDown:0  Rel'd:1
WM_KEYDOWN  Code: 66 'B'  Repeat:1  Oem: 48  Ext'd:0  IsAlt:0  WasDown:0  Rel'd:0
WM_CHAR     Code: 98 'b'  Repeat:1  Oem: 48  Ext'd:0  IsAlt:0  WasDown:0  Rel'd:0
WM_KEYUP    Code: 66 'B'  Repeat:1  Oem: 48  Ext'd:0  IsAlt:0  WasDown:0  Rel'd:1
WM_KEYDOWN  Code: 67 'C'  Repeat:1  Oem: 46  Ext'd:0  IsAlt:0  WasDown:0  Rel'd:0
WM_CHAR     Code: 99 'c'  Repeat:1  Oem: 46  Ext'd:0  IsAlt:0  WasDown:0  Rel'd:0
WM_KEYUP    Code: 67 'C'  Repeat:1  Oem: 46  Ext'd:0  IsAlt:0  WasDown:0  Rel'd:1
```

You'll first notice that the message pipe gets the sequence of WM_KEYDOWN, WM_CHAR, and WM_KEYUP for each key pressed and released. The next thing you'll notice is that the code returned by WM_CHAR is different from the other messages when characters are lower case.

This should give you a clue that you can use WM_CHAR for simple character input when all you care about is getting the right character code. What happens if a key is held down? Let's find out. The next table shows the output I received by first pressing and holding an 'a' and then the left Shift key:

```
WM_KEYDOWN  Code: 65 'A'  Repeat:1  Oem: 30  Ext'd:0  IsAlt:0  WasDown:0  Rel'd:1
WM_CHAR     Code: 97 'a'  Repeat:1  Oem: 30  Ext'd:0  IsAlt:0  WasDown:0  Rel'd:1
WM_KEYDOWN  Code: 65 'A'  Repeat:1  Oem: 30  Ext'd:0  IsAlt:0  WasDown:0  Rel'd:1
WM_CHAR     Code: 97 'a'  Repeat:1  Oem: 30  Ext'd:0  IsAlt:0  WasDown:0  Rel'd:1
WM_KEYDOWN  Code: 65 'A'  Repeat:1  Oem: 30  Ext'd:0  IsAlt:0  WasDown:0  Rel'd:1
WM_CHAR     Code: 97 'a'  Repeat:1  Oem: 30  Ext'd:0  IsAlt:0  WasDown:0  Rel'd:1
WM_KEYDOWN  Code: 65 'A'  Repeat:1  Oem: 30  Ext'd:0  IsAlt:0  WasDown:0  Rel'd:1
WM_CHAR     Code: 97 'a'  Repeat:1  Oem: 30  Ext'd:0  IsAlt:0  WasDown:0  Rel'd:1
WM_KEYDOWN  Code: 65 'A'  Repeat:1  Oem: 30  Ext'd:0  IsAlt:0  WasDown:0  Rel'd:1
WM_CHAR     Code: 97 'a'  Repeat:1  Oem: 30  Ext'd:0  IsAlt:0  WasDown:0  Rel'd:1
WM_KEYUP    Code: 65 'A'  Repeat:1  Oem: 30  Ext'd:0  IsAlt:0  WasDown:0  Rel'd:1
```

5

```
WM_KEYDOWN  Code: 16 '_'  Repeat:1  Oem: 42  Ext'd:0  IsAlt:0  WasDown:0  Rel'd:0
WM_KEYDOWN  Code: 16 '_'  Repeat:1  Oem: 42  Ext'd:0  IsAlt:0  WasDown:0  Rel'd:1
WM_KEYDOWN  Code: 16 '_'  Repeat:1  Oem: 42  Ext'd:0  IsAlt:0  WasDown:0  Rel'd:1
WM_KEYDOWN  Code: 16 '_'  Repeat:1  Oem: 42  Ext'd:0  IsAlt:0  WasDown:0  Rel'd:1
WM_KEYDOWN  Code: 16 '_'  Repeat:1  Oem: 42  Ext'd:0  IsAlt:0  WasDown:0  Rel'd:1
WM_KEYUP    Code: 16 '_'  Repeat:1  Oem: 42  Ext'd:0  IsAlt:0  WasDown:0  Rel'd:1
```

It seems that I can't count on the repeat value as shown here. It is completely dependent on your equipment manufacturer and keyboard driver software. You may get repeat values and you may not. You need to make sure your code will work either way.

For the next sequence, I held the left Shift key and typed the same original sequence: 1 2 3 a b c:

```
WM_KEYDOWN  Code: 16 '_'  Repeat:1  Oem: 42  Ext'd:0  IsAlt:0  WasDown:0  Rel'd:0
WM_KEYDOWN  Code: 16 '_'  Repeat:1  Oem: 42  Ext'd:0  IsAlt:0  WasDown:0  Rel'd:1
WM_KEYDOWN  Code: 16 '_'  Repeat:1  Oem: 42  Ext'd:0  IsAlt:0  WasDown:0  Rel'd:1
WM_KEYDOWN  Code: 16 '_'  Repeat:1  Oem: 42  Ext'd:0  IsAlt:0  WasDown:0  Rel'd:1
WM_KEYDOWN  Code: 16 '_'  Repeat:1  Oem: 42  Ext'd:0  IsAlt:0  WasDown:0  Rel'd:1
WM_KEYDOWN  Code: 49 '1'  Repeat:1  Oem:  2  Ext'd:0  IsAlt:0  WasDown:0  Rel'd:0
WM_CHAR     Code: 33 '!'  Repeat:1  Oem:  2  Ext'd:0  IsAlt:0  WasDown:0  Rel'd:0
WM_KEYUP    Code: 49 '1'  Repeat:1  Oem:  2  Ext'd:0  IsAlt:0  WasDown:0  Rel'd:1
WM_KEYDOWN  Code: 50 '2'  Repeat:1  Oem:  3  Ext'd:0  IsAlt:0  WasDown:0  Rel'd:0
WM_CHAR     Code: 64 '@'  Repeat:1  Oem:  3  Ext'd:0  IsAlt:0  WasDown:0  Rel'd:0
WM_KEYUP    Code: 50 '2'  Repeat:1  Oem:  3  Ext'd:0  IsAlt:0  WasDown:0  Rel'd:1
WM_KEYDOWN  Code: 51 '3'  Repeat:1  Oem:  4  Ext'd:0  IsAlt:0  WasDown:0  Rel'd:0
WM_CHAR     Code: 35 '#'  Repeat:1  Oem:  4  Ext'd:0  IsAlt:0  WasDown:0  Rel'd:0
WM_KEYUP    Code: 51 '3'  Repeat:1  Oem:  4  Ext'd:0  IsAlt:0  WasDown:0  Rel'd:1
WM_KEYDOWN  Code: 65 'A'  Repeat:1  Oem: 30  Ext'd:0  IsAlt:0  WasDown:0  Rel'd:0
WM_CHAR     Code: 65 'A'  Repeat:1  Oem: 30  Ext'd:0  IsAlt:0  WasDown:0  Rel'd:0
WM_KEYUP    Code: 65 'A'  Repeat:1  Oem: 30  Ext'd:0  IsAlt:0  WasDown:0  Rel'd:1
WM_KEYDOWN  Code: 66 'B'  Repeat:1  Oem: 48  Ext'd:0  IsAlt:0  WasDown:0  Rel'd:0
WM_CHAR     Code: 66 'B'  Repeat:1  Oem: 48  Ext'd:0  IsAlt:0  WasDown:0  Rel'd:0
WM_KEYUP    Code: 66 'B'  Repeat:1  Oem: 48  Ext'd:0  IsAlt:0  WasDown:0  Rel'd:1
WM_KEYDOWN  Code: 67 'C'  Repeat:1  Oem: 46  Ext'd:0  IsAlt:0  WasDown:0  Rel'd:0
WM_CHAR     Code: 67 'C'  Repeat:1  Oem: 46  Ext'd:0  IsAlt:0  WasDown:0  Rel'd:0
WM_KEYUP    Code: 67 'C'  Repeat:1  Oem: 46  Ext'd:0  IsAlt:0  WasDown:0  Rel'd:1
WM_KEYUP    Code: 16 '_'  Repeat:1  Oem: 42  Ext'd:0  IsAlt:0  WasDown:0  Rel'd:1
```

There's nothing too surprising here; the Shift key will repeat until the next key is pressed. Note that the repeats on the Shift key don't continue. Just as in the first sequence, only the `WM_CHAR` message gives you your expected character.

You should realize by now that if you want to use keys on the keyboard for hotkeys, you can use the WM_KEYDOWN message, and you won't have to care if the Shift key (or even the Caps Lock key) is pressed. Pressing the Caps Lock key gives you this output:

```
WM_KEYDOWN  Code: 20 '_'  Repeat:1  Oem: 58  Ext'd:0  IsAlt:0  WasDown:0  Rel'd:0
WM_KEYUP    Code: 20 '_'  Repeat:1  Oem: 58  Ext'd:0  IsAlt:0  WasDown:0  Rel'd:1
```

The messages that come though for WM_CHAR will operate as if the Shift key is pressed down.

Let's try some function keys including, F1, F2, F3, and the shifted versions also:

```
WM_KEYDOWN  Code:112 'p'  Repeat:1  Oem: 59  Ext'd:0  IsAlt:0  WasDown:0  Rel'd:0
WM_KEYUP    Code:112 'p'  Repeat:1  Oem: 59  Ext'd:0  IsAlt:0  WasDown:0  Rel'd:1
WM_KEYDOWN  Code:113 'q'  Repeat:1  Oem: 60  Ext'd:0  IsAlt:0  WasDown:0  Rel'd:0
WM_KEYUP    Code:113 'q'  Repeat:1  Oem: 60  Ext'd:0  IsAlt:0  WasDown:0  Rel'd:1
WM_KEYDOWN  Code:114 'r'  Repeat:1  Oem: 61  Ext'd:0  IsAlt:0  WasDown:0  Rel'd:0
WM_KEYUP    Code:114 'r'  Repeat:1  Oem: 61  Ext'd:0  IsAlt:0  WasDown:0  Rel'd:1
WM_KEYDOWN  Code: 16 '_'  Repeat:1  Oem: 42  Ext'd:0  IsAlt:0  WasDown:0  Rel'd:0
WM_KEYDOWN  Code:112 'p'  Repeat:1  Oem: 59  Ext'd:0  IsAlt:0  WasDown:0  Rel'd:0
WM_KEYUP    Code:112 'p'  Repeat:1  Oem: 59  Ext'd:0  IsAlt:0  WasDown:0  Rel'd:1
WM_KEYDOWN  Code:113 'q'  Repeat:1  Oem: 60  Ext'd:0  IsAlt:0  WasDown:0  Rel'd:0
WM_KEYUP    Code:113 'q'  Repeat:1  Oem: 60  Ext'd:0  IsAlt:0  WasDown:0  Rel'd:1
WM_KEYDOWN  Code:114 'r'  Repeat:1  Oem: 61  Ext'd:0  IsAlt:0  WasDown:0  Rel'd:0
WM_KEYUP    Code:114 'r'  Repeat:1  Oem: 61  Ext'd:0  IsAlt:0  WasDown:0  Rel'd:1
WM_KEYUP    Code: 16 '_'  Repeat:1  Oem: 42  Ext'd:0  IsAlt:0  WasDown:0  Rel'd:1
```

There's a distinct lack of WM_CHAR messages, isn't there? Also, notice that the code returned by the F1 key is the same as the lower case 'p' character. So, what does 'p' look like?

```
WM_KEYDOWN  Code: 80 'P'  Repeat:1  Oem: 25  Ext'd:0  IsAlt:0  WasDown:0  Rel'd:0
WM_CHAR     Code:112 'p'  Repeat:1  Oem: 25  Ext'd:0  IsAlt:0  WasDown:0  Rel'd:0
WM_KEYUP    Code: 80 'P'  Repeat:1  Oem: 25  Ext'd:0  IsAlt:0  WasDown:0  Rel'd:1
```

Isn't that interesting? The virtual scan code for 'p' as encoded for WM_CHAR is exactly the same as the code for WM_KEYUP and WM_KEYDOWN. This funky design leads to some buggy misinterpretations of these two messages, if you are looking at nothing but the virtual scan code. I've seen some games where you could use the function keys to enter your character name!

You can't use WM_CHAR to grab function key input, or any other keyboard key not associated with a typeable character. It is confusing that the ASCII value for the lower case 'p' character is also the VK_F1. If you were beginning to suspect that you can't use the wParam value from all these messages in the same way, you're right.

If you want to figure out the difference between keys you should use the OEM scan code. There's a Win32 helper function to translate it into something useful:

```
// grab bits 16-23 from LPARAM
unsigned int oemScan = int(lParam & (0xff << 16))>>16;
UINT vk = MapVirtualKey(oemScan, 1);
if (vk == VK_F1)
{
   // we've got someone pressing the F1 key!
}
```

The `VK_F1` is a `#define` in WinUser.h, where you'll find definitions for every other virtual key you'll need: VK_ESCAPE, VK_TAB, VK_SPACE, and so on.

Processing different keyboard inputs seems messy, doesn't it? Hold on, it gets better. The next sequence shows the left Shift key, right Shift key, left Ctrl key, and right Ctrl key:

```
WM_KEYDOWN  Code: 16 '_'  Repeat:1  Oem: 42  Ext'd:0  IsAlt:0  WasDown:0  Rel'd:0
WM_KEYUP    Code: 16 '_'  Repeat:1  Oem: 42  Ext'd:0  IsAlt:0  WasDown:0  Rel'd:1
WM_KEYDOWN  Code: 16 '_'  Repeat:1  Oem: 54  Ext'd:0  IsAlt:0  WasDown:0  Rel'd:0
WM_KEYUP    Code: 16 '_'  Repeat:1  Oem: 54  Ext'd:0  IsAlt:0  WasDown:0  Rel'd:1
WM_KEYDOWN  Code: 17 '_'  Repeat:1  Oem: 29  Ext'd:0  IsAlt:0  WasDown:0  Rel'd:0
WM_KEYUP    Code: 17 '_'  Repeat:1  Oem: 29  Ext'd:0  IsAlt:0  WasDown:0  Rel'd:1
WM_KEYDOWN  Code: 17 '_'  Repeat:1  Oem: 29  Ext'd:1  IsAlt:0  WasDown:0  Rel'd:0
WM_KEYUP    Code: 17 '_'  Repeat:1  Oem: 29  Ext'd:1  IsAlt:0  WasDown:0  Rel'd:1
```

The only way to distinguish the left Shift key from the right Shift key is to look at the OEM scan code. On the other hand, the only way to distinguish the left Ctrl key from the right Ctrl key is to look at the extended key bit to see if it is set for the right Ctrl key. This insane cobbler of aggregate design is the best example of what happens if you have a mandate to create new technology while supporting stuff as old as my high school diploma (or is that my grade school one?)

To get around the problems of processing keyboard inputs that look the same as I've outlined in this section, you'll want to write your own handler for accepting the `WM_KEYDOWN` and `WM_KEYUP` messages. If your game is going to have a complicated enough interface to distinguish between left and right Ctrl or Shift keys, and use these keys in combination with others, you've got an interesting road ahead. My best advice is to try to keep things as simple as possible. It's a bad idea to assign different actions to both Ctrl or Shift keys anyway. If your game only needs some hotkeys, and no fancy combinations, `WM_KEYDOWN` will work fine all by itself.

Here's a summary of how to get the right data out of these keyboard messages:

- WM_CHAR: Use this message only if your game cares about printable characters: no function keys, Ctrl keys, or Shift keys as a single input.
- **WM_KEYDOWN/WM_KEYUP:** Grabs each key as you press it, but makes no distinction between upper and lower case characters. Use this to grab function key input – and compare the OEM scan codes with `MapVirtualKey()`. You won't get upper and lower case characters without tracking the status of the shift keys yourself.

It's almost like this system was engineered by a Congressional conference committee.

GetAsyncKeyState() and Other Evils

There's a Win32 function that will return the status of any key. It's tempting to use, especially given the morass of weirdness you have to deal with going a more traditional route with Windows keyboard messages. Unfortunately, there's a dark side to these functions, and other functions that poll the state of device hardware outside of the message loop.

Most testing scripts or replay features pump recorded messages into the normal message pump, making sure that actual hardware messages are shunted away. Polling functions like `GetAsyncKeyState()` can't be fooled or trapped in the same way. They also make debugging and testing more difficult, since timing of keyboard input could be crucial to recreating a weird bug.

There are other polled functions are equally evil, and one of them is the polled device status functions in DirectInput, such as `IDirectInputDevice8::GetDeviceState()`. The only way I'd consider using these functions is if I wrote my own mini-message pump, where polled device status was converted into messages sent into my game logic. That, of course, is a lot more work.

Handling the Alt Key Under Windows

If I use the same program to monitor keyboard messages related to pressing the right and left Alt keys, I get nothing. No output at all. Windows keeps the Alt key for itself, and uses it to send special commands to your application. You should listen to `WM_SYSCOMMAND` to find out what's going on. Some of these messages are important to handle and I'll be covering them in Chapter 11.

You could use the polling functions to find out if the Alt keys have been pressed, but not only does that go against some recent advice it's not considered "polite" Windows behavior. Microsoft has guidelines that well behaved applications should follow, including games. The Alt key is reserved for commands sent to Windows. Users will not expect your game to launch missiles when all they want to do is switch over to Excel, and try to look busy for the boss.

User Interface Components

Now that you've put a tap into the private lives of your input devices, you've got to do something with their messages. Games usually have a small set of user interface components and they are almost always custom coded. MFC and straight Win32 GDI calls just don't cut it, as far as I'm concerned. Sure, the number of controls you can attach to dialog boxes and screens is overwhelming, but most games don't need rich text editors, grid controls, OLE containers, property pages, and so on. Rather, the lack of control over position, animation and sounds usually compel game programmers to roll their own simple user interface.

These simple interfaces break the job into two parts: controls and containers for controls. Some user interface designs, such as Windows, don't distinguish between controls and control containers. Everything in the Win32 GDI has an `HWND`, or if you code in MFC everything derives from `CWnd`. This might seem a little weird because it would be unlikely that a button in your game would have other little buttons attached to it.

Instead of proposing any specific design, it's best to discuss some of the implementation issues and features any game will need in a user interface. I'll talk about control containers first, and then move to individual control types.

Screens

The highest level component of any user interface is analogous to the window, although I prefer to use my older nomenclature since I was coding screen based user interfaces long before Windows 95 came about. It's also easier for game programmers to see each screen as a self-contained unit, whether you are coding a PC game or a console game.

If your game has multiple screens, and even simple games have many, it's wise to manage them and the transitions between them in a high level API. This might seem a little strange to Windows programmers but it's a little like programming multiple applications for the same window, and you can freely move from one screen to another by selecting the right controls.

If your screens are fairly small "memory-wise" consider preloading them. Any transitions that happen will be blazingly fast, and players like responsive transitions. If your screens have tons of controls, graphics, and sounds, you won't necessarily be able to preload them because of memory constraints but you might consider loading a small transition screen to give your players something to look at while you load your bigger screens. Lots of console games do this, and they usually display a bit of the next mission in the background while a nice animation plays, showing the load progress.

Games such as Myst use a screen architecture like the one shown in Figure 5.2 throughout the entire game. Lots of kids games and mass market titles have a similar architecture.

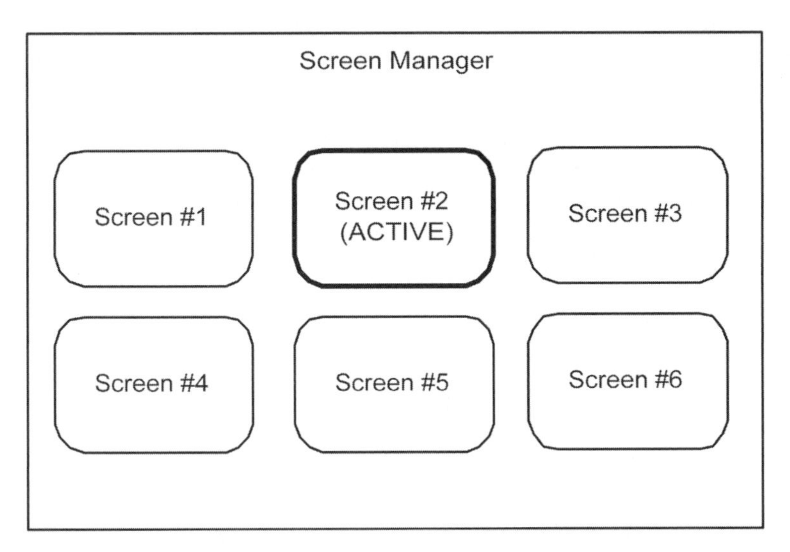

Figure 5.2
A Screen Manager Is a Container for Game Screens.

5

When the right controls are activated in the right order, the current screen is replaced by a new one with different controls.

Other games use multiple screens to set up the characters or missions. When everything is set up for the player, the game transitions to the game screen where most, if not all, the game is played. Almost every console game uses this model.

How do the device messages get to your game code? Again, it depends on a lot of things. Let's look at a simple example, such as keyboard input. Every time a player presses a keyboard key a `WM_KEYDOWN` event is sent to the top-level window via a call to your main window procedure. We'll make a reasonable assumption that you've encapsulated the normal `WndProc` routine into a game application class, and that one member of this class is the active screen:

```
LRESULT APIENTRY MyGameApp::WndProc(HWND hwndMain, UINT uMsg, WPARAM wParam,
                                    LPARAM lParam)
{
   switch (uMsg)
   {
      case WM_KEYDOWN:

         // A key is down! Holy crap what do I do now???

         // First, translate the raw event into something I like.
```

```
        yourcode::KeyboardEvent event = yourcode::TranslateKeyboardEvent(wParam,
        lParam);

        // Send the event into my active screenÖ
        if (m_activeScreen)
          m_activeScreen->OnKeydown(event);

        break;
    }
}
```

The first thing you'll do is translate the raw device event into something you'll use directly for your game. If you care about nothing more than printable ASCII characters, all you need to do is store an unsigned char in the event. If your game wants to know the current status of the left and right Ctrl keys in addition to the key that triggered the event, you'll have to create a more complicated event structure. You'll also have to put more logic in the `yourcode::TranslateKeyboardEvent` method to remember the status of previous key presses. Either way, by writing an event translator you've just successfully decoupled the operating system and device details from your game code.

The second task is detecting the active screen, and forwarding your translated event into the screen's implementation of `OnKeydown()`. The screen is a control container and it must iterate through the list of controls and send the message to each one until a control responds and handles the event:

```
bool CScreen::OnKeyDown(MyKeyboardEvent const &event)
{
    ControlList::reverse_iterator j=m_ControlList.rbegin();
    while(j!=m_ControlList.rend())
    {
      if((*j)->OnKeyDown( event ))
        return true;
      ++j;
    }

    return false;
}
```

Did you notice that the STL list was traversed in reverse order? Assuming the list is sorted in the order in which controls are actually drawn—back to front—the user interface code must ask controls about messages in the reverse order. The controls that appear on top of everything will get messages before their brethren (see Figure 5.3).

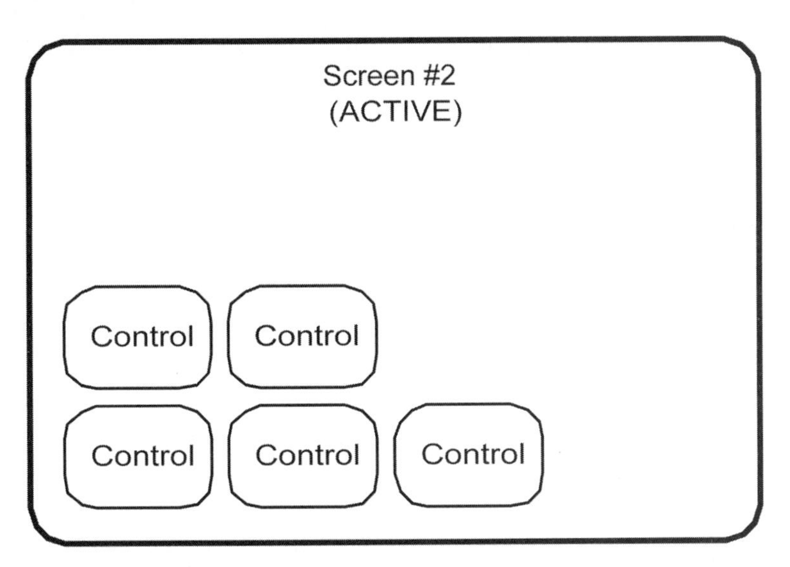

Figure 5.3
A Screen Is a Container for Controls.

The STL reverse iterator works its way through the list of controls from the tail of the list to the head. The first control to accept the message, signifying by returning true from `OnKeyDown()`, terminates the loop.

The screen class shouldn't care about anything except that the controls exist and that each one attached to the screen is a candidate to receive a particular kind of message. The control class implements code to determine whether it should care about the event:

```
bool Control::OnKeyDown(MyKeyboardEvent const &event)
{
   if ( IsActive() )
   {
      if ( CareAbout(event) )
      {
         OnChangeState();    // No Meat Here!
         return true;
      }
   }
   return false;
};
```

In the case of a control that processes keyboard events, it only needs to determine if it is currently active—since controls can be disabled—and whether the events match keys on its dance card.

You might think that the meat of the control code is really inside `OnChangeState()`. You'd be wrong, but I wouldn't blame you for guessing. `OnChangeState()` might perform some minor graphical or audio tasks but it doesn't call your game logic. Think about where we are in the overall call stack for your game. We're deep inside the message pump if you're coding in Windows, or you're in some callback function sending you device input.

That is the last place you want to change game logic or do anything drastic, like flip your game to fullscreen from windowed mode. I use that example because it's exactly what you might hook up to a hotkey, and you really don't want the message pump stalled out while your game is flipping graphics modes. Instead, do something simple like add the control a list that tracks activated controls. The list can be processed when your game is outside the callbacks and message pumps, and can safely do whatever madness it must:

```
void CScreen::ProcessActivatedControls()
{
   while( ! m_activatedControlList.empty() )
   {
      OnControl(* (m_activatedControlList.begin()) );
      m_activatedControlList.pop_front();
   }
}
```

There's much more discussion about what goes on in the main loop of the game in Chapter 7. Until then, you'll have to take my word that `ProcessActivatedControls()` gets called once per game loop.

Every screen in your game implements an `OnControl()`, which is somewhat analogous to Win32's processing of the `WM_COMMAND` message. Each control has an identifier, and the `OnControl` switches on the value of that ID. You can define these IDs in something as simple as an enumeration. Since user interface code can have a relatively slow reaction time—less than 80ms is adequate—you can even use a more complicated scheme that matches controls with text strings. Whatever you choose, make it easy for programmers to change, and try to keep these IDs out of header files; they'll change often.

Here's an imaginary implementation of a screen's `OnControl()` method:

```
bool CScreen::OnControl(const CControl* pControl)
{
   switch( pControl->GetID() )
   {
      case CID_PLAY:
         Play();
         return true;
```

```
      case CID_PAUSE:
         Pause();
         return true;

      case CID_REWIND:
         Rewind();
         return true;

      case CID_FASTFORWARD:
         FastForward();
         return true;

      case CID_EXIT:
         Exit();
         break;

      default:
         assert(0 && _T("Unknown control!"));
         break;
   }
   return false;
}
```


There are five controls on this screen, each distinguishing itself with a control identifier. The controls might be buttons, hidden hot areas sensitive to mouse movement, or hot key detectors. By the time the device input gets to the screen the input is translated into a command.

Dialog Boxes: Modal vs. Modeless

Dialog boxes usually present the player with a question, such as "Do you really want to quit?" In most cases, the game stops while the dialog box is displayed so the player can answer the question (see Figure 5.4). The answer is usually immediately accepted by the game.

This might seem easy to code, but it's actually fraught with pain and suffering. Why? Let's look at the anatomy of the "quit" dialog. The code to bring up a message box in Win32 looks like this:

```
int answer =
   MessageBox(_T("Do you really want to quit?"),
              _T("Question"),
              MB_YESNO | MB_ICONEXCLAMATION);
```

When this code is executed, a message box appears over the active window and stays there until one of the buttons is pressed. The window disappears and the button ID is sent back

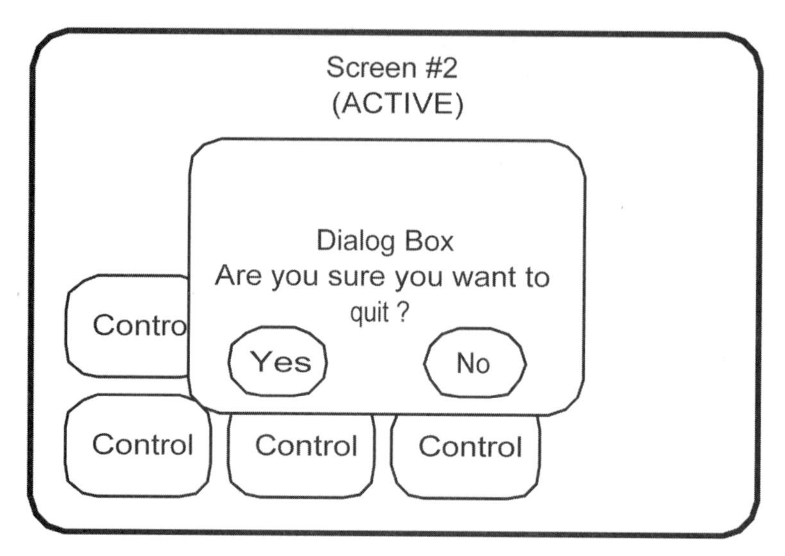

Figure 5.4
A Modal Dialog Box.

to the calling code. If you haven't thought about this before, you should realize that the regular message pump can't be working, but clearly *some* message pump is active. How else could mouse and keyboard messages activate the dialog box? How does that work?

The code to `MessageBox` has its own version of the message pump inside it, and similar to the main loop of your game, it doesn't exit until the dialog box destroys itself. The function that solves this problem is shown here:

```
int MyApp::PumpUntilMessage (UINT msgEnd, LPARAM* pLParam, WPARAM* pWParam)
{
   MSG msg;
   for ( ;; )
   {
      if ( PeekMessage( &msg, NULL, 0, 0, PM_NOREMOVE ) )
      {
         // If the WM_CLOSE comes through, we've got to close
         // no matter what - your game should begin its shut down
         // code even if the dialog is up.

         if (msg.message == WM_CLOSE)
         {
            // a member variable of MyApp
            m_CloseReceived = true;
            GetMessage(& msg, NULL, 0, 0);
            break;
```

```
        }
        else
        {
            // Default processing
            if ( !PumpMessage() )
                return ExitInstance();

            // Are we done?
            if ( msg.message == msgEnd)
                break;
        }
    }
    else
    {
        // Process
        MyGameIdle(1);              // this is your idle function
    }
  }
  if (pLParam)
      *pLParam = msg.lParam;
  if (pWParam)
      *pWParam = msg.wParam;

  return 0;
}
```

5

The PumpUntilMessage function works similar to the message pump in your main loop, but it is a special one meant for modal dialog boxes. One message, WM_CLOSE, gets special treatment since they must terminate the dialog and begin the game close process. Other than close, the loop continues until the target message is seen in the message queue—although it could look for anything it will usually look for MSG_END_MODAL, something you'll need to define yourself:

```
#define MSG_END_MODAL       WM_USER + 100
```

Your application will need more than an internal message pump. It needs something to handle the logistics of preparing the screen for a model dialog. If the game is processing a drag command, weird things will happen if a dialog interrupts the drag. You'll want to abort the drag before the dialog appears:

```
int MyApp::DoModal(MyScreen* modalScreen)
{
   //Abort all drag operations - you write these yourself
   if (IsSomeoneDraggingSomething())
   {
      AbortTheDragToAvertStrangeness();
   }

   PushActiveScreen(modalScreen);

   LPARAM lParam = 0;
   int result = PumpUntilMessage(MSG_END_MODAL, &lParam);
   if (lParam != 0)
      result = (int)lParam;

   PopActiveScreen();
   if (mCloseReceived)
   {
      QuitMyGame();                  // Call your quit code here!
   }

   return result;
}
```

There's special code in here to handle the case of `WM_CLOSE` coming through while your game is asking a question like, "Would you like fries with that?" The message terminates the modal dialog and begins the process of the quit code. This implies that each dialog must have a default answer, which is true. The code that calls `DoModal` with your dialog screen needs a rational way to interpret the answer.

Notice the calls to `PushActiveScreen()` and `PopActiveScreen()`. You'll write those to make your modal screen the top level screen. This allows a smaller dialog box to appear over another screen. It wouldn't do to have your game screen completely disappear just because a message box pops up.

Your dialog code can work exactly like one of your normal screens, with one exception. Instead of using the root screen manager to transition from one screen to another, it sends `MSG_END_MODAL` to the internal message pump:

```
PostMessage( m_myGameWindow, MSG_END_MODAL, 0, result );
```

The value in `result` is sent back to the code that called the modal dialog.

Modeless dialog boxes are usually status screens, object palettes, or anything else that needs to overlay the main game screen. Attach these screens to the root screen and make them active, so they'll be drawn and accept events. Just like controls, screens have a Z-order, and they draw from back to front but accept events from front to back. Other than that, they don't need any special treatment. Don't you wish we could say that about game programmers!

Controls

Controls have lots of permutations, but most of them share similar properties. I've seen push buttons, radio buttons, checkboxes, combo boxes, edit boxes, expandable menus, and all sorts of stuff. I've also coded quite a few of them, I'm sad to say.

The tough thing about implementing a new kind of control in your game isn't how to draw a little 'x' in the checkbox; good grief if you can't do that you should give up programming and become an attorney or a truck driver. Rather, the tough thing is knowing what features your controls will need beyond simple push button animations. You also need to be aware of the important gotchas you'll need to avoid. Let's start with the easy stuff first:

- *Message sensitivity*: Which device messages do the controls care about?
- *Identification*: How is the control distinguished from others on the same screen?
- *Hit Testing/Focus Order*: Which control gets messages, especially if they overlap graphically?
- *State*: What states should controls support?

I suggest you approach the first problem from a device-centric point of view. Each device is going to send input to a game, some of which will be mapped to the same game functions. In other words, you might be able to select a button with the mouse to perform some game action, like firing a missile. You might also use a hot key to do the same thing.

First, model the devices and their physical design: buttons, one-axis, and two-axis controls. Then, create some helper interface classes for each device, that take as input the translated events that you received from messages, callbacks, or even polling. You can write these any way you want, but here are some examples:

```
class IKeyboardSensitive
{
   virtual bool OnKeyDown(unsigned int const kcode)=0;
   virtual bool OnKeyUp(unsigned int const kcode)=0;
};
```

```
class IMouseSensitive
{
    virtual bool OnLMouseDown(int const x, int const y)=0;
    virtual bool OnLMouseUp  (int const x, int const y)=0;
    virtual bool OnRMouseDown(int const x, int const y)=0;
    virtual bool OnRMouseUp  (int const x, int const y)=0;
    virtual bool OnMouseMove (int const x, int const y)=0;
};

class IJoystickSensitive
{
    virtual bool OnButtonDown(int const button, int const pressure)=0;
    virtual bool OnButtonUp(int const button)=0;
    virtual bool OnJoystick(float const x, float const y)=0;
};

class IGamepadSensitive
{
    virtual bool OnTrigger(bool const left, float const pressure)=0;
    virtual bool OnButtonDown(int const button, int const pressure)=0;
    virtual bool OnButtonUp(int const button)=0;
    virtual bool OnDirectionalPad(int directionFlags)=0;
    virtual bool OnThumbstick(int const stickNum, float const x,
                              float const y)=0;
};
```

Each function represents an action taken by a control when something happens to an input device. Here's how the return values work: If the message is handled, the functions return `true`; otherwise they return `false`.

Your control classes, such as a push button class or a menu class, will implement the interfaces for the devices they care about. Control objects in your game are guaranteed to receive device input in a standard and predictable way. Thus, it should be a simple matter to modify and change the interface of your game by attaching new control objects that care about any device you've installed.

The interface classes described previously are simple examples and they should be coded as to fit the unique needs of your game. You can easily remove or add functions at will. Clearly, not every game will use input exactly the same way.

Don't add parameters to distinguish between multiple joysticks or gamepads. A better solution is to create controls that map directly to the object they are controlling. For example, if multiple gamepads control multiple human drivers, the control code shouldn't need to be aware of any other driver but the one it is controlling. Set all this up in a factory that creates the driver, the controller, and informs the input device code where to send the input from each gamepad.

If you follow a modular design, your game objects can be controlled via the same interface whether the source of that control is a gamepad or an AI character. The AI character sends commands like "brake 75%" or "steer 45%" into a car controller, where the human player touches a few gamepad keys, generating translated events that eventually result in exactly the same calls, but to a different car.

This design should always exist in any game where AI characters and humans are essentially interchangeable. If humans and AI characters use completely different interfaces to game objects it becomes difficult to port a single player game to multiplayer. You'll soon discover that none of the "plugs" fit.

Control Identification

Every control needs an identifier—something the game uses to distinguish it from the other controls on the screen. The easiest way to do this is define an `enum`, and when the controls are created they retain the unique identifier they were assigned in their construction:

```
enum MAINSCREEN_CONTROL_IDS
{
   CID_EXIT,
   CID_EXIT_DESKTOP,
   CID_PREVIOUS_SCREEN,
   CID_MAIN_MENU,
   CID_OPTIONS
};

bool MyMainScreen::OnControl(const MyControl* pControl)
{
   switch(pControl->GetID())
   {
      case CID_EXIT:
         // exit this screen
         break;

      case CID_EXIT_DESKTOP:
         // exit to the desktop
         break;

      // etc. etc.
   }
}
```

Each screen should define a method that accepts messages from controls. A control will send the message to the screen when it is selected. This is very similar to the way Win32 sends messages from controls to windows via the `WM_COMMAND` message, but simplified. The only problem with defining control IDs in this manner is keeping them straight, especially if you create screen classes that inherit from other screen classes, each with their own set of controls.

There's almost no end to the religious arguments about creating new screens by inheriting from existing screen classes. Object oriented coding techniques make it easy to extend one class into another but there is a risk of confusion and error when the new class is so different from the original that it might as well be a completely new class. This is why it's better to define functionality in terms of interfaces and helper functions, and flatten your class hierarchy into functional nuggets. A deep inheritance tree complicates the problems of changing something in a base class without adversely affecting many classes that inherit from it.

Some games define controls in terms of text strings, assigning each control a unique string. The downside is the more expensive string compare every time you want to figure out what control is talking to the screen. It does make things easy to debug, but there's nothing stopping you from including a string member in the debug build of the class. You can solve this problem by writing a bit of debug code that detects multiple controls with the same ID. Your code should simply assert so you can go find the problem and redefine the offending identifier.

Hit Testing and Focus Order

There are two ways controls know they are the center of your attention. The first way is via a hit test. This is where you use a pointer or cursor and position it over the control by an analog device such as a mouse. This method is prevalent in PC games, and especially games that have a large number of controls on the screen.

The second method uses a focus order. Only one control has the focus at any one time, and each control can get the focus by an appropriate movement of the input device. If the right key or button is pressed, the control with focus sends a message to the parent screen. This is how most console games are designed, and it clearly limits the number and density of controls on each screen.

Hit testing usually falls into three categories: rectangular hit testing, polygonal hit testing, and bitmap collision testing. The rectangle hit test is brain dead simple. You just make sure your hit test includes the entire rectangle, not just the inside. If a rectangle's coordinates were (15,4) and (30,35), then a hit should be registered both at (15,4) and (30,35).

The hit test for a 2D polygon is not too complicated. The following algorithm was adapted from Graphics Gems, and assumes the polygon is closed. This adaptation uses a `Point` structure and STL to clarify the original algorithm. It will work on any arbitrary polygons, convex or concave:

```
#include <vector>

struct Point
{
   int x, y;
   Point() { x = y = 0; }
   Point(int _x, int _y) { x = _x; y = _y; }
};

typedef std::vector<Point> Polygon;

bool PointInPoly( Point const &test, const Polygon & polygon)
{
   Point newPoint, oldPoint;
   Point left, right;

   bool inside=false;

   size_t points = polygon.size();

   // The polygon must at least be a triangle
   if (points < 3)
         return false;

   oldPoint = polygon[points-1];

   for (unsigned int i=0 ; i < points; i++)
   {
      newPoint = polygon[i];
      if (newPoint.x > oldPoint.x)
      {
         left = oldPoint;
         right = newPoint;
      }
      else
      {
         left = newPoint;
         right = oldPoint;
      }
```

```
        // A point exactly on the left side of the polygon
        // will not intersect - as if it were "open"
        if ((newPoint.x < test.x) == (test.x <= oldPoint.x)
          && (test.y-left.y) * (right.x-left.x)
            < (right.y-left.y) * (test.x-left.x) )
        {
          inside=!inside;
        }

        oldPoint = newPoint;
    }
    return(inside);
}
```

Bitmap collision is easy. You simply compare the pixel value at the (x,y) coordinate with your definition of the transparent color.

Control State

Controls have four states: active, highlighted, pressed, and disabled. These states are shown in Figure 5.5. An active control is able to receive events but isn't the center of attention. When the control gets the focus or passes a hit test from the pointing device, its state changes to highlighted. Its common for highlighted controls to have separate art or even a looping animation that plays as long as it has focus.

When the player presses an activation button on their mouse or controller the button changes state again to pressed. The art for this state usually depicts the control in a visually pressed state so that the player can tell what's going on. If the cursor moves away from the control it will change state to active again, giving the player a clue that if the activation button is released, nothing will happen.

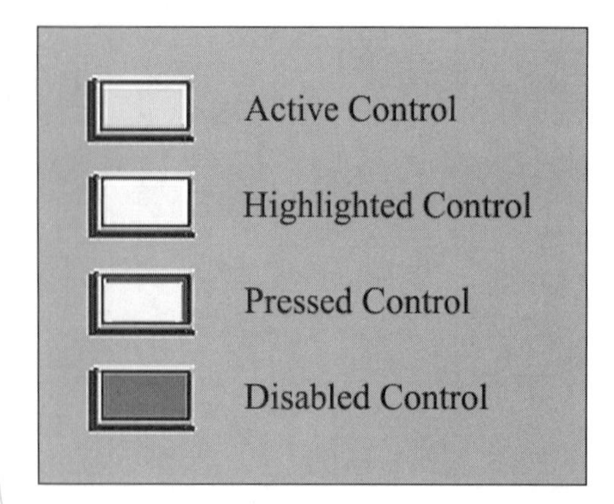

Figure 5.5
The Four States Used with Controls.

Disabled controls are usually drawn darkened, giving the impression that no one is home. I know that Windows does this all over the place, but there is one thing about it that really bothers me: I can never tell *why* the control is disabled. It's fine to have a disabled state, but make sure that the player can figure out why it's disabled or you'll just cause a lot of frustration.

If your interface uses a mouse, change the mouse cursor to a hand when you are over an active control. This approach will give the player another clue that something will happen when he or she clicks the button. Use the Win32 `LoadCursor()` API to grab a handle to the right mouse cursor, and call `SetCursor()` with the cursor handle. If you want a good package to create animated mouse pointers try Microangelo by Impact Software, **www.impactsoftware.com**.

Don't get confused about the control states mentioned here and control activation. Control activation results in a command message that propagates though to the screen's `OnControl()` function. For a standard push button control, this only happens if the mouse button is pressed and released over the button's hit area.

More Control Properties

There are some additional properties you can attach to controls, mostly to give the player a more flexible and informative interface.

Hotkeys

An excellent property to attach to any control is a hotkey. As players become more familiar with the game they'll want to ditch the mouse control in favor of pressing a single key on the keyboard. It's faster, which makes hardcore players really happy. You can distinguish between a hotkey command and a normal keyboard input by checking the keyboard focus. The focus is something your screen class keeps track of itself, since it is an object that moves from control to control. Let's assume you have a bunch of button controls on a game screen, as well as a chat window. Normally, every key down and up event will get sent to the controls to see if any of their hotkeys match. If they do match, the `OnControl()` method of the screen will get called. The only way to get enable the chat window is to click on it with the mouse or provide a hotkey for it that will set the keyboard focus for the screen.

As long as the keyboard focus points to the chat control, every keyboard event will be sent there, hotkeys are essentially disabled. Usually the focus is released when the edit control decides it's done with keyboard input, such as when the Enter key is pressed. The focus can also be taken away by the screen, such as if a different control were to be activated by the mouse.

Tooltips

Tooltips are usually controlled by the containing screen, since it has to be aware of moving the tooltip around as different controls are highlighted. Tooltips are trickier than you'd think, because there's much more to enabling them than creating a bit of text on your screen for each control.

For one thing, every tooltip needs to have a good position relative to the control it describes. You can't just assume that every tooltip will look right if you place them in the same relative position to every control. If you decide that every tooltip will be placed in the upper right area of every control, what happens when a control is already at the upper right border of the screen? Also, you'll want to make sure tooltips don't cover other important information on the screen when they appear. You don't want to annoy the heck out of your users.

Even if you provide a placement hint, such as above or beside a control, you'll still need to tweak the placement of the tooltip to make sure it doesn't clip on the screen edge. Also, make sure that screens can erase tooltips prematurely, such as when a dialog box appears or when a drag begins.

Context Sensitive Help

Context sensitive help is useful if you have a complicated game with lots of controls. If the player presses a hotkey to launch the help window when a control is highlighted, the help system can bring up help text that describes what the control will do. An easy way to do this is to associate an identifier with each control that has context sensitive help. In one game this identifier was the name of the HTML file associated with that control. When the screen gets the hot key event for help, it first finds any highlighted control and asks it if it has an associated help file.

Dragging

Controls can initiate a drag event or accept drag events. Drag initiation is simply a `boolean` value that is used to indicate if a drag event can start on top of the control or not. Drag acceptance is a little more complicated. Most drag events have a source type, as discussed at the beginning of this chapter. Some controls might accept drags of different types given only particular game states. An example of this might be dragging items around in a fantasy role playing game. A character in the game might not be able to accept a dragged object because he's already carrying too much, and thus not be a legal target for the drag event.

Sounds and Animation

Most controls have a sound effect that launches when the button changes state. Some games associate a single sound effect for every button, but it's not crazy to give each control their own sound effect. Animation frames for buttons and other controls are usually associated with the highlighted state. Instead of a single bitmap, you should use a bitmap series that loops while the control is highlighted. You'll find out more about animations and animating processes in this book. (For more information see Chapter 6 and Chapter 8.)

Some Final User Interface Tips

As parting advice, there are a few random, but important, tips I can give you on user interface work.

- All rectangular interfaces are boring.
- Localization can make a mess of your UI.
- UI code is easy to write, but making a good UI is a black art.

If your interface code doesn't use polygonal hit testing or bitmap collision, you are destined to have legions of square buttons and other controls populating your interface. That's not only a dull and uncreative look, but your artists will probably strangle you before you ever finish your game. Artists need the freedom to grow organic shapes in the interface, and will resist all those vertical and horizontal lines.

Localization is a huge subject, but a significant part of that subject is interface design. You may hear things like, "make all your buttons 50% wider for German text," as the end all, be all for localization. While that statement is certainly true, there's a lot more to it than that. It's difficult to achieve an excellent interface using nothing but icons, instead of clear text labels. We attempted that on one of the casino games we developed, and we were completely stymied with the problem of choosing an international icon for features like blackjack insurance and placing a repeat bet on a roulette table. The fact is that international symbols are used and recognized for men and women's bathrooms and locating baggage claim, but they are only recognized because they are advertised much more aggressively than the unique features you use in your games. If you use icons, more power to you, but you'd better provide some tooltips to go along with them.

A truly international application has to conform with much more than left to right, top to bottom blocks of text. Asian and Middle Eastern languages don't always follow western European "sensibility." All you can really count on is being able to print text to a definable rectangle. If you have to print lots of text, consider using a well-known format like HTML and be done with it.

When you design your user interface, know your audience. Older players are more comfortable with menus and labeled buttons. Younger players enjoy the experience of exploring a graphical environment with their mouse and clicking where they see highlights. This is extremely problematic if you are a youngish programmer writing games for little kids or your parents. They simply don't think the same way you do, and nothing you do in your interface code will change that. Mimic proven solutions if you can, but always get a random sample of your target audience by taking your interface design for a test drive.

There's nothing more humbling when you stand behind someone playing your game and silently watch them struggle with the simplest task. You want to scream at the top of your lungs, "Simpleton! How do you find enough neurons to respirate?" In a calmer moment, perhaps you'll realize that the one with missing neurons looks back at you from mirrors.

Chapter 6

2D Stuff Every Game Programmer Should Know

I used to play a great kid's game called Lite Brite that let me create pictures by pushing little pieces of colored plastic into a black screen brightly backlit with a light bulb. I made some pretty bizarre stuff with this game. I'm sure my parents never realized that more than thirty years later I'd be still playing with little bits of color on a screen. The bits of color are now moving a whole hell of a lot faster, and there are millions more of them. I remember finding out how graphical displays worked, and I recall being surprised at how easy it seemed. Each pixel is drawn using the contents of a range of video memory. If I change the value stored in that memory, I'll notice a color change in one of the pixels. How elegant and cool! What can I say, I was a geek.

After my initial joy wore off, I discovered that getting the right pixel to change or getting the right color was easy but the system had some tricks to it. Not every video card stored pixels in the same format and accessing each pixel wasn't as simple as tweaking values in a two dimensional array of values. Then the hard stuff began. I wanted to draw shapes, text, and scenes all blended together with nice translucent effects. This stuff is also not hard, but my trivial implementations also dropped the frame rate to embarrassing levels. In other words, making pretty pictures is still easy; making them at 60+ frames per second is trickier than you'd think.

For those of you who are already thinking of skipping this chapter in favor of reading some juicy 3D tricks, hang tight. One of the fastest growing areas of the computer game industry is handheld stuff. Games are being written for cell phones, Pocket PCs, and the GameBoy Advance. There's a renaissance of retro 2D gaming out there so don't think for a second that pushing pixels instead of polygons is a waste of your time. Besides, every 3D game I see still has plenty of 2D screens, animations, and other goodies. You need to walk before you can run, so we'll start back with drawing little blobs of color in this chapter, and see where it goes.

Let me say this again for emphasis: 2D is far from dead, as much as DirectX 8 would have you believe. 2D is coming back with a vengeance, and if all you know how to do is push polys, you're going to miss out on some of the best stuff that has happened to computer gaming in a long time. Nintendo's Game Boy Advance and Nokia's latest cell phones do not have 3D hardware acceleration.

2D Drawing and DirectX

I mentioned DirectX 8 a moment ago and you may have wondered why. 2D drawing and DirectX have had a shaky relationship for the past few years. Since DirectX version 8 has been introduced, the entire drawing pipeline is 3D. The DirectX team at Microsoft was motivated to simplify the DirectDraw and Direct3D APIs, specifically concerning textures and DirectDraw surfaces, both essentially 2D arrays of pixels. DirectX 8 eliminated the entire interface for DirectDraw, leaving any 2D games to stay with DirectX 7 or port their code to a 3D engine. DirectX 9 corrected this problem, but only somewhat. The DirectDraw API is part of DirectShow, and can't be readily used with Direct3D.

When I wrote this chapter I considered writing it using DirectX 9, since it is the API that is the latest and greatest from Microsoft. After about 50ms, I decided to use the DirectX 7 interface with the examples. The DirectX 7 code in this chapter is well tested and shows important concepts that will be useful for any game that needs to manipulate pixel surfaces. Just so you know, DirectX 7 is old, but these calls will still work fine on any machine with DirectX 7, 8, 9, and so on.

Pixels and Video Hardware

Here's a bit of inane trivia: "Pixel" is shorthand for "picture element." The term was coined when video displays were more than oscilloscopes but something less than flat plasma displays. It's not surprising that since humans developed video displays they are uniquely tuned to human physiology, but governed by physics. What humans perceive as color is light, or more specifically, electromagnetic radiation, in a narrow band of wavelengths. Humans can perceive color from deep reds at longer wavelengths to violet at shorter wavelengths. Not surprisingly, the color we call yellow is almost in the exact center of these two extremes, and it is almost exactly the color of our sun.

Two or more different colors of light can blend to form a new color. To represent the widest possible color range, you need to choose three colors: red, green, and blue. Mix these colors in varying proportions and you'll cover most, but not all, of the perceivable colors visible to the human eye.

Color depth is the term that describes the number of different values that can be assigned to a single pixel. Table 6.1 lists the three common formats for color depth.

Table 6.1 The Three Common Formats for Color Depth.

Channel Depth	Colors	Bit Depth
R-8 G-8 B-8 Masks: 0x00FF0000, 0x0000FF00, 0x000000FF	16.7 million	32-bit
R-5 G-5 B-5 Masks: 0x7C00, 0x03E0, 0x001F	32,768	16-bit
R-5 G-6 B-5 Masks: 0xF800, 0x07E0, 0x001F	65,536	16-bit

The sequence of bits represent the intensity of the different colors. For example, the 32-bit pixel contains 8-bits each for red, green, and blue. If all of the bits for red are set to zero, the resulting color will have absolutely no red component at all. If the bits were set to a binary value of 10000000b, the red component would be at exactly 50% intensity.

The number of bits for each component affect the number of discrete values of intensity from 0% to 100%. If the red component has 8 bits, red can have 256 intensity settings. If the red component had 5 bits, it could only have 32 different values. Another way to describe this is that pure black and white can always be represented, since all the color bits can be either zero or one, but if you want to get an exact match for Barbie pink, it might be troublesome if you only have 5 bits for red.

Believe it or not, there are some video cards that support a 48-bit mode, 16 bits per color channel. This gives you more than 281 trillion colors, and an uncompressed 800x600 screen would take 2.74Mb! I'm sure an artist had something to do with the design of that video card.

We also still have palettized, or indexed formats to deal with. Here programmers and artists are forced to choose 256 colors, each color 24-bit, with which they can use to draw their screen. Palettized modes are a pain to work with and generally don't look very good if they have to be applied to an entire screen. When we moved to 16- and 32-bit displays all you heard was cheering from every programmer and artist I knew. It is still common practice to store individual pieces of art for backgrounds, textures, or sprites in an 8-bit palletized format, since it keeps a high degree of accuracy in the art and saves space at the same time.

Now that you know how each pixel is stored, let's move on and learn a little about video hardware.

Video Hardware and Buffers

A video card is essentially a tool to manipulate and examine two-dimensional arrays of pixels. At their simplest, video cards simply scan the contents of their memory and convert each pixel to an electrical signal sent to a CRT. The scan rate is usually 60Hz or faster; 50Hz if you happen to live abroad in Europe, which uses the PAL standard. The scan rate is timed to coincide exactly with the scan rate of the electron guns in the CRT. When the contents of the video memory change, the results are displayed the next time the pixel is scanned.

You might have heard the term "vertical blank" and wondered what it meant. The vertical blank is a signal sent from the monitor to the video card each time the electron guns skip back to the top of the display. It's important to change the screen pixels only when the electron guns aren't drawing pixels, and the vertical blank is your signal to make any screen changes. If you don't, you'll witness an effect called "tearing." This is what happens when you change pixels in video memory while the electron guns are scanning the image. You'll notice a small discontinuity in your shapes as shown in Figure 6.1.

This happens because you're not changing all the pixels fast enough. Since you can't change all the pixels at once, the electron guns will inevitably draw some pixels of the old frame and some pixels of the new frame. This drawing technique is called *single buffering*, since there's one and only one buffer that holds your pixels. In a single buffering solution, your only hope of avoiding tearing is to change all of the pixels in the video buffer in one lightning quick move, while the electron guns are moving back to the top of the screen. Even in the dark ages (circa 1990), an off-screen buffer held the contents of the next frame. This buffer was stored in regular system memory. All the draw code changed the off-screen buffer while the video card drew the contents of video memory over and over again.

Figure 6.1
How Tearing Can Impact a Display.

When the off-screen buffer, sometimes called a *backbuffer*, was completely rendered it was copied to the video memory or *frontbuffer*. Copying the bits from the backbuffer to the front buffer is fast enough to happen completely during the vertical blank, so all the programmer had to do was wait for the vertical blank signal and copy the bits. Old Origin lingo called this process "slamming" but today's vernacular calls it "blitting."

DirectX's `WaitForVerticalBlank()` method is used to tap into the monitor signal:

```
m_pDD->WaitForVerticalBlank(DDWAITVB_BLOCKBEGIN, NULL);
```

The problem with this method is that copying the bits from the backbuffer to the front buffer was dependant on waiting for the vertical blank signal. On average, the system would wait 1/120th of a second every frame, if the monitor scanned at 60Hz. A few hardware solutions attempted to minimize this problem by providing faster bit transfer rates over better bus architectures or even direct memory access—video cards could "pull" the bits out of main memory without the CPU's involvement.

These solutions were ok, but still fell short. Video cards soon installed more memory on their boards, enough to keep more than two full screens of pixels. The pixel scanning could be programmed via the video driver to begin scanning at any point in video memory. Thus it became possible to construct the backbuffer on the video card and when it was done, change the scanning start address to the backbuffer. The area of memory that was previously displayed was now free to be the scratchpad for the next frame.

Reassigning the front and backbuffers each frame is known as *flipping*. The best part about it is how fast it is; the huge bit transfers from the back buffer to the front buffer are a thing of the past. The CPU does have to wait for the go ahead to begin modifying the backbuffer. The vertical blank signal is still the green light to change pixels, until the flip actually occurs you might be changing pixels the player can see.

One quick aside for beleaguered DirectX programmers: The flipping chain is smart enough to reassign internal data so you don't have to. The member variable that points to your front buffer always points to your front buffer; it doesn't matter how many times you call `Flip()`. I think this confused me when I first saw it. I had an incredible urge to do something like this:

```
hr = m_pddsFrontBuffer->Flip( NULL, 0 );

LPDIRECTDRAWSURFACE7 temp = m_pddsFrontBuffer;
m_pddsFrontBuffer = m_pddsBackBuffer;
m_pddsBackBuffer = temp;
```

Don't go down that road because it is completely incorrect. DirectX flipping chains take care of this for you—your back buffer is always your back buffer, and your front buffer is always your front buffer, no matter how many times you flip.

Now you know about single buffers, double buffering, and double buffered flipping, but there's still one more technique: *triple buffering*. Triple buffering adds one more screen to the flipping chain, so that after three flips the original buffer is the front buffer. The advantage to triple buffering is that after the flip, the CPU can move directly to constructing the pixels for the next frame. You don't have to wait for the vertical blank. The newly constructed frame and the previously constructed frame exist on the other two buffers—the scratch buffer hasn't seen the light of day for two flips.

What's the downside? Double and triple buffered surfaces require more memory, that's pretty clear. Since they take more video memory, there's less left over for other things such as commonly used sprites or textures that need to exist in video memory for ultra fast drawing.

One more note about flipping surfaces: the Windows GDI only draws to one surface. If you ever call a GDI function, such as `MessageBox()`, you must call the DirectX method `FlipToGDISurface()` beforehand. If you don't, you take your chances that the GDI will draw to the wrong surface. One more thing: The surface that you are about to flip to, the one that GDI draws on, had better look right. If it has an old frame from two flips ago, your player will notice.

Video and Memory Surfaces

Video and memory surfaces are two-dimensional arrays of pixels. They differ only in the details of their internal structure, which is usually hidden from the programmer by a class. While the structure may be, and should be, hidden it's important to understand their differences so you'll recognize the source of problems.

Video surfaces don't organize pixels for memory efficiency; they organize them for speed. This effects two things: the effective space taken up by a pixel, and the effective space used by a scan line. 24-bit color isn't really 24-bit when it gets to the video card. Video hardware stores 24-bit pixels in 32 bits, or four bytes. It may seem like a waste of memory but the added speed is well worth it. Dividing by three is a lot slower than shifting by two, which is what the hardware would have to do to find pixel addresses in a 24-bit system.

Scan line width is not necessarily the same as the number of bytes per pixel multiplied by the number of pixels on the scan line. Scan lines are aligned on convenient boundaries, defined by the video card engineers. This boundary might be four bytes, eight bytes, or more. The number of bytes actually used by a scan line, which includes the pixel data and zero or more bytes at the end, is called *pitch*. Figure 6.2 provides an image to help you detect the difference.

Our friend from Diablo II is sitting on a DirectDraw surface with a width of 78 bytes. When the surface was created, the DirectDraw system saw fit to allocate the surface with

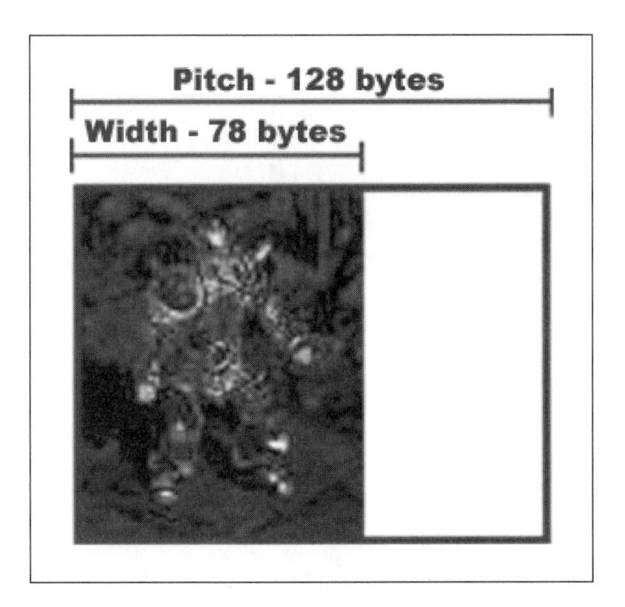

Figure 6.2
The Difference between Width and Pitch.

a pitch of 128 bytes. If you think this is a colossal waste of memory, you're right. Depending on your display driver, it might assign surface memory only in byte widths that conform to powers of two. In any case, always be aware that your pitch might be vastly different than your width.

If you ever see a piece of art that looks like an old TV set with a scrambled and slanted picture, you've copied the pixels without taking the pitch into account. The slant will go from top-left to bottom-right if the destination pitch is bigger than the source, and from top-right to bottom-left if the destination pitch is smaller than the source.

Window's BMP format also does this. Each line of the BMP aligns on four byte boundaries. If you can't seem to parse bitmap files and all you get is funny slanted art, check your code and I'll bet it assumes that the pitch is equal to the width, which it's not.

Memory surfaces are organized any way the programmer chooses. They might reflect the bigger but speedier arrangement of video memory or they might compress the image into as small a memory space as possible. How do you go about creating a surface? You can look at DirectX samples all day if you just need to know how to fill in a DDSURFACEDESC but there are a few tricks you should know. The following code should puts these tricks to work:

```
LPDIRECTDRAWSURFACE7 CreateSurface( DWORD dwWidth, DWORD dwHeight,
                                    DWORD dwCaps, BOOL favorVRAM )
{
   if( NULL == g_pDD )                       // pointer to the direct draw object
   return NULL;

   HRESULT        hr;
   LPDIRECTDRAWSURFACE7 pSurface = NULL;
   DDSURFACEDESC2 ddsd;

   ZeroMemory( &ddsd, sizeof( ddsd ) );
   ddsd.dwSize          = sizeof( ddsd );
   ddsd.dwFlags         = DDSD_CAPS | DDSD_WIDTH | DDSD_HEIGHT;

   if (favorVRAM && dwHeight<=g_ScreenHeight && dwWidth<=g_ScreenWidth )
   {
      ddsd.ddsCaps.dwCaps = DDSCAPS_VIDEOMEMORY;
   }
   else
   {
      ddsd.ddsCaps.dwCaps = DDSCAPS_SYSTEMMEMORY | DDSCAPS_OFFSCREENPLAIN;
   }
```

```
    ddsd.ddsCaps.dwCaps |= dwCaps;

    ddsd.dwWidth = dwWidth;
    ddsd.dwHeight = dwHeight;

    if(FAILED (hr= g_pDD->CreateSurface( &pSurface, &ddsd, NULL ) ) )
    {
    ddsd.ddsCaps.dwCaps =
      dwCaps | DDSCAPS_OFFSCREENPLAIN | DDSCAPS_SYSTEMMEMORY;

    if(FAILED (hr= g_pDD->CreateSurface( &pSurface, &ddsd, NULL ) ) )
    {
      return NULL;
      }
    }

    return pSurface;
}
```


There are a few critical things in this function. First, the function is smart enough to check the validity of the width and height of a surface that wants to live in video memory. There are a few video cards out there that freak out when you allocate a surface wider or higher than the current screen resolution. Second, if an attempt to create a surface in video memory fails, the function will attempt to load the surface into system memory. The only problem with system memory surfaces is that they'll run slower on some machines, sometimes much slower. Your game might follow the above code sample and fail over to the system memory surface, but another valid solution is to fail entirely. You might have a video memory leak, use too much video memory, or are running on a machine with a lame video card.

Now that you've got a surface to draw to, you'll want some nice drawing functions.

Basic 2D Drawing Concepts

If you need to find fast algorithms to draw lines, ellipses, or other simple shapes there's no better reference series than *Graphics Gems*. Every programmer should have all but one on their bookshelf. The one not on your bookshelf will be open on your desk. I hope you'll forgive me for de-referencing those algorithms instead of regurgitating them here, but I simply can't add anything new to that venerable body of knowledge and I'd like to spend time and trees on other things. This is not going to be one of those books where I reinvent the wheel.

Windows Bitmaps and Other GDI Doodads

If you have a DirectX surface, you can grab a device context, or DC, and use the Windows GDI to draw to your surface. This is pretty convenient if you want to use the GDI for one shot stuff, but don't forget that it's way too slow for things you'll be doing every game loop. Here's an example of how you would go about drawing a bitmap:

```
HRESULT DrawBitmap(
        LPDIRECTDRAWSURFACE7 pdds,
        HBITMAP hBMP,
   DWORD dwBMPOriginX, DWORD dwBMPOriginY,
   DWORD dwBMPWidth, DWORD dwBMPHeight,
        bool stretch)
{
   HDC            hDCImage;
   HDC            hDC;
   BITMAP         bmp;
   DDSURFACEDESC2 ddsd;
   HRESULT        hr;

   if( hBMP == NULL || pdds == NULL )
       return E_INVALIDARG;

   // Make sure this surface is restored.
      if ( (pdds->IsLost() != DD_OK) )
   {
        if( FAILED( hr = pdds->Restore() ) )
          return hr;
   }

    // Get the surface.description
    ddsd.dwSize  = sizeof(ddsd);
    m_pdds->GetSurfaceDesc( &ddsd );

    if( ddsd.ddpfPixelFormat.dwFlags == DDPF_FOURCC )
        return E_NOTIMPL;

    // Select bitmap into a memoryDC so we can use it.
    hDCImage = CreateCompatibleDC( NULL );
    if( NULL == hDCImage )
        return E_FAIL;

    SelectObject( hDCImage, hBMP );

   // Get size of the bitmap
```

```
    GetObject( hBMP, sizeof(bmp), &bmp );

    // Use the passed size, unless zero

    dwBMPWidth  = ( dwBMPWidth  == 0 ) ? bmp.bmWidth  : dwBMPWidth;
    dwBMPHeight = ( dwBMPHeight == 0 ) ? bmp.bmHeight : dwBMPHeight;

    // Stretch the bitmap to cover this surface
    if(  FAILED( hr = pdds->GetDC( &hDC ) ) )\
         return hr;

         if(stretch)
         {
                      StretchBlt( hDC, 0, 0,
                              ddsd.dwWidth, ddsd.dwHeight,
                              hDCImage, dwBMPOriginX, dwBMPOriginY,
                              dwBMPWidth, dwBMPHeight, SRCCOPY );
    }
    else
    {
                      BitBlt(hDC, dwBMPOriginX, dwBMPOriginY,
                              dwBMPWidth, dwBMPHeight,
                              hDCImage, 0, 0, SRCCOPY);
    }

    if( FAILED( hr = pdds->ReleaseDC( hDC ) ) )
         return hr;

    DeleteDC( hDCImage );

    return S_OK;
}
```

Notice that the first thing this function does is check to see if the surface is lost and needs restoring. This is critical and failure to do it every time you access a DirectX surface is asking for trouble. The Win32 calls to `StrectchBlt` and `BitBlt` are inside the predicate that grabs a DC from the DirectX surface. You could replace these calls with any GDI function: `LineTo`, `MoveTo`, `TextOut`, whatever you want.

You should note one thing about grabbing a DC from any DirectDraw surface. This effectively locks the surface until the device context is released. If the surface happens to be a texture or otherwise inserted in the draw pipeline, it can't be used to draw anything until the DC is released. If you really want to use GDI functions to draw to a DirectDraw surface, the best thing to do is create it in off-screen memory, perform the GDI drawing, and copy the surface to something in the draw pipeline like a surface in video RAM. This seems like going out of your way, but your game will run faster.

Color Key or Chroma Key

A color key, or as artists call it "chroma key" is a special pixel value that means, "Don't copy me." Actually there's a more specific name for that kind of color key—it's a source color key. There are destination color keys, too, which are neat for creating interesting effects but they are only rarely used. The source color key, on the other hand, is used all the time. In case you were wondering, this technology is exactly the same as the technology used to make weather forecasters appear on weather maps. They actually stand in front of a green background, watching their own image on a monitor after it has been blended with the weather map. Have you ever noticed that they never wear anything green? If they did, that part of their wardrobe would appear completely transparent.

When you set a color key for a surface, you use a pixel value that matches exactly with the pixel format of that surface (see Figure 6.3). Most colors are expressed in full are expressed in full 8-bit RGB values, which you can only use if the surface's pixel format happens to be 32-bit. Artists need to know the exact RGB value so they can fill the areas that should be transparent, but when the art is converted to the screen's pixel format, the bits that map to the color key don't match the original definition! You solve this problem in one of two ways.

First, your artists must be aware that any art with a color key must be stored in a convenient format that doesn't mess up the color key value. For example, a slightly lossy JPG will most certainly tweak some of your transparent pixel values to something other than the exact RGB value you expect. This will create weird colored halos around your art at best or completely disable the transparency at worst.

Figure 6.3
A Background, a Sprite with a Color Key, and the Intended Result.

There's another insidious problem that artists will unknowingly create in their art. Many art packages like Photoshop and 3D Studio Max can antialias the art to a specific color. It might seem like antialiasing to the color key would smooth the edges of your art into the background, but it won't. Instead, you'll get a nasty colored outline that somewhat matches the color key color. If you want to have a smooth transition from your sprite to a background, the only solution is to use a separate alpha channel, something you'll learn shortly.

Second, the programmer needs to find out what pixel value maps to the RGB color key definition, given the destination surface's pixel format. Under Win32, you get to use a GDI function, because you can't count on performing the conversion yourself. The resulting pixel must be exactly the same as what will be drawn by the video driver, and unless you've seen the video driver code, you can't predict its behavior. You only have to do this once for any destination surface. Here's a code example that performs this task:

```
//-----------------------------------
// Name: ConvertGDIColor()
// Desc: Converts a GDI color (0x00bbggrr) into the equivalent color on a
//       DirectDrawSurface using its pixel format.
//-----------------------------------
DWORD ConvertGDIColor( LPDIRECTDRAWSURFACE7 pdds, COLORREF dwGDIColor )
{
    if( pdds == NULL )
       return 0x00000000;

    COLORREF       rgbT;
    HDC            hdc;
    DWORD          dw = CLR_INVALID;
    DDSURFACEDESC2 ddsd;
    HRESULT        hr;

    //  Use GDI SetPixel to color match for us
    if( pdds->GetDC(&hdc) == DD_OK)
    {
        rgbT = GetPixel(hdc, 0, 0);            // Save current pixel value
        SetPixel(hdc, 0, 0, dwGDIColor);       // Set our value
        pdds->ReleaseDC(hdc);
    }

    // Now lock the surface so we can read back the converted color
    ddsd.dwSize = sizeof(ddsd);
    hr = pdds->Lock( NULL, &ddsd, DDLOCK_WAIT, NULL );
    if( hr == DD_OK)
    {
```

```
        dw = *(DWORD *) ddsd.lpSurface;
        if( ddsd.ddpfPixelFormat.dwRGBBitCount < 32 ) // Mask it to bpp
             dw &= ( 1 << ddsd.ddpfPixelFormat.dwRGBBitCount ) - 1;
        pdds->Unlock(NULL);
    }

    //  Now put the color that was there back.
    if( pdds->GetDC(&hdc) == DD_OK )
    {
        SetPixel( hdc, 0, 0, rgbT );
        pdds->ReleaseDC(hdc);
    }

    return dw;
}
```

This code grabs a DC from the DirectX surface and uses the GDI's `GetPixel` and `SetPixel` to save the current pixel and draw the target color to the upper left-hand pixel. The resulting pixel value is obtained using DirectX's `Lock` to get a pointer to the surface. Once this is done, the old pixel value is restored. Clearly, this function isn't very speedy so you should only call it once per destination surface. If every surface has the same pixel format, you should only call it once for your whole game. You'll have to call this function again if these surfaces are lost, because they usually get lost when the player does something crazy like changing their desktop settings or switching from fullscreen mode to windowed mode.

The source color key is set for the surface that has the transparent pixels. Here's how you do that:

```
HRESULT SetColorKey( LPDIRECTDRAWSURFACE7 pdds, DWORD dwColorKey,
                     DDCOLORKEY &ddck )
{
    if( NULL == pdds )
        return E_POINTER;

    ddck.dwColorSpaceLowValue =
      ddck.dwColorSpaceHighValue = ConvertGDIColor( pdds, dwColorKey );

    return pdds->SetColorKey( DDCKEY_SRCBLT, &m_ddck );
}
```

Notice that the last value, DDCOLORKEY, is actually an output of this function. It's convenient to keep it around in case you have other surfaces with the same pixel format; you won't have to call ConvertGDIColor again.

How do you choose color key color? It should be a color that is not only rarely used, but located in the color space in a group of rarely used colors. This will avoid any unintentional misuse of the color key. After years of study and many opinions of artists, it seems that the first prize for the "ugliest color contest" goes to a setting of RGB (255, 0, 255). I think the only development group in the industry that can't use it is Mattel. This color is just too close to Barbie's favorite color. Maybe they use "vomit green;" I have no idea.

Copying Surfaces

Copying a surface should be straightforward. The hard part is figuring out what to do when the copy fails, or how to detect it:


```
HRESULT Copy(LPDIRECTDRAWSURFACE7 dest, LPDIRECTDRAWSURFACE7 src,
          CPoint &destPoint, CRect &srcRect, BOOL isColorKeyed)
{
   if ( !dest || !src )
   {
      return DDERR_SURFACELOST;
   }

   HRESULT hr;

   for ( ;; )
   {
      // Copy the surface

      hr = dest->BltFast(
         destPoint.x, destPoint.y,
         src,
         srcRect,
         isColorKeyed ? DDBLTFAST_SRCCOLORKEY : 0 );

      if( hr != DDERR_WASSTILLDRAWING )
      {
         /***
         Note: Surfaces should not restore themselves because they don't know how
         to recreate their graphics. If they fail to draw, just return the result
         and let the caller figure it out.
         ***/
```

```
            return hr;
        }
    };
    return hr;
}
```

The code enters a loop and attempts to copy the source surface to the destination. If it fails because the surface was busy, it tries again. If the failure was for any other reason, such as an invalid surface, the code exits with an error.

You might think that it would be a good idea to attempt a surface restore before bailing but that would be a mistake in this piece of code. A surface to surface copy will get used heavily in the screen render. Don't forget that the backbuffer is a surface also. If either the source or destination surface can't render, the most likely cause is an invalid surface. This would happen if the player flipped screen modes, which can happen at any time. It is likely that every other surface will fail a `BltFast` call, so the best course of action is to exit the draw entirely and restore every surface at once. After you do that you can try to draw everything again. This time it will work.

Copying Surfaces Using an Alpha Channel

Color keys are convenient and cheap. Almost all video hardware accelerates surface to surface copies with a color key. The problem is that they don't look good. It's easy to pick out color keyed sprites because their edges are harsh and aliased. I mentioned before that you could use an alpha channel to fix this problem, but be aware that there's no hardware acceleration. That should surprise you; it has certainly confused me. Video cards clearly have the hardware to blend pixel values. This is evident whenever you see a semi-transparent 3D object. This same technology though has *never* been exposed in DirectDraw, even though the flags are there! We are left to compose our alpha blended surfaces with nothing more than stone knifes and bear skins.

Here's the basic formula for alpha blending two values in the same color channel:

```
Result = Destination + ( Alpha * ( Source - Destination ) )
```

It might not be obvious, but this formula works on color channels, not pixels. A pixel has three color channels: red, green, and blue. When you implement this formula, you must calculate each color separately. You have to perform a little trickery to keep masked integer values from overflowing their boundaries. Here's the code that implements this formula for an 8-bit color channel:

```
// rd is the destination pixel's red component
// rs is the source pixel's red component
// rd2 holds the result of the blending operation

rd = (*lpDestPixel & REDMASK);
rs = (*lpSrcPixel & REDMASK);
rd2 = rd + ((alphaPixel * ( rs - rd ) ) >> 8);
rd2 &= REDMASK;
```

The first two lines isolate the color channel from the pixel values of both the destination and source surface. The third line implements the formula, shifting the bit values back into place after the multiplication. The last line masks any overflow bits from the result.

Now you're ready to see the entire `CopyAlpha` function. There are three surfaces sent into `CopyAlpha`: the source and destination surfaces accompany a surface that stores the alpha channel. There are a number of ways to store the alpha channel values, even including it within a full 32-bit source surface. The code below stores alphas in a completely separate surface, encoded in the blue channel, which has exactly the same pixel format as the other two surfaces. Why? The blue channel doesn't require any shifting to grab the value. It also has to do with how the surface is created and cached into the game.

First, most 3D art tools like 3D Studio can create art with an alpha channel, but for it to have a reasonable resolution the whole piece of art will be stored as ARGB, each channel taking eight bits. It's a good idea to split this into two surfaces: one for RGB art and the other for the alpha channel, preferably stored in an 8-bit image. Splitting the art has the advantage of reducing its size and memory requirements, but more importantly it gives your game the ability to disable the alpha map entirely. A player with a slower machine might turn off the alpha map to speed up their game.

No more stalling, here's `CopyAlpha`:

```
HRESULT CopyAlpha(const LPDIRECTDRAWSURFACE7 dest,
   const LPDIRECTDRAWSURFACE7 src,
   const LPDIRECTDRAWSURFACE7 alphaSurf,
   const LPPOINT destPoint,
   const LPRECT srcRect,
   const bool isColorKeyed )
{
   HRESULT hr = DDERR_UNSUPPORTED;

   // Check if it is colorKeyed
   int colorKey = 0;
   if ( isColorKeyed )
```

```
{
    DDCOLORKEY ddck;
    src->GetColorKey( DDCKEY_SRCBLT, &ddck );
    colorKey = ddck.dwColorSpaceLowValue;
}

//Prepare the surface descriptors
DDSURFACEDESC2 sdSrc, sdDest, sdAlpha;

// Lock the source and obtain its descriptor
ZeroMemory( &sdSrc, sizeof( sdSrc ) );
sdSrc.dwSize = sizeof( sdSrc );

hr = src->Lock( NULL, &sdSrc, DDLOCK_WAIT, NULL );
if ( (hr != DD_OK) )
{
    return hr;              // Failed to lock
}

// Lock the source and obtain its descriptor
ZeroMemory( &sdDest, sizeof( sdDest ) );
sdDest.dwSize = sizeof( sdDest );

hr = dest->Lock( NULL, &sdDest, DDLOCK_WAIT, NULL );
if ( (hr != DD_OK) )
{
    src->Unlock( NULL );
    return hr;              // Failed to lock
}

// Lock the source and obtain its descriptor
ZeroMemory( &sdAlpha, sizeof( sdAlpha ) );
sdAlpha.dwSize = sizeof( sdAlpha );

hr = alphaSurf->Lock( NULL, &sdAlpha, DDLOCK_WAIT, NULL );
if ( hr != DD_OK )
{
    src->Unlock( NULL );
    dest->Unlock( NULL );
    return hr;              // Failed to lock
}

// Note:
// Alpha blitting requires that both the source and destination exist
// in system memory, not video memory. It will freeze windows 98 machines
// and slow down win2K machines if a source or destination
```

```
   // live in video memory

if ((sdSrc.ddpfPixelFormat.dwRGBBitCount!=sdDest.ddpfPixelFormat.dwRGBBitCount) ||
(sdSrc.ddpfPixelFormat.dwRBitMask!=sdDest.ddpfPixelFormat.dwRBitMask) ||
(sdSrc.ddpfPixelFormat.dwGBitMask!=sdDest.ddpfPixelFormat.dwGBitMask) ||
(sdSrc.ddpfPixelFormat.dwBBitMask!=sdDest.ddpfPixelFormat.dwBBitMask) )
   {
     src->Unlock( NULL );
     dest->Unlock( NULL );
     alphaSurf->Unlock( NULL );
     return DDERR_WRONGMODE;             // Incompatible surfaces
   }

   // Grab the mask values
   const unsigned int REDMASK = sdSrc.ddpfPixelFormat.dwRBitMask;
   const unsigned int GREENMASK = sdSrc.ddpfPixelFormat.dwGBitMask;
   const unsigned int BLUEMASK = sdSrc.ddpfPixelFormat.dwBBitMask;

   // Determine how to blend based on source RGBBitCount
   switch( sdSrc.ddpfPixelFormat.dwRGBBitCount )
   {

   // 16 bit blend
   case 16 :
   {
     const int iSrcWidth = sdSrc.lPitch / sizeof( short unsigned int );
     const int iDstWidth = sdDest.lPitch / sizeof( short unsigned int );

     // It will be assumed that the alpha surface shares
     // the same dimensions as the source
     short unsigned int * lpAlpha =
       &((short unsigned int *)sdAlpha.lpSurface)[ srcRect->left +
         srcRect->top * iSrcWidth ];
     short unsigned int * lpSrc =
       &((short unsigned int *)sdSrc.lpSurface)[ srcRect->left +
         srcRect->top * iSrcWidth ];
     short unsigned int * lpDest =
       &((short unsigned int *)sdDest.lpSurface)[ destPoint->x +
         destPoint->y * iDstWidth ];

     assert(sdSrc.lPitch == sdAlpha.lPitch && "It is assumed that the alpha
       mask will have the same dimensions as the source sprite");

     int rectH = srcRect->bottom - srcRect->top;
     int rectW = srcRect->right - srcRect->left;
     const int sskip = iSrcWidth - rectW;
```

6

```
const int dskip = iDstWidth - rectW;

int x,y;
unsigned int alpha;           //alpha pixel component
unsigned int rs,gs,bs;        //source pixel components
unsigned int rd,gd,bd;        //destination pixel components
unsigned int rd2,gd2,bd2;     //destination pixel components used to
                              // avoid stalling due to read-write conflict
for(y=0; y<rectH; y++)
{
  for(x=0; x<rectW; x++, lpDest++, lpSrc++, lpAlpha++)
  {
    if ( colorKey && (*lpSrc)==(short unsigned int)colorKey )
    {
      continue;
    }

    // Alpha channel will be based on the blue intensity because
    // reading blue requires no shifting
    alpha = *lpAlpha & BLUEMASK;

    if(BLUEMASK == alpha)
    {
      // Trivial case 1: full intensity, nothing but source shows
      *lpDest = *lpSrc;
      continue;
    }
    else if(0 == alpha)
    {
      // Trivial case 2: No intensity, background all the way
      continue;
    }

    rd = (*lpDest & REDMASK);
    gd = (*lpDest & GREENMASK);
    bd = (*lpDest & BLUEMASK);

    rs = (*lpSrc & REDMASK);
    gs = (*lpSrc & GREENMASK);
    bs = (*lpSrc & BLUEMASK);

    rd2 = rd + ((alpha*(rs-rd))>>5);
    gd2 = gd + ((alpha*(gs-gd))>>5);
    bd2 = bd + ((alpha*(bs-bd))>>5);
    rd2 &= REDMASK;
```

```
            gd2 &= GREENMASK;
            bd2 &= BLUEMASK;

            *lpDest = rd2 | gd2 | bd2;
        }

        lpDest += dskip;
        lpSrc += sskip;
        lpAlpha += sskip;
    }

    hr = DD_OK;
}
break;

// 32 bit blend
case 32 :
{
    const int iSrcWidth = sdSrc.lPitch / sizeof( unsigned int );
    const int iDstWidth = sdDest.lPitch / sizeof( unsigned int );

    //It will be assumed that the alpha surface shares the same
    //dimensions as the source

    unsigned int * lpAlpha = &((unsigned int *)sdAlpha.lpSurface)
        [ srcRect->left + srcRect->top * iSrcWidth ];
    unsigned int * lpSrc = &((unsigned int *)sdSrc.lpSurface)
        [ srcRect->left + srcRect->top * iSrcWidth ];
    unsigned int * lpDest = &((unsigned int *)sdDest.lpSurface)
        [ destPoint->x + destPoint->y * iDstWidth ];

    assert(sdSrc.lPitch == sdAlpha.lPitch && "It is assumed that the
        alpha mask will have the same dimensions as the source sprite");

    int rectH = srcRect->bottom - srcRect->top;
    int rectW = srcRect->right - srcRect->left;
    const int sskip = iSrcWidth - rectW;
    const int dskip = iDstWidth - rectW;

    int x,y;
    unsigned int alpha;          //alpha pixel component
    unsigned int rs,gs,bs;       //source pixel components
    unsigned int rd,gd,bd;       //destination pixel components
    unsigned int rd2,gd2,bd2;    //destination pixel components used to
                                 //avoid stalling due to read-write conflict
```

6

```
for(y=0; y<rectH; y++)
{
  for(x=0; x<rectW; x++, lpDest++, lpSrc++, lpAlpha++)
  {
    if (colorKey && (*lpSrc)==(unsigned int)colorKey)
    {
      continue;
    }

    //Alpha channel will be based on the blue intensity
    //because reading blue requires no shifting
    alpha = *lpAlpha & BLUEMASK;
    if(BLUEMASK == alpha)
    {
      // Trivial case 1: full intensity, nothing but source shows
      *lpDest = *lpSrc;
      continue;
    }
    else if(0 == alpha)
    {
      // Trivial case 2: No intensity, background all the way
      continue;
    }

    rd = (*lpDest & REDMASK);
    gd = (*lpDest & GREENMASK);
    bd = (*lpDest & BLUEMASK);

    rs = (*lpSrc & REDMASK);
    gs = (*lpSrc & GREENMASK);
    bs = (*lpSrc & BLUEMASK);

    rd2 = rd + ((alpha*(rs-rd))>>8);
    gd2 = gd + ((alpha*(gs-gd))>>8);
    bd2 = bd + ((alpha*(bs-bd))>>8);

    rd2 &= REDMASK;
    gd2 &= GREENMASK;
    bd2 &= BLUEMASK;

    *lpDest = rd2 | gd2 | bd2;
  }

  lpDest += dskip;
  lpSrc += sskip;
  lpAlpha += sskip;
```

```
        }

        hr = DD_OK;
    }
    break;

    // no alpha blending on palettized surface
    case 8 :
    // unsupported
    default :
        hr = S_FALSE;
        break;
    }

    // Cleanup
    src->Unlock( NULL );
    dest->Unlock( NULL );
    alphaSurf->Unlock( NULL );

    return hr;
}
```

You should pay some special attention to a few things in this function. It distinguishes between 16-bit and 32-bit surfaces. Rather than writing one piece of code that handles both cases it's a better idea to write optimal code for each case. The function handles the case where the source surface has a color key. Any source pixel that matches the color key causes the loop to skip ahead to the next pixel. You'll also notice that this code doesn't support 8-bit surfaces. You're free to write that code yourself!

There's another significant warning in this code: It doesn't support video memory surfaces of any kind. While there's no theoretical barrier to performing blends of video memory surfaces, it simply won't work well under WinXP or Win98. This is most likely a driver related issue, so take the warning seriously. Reading and writing individual pixels from video memory is painfully slow anyway, so this limitation shouldn't be a huge burden. If you want to blend to a surface in video RAM, like your backbuffer, make a temporary copy of the target area in system RAM, perform the blend, and copy it back when you're done.

You can modify `CopyAlpha` to accept a single alpha value instead of an entire surface. This would be useful to create a fade-in or fade-out effect over multiple frames. You can write this function yourself; just take the `CopyAlpha` code you saw a moment ago and remove all references to `alphaSurf`. Recompile, fix the errors, and you'll have what you need:

```
HRESULT CopyAlpha(   const LPDIRECTDRAWSURFACE7 dest,
```

```
                const LPDIRECTDRAWSURFACE7 src,
                const unsigned char alpha,
                const LPPOINT destPoint,
                const LPRECT srcRect,
                const bool isColorKeyed )
{

   // Same code as before, just eliminate all references to alphaSurf
}
```

Drawing Text

I've seen two fundamental solutions for drawing text in computer games.

- Pre-draw the character set into a surface, and copy each character
- Draw text with a font

Each solution has strengths and weaknesses.

The surface method requires you to put the entire character set into a surface. This is fairly doable for a western European language. I've see the character sets generated in two ways: They can be drawn by hand or you can write a simple tool to use a font to draw each character into a grid. When you get ready to draw a text string, you simply run through the characters in the string and copy the corresponding bits from the surface.

The downside of the pre-drawn solution is that each character must exist on the grid, which means that languages like Mandarin Chinese are right out—their character set has thousands of symbols. It's just not a good idea to store a few megabytes of thousands of characters in a pre-drawn bitmap. It's too big. If we're talking about a western European language, the solution is more viable because there aren't that many symbols—less than 200. You also don't have the freedom of changing their size. Unless you stretch or squash the characters, you only get the size that was drawn originally.

The upside of this solution is its speed: character strings can easily be drawn in real time. Another upside is the high quality of the graphics, which can be custom tweaked and appear in multiple colors.

When I speak of a grid, it's important to note that the grid isn't necessarily a regular one. Most fonts have characters that are different widths. The font used in this book is a good example. The sequence "iiiiiiiii" takes up a lot less space than "wwwwwwwwwww" even though there are the same number of characters in each string. Figure 6.4 shows an example of a character set that covers the first few rows of the Unicode character set. If you want to see all of it you can open the Character Map tool in Windows, Accessories, System Tools.

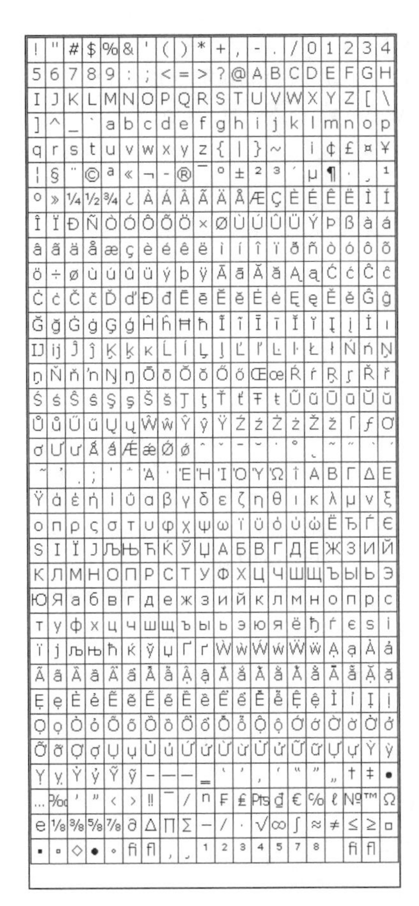

Figure 6.4
A Typical Character Set.

You can order these characters any way you want, but sticking to standards like ASCII or UNICODE is a pretty good idea. It sure makes your code look a lot better. Each character is "cut" into its own rectangular graphic. You'll have to do this by finding the rectangle coordinates for each character. It's not too hard to write a tool to do this, which is very common. Win32 has an API called `GetTextExtentPoint32`, which you can use to find the exact width and height of a character. Iterate through the character set, find the dimensions of each character, and use those dimensions to plan your grid. You'll also want to store the grid coordinates somewhere so you can find the exact location and size of each character. You'll learn more about how to manipulate graphic elements like this when we discuss sprites a little later in this chapter.

The second solution, using a font, has exactly opposite characteristics. Fonts are single color entities and are very slow to draw. Their strong point is their memory efficiency, ability to draw foreign languages, and amazing flexibility. A Win32 font is created by filling in a LOGFONT structure, and calling `CreateFontIndirect`. Win32 examples on exactly how to do this are quite terrible, and always seem to fill the `LOGFONT` structure by asking the `ChooseFont` dialog to do all the dirty work. It turns out that the `LOGFONT` structure is nearly impossible to fill out by hand and be 100% sure you will get the same thing on every computer. Don't believe me? Take a look at Figure 6.5 to see the values `LOGFONT` requires for some fonts we used in the Microsoft products.

If you think the #`defined` constants that you see in the LOGFONT documentation would make more sense than these hard coded numbers, you are somewhat correct. They end up justifying the numbers, but you can't necessarily guess the exact values that will result in the exact font you want. Here's our solution: We wrote a little tool that used the `ChooseFont()` dialog in Win32 to select the font, weight, height, and effects and wrote out the resulting LOGFONT structure into a CSV file. Our game read the CSV file to initialize the fonts it used to draw all the text in the game. I suggest you do exactly the same thing. The steps involved include.

1. Initialize an array of LOGFONT structures from a data file.

2. Send each one of these structures into the Win32 `CreateFontIndirect() function.`

3. Store the resulting HFONT for future use.

#	lfHeight	lfWidth	lfEscapement	lfOrientation	lfWeight	lfItalic	lfUnderline	lfStrikeOut	lfCharSet	lfOutPrecision	lfClipPrecision	lfQuality	lfPitchAndFamily	lfFaceName
0	-21	0	0	0	400	0	0	0	0	3	2	1	66	(Forte)
1	-16	0	0	0	400	0	0	0	0	3	2	1	34	(Gill Sans MT Condensed Bold)
2	-21	0	0	0	700	0	0	0	0	3	2	1	34	(Gill Sans MT Condensed)
3	-11	0	0	0	400	0	0	0	0	3	2	1	34	(Gill Sans MT Condensed)
4	-19	0	0	0	700	0	0	0	0	3	2	1	34	(Gill Sans MT)
5	-16	0	0	0	400	0	0	0	0	3	2	1	34	(Gill Sans MT)
6	-16	0	0	0	700	0	0	0	0	3	2	1	18	(Gill Sans MT)
7	-14	0	0	0	400	0	0	0	0	3	2	1	34	(Gill Sans MT)
8	-13	0	0	0	700	0	0	0	0	3	2	1	18	(Gill Sans MT)
9	-12	0	0	0	700	0	0	0	0	3	2	1	34	(Gill Sans MT)
10	-11	0	0	0	700	0	0	0	0	3	2	1	34	(Gill Sans MT)
11	-11	0	0	0	700	0	0	0	0	3	2	1	18	(Gill Sans MT)
12	-48	0	0	0	400	1	0	0	0	3	2	1	34	(Gill Sans Ultra Bold Condensed)
13	-11	0	0	0	400	0	0	0	0	3	2	1	34	(Gill Sans Ultra Bold Condensed)
14	-37	0	0	0	400	0	0	0	0	3	2	1	34	(Gill Sans Ultra Bold)
15	-13	0	0	0	700	0	0	0	0	3	2	1	50	(OCR A Extended)
16	-19	0	0	0	400	0	0	0	0	3	2	1	49	(OCRB)
17	-16	0	0	0	400	0	0	0	0	3	2	1	81	(Quartz)
18	-17	0	0	0	400	0	0	0	2	3	2	1	2	(Wingdings)
19	-12	0	0	0	400	0	0	0	2	3	2	1	2	(Wingdings)

Figure 6.5
Values for LOGFONT to Display Different Fonts.

When you're ready to draw the font to a surface, here is the function you can use:

```
static const COLORREF COLOR_TRANSPARENT( RGB( 255, 0, 255 ) ) ;

HRESULT DrawText( HFONT hFont, const TCHAR* strText,
                  DWORD dwOriginX, DWORD dwOriginY,
                  COLORREF crBackground, COLORREF crForeground,
                  COLORREF crShadow,const CPoint& shadowOffset)
{
        HDC      hDC = NULL;
    HRESULT hr;

    if( m_pdds == NULL || strText == NULL )
        return E_INVALIDARG;

    // Make sure this surface is restored.
        if ( m_pdds->IsLost() != DD_OK )
    {
    if( FAILED( hr = m_pdds->Restore() ) )
        return hr;
    }

    if( FAILED( hr = m_pdds->GetDC( &hDC ) ) )
        return hr;

    // Transparency
    if ( COLOR_TRANSPARENT==crBackground )
    {
          SetBkMode(hDC, TRANSPARENT);
    }
    else
    {
          SetBkColor( hDC, crBackground );
    }

    void *pOld = NULL;
if( hFont )
    pOld = SelectObject( hDC, hFont );

    if(COLOR_TRANSPARENT != crShadow)//Draw the shadow if you must"
    {
          //The shadow text gets drawn first, with the background color intact

          SetTextColor( hDC, crShadow );
                    TextOut( hDC,
```

```
            dwOriginX+shadowOffset.x,
            dwOriginY+shadowOffset.y, strText, 1 );

        //The main text gets drawn with a transparent background
        SetBkMode(hDC, TRANSPARENT);
    }

    SetTextColor( hDC, crForeground );
    TextOut( hDC, dwOriginX, dwOriginY, strText, 1 );

    if ( pOld )
            SelectObject( hDC, (HFONT) pOld );

  if( FAILED( hr = m_pdds->ReleaseDC( hDC ) ) )
      return hr;

  return S_OK;
}
```

There are two important things going on in this function. Right after the DC is grabbed, the `cdBackground` color is checked to see if it is transparent. This is important if your font is antialiased to the background pixels instead of a particular color. Figure 6.6 shows the difference.

The antialiased font blends the edges of the letters with the background color or the pixel values that are already there. There is a processor cost to using antialiased fonts, since they must read the background pixel values as the calculated blended colors. Fonts aren't cheap to draw, aliased or not so you might as well make sure your fonts are all drawn antialiased. One thing is clear, they look much better. Another feature of this function is a colored drop shadow. A drop shadow clarifies text and sharpens its image, especially on busy or light colored backgrounds. Figure 6.7 shows an example.

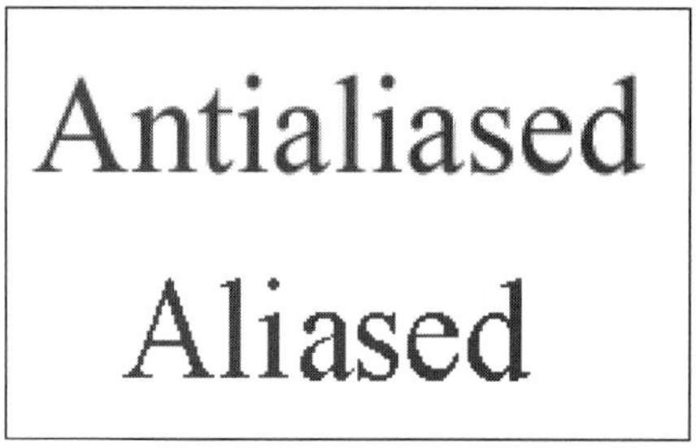

Antialiased

Aliased

Figure 6.6
Displaying Fonts with Antialiasing Effects.

No Drop Shadow

Drop Shadow

Figure 6.7
Using a Drop Shadow to Display Text.

Drop shadows are not native to Win32 fonts: You have to draw yours the hard way. You do this by drawing the text string twice, first with the drop shadow color, and then with a small (x,y) offset and second with the nominal color. Yes, it's expensive. Yes, you should do it.

Did I mention that fonts were expensive to draw? I could say this hundreds of times and it would still lack punch. On one of our games there was a bit of text that was supposed to flash red, green, yellow and back to red in a looping animation. Hey, this was a casino game, what did you expect? Taste? Anyway, my first implementation simply redrew the font every second. Even this seemingly vast amount of time—
1,000 ms is a near eternity to a modern CPU—was not enough. The game's framerate was brought to its knees. The solution to the problem was to pre-draw the text string in all three colors, and save off the result. A font draw every 1,000 ms was replaced with a smallish memory copy. The game's framerate was thankfully restored.

A more insidious problem has to do with an antialiased font with a transparent background color—it is supposed to antialias to the destination surface. This implies that if the destination surface changes, as it might if something were to animate underneath the text string, that the font would need to be redrawn. That's absolutely true. If you fail to redraw the font you'll get some odd pixel artifacts around the outside of the letters. Needless to say, you should avoid screen designs that have antialiased fonts overlap background animations.

One more clue about fonts: Not every font that comes default on Windows machines can be drawn antialiased. Documentation on font attributes is pretty tough to come by, including which fonts are included with all the different Windows operating systems. I suggest you perform empirical experiments, and keep good records. Whenever I need this data I just call a friend at Microsoft! I know, I cheat. So what?

Never forget that fonts are creative works and must be licensed. If you include a font file in your game you must have permission from the font company or your game will be in breach of copyright laws. Some font companies have special terms of use in multimedia content. Before you use a font that you didn't create in-house make sure you lawyer up and cover your butt. The last thing you need is a font company suing you because you didn't buy the right license, which can run as high as $15,000 for a single font family.

Working with Sprites

A surface is simply a two dimensional array of pixels. This isn't enough information to create a complicated screen that has layered backgrounds and multiple elements moving around and animating. You need a construct that contains references to a surface that contains every animation frame, knows its current location on the screen, and can be sorted.

A Basic Sprite Class

The sprite class is the foundation of every 2D computer game, and certainly many 3D games. At a minimum, a sprite contains a Z-order for sorting, a position, a special offset called a *hotspot*, a surface, a width and height, a frame number to identify the current animation frame, and the total number of frames that the surface holds. Here's a model sprite class you can use right out of the box or alter to work for your needs:

```
class Sprite
{
protected:
   // Position and Pixel data
   // ---------------
   LPDIRECTDRAWSURFACE7 m_Surface;  // the surface bits
   CPoint m_Position, m_Hotspot;    // subtract HS from pos to get origin
   int m_ZOrder;                    // the sort order of the sprite
   int m_Width, m_Height;           // dimensions of one frame
   int m_CurrentFrame, m_NumFrames; // current frame and total frames
   int m_Alpha;                     // range 0x0-0xFF, 0xFF is totally opaque
   bool m_HasColorKey;              // set to true if the sprite has a color key
   bool m_IsVisible;                // set to true if you want the sprite to draw

   // Members that control animation
   // ---------------
   bool m_IsPaused;         // set to true if the animation has been paused
   bool m_LoopingAnim;      // set to true if the animation loops
   int m_ElapsedTime;       // the measure of total elapsed time in ms
   int m_MSPerFrame         // ms per frame (1000 / desired frames per second)
```

```
public:
   Sprite();
   void Update(const int deltaMS);
   HRESULT Draw(LPDIRECTDRAWSURFACE7 dest, const CRect& screenRect)
   virtual HRESULT Restore();

   // the method that sets the current frame

   void SetFrame() { m_CurrentFrame = desiredFrame % m_NumFrames; }

   // the method that retrieves the current frame
   int GetFrame() const { return m_CurrentFrame; }

   // the method that returns the number of frames in this animation
   int GetFrameCount() const       { return m_TotalFrames; }

};

Sprite::Sprite()
{
   m_Surface = NULL;
   m_Position = m_Hotspot = CPoint(0,0);
   m_Width = m_Height = 0;
   m_CurrentFrame = m_NumFrames = 0;
   m_Alpha = ALPHA_LEVEL_OPAQUE;            // 0xFF is totally opaque
   m_HasColorKey = TRUE;

   m_IsPaused = FALSE;
   m_LoopingAnim = FALSE;
   m_ElapsedTime = 0;
   m_MSPerFrame = 0;
};
```

6

Sprites can also control how they draw and how they animate, but before you learn how that works we'll go over the simple stuff. As you read the next few sections, you'll find out exactly how this Sprite class works.

Sorting Order and Position

Sprites are usually stored in ordered lists so that the screen they are attached to can easily iterate through the list of sprites and draw them. This order is call the *Z-order*. It is the value used to sort the sprite into the sprite list.

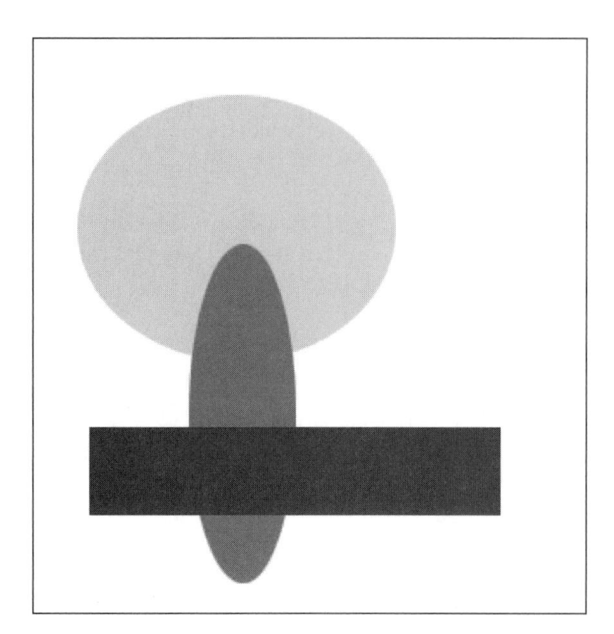

Figure 6.8
Z-Order Sprites.

Figure 6.8, shows three sprites. The black rectangle sorts on top of the other sprites because it is drawn last. When the black rectangle sprite is defined, the programmer assigns a Z-order such that it is inserted in the sprite list at the very end. The Z-order determines where sprites are inserted into the list, and therefore the order in which they will draw.

In most games, a list of constants are used to define different Z-orders. Background layers have the lowest Z-order, assuming the list is ordered from back to front. Different layers are given "higher Zs" so that they always sort on top of the background and other sprites that have lower Zs. Sprites, like tooltips, get the highest Zs, so they'll be guaranteed to be drawn on top of everything.

It's a good idea to define a number of different Z layers such as `ZORDER_BACKGROUND`, `ZORDER_FOREGROUND`, `ZORDER_TOOLTIP`, and sort other sprites by using offsets from these layers. For example, if you wanted a special layer of sprites to sort just underneath the tooltips you could set their Z-order at `(ZORDER_TOOLTIP-1)`. This lets you easily redefine the sort order of different layers of similar sprites. Two sprites that have exactly the same Z will sort in the order in which they appear in the sprite list.

The position of the sprite is expressed in pixel coordinates where (0,0) is the upper left-hand corner of the screen and coordinates increase as you move right and down. Not every sprite is positioned relative to its upper left-hand corner. Instead, sprites use a special offset called a *hotspot* (see Figure 6.9).

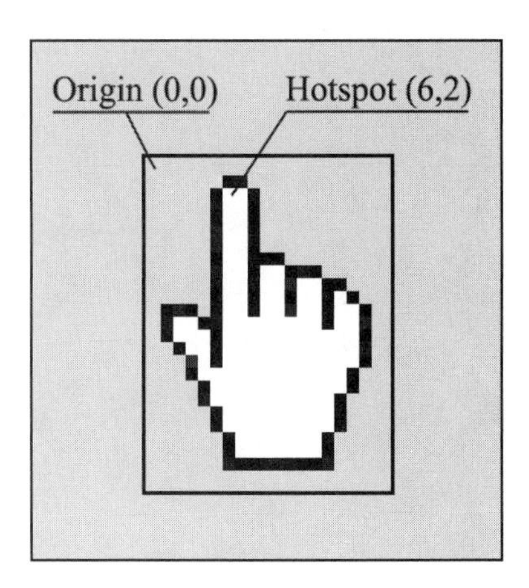

Figure 6.9
A Hand Pointer's Hot Spot Is at the Tip of the Finger.

Some shapes, such as a tip of a finger in a mouse pointer, have a natural target position other than the top left-hand corner of the surface. Sprites store this offset internally so programmers can position the sprite exactly. The origin of the sprite, its (0,0) pixel, is always drawn at the stored position minus the hotspot offset.

The Sprite class stores these values here:

```
CPoint m_Position, m_Hotspot;       // subtract HS from pos to get origin
```

Assuming you store the hotspot as a positive pixel value, you'll draw the sprite at a screen location calculated by subtracting the hotspot value from the current position.

Drawing and Animation

A sprite animates by drawing slightly different versions of itself in a smooth sequence. A single surface can store all the animation frames, with a few caveats. Most of the problems come from attempting to store large animations; either from a large dimension or a long sequence of frames. More problems come from storing one of these large frame sequences in video memory.

The best organization for a multi-frame animation sequence in a single surface is a filmstrip (see Figure 6.10). This method guarantees that all the pixels in a single frame are located in contiguous memory addresses. If the animation frames were stored side-by-side, the first "row" of pixels would contain the first row of each frame of the animation, virtually guaranteeing cache misses when the CPU copies any frame of the sprite to the screen. This is why sprites also store their width and height: It is the width and height of one frame, not the width and height of the surface. The frame number is

Figure 6.10
Store Multi-Frame Animations in a Filmstrip.

the current frame of the animation—the first frame is always frame zero. The width, height, and frame can be used to find the inclusive rectangle of the current frame within the larger surface.

In the sprite class definition I presented, I defined methods to get and set the current frame number, as well as get the total number of frames in the surface. `SetFrame()` is smart enough to wrap around using a modulo operation. This is convenient for coding simple animations that always loop around to the beginning by calling `SetFrame(GetFrame()+1)`.

You can see how all this works together in the code that a sprite uses to draw itself to a destination surface:

```
HRESULT Sprite::Draw(LPDIRECTDRAWSURFACE7 dest, const CRect& screenRect)
{
   if ( ! m_IsVisible )
      return DD_OK;

   HRESULT hr;

   // Convert to point to screen coordinates
   CPoint actualPos( m_Position - m_Hotspot );
   actualPos.Offset( screenRect.TopLeft() );

   // Source and dest rects
   CRect sourceRect( actualPos,
```

```
    CPoint( actualPos.x + m_Width, actualPos.y + m_Height ) );
CRect destRect = screenRect;

// Modify destination rect - make it valid
if ( ! destRect.IntersectRect( sourceRect, destRect ) )
    return DD_OK;

// Find the real source rectangle - from the DX surface
CPoint srcOffset = ( destRect.TopLeft() - actualPos );

// Convert to image coordinates
sourceRect.left = srcOffset.x;
sourceRect.top = srcOffset.y;
sourceRect.right = sourceRect.left + min( destRect.Width(), m_Width );
sourceRect.bottom = sourceRect.top + min( destRect.Height(), m_Height );

// Adjust for the frame
sourceRect.top += ( m_CurrentFrame * m_Height );
sourceRect.bottom += ( m_CurrentFrame * m_Height );

//Blit from Bitmap Surface to the Offscreen surface
for ( ;; )
{
     //Blit to the appropriate display
     if (m_Alpha!=0xFF)
     {
          hr = CopyAlpha(
                         dest, m_Surface, m_Alpha,
                         destRect.TopLeft(), sourceRect, m_HasColorKey);
    }
    else
    {
          hr = Copy(dest, m_Surface,
                         destRect.TopLeft(), sourceRect, m_HasColorKey);
    }

    if( SUCCEEDED(hr) )
          break;

    if ( hr == DDERR_SURFACELOST )
    {
          if ( FAILED( hr = Restore() ) )
               return hr;
    else
    {
               continue;
```

6

```
            }
        }

    if(  hr != DDERR_WASSTILLDRAWING )
            {
                    return hr;
        }
}

return DD_OK;

}
```

Here's what's happening in this code: The "homework" section at the top checks to see if the sprite is visible. The next section of code, which deals with pixel coordinates and rectangles, looks a little confusing, but it's not as bad as it looks.

If you remember the discussion about screens, you'll recall that a dialog box is a screen, positioned at some positive offset from the background screen's origin. The first two lines of code take the sprite's position, subtract the hot spot, and add the screen's top left corner. If the screen isn't a dialog box the top left point will be (0,0). Then we start calculating the clipping rectangle, if the destination of the sprite would place the right hand or lower portion of the sprite off the screen.

The final adjustment for finding the right animation frame pixels is just before the `for` loop, where the top and bottom coordinates of the source rectangle are moved relative to the current frame number and the height of an individual frame. The `for` loop attempts to copy the source frame to the destination surface until it succeeds, or an error other than `DDERR_WASSTILLDRAWING` is received. The two copy functions assume that the sprite has a color key. If the sprite's surface was lost, it can attempt a restore in the middle of the loop.

Now you need to know how to set the frame counter. You could set it to any legal value and just leave it there; not every sprite animates all the time. Buttons on the user interface usually animate only when they are in a highlighted or rollover state. Another example would be a sprite that shows increasing levels of damage, like the head shot in Doom. Every time damage increases, so does the current frame of the sprite.

Sprite animation is different. An animating sprite changes frames constantly, usually looping back to the beginning and playing again as long as the sprite is in view. A trivial solution would simply involve advancing the frame counter each time the sprite was updated by the game logic, but that's not a very wise choice.

Most artists will design animations with a particular framerate in mind. You should always check with the artist to see what the framerate is for two reasons. First, you want the animation to look as if the artist designed it. It will look wrong if it's played back too fast or too slow. Second, some artists will send you an animation with an insane framerate. I've seen 60fps animations coming from artists who simply didn't check their rendering settings. Most animations can be set at 15fps with little or no degradation in look and feel.

Different computers run through the draw code at vastly different rates. If you used the trivial solution a fast computer would run through the animation frames instantly, where a slow computer could take forever to run through the same animation. Even more importantly, some animations are accompanied by sound effects which always finish in the same amount of time on all machines. How do you synchronize these things?

You need a sprite that runs through its animation in a given amount of time. Most programmers and artists think in terms of FPS, or frames per second. Animation code is written in terms of milliseconds per frame because the algorithm is easier. Milliseconds per frame is simple to calculate from either a given FPS or a given animation time and total animation frames:


```
msPerFrame = 1000 / framesPerSecond;

msPerFrame = ( totalSeconds * 1000 ) / totalAnimationFrames;
```

An update function is all you need to animate the sprite. You'll learn how to set up the architecture to call this function in Chapter 7.

For now, you can assume that this function will get called frequently, with the input parameter set to the number of milliseconds since the last time the method was called:

```
void Sprite::Update(const int deltaMS)
{
   if (m_IsPaused)
   {
      return;
   }

   m_ElapsedTime += deltaMS;

   // Only call SetFrame() if we have to.
   // We're guaranteed to have to advance at least one frame...
```

```
    if (m_ElapsedTime >= mMSperFrame)
    {
        DWORD const numFramesToAdvance = (m_ElapsedTime / mMSPerFrame);
        m_ElapsedTime -= (numFramesToAdvance * mMSPerFrame);

        int desiredFrame = GetFrame() + numFramesToAdvance;

        //Check if we're looping...
        if ((false==mLoop) && (desiredFrame >= GetFrameCount()))
        {
            desiredFrame = GetFrameCount() - 1;        //Stay on last frame...
        }

        //Now advance our frame properly...
        SetFrame(desiredFrame);
    }
}
```

The first thing you'll notice is a simple predicate that checks to see if the sprite is actually animating. If the animation is paused, the method returns. The second predicate checks to see if enough time has elapsed to change the current frame. The code inside the second predicate calculates the next frame number given the elapsed time. If the animation does not loop, there's a special case that sets the current frame to the last frame of the animation.

Initializing Sprites

You've got most of a working sprite class with the code you've already seen, but you still lack an important part. How does a sprite get initialized? Initialization needs to be very specific for your game. It depends completely on how you store the data that goes along with the surface bits. You might create surfaces and initialize them from graphics files like JPGs, BMPs, or GIFs, but these formats don't hold all the additional data that a sprite needs to function: position, hotspot, frame information, animation data, and everything else. Something has to associate a single graphics file with all this extra data.

One possible solution is to store this data in an XML file. Every sprite definition can have a unique identifier, a graphic source file, and all the extra bits and pieces that make up a sprite. That would certainly work and it would be a snap to edit, but before you get too excited I should tell you that that solution isn't the best choice. You'll learn more about this solution in Chapter 8, but it makes sense to give you a little peek.

Most games store all their game data in resource files. A resource file stores any kind of game data and associates this data with a unique identifier. A resource manager, or perhaps a better description would be resource cache, would be responsible for taking those identifiers and handing back a pointer to a game object:

```
Sprite *kaboom = ResourceCache::Use(SPRITE_KABOOM);
```

This implies that the resource cache is smart enough to create a sprite, or anything else for that matter. The block of data that is read to create a sprite resource contains all the extra information to properly initialize the member variables of the sprite, followed by the surface bits.

One question you might have at this point is how in the hell that information gets saved to the resource file. It clearly didn't use the random junk on your hard drive. The resource file is created and maintained with a special builder tool that you'll end up writing yourself. That XML solution I mentioned before might be looking a little better to you right about now, given the inertia of writing an entire tool. Trust me, get to the end of the discussion on resource files before you issue a final judgement; there's a good reason I'm sending you down this road.

Restore()

Restoring is simply the process of throwing out the current surface and reinitializing it, probably by reloading the graphic resource through whatever initialization scheme you've cooked up. This might not always be the case, which is why the `Restore()` method is virtual. Some sprites don't have a resource file based beginning. A good example might be a sprite that is drawn with an algorithm instead of a resource. This might be a fractal pattern. An even better example is a text sprite, something that you'll initialize by drawing a font to a surface when it is created.

In these cases, you'll want to create classes that overload `Restore()`. When crazy game players change their game display options or reset their desktop settings, you can iterate through every sprite and reinitialize them.

Dirty Rectangle Drawing

Drawing complicated screens is slow, even for fast machines. There are two primary culprits: pixel overdraw and fonts. Fonts are so slow that it would take a liquid nitrogen cooled CPU to get any framerate if you ever attempted to draw them every frame. Even without fonts, a multilayered sprite screen with tons of pixel overdraw will still bring a flamethrower to its knees, especially if you can't fit everything into video memory. *Dirty rectangle drawing* refers to something very familiar to programmers unlucky enough to spend any amount of time with Win32's GDI. It refers to redrawing only the portion of the screen that changes, and leaving everything else alone.

If your game uses a 3D engine you can stop reading right now because you can't use dirty rectangle drawing. Actually I lied. Ultima IX's software rasterizer used dirty rectangles, and it was only possible because the screen was drawn without perspective. Everything on the screen appeared just like the old sprite-based Ultima games, which meant that things nearer the viewer scrolled across the screen as the grass under the Avatar's feet. Hardware acceleration did away with all that nastiness. So follow my original advice and don't bother using a dirty rectangle scheme to speed up your 3D game.

A simple dirty rectangle scheme creates a list of rectangles that will be drawn when the screen updates. It might not be completely obvious, but you can't use a flipping screen surface with dirty rectangles. This is because it would be onerous to keep track of which screen areas are dirty from frame to frame. The smallest and simplest flipping chain has a front buffer and a back buffer. A dirty rectangle list would have to be kept for each screen separately, which would also tend to cover more pixels since each buffer only gets updated once every other frame. A non-flipping back buffer is much easier to manage.

Let's assume that your game uses something similar to the sprite class. During the game's update loop, changes to any sprites will be reflected in a managed list of rectangles that describe the areas of the screen that have been touched:

- *Sprite creation/deletion*: Add the sprite's screen area to the list.
- *Sprite frame change*: Add the sprite's screen area to the list.
- *Sprite movement*: Add a set of rectangles that describe the minimum surface area of the old and new screen areas.

You'll end up with a list of rectangles that describe the areas of the screen that have been "dirtied." If your game's list of rectangles is sparse, you can simply run through your sprite list and draw them if they intersect with any of the rectangles. Most games aren't this lucky. The list of rectangles probably has significant overlap and could use some pre-processing to create a list of sprites and rectangles that minimize overdraw. Lucky for you Michael Abrash solved this problem in the *Zen of Graphics Programming*. Go buy his book and use his solution. I did.

Graphics Files Formats

I just need to say this: - The internet is pretty freaking amazing. If you want some utilities or source code to read virtually any file format, don't waste any time and go to **http://myfileformats.com/**. There are multiple resources at this site that, at a minimum, document the file format. Most of the resources actually provide source code to read and write graphics files.

Most file formats have the flexibility to store art in a wide variety of bit depths. The contents of each piece of art will dictate whether you should use 8-bit, 16-bit or 24-bit formats. The only format to watch out for is 16-bit, because not every video card uses the same pixel format for 16-bit modes. Most video cards on the market use a 565 format for storing RGB in 16 bits: 5 bits for red, 6 bits for green, 5 bits for blue. Some video cards, such as old 3Dfx cards, use a 555 format.

There's a great interview question I asked for many years that asked the interviewee to write the code to convert a 555 rectangular video buffer to a 565 buffer. Anyone who answered the question knows that there's an optimized solution for this question, but it still requires a few adds and shifts for each pixel, and therefore it wasn't too incredibly speedy. This means that you don't need to be converting your 565 art to 555 art every time you draw it; that would bring your game to a complete halt.

Since you can't count on either the 565 or 555 video card, you have to make a choice about how your art assets are stored, and what you want to do when your assets are stored in one format but the video card is the other. There are really three solutions and one fake solution:

- Choose one format and convert if needed on loading the asset.
- Choose one format and convert if needed on installation.
- Store both formats.
- Store every asset in 8-bit, and convert to 16 bit at load time.

The first solution is a pretty good one but you'll find that the conversion process will increase your load times. This actually got pretty bad on one project I was on because not only were we converting from 565 to 555 but we were also decompressing the asset as well, and it was a multiframe animation. The load time was pretty dismal on-low end machines, but there wasn't anything else we could do. The asset had to be compressed due to CD-ROM space constraints and we didn't want to penalize the vast majority of players that had 565 video cards.

If you ever thought about using Microsoft's BMP format to store graphics data, think again. The 16-bit format is a 555 format which will require conversion for quick display on most video cards. Of course, you can cheat and use the format for convenience and simply store 565 pixel data. You'll get some funky looking art if you load that munged BMP into MS Paint!

The second solution is really a non-solution, especially if your game runs in windowed mode. If your game player decides to change their desktop to a different pixel format you'll have to reinstall your whole game and reconvert everything to the new pixel format. That's just plain stupid. The third solution is a great solution if you have enough space on your CD-ROM and you've got some reasonable mechanism for keeping all these art assets in sync. If you rely on some manual process, you'll have thousands of bugs proclaiming that the art looks wrong, and you'll waste tons of time figuring out why.

The last solution is a good one too, if your art looks good in 8-bit. This can be a judgement call and can require a picky art director to lead you in the right direction. Look carefully at your largest art assets such as backgrounds, and convert them to 8-bit in something like Photoshop. If you still like what you see you can store it in 8-bit. Remember that storing 8-bit art is really storing art using 256 24-bit colors, so in many ways it's a better art format than 16-bit which uses two or three fewer bits. Also, you get the added benefit that if you want to support 32-bit resolutions your art will support that easily and you'll get the full monty! Converting the art to either 16- or 32-bit resolutions can be done with a simple lookup table, since you're only worried about a maximum of 256 different values for each asset.

The first solution is a good compromise, and it's the method I've used on every game I've worked on since I had to worry about it. We chose this solution because our backgrounds looked terrible when palettized, and the artists were really happy going to 16-bit art. There's no hard and fast rule, as with many things in game development, only tradeoffs.

Conclusion

There are plenty of programmers who jump into 3D without ever fully understanding some of the critical 2D concepts. They think 2D is passé. They're wrong. I hope you see the light now—all three of them. I can teach someone how to take the square root of a number with a calculator. I could teach someone else how to derive the square root themselves. The difference between these two people is that one knows how to push a button and the other knows what that button does behind the scenes. By looking under the hood, they probably will also figure out how most of the other buttons work as well.

After reading this chapter you'll know how to create textures with a color key or an alpha channel. You'll now know that even in 2D you must avoid pixel overdraw at all costs to keep your framerate high. Since 3D textures are very similar to 2D surfaces, you also know how to create a texture with dynamic text; perhaps you'll use it to draw a texture for a computer screen or a book. You'll know how to animate something in real time. After all there's not much difference between the concept of a sprite's current frame and the next keyframe of an animating 3D object.

It is better to know how things work instead of which buttons to push, certainly if you have to make some buttons no one has ever made before.

Chapter 7

Initialization and the Main Loop

As you are about to learn in this chapter, there are a million little details about writing games that no one talks about. It's a simple matter to surf the web or read one of the run-of-the-mill game programming books to find a few different ways to draw textured polygons in Direct3D, but when it comes to figuring out your initialization sequence or controlling your main loop you'll find little discussion. Most programmers who haven't performed these tasks are left with making some initial assumptions and they usually come up with less than perfect solutions only after time-consuming experimentation. In other words, they waste a lot of precious development time.

I've written this chapter to show you the ins and outs of writing code to initialize your games and controlling a main loop. As you check out the code in this chapter, keep in mind that the solutions provided shouldn't always be used verbatim. It's really important that you develop an understanding of how and why they work, and, if you do, you'll have some neat bits and pieces to add to your toolbox. What's even more likely is you'll make some significant improvements after you try some of these ideas. More power to you. Truly elegant solutions and algorithms never just fall out of the sky; they usually come to you after seeing some code that falls slightly short of what is needed.

With any luck you'll view some of the code in this chapter as slightly less than elegant and upon tweaking or rewriting it you'll send me an email gloating about your improvements. Don't bother because I'll just send you an email in return to inform you that you were always a pawn in my master plan.

Every piece of software, including games, has three key functional parts: initialization, the core or main loop, and clean up. Initialization prepares your canvas for painting pixels. The main loop accepts and translates user input, changes the game state, and renders the game state until the loop is broken. This loop is broken by a user input or some kind of failure. The clean up code releases key system resources, closes files, and exits back to the operating system.

Initialization 101

Initializing games involves performing setup tasks in a particular order, especially on Windows platforms. Initialization tasks for Windows games are a superset of console games. Consoles, due to their predictable architecture, have no need of determining how much VRAM is installed and many other things that are user configurable on a Wintel platform. There are some tasks you must perform before creating your window, and others that must have a valid window handle or HWND, and therefore happen after you create your window. Initialization tasks for a Windows game should happen in this order:

- Check system resources: hard drive space, memory, input and output devices
- Check the CPU speed
- Estimate available VRAM
- Initialize your random number generator (this was covered in Chapter 3)
- Load programmer's options for debugging purposes
- Initialize your memory cache
- Create your window
- Initialize the audio system
- Load the player's game options and saved game files
- Create your drawing surface
- Perform initialization for game systems: physics, AI, and so on

Some C++ Initialization Pitfalls

Before we work through our initialization checklist, let's get some critical initialization pitfalls out of the way. I've heard that power corrupts, and absolute power corrupts absolutely. You might get some disagreement from Electonic Art's executives on this point. I'll prove it to you by showing you some problems with going too far using C++ constructors to perform initialization. It turns out that C++ constructors are horrible at initializing game objects, especially if you declare your C++ objects globally.

Programming in C++ gives you plenty of options for initializing objects and subsystems. Since the constructor runs when an object comes into scope, you might believe that you *can* write your initialization code like this:

```
// Main.cpp - initialization using globals
//
```

```
DataFiles g_DataFiles;
AudioSystem g_AudioSystem;
VideoSystem g_VideoSystem;

int main(void)
{
   BOOL done = false;
   while (! done)
   {
      // imagine a cool main loop here
   }
   return 0;
}
```

The global objects in this source code example are all complicated objects that could encapsulate most game subsystems. The fledgling game programmer might briefly enjoy the elegant look of this code, but that love affair will be quite short lived. When any of these initialization tasks fail, and they will, there's no way to recover.

Global objects under C++ are initialized before the entry point, in this case `main(void)`. One problem with this is ordering; you can't control the order in which global objects are instantiated. Under Visual Studio.NET and other Microsoft compilers, the objects are instantiated in the order of the link, but you can't count on that being the case with all compilers. In other words, don't count on it. What makes this problem worse is that since C++ constructors have no return value, you are forced to do something ugly to find out if anything went wrong. One option, if you can call it that, is to check a member variable of the class to see if the initialization completed properly:

```
// Main.cpp - initialization using globals
//

DataFiles g_DataFiles;
AudioSystem g_AudioSystem;
VideoSystem g_VideoSystem;

int main(void)
{
   // check all the global objects for initialization failure
   if (! g_DataFiles.Initialized() ||
       ! g_AudioSystem.Initialized() ||
       ! g_VideoSystem.Initialized() )
   {
      printf("Something went horribly wrong. Please return this game to the "
         "store in a fit of anger and write scathing emails to FatBabies "
```

```
        "about the company that would hire such idiots.");

      return (1);
   }

   BOOL done = false;
   while (! done)
   {
      // imagine a cool main loop here
   }
   return (0);
}
```

This code is suddenly looking less elegant. But wait, there's more! The wise programmer will inform their game players about what has gone wrong so they can have some possibility of fixing the problem. The simpler alternative of failing and dropping back to the operating system with some lame error message is sure to provoke a strong reaction.

If you want to inform the player you might want to do it with a simple dialog box. This assumes that you've already initialized the systems that make the dialog box function: video, user interface, data files that contain the button art, font system, and so on. This is certainly not always possible. What if your brilliant game player hacked into the art data files and screwed them up? You won't have any button art to display your nice dialog box telling the hacker they've screwed themselves. You have no choice but to use the system UI, such as the ugly message box under Windows. It's better than nothing.

Initialize your text cache, or whatever you use to store text strings, very early. You can present any errors about initialization failures in te right language. If the initialization of the text cache fails, present an error with a number. It's easier for foreign language speakers almost anywhere in the world to use the number to find a solution from a customer service person or a web site.

There are some good reasons to use global objects. One of the best ones is to trap the general exception handler; your code then has control over how the game will handle failures during initialization. If you write applications in MFC, the application object, `CApp()`, is global. These global objects have one important thing in common: They cannot fail. Make sure that any global object you create has the same quality: It cannot fail on construction.

Global object pointers are much better than global objects. Singleton objects such as the instantiation of the class that handles the audio system or perhaps your application object are naturally global, and if you're like me you hate passing pointers or references to these objects in every single method call from your entry point to the lowest level code.

Declare global pointers to these objects, initialize them when you're good and ready, and free them under your complete control. Here's an example of a more secure way to initialize:

```
// Main.cpp - initialization using pointers to global objects
//

// A useful macro
#define SAFE_DELETE(p)       { if (p) { delete (p); (p)=NULL; } }

DataFiles *gp_DataFiles = NULL;
AudioSystem *gp_AudioSystem = NULL;
VideoSystem *gp_VideoSystem = NULL;

int main(void)
{
   gp_DataFiles = new DataFiles;
   if ( (NULL==gp_DataFiles) || (!gp_DataFiles->Initialized() ) )
   {
      // Please excuse the use of naked text strings! They are better for
      // examples, but in practice I'd use a text cache for localization.
      // Not everyone speaks English, you know.

      printf("The data files are somehow screwed. Try to reinstall before you "
         "freak out and return the game.");
      return (1);
   }

   gp_AudioSystem = new AudioSystem;
   if ( (NULL==gp_AudioSystem) || (!gp_AudioSystem ->Initialized() ) )
   {
      printf("The audio system is somehow screwed. Reboot and try running the "
      "game again. That almost always works. ");
      return (1);
   }

   gp_VideoSystem = new VideoSystem;
   if ( (NULL==gp_VideoSystem) || (!gp_VideoSystem ->Initialized() ) )
   {
      printf("The video system is somehow screwed. Go get a real video "
      "card before you even think of trying to run this game.");
      return (1);
   }

   BOOL done = false;
```

```
    while (! done)
    {
       // imagine a cool main loop here
    }

    SAFE_DELETE(gp_VideoSystem);              // AVOID DEADLOCK!!!
    SAFE_DELETE(gp_AudioSystem);
    SAFE_DELETE(gp_DataFiles);
    return (0);
}
```

Note that the objects are released in the reverse order in which they are instantiated. This is no mistake, and it is a great practice whenever you need to grab a bunch of resources of different kinds in order to do something. In multithreaded operating systems with limited resources, you can avoid deadlock by allocating and deallocating your resources in this way. Deadlock is a nasty situation whereby two processes are attempting to gain access to the same resources at the same time, and cannot because they each have access to the resource the other process needs to continue. Computers are very patient, and will happily wait until the sun explodes. Get in the habit of programming with that problem in mind, even if your code will never run on an operating system where that will be a problem. It's a great habit and you'll avoid some nasty bugs.

Exception Handling

Sometimes you have no choice but to write code in a C++ constructor that has the possibility of failing. Certainly if you wrap the creation of some DirectX objects in a nice class you'll have plenty of places you'd wish a constructor can return an HRESULT. Instead of rewriting all your code to cripple the constructor and replace it with the ubiquitous `Init()` method that returns success or failure, use exception handling as shown here.

```
// Main.cpp - nitialization using pointers to global objects and
exception handling
//

// A useful macro
#define SAFE_DELETE(p)              { if (p) { delete (p); (p)=NULL; } }


DataFiles::DataFiles()
{
   // Imagine some code up here…
   {
      // blah blah blah
   }
```

```
    if (somethingWentWrong)
    {
        // You can throw anything you want, I'm throwing a custom class that
        // defines errors, so don't go looking in MSDN for the ErrorCode
        // class; it's mine!
        throw ErrorCode(EC_DATAFILES_PROBLEM);
    }
}

DataFiles *gp_DataFiles = NULL;
AudioSystem *gp_AudioSystem = NULL;
VideoSystem *gp_VideoSystem = NULL;

int main(void)
{
    BOOL returnCode = 0;
    try
    {
        // initialize everything in this try block
        gp_DataFiles = new DataFiles;
        gp_AudioSystem = new AudioSystem;
        gp_VideoSystem = new VideoSystem;

        BOOL done = false;
        while (! done)
        {
            // imagine a cool main loop here
        }
    }

    catch(ErrorCode e)
    {
        e.InformUser();       // ErrorCode can inform the user itself
        returnCode = 1;
    }

    SAFE_DELETE(gp_VideoSystem);                  // AVOID DEADLOCK!!!
    SAFE_DELETE(gp_AudioSystem);
    SAFE_DELETE(gp_DataFiles);

    return (returnCode);
}
```

That code is looking much nicer, and it's beginning to appeal to my sense of elegance. Any problem in initialization is going to throw an exception, jumping past the main loop entirely. The `ErrorCode` class, the design of which I'll leave as an exercise for the reader, simply reports the error back to the user in the best way possible given what systems are up and running. Perhaps the only thing it can do is send a text string out to `stdout`, or maybe it can bring up a nice dialog box using your game's graphics. After the error is reported to the player a useful macro frees the global objects that have been constructed. Finally, a return code is sent back to the operating system.

Initializing Your Game

We're now ready to work our way through the initialization checklist. There are a number of details to work through thus you might find you'll need to read through this section once and then go back and review some of the specifics. After I get through all of the initialization tasks, I'll dig into the main loop.

Checking System Resources

Checking system resources is especially important for Windows games, but console developers don't get off scott-free. Permanent storage, whether it is a hard disk or a memory card, should be checked for enough space to store game data before the player begins. Windows and console games that support special hardware like steering wheels or other input devices must check for their existence and fall back to another option, like the Gamepad, if nothing is found. System RAM and VRAM checks or calculating the CPU speed is clearly a job for the Windows programmer.

Here is code you can use to check the available disk space on the current drive:

```
// Check for enough free disk space on the current disk.
int const drive = _getdrive();
struct _diskfree_t diskfree;

_getdiskfree(drive, &diskfree);

unsigned int const neededClusters =
   DISK_SPACE_NEEDED /(diskfree.sectors_per_cluster*diskfree.bytes_per_sector);

if (diskfree.avail_clusters < neededClusters)
{
   // if you get here you don't have enough disk space!
}
```

This code will work on any ANSI compatible system. Since disk space is calculated in clusters and not bytes you have to do a little legwork. You must set `DISK_SPACE_NEEDED` to the number of bytes you need.

Checking for system RAM under Windows is a little trickier; sadly you need to leave ANSI behind. You should check the total physical memory installed, as well as the available virtual memory using Win32 calls. Virtual memory is a great thing to have on your side. You can think of it as having a near infinite bank account, with a very slow bank. If your game uses virtual memory in the wrong way, it will slow to a crawl. You might as well grab a pencil and sketch a storyboard of the next few minutes of your game; you'll see it faster. You can check both kinds of memory using this code:

```
MEMORYSTATUS status;
GlobalMemoryStatus(&status);
if (status.dwTotalPhys < (TOTAL_PHYSICAL_MEMORY_NEEDED))
{
   // You don't have enough physical memory. Tell the player to go get a real
   // computer and give this one to his mother.
}

// Check for enough free memory.
if (status.dwAvailVirtual < AVAILABLE_VIRTUAL_MEMORY_NEEDED)
{
   // You don't have enough virtual memory available.
   // Tell the player to shut down the copy of Visual Studio running in the
   // background, or whatever seems to be sucking the memory dry.
}

char *buff = new char[AVAILABLE_VIRTUAL_MEMORY_NEEDED];
if (buff)
   delete[] buff;
else
{
   // The system lied to you. When you attempted to grab a block as big
   // as you need the system failed to do so. Something else is eating
   // memory in the background; tell them to shut down all other apps
   // and concentrate on your game.
}
```

The call to `GlobalMemoryStatus()` is supported under Win9x, but it can return incorrect information if there is more than 2Gb of RAM installed. You could call `GlobalMemoryStatusEx()` instead, but that call is not supported on Win9x operating systems like Win98 and WinME. Lovely. Luckily there are very few machines out there with that much memory installed, and by the time there are we'll be able to put Win9x machines out to pasture. Until then, you'd better stick with the older API.

The last paragraph of code is actually allocating and immediately releasing a huge block of memory. This has the effect of making Windows clean up any garbage that has accumulated in the memory manager and double checks that you can allocate a contiguous block as large as you need. If the call succeeds, you've essentially run the equivalent of a Zamboni machine through your systems memory, getting it ready for your game to hit the ice.

Calculating CPU Speed

You'd think that grabbing the CPU speed from a Wintel box would be as easy as reading the system information. It seems completely crazy that this value has to be calculated. Here's a great piece of code to do just that:

```
//========================================================
// CPUSPEED
//
// CPU Timer for the Action, Arcade, Strategy Games Group, a part of
// the Entertainment Business Unit at Microsoft.
//
// (c) Copyright 1999-2000 Microsoft Corporation.
// Written by Michael Lyons (mlyons@microsoft.com)
//
//========================================================
#include "cpu.h"

#include <windows.h>
#define SLEEPTIME    0

//========================================================
// define static variables
//========================================================
static int s_milliseconds;
static __int64       s_ticks;

static int s_milliseconds0;
static __int64       s_ticks0;

//========================================================
// fabs
//
// floating point absolute value function
//========================================================
float inline fabs(float a)
{
```

```
    if (a < 0.0f)
        return -a;
    else
        return a;
}

//========================================================================
// StartTimingCPU
//
// Call this function to start timing the CPU. It takes the CPU tick
// count and the current time and stores it. Then, while you do other
// things, and the OS task switches, the counters continue to count, and
// when you call UpdateCPUTime, the measured speed is accurate.
//
//========================================================================
int StartTimingCPU()
{
    //
    // detect ability to get info
    //
    __asm
    {
        pushfd                  ; push extended flags
        pop     eax             ; store eflags into eax
        mov     ebx, eax        ; save EBX for testing later
        xor     eax, (1<<21)    ; switch bit 21
        push eax                ; push eflags
        popfd                   ; pop them again
        pushfd                  ; push extended flags
        pop     eax             ; store eflags into eax
        cmp     eax, ebx        ; see if bit 21 has changed
        jz   no_cpuid           ; make sure it's now on
    }

    //
    // make ourselves high priority just for the time between
    // when we measure the time and the CPU ticks
    //
    DWORD dwPriorityClass = GetPriorityClass(GetCurrentProcess());
    int dwThreadPriority = GetThreadPriority(GetCurrentThread());
    SetPriorityClass(GetCurrentProcess(), REALTIME_PRIORITY_CLASS);
    SetThreadPriority(GetCurrentThread(), THREAD_PRIORITY_TIME_CRITICAL);
    //
    // start timing
    //
```

7

```
    s_milliseconds0 = (int)timeGetTime();

    __asm
    {
       lea     ecx, s_ticks0          ; get the offset
       mov     dword ptr [ecx], 0     ; zero the memory
       mov     dword ptr [ecx+4], 0   ;
       rdtsc                          ; read time-stamp counter
       mov     [ecx], eax             ; store the negative
       mov     [ecx+4], edx           ; in the variable
    }

    //
    // restore thread priority
    //
    SetThreadPriority(GetCurrentThread(), dwThreadPriority);
    SetPriorityClass(GetCurrentProcess(), dwPriorityClass);

    return 0;

no_cpuid:
    return -1;
}

//==========================================================
// UpdateCPUTime
//
// This function stops timing the CPU by adjusting the timers to account
// for the amount of elapsed time and the number of CPU cycles taked
// during the timing period.
//==========================================================
void UpdateCPUTime()
{
    //
    // make ourselves high priority just for the time between
    // when we measure the time and the CPU ticks
    //
    DWORD dwPriorityClass = GetPriorityClass(GetCurrentProcess());
    int dwThreadPriority = GetThreadPriority(GetCurrentThread());
    SetPriorityClass(GetCurrentProcess(), REALTIME_PRIORITY_CLASS);
    SetThreadPriority(GetCurrentThread(), THREAD_PRIORITY_TIME_CRITICAL);

    //
    // get the times
    //
    s_milliseconds    = -s_milliseconds0;
```

```
    s_ticks          = -s_ticks0;

    s_milliseconds   += (int)timeGetTime();

    __asm
    {
        lea     ecx, s_ticks            ; get the offset
        rdtsc                           ; read time-stamp counter
        add     [ecx], eax              ; add the tick count
        adc     [ecx+4], edx            ;
    }

    //
    // restore thread priority
    //
    SetThreadPriority(GetCurrentThread(), dwThreadPriority);
    SetPriorityClass(GetCurrentProcess(), dwPriorityClass);

    return;
}

//=========================================================================
// CalcCPUSpeed
//
// This function takes the measured values and returns a speed that
// represents a common possible CPU speed.
//=========================================================================
int CalcCPUSpeed()
{
    //
    // get the actual cpu speed in MHz, and
    // then find the one in the CPU speed list
    // that is closest
    //
    const struct tagCPUSPEEDS
    {
        float   fSpeed;
        int     iSpeed;
    } cpu_speeds[] =
    {
        //
        // valid CPU speeds that are not integrally divisible by
        // 16.67 MHz
        //
        {  60.00f,     60 },
        {  75.00f,     75 },
```

```
    {  90.00f,      90 },
    { 120.00f,     120 },
    { 180.00f,     180 },
};

//
// find the closest one
//
float   fSpeed=((float)s_ticks)/((float)s_milliseconds*1000.0f);
int   iSpeed=cpu_speeds[0].iSpeed;
float   fDiff=(float)fabs(fSpeed-cpu_speeds[0].fSpeed);

for (int i=1 ; i<sizeof(cpu_speeds)/sizeof(cpu_speeds[0]) ; i++)
{
    float fTmpDiff = (float)fabs(fSpeed-cpu_speeds[i].fSpeed);

    if (fTmpDiff < fDiff)
    {
        iSpeed=cpu_speeds[i].iSpeed;
        fDiff=fTmpDiff;
    }
}

//
// now, calculate the nearest multiple of fIncr
// speed
//

//
// now, if the closest one is not within one incr, calculate
// the nearest multiple of fIncr speed and see if that's
// closer
//
const float fIncr=16.66666666666666666666667f;
const int iIncr=4267; // fIncr << 8

//if (fDiff > fIncr)
{
    //
    // get the number of fIncr quantums the speed is
    //
    int   iQuantums = (int)((fSpeed / fIncr) + 0.5f);
    float   fQuantumSpeed  = (float)iQuantums * fIncr;
```

```
        float   fTmpDiff = (float)fabs(fQuantumSpeed - fSpeed);

        if (fTmpDiff < fDiff)
        {
                iSpeed = (iQuantums * iIncr) >> 8;
          ifDiff=fTmpDiff;
        }
    }

    return iSpeed;
}


//=========================================================
// GetCPUSpeed
//
// Gets the CPU speed by timing it for 3 seconds.
//=========================================================
int GetCPUSpeed()
{
    static int CPU_SPEED = 0;

    if(CPU_SPEED!=0)
    {
        //This will assure that the 0.5 second delay happens only once
        return CPU_SPEED;
    }

    if (StartTimingCPU())
        return 0;

    //This will lock the application for 1 second
    do
    {
        UpdateCPUTime();
        Sleep(SLEEPTIME);
    } while (s_milliseconds < 1000);

    CPU_SPEED = CalcCPUSpeed();
    return CPU_SPEED;
}
```

The only thing you have to do is call `GetCPUSpeed()`. The first call will start the timer, which takes a few seconds to run. The longer it runs the more accurate the timing, but there's no reason to run it any longer than two seconds, and one second will provide a pretty accurate count. You can use the results of this calculation to turn off certain CPU sucking activities like decompressing MP3 files or drawing detailed animations. It's not completely crazy to save the value off in a game options setting, so you don't have to calculate it each time your game runs.

Estimating VRAM

Something every game must do on Windows platforms is estimate the size of VRAM. From DirectX 4 to DirectX 7, an API is available to get this through the IDirectDraw interface, `GetAvailableVidMem`. Here's an example of how you can use this API to estimate VRAM size:

```
DDSCAPS2 ddsCaps;
ZeroMemory(&ddsCaps, sizeof(ddsCaps));

ddsCaps.dwCaps = DDSCAPS_VIDEOMEMORY;
DWORD dwUsedVRAM = 0;
DWORD dwTotal=0;
DWORD dwFree=0;

// lp_DD points to the IDirectDraw object
HRESULT hr = lp_DD->GetAvailableVidMem(&ddsCaps, &dwTotal, &dwFree);

// dwUsedVRAM holds the number of bytes of VRAM used
dwUsedVRAM = dwTotal-dwFree;
```

In DirectX 9, however, this useful API was replaced. The DirectX 9 documentation advertises that the best way to gain access to the amount of available video RAM is to use a method of the `IDirect3DDevice9` interface, `GetAvailableTextureMem` as shown here:

```
UINT free=0;

// lp_D3DDev points to the IDirect3DDevice9 object,
// and returns free VRAM in MB
free = lp_D3DDev->GetAvailableTextureMem();
```

Don't be fooled. Read the docs more carefully and you'll se that this API returns the amount of available texture memory, which turns out to be completely different from the amount of VRAM. Not exactly an improvement, is it? I'm sticking with using the old DX7 API, even if all I'm doing is making this one call. Don't forget that even if you are using DX9, you can always grab the useful bits of DX7, DX6, and so on, if you find a good enough reason to do it.

Just because you can call `QueryInterface` and grab an ancient DirectX 4 object, it doesn't mean that it is safe to do it. The word from some hardware manufacturers and driver writers is this—they aren't proactively testing their latest drivers to support old DirectX code. In other words, make sure you test your code against the newest cards and the newest drivers, which is always a good idea anyway.

Loading Game Options for Debugging

I may be completely old school but I still like using INI files. As long as you only use them for loading options or some other rare event, they work just fine and you can edit INI files with any text editor. The exact contents of this file are completely up to you, but it should definitely hold anything that you would want to switch from run to run without recompiling. Here's an example:

```
; game.ini
;
;

[OPTIONS]

; Run at full speed (default 0) instead of frame limiting artificially
Fullspeed=0

; Use hardware acceleration ( default software = 0)
Hardware_Acceleration=1

; Page Flipping (default 1)
PageFlip=1

; Antialias primitive edges (default 1)
Antialias=1

; Edge antialiasing (default 0)
Edge_AntiAliasing=0

; Dithering (default 1)
Dithering=1

; Texture Perspective (default 1)
Texture_Perspective=1
```

Windows programmers can use the `GetPrivateProfileInt` API to easily read this file. The rest of you can write the parser yourself. Since the default values are sent into the function call, the INI file doesn't even have to exist. That can be really convenient. Here's an example:

```
m_useHardwareAccel = ::GetPrivateProfileInt(
   _T("OPTIONS"), _T("Hardware_Acceleration"), false, path ) ? true : false;

m_usePageFlipping = ::GetPrivateProfileInt(
   _T("OPTIONS"), _T("PageFlip"), true, path ) ? true : false;

m_useDithering = ::GetPrivateProfileInt(
   _T("OPTIONS"), _T("Dithering"), true, path ) ? true : false;

m_useAntialiasing = ::GetPrivateProfileInt(
    _T("OPTIONS"), _T("AntiAliasing"), true, path ) ? true : false;

m_useEgdeAntiAliasing = ::GetPrivateProfileInt(
   _T("OPTIONS"), _T("Edge_AntiAliasing"), false, path ) ? true : false;

m_useVRAM = ::GetPrivateProfileInt(
   _T("OPTIONS"), _T("Enable_VRAM"), true, path ) ? true : false;

m_runFullSpeed = ::GetPrivateProfileInt(
   _T("OPTIONS"), _T("Fullspeed"), false, path ) ? true : false;

m_useTexturePerspective = ::GetPrivateProfileInt(
   _T("OPTIONS"), _T("Texture_Perspective"), true, path ) ? true : false;
```

I've used these settings to debug hardware compatibility issues, and easily control what settings are on by default for demos. I hate recompiles, so making data-driven debug settings like these is a winning proposition all around.

Do You Have a Dirtbag on Your Hands?

If you are lucky (or probably unlucky) enough to be working on a mass-market title, you have to support computers that should really be at the business end of a boat's anchor chain. Everyone wants a game to look really good, but when you have to support machines that have only 15% of the CPU speed as the top end rigs something has to give. You can use any benchmark to determine what makes a computer a dirtbag and what doesn't. For 2003 products, a dirtbag CPU is anything less than a 300MHz or anything that had less than 32Mb of system RAM. For your game, a dirtbag CPU might have to rely on the streaming speed of the DVD or whether the video card has hardware transform and lighting. Whatever you use, it is important to set your standards and determine if the computer the player is using is at the shallow end of the wading pool.

Once you figure the computer is at the bottom end, you should set your game defaults for new players accordingly. A good start would be to turn off any CPU intensive activities like decompressing MP3 streams or scale back animations. If the player decides to bring up the options screen and turn some of these features back on, my suggestion is to let him do it if it's possible. Maybe they'll be inclined to retire their old machine.

Initializing Your Resource Cache

I covered general memory management in Chapter 3 and resource caching is covered in Chapter 8. Make sure that you bone up on these topics. Initializing the resource cache will be a gateway to getting your game up and running. The size of your resource cache is totally up to your game design and the bottom end hardware you intend to support. It's a good idea to figure out if your player's computer is a dirtbag or flamethrower and set your resource cache memory accordingly.

You can't impress a player with fantastic graphics until you reserve a nice spot in system and video memory for your textures, models, and sprites. You can't even bring up a nice dialog box telling a loser player they are low on memory. If your resource cache allocation fails, you know there's something horribly wrong. The game should fail as elegantly as possible.

Using CreateWindow to Create Your Window

Win32 programmers can't put off the task of creating their window any longer. Creating a game window is easy enough, every DirectX sample shows you how to do it. What they don't show you is how to make sure you only create one instance of your game.

If your game takes a moment to get around to creating a window, a player might get a little impatient and double click the game's icon a few times. If you don't take the precaution of handling this problem, multiple copies of your game initializing code will overwhelm the computer system. Here's a piece of code that will take care of this problem under Win32:

```
// Find the window.  If active, set and return false
// Only one game instance may have this mutex at a time...

const char *GAME_TITLE = "Yet Another Shooter v3.141";

HANDLE handle = CreateMutex(NULL, TRUE, GAME_TITLE);

// Does anyone else think 'ERROR_SUCCESS' is a bit of a dichotomy?
if (GetLastError() != ERROR_SUCCESS)
{
   CWnd *pWnd = CWnd::FindWindow(NULL, GAME_TITLE);
```

```
    if (pWnd)
    {
        // An instance of your game is already running.
        pWnd->ShowWindow(SW_SHOWNORMAL);
        pWnd->SetFocus();
        pWnd->SetForegroundWindow();
        pWnd->SetActiveWindow();
        return false;
    }

    // There can be only one!

    // Imagine cool window creation code here

    return true;
}
```

Make sure the `GAME_TITLE` is a string that uniquely identifies your game. A mutex is a process synchronization mechanism and is common to any multitasking operating system. This code is guaranteed to create one mutex with the identifier `GAME_TITLE` for all processes running on the system. If it can't be created, then another process has already created it.

The very next thing a Windows game needs to do is create a window class. Here's a good example that creates a simple window with no frills.

```
WNDCLASS wndcls;
memset(&wndcls, 0, sizeof(WNDCLASS));   // start with NULLS

wndcls.style = CS_HREDRAW|CS_VREDRAW|CS_DBLCLKS;
wndcls.hIcon = NULL;                   // icons and cursors can be loaded laterÖ
wndcls.hCursor = NULL;
wndcls.hbrBackground = HBRUSH(GetStockObject(NULL_BRUSH));
wndcls.lpszMenuName = NULL;

// Specify your own class name for using FindWindow later
wndcls.lpszClassName = GAME_TITLE;


#ifdef MFC_VER
   wndcls.lpfnWndProc = ::DefWindowProc;   // MFC has their own functions.
   wndcls.hInstance = AfxGetInstanceHandle();

   // Register the new class and exit if it fails
```

```
    if(!AfxRegisterClass(&wndcls))
    {
        // Yikes! Try to fail elegantly. You are doomed.
    }

#else
    wndcls.lpfnWndProc = MyWindowProc;// you can specify your own window procedure
    wndcls.hInstance = hInstance;     // get hInstance from WinMain

    // Register the new class and exit if it fails
    if(!RegisterClass(&wndcls))
    {
        // Yikes! Try to fail elegantly. You are doomed.
    }

#endif
```

This code will work just fine for MFC apps or plain Win32 apps. If you are working in MFC, the code that registers the window class and tweaks the values of the `CREATESTRUCT` should appear in the `PreCreateWindow` method of your main frame. Plain old Win32 programmers can put this code right above the call to `CreateWindow`:

```
// This fixes the problem of running 800x600 going into the
// game, and not having controls aligned with the screen.

cs.cx = min( SCREEN_WIDTH, ::GetSystemMetrics( SM_CXFULLSCREEN ) );
cs.cy = min( SCREEN_HEIGHT, ::GetSystemMetrics( SM_CYFULLSCREEN ) );

cs.x = 0;  //Set the position to the origin
cs.y = 0;

cs.dwExStyle &= ~WS_EX_CLIENTEDGE;
cs.lpszClass = GAME_TITLE;
```

Notice that the size of the window is set to the smaller of the expected screen size or the maximum width of the screen. If your player has done something stupid and set their desktop to 640x480 and your game is assuming an 800x600 window minimum, then any dialog box on an 800x600 window will appear cut off on the right side. Win32 will happily create a window of any size, 8000x6000 perhaps, and any dialog box appearing in the center of that huge window will never be seen by man or beast.

There's one more trick to making a perfect MFC game window. An MFC application is really two windows at a minimum. The main application window is called a main frame, and the client area is called a child view. The child view for a game needs a special window class. You can accomplish this by overloading the call to `PreCreateWindow` and create a game friendly window class as shown here:

```
BOOL CChildView::PreCreateWindow(CREATESTRUCT& cs)
{
   if (!CWnd::PreCreateWindow(cs))
     return FALSE;

   cs.style &= ~WS_BORDER;
   cs.lpszClass = AfxRegisterWndClass(CS_HREDRAW|CS_VREDRAW|CS_DBLCLKS,
     NULL, HBRUSH(GetStockObject(NULL_BRUSH)), NULL);

   return TRUE;
}
```

The `CChildView` class will be the main receiver of all the MFC messages for keyboard and mouse input. You'll most likely translate these messages into something useful for your game.

Now that your application has a window handle you can initialize all the other parts of your game that require it such as your audio system or graphics system.

Initializing Your Audio

Audio systems are usually multithreaded at the lowest level. This is one of the reasons you have to wait until you are sure your game isn't running multiple instances of itself when your game initializes. The only thing you want to do at the initialization stage is get your audio system ready to play; don't start playing anything just yet. Most games have user settable game options, which will be read next if they exist. Those game options will definitely set audio options such as turning music or character speech off. If the gamer has turned all the audio options off in favor of playing some old Pink Floyd, you don't want a few milliseconds of audio to chirp the speaker before the options are loaded.

Loading User Settable Game Options

Finding the right directory for user settable game options used to be easy. A programmer would simply store user data files close to the EXE and use the `GetModuleFileName` API. Windows XP Home makes the `Program Files` directory off limits by default, and applications are not allowed to write directly to this directory tree. Instead, applications must write user data to the `C:\Documents and Settings\{User name}\Application Data` directory. This directory is completely different from one version of Windows to another, so you have to use a special API to find it: `SHGetSpecialFolderPath`. Windows XP Pro is more forgiving, and doesn't limit access to these directories by default. XP Home was designed this way to keep the casual, home user from stomping though the Program Files directory in a ham-fisted attempt to solve various problems.

If it were that easy I wouldn't have to show you the next code block. If you open Windows Explorer to your application data directory, you'll see plenty of companies who play by the rules, writing application data in the spot that will keep Windows XP from freaking out. Clearly you can't just stick your data files in the top level. Our last Microsoft product used this path:

```
GAME_APP_DIRECTORY = "Microsoft\\Microsoft Games\\Bicycle Casino\\2.0";
```

The value for your `GAME_APP_DIRECTORY` is also a great value for a registry key. Don't forget to add the version number at the end. You might as well hope for a gravy train: 2.0, 3.0, 4.0, and so on.

7

It's up to you to make sure you create the directory if it doesn't exist. This can be a hassle, since you have to walk down the directory tree, creating all the way down. Since I already went to the trouble of writing this code for you, feel free to take it. Your time is better spent writing something fun instead of annoying Windows homework:

```
CString m_ProfilesDirectory;

HRESULT hr;
TCHAR userDataPath[MAX_PATH];

Hr = SHGetSpecialFolderPath(hWnd, userDataPath, CSIDL_APPDATA, true);

m_ProfilesDirectory = profilesPath;
m_ProfilesDirectory += "\\";
m_ProfilesDirectory += GAME_APP_DIRECTORY;

// Does our directory exist?
if (0xffffffff == GetFileAttributes(m_ProfilesDirectory))
{
   // Nope - we have to go make a new directory to store application data.
   CString current = profilesPath;
   CString myAppData = GAME_APP_DIRECTORY;
   CString token;

   do {
```

```
        int left = myAppData.Find('\\');
        if (left==-1)
        {
            token = myAppData;
            myAppData = _T("");
        }
        else
        {
            assert(myAppData.GetLength()>=left);
            token = myAppData.Left(left);
            myAppData = myAppData.Right(myAppData.GetLength()-(left+1));
        }

        if (token.GetLength())
        {
            current += "\\";
            current += token;
            if (false == CreateDirectory(current, NULL))
            {
                int error = GetLastError();
                if (error != ERROR_ALREADY_EXISTS)
                {
                    return false;
                }
            }
        }

    } while (myAppData.GetLength());
}

m_ProfilesDirectory += _T("\\");
```

This code will make sure your application data directory exists, and set the value of `m_ProfilesDirectory` to the name of that directory—drive letter and all.

Your game options are completely up to you and the design of your game. There's no hard and fast rule of what game options you need to provide. You can count on needing volume controls for various audio tracks in your game such as music or sound effects. It's also a great idea to store a game option for fullscreen mode.

Make sure that the DEBUG game.ini file has some way to override the fullscreen option in the user settings. If you need to debug a saved game and you don't happen to have a multi-monitor setup, any breakpoints will cause trouble if the game is in fullscreen mode. Any programmer who attempts to debug a fullscreen game with only one monitor is sure to lose their mind and start a killing spree.

Creating Your Drawing Surfaces

It's finally time to create the drawing surfaces. If your game can run in a window, the first thing you need to check is whether or not the current display settings are compatible with the drawing surface your game will use. There are two things you need to check: display size and bit depth. If your game assumes an 800x600 drawing surface, the display settings must be set to anything higher than 800x600 such as 1024x768. In a windowed mode, you have to leave some room for the window border and title bar. If you don't, the player will be forced to use the keyboard to move the window around, because the only part of the window that can accept a drag command from the mouse is displayed offscreen.

Bit depth is easier. The only incompatibility is in 24-bit mode because you can't count on enumerating a 24-bit Direct3D device because very few cards support it. 3D hardware draws optimally onto 16- or 32-bit render targets. Of course, you could create a 32-bit Direct3D device and have Windows do the translation from 32-bit to 24-bit, but that isn't going to make your game faster.

If either of these incompatibilities exist the best thing to do is notify the player with a dialog box. You'll have to use a nasty GDI dialog, of course since you don't have your drawing surface up, so just call the Win32 `MessageBox API`. Tell them that they can't run in windowed mode with their current display settings and reinitialize the drawing surface in fullscreen mode.

Initializing Your Game Objects

Everything is ready for your game to start. The hardware checks out, your data files are open, the resource cache is running, and the audio and video systems are ready to play. Most likely you'll have some special systems such as physics, user interface, or AI to initialize depending on your game architecture. The order in which you create these objects is entirely up to you and your game design.

With initialization done control passes to the main loop.

The Main Loop

The main difference between games and most other applications is that games are constantly busy doing something in the background. Other applications will patiently wait until you move the mouse or mash keys on the keyboard before they do anything. If games did this they would be as boring as Microsoft Word or Excel. The main loop of a game should accomplish the following tasks until the player quits the game or deactivates the window:

- Update your game logic
- Render and present the scene

We'll start by taking an example of a classic Win32 message pump and build it up until it works for games. Taken straight from a DirectX 9 sample, the simplest game message pump looks like this:

```
MSG msg;
ZeroMemory( &msg, sizeof(msg) );
while( msg.message!=WM_QUIT )
{
   if( PeekMessage( &msg, NULL, 0U, 0U, PM_REMOVE ) )
   {
      TranslateMessage( &msg );
      DispatchMessage( &msg );
   }
   else
      MyRender();
}
```

Assume for a moment that the `MyRender()` method does nothing more than render and present the frame. You'll also have to assume that any game logic update occurs only as a result of messages appearing in the message queue. The problem with this message pump is that there's nothing in the code to change the game state if there are no messages in the queue. If you changed the game state only as a result of receiving messages, you would only see animations happen if you moved the mouse. A game with that kind of architecture would probably help hard core gamers get a little exercise, but I wouldn't suggest it.

Windows provides a message that seems like a good solution to this problem: `WM_TIMER`. This Win32 message can be sent at definite intervals. Using the Win32 `SetTimer()` API, you can cause your application to receive these `WM_TIMER` messages or you can specify a callback function. For those programmers like me who remember the old Windows 3.1 days, `WM_TIMER` was the only way games could get a semblance of background processing. Windows 3.1 was a cooperative multitasking system, which meant that the only time your application got CPU time was if it had a message to process and no other app was hogging the message pump.

The biggest problem with using `WM_TIMER` is resolution. Even though you specify `WM_TIMER` calls down to the millisecond, the timer doesn't actually have millisecond accuracy and you are not guaranteed to be called in the exact intervals you'd hope. Since Win32 operating systems are multitasking we can happily choose a better alternative. To see this, let's make a few changes to the main loop code:

```
MSG msg;
ZeroMemory( &msg, sizeof(msg) );
while( msg.message!=WM_QUIT )
{
   // Part 1: Do idle work until a message is seen in the message queue
   while (!PeekMessage(&msg, NULL, NULL, NULL, PM_NOREMOVE))
   {
      // call MyMainLoop while in bIdle state
      MyMainLoop();
   }

   // Part 2: Pump messages until the queue is empty
   do
   {
      if (GetMessage(&msg, NULL, NULL, NULL))
      {
         TranslateMessage(&msg);
         DispatchMessage(&msg);
      }

   } while (::PeekMessage(&msg), NULL, NULL, NULL, PM_NOREMOVE));
}
```


This is a much better main loop because it alternates between emptying the message queue and doing idle work, which is defined as anything that happens while the player isn't doing anything: game logic, AI, and rendering.

This code could be optimized but I'll leave that as an exercise for you. If you want to see a better version of this main loop take a look at the source code for `CWinThread::Run()` in the MFC library. It does a pretty fair job of filtering out certain messages that should not affect the state of the user interface, such as redundant `WM_MOUSEMOVE` messages. Still, the code above is good enough for government work.

Let's take a look at the inside of the `MyMainLoop()` method. Those of you coding in MFC will put this code into an overloaded `CMainFrame::OnIdle()`:

```
bool MyMainLoop()
{
   if ( !m_bInitialized || m_bMinimized  )
      return false;

   HRESULT hr;

   if( m_bActive )
   {
```

```
        // MyProcessNextFrame is the call that processes game logic
        if( FAILED( hr = MyProcessNextFrame() ) )
        {
            MyReinitializeDisplay();
            return false;
        }

        Sleep(2); // Pause a bit to keep from sucking all the CPU

        return true;
    }
    else
    {
        // Note! Never ever paint if the app isn't active.

        // Turn off audio, since the boss doesn't like game music.
        MyPauseAudio();

        // Go to sleep until a message appears in the queue
        WaitMessage();

        return false;
    }

    if (m_bQuitting)
    {
        PostMessage(WM_CLOSE, 0, 0);
        return ret;
    }

    return false;
}
```

The first predicate in the main loop handles the trivial case where the main loop should return instantly. It is possible that the main loop will run before the game is fully initialized. In Windows, there are plenty of messages that get pumped before you are really ready to run your main loop, `WM_CREATE` is a great example. If you want to see all of them sometime, I suggest you run Spy++ and see for yourself.

Another trivial case is easy to fathom; if the window is minimized you shouldn't do anything. This is true for most games, but perhaps a case could be made for massively multiplayer games that support background activity of some kind. Perhaps you'll need to write some code that will maximize the window automatically upon some event or trigger. It's purely up to you.

This main loop has two branches, which run depending on whether the window is active. An active game should do three things: call the business end of the game code, `MyProcessNextFrame()`, check to see if the display needs to be reinitialized, and finally call `Sleep()`. `MyProcessNextFrame()` is what you'll code to change your game state and render the display, and you can assume that the only reason it will fail and return control back to the main loop is upon a draw failure. It's totally possible that in the middle of this call the player will do something crazy like change their desktop settings or switch to fullscreen mode, invalidating the display. You'll call the Win32 API `Sleep()` for a really short time, two milliseconds in fact, to relinquish some CPU time to other applications. Otherwise, your game will constantly peg the CPU at 100%, making running anything else, including a debugger, a pain in the ass.

If the player Alt-Tabs away to look at email or something, the window will go inactive and you should do a little homework to make your game Windows friendly. The first thing you should do is pause your audio system. If someone is playing a game at the office and the boss walks in the door the last thing that needs to happen after an Alt-Tab is some grunt warrior in your game yelling, "Who's your daddy!" An Alt-Tab should bury your game instantly, thus the necessity of pausing your audio system. When the game is reactivated, the audio system can pick up where it left off.

The call to the Win32 API `WaitMessage()` guarantees that the game won't get any more attention from the process scheduler until a message is inserted into the message queue. Essentially it instructs Windows to let this application lie dormant until something wakes it up, such as a mouse click or another window being dragged over the inactive window. This is friendly Windows application behavior, as it allows your game to relinquish its stranglehold on the CPU when the player wants to activate another application.

The code inside `MyProcessNextFrame()` decouples the processing of game logic and updating the screen. Rendering the display is extremely time-consuming and it makes little sense to update the screen at a high refresh rate. A good rule of thumb says that games shouldn't need to refresh their screens any more than 60fps. Why? That happens to coincide with the default scan rate of most monitors, and it turns out that humans can't really perceive a framerate any faster than about 22fps.

```
#include <mmsystem.h>
const unsigned int SCREEN_REFRESH_RATE(1000/60);

HRESULT MyProcessNextFrame()
{
   // The wise C++ programmer would put these nasty static variables in
```

```
    // a nice class.

    static DWORD currTick = 0;          // time right now
    static DWORD lastUpdate = 0;        // previous time
    static DWORD lastDraw = 0;          // last time the game rendered
    static bool runFullSpeed = false; // set to true if you want to run full speed

    // Figure how much time has passed since the last time
    currTick = timeGetTime();

    MyUpdateGameLogic(currTick - lastUpdate);
    lastUpdate = currTick;

    // It is time to draw ?
    if( runFullSpeed || ( (currTick - lastDraw) > SCREEN_REFRESH_RATE) )
    {
      if (S_OK == MyPaint())
      {
        // record the last successful paint
        lastDraw = currTick;
      }
    }

     return S_OK;
}
```

The call to `timeGetTime()` returns the current system time in milliseconds. There are more accurate timers available in Intel based machines, but the Windows multimedia timer is an excellent workhorse timer. The call to `MyUpdateGame()` is made with the number of milliseconds that have passed since the last game loop. Any time dependant game logic, such as the distance an object should move given a certain speed in the game world, will use this value as the master clock. The call to `MyPaint()` is made within a predicate that limits the frame rate to `SCREEN_REFRESH_RATE`. A boolean value, `runFullSpeed`, can be set to true if you are interested in watching your game run without the "governor."

The funny part of all this is that most console games only worry about this last method, and simply stick it into a while loop. Console games are never inactive and they never have to worry about working and playing well with other apps like Microsoft Word. This is yet another case where I shake my head at producers that think programming Windows games is somehow trivial compared to console games.

The guts of `MyUpdateGameLogic()`will take up the rest of this chapter, so for clarity I'll skip that for a moment and show you how to render and present your display.

Rendering and Presenting the Display

The method `MyPaint()` attempts to draw the next frame, get the results to the front buffer, and handle any problems if a failure occurs:

```
HRESULT MyPaint()
{
   HRESULT hr;

   if( FAILED( hr = MyDraw() ) || FAILED( hr = MyPresent() )
   {
      // insert code to handle drawing problems hereÖsuch as mode changes…
      return hr;
   }

    return S_OK;
}
```


Every game's draw routine will look something like this:

```
//Draw everything
HRESULT MyDraw() const
{
   HRESULT result = S_OK;

   for(MyDrawableList::iterator i=pDrawList->begin(); i!=pDrawList->end(); ++i)
   {
      result = (*i)->Draw();

      if(result != S_OK)
         return result;
   }

   return result;
}
```

I've implemented my draw list in STL. Drawable objects can be anything from a background sprite to an off-screen surface that is the destination surface of a render target. Each drawable object knows how to draw itself via the implementation of the `Draw()` method. If you think there's plenty missing from this little example, you're right. First, the incredibly tricky task of managing and sorting the draw list is handled in the game update code. As drawable objects come into and out of view, the object will get added to or removed from the draw list. One of the hardest tasks in all of game programming is minimizing the size and sorting of this list. One more thing: Some games actually use a tree structure instead of a list. Secondly, the code to actually draw the objects themselves is completely dependent on the object. These topics are covered in the graphics chapters.

`MyDraw()` composes a new frame in a back buffer. The contents are either copied to the front buffer or the front and back buffers are flipped, assuming the appropriate video hardware is installed. This process is commonly called presenting, thus the name for the next function, `MyPresent()`:

```
HRESULT MyPresent()
{
    HRESULT hr;

    while( 1 )
    {
      // Windowed mode - nothing special - full BLIT
      if ( m_bWindowed )
      {
        m_pDD->WaitForVerticalBlank(DDWAITVB_BLOCKBEGIN, NULL);
        hr = m_pddsFrontBuffer->Blt(
           &m_rcWindow,
           m_pddsBackBuffer,
           NULL, DDBLT_WAIT, NULL );
      }
      else // Fullscreen modes
      {
        // There are modals up and fullscreen, wait and blit directly
        // Fullscreen BLIT
        if ( ! m_bFlipping )
        {
          m_pDD->WaitForVerticalBlank(DDWAITVB_BLOCKBEGIN, NULL);
          hr = m_pddsFrontBuffer->Blt(
            CRect( 0, 0, SCREEN_WIDTH, SCREEN_HEIGHT ),
            m_pddsBackBuffer,
            NULL, DDBLT_WAIT, NULL );
        }
        else
        {
          // Fullscreen FLIP
          hr = m_pddsFrontBuffer->Flip( NULL, 0 );
        }
      }
```

```
    if ( FAILED( hr ) )
       TRACE( _T("Present() failed to FLIP/BLIT m_surface.\n" ) );

    if( hr == DDERR_SURFACELOST )
    {
      if (FAILED (hr = MyRestore() ) )
      {
          return hr;
      }
    }
    else if( hr != DDERR_WASSTILLDRAWING )
      {
         return hr;
      }
    }

    return hr;
}
```


If the game is not running a flipping front and back buffer, all you need to do is wait for the vertical blank signal and copy the back buffer to the front buffer. If the video hardware supports flipping, waiting for the vertical blank is not necessary since the video card won't flip until the vertical blank is signaled.

As always, if the call to `Blt()` or `Flip()` fails, you'll want to restore your drawing surfaces since it is likely that something like a mode change has occurred. If the call fails because another draw is still in progress, the whole process repeats.

Updating the Game State

Anything that's not input or output falls into this huge category of game logic. This could include AI, physics, animations, triggers, etc. Games tend to handle an enormous amount of seemingly autonomous entities that come to life, stomp around the game world, and die off. Each of these game objects can affect the life cycle of other objects, such as a missile colliding and destroying an enemy vehicle. Back in the dark ages, circa 1991, each major subsystem of the game had a handler function.

```
void MyUpdateGameLogic(unsigned int ms)
{
   PollInputDevices();
   HandleUserInput(ms);
   CalculateAI(ms);
   ReticulateSplines(ms);
   RunPhysicsSimulation(ms);
```

```
    PokeAudioSystem(ms);
    UpdateDisplayList(ms);
}
```

Each of these subsystems was called in a simple linear fashion. The internals of each function were completely customized, but generally they manipulated lists of objects and ran some code on each one, sometimes changing the members of the lists in the process.

This design wasn't very flexible. For example, if the audio system is disabled there is no reason to call `PokeAudioSystem()`. Perhaps the `ReticulateSplines()` call needs to happen at a different frequency than once per main loop. A more general system could be easily devised, that is based on cooperative multitasking.

Cooperative multitasking is a mechanism where each process gets a little CPU time in a round robin fashion. It's called cooperative because each process is responsible for releasing control back to the calling entity. If a process goes into an infinite loop the entire system will hang. The tradeoff for that weakness is that the system is simple to design and extremely efficient.

Imagine a simple class called `CProcess` with a single virtual method, `OnUpdate()`:

```
class CProcess
{
public:
    virtual void OnUpdate(const int deltaMilliseconds);
};
```

You could create objects inheriting from this class and stick them in a master process list. Every game loop, your code could traverse this list and call `OnUpdate()` for each object:

```
typedef std::list<CProcess*> ProcessList;
ProcessList g_ProcessList;

void UpdateProcesses(int deltaMilliseconds)
{
    ProcessList::iterator i = g_ProcessList.begin();

    while ( i != m_ProcessList.end() )
    {
        CProcess* p = *i;
        p->OnUpdate( deltaMilliseconds );
        ++i;
    }
}
```

The contents of the `OnUpdate()` overload could be anything. It could move the object on a spline, it could monitor the contents of a buffer stream and update it accordingly, it could run some AI code. It could render your screen, or monitor user interface objects like screens and buttons. At the highest level, your top-level function could look something like this:

```
void main()
{
   if (CreateProcesses())
   {
      RunProcesses();
   }
   ShutdownProcesses();
}
```

It may sound crazy, but Ultima VIII's main loop looked almost exactly like that, give or take a few lines.

There are a few wrinkles to this wonderful design that you should know about. If creating a system to handle your main loop were so easy as all that that I wouldn't bother devoting so much time to it. The first big problem comes when one process's `OnUpdate()` can destroy other processes, or even worse cause a recursive call to indirectly cause itself to be destroyed. Think of the likely code for a hand grenade exploding. The `OnUpdate()` would likely query the game object lists for every object in a certain range, and then cause all those objects to be destroyed in a nice fireball. The grenade object would be included in the list of objects in range, wouldn't it?

The solution to this problem involves some kind of reference counting system, or maybe a smart pointer. The `SmartPtr class` in Chapter 3 solves this problem well, and it will be used in the next section.

A Simple Cooperative Multitasker

A good process class should contain some additional data members and methods to make it interesting and flexible. There are as many ways to create this class as there are programmers, but this should give you a good start. There are three classes in this nugget of code:

- `class SmartPtr`: A smart pointer class. The source code for this class was presented in Chapter 3. If you can't remember what a smart pointer is you'd better go back now and review.

- `class Cprocess`: A base class for processes. You'll inherit from this class and redefine the `OnUpdate()` method.
- `class CprocessManager`: This is a container and manager for running all your cooperative processes.

Here's the header file:

```
#ifndef CPROCESS_H
#define CPROCESS_H

#include <list>
#include "SmartPtr.h"

//////////////////////////////////////////////////////////////////////
// Enums
//////////////////////////////////////////////////////////////////////

// This process type enumeration is obviously subject to changes
// based on the game design, for example, we are assuming the game will
// have separate behaviors for voice, music, and sound effects
// when in actuality, this engine will play all sound processes the same way

enum PROCESS_TYPE
{
   PROC_NONE,
   PROC_WAIT,
   PROC_SPRITE,
   PROC_CONTROL,
   PROC_SCREEN,
   PROC_MUSIC,
   PROC_SOUNDFX,
   PROC_GAMESPECIFIC
};


//////////////////////////////////////////////////////////////////////
// Flags
//////////////////////////////////////////////////////////////////////

static const int PROCESS_FLAG_ATTACHED            = 0x00000001;

//////////////////////////////////////////////////////////////////////
// CProcess Implementation
//////////////////////////////////////////////////////////////////////
```

```
class CProcess
{
   friend class CProcessManager;

protected:
   int                     m_iType;        // type of process running
   bool            m_bKill;                // tells manager to kill and remove
   bool            m_bActive;
   bool            m_bPaused;
   bool            m_bInitialUpdate;       // initial update?
   SmartPtr<CProcess>      m_pNext;

private:
   unsigned int    m_uProcessFlags;

public:
   CProcess(int ntype, unsigned int uOrder = 0);
   virtual ~CProcess();

public:

   virtual bool            IsDead(void) const { return(m_bKill);};
   virtual void            Kill();

   virtual int             GetType(void) const { return(m_iType); };
   virtual void            SetType(const int t) { m_iType = t; };

   virtual bool            IsActive(void) const { return m_bActive; };
   virtual void            SetActive(const bool b) { m_bActive = b; };
   virtual bool            IsAttached()const;
   virtual void            SetAttached(const bool wantAttached);

   virtual bool            IsPaused(void) const { return m_bPaused; };
   // call to pause a process
   virtual void            TogglePause() {m_bPaused = !m_bPaused;}

   bool                    IsInitialized()const { return ! m_bInitialUpdate; };

   SmartPtr<CProcess> const GetNext(void) const { return(m_pNext);}
   virtual void            SetNext(SmartPtr<CProcess> nnext);

   virtual void            OnUpdate(const int deltaMilliseconds);
   virtual void            OnInitialize(){};

private:
```

7

```
    CProcess();                         //disable default construction
    CProcess(const CProcess& rhs);      //disable copy construction
};

inline void CProcess::OnUpdate( const int deltaMilliseconds )
{
    if ( m_bInitialUpdate )
    {
        OnInitialize();
        m_bInitialUpdate = false;
    }
}


/////////////////////////////////////////////////////////////////////
// ProcessList is a list of smart CProcess pointers.
/////////////////////////////////////////////////////////////////////

typedef std::list<SmartPtr<CProcess> > ProcessList;


/////////////////////////////////////////////////////////////////////
// CProcessManager is a container for CProcess objects
/////////////////////////////////////////////////////////////////////

class CProcessManager
{
public:
    void UpdateProcesses(int deltaMilliseconds);
    void DeleteProcessList();
    bool IsProcessActive( int nType );
    void Attach( SmartPtr<CProcess> pProcess );
    bool HasProcesses();

protected:
    ProcessList      m_ProcessList;

private:
    void Detach( SmartPtr<CProcess> pProcess );
};

#endif
```

The source code for the `CProcess` base class and the `CProcessManager` follows:

```
#include "stdafx.h"
#include "CProcess.h"

//////////////////////////////////////////////////////////////////////
// CProcess constructor
//
CProcess::CProcess( int ntype, unsigned int uOrder ) :
   m_iType( ntype ),
   m_bKill( false ),
   m_bActive( true ),
   m_uProcessFlags( 0 ),
   m_pNext( NULL ),
   m_bPaused( false ),
   m_bInitialUpdate( true )
{
}

//////////////////////////////////////////////////////////////////////
// CProcess destructor -
//   Note: always call Kill(), never delete.
//
CProcess::~CProcess()
{
   if (m_pNext)
   {
      m_pNext = NULL;
   }
}

//////////////////////////////////////////////////////////////////////
// CProcess::Kill() - marks the process for cleanup
//
void CProcess::Kill()
{
   m_bKill=true;
}

//////////////////////////////////////////////////////////////////////
// CProcess::SetNext - sets a process dependancy
//
// A->SetNext(B)  means that B will wait until A is finished
//
void CProcess::SetNext(SmartPtr<CProcess> nnext)
{
   if (m_pNext)
   {
```

7

```
        m_pNext = NULL;
    }

    m_pNext = nnext;
}


//////////////////////////////////////////////////////////////////
// CProcess attachement methods
//
// IsAttached() - Is this process attached to the manager?
// SetAttached() - Marks it as attached. Called only by the manager.
//
bool CProcess::IsAttached() const
{
    return (m_uProcessFlags & PROCESS_FLAG_ATTACHED) ? true : false;
}

void CProcess::SetAttached(const bool wantAttached)
{
    if(wantAttached)
    {
        m_uProcessFlags |= PROCESS_FLAG_ATTACHED;
    }
    else
    {
        m_uProcessFlags &= ~PROCESS_FLAG_ATTACHED;
    }
}

//////////////////////////////////////////////////////////////////
// CProcessManager::Attach - gets a process to run
//
void CProcessManager::Attach( SmartPtr<CProcess> pProcess )
{
    m_ProcessList.push_back(pProcess);
    pProcess->SetAttached(true);
}

//////////////////////////////////////////////////////////////////
// CProcessManager::Detach
//  - Detach a process from the process list, but don't delete it
//
void CProcessManager::Detach( SmartPtr<CProcess> pProcess )
{
    m_ProcessList.remove(pProcess);
```

```
    pProcess->SetAttached(false);
}

/////////////////////////////////////////////////////////////////////
// CProcessManager::IsProcessActive
//   - Are there any active processes of this type?
//
bool CProcessManager::IsProcessActive( int nType )
{
    for(ProcessList::iterator i=m_ProcessList.begin();
        i!=m_ProcessList.end(); ++i)
    {
        // Check for living processes.  If they are dead, make sure no children
        // are attached as they will be brought to life on next cycle.
        if ( ( *i )->GetType() == nType &&
            ( ( *i )->IsDead() == false || ( *i )->m_pNext ) )
          return true;
    }
    return false;
}

/////////////////////////////////////////////////////////////////////
// CProcessManager::HasProcesses
//   - Are there any processes at all?
//
bool CProcessManager::HasProcesses()
{
    return !m_ProcessList.empty();
}

/////////////////////////////////////////////////////////////////////
// CProcessManager::DeleteProcessList
//   - run through the list of processes and detach them
//
void CProcessManager::DeleteProcessList()
{
    for(ProcessList::iterator i = m_ProcessList.begin();
        i != m_ProcessList.end(); )
    {
        Detach(* (i++) );
    }
}

/////////////////////////////////////////////////////////////////////
// CProcessManager::DeleteProcessList
```

```
//  - run through the list of processes and update them
//
void CProcessManager::UpdateProcesses(int deltaMilliseconds)
{
   ProcessList::iterator i = m_ProcessList.begin();
   SmartPtr<CProcess> pNext(NULL);

   while ( i != m_ProcessList.end() )
   {
      SmartPtr<CProcess> p = *i;
      ++i;

      if ( p->IsDead() )
      {
         // Check for a child process and add if exists
         pNext = p->GetNext();
         if ( pNext )
         {
            p->SetNext(SmartPtr<CProcess>(NULL));
            Attach( pNext );
         }
         Detach( p );
      }
      else if ( p->IsActive() && !p->IsPaused() )
      {
         p->OnUpdate( deltaMilliseconds );
      }
   }
}
```

Most of the methods are self-explanatory. When you overload `CProcess::OnUpdate()` in the derived class, you'll call `CProcess::Kill()` on itself to mark the process for termination and cleanup—a process marked to be killed is a dead process. I'll show you a couple of examples in a moment.

Note the use of the `SmartPtr` class throughout. This is an excellent example of using smart pointers in a class that uses an STL list. Any reference to a `SmartPtr <CProcess>` object is managed by the smart pointer class, ensuring that the process object will remain in memory as long as there is a valid reference to it. The moment the last reference is cleared or reassigned, the process memory is finally freed. That's why the `CProcessManager` has a list of `SmartPtr <CProcess>` instead of a list of `CProcess` pointers.

CProcessManager::Attach() implements the insertion of a new process into an ordered process list. CProcessManager::UpdateProcesses() deserves some special attention. Recall that nearly 100% of the game code could be inside various overloads of CProcess::OnUpdate(). This game code can, and will cause game processes and objects to be deleted, all the more reason that this system uses smart pointers.

These classes and the classes that inherit from CProcess can run your entire game. Assuming we use the code from MyProcessNextFrame() described previously, it can use the CProcessManager class by changing one line of code:

```
#include <mmsystem.h>
const unsigned int SCREEN_REFRESH_RATE(1000/30);

HRESULT MyProcessNextFrame()
{
   // Figure how much time has passed since the last time
   m_dwCurrTick = timeGetTime();

   // THIS LINE IS DIFFERENT! Call CProcessManager::UpdateProcesses()
   g_pProcessManager->UpdateProcesses(m_dwCurrTick - m_dwLastUpdate);
   m_dwLastUpdate = m_dwCurrTick;

   // It is time to draw ?
   if( m_runFullSpeed || ( (m_dwCurrTick - m_dwLastDraw) > SCREEN_REFRESH_RATE) )
   {
      if (S_OK == MyPaint())
      {
         // record the last successful paint
         m_dwLastDraw = m_dwCurrTick;
      }
   }

    return S_OK;
}
```


You could take the process manager a few steps further. Ultima VIII and Origin's Crusader: No Remorse had an extremely robust and complicated process management system that allowed processes to depend on the completion or failure of other processes. A process with a dependent would signal the waiting process when it could become active. It was possible to create code in Ultima VIII that looked like this:

```
CWalkProcess *walk = new CWalkProcess(avatar, door);
CAnimProcess *openDoor = new CAnimProcess(OPEN_DOOR, avatar, door);
CAnimProcess *drawSword = new CAnimProcess(DRAW_WEAPON, avatar, sword);
```

```
CCombatProcess *goBerserk = CCombatProcess(BERSERK, avatar);

walk->then(openDoor)->then(drawSword)->then(goBerserk);
```

It is easy to see that this code would begin a sequence of events that started with the Avatar walking to the door and finally going berserk with his sword out. The best part of this design was that if something got in the Avatar's way and abruptly ended the original walk animation, all the other processes would be cancelled.

One of the worst bugs I ever had the pleasure of finding was a bug in the core of the Ultima VIII process manager. Ultima VIII processes could attach their `OnUpdate()` calls to a real time interrupt, which was pretty cool. Animations and other events could happen smoothly without worrying about the exact CPU speed of the machine. The process table was getting corrupted somehow, and no one was sure how to find it as the bug occurred completely randomly—or so we thought. After tons of QA time and late nights we eventually found that jumping from map to map made the problem happen relatively frequently. We were able to track the bug down to the code that removed processes from the main process list. It turned out that the real time processes were accessing the process list at the same moment the list was being changed. Thank goodness we weren't on multiple processors; we never would have found it.

Examples of Classes that Inherit from CProcess

A very simple example of a useful process using this cooperative design is a wait process. This process is useful for inserting timed delays as the code example here shows:

```
///////////////////////////////////////////////////////////////////////
// CWaitProcess
///////////////////////////////////////////////////////////////////////

class CWaitProcess : public CProcess
{
protected:
   unsigned int      m_uStart;
   unsigned int      m_uStop;

public:
   CWaitProcess(CProcess* pParent, unsigned int iNumMill );

   virtual void OnUpdate(const int deltaMilliseconds);
};
```

```
CWaitProcess::CWaitProcess(CProcess* pParent, unsigned int iNumMill ) :
   CProcess( PROC_WAIT, 0, pParent ),
   m_uStart( 0 ),
   m_uStop( iNumMill )
{
}

void CWaitProcess::OnUpdate( const int deltaMilliseconds )
{
   CProcess::OnUpdate( deltaMilliseconds );

   if ( m_bActive )
   {
      m_uStart += deltaMilliseconds;

      if ( m_uStart >= m_uStop )
         Kill();
   }
}
```

Create an instance of `CWaitProcess` in this way:

```
{
   SmartPtr<CProcess> wait(new CWaitProcess(3000));
   processManager.Attach(wait);
}
```

Take note of two things. First, you don't just "new up" a `CWaitProcess` and attach it to the `CProcessManager`. You have to use the `SmartPtr` template to manage `CProcess` objects. The second thing you'll notice is that the object, `wait`, is declared in a local scope. If you don't do this, the smart pointer will retain a reference as long as `wait` exists, and you probably don't want that, since the `CProcessManager` will manage the process object from here on out.

The wait process will hang out for three seconds and kill itself off. By itself it's a little underwhelming. Let's assume you've defined another process, called `CKaboomProcess`. You can then create a nuclear explosion with a three-second fuse, without a physics degree:

```
{
   // Open a local scope, create some processes,
   // and set up their linkage. Since CProcess uses
   // smart pointers to manage their life, we use a
   // local scope to declare them

   // The wait process will stay alive for three seconds
```

```
    SmartPtr<CProcess> wait(new CWaitProcess(3000));
    processManager.Attach(wait);

    // The CKaboomProcess will wait for the CWaitProcess
    //   Note - it is not attached

    SmartPtr<CProcess> kaboom(new CKaboomProcess());
    wait->SetNext(kaboom);

}
```

The `CProcess::SetNext()` method sets up a simple dependency between the `CWaitProcess` and the `CKaboomProcess`. `CKaboomProcess` will remain inactive until the `CWaitProcess` is killed.

More Uses of CProcess Derivatives

Every updatable game object can inherit from `CProcess`. This includes display objects like screens, sprites, or animated characters. User interface objects such as buttons, edit boxes, or menus can inherit from `CProcess`. Audio objects such as sound effects, speech, or music make great use of this design because of the dependency and timing features.

Stick the Landing: A Nice Clean Exit

Your game won't run forever. Even the best games will take a back seat to food and water, regardless of what Microsoft's XBox ads seem to imply. There may be a temptation to simply call `exit(0)` and be done with it. This isn't a wise choice because system resources won't be released properly.

DirectX drivers sometimes handle hard exits badly, causing VRAM or other limited resources to remain tied up by a half dead application. When the player attempts to restart the game they find that it won't start, due to a lack of VRAM or perhaps something else. The player might have to reboot their machine. Rebooting used to be a normal thing and every gamer was used to multiple reboots every day. The latest operating systems like Windows XP are much more resilient and reboots are very rare. Players who find that your game requires a reboot after they're done will get pretty annoyed and most likely return your game.

If you don't have a decent exit mechanism you'll also find it impossible to determine where your game is leaking memory or other resources. After all, a hard exit is basically a huge memory leak. A tight exit mechanism will show you a single byte of leaked memory before returning control to the operating system. This is important for all games, but it is especially true for console games.

Console games are not allowed to leak memory. Period. To be honest, Windows games shouldn't be given any slack either. The reality of it is that some Win32 calls leak resources and you just have to live with it. That's no reason your game code should be sloppy; hold yourself to a high standard and you won't get a reputation for crappy software.

How Do I Get Out of Here?

There are two ways to stop a game from executing without yanking the power or causing some kind of exception:

- The player quits the game on purpose.
- The system shuts the application down (Win32).

If the player chooses to stop playing, the first thing you should do is ask the player if he or she wants to save their game. The last thing someone needs is to lose six hours of progress only to hit the wrong button by accident. A good standard detects if the current state of the game has changed since the last time the user saved, and only if the state is different does the system ask if the player wants to save his or her game. It is equally annoying to save your game, quit, and have the idiot application ask if the game needs saving all over again.

Remember the piece of code just outside the main message pump:

```
if (m_bQuitting)
{
   PostMessage(WM_CLOSE, 0, 0);
   return ret;
}
```

This code implies that you shouldn't perform any quit mechanism while you are pumping messages. This little trick solves the problem of hitting the quit hotkey fifteen times really fast, where a badly engineered game might recursively call the quit code. The user interface control that receives the quit button click event or the hotkey event should simply set a Boolean variable to true, which will be checked after the last message in the queue has been handled.

Console programmers can stop here and simply run their exit code, destroying all the game systems generally in the reverse order in which they were created. Windows programmers, as usual, don't get off nearly that easy.

When the Win32 OS decides your game has to shut down, it sends a different message. Win32 apps should intercept the `WM_SYSCOMMAND` message, and look for `SC_CLOSE` in the `wParam`. MFC applications can overload the `CWnd::OnSysCommand()` to grab the same message. This is what Win32 sends to applications that are being closed, perhaps against their will. This can happen if the machine is shut down or if the player hits ALT-F4.

The problem with this message is that Alt-F4 should act just like your normal exit, asking you if you want to quit and all of that. If you can save to a temporary location and load that state the next time the player starts, your players will thank you. Most likely they were just getting to the boss monster and the batteries on their laptop finally ran out of motivated electrons.

Again, you have to double check for multiple entries into this code with a Boolean variable. If the player hits Alt-F4 and brings up a dialog box in your game asking if they want to quit, nothing is keeping them from hitting Alt-F4 again. If your players are like the folks at Microsoft's test labs they'll hit it about fifty times. Your game is still pumping messages, so the `WM_SYSCOMMAND` will get through every time a player hits Alt-F4. Make sure you handle that by filtering it out.

If your game is minimized you have to do something to catch the player's attention. If your game runs in full-screen mode and you've tabbed away to another app, your game will act just as if it is minimized. If your player uses the system menu, by right clicking on the game in the start bar, your game should exhibit standard windows behavior and flash. This is what well-behaved windows applications do when they are minimized but require some attention from a human being. Call the following function to flash your window until it is maximized:

```
// Wait for the application to be restored
// before going any further with the new
// screen.  Flash until the person selects
// that they want to restore the game.
void CMyApp::FlashWhileMinimized()
{
   // Flash the application on the taskbar
   // until it's restored.
   if ( ! m_pMainWnd )
      return;

   // Blink the application if we are minimized,
   // waiting until we are no longer minimized
   if ( m_pMainWnd->IsIconic() )
   {
      // Make sure the app is up when creating a new screen
```

```
      // Make sure the app is up when creating a new screen
      // this should be the case most of the time, but when
      // we close the app down, minimized, and a confirmation
      // dialog appears, we need to restore
      DWORD now = timeGetTime();
      DWORD then = now;
      MSG msg;

      m_pMainWnd->FlashWindow( true );

      for (;;)
      {
         if ( PeekMessage( &msg, NULL, 0, 0, PM_NOREMOVE ) )
         {
            // Bug with closing the game multiple times while minimized
            // Uncomment this to fix the problem
            if ( msg.message == WM_SYSCOMMAND && msg.wParam == SC_CLOSE )
            {
               // Swallow close messages
               // (we are already minimized and closing)
               GetMessage( &msg, NULL, 0, 0 );
            }
            else
            {
               // Default processing
               PumpMessage();
            }

            // Are we done?
            if ( ! m_pMainWnd->IsIconic() )
            {
               m_pMainWnd->FlashWindow( false );
               break;
            }
         }
         else
         {
            now = timeGetTime();
            if ( abs( now - then ) > 1000 )
            {
               then = now;
               m_pMainWnd->FlashWindow( true );
            }
         }
      }
   }
}
```

Shutting the Game Down

With some exceptions, you should shut down or deallocate game systems in the reverse order from which they were created. This is a good rule of thumb to use whenever you are grabbing and releasing multiple resources that depend on each other. Each data structure should be traversed and freed. Take care that any code that is run inside destructors has the resources it needs to properly execute. It's pretty easy to imagine a situation where the careless programmer has uninitialized something in the wrong order and a destructor somewhere fails catastrophically. Be extremely aware of your dependencies, and where multiple dependencies exist, lean on a reference counting mechanism to hold on to resources until they really aren't needed anymore.

After big systems shut down check the heap for corruption. ANSI C applications can do this with `_CrtCheckMemory`. Heap walkers are excellent for finding problems when memory is being released en masse. Close all your open files, release any system resources, and unload DLLs. Finally get rid of DirectX objects and restore the desktop to its natural state.

Can I Make a Game Yet?

By now you've learned a lot about some of the hidden superstructure of game code, most notably about `CProcess` and `CProcessManager`. You've probably figured out by now that most of the subsystems discussed so far can benefit from cooperative multitasking: animated objects, user interface code, and more. If you're like me you've already played with writing your own games, and your itching to put everything together in a tight little game engine. If you want to make a relatively small game, you've got everything you need right now. Get to it. The more ambitious programmer turned game designer should read on. The next chapter discusses how tiny games turn into mammoth worlds.

You probably never thought about how game engines stuff a few gigabytes of game art and sounds through a much smaller memory space. Read the next chapter and find out.

Chapter 8

Loading and Caching Game Resources

Once you get a nice bitmap or sound, how do you actually get it into your game? Most game books show code examples where the game loads BMP, WAV, or MP3 files directly. This doesn't work in real games. Real games have thousands of bitmaps, sounds, models, and other bits of data. They don't all fit into memory at the same time either. A DVD can store 4.7Gb and the last time I looked my PC had only a fraction of that amount of RAM. So how do developers really incorporate sounds and bitmaps into their games?

They convert them to the smallest possible useable format, and pack them all into a simple flat file, usually called a *resource file.* By the way, just in case I haven't mentioned it, I tend to use the terms *game assets* and *game resources* to mean the same thing—they are all game data. Art, sounds, AI, map levels, are all game assets.

Each game resource you use must be converted to the smallest possible format without compromising its quality. This is pretty easy for sounds, since you can easily predict the quality and size delta of a 44KHz stereo WAV versus an 11KHZ mono WAV stream. Bitmaps are trickier to work with, on the other hand, because the best storage format is completely dependent on its use in the game and what it looks like.

That's only the first part as you'll learn in this chapter. Since these resources are usually packed into a resource file or resource database, game companies usually write their own tools to create these files. You'll see an example of one I've used for the last few years, and while they aren't terribly complicated to write they always mirror the particular needs of your game.

Finally, a game has to have some internal mechanism to load desired resources. Depending on the game design it might also need a resource cache, a technology that can keep common resources resident in memory but also predict what resources are about to be needed by the game.

Art and Sound Formats

Left to their own devices, artists would hand you every sprite and texture they create in a TIF or TGA file. The uncompressed 32-bit art would look exactly like the artist envisioned. When you consider that a raw 32-bit 1024x768 bitmap tips the scales at just over 3Mb you'll quickly decide to use a more efficient format. The same is true for sound files and cinematics.

As always, you'll generally need to trade quality for size, and sometimes load time will need to be considered. The best games choose the right format and size for each asset. You'll be better at doing this if you understand how bitmaps, textures, and audio files are stored and processed, and what happens to them under different compression scenarios.

Bitmaps and Textures

Different bitmap formats allocate a certain number of bits for red, green, blue, and alpha channels. Some formats are indexed, meaning that the pixel data is actually an index into a color table that stores the actual RGBA values. Here's a list of the most common formats:

- *32-bit (8888 RGBA)*: The least compact way to store bitmaps, but retains the most information.
- *24-bit (888 RGB)*: This format is common for storing backgrounds that have too much color data to be represented in either 8-bit indexed or 16-bit formats, and no need for an alpha channel.
- *24-bit (565 RGB, 8 A)*: This format is great for making nice looking bitmaps with a good alpha channel.
- *16-bit (565 RGB)*: This compact format is used for storing bitmaps with more varieties of color and no alpha channel.
- *16-bit (555 RGB, 1 A)*: This compact format leaves one bit for translucency, which is essentially a chroma-key.
- *8-bit indexed*: A compact way to store bitmaps that have large areas of subtly shaded colors; some of the indexes can be reserved for different levels of translucency.

DirectX supports virtually any combination of pixel depth in each red, blue, green, and alpha channel. While it would be possible to store some oddball 24-bit format like 954 RGB and 6 bits for alpha, there's no art tool in the world that would let an artist look at that art and edit it.

If you write your game to make it difficult for artists to do their job, your game art will suck. Instead, spend some time to make your game use the same art formats used by popular art tools like Photoshop. Your game will look exactly the way the artists intended it to look. You'll also be able to find artists who can work on your game if you stick to the standard formats and tools.

Which Is Better: 24-, 16-, or 8-Bit Art?

It's virtually impossible to choose a single format to store every bitmap in your game and have all your bitmaps come through looking great. In fact, I can assure you that some of your bitmaps will end up looking like they should be in your laundry pile.

Figure 8.1 shows three different bitmaps that were created by drawing a grayscale image in Photoshop. The bitmap on the far left uses 256 colors. The center bitmap is stored using 32 different colors, while the one on the right is stored using 16 colors. If you attempt to store a subtly shaded image using too few colors you'll see results closer to the right bitmap, which looks crummy.

The image in the middle is analogous to a 16-bit image, in that these images have five or six bits to store their colors, and you'll likely see some banding. One the other hand, if you can use an 8-bit color range for each color channel, you'll see the best result, but you'll trade this quality for bigger art assets. Needless to say, if your artist storms into your office and wonders why her beautiful bitmaps are banded all to hell you've likely forced them into a bad color space.

Using Lossy Compression

A discussion of art storage wouldn't be complete without taking a look at the effects of using a lossy compression scheme, such as JPG. The compression algorithm tweaks some values in the original art to achieve a higher compression ratio, hence the term "lossy." It's not a mistake that if you spell-check the word lossy you get "lousy" as one of your choices. Beyond a certain threshold, the art degrades too much to get past your QA department, and it certainly won't get past the artist that spent so much time creating it.

Figure 8.1
Grayscale Banding Patterns for Different Bit Depths.

Perhaps the best approach is to get artists to decide how they'll save their own bitmaps, using the highest lossiness they can stand. It still won't be enough, I guarantee you, but it's a start.

Sound and Music

Sound formats in digital audio are commonly stored in either mono or stereo, sampled at different frequencies, and accurate to either 8 or 16 bits per sample. The effect of mono or stereo on the resulting playback and storage size is obvious: Stereo sound takes twice as much space to store but provides left and right channel waveforms. The different frequencies and bit depths have an interesting and quite drastic effect on the sound.

Digital audio is created by sampling a waveform and converting it into discrete 8- or 16-bit values that approximate the original waveform. This works because the human ear has a relatively narrow range of sensitivity: 20Hz to 20,000Hz. It's no surprise that the common frequencies for storing WAV files is 44KHz, 22KHz, and 11KHz.

It turns out that telephone conversations are 8 bit values sampled at 8Khz, after the original waveform has been filtered to remove frequencies higher than 3.4Mhz. Music on CDs is first filtered to remove sounds higher than 22Khz, and then sampled at 16-bit 44Khz. Just to summarize, Table 8.1 shows how you would use the different frequencies in digital audio.

Table 8.1 Using Different Audio Frequencies with Digital Formats.

Format	Quality	Size per Second	Size per Minute
44.1 KHz 16 bit stereo WAV	CD quality	172Kb / second	10Mb / minute
128 Kbps stereo MP3	Near CD quality	17Kb / second	1Mb / minute
22.05 KHz 16 bit stereo WAV	FM Radio	86Kb / second	5Mb / minute
64 Kbps stereo MP3	FM Radio	9Kb / second	540Kb / minute
11.025 KHz 16 bit mono WAV	AM Radio	43Kb / second	2.5Mb / minute
11.025 KHz 8 bit mono WAV	Telephone	21Kb / second	1.25Mb / minute

Use lower sampling rates for digital audio in your game to simulate telephone conversations or talking over shortwave radio.

Video and Cinematics

Animated sequences in games goes as far back as Pac Man, when after every few levels you'd see a little cartoon featuring the little yellow guy and his friends. The cartoons had little or nothing to do with the game; but they were fun to watch and gave players a reward. One of the first companies to use large amounts of video footage in games was Origin Systems in the Wing Commander series, and more than giving players a reward they actually told a story. Introductions, midgame, and endgame cinematics are not only common in today's games, they are expected.

There are two techniques worth considering for incorporating cinematic sequences. Some games like Wing Commander III will shoot live video segments and mix them into 3D rendered backgrounds using digital editing software like Adobe Premiere. The result is usually an enormous .AVI file that would fill up a good portion of your optical media. That file is usually compressed into something more usable by the game.

The second approach uses a game engine. For example, Grand Theft Auto: Vice City used the Renderware Engine from Criterion Studios to create all their sequences in 3D Studio Max or Maya and exported the animations. The animations can be played back by loading a tiny animation file and pumping the animations through the rendering engine. They only media you have to store beyond that is the sound. If you have tons of cinematic sequences, doing them *in-game* like this is the way to go.

The biggest difference your players will notice is the look of the cinematic. If a animation uses the engine your players won't be mentally pulled out of the game world. The in-game cut-scenes will also flow perfectly between the action and the narrative as compared to the pre-rendered cut-scenes which usually force some sort of slight delay and interruption as the game-engine switches back and forth between in-game action and retrieving the cut-scene from the disc or hard drive. As a technologist, the biggest difference you'll notice is the smaller resulting cinematic data files. The animation data is tiny compared to digital video.

Sometimes you'll want to show a cinematic that simply can't be rendered in real time by your graphics engine—perhaps something you need Maya to chew on for a few hours in a huge render farm. In that case you'll need to understand a little about streaming video and compression.

Streaming Video and Compression

Each video frame in your cinematic should pass through compression only once. Every compression pass will degrade the art quality. Prove this to yourself by compressing a piece of video two or three times and you'll see how bad it gets even with the second pass. If you can store your video completely uncompressed on a big RAID array on your network you'll also get a side benefit. Unless you have some hot video editing rig, it's really the only way you can manipulate your video frame-by-frame, or in groups of frames. Here are some settings I recommend:

- *Source Art and Sound*: Leave it uncompressed, 30fps; store art in TGAs or TIFs, and all audio tracks in 44KHz WAV.
- *Compression Settings*: Balance the tradeoff between data size and accuracy.

One drawback to storing video uncompressed is the size. A two-minute, 30fps video sequence at 800x600 resolution and 24-bit color will weigh in at just under 5Gb. You'll realize that simply moving the frames from one computer to another will be a royal pain in the ass.

If you need to move a large dataset like uncompressed video from one network to another, use a portable computer. It might make security conscious IT guys freak out, but it's a useful alternative if you don't already have a DAT drive or DVD burner around. This is modern day "Sneakernet."

Don't waste your time backing up uncompressed video files. Instead, make sure you have everything you need to recreate them such as a 3DStudio MAX scene file, or even raw video tape. Make sure the source is backed up, and the final compressed files are backed up.

Compression settings for streaming video can get complicated. Predicting how a setting will change the output is also tricky. Getting a grasp of how it works will help you understand which settings will work best for your footage. Video compression uses two main strategies to take a 5Gb two minute movie and boil it down into a 10Mb or so file. Just because the resolution drops doesn't mean you have to watch a postage stamp sized piece of video. Most playback APIs will allow a stretching parameter for the height, width, or both.

The first strategy for compressing video is to simply remove unneeded information by reducing the resolution or interlacing the video. Reducing resolution from 800x600 to 400x300 would shave 3Gb from a 4Gb movie, or 25% of the original size. An interlaced video alternates drawing the even and odd scanlines every other frame. This is exactly how television works; the electron gun completes a round trip from the top of the screen to the bottom and back at 60Hz, but it only draws every other scanline. The activated phosphors on the inside of the picture tube persist longer than 1/30th of a second after they've been hit with the electron gun, and can therefore be refreshed or changed at that rate without noticeable degradation in the picture. Interlacing the video will drop the dataset down to one-half of its original size. Using interlacing and resolution reduction can make a huge difference in your video size, even before the compression system kicks in.

Video compression can be lossless, but in practice you should always take advantage of the compression ratios even a small amount of lossiness can give you. If you're planning on streaming the video from optical media you'll probably be forced to accept some lossiness simply to get your peak and average data rates down low enough for your minimum specification CD-ROMs. In any case, you'll want to check the maximum bit-rate you can live with if the video stream is going to live on optical media. Most compression utilities give you the option of entering your maximum bit-rate. The resulting compression will attempt to satisfy your bit-rate limitations while keeping the resulting video as accurate to the original as possible. Table 8.2 shows the ideal bit rate that should be used for different CD-ROM and DVD speeds.

Table 8.2 Matching Bit Rates with CD-ROM/DVD Speeds.

Technology	Bit Rate
1x CD	150 Kbps
1x DVD	1,385 Kbps
32x CD	4,800 Kbps
16x DVD	2.21 Mbps

Resource Files

Many hard disks rotate as fast as 7200rpm. This means that on average, the processor must wait an average of 4ms for a desired piece of data to be located in the right position to be read, assuming the read/write head doesn't have to seek to a new track. For a modern day processor operating at 2GHz or more, this time is interminable. It's a good thing processors aren't conscious because they'd go mad waiting for hard disks all the time. Seeking time is much slower. The head must accelerate, move, stop, and become stable enough to accurately read the magnetic media. For a CPU, that wait is an eternity.

Optical media is even worse. Their physical organization is a continuous spiral from the inside of the disc to the outside, and the read laser must traverse this spiral at a constant linear velocity. This means that not only does the laser read head have to seek to an approximate location instead of an exact location, but the rotational velocity of the disc must change to the right speed before reading can begin. If the approximate location was wrong, the head will re-seek. All this mechanical movement makes optical media exceedingly slow. This is why Microsoft put a hard drive in the Xbox. If you really want to know why play Halo. Halo uses the hard drive to cache level files from the DVD-ROM enabling huge levels without any noticeable load time.

The only thing slower than reading data from a hard drive or optical media is to have an intern actually type the data in manually from the keyboard.

Needless to say you want to treat data in your files like I treat baubles in stores like Pier One. I do everything in my power to stay away from these establishments (my wife loves them) until I have a big list of things to buy. When I can't put it off any longer I make my shopping trip a surgical strike. I go in, get my stuff, and get out as fast as I can. When your game needs to grab data from the hard drive or DVD, it should follow the same philosophy.

The best solution would completely compartmentalize game assets into a single block of data that could be read in one operation with a minimum of movement of the read/write head. Everything needed for a screen or a level would be completely covered by this single read. This is usually impractical because some common data would have to be duplicated in each block. A fine compromise factors the common data in one block leaving and the data specific for each level or screen in their own blocks. When the game loads it is likely you'll notice two seeks—one for the common data block and one for the level specific block. You should make sure the common data stays in memory even if new levels are loaded.

Knowing how hardware works is critical to writing any kind of software. You don't have to be a guru writing device drivers to crack the books and learn exactly how everything works and how you can take advantage of it. This same lesson applies to the operating system and how the hardware APIs work under the hood. This knowledge separates armchair game programmers from professional game programmers.

Packaging Resources into a Single File

It's a serious mistake to store every game asset such as a bitmap or sound effect in their own file. You might want to do this to keep your game architecture open so that your players can add their own player skins, but separating thousands of assets in their own files wastes valuable storage space and makes it impossible to get your load times fast.

It turns out that hard drives are logically organized into blocks or clusters that have surprisingly large sizes. Most hard drives in the gigabit range have cluster sizes of 16Kb-32Kb. File systems like FAT32 and NTFS were written to store a maximum of one file per cluster to enable optimal storage of the directory structure. This means that if you had 500 sound effect files, each $^1/_2$ second long and recorded at 44KHz mono, you'd have 5.13Mb of wasted space on the hard disk:

```
0.5 seconds * 44KHz mono = 22,000 bytes
```

```
32,768 bytes minimum cluster size - 22,000 bytes in each file = 10,768 bytes
wasted per file
```

```
10,768 bytes wasted in each file * 500 files = 5.13Mb wasted space
```

You can easily get around this problem by packing your game assets into a single file. If you've ever played with DOOM level editors you're familiar with WAD files; they are a perfect example of this technique. These packed file formats are file systems in miniature, although most are read only. Ultima VIII and Ultima IX had a read/write version (FLX files) that had multiuser locking abilities for development. Almost every game on the market uses some custom packing scheme for more reasons than saving hard drive space.

Other Benefits of Packaging Resources

The biggest advantage of combining your resources by far is load time optimization. Opening files is an extremely slow operation on most operating systems, and Windows is no exception. At worst you'll incur the cost of an extra hard disk seek to read the directory structure to find the physical location of the file.

Another advantage is security. You can use a proprietary logical organization of the file that will hamper arm chair hackers from getting to your art and sounds. While this security is quite light and serious hackers will usually break it before the sun sets the first day your game is on the shelves, it's better than nothing.

Another advantage is managing production. You can track where the original assets are on your internal network and whether they've been locked down against changes. You can even track who was the last person to import them. Of course, you'll want to store this information in a separate file that doesn't ship with your product.

During development keep your ear tuned to the sounds your hard drive makes while you play your game. At worst you should hear a "tick" every few seconds or so as new data is cached in. This would be common in a game like Ultima IX, where the player could walk anywhere on an enormous outdoor map. At best your game will have a level design that grabs all the data in one read.

A great trick is to keep indexes or file headers in memory while the file is open. These are usually placed at the beginning of a file, and on large files the index might be a considerable physical distance away from your data. Read the index once and keep it around to save yourself that extra seek.

Data Compression

Compression is a double-edged sword. Every game scrambles to store as much content on the distribution media and the hard drive as possible. Compression can achieve some impressive space ratios for storing text, graphics, and sound at the cost of increasing the load on the CPU and your RAM budget to decompress everything. The actual compression ratios you'll get from using different utilities is completely dependant on the algorithm and the data to be compressed. Use algorithms like ZLIB or LZH for general compression that can't afford lossiness. Use JPG or MPEG compression for anything that can stand lossiness such as graphics and sound.

Consider the cost of decompressing MP3 files for music, speech, or sound effects. On the upper end, each stream of 128K stereo MP3 under the Miles Sound System from RAD Game Tools, Inc. will suck about 25Mhz from your CPU budget, depending on your processor. If you design your audio system to handle 16 simultaneous streams, a 2GHz desktop will only have 1.6GHz left, losing 400Mhz to decompressing audio.

You can always trade some loading time and system RAM for real time decompression. Instead of decoding MP3 streams in real time, decompress them into a WAV buffer (Miles Sound will let you do this) and keep it in memory. You can use this trick for almost any compressed data stream.

Decompression limits overall performance because of all the extra RAM it uses. The compressed data stream must be read into memory and decompressed in chunks into a temporary buffer, usually allocated by the decompressor. These decompressed blocks are usually copied into the destination buffer. Copying this data around takes time. On operating systems that use virtual memory, this copying can cause page faulting in virtual memory—a real nightmare.

Whether or not you'll use compression is not the question. Almost every game compresses some data to get the most out of permanent storage. Be careful about monitoring the costs of using compression in your data files; loading files can be choppy and decoding compressed streams of data in real time can use more CPU budget than you have to give.

If your decompressor API uses a callback it is quite likely that the decompression will forward Windows system messages into your message pump. This can create a real nightmare since mouse clicks or hotkeys can cause new art and sounds to be recursively sent into the decompression system. Callbacks are necessary for proving user feedback like a progress bar, but they can also play havoc with your message pump. If this is happening to your application, trap the offending messages and hold them in a temporary queue until the primary decompression is finished.

Zlib: Open Source Compression

If you need a lossless compression/decompression system for your game, don't look any further than Zlib which is found at **http://www.gzip.org/zlib/**. It's free, open source, legally unencumbered and simple to integrate into almost any platform. Typical compression ratios with Zlib are 2:1 to 5:1, depending on the data stream.

iPac: A Resource File Builder

The case for resource files is an easy one to make; but how do you go about building your own resource files? Every game company I know builds their own tools for this mundane job, but they all share similar features and even data file formats.

For the last few years, all the products I managed used a proprietary tool, iPac, to create and manage resource files. It stores graphics, sounds, and anything else the game needs in a single packed file. In practice the games use multiple iPac files to factor common game data from data that is only used when the game is in a certain state, like when particular game screens are up. Sometimes the best way to learn how to do something is by watching someone else. In this case, if you learn how the guts of iPac work you'll probably come up with some good ideas about your own resource file system.

Overview of iPac

iPac is an MDI MFC application complete with all the drag and drop features you'd expect. The look and feel is very similar to the Windows Explorer as shown in Figure 8.2. The tool's main audience is artists and designers who enjoy a familiar interface. Face it, if you make a strange command line tool that only programmers can understand, they are the only ones who will use it.

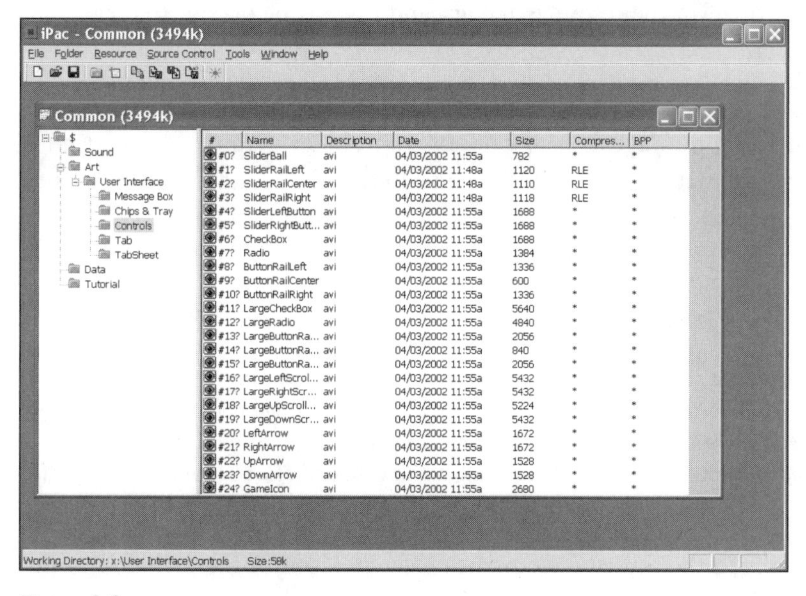

Figure 8.2
iPac Application Window.

If artists, sound engineers, and other folks outside of the programming team can use a simple tool to import their work into a game, the quality of their work will rise dramatically, and reduce the workload on the programmers. Imagine how tough it would be if programmers couldn't compile their own programs, and they needed someone else to put their code into the game.

The left pane shows the resource hierarchy, which generally maps one-to-one with the structure of the raw data files on our network. The right pane displays the list of resources in the left pane's selected folder. Unlike the Windows Explorer, iPac orders the contents of each folder and assigns each resource a number. This order dependant scheme can save programmers and the team plenty of time. If you sort animations and sounds with some rationale, the code doesn't have to use the identifier for each and every resource in the file. Imagine a resource folder that holds speech files of an actor counting from zero to one hundred; it would be much easier to access the right resource with an index from the resource "zero."

Each resource has a name and a description. The name is an identifier that is written to a C++ header file, so iPac checks it to make sure the name is a legal one. The description is hidden from the game API, and is a convenience for people building iPac files.

The date is the last date when the resource was imported. iPac is smart enough to detect when resources have changed—they are displayed in a different color. iPac can also lock out resources—a really important feature. As the development team locks down source code late in the development cycle the team should lock down the game data as well. A resource can be set to "final" in the resource dialogs, and it won't be overwritten even if the entire iPac file is refreshed.

The iPac file also monitors the size of each resource and the size of the entire file. It's very easy to let the size of a resource file grow out of control. For example, an artist might mistakenly add a 60fps animation when a 15fps one will do, or a sound engineer might import 44KHz stereo sound when 22KHz mono will work just fine. The size of the file is so important it's displayed in the window title bar.

Don't let developers get carried away. Huge resource files will fill up memory in a heartbeat and cause your game performance to plummet. If your game has to constantly hit the disk to swap resources the game will stutter, pause, and fail to run smoothly. Nothing will frustrate a player more than see a stuttering game on bleeding edge hardware. Make sure that custom tools or a DEBUG build of the game has a monitor that detects obese game data. It should send out some kind of annoying alarm or sound effect. Our game sent a message to `stderr` for any resource that takes longer than 50ms to load.

Each resource folder stored the source directory for the raw resource files, which is called the working directory. An example is shown in Figure 8.3.

Figure 8.3
Creating a Working Directory.

Folders within folders inherit the working directory by default and add their own name. This mechanism makes it easy to construct an arbitrary folder hierarchy that could mirror the folder hierarchy of the network or point to completely different areas.

Always use drive mappings to locate raw resource files on a network, and never store resources locally unless they are under source control. Network topologies change and servers get reassigned to other projects. For example, if every sound resource was mapped to \\Audio\Sfx and the server disappeared, someone would have a lot of work to do to reassign the working directory. If a raw resource is stored only on a developer's hard disk it can evaporate entirely.

iPac distinguishes graphics from other data. A single JPG or BMP file might contain a huge set of buttons or dialog edges. Bitmap sequences are cut from AVI files generated from hand drawn animations, flash animations, or pre-rendered 3D Studio Max files. Since the raw files can store multiple resources, iPac has to know about the boundaries of each resource and how many frames to assemble.

Any resource tool needs to be able to grab multiple resources from the same file. If the graphic has more than one frame, such as a button with rollover or disabled states, iPac has to know where the button art is located within the larger file. The Resource Properties dialog of a graphics element stores enough data to cut exactly the right pixels from a BMP or JPG, or a multiframe sequence from an AVI. Figure 8.4 shows an example of the Resource Properties dialog.

One of the important selections on the dialog is the compression type. Compressed resources take less space in the game file but they take longer to load. You must be able to choose whether the resource is compressed, and what type of compression algorithm you want to use.

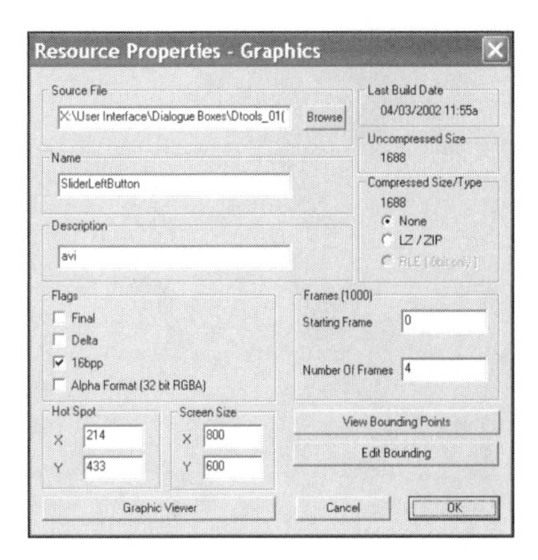

Figure 8.4
The Resource Properties Dialog.

The graphic viewer button on the lower left of the resource dialog launches a viewer window, with the raw resource file in view. The boundary of the desired graphic is outlined with a rectangle or polygon tool. It's a common practice for artists to create user interface components, like buttons and dialogs, in a single bitmap file, laid out in a regular grid. This allows them to make sure everything fits together with no visible seams. If there's animation, such as a button highlight, the art is stored in multiple frames of a single AVI. The animated button is "cut" out of the original animation with a rectangle tool. The resulting button animation contains the exact pixels necessary to draw the animating button.

iPac Data Files

iPac has two data files, one for development and one for the game. The game only needs enough data to locate and read resources. The iPac development file is actually a simple text file, and stores things the game doesn't need such as the source file, name, description, bounding points, and whether the resource has been marked final. A text file is a good format because it's easy to edit by hand or perform global search and replace operations.

The file that ships with the game is called a *PAD file*. It is a flat, indexed file with each index pointing to the bits of data contained in the file: sounds, art, map levels, whatever. Each indexed component may or may not be compressed. If disk space is critical you can trade some loading time by compressing the bits. It should always be possible for some bits to be compressed, and others to be stored in their raw form. In other words, it should be your choice. PAD files start with a short header as shown in Figure 8.5.

The header stores the size of the header and the version number of the file format. These help iPac determine what to do if it opens a file that is either newer or older than the version of the tool.

PAD File Header

int totalHeadingSize;	// Size of the heading area of this file
int padFileVersionNumber;	// Detect old file formats
int numberOfFolders;	// Holds the number of folders in the file
int folderOffsets[numberOfFolders];	// Stores the file offset for each folder definition

Figure 8.5
The PAD File Header.

Any internal tool should be able to detect legacy file formats and either convert them to the latest format or at least inform the user. A tool that doesn't detect file format changes can corrupt game files in development.

The number of folders and the folder offsets are stored next. The folder data is stored because a programmer might use the internal organization of the iPac file to their advantage. This is more flexible than storing the resources in a completely flat file.

Origin Systems used to use a game file format called FLX files, mostly on the last few Ultima games. FLX files were similar to a single folder of the PAD file format. Resources within FLX files were located using just the resource number. There's nothing wrong with this approach—it certainly worked on Ultima VIII and Ultima IX.

Assume for a moment that your game had twenty different characters, each of which had exactly the same kind of data. It might be convenient to store all of the character data in one file, each character organized into their own top level folder. As long as the contents of the folders were organized the same way, the code could access the character data with the folder number and a given resource such as AI with the resource number. Each folder has a short header that stores the number of resources it contains and offsets to the resource data as shown in Figure 8.6.

Since each folder knows how many resources it contains, the game can use that information to choose a random resource from a set. The Bicycle Casino project used this feature to store speech files. Each folder contained a number of MP3 data streams that said the same thing multiple ways. The game picked one of these MP3 streams at random and kept the speech from becoming monotonous.

The resource data included enough information to load resources based on their type and compression setting (see Figure 8.7). Compressed resources had a different actual size than their stored size, so the uncompressed size was stored rather than calculated.

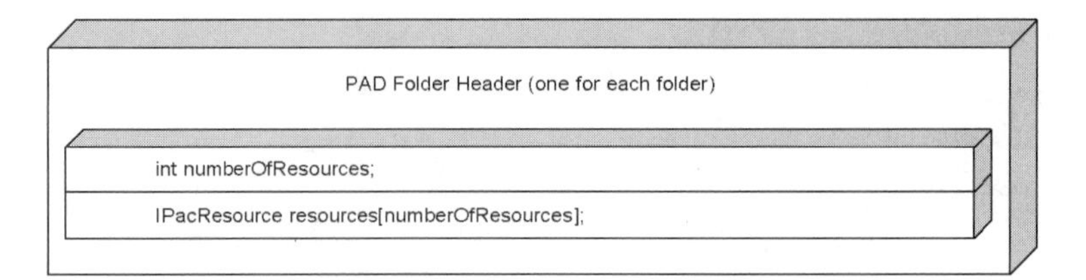

Figure 8.6
The PAD Folder Header.

IPacResource (one for each resource)

IPacResourceType resourceType;	// 0=Graphic, 1=Sound, 2=Misc
IPacCompressionType compressionType;	// 0=None, 1=LZ, 2=RLE
int uncompressedSize;	
int resourceSize;	// size of the resource in the file
int resourceOffset;	// file offset to the start of the data

Figure 8.7
The PAD Resource Header.

IPacGraphicResource (stored in the resource data)

int numberOfFrames;	// how many bitmaps are there
IPacPoint hotspot;	// the bitmap anchor point
IPacPoint screenSize;	// imported screen resolution
int numberOfPoints;	// points that define the bounding region
IPacPoint points[numberOfPoints];	// the bounding points
int frameOffsets[numberOfFrames];	// byte offset to each frame
char *framedata;	// frame bytes follow...

Figure 8.8
The PAD Graphic Source Header.

Graphic resources had an extra header before the data stream as shown in Figure 8.8.

Graphic resources can have multiple frames. Each frame is assumed to be the same size or shape and anchor at the same position from frame to frame. As long as you're not talking about 3D textures, 2D sprites can be any shape. In fact, most modern user interfaces are quite organic and there's rarely anything square about them.

The bits that make up the graphics data for each frame immediately follow the resource header.

Generated Header Files

A game's source code includes header files that iPac generates each time a new resource is created or the folder format changes. Each .PAD file has a companion .H file, which contains two enumerations:

```
//
// iPac generated header file
// C:\Projects\Casino_Publish\Jokerz\Bin\Data\GamePacs\Common.pac
//

#if !defined(IPAC_COMMON_H)
#define IPAC_COMMON_H

enum CommonFolders
{
   COMMON_FOLDER                                    = 1,
   COMMON_FOLDER_SOUND                              = 2,
   COMMON_FOLDER_ART                                = 3,
   COMMON_FOLDER_ART_USER_INTERFACE                 = 4,
   COMMON_FOLDER_ART_USER_INTERFACE_MESSAGE_BOX     = 5,
};

enum CommonResources
{
   COMMON_LISTSTART                                 = 0,
   COMMON_LISTCOUNT                                 = 0,

   COMMON_SOUND_LISTSTART                           = 0,
   COMMON_SOUND_BUTTONPUSHED                        = 0,
   COMMON_SOUND_LISTCOUNT                           = 1,

   COMMON_ART_LISTSTART                             = 0,
   COMMON_ART_LISTCOUNT                             = 0,

   COMMON_ART_USER_INTERFACE_LISTSTART              = 0,
   COMMON_ART_USER_INTERFACE_SPOT                   = 0,
   COMMON_ART_USER_INTERFACE_LISTCOUNT              = 1,

   COMMON_ART_USER_INTERFACE_MESSAGE_BOX_LISTSTART = 0,
   COMMON_ART_USER_INTERFACE_MESSAGE_BOX_TL         = 0,
   COMMON_ART_USER_INTERFACE_MESSAGE_BOX_TL2        = 1,
   COMMON_ART_USER_INTERFACE_MESSAGE_BOX_TC         = 2,
```

8

```
    COMMON_ART_USER_INTERFACE_MESSAGE_BOX_TC2       = 3,
    COMMON_ART_USER_INTERFACE_MESSAGE_BOX_LISTCOUNT = 4,
};
#endif //IPAC_COMMON_H
```

The names are concatenations of the various resource and folder names. This is important because name collisions between two similar folders or resources will keep a game from compiling.

If you write a tool that generates header files of any kind (especially for resources), make sure the tool updates the header file only when it absolutely must. Earlier versions of iPac wrote the header file out every time an iPac file was opened, even if no changes were made to the file. This caused much recompiling and gnashing of teeth.

Every resource in a game is uniquely identified by the iPac file name, the folder number, and the resource number as shown here:

```
IPacResource buttonPushed =
IPacResource(_T("common.pad"),                    // iPac file name
                    COMMON_FOLDER_SOUND,          // iPac folder
                    COMMON_SOUND_BUTTONPUSHED);   // iPac resource
```

Other Features for Managing Resources

There are a couple of other important features any resource builder needs:

- *Command line interface*: All the major features should be exposed via the command line, so that build tools or batch files can change the resource files.
- *Resource finalization*: Each resource can be locked from further changes. When a game goes into final lockdown, this will keep unwanted resource changes out of the game.
- *Checking/viewing resources*: If there's a bad or corrupted resource in the file it can be impossible to find manually. If each resource can be automatically checked it will save a lot of debugging time.
- *Resource extraction*: Some publishers, like Microsoft, require all compressed or concatenated files to be extracted in full so they can be scanned for viruses or unwanted content. Make sure your resources can be dumped, preferably into standard file formats for graphics or sound data.

The Resource Cache

Resource files need a resource cache. If your game has a tiny set of graphics and sounds small enough to exist completely in memory for the life of your game, you don't need a cache. It's still a good idea to use resource files to pack everything into one file; you'll save disk space and speed up your game's load time.

Most games are bigger. If your game is going to ship on a DVD you'll have almost five gigabytes to play around in, and I doubt your minimum RAM specification will require 5Gb. What you'll need is a resource cache—a piece of technology that will sit on top of your resource files and manage the memory and the process of loading resources when you need them. Even better, a resource cache should be able to predict resource requirements before you need them.

Resource caches work on similar principles as any other memory cache. Most of the bits you'll need to display the next frame or play the next set of sounds are probably ones you've used recently. As the game progresses from one state to the next, new resources are cached in. They might be needed, for example, to play sound effects for the first time. Since memory isn't available in infinite quantities, eventually your game will run out of memory, and you'll have to throw something out of the cache.

Caches have two degenerate cases: cache misses and thrashing. A cache miss occurs when a game asks for the data associated with a resource and it isn't there—the game has to wait while the hard drive or the CD-ROM wakes up and reads the data. A cache miss is bad, but thrashing is fatal.

Cache thrashing occurs when your game consistently needs more resource data than can fit in the available memory space. The cache is forced to throw out resources that are still frequently referenced by the game. The disk drives spin up and run constantly and your game goes into semi-permanent hibernation.

The only way to avoid thrashing is to decrease the memory needed or increase the memory requirements. It's rare that you'll get the go ahead to increase the memory requirements, so you're left with slimming down the game data. You'll probably have to use smaller textures, fewer sounds, or decrease the object or map density of your game to fix things.

Most of the interesting work in resource cache systems involve predictive analysis of your game data in an attempt to avoid cache misses. There are some tricks to reduce this problem, some of which reach into your level design by adding pinch points such as doors, elevators, or barren hallways. Some games with open maps, like flight simulators, can't do this. They have to work a lot harder. I'll show you a very simple resource cache so you can get your bearings. Then, I'll discuss why this problem generally gets its own programmer–and a good one.

For the sake of simplicity, I'm going to assume that the cache only handles one resource file. It's easy enough to make the modifications to track resources across multiple files. You'd need to attach a file identifier of some sort to each resource to track which resources came from which file. There's no need to create a monolithic file that holds all the game assets. You should just break them up into manageable chunks.

Resources might not exist in memory if they've never been loaded or if they've been thrown out to make room for other resources. You need a way to reference them whether they are loaded or not. You need a mechanism to uniquely identify each resource. A resource identifier for an iPac resource looks like this:

```
struct IPacResource
{
   union
   {
      struct
      {
         short int m_folder;
         short int m_resource;
      };
      int m_id;
   };

   IPacResource(int f=0, int r=0) { m_folder=f;  m_resource=r; }
};
```

For any resource in an iPac file, it is uniquely identified by combining the folder number and resource number into a single integer. Since iPac generates header files with enumerations for the folders and resources, you include the generated header file and declare a resource like this:

```
#include "art.h"                    // This header is generated by iPac
IPacResource r(ART_FOLDER, ART_PHOTOSHOP_32);
```

A resource cache takes valid identifiers and returns pointers to the loaded resource. The top level API, `Get()`, usually returns a `(void *)`, since the cache can hold anything:

```
char *data =
   (char *)cache.Get(IPacResource(ART_FOLDER, ART_PHOTOSHOP_32));
```

In a resource cache that manages multiple files, you would add a file identifier to the `IPacResource` structure. For speed use an integer that references an array of open resource files.

For the cache to do its work, it must keep track of all the loaded resources. A useful class, `ResHandle`, encapsulates the resource identifier with the resource data:

```
class ResHandle
{
   friend class ResCache;                    // You'll see this in a minute

protected:
   IPacResource m_resource;
   char *m_buffer;
   unsigned int m_size;

public:
   ResHandle(const IPacResource & resource, int size, char *buffer);
   ~ResHandle();
};

ResHandle::ResHandle(const IPacResource & resource, int size, char *buffer)
{
   m_resource = resource;
   m_size = size;
   m_buffer = buffer;
}

ResHandle::~ResHandle()
{
   if (m_buffer) delete [] m_buffer;
}
```

The `ResHandle` also tracks the size of the memory block. When the cache loads a resource it dynamically creates a `ResHandle`, allocates a buffer of the right size, and reads the resource from the resource file. The `ResHandle` class exists in memory as long as the resource caches it in.

A pointer to the `ResHandle` is inserted into two data structures. The first, a linked list, is managed such that the nodes appear in the order in which the resource was last used. Every time a resource is queried from the cache with `Get()`, the node in the least recently used list is removed from its current position and reinserted at the head of the list.

The second data structure, and STL map, provides a way to quickly find resource data with the unique resource identifier:

```
typedef std::list<ResHandle *> ResHandleList;     // lru list
typedef std::map<int, ResHandle *> ResHandleMap;  // maps identifiers to data
```

Since most of the players are already on the stage, it's time to bring out the ResCache class, an ultra simple resource cache:

```
class ResCache
{
   ResHandleList m_lru;
   ResHandleMap m_resources;

   IPacGameInterface *m_file;        // The resource file interface

   unsigned int      m_cacheSize;   // total memory size
   unsigned int      m_allocated;   // total memory allocated

protected:

   char *Allocate(unsigned int size);

   void *Load(const IPacResource & r);
   ResHandle *Find(const IPacResource & r);

   void Free(void);
   void *Update(ResHandle *handle);

public:
   ResCache(const unsigned int sizeInMb, const _TCHAR *iPacFile);
   ~ResCache();

   void *Get(const IPacResource & r);
};
```

The first two members of the class have already been introduced; they are the LRU list and the STL map.

The `IPacGameInterface` class is an interface to the resource file, the nature of which is completely dependant on your game's data files. As far as `ResCache` is concerned, it only needs a few member functions:

```
class IPacGameInterface
{
   // opens and closes the resource file
   IPacGameInterface(const _TCHAR *iPacFile);
   ~IPacGameInterface();
   // finds the uncompressed resource size
   int GetResourceSize(int folder, int resource);

   // loads the resource into a pre-allocated buffer
   int GetResource(int folder, int resource, char *buffer);
};
```

Since the resource file is specific to each game, I won't waste time going over the details of writing code to make it work. I'm sure you can do that yourself. Let's concentrate on the guts of `ResCache`, starting with `ResCache::Get()` and working through the protected member functions:

```
void *ResCache::Get(const IPacResource & r)
{
   ResHandle *handle = Find(r);
   return (handle!=NULL) ? Update(handle) : Load(r);
}
```

`ResCache::Get()` is brain-dead simple: If the resource is already loaded in the cache, update it. If it's not there, you have to take a cache miss and load the resource from the file.

Finding, updating, and loading resources is easy. `ResCache::Find()` uses an STL map, `m_resources`, to locate the right `ResHandle` given a `IPacResource`. `ResCache::Update()` removes a `ResHandle` from the LRU list and promotes it to the front making sure that the LRU is always sorted properly. `ResCache::Load()` grabs the size of the resource from the file, allocates space in the cache, plugs the new resource into the cache, and reads the resource from the file:

```
ResHandle *ResCache::Find(const IPacResource & r)
{
   ResHandleMap::iterator i = m_resources.find(r.m_id);
   if (i==m_resources.end())
      return NULL;

   return (*i).second;
}

void *ResCache::Update(ResHandle *handle)
```

```
{
   m_lru.remove(handle);                    // REALLY REALLY SLOW!!!!
   m_lru.push_front(handle);

   return handle->m_buffer;
}

void * ResCache::Load(const IPacResource & r)
{
   // find the resource size
   int size = m_file->GetResourceSize(r.m_folder, r.m_resource);
   char *buffer = Allocate(size);
   if (buffer==NULL)
   {
      return NULL;           // ResCache is out of memory!
   }

   // Create a new resource and add it to the lru list and map
   ResHandle *handle = new ResHandle(r, size, buffer);

   // Add the new handle to the STL data structures
   m_lru.push_front(handle);
   m_resources[r.m_id] = handle;

   // read the resource from the file
   m_file->GetResource(r.m_folder, r.m_resource, buffer);
   return buffer;
}
```

The implementation of the LRU list as a naked STL list is a horrible choice, by the way. The call to `m_lru.remove()` in `Update()` has linear complexity, which is an ivy league way of saying that the more resources that exist in the list, the longer it will take to remove the `ResHandle`.

I considered a better method, but it bloated the example somewhat and made it harder to understand. I figured it would be just as good to leave the heinous abuse of `STL <list>` in there as an example to you all that abusing STL isn't a good idea!

Enough kid stuff. Here's `ResCache::Allocate()` and `ResCache::Free()`:

```
char *ResCache::Allocate(unsigned int size)
{
   if (size > m_cacheSize)
   {
```

```
        return(NULL);
    }
    // return null if there's no possible way to allocate the memory
    while (size > (m_cacheSize - m_allocated))
    {
        // The cache is empty, and there's still not enough room.
        if (m_lru.empty())
            return NULL;

        Free();
    }

    char *mem = new char[size];
    if (mem)
    {
        m_allocated += size;
    }

    return mem;
}


void ResCache::Free()
{
    // find the oldest resource
    ResHandleList::iterator gonner = m_lru.end();
    gonner--;

    ResHandle *handle = *gonner;

    // remove the ResHandle from the LRU list and the map
    m_lru.pop_back();
    m_resources.erase(handle->m_resource.m_id);

    // update the cache size
    m_allocated -= handle->m_size;

    // delete the resource
    delete handle;
}
```

After the initial sanity check, the while loop performs the work of removing enough resources from the cache to load the new resource. If there's already enough room, the loop is skipped.

ResCache::Free() removes the oldest resource and updates the cache data members. The only thing you haven't seen you could write yourself, but I'll be nice and give you the constructor and destructor:

```
ResCache::ResCache(const unsigned int sizeInMb, const _TCHAR *iPacFile )
{
   m_cacheSize = sizeInMb * 1024 * 1024;          // total memory size
   m_allocated = 0;

   m_file = new IPacGameInterface(iPacFile, true);
}


ResCache::~ResCache()
{
   while (!m_lru.empty())
   {
      Free();
   }
   delete m_file;
}
```

Once you replace IPacGameInterface and IPacResource with the analogs to your game's data files you've got a simple resource cache. If you want to use this in a real game, you've got more work to do.

First of all, there's hardly a line of defensive or debugging code in ResCache. Resource caches are a significant source of bugs and other mayhem. Data corruption from buggy cache code or something else trashing the cache internals will cause your game to simply freak out.

A functional cache will need to be aware of more than one resource file. It's not reasonable to assume that a game can stuff every resource into a single file, especially since it makes it impossible for teams to work on different parts of the game simultaneously. Associate a file name or number with each resource, and store an array of open resource files in ResCache.

Consider implementing your own memory allocator. Many resource caches allocate one contiguous block of memory when they initialize, and manage the block internally. Some even have garbage collection, where the resources are moved around as the internal block becomes fragmented. A garbage collection scheme is an interesting problem, but it is extremely difficult to implement a good one that doesn't make the game stutter. Ultima VIII used this scheme.

That brings us to the idea of making the cache multithread compliant. Why not have the cache defrag itself if there's some extra time in the main loop, or perhaps allow a reader in a different thread to fill the cache with resources that might be used in the near future? This is a likely solution for games with an open map, and the game will constantly cache new resources in and out of the game. Games that use closed maps or pinch points may get away with a single threaded version.

It's also not unusual to use separate resource caches for different resources such as textures, objects, and sounds. This is especially true for textures, since they can exist in two different kinds of memory: video memory or system memory. A good texture cache needs to take that into account.

World Design and Cache Prediction

Perhaps you've just finished a supercharged version of `ResCache`—good for you. You're not done yet. If you load resources the moment you need them, you'll probably suffer a wildly fluctuating frame rate. The moment your game asks for resources outside of the cache, the flickering hard disk light will be the most exciting thing your players will be able to watch.

First, classify your game design into one of the following categories:

- *Load Everything at Once*: This is for any game that caches resources on a screen-by-screen basis or level-by-level. Each screen of Myst is a good example, as well as Grim Fandango. Most fighting and racing games work under this model for each event.
- *Load Only at Pinch Points*: Almost every shooter utilizes this design, where resources are cached in during elevator rides or in small barren hallways.
- *Load Constantly*: This is for open map games where the player can go anywhere they like. Examples include flight simulators, massively multiplayer games, and action/adventure games like Grand Theft Auto: Vice City.

The first scheme trades one huge loading pause for lightning fast action during the game. These games have small levels or arenas that can fit entirely in memory. Thus, there's never a cache miss. The game designers can count on every CPU cycle spent on the game world instead of loading resources. The downside is since your entire playing area has to fit entirely in memory, it can't be that big.

Shooters like Halo on the Xbox load resources at pinch points. The designers add buffer zones between the action where relatively little is happening in the game. Elevators are perfect examples of this technique. The CPU spends almost no time rendering the tiny environment inside the elevator, and uses the left over cycles to load the next hot zone. The player can't change his or her mind in the middle of the trip until the elevator gets to the right floor.

These buffer zones will exist in many places throughout the game, providing the player with a brief moment to load weapons and rest happy trigger fingers. The designers at Bungie took advantage of this and placed a few surprise encounters in these buffer zones, something that always made me freak out when I was playing Halo.

Hallways are another good example of buffer zones. If you ever wondered why the Master Chief in Halo spends a lot of time in abandoned hallways it's because the Xbox is busy loading the next section of the map. The bigger the map, the longer the hallway. It's a great design conceit because the player is moving, making it feel like the action is still there. Even better, the folks at Bungie were wise enough to use the hallways to set the tone for the next fight with Covenant forces or The Flood—sometimes it was as simple as painting the walls with enemy blood or playing some gruesome sound effects.

Don't make the player read a bunch of text in between levels just to give yourself time to cache resources. Players figure this out right away, and want to click past the text they've read five or six times. They won't be able to since you've got to spend a few more seconds loading resources and they'll click like mad and curse your name. If you're lucky, the worst thing they'll do is return your game. Don't open any suspicious packages you get sent in the mail.

Open mapped games such as flight simulators, fantasy role playing games, or action/ adventure games have a much tougher problem. The maps are huge, relatively open, and the game designers have little or no control over where the player will go next. Players also expect an incredible level of detail in these games. They want to read the headlines in newspapers or see individual leaves on the trees, while tall buildings across the river are in plain view. Players like that alternate reality. One of the best games that uses this open world design is Grand Theft Auto: Vice City.

Of these kinds of games, the third person over-the-shoulder camera like you see in Ultima or Diablo is the easiest to handle. The viewable area may be small, but very densely populated with detail.

Ultima VII used a simple approach. The main map was broken into segments approximately 16 meters square as shown in Figure 8.9.

Enough area was cached in to keep the game rendering smoothly. When the player walks across the map, the areas behind the player are cached out to make room for new areas in the direction of travel. Every time the player walked across a map boundary, the game froze for half a second. This pause wasn't a fatal flaw by any means, since the year was

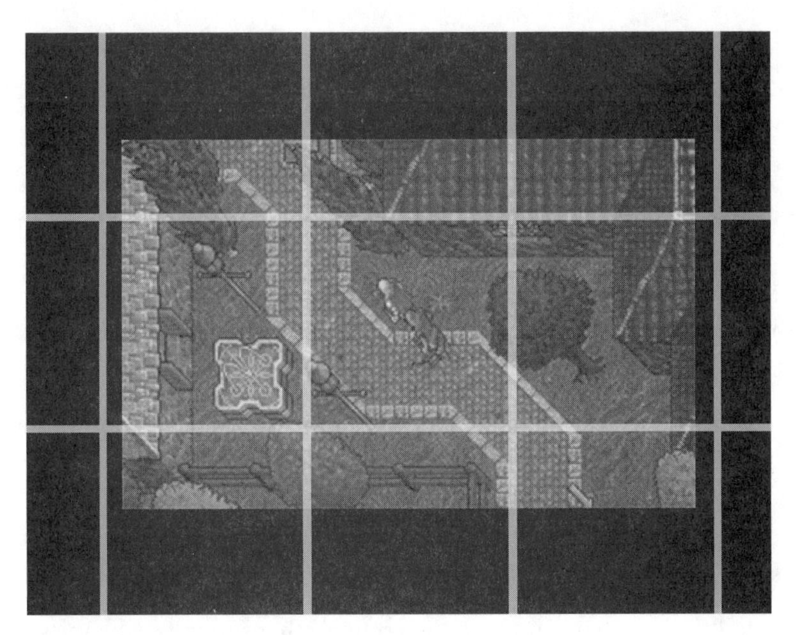

Figure 8.9
Ultima VII's Main Map.

1992, and players were willing to accept a little frame stutter in exchange for the densely populated world. Solving the frame stutter would have been non-trivial in Ultima VII's single threaded environment.

Modern operating systems have more options for multithreading, especially for caching in game areas while the CPU has some extra time. Use the players direction of travel to predict the most likely areas that will be needed shortly, and add those resources to a list that is loaded on an ad hoc basis as the cache gets some time to extra work. This is especially beneficial if the game designers can give the cache some hints, such as the destination of a path or the existence of a mountain pass, if it is clear that the player is likely heading in a predictable direction. These map elements almost serve as pinch points like the hallways in Halo, although players can always turn around and go the other direction.

Create your cache to load multiple resources at one time, and sort your cache reads in the order in which they appear in the file. This will minimize any seeking activity on the part of the drive's read head. If you're resource file is organized properly, the most used resources will appear close together at the beginning of the file. It will then be probable that resource loads will be accomplished in a single read block with as few seeks as possible.

If you want to find out which resources are used most frequently, you should *instrument your build*. That's a complicated way of saying you'll create a debug build with special code that creates a log file every time a resource is used. Use this log as a secondary data file to your resource file packing tool. The most used resources should sort to the beginning of the file, and attempt to exist as a contiguous block.

The maximum map density should always leave a little CPU time to perform some cache chores in open map game designs. Denser areas will spend most of their CPU time on game tasks for rendering, sound, and AI. Sparse areas will spend more time preparing the cache for denser areas about to reach the display. The trick is to balance these areas carefully, guiding the player through pinch points where it's possible, and never overloading the cache.

If the CPU can't keep up with cache requests and other game tasks, you'll probably suffer a cache miss and risk the player detecting a pause in the game. Not all is lost, however, since a cache miss is a good opportunity to catch up on the entire list of resources that will be needed all at once. This should be considered a worst case scenario—because if your game does this all the time it will frustrate players.

A better solution is a fallback mechanism for some resources that suffer a cache miss. Flight simulators and other open architecture games can sometimes get away with keeping the uncached resource hidden until the cache can load it. Imagine a flight simulator game that caches in architecture as the plane gets close. If the game attempts to draw a building that hasn't been cached in then the building simply won't show up. Think for a moment what is more important to the player: a piece of architecture that will likely show up in 100ms or so anyway, or a frustrating pause in the action.

It's a good idea to associate a priority with each resource. Some resources are so important to the game that it must suffer a cache miss rather than fail to render it. This is critical for sound effects, which must sometimes be timed exactly with visual events such as explosions.

The really tough open map problems are those games that add level of detail on top of an open map design. This approach is common with flight simulators and action adventure games. Each map segment has multiple levels of detail for static and dynamic objects. It's not a horrible problem to figure out how to create different levels of detail for each segment. The problem is how to switch from one level of detail to another without the player noticing. This is much easier in action/adventure games where the player is on the ground and most objects are obscured from view when they flip to a new level of detail.

Flight simulators don't have that luxury. Of all the games on the market, flight simulators spend more time on caching continuous levels of detail than any other non-rendering task. Players want the experience of flying high enough to see the mountains on the horizon and diving low enough to see individual trees and ground clutter whiz by at Mach 1.

This subject is way beyond the scope of this book, but I won't leave you hanging. There is some amazing work done in this area, not the least of which was published in *Level of Detail for 3D Graphics* by D. Luebke, M. Reddy, J. Cohen, A. Varshney, B. Watson, and R. Huebner. They also have a web site at: **http://lodbook.com/**.

I'm Out of Cache

Smart game programmers realize early on that some problems are harder than others. If you thought that creating a good flight simulator was a piece of cake, I'd tell you that the part that's a bitch isn't simulating the airplane, but simulating the ground. The newbie game programmer could spend all his time creating a great flight model, and when he started the enormous task of representing undulating terrain with smooth detail levels he would fold like laundry.

Games need enormous amounts of data to suspend disbelief on the part of players. No one, not even Rockstar Games, can set their system RAM requirements to hold the entire contents of even one disk of current day optical media. It's also not enough to simply assume that a game will load resources as needed, and the game designers can do what they want. That is a tragic road traveled by many games that never shipped. Most games that suffer fatal frame rate issues ignored their cache constraints.

It's up to programmers to code the best cache they can, and figure out a way to get game level designers, artists, and sound engineers to plan the density of game areas carefully. If everyone succeeds in their task, you get a smooth game that plays well. If you succeed brilliantly you'll get a game that even predicts the future.

Chapter 9

3D Graphics All Game Programmers Must Master

I want to tell you up front that this chapter won't teach you everything you need to know about 3D graphics—actually far from it. Walk the aisle of any decent computer bookstore and you'll see racks of books devoted entirely to 3D graphics. I'm only including two 3D chapters in this book so I can't compete with the classics on 3D graphics. What's lacking in volume I'll try to make up in focus and content. My job in the next two chapters is to open the door to 3D graphics, especially in the way game programmers utilize 3D techniques. Once inside, I'll hand you a map of the place and send you on your way. I hope you are wearing comfortable shoes because we have a lot of ground to cover.
In this chapter I'll focus on the essentials, which is a nice way of saying that I'm going to load you down with some math you'll need to know. This will set the foundation so that we can start manipulating objects and perform some of the fun stuff I have planned for later in this chapter and Chapter 10.

3D Graphics Pipeline

The word *pipeline* describes the process of getting a 3D scene up on a screen. It's a great word because it implies a beginning that accepts raw materials, a process that occurs along the way, and a conclusion from which pours the refined result. This is almost exactly what happens inside 3D game engines. The raw materials at the beginning include collections of the following components:

- *Geometry*: Everything you see on the screen starts with descriptions of their shape. Each shape is broken down into triangles, which is a basic drawable element in 3D engines. Meshes and polygons are different types of geometry.
- *Materials*: These elements describe appearance. You can imagine materials as paint or wallpaper that you apply to the geometry. Each material can describe colors, translucency, and how the material reflects light.
- *Textures*: These are images that can be applied to objects, just as you might have applied decals to plastic models.

- *Lights*: You must have light to see anything. Light can affect an entire scene or have a local effect that mimics a spotlight.
- *Camera*: Records the scene onto a render target such as the display. It even describes what kind of lens is used, such as a wide or narrow angle lens. You can have multiple cameras to split the screen for a multiplayer game or render a different view to create a rear view mirror.
- *World*: A data structure that organizes the raw materials so that a minimum set of the above collections can be presented to the rendering hardware. These data structures also relate objects hierarchically to create complicated shapes such as human figures.

Some of the processes applied to the raw materials include:

- *Transformations*: The same object can appear in the world in different orientations and locations. Objects are manipulated in 3D space via matrix multiplications.
- *Culling*: A list of objects is selected based on their visibility.
- *Lighting*: Each object in range of a light source is illuminated by calculating additional colors applied to each vertex.
- *Rasterization:* Polygons are drawn.

We'll start to see how all of these components and processes act together shortly. I'm going to take a quick shortcut through two math classes you probably slept though in high school or college. I know that because I slept through the same classes—trigonometry and linear algebra.

Your DirectX 9 Playground

There's a useful feature added to Visual Studio.NET supplied by the DirectX 9 SDK: The DirectX 9 Visual C++ Wizard. It creates a framework for building DirectX 9 projects. As you read this chapter and the next one, you can cut and paste the code examples into your playground project and see how they work for yourself. To create the playground project, follow these steps:

- Open Visual Studio.NET and select File, New Project.
- Select Visual C++ Projects in the left pane listing project types.
- Find DirectX 9 Visual C++ Project Wizard and select it.
- Choose a good name and location for your new project, and hit the OK button.

- Clear the DirectInput support if you want to grab WM_CHAR messages—that's an easy place to install bits of test code. Otherwise, you'll need to learn a little DirectInput, and then you'll be on your own!
- Hit Finish and create your project.

If you choose "Playground" as the name of your project you'll find the main entry point in Playground.cpp, which is where you'll plug in most of your test code.

3D Math 101

I'll try my best to make this topic interesting. I'll know I've succeeded if I get through writing it without losing consciousness. This stuff can make your eyes glaze over. Remember one thing: You must understand the math or you'll be hopelessly confused if you attempt any 3D programming. Sure, you'll be able to compile a DirectX sample program, tweak some parameters, and make some pretty pictures. Once you leave "Sampleland" and start writing your own 3D code, however, you won't have a freaking clue why your screen is black and none of the pretty pictures show up. You'll attempt to fix the problem with random tweaks of various numbers in your code, mostly by adding and removing minus signs, and you'll end up with the same black screen and a mountain of frustration.

My advice is to start small. Make sure you understand each component fully, and move to the next. Have patience, and you'll never tweak a negative sign in anger again.

3D programming is easier to get wrong than right, and the difficult part is that a completely miscoded system can look and feel correct. There will be a point where things will begin to break down, but by that time you might have hundreds or thousands of lines of bogus code. If something is wrong, and you randomly apply a negative sign to something to fix it, and don't understand why it fixed it, you should back up and review the math.

Coordinates and Coordinate Systems

In a 2D graphics system you express pixel coordinates with two numbers: (x,y). These are screen coordinates to indicate that each integer number *x* and *y* corresponds to a row and column of pixels, respectively. Taken together as a pair, they describe the screen location of exactly one pixel. If you want to describe a 2D coordinate system fully, you need a little more data, such as where (0,0) is on the screen, whether the x coordinate describes rows or columns, and in which direction the coordinates grow—to the left or right. Those choices are made somewhat arbitrarily. There's nothing that says we couldn't create a 2D graphics engine that used the lower right-hand corner of the screen as our (0,0) point—our origin. There's nothing that would keep us from describing the x-axis as vertical and y as horizontal, and both coordinates grow positive toward the upper left-hand side of the screen.

Nothing would keep us from doing this, except perhaps the risk of industry-wide embarrassment. I said that these choices of coordinate system are somewhat arbitrary, but they do have a basis in tradition or programming convenience. Here's an example: Since the display memory is organized in row order it makes sense to locate the origin at the top left-hand side of the screen. Traditional Cartesian mathematics sets the horizontal as the X-axis and the vertical as the Y-axis, which means that programmers can relate to the graphics coordinates with ease. If these were reversed, programmers would be constantly slapping their foreheads and saying, "oh yeah, those idiots made the X-axis vertical!"

A 3D world requires a 3D coordinate system. Each coordinate is expressed as a triplet: (x,y,z). This describes a position in a three dimensional universe. As you might expect, a location on any of the three axes is described with a floating-point number. The range that can be expressed in a 32-bit floating-point number in IEEE format is $\pm \sim 10^{-44.85}$ to $\sim 10^{38.53}$. The diameter of the known universe is on the order of 10^{26} meters. The smallest theoretical structures of the universe, *superstrings*, have an estimated length of 10^{-35} meters. You might believe that a 32-bit floating-point number is more than sufficient to create a 3D simulation of everything in our universe, but you'd be wrong, because even though the range is up to the task the precision is not. Oddly enough, we may one day find out that the universe is best expressed in terms of 256-bit integers, which would give enough range and precision to represent a number from 0 to $\sim 10^{76}$, plenty to represent the known universe, ignoring irrational or transcendental numbers like π.

So where does that leave you and your 32-bit IEEE floating-point number with its decent range and lacking precision? The IEEE format stores an effective 24 bits of resolution in the mastissa. This gives you a range of 1.67×10^7. How much is that? As Table 9.1 indicates, you should set your smallest unit based on your game design. Most games can safely use the 100 micrometer basis since your sandbox can be as big as downtown San Francisco. The human eye can barely detect objects 100 micrometers across, but can't discern any detail.

This is why most games set their basic unit of measurement as the meter, and constrain the precision to 1mm and set their maximum range to 100 kilometers. Most art packages like 3D Studio Max allow artists to set their basic unit of measurement. If you use such a package you need to make sure they set it to the right value for your game.

A common source of problems in computer game development is when artists can't seem to get their units of measurement correct. Either they'll create models with different units of measurement, such as feet instead of meters. One clue: If things in your game appear either three times too big or three times too small, your artist is using the wrong unit of measurement.

Table 9.1 Guidelines for Setting Coordinate Units.

Smallest Unit	Physical Description of Smallest Representable Object (as a Textured Polygon)	Upper Range In Meters	Physical Description of Area in the Upper Range
100m	A group of redwood trees.	1.67×10^9	Earth/Moon System
1m	A human being	1.67×10^7	North and South America
1cm	A coin	1.67×10^6	California
1mm	A flea	1.67×10^5	San Francisco Bay Area
100 μm	A grain of pollen	1.67×10^4	Downtown San Francisco

Now that we've nailed the range and precision of the 3D coordinates, let's take a few moments to consider those arbitrary decisions about origin and axes directions. You've probably heard of 3D coordinate systems described as either left or right handed, and if you're like me you tend to forget which is which, and the explanation with your fingers and thumbs was always just a little confusing because I couldn't remember how to hold my hands! Here's another way to visualize it. Imagine that you are standing at the origin of a classic 3D Cartesian coordinate system and you are looking down the positive X-axis. The positive Y-axis points straight up. If the coordinate system is right handed, the Z-axis will point to your right. A left-handed coordinate system will have a positive Z-axis pointed to the left.

Why is *handedness* important? For one thing, when you move objects around your world you'll want to know where your positive Z-axis is and how it relates to the other two, or you might have things zig instead of zag. The tougher answer is that it effects the formulas for calculating important 3D equations such as a cross product. I'm extremely glad I don't have to explain a 4D coordinate system. I don't think I have it in me.

Since some art packages have different handedness than 3D rendering engines, you have to know how to convert the handedness of objects from one coordinate system to another. Here how you do it:

1. Reverse the order of the vertices on each triangle. If a triangle started with vertices v0, v1, and v2, they need to be flipped to v2, v1, and v0.

2. Multiply each z coordinate in the model by -1.

Here's an example:
Original:
V0 = (2.3, 5.6, 1.2)   V1 = (1.0, 2.0, 3.0)   V2 = (30.0, 20.0, 10.0)

Becomes:
V0 = (30.0, 20.0, -10.0) V1 = (1.0, 2.0, -3.0)   V2 = (2.3, 5.6, -1.2)

Vector Mathematics

Vector and matrix math was always the sleepiest part of linear algebra for me. Rather than just show you the guts of the dot product or cross product for the umpteeth time, I'll also tell you what they do. That's more important anyway. I'll also show you some safety rules regarding matrix mathematics because they don't act like regular numbers.

Before we go any further you need to know what a unit vector is because it is something you'll use all the time in 3D graphics programming. A unit vector is any vector that has a length of 1.0. If you have a vector of arbitrary length, you can create a unit vector that points in the same direction by dividing the vector by its length. This is also known as "normalizing" a vector:

```
float length = sqrt ( v.x * v.x + v.y * v.y + v.z * v.z)

Vector unit = Vector(v.x / length, v.y / length, v.z / length)

Example: V(x,y,z) = V(3, 4, 0)

Length = Sqrt ( 9 + 16 + 0 ) = Sqrt ( 25 ) = 5;

Unit Vector U(x,y,z) = U( 3/5, 4/5, 0/5) = U(0.6, 0.8, 0)
```

When we talk about dot and cross products, their inputs are always unit vectors. The formulas certainly work on any arbitrary vector, but the results are relatively meaningless. Take the same formulas and apply unit vectors to them, and you'll find some interesting results that you can use to calculate critical angles and directions in your 3D world. A dot product of two vectors is a number, sometimes called a *scalar*. The cross product of two vectors is another vector. Remember these two important facts and you'll never get one confused with the other again. Another way to say this is dot products calculate angles, and cross products calculate direction. The dot product is calculated with the following formula:

```
float dotProduct = ( v1.x * v2.x ) + ( v1.y * v2.y ) + (v1.z * v2.z);
```

Unit vectors never have any coordinate with an absolute value greater than 1.0. Given that, you'll notice that the results of plugging various numbers into the dot product formula have interesting effects. Here are a few:

- *V1 equals V2*: If you calculate the dot product of a vector with itself, the value of the dot product is always 1.0.

- *V1 is orthogonal to V2*: If the two vectors form a right angle to each other, the result of the dot product is always zero.
- *V1 points in the opposite direction to V2*: Two vectors pointing exactly away from each other have a dot product of -1.0.

If this relationship between vectors, right angles, and the range [-1.0, 1.0] is stirring some deep dark memory, you're correct. The dark memory is trigonometry, and the function you are remembering is the cosine. It turns out that the dot product of two unit vectors calculates the cosine of the angle between the two vectors. Another way to visualize the dot product graphically is that the dot product projects one vector onto the other, and calculates the length of that vector. This dot product relationship is shown in Figure 9.1, where the dot product equals the length of the projection of vector A onto B. As it turns out, this length is exactly the same as the projection of vector B onto vector A. Weird, huh?

The dot product can be useful by itself, since it can determine whether the angle between two vectors is acute, a right angle, or obtuse. The classic application of the dot product in 3D graphics is determining whether a polygon is facing towards or away from the camera.

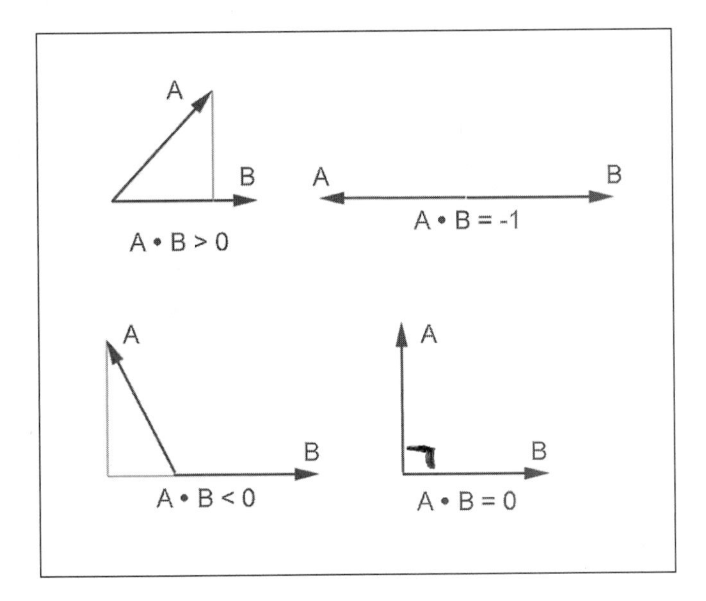

Figure 9.1
Dot Products.

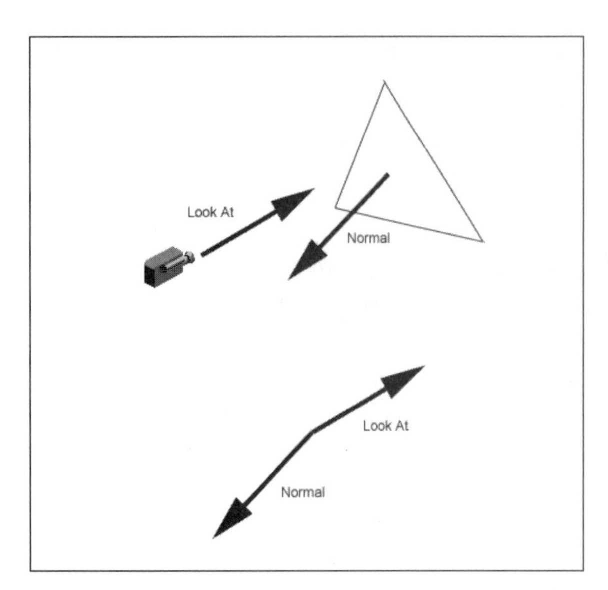

Figure 9.2
Dot Products Used for Backfacing.

In Figure 9.2, the camera has a unit vector called the "look at" vector and it points in the same direction as the camera. Each polygon has a normal vector that is orthogonal to the plane of the polygon. If the dot product between these two vectors is less than zero, the polygon is facing the camera and should be added to the draw list. In the case of Figure 9.2, the dot product for these two vectors is close to -1.0, so the polygon will be drawn.

If you want the actual angle represented by the dot product, you must perform an arccosine operation. If you remember those hazy trig classes at all you'll know that the arccosine isn't defined everywhere, only between values [-1.0, 1.0]. That's lucky, because dot products from unit vectors have exactly the same range. So where's the problem? The arccosine will always return positive numbers.

The dot product is directionless, giving you the same result no matter which vector you send in first: A dot B is the same as B dot A. Still not convinced this is a problem? Let's assume you are using the dot product to determine the angle between your current direction and the direction vector that points to something you are targeting.

In Figure 9.3, the white arrow is the current direction, and the grey arrows are oriented 45 degrees away about the y-axis. Notice that one of the grey arrows is pointing straight to our teapot target, but the other one is pointing in a completely wrong direction. The dot products between the white direction vector and both grey vectors are the same!

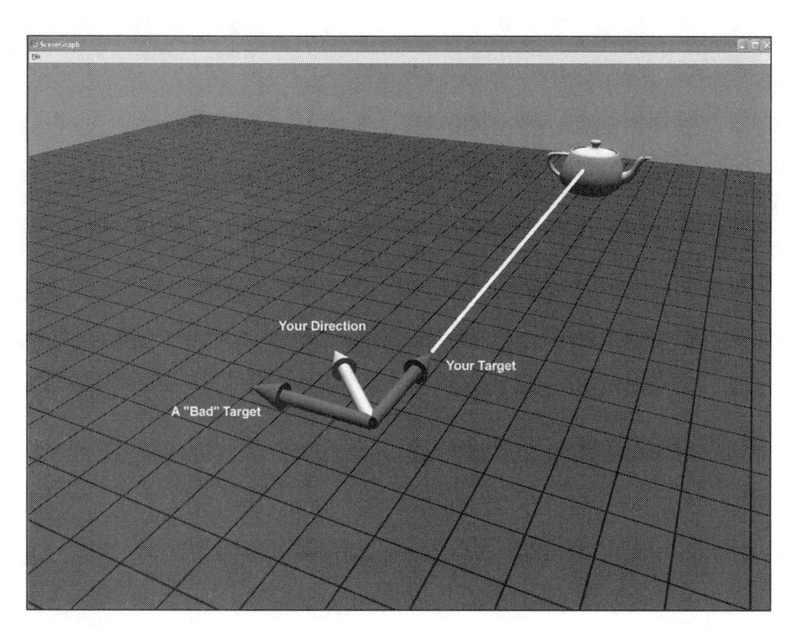

Figure 9.3
Dot Products Can't Find Targets.

Remember that the dot product measures angles and not direction. As you can see from the diagram, the dot product won't tell you which way to turn, only how much to turn. You need a *cross product.*

Graphically, the cross product returns a vector that is orthogonal to the plane formed by the two input vectors. The cross product vector should be normalized before you use it. Planes have two sides, and the resulting normal vector can only point in one direction. How does it know which way to point? It turns out that cross products are sensitive to the order of their input vectors. In other words, A cross B is not equal to B cross A. As you might expect, it is exactly negative. This is where the handedness of the coordinate system comes back into play. The cross product is always calculated with this formula:

```
cross.x = (A.y * B.z) - (B.y * A.z)

cross.y = (A.z * B.x) - (B.z * A.x)

cross.z = (A.x * B.y) - (B.x * A.y)
```

I'm going to borrow your right hand for a moment. Hold your right hand out in front of you, fingers together, and totally flat. Make sure you are looking at your palm. Extend your thumb out, keeping your hand flat. Your thumb is vector A and your forefinger is vector B. The result of the cross product, A cross B, is a vector pointing up out of your palm. If you did it backwards, B cross A, the vector would be pointing away from you. This is the fundamental difference between left and right handed coordinate systems—determining which vectors get sent into the cross product in which order. It matters!

The classic use of the cross product is figuring out the normal vector of a polygon (see Figure 9.4). The normal vector is fundamental to calculating which polygons are facing the camera, and therefore, which polygons are drawn and which can be ignored.

For any polygon that has three vertices, V0, V1, and V2, the normal vector is calculated using a cross product:

```
Vector A = V1 - V0;

Vector B = V2 - V1;

Vector Cross = A X B;
```

In a right-handed coordinate system, the vertices are arranged in a counter clockwise order as they are seen when looking at the drawn side of the polygon.

Another use is figuring the direction. Returning to our chase problem, we have a dot product that tells us that we need to steer either left or right, but we can't figure out which. It turns out that the cross product between the direction vectors will tell us.

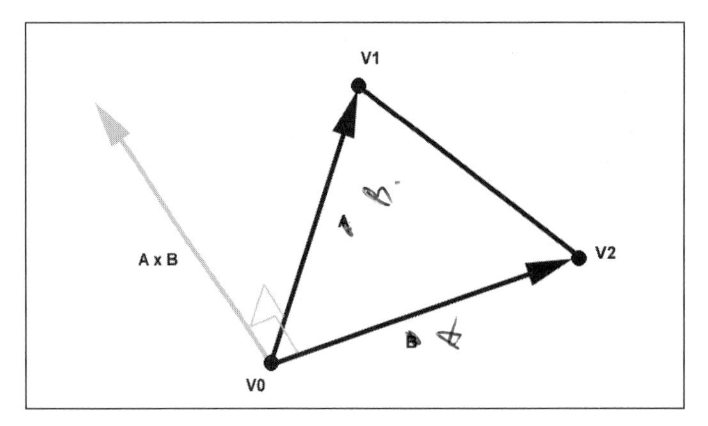

Figure 9.4
A Cross Product.

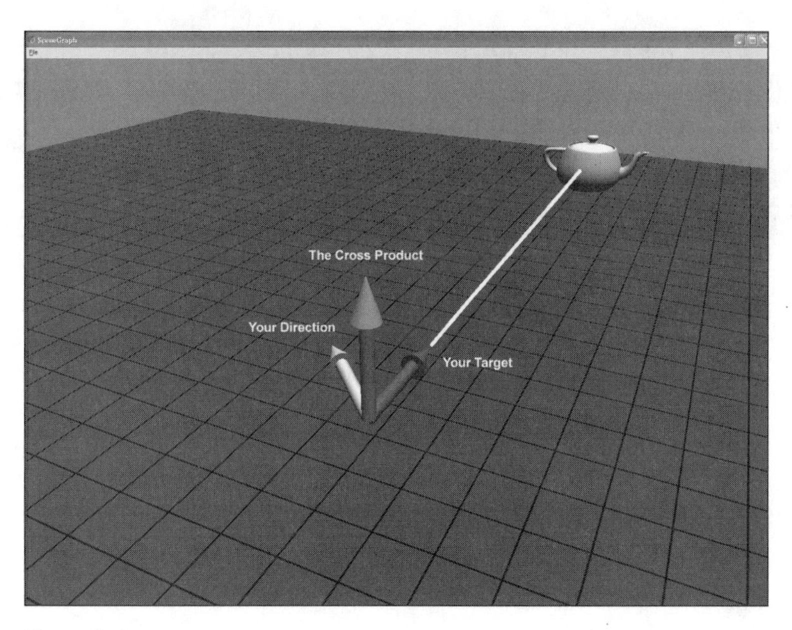

Figure 9.5
A Cross Product and A Dot Product Can Find a Target.

The cross product between the target vector and your direction vector points up, indicating we should steer right (see Figure 9.5). If the cross product pointed down, the target would have been off to our left. The target example is somewhat contrived because you don't actually need the cross product at all. It makes a good example because it's a useful experiment to visualize the usefulness of the cross product. Through a little trickery, you can do it solely with the dot product, as long as you choose the correct vectors. If you use a vector that points to your right instead of straight ahead, your dot product will yield a positive number if you need to steer right and a negative number if you need to steer left, and something close to zero if your target is right in front of you. Even better, if your steering parameters range from -1.0 to steer hard left and 1.0 to lock it all the way to the right, you can send this dot product straight into your steering code. Cool, huh?

Matrix Mathematics

A 3D world is filled with objects that move around. It would seem like an impossible task to set each vertex and surface normal of every polygon each time an object moved. There's a shortcut, it turns out, and it concerns matrices. Vertices and surface normals for objects in your 3D world are stored in object space. As the object moves and rotates, the only thing that changes is the object's transform matrix. The original vertices and normals remain exactly the same. The object's transform matrix holds information about its position in the world and its rotation about the X, Y, and Z-axis.

Multiple instances of an object need not duplicate the geometry data. Each object instance only needs a different transform matrix and a reference to the original geometry. As each object moves the only things that change are the values of each transform matrix. A transform matrix for a 3D engine is represented by a 4x4 array of floating point numbers. The matrix elements are set in specific ways to perform translations and different rotations. For each kind of matrix, I'll show you how to set the elements yourself or how to call a DirectX function to initialize it.

A translation matrix moves vectors linearly. Assuming you have a displacement vector T, which describes the translation along each axis, you'll initialize the translation matrix with the values shown in Table 9.2.

Here's how to do the same thing in DirectX:

```
// Create a DirectX matrix that will translate vectors
// +3 units along X and -2 units along Z
D3DXVECTOR3 t(3,0,-2);
D3DXMATRIX transMatrix;
D3DXMatrixTranslation(&transMatrix, t.x,t.y,t.z);
```

Let's look at a quick example.

```
D3DXVECTOR4 original(1, 1, 1, 1);
D3DXVECTOR4 result;
D3DXVec4Transform(&result, &original, &transMatrix);
```

The transform creates a new vector with values (4, 1, -1, 1). The DirectX function `D3DXVec4Transform` multiplies the input vector with the transform matrix. The result is a transformed vector.

Table 9.2 Translation Matrix for Moving Vectors Linearly.

1	0	0	0
0	1	0	0
0	0	1	0
T.x	T.y	T.z	1

Did you notice my underhanded use of the D3DXVECTOR4 structure without giving you a clue about its use? Matrix mathematics is very picky about the dimensions of vectors and matrices that you multiply. It turns out that you can only multiply matrices where the number of rows matches the number of columns. This is why a 4x4 matrix must be multiplied with a 4 dimensional vector. Also, the last value of that 4D vector, w, should be set at 1.0, or you'll get odd results.

There are three kinds of rotation matrices, one for rotation about each axis. The most critical thing you must get through your math-addled brain is this: rotations always happen around the origin. What in the hell did that mean? You'll understand it better after you see an example. First, you need to get your bearings. Figure 9.6 shows an image of a teapot, sitting at the origin. The squares are one unit across. We are looking at the origin from (x=6, y=6, z=6). The Y-axis points up. The X-axis points off to the lower left, and the Z-axis points to the lower right.

If you look along the axis of rotation, an object will appear to rotate counter clockwise if you rotate it in a positive angle. One way to remember this is by going back to the unit circle in trig as shown in Figure 9.7.

A special note to my high school geometry teacher, Mrs. Connally: You were right all along—I did have use for the unit circle after all…

Figure 9.6
Displaying a Teapot in 3D.

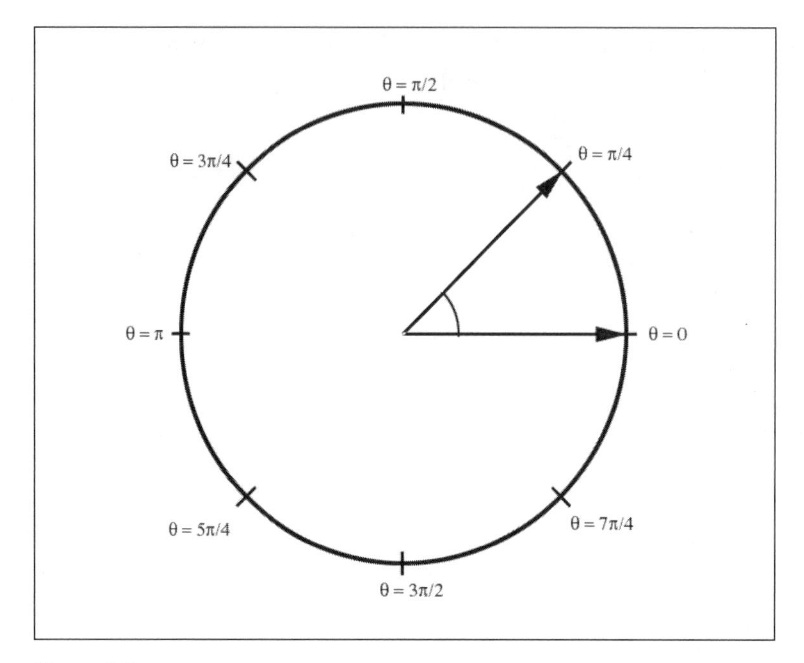

Figure 9.7
The Infamous Unit Circle.

That means if we want to rotate the teapot so that the spout is pointing straight at us, we'll need to rotate it about the Y-axis. The Y-axis points up, so any rotation about that axis will make the teapot appear as if it is sitting on a potter's wheel. How do you calculate the angle? Go back to your unit circle to figure it out. The angle we want is 45 degrees, or $\pi/4$. We also know that the angle should be negative. Here's why: If we are looking along the Y-axis, we'd be underneath the teapot looking straight up. The teapot's spout needs to twist clockwise to achieve our desired result, so the angle is negative.

A rotation matrix for the Y-axis looks like the one shown in Table 9.3.

Here's the code to create this matrix in DirectX:

```
float angle = -D3DX_PI / 4.0f;
D3DXMATRIX rotateY;
D3DXMatrixRotationY(&rotateY, angle);
```

Table 9.3 Rotate θ Degrees About the Y-Axis.

cos(θ)	0	-sin(θ)	0
0	1	0	0
sin(θ)	0	cos(θ)	0
0	0	0	1

Let's transform a vector with this matrix and see what happens. Since the teapot's spout is pointing down the X-axis, let's transform (x=1, y=0, z=0):

```
D3DXVECTOR4 original(1, 0, 0, 1);
D3DXVECTOR4 result(0,0,0,0);
D3DXVec4Transform(&result, &original, &rotateY);
```

Here's the result:

```
result  {...}          D3DXVECTOR4
   x 0.70710677        float
   y 0.00000000        float
   z 0.70710677        float
   w 1.0000000         float
```

Excellent, that's exactly what we want. The new vector is sitting on the X-Z plane, both coordinates in the positive. If we take that same transform and apply it to every vertex of the teapot, and redraw it, we'll get the picture shown in Figure 9.8.

Table 9.4 shows how to create a rotation about the X-axis and Table 9.5 shows how to create a rotation about the Z-axis.

Figure 9.8
The Teapot: Rotated†–π/4 Degrees about the Y-Axis.

Table 9.4 Rotate θ Degrees About the X-Axis.

1	0	0	0
0	cos(θ)	Sin(θ)	0
0	sin(θ)	Cos(θ)	0
0	0	0	1

Table 9.5 Rotate θ Degrees About the Z-Axis.

cos(θ)	sin(θ)	0	0
-sin(θ)	cos(θ)	0	0
0	0	1	0
0	0	0	1

The DirectX code to create those two rotations is exactly what you'd expect:

```
float angle = -D3DX_PI / 4.0f;
D3DXMATRIX rotateX, rotateZ;
D3DXMatrixRotationX(…rotateX, angle);
D3DXMatrixRotationZ(…rotateZ, angle);
```

That handles simple translation and rotation transforms. Now you need to learn how to put multiple transforms into action. It turns out that you can multiply, or concatenate, matrices. The result encodes every operation into a single matrix. I know, it seems like magic. There's one important part of this wizardry: The concatenated matrix is sensitive to the order in which you did the original multiplication. Let's look at two examples, starting with two matrices you should be able to visualize:

```
D3DXMATRIX trans, rotateY;
D3DXMatrixTranslation(&trans, 3,0,0);
D3DXMatrixRotationY(&rotateY, -D3DX_PI / 4.0f);
```

The translation matrix will push our teapot down the X-axis, or to the lower left in our current view. The negative angle rotation about the Y-axis you've already seen.

In DirectX, you can multiply two matrices with a function call. I'm not going to bother showing you the actual formula for two reasons. First, you can find it for yourself on the Internet and second, no one codes this from scratch. There's always an optimized version of a matrix multiply in any 3D engine you find, including DirectX:

```
D3DXMATRIX result;
D3DXMatrixMultiply(&result, &trans, &rotateY);
```

Figure 9.9
The Teapot: Rotation Applied after Translation.

Note the order. This should create a transform matrix that will push the teapot down the X-axis and rotate it about the Y-axis, in that order. Figure 9.9 shows the results.

If you expected the teapot to be sitting on the X-axis you must remember that any rotation happens about the origin, not the center of the object! This is a common mistake, and I've spent much of my 3D debugging time getting my matrices in the right order.

Always translate last. If you want to place an object in a 3D world, you always perform your rotations first and translations afterwards.

Let's follow my own best practice and see if we get a better result. First we reverse the order of the parameters into the matrix multiplication API:

```
D3DXMATRIX result;
D3DXMatrixMultiply(&result, &rotateY, &trans );
```

Figure 9.10 shows the result.

I'll show you one more, just to make sure you get it. The goal of this transformation is two rotations and one translation. I want the teapot to sit four units down the Z-axis, on its side with the top towards us and the spout straight up in the air. Here's the code:

Figure 9.10
The Teapot: Translation Applied after Rotation.

```
D3DXMATRIX rotateX, rotateZ, trans;
D3DXMatrixRotationZ(&rotateZ, -D3DX_PI / 2.0f);
D3DXMatrixRotationX(&rotateX, -D3DX_PI );
D3DXMatrixTranslation(&trans, 0,0,4);
D3DXMATRIX temp, result;
D3DXMatrixMultiply(&temp, &rotateZ, &rotateX);
D3DXMatrixMultiply(&result, &temp, &trans);
```

The first rotation about the Z-axis points our teapot's spout down the negative Y-axis, and the second rotation twists the whole thing around the X-axis to get the spout pointing straight up. The final translation moves it to its resting spot on the Z-axis (see Figure 9.11).

I hope you've followed these bits about rotating things around an axis because it's a critical concept you need to understand before we talk about *quaternions*. If you think you might be hazy on the whole rotation thing, perhaps you'd better reread the previous section.

Quaternion Mathematics

Orientation can be expressed as three angles: yaw, pitch, and roll. In our teapot example yaw would be around the Y-axis, pitch would be around the Z-axis, and roll would be around the X-axis. By the way, this happens to be called the Euler representation, or

Figure 9.11
The Teapot: Two Rotations and One Translation.

Euler angles. This method has a critical weakness. Imagine you want to interpolate smoothly between two orientations. This would make sense if you had an object like an automated cannon that slowly tracked moving objects. It would know its current orientation and the target orientation, but getting from one to the other might be problematic with Euler angles.

There a special mathematical construct known as a quaternion and most every 3D engine supports its use. A quaternion is a fourth dimensional vector, and it can be visualized as a rotation about an arbitrary axis. Let's look at an example:

```
D3DXQUATERNION q;
D3DXQuaternionIdentity(&q);
D3DXVECTOR3 axis(0,1,0);
float angle = -D3DX_PI / 4.0;
D3DXQuaternionRotationAxis(&q, &axis, angle);
D3DXMATRIX result;
D3DXMatrixRotationQuaternion(&result, &q);
```

This code has exactly the same effect on our teapot at the first rotation example. The teapot rotates around the Y-axis, $-\pi/4$ degrees. Notice that I'm not setting the values of the quaternion directly, I'm using a DirectX API. I do this because the actual values of the quaternion are not intuitive at all. Take a look at the resulting values from our simple twist around the Y-axis:

```
q  {...}   D3DXQUATERNION
   x  0.00000000      float
   y  -0.38268343     float
   z  0.00000000      float
   w  0.92387950      float
```

Not exactly the easiest thing to read naked, is it?

The quaternion is sent into another DirectX function to create a transformation matrix. This is done because vectors can't be transformed directly with quaternions—you still have to use a transform matrix.

If you think this seems like a whole lot of work with little gain, let's look at the interpolation problem. Let's assume that I want the teapot to turn such that the spout is pointing down the Z-axis—this would mean a rotation about the Y-axis with an angle of– $\pi/2$ degrees. Let's also assume I want to know what the transformation matrix is at 2/3 of the way through the turn as shown in Figure 9.12.

Here's the code:

```
D3DXQUATERNION start, middle, end;
D3DXQuaternionIdentity(&start);
D3DXQuaternionIdentity(&middle);
D3DXQuaternionIdentity(&end);

D3DXVECTOR3 axis(0,1,0);
float angle = -D3DX_PI / 2.0;
D3DXQuaternionRotationAxis(&start, &axis, 0);
D3DXQuaternionRotationAxis(&end, &axis, angle);

D3DXQuaternionSlerp(&middle, &end, &start, 0.66f);

D3DXMATRIX result;
D3DXMatrixRotationQuaternion(&result, &middle);
```

The two boundary quaternions, start and end, are initialized in the same way. The target orientation quaternion, `middle`, is calculated with the DirectX method `D3DXQuaternionSlerp`. This creates a quaternion 66% of the way between our start and end quaternions.

I might not quite have convinced you yet but only because I used a trivial rotation that was easy to display. Face it, anyone can interpolate a rotation around a single axis. Since quaternions can represent a rotation about a completely arbitrary axis, like (x=3.5, y=-2.1, z=0.04), they can be much more useful than Euler angles.

Figure 9.12
The Teapot Oriented with Quaternions.

We've just exposed the first step in getting objects to your screen. All of the matrix concatentation, quaternions, and translations you just learned were used to place a single object in a 3D world, with an orientation we wanted and the exact position we desired. This step is called *transforming object space into world space.* Object space is totally untransformed. The vertices exist in exactly the same spots the artist or the programmer placed them. The transform that placed the teapot exactly where we wanted it placed transformed the object space to world space, and is generally called a *world transform.*

In DirectX, you set the current world transform with this line of code:

```
pD3DDevice->SetTransform( D3DTS_WORLD,  &result );
```

Any untransformed polygons sent into the renderer will use this transform. Your teapot will be exactly where you want it. I say untransformed polygons because it is possible to transform polygons yourself, and have the renderer do its magic with polygons in screen space. We'll learn more about that in a moment.

First, there are two more transforms to add into the mix. The addition of these two transforms is what you'll need to set a camera in the world to view the teapot and project its vertices onto a flat pane of glass—your computer's display. The first one is the *view transformation.*

View Transformation

If we are going to render the scene we need to have a camera. That camera must have an orientation and a position just like any other object in the world. Similar to any other object, the camera needs a transform matrix that converts world space vertices to camera space.

Calculating the transform matrix for a camera can be tricky. In many cases you want the camera to look at something, like a teapot. If you have a desired camera position and a target to look at, you don't quite have enough information to place the camera. The missing data is a definition of the *up* direction for your world. This last bit of data gives the camera a hint about how to orient itself. The view matrix for our previous teapot experiment used a DirectX function, `D3DXMatrixLookAtLH`:

```
D3DXMATRIX matView;
D3DXVECTOR3 vFromPt   = D3DXVECTOR3( 6.0f, 6.0f, 6.0f );
D3DXVECTOR3 vLookatPt = D3DXVECTOR3( 0.0f, 0.0f, 0.0f );
D3DXVECTOR3 vUpVec    = D3DXVECTOR3( 0.0f, 1.0f, 0.0f );
D3DXMatrixLookAtLH( &matView, &vFromPt, &vLookatPt, &vUpVec );
m_pd3dDevice->SetTransform( D3DTS_VIEW, &matView );
```

By the way, the `LH` at the end of the DirectX function's name is a hint that this function assumes a left-handed coordinate system. There is a right-handed version of this, and most other matrix functions, as well.

The from point was out along the positive values of X, Y, and Z, and the look-at point was right back at the origin. The last parameter defines the up direction. If you think about a camera as having an orientation constraint similar to a camera boom like you see on ESPN, it can move anywhere, pan around to see its surroundings, and pitch up or down. It doesn't tilt, at least not normally. This is important, If tilting were allowed in constructing a valid view transform, there could be many different orientations that will satisfy your input data.

This system isn't completely perfect because there are two degenerate orientations. Given the definition of up as (x=0, y=1, z=0) in world space, the two places you can't easily look is straight up and straight down. You can construct the view transform yourself quite easily but don't expect the look-at function to do it for you.

Remember that the camera's view transform is a matrix, just like any other. You don't have to use the look-at function to calculate it, but it tends to be the most effective camera positioning function there is.

Projection Transformation

So far, we've taken vertices from object space and transformed them into world space, and taken world space and transformed them into camera space. Now we need to take all those 3D vertices sitting in camera space and figure out where they belong on your computer screen, and which objects sit in front of other objects.

Imagine sitting in front of a computer screen, and seeing four lines coming from your eyeball and intersecting with the corners of the screen. For he sake of simplicity I'll assume you have only one eyeball in the center of your head. These lines continue into the 3D world of your favorite game. You have a pyramid shape with the point at your eyeball and its base somewhere out in infinity somewhere. Clip the pointy end of the pyramid with the plane of your computer screen, and form a base of your pyramid at some arbitrary place in the distance. This odd clipped pyramid shape is called the viewing *frustum*. The shape is actually a cuboid, since it is topologically equivalent to a cube, although cruelly pushed out of shape.

Every object inside this shape, the viewing frustum, will be drawn on your screen. The projection transformation takes the camera space (x,y,z) of every vertex and transforms it into a new vector that holds the screen pixel (x,y) location and a measure of the vertices' distance into the scene.

Here's the code to create the viewing frustum of the teapot experiments:

```
D3DXMATRIX matProj;
FLOAT fAspect = ((FLOAT)m_d3dsdBackBuffer.Width) / m_d3dsdBackBuffer.Height;
D3DXMatrixPerspectiveFovLH( &matProj, D3DX_PI/4, fAspect, 1.0f, 100.0f );
m_pd3dDevice->SetTransform( D3DTS_PROJECTION, &matProj );
```

The DirectX function that helps you calculate a projection matrix—something you don't want to do by yourself—accepts four parameters after the address of the matrix:

- *Field of view*: Expressed in radians, this is the width of the view angle. $\pi/4$ is a pretty standard angle. Wider angles such as $3\pi/4$ make for some weird results. Try it and see what happens.
- *Aspect ratio*: This is the aspect ratio of your screen. If this ratio were 1.0, the projection transform would assume you had a square screen. A 640x480 screen has a 1.333 aspect ratio.
- *Near clipping plane*: This is the distance between your eye and the near view plane. Any object closer will get clipped. The units are usually meters, but feel free to set them to whatever standard makes sense for your game.

- *Far clipping plane*: The distance between your eye and the far clipping plane. Anything farther away will be clipped.

Don't set your far clipping plane to some arbitrarily large number in the hopes that nothing in your huge 3D world will get clipped. The tradeoff is that the huge distance between your near and far clipping plane will create sorting problems in objects close to the camera. These weird sorting problems manifest themselves as if two polygons were run through a paper shredder, since the individual pixels on two coincident polygons will sort incorrectly. If you see this problem, check your far clipping plane distance.

Also, don't set your near clipping plane to zero, in the hopes that you'll be able to see things very close to the camera. There's a relationship between the near clipping plane and the field of view: If you arbitrarily move the near clipping plane closer to the camera without changing the field of view, weird things begin to happen. My suggestion is to write a little code and see for yourself.

Enough Math—Please Stop

I'm done torturing you with linear algebra, but I'm not quite done with geometry. Hang in there because you'll soon find out some interesting things about triangles.

Triangles

Did you know that everything from teapots to cars to volleyball-playing beach bunnies can be made out of triangles? We all know that a geometric triangle is made up of three points. In a 3D world, a triangle is composed of three vertices. A vertex holds all of the information the renderer will use to draw the triangle, and as you might expect there can be a lot more than its location in a 3D space.

Different renderers will support different kinds of triangles, and therefore different kinds of vertices that create those triangles. Once you get your feet wet with one rendering technology, such as DirectX 9, you'll quickly find analogs in any other rendering technology, such as OpenGL. Since I've already sold my soul to Bill Gates, I'll show you how you create vertices in DirectX 9. A DirectX 9 vertex is a structure you define yourself. When you send your vertex data to the renderer you send in a set of flags that inform it about the contents of the vertex data.

You may define the structure yourself, but DirectX 9 expects the data in the structure to exist in a particular order. Search for "Vertex Formats" in the DirectX SDK to see this order. All hell will break loose if you don't.

First, you should understand the concepts of a *transformed vertex* versus an *untransformed vertex*. A transformed vertex is defined directly in screen space. It doesn't need the transformations we discussed in the last section—object to world, world to camera, camera to screen. You would use this kind of vertex to build triangles that create user interface components, since they don't need to exist in anything else but screen space.

Don't think that you can easily get away with defining triangles in screen space that "look" like they exist in world space. On the first Microsoft Casino project, we defined our card animations in screen space. Every corner of every card was painstakingly recorded and entered into the card animation code. These coordinates looked fairly good, but the second we needed to tweak the camera angle all the coordinates had to be recomputed, rerecorded, and entered into the code by hand. It seemed like a good idea at the time but we finally ditched this approach in favor of real cards animating through world space.

An untransformed vertex exists in object space, like the triangles that make up our teapot. Before the triangles are drawn, they'll be multiplied with the concatenated matrix that represents the transformations that will change a location in object space to projected screen space. Here's how you define a DirectX 9 vertex structure for a transformed vertex, and an untransformed vertex:

```
struct TRANSFORMED_VERTEX
{
   D3DXVECTOR3 position;     // The screen x, y, z - x,y are pixel coordinates
   float rhw;                // always 1.0, the reciprocal of homogeneous w
};
#define D3DFVF_TRANSFORMED_VERTEX (D3DFVF_XYZRHW)

struct UNTRANSFORMED_VERTEX
{
    D3DXVECTOR3 position;   // The position in 3D space
};
#define D3DFVF_UNTRANSFORMED_VERTEX (D3DFVF_XYZ)
```

The #defines below the vertex definitions are the flags that you send into renderer calls that inform the renderer how to treat the vertex data. A renderer needs to know more than the location of a vertex in 3D space or screen space. It needs to know what it looks like. There are a few categories of this appearance information, but the first one on your list is lighting and color.

9

Lighting, Normals, and Color

In DirectX 9 and many other rendering technologies you can assign colors to vertices yourself, or you can instruct the renderer to calculate those colors by looking at vertex data and the lights that illuminate the vertex. You can even do both. Everyone has seen games that show subtle light pools shining on walls and floors—a nice effect but completely static and unmoving. Other illumination is calculated in real time, such as when your character shines a flashlight around a scene. Multiple lights can affect individual vertices, each light adding a color component to the vertex color calculation.

Two flavors of dynamic lighting effects are *diffuse* and *specular* lighting. DirectX 9 can calculate these values for you if you want to send unlit vertices to the renderer, but you can also set the diffuse and specular colors directly. If you want the renderer to calculate the lighting values—a good idea because many 3D cards have hardware acceleration for lighting—you have to create a *normal* vector as a component of your vertex.

When light hits an object, the color of light becomes a component of the object's appearance. Perform a little experiment to see this in action: Take a playing card, like the ace of spades, and place it flat on a table lit by a ceiling lamp. The card takes on a color component that reflects the color of that lamp. If your lamp is a fluorescent light the card will appear white with a slight greenish tint. If your lamp is incandescent the card will take on a slightly yellowish color.

If you take the card in your hand and slowly turn it over, the brightness and color of the card changes. As the card approaches an edge on orientation to the lamp, the effects of the lighting diminish to their minimum. The light has its maximum effect when the card is flat on the table, and its minimum effect when the card is edged on to the light. This happens because when light hits a surface at a low angle it spreads out and has to cover a larger area with the same number of photons. This gives you a dimming effect.

Diffuse lighting attempts to simulate this effect. With the ace sitting flat on the table again, take a pencil and put the eraser end in the middle of the card and point the tip of the pencil straight up in the air, towards your ceiling lamp. You've just created a normal vector. Turn the card as before, but hold the pencil and turn it as well, as if it were glued to the card. Notice that the light has a maximum effect when the angle between the pencil and the light is 180 degrees and minimum effect when the angle between the light and the pencil is 90 degrees, and no effect when the card faces away from the light.

Each vertex gets its own normal vector. This might seem like a waste of memory, but consider this: If each vertex has its own normal, you can change the direction of the normal vectors to "fool" the lighting system. You can make the 3D object take on a smoother shading effect. This is a common technique to blend the edges of coincident triangles. The illusion you create allows artists to create 3D models with fewer polygons.

The normals on the teapot model are calculated to create the illusion of a smooth shape as shown in Figure 9.13.

Now that you know what a normal vector is, you need to know how to calculate one. If you want to find the normal vector for a triangle you'll need to use a cross product as shown here:

```
D3DXVECTOR3 triangle[3];
triangle[0] = D3DXVECTOR3(0,0,0);
triangle[1] = D3DXVECTOR3(5,0,0);
triangle[2] = D3DXVECTOR3(5,5,0);

D3DXVECTOR3 edge1 = triangle[1]-triangle[0];
D3DXVECTOR3 edge2 = triangle[2]-triangle[0];

D3DXVECTOR3 temp, normal;
D3DXVec3Cross(&temp, &edge1, &edge2);
D3DXVec3Normalize(&normal, &temp);
```

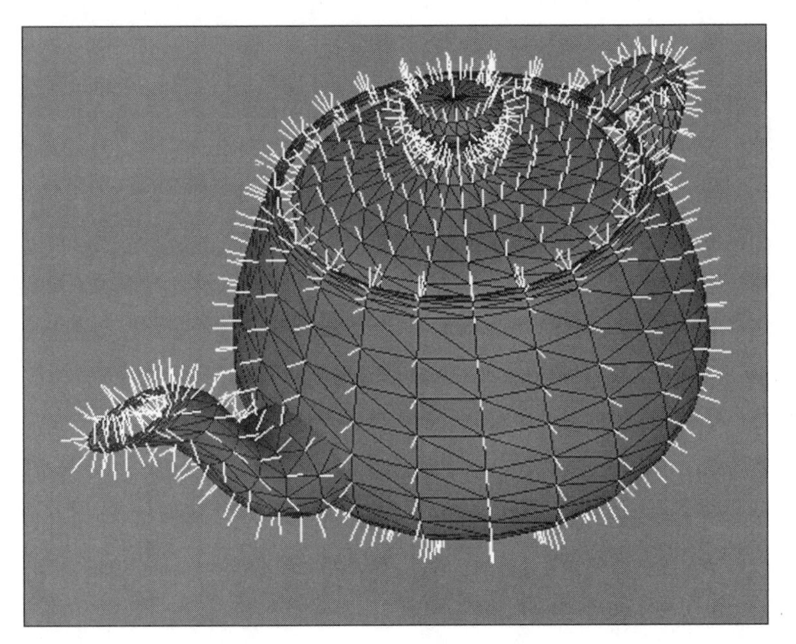

Figure 9.13
Vertex Normals on the Teapot.

Our triangle is defined with three positions in 3D space. These positions are used to construct two edge vectors, both pointing away from the same vertex. The two edges are sent into the cross product function, which returns a vector that is pointing in the right direction, but the wrong size. All normal vectors must be exactly one unit in length to be useful in other calculations, such as the dot product. The `D3DXVec3Normalize` function calculates the unit vector by dividing the temp vector by its length. The result is a normal vector you can apply to a vertex.

If you take a closer look at the teapot figure, you'll notice that the normal vectors are really the normals of multiple triangles, not just a single triangle. You calculate this by averaging the normals of each triangle that shares your vertex. Calculate the average of multiple vectors by adding them together, and dividing by the number of vectors, exactly as you would calculate the average of any other number.

Calculating a normal is an expensive operation. Each triangle will require two subtractions, a cross product, a square root, and three divisions. If you create 3D meshes at run time, try to calculate your normals once, store them in object space, and use transforms to reorient them.

Specular lighting is calculated slightly differently. It adds "shinyness" to an object by simulating the reflection of the light on the object. The light calculation takes the angle of the camera into account along with the normal vector of the polygon and the light direction.

You might be wondering why I didn't mention ambient lighting—a color value that is universally applied to every vertex in the scene. This has the effect of making an object glow like a light bulb, and isn't very realistic. Ambient lighting values are a necessary evil in today's 3D games, because they simulate low light levels on the back or underside of objects due to light reflecting all about the scene. In the next few years, I expect this light hack to be discarded completely in favor of the latest work with pixel shaders and environment based lighting effects. I can't wait!

Here are the DirectX 9 vertex definitions for lit and unlit vertices:

```
struct UNTRANSFORMED_LIT_VERTEX
{
    D3DXVECTOR3 position;   // The position in 3D space
    D3DCOLOR    diffuse;    // The diffuse color
    D3DCOLOR    specular;   // The specular color
};
#define D3DFVF_UNTRANS_LIT_VERTEX (D3DFVF_XYZ | D3DFVF_DIFFUSE |
                                    D3DFVF_SPECULAR)
```

```
struct UNTRANSFORMED_UNLIT_VERTEX
{
    D3DXVECTOR3 position;   // The position in 3D space
    D3DXVECTOR3 normal;     // The normal vector (must be 1.0 units in length)
    D3DCOLOR    diffuse;    // The diffuse color
    D3DCOLOR    specular;   // The specular color
};
#define FVF_UNTRANS_UNLIT_VERT      \
   (D3DFVF_XYZ | D3DFVF_NORMAL | D3DFVF_DIFFUSE | D3DFVF_SPECULAR)
```

Notice that both vertex definitions were of the untransformed variety, but there's nothing keeping you from making the transformed versions of these things. It's entirely up to you and what you need for your game. Remeber that the transformed versions will bypass the transformation and lighting pipeline entirely. The transformation and lighting pipeline are inseparable.

Note also that the unlit vertex still had definitions for diffuse and specular color information. This is kind of like having the best of both worlds. You can set specific diffuse and specular lighting on each vertex for static lights and the renderer will add any dynamic lights if they affect the vertex.

Textured Vertices

A texture is a piece of two-dimensional art that is applied to a model. Each vertex gets a texture coordinate. Texture coordinates are conventionally defined as (U,V) coordinates, where U is the horizontal component and V is the vertical component. Classically these coordinates are described as floating-point numbers where (0.0f,0.0f) signifies the top left of the texture and grows to the left and down. The coordinate (0.5f, 0.5f) would signify the exact center of the texture. Each vertex gets a texture coordinate for every texture. DirectX 9 supports up to eight textures on a single vertex.

Here's an example of a vertex with a texture coordinate:

```
// A structure for our custom vertex type. We added texture coordinates
struct COLORED_TEXTURED_VERTEX
{
    D3DXVECTOR3 position; // The position
    D3DCOLOR    color;    // The color
    FLOAT       tu, tv;   // The texture coordinates
};

// Our custom FVF, which describes our custom vertex structure
#define D3DFVF_COLORED_TEXTURED_VERTEX (D3DFVF_XYZ|D3DFVF_DIFFUSE|D3DFVF_TEX1)
```

This vertex happens to include a diffuse color component as well, and you should also be able to tell by the flags that this vertex is untransformed, which means it exists in 3D world space, as opposed to screen space. This kind of vertex is not effected by any dynamic lighting in a scene, but it can be prelit by an artist, creating nicely lit environments. This vertex is also extremely efficient, since it isn't sent into the lighting equations.

Numbers greater than 1.0 can tile the texture, mirror it, or clamp it depending on the addressing mode of the renderer. If you wanted a texture to tile three times in the horizontal direction and four times in the vertical direction on the surface of a single polygon, the texture (U,V) coordinate that would accomplish that task would be (3.0f, 4.0f). Numbers less than 0.0f are also supported. They have the effect of mirroring the texture.

Other Vertex Data

If you happen to have the DirectX SDK documentation open and you are following along, you'll notice that I skipped over a few additional vertex data components such as blending weight and vertex point size, and also tons of texturing minutia. All I can say is that these topics are beyond the scope of this simple 3D primer. I hope you'll forgive me and perhaps write a note to my publisher begging for me to write a more comprehensive book on the subject. That is, of course, if my wife ever lets me write another book. You have no idea how much housework I've been able to get out of by writing.

Triangle Meshes

We've been talking so far about individual vertices. Its time to take that knowledge and create some triangle meshes. There are three common approaches to defining sets of triangles:

- *Triangle List*: A group of vertices defines individual triangles, each set of three vertices defines a single triangle.
- *Triangle Strip*: A set of vertices that define a strip of connected triangles; this is more efficient than a triangle list because fewer vertices are duplicated. This is probably the most popular primitive because it is efficient and can create a wide variety of shapes.
- *Triangle Fan*: Similar to a triangle strip, but all the triangles share one central vertex; also very efficient.

When you define sets of vertices in DirectX 9, you put them in a *vertex buffer*. The vertex buffer is sent to the renderer in one atomic piece, which implies that every triangle defined in the buffer is rendered with the current state of the renderer. Every triangle will have the same texture, be affected by the same lights, and so on.

This turns out to be a staggeringly good optimization. The teapot you saw earlier in this chapter required 2,256 triangles and 1,178 vertices but it could be drawn with around 50 triangle strips. It turns out that DirectX meshes are always triangle lists. Lists or strips are much faster than sending each triangle to the card and rendering it individually, which is what happened in the dark ages—circa 1996.

In DirectX 9, you create a vertex buffer, fill it with your triangle data, and then use it for rendering at a time of your choosing:

```
class Triangle
{
   LPDIRECT3DVERTEXBUFFER9 m_pVerts;
   DWORD m_numVerts;

public:
   Triangle() { m_pVerts = NULL;    m_numVerts = 3; }
   ~Triangle() { SAFE_RELEASE(m_pVerts); }

   HRESULT Create(LPDIRECT3DDEVICE9 pDevice);
   HRESULT Render(LPDIRECT3DDEVICE9 pDevice);
};


HRESULT Triangle::Create(LPDIRECT3DDEVICE9 pDevice)
{
    // Create the vertex buffer.
   m_numVerts = 3;
    if( FAILED( pDevice->CreateVertexBuffer(
        m_numVerts*sizeof(TRANSFORMED_VERTEX),
           D3DUSAGE_WRITEONLY, D3DFVF_TRANSFORMED_VERTEX,
           D3DPOOL_MANAGED, &m_pVerts, NULL ) ) )
    {
        return E_FAIL;
    }

    // Fill the vertex buffer. We are setting the tu and tv texture
    // coordinates, which range from 0.0 to 1.0
    TRANSFORMED_VERTEX* pVertices;
    if( FAILED( m_pVerts->Lock( 0, 0, (void**)&pVertices, 0 ) ) )
        return E_FAIL;

   pVertices[0].position = D3DXVECTOR3(0,0,0);
   pVertices[0].rhw = 1.0;
   pVertices[1].position = D3DXVECTOR3(0,50,0);
   pVertices[1].rhw = 1.0;
   pVertices[2].position = D3DXVECTOR3(50,50,0);
   pVertices[2].rhw = 1.0;
```

```
    m_pVerts->Unlock();

    return S_OK;
}
```

This is a simple example of creating a vertex buffer with a single triangle, and a transformed one at that. The call to `CreateVertexBuffer` is somewhat scary looking, but all it does is set up a piece of memory the right size, the kind of vertex that will inhabit the buffer, and how the memory will be managed.

Once the buffer is created, you have to lock it before writing data values. This should remind you somewhat of locking a 2D surface. The single triangle has three vertices—no surprise there. Take a quick look at the position values and you'll see that I've defined a triangle that will sit in the upper left-hand corner of the screen with a base and height of 50 pixels. This triangle is defined in screen space, since the vector is defined as a transformed vertex.

When I'm ready to render this vertex buffer, I call this code:

```
HRESULT Triangle::VRender(LPDIRECT3DDEVICE9 pDevice)
{
    pDevice->SetStreamSource( 0, m_pVerts, 0, sizeof(TRANSFORMED_VERTEX) );
    pDevice->SetFVF( D3DFVF_TRANSFORMED_VERTEX );
    pDevice->DrawPrimitive( D3DPT_TRIANGLELIST , 0, 1 );
    return S_OK;
}
```

The first call sets the stream source, or vertex buffer to our triangle. The second call tells D3D what kind of vertices to expect in the stream buffer, using the flags that you or'ed together when you defined the vertex structure. The last call to `DrawPrimitive` actually renders the triangle.

You can't call any drawing functions in Direct3D without first calling `IDirect3D9Device::BeginScene`, and you must call `IDirect3DDevice::EndScene` when you are done drawing! The example above encapsulates the rendering of a single triangle and would be called only from within the context of the beginning and ending of a scene.

Indexed Triangle Meshes

There's one more wrinkle to the defining triangle meshes: Instead of sending vertex data to the renderer alone you can send an index along with it. This index is an array of 16- or 32-bit numbers that define the vertex order, allowing you to avoid serious vertex duplication and therefore save memory. Let's take a look at a slightly more complicated mesh example. Here's the code that created the grid mesh in the teapot example:

```
class Grid
{
protected:
   LPDIRECT3DTEXTURE9       m_pTexture;    // the grid texture
   LPDIRECT3DVERTEXBUFFER9  m_pVerts;      // the grid verts
   LPDIRECT3DINDEXBUFFER9   m_pIndices;    // the grid index
   DWORD                    m_numVerts;
   DWORD                    m_numPolys;

public:
   Grid();
   ~Grid();
   HRESULT Create(LPDIRECT3DDEVICE9 pDevice,
             const DWORD gridSize,
             const DWORD color);
   HRESULT Render(LPDIRECT3DDEVICE9 pDevice);
};

Grid::Grid()
{
   m_pTexture = NULL;
   m_pVerts = NULL;
   m_pIndices = NULL;
   m_numVerts = m_numPolys = 0;
}

Grid::~Grid()
{
   SAFE_RELEASE(m_pTexture);
   SAFE_RELEASE(m_pVerts);
   SAFE_RELEASE(m_pIndices);
}

HRESULT Grid::Create(
   LPDIRECT3DDEVICE9 pDevice,
   const DWORD gridSize,
   const DWORD color)
{
   if( FAILED( D3DUtil_CreateTexture(
        pDevice, "Textures\\Grid.dds", &m_pTexture ) ) )
   {
      return E_FAIL;
```

9

```
}

// Create the vertex buffer - we'll need enough verts
// to populate the grid. If we want a 2x2 grid, we'll
// need 3x3 set of verts.
m_numVerts = (gridSize+1)*(gridSize+1);

if( FAILED( pDevice->CreateVertexBuffer(
  m_numVerts*sizeof(COLORED_TEXTURED_VERTEX),
    D3DUSAGE_WRITEONLY, D3DFVF_COLORED_TEXTURED_VERTEX,
    D3DPOOL_MANAGED, &m_pVerts, NULL ) ) )
{
    return E_FAIL;
}

// Fill the vertex buffer. We are setting the tu and tv texture
// coordinates, which range from 0.0 to 1.0
COLORED_TEXTURED_VERTEX* pVertices;
if( FAILED( m_pVerts->Lock( 0, 0, (void**)&pVertices, 0 ) ) )
    return E_FAIL;

for( DWORD j=0; j<(gridSize+1); j++ )
{
  for (DWORD i=0; i<(gridSize+1); i++)
  {
    // Which vertex are we setting?
    int index = i + (j * (gridSize+1) );
    COLORED_TEXTURED_VERTEX *vert = &pVertices[index];

    // Default position of the grid is at the origin, flat on
    // the XZ plane.
    float x = (float)i;
    float y = (float)j;
    vert->position =
      ( x * D3DXVECTOR3(1,0,0) ) + ( y * D3DXVECTOR3(0,0,1) );
    vert->color    = color;

    // The texture coordinates are set to x,y to make the
    // texture tile along with units - 1.0, 2.0, 3.0, etc.
    vert->tu       = x;
    vert->tv       = y;
  }
}
m_pVerts->Unlock();
```

```
    // The number of indicies equals the number of polygons times 3
    // since there are 3 indicies per polygon. Each grid square contains
    // two polygons. The indicies are 16 bit, since our grids won't
    // be that big!
    m_numPolys = gridSize*gridSize*2;
    if( FAILED( pDevice->CreateIndexBuffer(
              sizeof(WORD) * m_numPolys * 3,
              D3DUSAGE_WRITEONLY, D3DFMT_INDEX16,
              D3DPOOL_MANAGED, &m_pIndices, NULL ) ) )
    {
      return E_FAIL;
    }

     WORD *pIndices;
     if( FAILED( m_pIndices->Lock( 0, 0, (void**)&pIndices, 0 ) ) )
         return E_FAIL;

    // Loop through the grid squares and calc the values
    // of each index. Each grid square has two triangles:
    //
    //    A - B
    //    | / |
    //    C - D

    for( DWORD j=0; j<gridSize; j++ )
     {
      for (DWORD i=0; i<gridSize; i++)
      {
         // Triangle #1  ACB
         *(pIndices) = WORD(i + (j*(gridSize+1)));
         *(pIndices+1) = WORD(i + ((j+1)*(gridSize+1)));
         *(pIndices+2) = WORD((i+1) + (j*(gridSize+1)));

         // Triangle #2  BCD
         *(pIndices+3) = WORD((i+1) + (j*(gridSize+1)));
         *(pIndices+4) = WORD(i + ((j+1)*(gridSize+1)));
         *(pIndices+5) = WORD((i+1) + ((j+1)*(gridSize+1)));
         pIndices+=6;
      }
    }

     m_pIndices->Unlock();
    return S_OK;
}
```

I've commented the code pretty heavily to help you understand what's going on. An index buffer is created and filled in much the same way as vertex buffers. Take a few minutes to stare at the code that assigns the index numbers—it's the last nested `for` loop. If you have trouble figuring it out, trace the code with a 2x2 grid and you'll get it.

This code creates an indexed triangle list. If you wanted to be truly efficient you'd rewrite the code to create an indexed triangle strip. All you have to do is change the index buffer. I'll leave that to you. If you can get that working you'll know you have no trouble understanding index buffers. The code that renders the grid looks very similar to the triangle example:

```
HRESULT Grid::Render(LPDIRECT3DDEVICE9 pDevice)
{
    // Setup our texture. Using textures introduces the texture stage states,
    // which govern how textures get blended together (in the case of multiple
    // textures) and lighting information. In this case, we are modulating
    // (blending) our texture with the diffuse color of the vertices.
    pDevice->SetTexture( 0, m_pTexture );
    pDevice->SetTextureStageState( 0, D3DTSS_COLOROP,   D3DTOP_MODULATE );
    pDevice->SetTextureStageState( 0, D3DTSS_COLORARG1, D3DTA_TEXTURE );
    pDevice->SetTextureStageState( 0, D3DTSS_COLORARG2, D3DTA_DIFFUSE );

   pDevice->SetStreamSource( 0, m_pVerts, 0, sizeof(COLORED_TEXTURED_VERTEX) );
   pDevice->SetIndices(m_pIndices);
   pDevice->SetFVF( D3DFVF_COLORED_TEXTURED_VERTEX );
   pDevice->DrawIndexedPrimitive(
     D3DPT_TRIANGLELIST , 0, 0, m_numVerts, 0, m_numPolys );

   return S_OK;
}
```

You'll note the few extra calls to let the renderer know that the triangles in the mesh are textured, and that the texture is affected by the diffuse color of the vertex. This means that a black and white texture will take on a colored hue based on the diffuse color setting of the vertex. It's a little like choosing different colored wallpaper with the same pattern.

Materials

There's a lot more to texturing than the few calls you've seen so far. One thing you'll need to check out in DirectX 9 is *materials*. When you look at the structure of `D3DMATEIRAL9`, you'll see things that remind you of those color settings in vertex data:

```
typedef struct _D3DMATERIAL9†{
    D3DCOLORVALUE†Diffuse;
```

```
    D3DCOLORVALUE†Ambient;
    D3DCOLORVALUE†Specular;
    D3DCOLORVALUE†Emissive;
    float†Power;
} D3DMATERIAL9;
```

If the DirectX 9 renderer doesn't have any specific color data for vertices, it will use the current material to set the color of each vertex, composing all the material color information with the active lights illuminating the scene.

One common mistake with DirectX 9 is not setting a default material. If your vertex data doesn't include diffuse or specular color information your mesh will appear completely black. If your game has a black background, objects in your scene will completely disappear!

Other than the critical information about needing a default material and texture, the DirectX SDK documentation does a pretty fair job of showing you what happens when you play with the specular and power settings. They can turn a plastic ping pong ball into a ball bearing, highlights and everything.

Texturing

Back in `Grid::Create` I quietly included some texture calls into the code. Let's start with what I did to actually create the texture in the first place, and go through the calls that apply the texture to a set of vertices. The first thing you'll do to create a texture is pop into Photoshop, Paint, or any bitmap editing tool. That leaves out tools like Macromedia Flash or Illustrator because they are vector tools and are no good for bitmaps.

Go into one of these tools and create an image 128x128 pixels in size. Figure 9.14 shows my version.

Save the texture as a TIF, TGA, or BMP. If you are working in Photoshop you'll want to save the PSD file for future editing but our next step can't read PSDs. Open the DirectX Texture Tool and load your texture file. Save it as a DDS file where your game will be able to load it. Your game will load the texture by calling a DirectX utility function:

```
if( FAILED( D3DUtil_CreateTexture(
      pDevice, "Textures\\texture.dds", &m_pTexture ) ) )
{
      return E_FAIL;
}
```

Figure 9.14
A Sample Texture.

This function makes some assumptions about how you want to load your texture. The source code for this function is in the code created by the DirectX 9 Project Wizard:

```
HRESULT D3DUtil_CreateTexture(
   LPDIRECT3DDEVICE9 pd3dDevice, TCHAR* strTexture,
   LPDIRECT3DTEXTURE9* ppTexture, D3DFORMAT d3dFormat )
{
    HRESULT hr;
    TCHAR strPath[MAX_PATH];

    // Get the path to the texture
    if( FAILED( hr = DXUtil_FindMediaFileCb(
                     strPath, sizeof(strPath), strTexture ) ) )
        return hr;

    // Create the texture using D3DX
    return D3DXCreateTextureFromFileEx( pd3dDevice, strPath,
              D3DX_DEFAULT, D3DX_DEFAULT, D3DX_DEFAULT, 0, d3dFormat,
              D3DPOOL_MANAGED, D3DX_FILTER_TRIANGLE|D3DX_FILTER_MIRROR,
              D3DX_FILTER_TRIANGLE|D3DX_FILTER_MIRROR, 0, NULL, NULL,
                                   ppTexture );
}
```

If you ever thought that texturing was trivial the call to `D3DXCreateTextureFromFileEX` should make you think twice. If you look at the DirectX 9 documentation on this function, it's clear there's a lot to learn—way too much for an introduction.

There is one important concept, *mip-mapping*, that needs special attention. If you've ever seen old 3D games, or perhaps just really bad 3D games, you'll probably recall an odd effect that happens to textured objects as you back away from them. This effect, called *scintillation*, is especially noticeable on textures with a regular pattern, such as a black and white checkerboard pattern. As the textured objects recedes in the distance, you begin to notice that the texture seems to jump around in weird patterns. This is due to an effect called *subsampling*.

Subsampling

Assume for the moment that a texture appears on a polygon very close to its original size. If the texture is 128x128 pixels, the polygon on the screen will look almost exactly like the texture. If this polygon were reduced to half of this size, 64x64 pixels, the renderer must choose which pixels from the original texture must be applied to the polygon. So what happens if the original texture looks like the one shown in Figure 9.15?

This texture is 128x128 pixels, with alternating vertical lines exactly one pixel in width. If you reduced this texture in a simple paint program, you might get nothing but a 64x64 texture that is completely black. What's going on here?

When the texture is reduced to half its size, the naïve approach would select every other pixel in the grid, which in this case happens to be every black pixel on the texture. The original texture has a certain amount of information, or *frequency* in its data stream. The frequency above texture is the number of alternating lines. Each pair of black and white lines is considered one wave in a waveform that makes up the entire texture. The frequency of this texture is 64, since it takes 64 waves of black and white lines to make up the texture.

Subsampling is what occurs if any waveform is sampled at less than twice its frequency, in the above case any sample taken at less than 128 will drop critical information from the original data stream.

Figure 9.15
A 128x128 Texture with Alternating White and Black Vertical Lines.

It might seem weird to think of a texture having a frequency, but they do. A high frequency implies a high degree of information content. In the case of a texture it has to do with the number of undulations in the waveform that make up the data stream. If the texture were nothing more than a black square it has a minimal frequency, and therefore carries only the smallest amount of information. A texture that is a solid black square, no matter how large, can be sampled at any rate whatsoever. No information is lost because there wasn't that much information to begin with.

In case you were wondering whether or not this subject of subsampling can apply to audio waveforms, it can. Let's assume you have a high frequency sound, say a tone at 11KHz. If you attempt to sample this tone in a WAV file at 11KHz, exactly the frequency of the tone, you won't be happy with the results. You'll get a subsampled version of the original sound. Just as the texture turned completely black, you're subsampled sound will be a completely flat line, erasing the sound altogether.

It turns out there is a solution for this problem, and it involves processing and filtering the original data stream to preserve as much of the original waveform as possible. For sounds and textures, the new sample isn't just grabbed from an original piece of data in the waveform. The data closest to the sample is used to figure out what is happening to the waveform, instead of one value of the waveform at a discrete point in time.

In the case of our lined texture above, the waveform is alternating from black to white as you sample horizontally across the texture, so naturally if the texture diminishes in size the eye should begin to perceive a 50% gray surface. It's no surprise that if you combine black and white in equal amounts you get 50% gray.

For textures, each sample involves the surrounding neighborhood of pixels—a process known as *bi-linear filtering*. The process is a linear combination of the pixel values on all sides sampled pixel—nine values in all. These nine values are weighted and combined to create the new sample. The same approach can be used with sounds as well, as you might have expected.

This processing and filtering is pretty expensive so you don't want to do it in real time for textures or sounds. Instead, you'll want to create a set of reduced images for each texture in your game. This master texture is known as a *mip-map*.

Mip-Mapping

Mip-mapping is a set of textures that have been pre-processed to contain one or more levels of size reduction. In practice, the size reduction is in halves, all the way down to one pixel that represents the dominant color of the entire texture. You might think that this is a waste of memory but it's actually more efficient than you'd think. A mip-map uses only 1/3 more memory than the original texture, and considering the vast improvement in the quality of the rendered result, you should provide mip-maps for any texture that has a relatively high frequency of information. It is especially useful for textures with regular patterns, such as our black and white line texture.

The DirectX Texture Tool can generate mip-maps for you. To do this you just load your texture and select Format, Generate Mip Maps. You can then see the resulting reduced textures by pressing PageUp and PageDn.

One last thing about mip-maps: As you might expect, the renderer will choose which mip-map to display based on the screen size of the polygon. This means that it's not a good idea to create huge polygons on your geometry that can recede into the distance. The renderer might not be able to make a good choice that will satisfy the look of the polygon edge both closest to the camera and the one farthest away. Most modern hardware has no problem with this, and selects the mip-map on a per-pixel basis. You can't always count on every player having modern hardware. Do some research before jumping in.

Also, while we're on the subject, many other things can go wrong with huge polygons in world space, such as lighting and collision. It's always a good idea to *tessellate*, or break up, large surfaces into smaller polygons that will provide the renderer with a good balance between polygon size and vertex count.

You might have heard of something called *tri-linear filtering*. If the renderer switches between one mip-map level on the same polygon, it's likely that you'll notice the switch. Most renderers can sample the texels from more than one mip-map, and blend their color in real time. This creates a smooth transition from one mip-map level to another, a much more realistic effect. As you approach something like a newspaper, the mip-maps are sampled in such a way that eventually the blurry image of the headline can resolve into something you can read and react to.

3D Graphics—It's That Simple

You've seen enough to be dangerous in DirectX 9, and perhaps even be dangerous in any other renderer you choose, such as OpenGL. The concepts I presented are the same, the only thing different is the function calls, the coordinate systems, the texturing support, how they expect your geometry, and so on. This chapter's goal was really not much more than a vocabulary lesson, and a beginning one at that. We'll get to more 3D material in the next chapter, so don't worry.

I suggest that you go play around a bit in DirectX 9's sample projects and get your bearings. Don't feel frustrated when you get lost either. Even while writing this book you could see me holding my hands in front of myself twisted like some madman, attempting to visualize rotations and cross products. With any luck, you've got just enough knowledge in your head to perform some of your own twisting and cursing.

Chapter 10

3D Engines

In the previous chapter you learned something about how to draw 3D geometry, but there's a lot more to a 3D game than drawing a few triangles. Even a relatively boring 3D game has characters, interesting environments, dynamic objects, and a few special effects here and there.

In a way, this chapter brings many concepts and source code that you've seen throughout the book together in one piece. I'm not going to fool you into thinking that by the end of this chapter you'll have the beginnings of a game that will beat the pants off of Bungie's Halo—one of my favorite games by the way. You will, however, develop the knowledge on how a prototype for a 3D game engine gets its start. With any luck you'll end this chapter with a healthy respect for the programmers that build 3D engines.

Setting Up a Project

If you haven't done it already, create a new Direct X 9 Visual C++ project, and if you want your code to look just like mine, call the project *SceneGraph*. The code I'll be presenting in this chapter will plug straight into the project the DirectX 9 wizard spits out. When you create the project, make sure you create a single document window, and clear the checkboxes for everything except Direct3D. The project will be a little cleaner and we can concentrate on Direct3D.

When the project is created, follow these steps:

- Open SceneGraph.h, and delete all references to `m_UserInput`, `m_fWorldRotX`, `m_fWorldRotY`, `m_pD3DXMesh` and void `UpdateInput( UserInput* pUserInput )`.
- Recompile and fix all the errors. When you run your project you should see nothing but a blank blue field with yellow text.
- Using your favorite paint program and the DirectX Texture Tool; create a Grid.dds file into a new Textures directory. It should be a 128x128 texture, with a black outline and a white background.

- Use the smart pointer class described in Chapter 3. Put it in a SmartPtr.h file.

Now you are ready to create a scene graph based 3D engine, using the DirectX renderer.

Using a Scene Graph

A *scene graph* is a dynamic data structure, similar to a multiway tree. Each node represents an object in a 3D world or perhaps an instruction to the renderer. Every node can have zero or more children nodes. The scene graph is traversed every frame to draw the visible world. The code you'll see that describes the scene graph classes can be installed into one CPP and H file, and added to the SceneGraph project. We'll take a look at the scene graph classes in detail and then I'll show you how to change your SceneGraph.cpp and SceneGraph.h files to install your new toys.

```
////////////////////////////////////////////////////
//
// File: SceneNodes.h
//
//    Contains some basic definitions for a simple
//    scene graph for use with DirectX 9.
//
////////////////////////////////////////////////////
#pragma once


#include <list>
#include <d3d9.h>
#include <d3dx9math.h>
#include "assert.h"
#include "SmartPtr.h"
#include "dxutil.h"
#include "d3dutil.h"

// Forward declarations
class SceneNode;
class Scene;
class MovementController;


typedef std::list<SmartPtr<SceneNode> > SceneNodeList;

////////////////////////////////////////////////////
//
// SceneNode Definition
//
```

```
////////////////////////////////////////////////////

class SceneNode
{
public:
   SceneNodeList            m_children;

   virtual ~SceneNode();

   virtual HRESULT VRenderChildren(Scene *);
   virtual HRESULT VRestore(Scene *);
   virtual HRESULT VUpdate(Scene *, DWORD const elapsedMs);

   virtual HRESULT VPreRender(Scene *) { return S_OK; }
   virtual HRESULT VRender(Scene *) { return S_OK; }
   virtual HRESULT VPostRender(Scene *) { return S_OK; }

   virtual void VSetTransform(
      const D3DXMATRIX *toWorld,
      const D3DXMATRIX *fromWorld=NULL) { }

};
```

You can probably tell immediately that `SceneNode` is meant to be a base class. A bunch of trivial virtual functions is a clear give-away. The goal for this class design is to give some flexibility to programmers that create new objects that inherit from `SceneNode`. Here's the implementation of the non-trivial `SceneNode` methods:


```
////////////////////////////////////////////////////
// SceneNode Implementation
////////////////////////////////////////////////////

SceneNode::~SceneNode()
{
   // Get rid of all those pesky kids...
   while (!m_children.empty())
   {
      m_children.pop_front();
   }
}

HRESULT SceneNode::VRestore(Scene *pScene)
{
   // This is meant to be called from any class
   // that inherits from SceneNode and overloads
```

```
    // VRestore()

    SceneNodeList::iterator i = m_children.begin();
    while (i != m_children.end())
    {
        (*i)->VRestore(pScene);
        i++;
    }
    return S_OK;
}

HRESULT SceneNode::VUpdate(Scene *pScene, DWORD const elapsedMs)
{
    // This is meant to be called from any class
    // that inherits from SceneNode and overloads
    // VUpdate()

    SceneNodeList::iterator i = m_children.begin(); while (i != m_children.end())
    {
        (*i)->VUpdate(pScene, elapsedMs);
        i++;
    }
    return S_OK;
}

HRESULT SceneNode::VRenderChildren(Scene *pScene)
{
    // Iterate through the children....
    SceneNodeList::iterator i = m_children.begin();
    while (i != m_children.end())
    {
        if ((*i)->VPreRender(pScene)==S_OK)
        {
            // You could short-circuit rendering
            // if an object returns E_FAIL from
            // VPreRender()

            (*i)->VRender(pScene);
            (*i)->VRenderChildren(pScene);
        }
        (*i)->VPostRender(pScene);
        i++;
    }

    return S_OK;
}
```

The two methods, VRestore() and VUpdate(), simply traverse their children nodes and recursively call the same methods. When you inherit from SceneNode and create a new object, don't forget to call the base class's SceneNode::VRestore() or SceneNode::VUpdate() if you happen to overload them. If you fail to do this, your children nodes won't get these calls. VRestore() is meant to recreate any programmatically created data after it has been lost. This is a similar concept to the section on lost 2D DirectDraw surfaces.

VUpdate() is meant to handle game logic, animations, or anything else that is meant to be decoupled from the rendering traversal. That's why it is called with the elapsed time, measured in milliseconds. You can use the elapsed time to make sure animations or other movements happen at a consistent speed, regardless of computer processing power. A faster CPU should always create a smoother animation, not necessarily a faster one!

The VRenderChildren() iterates through the child nodes and calls virtual functions you are meant to overload in inherited classes. VPreRender() is meant to perform any task that must occur before the render, such as a visibility test. VRender() does exactly what it advertises: It renders the object. A recursive call to VRenderChildren() is made to tranverse the scene graph, performing all these actions for every node. VPostRender() is meant to perform a post-rendering action, such as restoring a render state to it's original value.

Don't even think of trying to attach a node to itself, or any of its descendants. Infinite recursion is not how I like to spend my off-time.

Here's the definition of the Scene, a container for SceneNodes of all shapes and sizes.

10

```
////////////////////////////////////////////////////
//
// Scene Definition   (declared in SceneNodes.h)
//
// A heirarchical container of scene nodes.
////////////////////////////////////////////////////

class Scene
{
public:
   IDirect3DDevice9 *m_pDevice;
   SmartPtr<SceneNode>  m_root;
   ID3DXMatrixStack *m_matrixStack;
   SmartPtr<MovementController> m_pMovementController;

   Scene(IDirect3DDevice9 *device, SmartPtr<SceneNode> root);
   ~Scene();
```

```
    HRESULT Render();
    HRESULT Restore();
    HRESULT Update();
};
```

The Scene knows about four kinds of data. The IDirect3DDevice9 is the interface to the DirectX rendering device, and is used throughout the SceneNodes. As you might expect, the scene also has a root node, the exact nature of which we'll get to in a moment.

The interesting bit that you might not have seen before is a Direct3D matrix stack. Back in the easy 3D chapter, we did plenty of work with matrix concatenation. Any number of matrices could be multiplied, or concatenated, to create any bizarre and twisted set of rotation and translation operations. In the case of a hierarchical model, like a human figure, these matrix concatenations can get tedious unless you can push them onto and pop them from a stack. Hang tight; examples are coming soon.

The last data item is a user interface object called a *movement controller*, which grabs input from the keyboard and mouse and can be used to move any object in the scene graph in arbitrary ways. In practice this controller affects the camera object, but there's nothing wrong with hooking it up to anything else. Here's the implementation of the Scene class:

```
////////////////////////////////////////////////////
// Scene Implementation (declared in SceneNodes.cpp)
////////////////////////////////////////////////////

Scene::Scene(IDirect3DDevice9 *device, SmartPtr<SceneNode> root)
: m_root(root)
 ,m_pMovementController(NULL)
{
    m_pDevice = device;
    m_pDevice->AddRef();

    D3DXCreateMatrixStack(0, &m_matrixStack);
}

Scene::~Scene()
{
    SAFE_RELEASE(m_pDevice);
    SAFE_RELEASE(m_matrixStack);
}


HRESULT Scene::Render()
```

```
{
   if (!m_root)
      return S_OK;

   // The scene root could be anything, but it
   // is usually a TransformNode with the identity
   // matrix

   if (m_root->VPreRender(this)==S_OK)
   {
      m_root->VRender(this);
      m_root->VRenderChildren(this);
      m_root->VPostRender(this);
   }

   return S_OK;
}

HRESULT Scene::Restore()
{
   if (!m_root)
      return S_OK;

   return m_root->VRestore(this);
}

HRESULT Scene::Update()
{
   static DWORD lastTime = 0;
   DWORD elapsedTime = 0;
   DWORD now = timeGetTime();

   if (!m_root)
      return S_OK;

   if (lastTime == 0)
   {
      lastTime = now;
   }

   elapsedTime = now - lastTime;
   lastTime = now;

   // There's one controller. But that isn't
   // very usefull, is it??? You should make a list
   // of them.
```

```
    if (m_pMovementController)
      m_pMovementController->Update(elapsedTime);

    return m_root->VUpdate(this, elapsedTime);
}
```

The scene is created with a valid `IDirect3DDevice9` interface and a root node. The movement controller doesn't have to exist at all until we want one, which we'll do when we actually create the scene later in the chapter.. The other calls to `Scene::Update()`, `Scene::Render()`, and `Scene::Restore()` kick start the hierarchical traversal of the entire scene graph starting at the root node. The call to `Scene::Update()` includes a call to the Win32 API `timeGetTime()`, a reasonably efficient timer, accurate to a few milliseconds.

Scene Graph Nodes

These data structures by themselves do absolutely nothing exciting. We need some classes that inherit from `SceneNode` to construct an interesting scene. We'll start with `TransformNode`, an object that encapsulates a frame of reference, or a transformation matrix. Any object in the scene will use the functionality of the `TransformNode` to position and orient itself in world space. You could even attach groups of objects as children of this node to move and orient them as a group, such as objects on a boat. If you add `TransformNodes` as children of existing `TransformNode` structures, you'll get an object hierarchy such as a human figure. It's a fundamental part of any scene graph. Here's the definition of the class:

```
////////////////////////////////////////////////////
//
// TransformNode Definition
//
//    This node changes the local object to world
//    transform by using D3D's Matrix Stack
//
////////////////////////////////////////////////////

class TransformNode : public SceneNode
{
public:
   D3DXMATRIX m_toWorld, m_fromWorld;
   TransformNode(const D3DXMATRIX *to, const D3DXMATRIX *from=NULL)
      { VSetTransform(to, from); }
   virtual HRESULT VPreRender(Scene *);
   virtual HRESULT VPostRender(Scene *);
```

```
    virtual void VSetTransform(
        const D3DXMATRIX *toWorld,
        const D3DXMATRIX *fromWorld=NULL);
};
```

Did you notice that there are two matrices in this data structure? You already know that you need a matrix that transforms vertices from object space to world space, if you want to draw the object at any arbitrary location and orientation. It turns out to be incredibly useful to have an inverse of this matrix as well so that you can transform a vector that exists in world space back to object space. This is critical for making things like movement controllers, since they apply rotations and translations in object space. We'll see more about that later. Here's the code that implements `TransformNode`:

```
////////////////////////////////////////////////////
// TransformNode Implementation
////////////////////////////////////////////////////

HRESULT TransformNode::VPreRender(Scene *pScene)
{
    // Note this code carefully!!!!! It is COMPLETELY different
    // from some DirectX 9 documentation out there....

    pScene->m_matrixStack->Push();
    pScene->m_matrixStack->MultMatrixLocal(&m_toWorld);
    pScene->m_pDevice->SetTransform(D3DTS_WORLD,
                pScene->m_matrixStack->GetTop());
    return S_OK;
}

HRESULT TransformNode::VPostRender(Scene *pScene)
{
    pScene->m_matrixStack->Pop();
    pScene->m_pDevice->SetTransform(D3DTS_WORLD,
                                   pScene->m_matrixStack->GetTop());
    return S_OK;
}

void TransformNode::VSetTransform(const D3DXMATRIX *toWorld,
                                  const D3DXMATRIX *fromWorld)
{
    m_toWorld = *toWorld;
    if (!fromWorld)
    {
```

10

```
        // Good god this is expensive...why bother????
        D3DXMatrixInverse(&m_fromWorld, NULL, &m_toWorld);
    }
    else
    {
        m_fromWorld = *fromWorld;
    }
}
```

Remember matrix concatenation? This class encapsulates matrix concatenation, and does it with a stack. The call to `VPreRender()` pushes a new matrix on the matrix stack. The next call is a little confusing, and I won't ask you to visualize it because when I tried I got a pounding headache—but here's the gist of it. The matrix that exists at the top of the stack is either the identity matrix or the result of all the concatenated matrices from the hierarchy in your parent nodes in the scene graph. As you traverse to child nodes deeper in the scene graph, they will push their own transform matrix on the stack and cause it to be concatenated with every transform up the chain, but by only doing one matrix multiplication. As you can see, this is quite efficient, and extremely flexible for implementing hierarchical objects.

You can imagine this by thinking about your hand as a self-contained hierarchical object. The root would be your palm, and attached to it are five children—the first segment of each of your five fingers. Each of those finger segments has one child, the segment without a fingernail. Finally, the segment with the fingernail attaches, making the palm its great-grandfather. If the transform matrix for one of those finger segments is rotated around the right axis, the finger should bend, carrying all the child segments with it. If I change the translation or rotation of the palm, the root object, everything moves. That is the basic notion of a hierarchical animation system.

It's common for artists to create human figures with the hips, or should I say, groin as the root node. It's convenient because it is close to the center of the human body, and has three children: the torso and the two legs. One fine day the Ultima VIII team went to the park for lunch, and played a little Ultimate Frisbee. As happens frequently in that game, two players went to catch the Frisbee at the same time, and collided. One of them was curled up on the ground writhing in pain, and when I asked what happened I was told that they caught an elbow right in the root of their hierarchy.

The call to `VSetTransform()` will calculate the inverse transform matrix for you if you didn't send it in. Yes it's somewhat expensive, if you've ever seen the formula for calculating the determinant of a 4x4 matrix you know what I'm talking about. If you've never seen it, just imagine an entire case of alphabet soup laid out on a recursive grid. It's gross.

But the inverse transform can be very useful, especially if you want to set a view matrix. If a camera were an object in a 3D world with a regular transform of its own, the view matrix that you would use to transform everything in the world to camera space is the inverse of the camera object's regular transform matrix. It can also be extremely useful for object picking, where you transform a screen space coordinate into world space, and finally into object space to find out what part of an object your mouse pointer is touching.

Another important scene graph node encapsulates the location and orientation of the camera. Here's the definition and implementation for the `CameraNode`:

```
////////////////////////////////////////////////////
//
// CameraNode Definition
//
//    A camera node controls the D3D view transform
//
////////////////////////////////////////////////////

class CameraNode : public TransformNode
{
public:
   CameraNode(const D3DXMATRIX *t) : TransformNode(t) { }
   virtual HRESULT VUpdate(Scene *, DWORD const elapsedMs);
};


HRESULT CameraNode::VUpdate(Scene *pScene, DWORD const )
{
   pScene->m_pDevice->SetTransform( D3DTS_VIEW, &m_fromWorld );
   return S_OK;
}
```

It inherits from `TransformNode` to take advantage of the matrix stack. If we wanted to, we could attach the camera node to any object in the scene, and as it moved around the camera would automatically follow. The call to `VUpdate()` sets the `IDirect3DDevice9`'s view transformation. A good thing to note right off is that scene graphs are tough to optimize. A robust version of this simpleton scene graph technology would be to check for changes in the `m_fromWorld` transform and if nothing changed, to leave Direct3D alone—every call takes time.

10

Avoid calling members of the `IDirect3DDevice9` class unless you absolutely have to. Unnecessary calls to the renderer will slow it down.

We still haven't seen anything that will actually draw a shape on the screen yet. Here's a class you'll recognize from earlier in the book–`Grid`:

```
////////////////////////////////////////////////////
//
// Grid Definition
//
//    A slightly modified version of Grid from
//       the beginning 3D chapter
//
////////////////////////////////////////////////////

class Grid : public TransformNode
{
protected:
   LPDIRECT3DTEXTURE9       m_pTexture;     // the grid texture
   LPDIRECT3DVERTEXBUFFER9  m_pVerts;       // the grid verts
   LPDIRECT3DINDEXBUFFER9   m_pIndices;     // the grid index
   DWORD                    m_numVerts;
   DWORD                    m_numPolys;
   DWORD                    m_gridSize;
   DWORD                    m_color;
   const TCHAR *            m_textureFile;

public:
   Grid(const DWORD gridSize, const DWORD color,
        const TCHAR *textureFile, const D3DXMATRIX *t);
   ~Grid();
   HRESULT VRestore(Scene *pScene);
   HRESULT VRender(Scene *pScene);
};

////////////////////////////////////////////////////
// Grid Implementation
////////////////////////////////////////////////////

Grid::Grid(const DWORD gridSize,
         const DWORD color,
         const TCHAR *textureFile,
         const D3DXMATRIX *t)
   : TransformNode(t)
```

```
{
   m_gridSize = gridSize;
   m_color = color;
   m_textureFile = textureFile;

   m_pTexture = NULL;
   m_pVerts = NULL;
   m_pIndices = NULL;
   m_numVerts = m_numPolys = 0;
}


Grid::~Grid()
{
   SAFE_RELEASE(m_pTexture);
   SAFE_RELEASE(m_pVerts);
   SAFE_RELEASE(m_pIndices);
}


HRESULT Grid::VRestore(Scene *pScene)
{
   // The code is exactly the same as in the Grid class
   //   you've seen - go grab the code you saw previously. . .
}


HRESULT Grid::VRender(Scene *pScene)
{
   // This is slightly different from the Chapter 7 implementation...
   // We take a little care to restore render states after we change them...

   LPDIRECT3DDEVICE9 pDevice = pScene->m_pDevice;

   DWORD oldLightMode;
   pDevice->GetRenderState( D3DRS_LIGHTING, &oldLightMode );
   pDevice->SetRenderState( D3DRS_LIGHTING, FALSE );

   DWORD oldCullMode;
   pDevice->GetRenderState( D3DRS_CULLMODE, &oldCullMode );
   pDevice->SetRenderState( D3DRS_CULLMODE, D3DCULL_NONE );

   // Setup our texture. Using textures introduces the texture stage states,
   // which govern how textures get blended together (in the case of multiple
   // textures) and lighting information. In this case, we are modulating
   // (blending) our texture with the diffuse color of the vertices.
```

```
    pDevice->SetTexture( 0, m_pTexture );
    pDevice->SetTextureStageState( 0, D3DTSS_COLOROP,   D3DTOP_MODULATE );
    pDevice->SetTextureStageState( 0, D3DTSS_COLORARG1, D3DTA_TEXTURE );
    pDevice->SetTextureStageState( 0, D3DTSS_COLORARG2, D3DTA_DIFFUSE );

    pDevice->SetStreamSource( 0, m_pVerts, 0,
                             sizeof(COLORED_TEXTURED_VERTEX) );
    pDevice->SetIndices(m_pIndices);
    pDevice->SetFVF( D3DFVF_COLORED_TEXTURED_VERTEX );
    pDevice->DrawIndexedPrimitive(
       D3DPT_TRIANGLELIST,0,0,m_numVerts,0,m_numPolys );

    // Notice that the render states are returned to
    // their original settings.....
    // Could there be a better way???

    pDevice->SetTexture (0, NULL);
    pDevice->SetRenderState( D3DRS_LIGHTING, oldLightMode );
    pDevice->SetRenderState( D3DRS_CULLMODE, oldCullMode );

    return S_OK;
}
```

The implementation of the `Grid` class is exactly the same as you remember from the first 3D chapter, with two exceptions. First, the names of the methods to have been changed to conform with the `SceneNode` base class. Second, the render method restores the render state after the geometry is sent to the card with `DrawIndexedPrimitive`.

This is one of the quirky things about a scene graph architecture: You can't be sure what the render state is at the beginning of a call to `VRender()`, so you tend to set the render states you absolutely need to render your object, and you restore settings after you're done with the render. If you think this will result in calling `SetRenderState` way too many times, you are absolutely right. You could encapsulate render states in an object of some kind, and create a utility function that figures out which render states need setting and which are good the way they are. Even better, this fictional `RenderStateDelta` object could be pre-calculated when nodes get added or removed from the scene graph, since they probably don't change much at run time. In any case, you should take the problem of minimizing the calls to renderer seriously.

A 3D game would be pretty boring with nothing but grids drawing at various positions and rotations. If you want interesting shapes you'll need to create them in a modeling tool like 3D Studio Max. Modeling tools are precise tools for creating shapes for your game levels or dynamic objects. DirectX can't read a ".MAX" or ".3DS" file directly, you'll need to convert it to a ".X" file with DirectX's conv3ds.exe utility. You can find help for this program in MSDN and elsewhere on the web.

Once you have a ".X" file, you can create a mesh object that DirectX can read natively, and all you need is a way to plug this object into the scene graph. The node you are looking for is `MeshNode`:

```
////////////////////////////////////////////////////
//
// MeshNode Definition
//
//    Attaches a D3D mesh object to the scene graph
//    with an accompanying material
//
////////////////////////////////////////////////////

class MeshNode : public TransformNode
{
protected:
   ID3DXMesh *m_mesh;
   D3DMATERIAL9 m_material;

public:
   MeshNode(ID3DXMesh *mesh, const D3DXMATRIX *t,
                       const D3DMATERIAL9 &material)
      : TransformNode(t)
      { m_mesh = mesh;  m_material = material; m_mesh->AddRef(); }

   virtual ~MeshNode() { SAFE_RELEASE(m_mesh); }
   virtual HRESULT VRender(Scene *);
};


HRESULT MeshNode::VRender(Scene *pScene)
{
   pScene->m_pDevice->SetMaterial( &m_material );
   return m_mesh->DrawSubset(0);
}
```

This node encapsulates `ID3DXMesh`, a D3D object that is created from a loaded ".X" file, DirectX's mesh file format. You can create simple meshes with the DirectX Mesh Viewer Utility, such as boxes, spheres, and all the teapots you could ever want. `MeshNode` inherits from `TransferNode` to utilize its position and orientation features, and adds `D3DMATERIAL9` so that the mesh objects can render with different color and light properties.

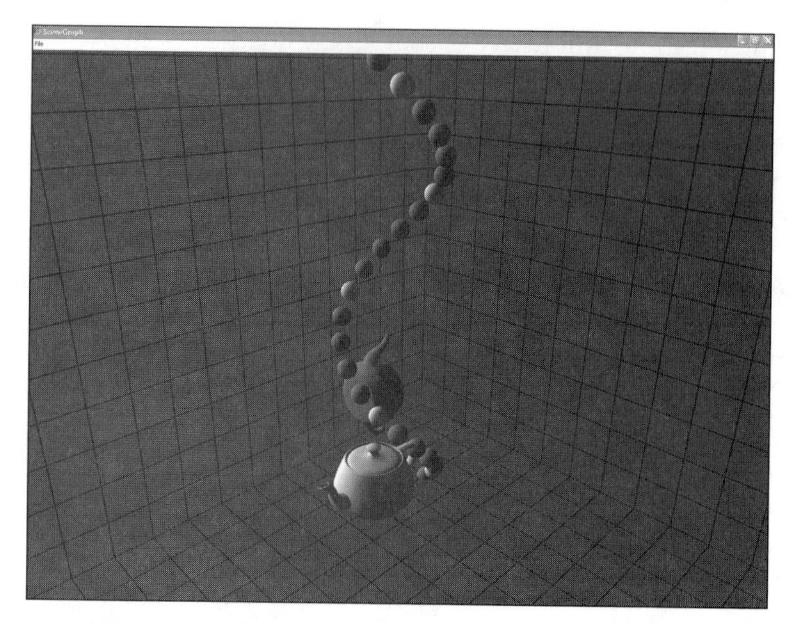

Figure 10.1
A Basic Scene: Teapots, Little Balls, and Some Grids.

Building Your Scene

With only the classes you've seen you can build a pretty complicated set of objects in a 3D world. I'll show you the code necessary to build the scene shown in Figure 10.1.

Something that isn't visible in the figure is that the balls are hierarchically linked with the lowest ball at the root. If this ball is moved or rotated the entire spiral structure would move with it. Any member of this structure could be rotated or translated without affecting any parent nodes—only the children. Here's the code to build this scene:

```
/////////////////////////////////////////////////////
// Free Function to Build the Scene
/////////////////////////////////////////////////////

Scene *BuildScene(IDirect3DDevice9 *d3dDevice)
{
   // Setup some materials - we'll use these for
   // making the same mesh appear in multiple
   // colors

   D3DMATERIAL9 colors[5];
   D3DUtil_InitMaterial( colors[0], 1.0f, 1.0f, 1.0f );   // white
   D3DUtil_InitMaterial( colors[1], 0.0f, 1.0f, 1.0f );   // cyan
   D3DUtil_InitMaterial( colors[2], 1.0f, 0.0f, 0.0f );   // red
```

```
D3DUtil_InitMaterial( colors[3], 0.0f, 1.0f, 0.0f );   // green
D3DUtil_InitMaterial( colors[4], 0.0f, 0.0f, 1.0f );   // blue

// The identity matrix is always useful
D3DXMATRIX ident;
D3DXMatrixIdentity(&ident);

// We'll use these rotations for some teapots and grid objects
D3DXMATRIX rotateX, rotateZ;
D3DXMatrixRotationZ(&rotateZ, D3DX_PI / 2.0f);
D3DXMatrixRotationX(&rotateX, -D3DX_PI / 2.0f);

// Create the root, and the camera.
// Remeber how to use smart pointers?? I hope so!

SmartPtr<SceneNode> root(new TransformNode(&ident));
SmartPtr<SceneNode> camera(new CameraNode(&ident));
root->m_children.push_back(camera);

ID3DXMesh *teapot;
 if( SUCCEEDED( D3DXCreateTeapot( d3dDevice, &teapot, NULL ) ) )
{
   // Teapot #1 - a white one at (x=6,y=2,z=4)
   D3DXMATRIX trans;
   D3DXMatrixTranslation(&trans,6,2,4);

   SmartPtr<SceneNode> mesh1(new MeshNode(teapot, &trans, colors[0]));
   root->m_children.push_back(mesh1);

   // Teapot #2 - a cyan one at (x=3,y=2,z=1)
   //   with a
   D3DXMatrixTranslation(&trans, 3,2,1);
   D3DXMATRIX result;
   D3DXMatrixMultiply(&result, &rotateZ, &trans);

   SmartPtr<SceneNode> mesh2(new MeshNode(teapot, &result, colors[1]));
   root->m_children.push_back(mesh2);

   // We can release the teapot now, mesh1 and mesh2 AddRef'd it.
   SAFE_RELEASE(teapot);
 }

 ID3DXMesh *sphere;
 if ( SUCCEEDED(
    D3DXCreateSphere(
       d3dDevice, .25, 16, 16, &sphere, NULL) ) )
```

10

```
    {
        // We're going to create a spiral of spheres...
        // starting at (x=3, y=0, z=3), and spiraling
        // upward about a local Y axis.

        D3DXMATRIX trans;
        D3DXMatrixTranslation(&trans, 3,0,3);

        SmartPtr<SceneNode> sphere1(new MeshNode(sphere, &trans,
                                                 colors[4]) );
        root->m_children.push_back(sphere1);

        // Here's the local rotation and translation.
        // We'll rotate about Y, and then translate
        // up (along Y) and forward (along Z).
        D3DXMATRIX rotateY;
        D3DXMatrixRotationY(&rotateY, D3DX_PI / 8.0f);
        D3DXMATRIX trans2;
        D3DXMatrixTranslation(&trans2, 0, 0.5, 0.5);
        D3DXMATRIX result;
        D3DXMatrixMultiply(&result, &trans2, &rotateY);

        for (int i=0; i<25; i++)
        {
            // If you didn't think smart pointers were cool -
            // watch this! No leaked memory....

            // Notice this is a heirarchy....
            SmartPtr<SceneNode> sphere2(
                new MeshNode(sphere, &result, colors[i%5]) );

            sphere1->m_children.push_back(sphere2);
            sphere1 = sphere2;
        }

        // We can release the sphere now, all the cylinders AddRef'd it.
        SAFE_RELEASE(sphere);
    }

    // Here are the grids...they make it easy for us to
    // see where the coordinates are in 3D space.

    SmartPtr<SceneNode> grid1(
        new Grid(40, 0x00400000, "Textures\\grid.dds", &ident));
    root->m_children.push_back(grid1);
```

```
    SmartPtr<SceneNode> grid2(
        new Grid(40, 0x00004000, "Textures\\grid.dds", &rotateX));
    root->m_children.push_back(grid2);

    SmartPtr<SceneNode> grid3(
        new Grid(40, 0x00000040, "Textures\\grid.dds", &rotateZ));
    root->m_children.push_back(grid3);

    // Everything has been attached to the root. Now
    // we attach the root to the scene.

    Scene *scene = new Scene(d3dDevice, root);
    scene->Restore();

    // A movement controller is going to control the camera,
    // but it could be constructed with any of the objects you see in this
    // function. You can have your very own remote controlled sphere.
    // What fun...
    SmartPtr<MovementController> m_pMovementController(
        new MovementController(camera));

    scene->m_pMovementController = m_pMovementController;
    return scene;
}
```

This code makes good use of the `SmartPtr` class you read about in Chapter 3. If we had to call a naïve reference counting mechanism explicitly this code would be a lot longer, and a lot less clearer.

10

The root node of the scene graph is a simple `TransformNode` with the identity as its transform matrix. Everything in the scene graph is attached to this node, including the camera node, which will be used to set the view transform matrix if the camera moves about the scene. After the camera is added to the scene, a teapot is created using the `D3DXCreateTeapot` call. Why would DirectX bother to have a special call to create a teapot? A little research on the web will find the answer:

"Aside from that, people have pointed out that it is a useful object to test with. It's instantly recognizable, it has complex topology, it self-shadows, there are hidden surface issues, it has both convex and concave surfaces, as well as 'saddle points.' It doesn't take much storage space—it's rumored that some of the early pioneers of computer graphics could type in the teapot from memory."
– quoted directly from http://sjbaker.org/teapot/.

Some 3D graphics professionals have even given this shape a special name—the "teapotahedron." It turns out that the original teapot that has come to be the official symbol of SIGGRAPH now lies in the Ephemera Collection of the Computer History Museum in Mountain View, California. Someday I should make a pilgrimage.

The code creates one teapot mesh, and attaches it to two `MeshNode` objects. This is perfectly fine and good, since the `ID3DXMesh` object is a COM based doo-dad and can therefore be reference counted.

The sphere objects are created next, but with a twist. I can't believe I wrote that! Once you're done rolling your eyes you'll see that I'm not kidding. The goal of the sphere creation is to make a complicated hierarchical object. If we animated the sphere's orientation randomly, the entire spiral structure would wag around like my dog's tail gone haywire.

The first sphere is attached to the root node just like the teapots. Then the code enters a loop, which creates a new sphere and attaches it to the first sphere. The last line of the loop does an odd thing. If you think it looks like a tail pointer in a linked list you aren't far from being wrong at all. Remember that `sphere1` and `sphere2` are essentially pointers to spheres. They don't seem like pointers because they are being managed by the `SmartPtr` template class, which does all the reference counting for you. As the loop iterates, new spheres are created and added to the deepening hierarchy.

Take a moment to look at the definition of the transform matrix, `result`. It rotates its target about the Y-axis by $\pi/8$ radians, then moves it up a half unit and forward a half unit. Stare at this transform a moment and you'll see that a deepening hierarchy of objects using this transform will resemble a single helix shape.

The grid objects are created next, and they are positioned to sit on the axis planes. Each grid object is attached directly to the root node. On another inspection it might have been wise to attach three grids to another `TransformNode`, and attach that node to the root. If I had done it that way I could have moved the grid objects as a single entity.

Once everything has been created and attached to the root node, the root node itself is attached to the scene, and the scene `Restore()` function is called to traverse each node and call it's overloaded `SceneNode::VRestore` method. This call will kick start your scene into action. In our case, the only node that happens to use `VRestore` is the `Grid` object, but there's nothing that would keep you from creating other nodes that did useful work outside of their constructors.

There's one important class I've failed to mention, the `MovementController` used in our scene to move the camera in and around the scene with a familiar interface from our many hours getting fragged in Quake.

A Useful Camera Controller

A camera controller needs to grab some keyboard and mouse input and translate that input into camera movement that people expect. The camera movement I'm speaking of performs the following tasks:

- Moves the camera straight ahead when the player presses 'W,' and straight backwards when the user presses 'S.'
- When the left mouse button is held, mouse movement will yaw and pitch the camera.
- The camera has total freedom of movement and can fly about the scene wherever we wish.

This controller class uses two interface classes from the user interface chapter:

```
////////////////////////////////////////////////////
//
// IKeyboardSensitive & IMouseSensitive
// Interface Definition
//
////////////////////////////////////////////////////

class IKeyboardSensitive
{
   virtual void OnKeyDown(const BYTE c)=0;
   virtual void OnKeyUp(const BYTE c)=0;
};

class IMouseSensitive
{
public:
   virtual void OnMouseMove(const POINTS &mousePos) = 0;
   virtual void OnLButtonDown(const POINTS &mousePos) = 0;
   virtual void OnLButtonUp(const POINTS &mousePos) = 0;
   virtual void OnRButtonDown(const POINTS &mousePos) = 0;
   virtual void OnRButtonUp(const POINTS &mousePos) = 0;
};


////////////////////////////////////////////////////
//
// MovementController Definition
//
//    Implements a quake-style movement controller
```

```
//
/////////////////////////////////////////////////////

class MovementController : public IMouseSensitive, public IKeyboardSensitive
{
protected:
   D3DXMATRIX m_matFromWorld;
   D3DXMATRIX       m_matToWorld;
   D3DXMATRIX m_matPosition;

   BOOL    m_bLeftMouseDown;
   POINTS     m_mousePos;            // The current mouse postion
   POINTS     m_mousePosOnDown;      // The position of the mouse on
                                     //   a down event
   BYTE    m_bKey[256];              // Which keys are up and down

   // Orientation Controls
   FLOAT      m_fTargetYaw;
   FLOAT      m_fTargetPitch;
   FLOAT      m_fYaw;
   FLOAT      m_fPitch;
   FLOAT      m_fPitchOnDown;
   FLOAT      m_fYawOnDown;

   SmartPtr<SceneNode> m_object;

public:
   MovementController(SmartPtr<SceneNode> object);
   void SetObject(SmartPtr<SceneNode> newObject);

   void Update(DWORD const elapsedMs);

public:
   void OnMouseMove(const POINTS &mousePos);
   void OnLButtonDown(const POINTS &mousePos);
   void OnLButtonUp(const POINTS &mousePos);
   void OnRButtonDown(const POINTS &mousePos) { }
   void OnRButtonUp(const POINTS &mousePos) { }

   void OnKeyDown(const BYTE c) { m_bKey[c] = true; }
   void OnKeyUp(const BYTE c) { m_bKey[c] = false; }

   const D3DXMATRIX *GetToWorld() { return &m_matToWorld; }
   const D3DXMATRIX *GetFromWorld() { return &m_matFromWorld; }
};
```

Note that the class has three transform matrices. You'll recognize the to-world and from-world transforms from the `TransformNode` class, but it also keeps a position transform matrix separate from the others. The `OnKeyDown()` and `OnKeyUp()` events simply record which buttons are being depressed in a Boolean matrix—nothing tough here.

Most of the member variables track the movement of the mouse and its effects. When the left mouse button goes down the current position is recorded and compared with movement events until the button is released. Horizontal movement of the mouse affects yaw of the object, and vertical movement affects pitch. The member variables that include pitch and yaw in their names are used to calculate the magnitude of the movement events, translated into rotations. Here's the implementation of the movement controller class:

```
////////////////////////////////////////////////////
// MovementController Implementation
////////////////////////////////////////////////////

#define MAX(a, b) ((a) >= (b) ? (a) : (b))
#define MIN(a, b) ((a) < (b) ? (a) : (b))

MovementController::MovementController(SmartPtr<SceneNode> object)
: m_object(object)
{
   D3DXMatrixIdentity(&m_matFromWorld);
   D3DXMatrixIdentity(&m_matToWorld);
   D3DXMatrixIdentity(&m_matPosition);

   m_fTargetYaw = m_fTargetPitch = 0.0f;
   m_fYaw = m_fPitch = 0.0f;

   m_bLeftMouseDown = false;

   memset(m_bKey, 0x00, sizeof(m_bKey));
}


void MovementController::OnMouseMove(const POINTS &mousePos)
{
   if (m_bLeftMouseDown)
   {
      // Every time the mouse moves, figure out how far and in
      // which direction. The X axis is for yaw, the Y axis is
      // for pitch.

      m_fTargetYaw = m_fYawOnDown + (m_mousePosOnDown.x - mousePos.x);
```

10

```
        m_fTargetPitch = m_fPitchOnDown + (mousePos.y - m_mousePosOnDown.y);
    }
}

void MovementController::OnLButtonDown(const POINTS &mousePos)
{
    // The mouse is down - record where it happened.
    m_bLeftMouseDown = true;
    m_mousePosOnDown = mousePos;
    m_fYawOnDown = m_fTargetYaw;
    m_fPitchOnDown = m_fTargetPitch;
}

void MovementController::OnLButtonUp(const POINTS &)
{
    m_bLeftMouseDown = false;
}


void MovementController::Update(DWORD const)
{
    if (m_bKey['W'] || m_bKey['S'])
    {
        // In D3D, the "look at" default is always
        // the positive Z axis.
        D3DXVECTOR4 at = D3DXVECTOR4(0.0f,0.0f,1.0f,0.0);
        if (m_bKey['S'])
            at *= -1;

        D3DXVECTOR4 atWorld(0,0,0,0);

        // This will give us the "look at" vector
        // in world space - we'll use that to move
        // the camera.
        D3DXVec4Transform(&atWorld, &at, &m_matToWorld);

        // But not an entire meter at a time!
        atWorld *= 0.1f;

        D3DXMATRIX camTranslate;
        D3DXMatrixTranslation(&camTranslate, atWorld.x, atWorld.y, atWorld.z);

        // The newly created delta position matrix, camTranslate,
        // is concatenated with the member position matrix.
        D3DXMatrixMultiply(&m_matPosition, &m_matPosition, &camTranslate);
    }
```

```
    if (m_bLeftMouseDown)
    {
        // The secret formula!!! Don't give it away!
        m_fYaw += (m_fTargetYaw - m_fYaw) * ( 0.35f );
        m_fTargetPitch = MAX(-90, MIN(90, m_fTargetPitch));
        m_fPitch += (m_fTargetPitch - m_fPitch) * ( 0.35f );

        // Calculate the new rotation matrix from the camera
        // yaw and pitch.
        D3DXMATRIX matRot;
        D3DXMatrixRotationYawPitchRoll(
            &matRot, -m_fYaw * D3DX_PI / 180,          // yaw
            m_fPitch * D3DX_PI / 180,                  // pitch
            0);                                        // roll

        // Create the new object-to-world matrix, and the
        // new world-to-object matrix.
        D3DXMatrixMultiply(&m_matToWorld, &matRot, &m_matPosition);
        D3DXMatrixInverse(&m_matFromWorld, NULL, &m_matToWorld);

        m_object->VSetTransform(&m_matToWorld, &m_matFromWorld);
    }
}
```

The first four methods: the constructor, `OnMouseMove`, `OnLButtonDown`, and `OnLButtonUp` are pretty self explanatory. The event based methods simply record what happened. The real meat of this function is inside `Update()`, which our scene graph will call whenever its `Update()` function is called. `Update()` has two independent sections. The first one handles object translation forward and backward along its "look-at" vector in world space. The second handles object rotations based on mouse movement.

If you want something to move forward, you must find out in which direction "forward" is. In DirectX, forward is always the positive Z-axis. Since you have a to-world transform, all you need to do is transform a unit Z vector into world space, and you'll be rewarded with a unit vector that points forward in the world for your object. Note that the unit vector is multiplied by -1 if we want to move backwards.

This implies something very serious about how your artists create their 3D models. In DirectX, "up" is always the Y-axis and "forward" is always the Z-axis. You'll want to make sure your artists are creating models that follow this scheme. An artist might create a rocket model in the classic pose, standing straight up, ready for launch. This would be wrong. The artist should create it with its body skewered on the Z-axis. When you move it "forward," along its transformed Z in world space, it will do exactly as you expect.

One more nit about model creation: Make sure that artists create models with convenient origins. Some artists might create a model of a door standing straight up, centered on the origin. This would also be wrong. The door should be able to rotate around its hinge without figuring out wacky interim translations so the artist should place a door hinge directly above the origin. When someone opens the door, all that will be needed in the game is a simple rotation about the Y-axis.

This kind of thing is very unintuitive for artists, and also isn't encouraged by many modeling tools. Most tools like 3D Studio Max tend to model things centered on the origin, and not every object has a natural rotation about its center of mass—a door being the best example.

Now we have a translation vector in world space, but it doesn't make sense to apply it directly to the object in question—it's not the right size. Usually you would calculate the maximum speed and acceleration of the object, and multiply the resulting world space vector with a scalar value to get something in the range you want. In this code, I'm simply limiting the vector to 1/10 of a unit. The resulting world space vector is used to construct a translation matrix, which is concatenated with the position matrix of the controller. Thus concludes the first part, and the easiest part, of this controller. Next come the rotations.

The first three lines of the rotation calculation are not that hard to visualize. Think of the yaw case, because it's easier and it doesn't have wacky limits. We arbitrarily limit the pitch to straight up and down. We'll break the yaw calculation down to an atomic level so you can see what's going on. When the left mouse button goes down, this code runs:

```
m_mousePosOnDown = mousePos;
m_fYawOnDown = m_fTargetYaw;
```

The current mouse position is recorded as well as the current target yaw. When the mouse moves around as shown here:

```
m_fTargetYaw = m_fYawOnDown + (m_mousePosOnDown.x - mousePos.x);
```

The target yaw becomes the sum of the yaw recorded when the mouse went down, which is the same value the first time the mouse moves, and the delta mouse horizontal movement. The target yaw therefore becomes a new yaw based on the difference between where we started and how far the mouse has been moved.

Finally, the update:

```
m_fYaw += (m_fTargetYaw - m_fYaw) * ( 0.35f );
```

This formula figures out how far to rotate the camera, in degrees, based on the number of pixels the mouse has moved. There's a mysterious `0.35f` multiplier in there. It alters the yaw calculation by a constant. The higher the constant, the farther your rotation will be for the same mouse movement. Notice that this constant cares nothing for screen width. Mouse movement is measured in pixels, but remember that the amount of physical movement it takes to move the mouse one pixel is pretty similar regardless of your current screen resolution.

The pitch calculation works in the same way, but it has an upper and lower limit. We don't want to deal with the camera pitching up and over—it would be upside down! The yaw and pitch are converted to radians and sent into a call that will create a transform matrix with yaw, pitch, and roll angles. Our roll angle is set to zero. The resulting matrix is concatenated with the to-world transformation matrix. An inverse matrix is calculated, and sent into the `VSetTransform()` of our controlled object. This implies that the movement controller can be used to control any object in the scene, which is completely true. Instead of attaching it to the camera node, I could have attached it to one of the sphere nodes, and watched them wiggle around as I activated the mouse.

Plugging the SceneGraph into the DirectX Playground

Here's exactly what you need to do to install your scene graph nodes into the SceneGraph.cpp and SceneGraph.h files that were automatically created with the DirectX 9 project wizard. First, go into the .h file and add the scene as a member of `CMyD3DApplication`:

```
class CMyD3DApplication : public CD3DApplication
{
   // Leave the class exactly the same!

   // ADD THIS CODE!  for the SceneGraph project...
    class Scene*            m_pScene;
};
```

The rest of the changes will be made to the .cpp file. First, add the `#include` for your scene node classes:

```
// ADD THIS CODE!  for the SceneGraph project...
#include "SceneNodes.h"
```

Second, set the scene member variable to `NULL` in the constructor for the application class:

```
CMyD3DApplication::CMyD3DApplication()
{
   // ... this code stays exactly as it was created.
```

```
    // ADD THIS CODE!  for the SceneGraph project...
    m_pScene = NULL;
}
```

Change `InitDeviceObjects()` to add a call to the free function that builds the scene:

```
HRESULT CMyD3DApplication::InitDeviceObjects()
{
     // Init the font
     m_pFont->InitDeviceObjects( m_pd3dDevice );

    // ADD THIS CODE!  for the SceneGraph project...
    m_pScene = BuildScene(m_pd3dDevice);
    return S_OK;
}
```

`FrameMove()` becomes a lot simpler—you only have to call `Scene::Update()`:

```
HRESULT CMyD3DApplication::FrameMove()
{
      // CHANGE THIS CODE!  for the SceneGraph project...

      m_pScene->Update();
       return S_OK;
}
```

`Render()` has a similar change. This is where `Scene::Render()` is called:

```
HRESULT CMyD3DApplication::Render()
{
      // Clear the viewport
      m_pd3dDevice->Clear( 0L, NULL, D3DCLEAR_TARGET|D3DCLEAR_ZBUFFER,
                           0x000000ff, 1.0f, 0L );

     // Begin the scene
     if( SUCCEEDED( m_pd3dDevice->BeginScene() ) )
     {
       // CHANGE THIS CODE!  for the SceneGraph project...
       if (m_pScene)
           m_pScene->Render();

       // Render stats and help text
       //RenderText();

       // End the scene.
```

```
        m_pd3dDevice->EndScene();
    }

    return S_OK;
}
```

MsgProc has some significant changes. The keyboard and mouse events are sent directly to the movement controller class:

```
LRESULT CMyD3DApplication::MsgProc(
    HWND hWnd, UINT msg, WPARAM wParam, LPARAM lParam )
{
    switch( msg )
    {
        case WM_PAINT:
        {
            if( m_bLoadingApp )
            {
                // Draw on the window tell the user that the app is loading
                // TODO: change as needed
                HDC hDC = GetDC( hWnd );
                TCHAR strMsg[MAX_PATH];
                wsprintf( strMsg, TEXT("Loading... Please wait") );
                RECT rct;
                GetClientRect( hWnd, &rct );
                DrawText(
                  hDC, strMsg, -1, &rct, DT_CENTER|DT_VCENTER|DT_SINGLELINE );
                ReleaseDC( hWnd, hDC );
            }
            break;
        }

      // ADD THIS CODE!  for the SceneGraph project...

      case WM_KEYDOWN:
         if (m_pScene && m_pScene->m_pMovementController)
             m_pScene->m_pMovementController->
                 OnKeyDown(static_cast<const BYTE>(wParam));
         break;

       case WM_KEYUP:
         if (m_pScene && m_pScene->m_pMovementController)
             m_pScene->m_pMovementController->
                 OnKeyUp(static_cast<const BYTE>(wParam));
         break;
```

```
        case WM_MOUSEMOVE:
          if (m_pScene && m_pScene->m_pMovementController)
              m_pScene->m_pMovementController->
                  OnMouseMove(MAKEPOINTS(lParam));
          break;

        case WM_LBUTTONDOWN:
          SetCapture(hWnd);
          if (m_pScene && m_pScene->m_pMovementController)
             m_pScene->m_pMovementController->
                  OnLButtonDown(MAKEPOINTS(lParam));
          break;
        case WM_LBUTTONUP:
          SetCapture(NULL);
          if (m_pScene && m_pScene->m_pMovementController)
             m_pScene->m_pMovementController->
                  OnLButtonUp(MAKEPOINTS(lParam));
          break;

        case WM_RBUTTONDOWN:
          SetCapture(hWnd);
          if (m_pScene && m_pScene->m_pMovementController)
             m_pScene->m_pMovementController->
                  OnRButtonDown(MAKEPOINTS(lParam));
          break;

        case WM_RBUTTONUP:
          SetCapture(NULL);
          if (m_pScene && m_pScene->m_pMovementController)
             m_pScene->m_pMovementController->
                  OnRButtonUp(MAKEPOINTS(lParam));
          break;

    }

    return CD3DApplication::MsgProc( hWnd, msg, wParam, lParam );
}
```

Finally, don't forget to delete your scene when the application exits:

```
HRESULT CMyD3DApplication::DeleteDeviceObjects()
{
    // TODO: Cleanup any objects created in InitDeviceObjects()
    m_pFont->DeleteDeviceObjects();
```

```
    // ADD THIS CODE!  for the SceneGraph project...
    SAFE_DELETE(m_pScene);
     return S_OK;
}
```

That is all you need to create a simple scene graph. It may seem like an extremely simplistic architecture but it's more flexible that you'd think. Each node you design can add functionality and special effects to all their children nodes. Here are some examples:

- *A billboard node*: Sets the transform matrix of all the child nodes such that they always face the camera. Use this for trees or light glare.
- *A sky node*: A huge box that sits over your scene and translates exactly in sync with the camera position. It creates the illusion that it exists at an extreme distance.
- *Level of detail node*: A node that chooses one node in its child list for rendering based on the node's distance from the camera.
- *A material node*: Sets the default material for all children nodes.
- *A world sector node*: Defines a 3D volume that completely contains all of its children nodes. You use it to determine if any children need to draw based on camera direction, or interposed opaque world sectors.
- *A mirror node*: Defines a portal through which the scene is rerendered from a different point of view, and stenciled onto a texture.

I'm sure you can come up with other cool stuff.

What's Missing?

The scene graph in this chapter is a fun toy. It's not nearly ready to install into a real game engine. You'll want tons of new nodes, articulated figures, and other visible objects. There are also a few other things you'll need to add to this system. The first and foremost is a better way of creating and editing your world. I'm pretty sure I mentioned somewhere in this book that any good game engine is a data driven creature, and then I show you a completely hard coded scene graph! No, I'm not a slacker—I opted for the cheap and easy route because it's also easy to understand. If I were to continue playing with this simple design, the first thing I'd add is an XML-based scene definition language.

The XML scene definition would only be used for development, of course, since the current XML implementation doesn't have a binary standard definition. By the time this book is in your hands, that will probably be fixed, which will boost XML from its current popularity into a staggeringly powerful data file standard. Then you could use it for a game.

In any case, your game needs a way to load and save this data. Each of the `SceneNode` descendants need a stream constructor to hook into a save game system. I'm going to make a broad assumption that whatever game in your head is going to have at least a few dynamic objects. After all, there aren't too many games based on a vacant art museum. Even if your game were a vacant art museum, the paintings, walls, and lights still need to load somehow.

Probably the most serious missing component to the scene graph is a collision system. No 3D game is complete without one, and believe me they are extremely complicated. To get an idea how complicated, go check out the latest work at the University of North Carolina, Chapel Hill's site devoted to the study of this problem: **www.cs.unc.edu/~geom/collide/index.shtml**. I've used ICOLLIDE in the past but I'm very interested to try VCOLLIDE and SWIFT++. When you look for a collision system, make sure that one of the features includes temporal coherence, which is a fancy way of saying that the system remembers the positions of geometry from frame to frame. Games typically have tons of static geometry, and a much smaller number of dynamic objects. If the collision system takes advantage of this fact, your game will run a lot faster.

The most trivial collision systems use axis aligned bounding boxes (AABB), and nothing more. These provide the most basic collision detection, and you've probably seen them installed in the nastier of the coin-op video games that have very fast moving objects that bounce around for a moment before they disappear. That's because they won't look right when the bouncing objects always seem to land right side up. Believe me if that worked in real life I'd be at the craps tables in Las Vegas.

More complicated systems seek to break objects down into their convex components, and perform collision detection on each of these components. These are probably the most common solution in games, because they provide a very realistic simulation. The only problem is creating and maintaining the collision geometry separate from the visible geometry. There are tons of tools to do this—rather I'm talking about the logistical problem of keeping all this extra data straight. Automatic tools are the key here. Don't assume that artists working in 3D Studio Max will always remember to create the collision geometry, save it to the right file, and keep everything organized.

Some of the most advanced work cares nothing for the geometry: convex or concave is just as good as anything else. These systems work on *polygon soups* and have the ability to determine which polygons are intersecting with each other, sometimes what forces are involved, and what your simulation should do to resolve the movement of the objects. Lucky for you there are some very smart people, and smart companies, working on this problem so you can spend more time on the important bits, like making a fun game.

3D Middleware Review

There are plenty of 3D engines and other middleware available for the taking. Some of them will expect you to pay large sums of money, and you'll have to weigh for yourself if you'd rather attempt to make a 3D engine yourself or if you'll sleep better at night knowing that you have something that works. Many companies in the middleware market like Epic (Unreal Engine) and Criterion (Renderware) are game companies as well as middleware providers. Other companies like Intrinsic are middleware companies through and through.

What you'll want from a licensed 3D engine is much more than the ability to draw triangles at blazing speed. After all, there are plenty of free technologies like OpenGL and DirectX that will draw triangles just fine. The problem is much deeper than drawing triangles.

Games don't read 3D Studio Max scene files (.MAX) because they aren't optimized for real time display and they certainly don't enforce certain limitations of 3D rendering hardware. The same is true for Maya or Softimage. Instead, you'll want to export these files into a format your game can use directly. These export plug-ins are fabulously tricky to write, especially if they support many types of hardware. The Xbox and the PS2 are extremely different architectures and an export tool must take that into account.

Beyond the export tools many companies provide secondary analysis tools to optimize and manipulate exported scenes and textures. Two examples are Renderware's PVS tool and Intrinsic's Finalizer. Both tools seek to restructure the geometry and textures of your static levels and dynamic objects in order to draw them as fast as possible on each target platform.

Its also important for middleware to support complicated objects and animations with a minimum of pain and suffering on your part. It's even better if the results of all this work look anything like what the artists created in their tools. I'll provide a quick summary of the top tier rendering engines next.

Renderware Graphics

Renderware by Criterion Software is an industry old hand. The technology can be trusted and you know there's a lot of people who've seen and solved virtually every problem you can create using Renderware. The fact that they've shipped fifty games means that they should be around for a long time to come. Their API is based in C, which seems a little backwards to me, and I found it a little difficult to learn because I think in C++. Their coordinate system is quite odd and differs from industry standard tools like 3DStudio Max. Their support system, probably one of the most important part of your decision, is excellent.

One interesting development out of Criterion is Renderware Studio, a completely integrated multi-platform game creation environment. Game designers use this tool to bring models, animations, sounds, and custom code together in one environment. Even more incredible it can show the newly created game environment on all four supported platforms simultaneously. It is even possible to customize the game environment so that one platform looks and acts differently than another.

- *API Support*: C API
- *Architecture*: World sectors define polygon sets for static geometry, world sectors are organized in a BSP tree.
- *Renderer Features*: Optimized tri-stripping and Bezier geometry, lightmaps, hardware-specific features such as mutitexturing, pixel shaders, and particle systems.
- *Exporters*: 3DStudio Max 4.x and Maya 4 are supported with a fully featured exporter that has a preview window.
- *Special Tools*: Light mapping tool, world sector editing tool for PVS (potentially visibly set), pre-instancing tool optimizes art assets for individual platforms, general animation toolkit for hierarchical and non-heirarchical animations, and a skin splitter to get around maximum bone limitations.
- *Platforms*: Playstation 2, Xbox, Gamecube, and PC
- *Games You Might Have Played*: Grand Theft Auto III, Tony Hawks Pro Skater 3, over 50 titles shipped in all

Intrinsic Alchemy

Intrinsic Alchemy by Intrinsic is one of the new kids on the block, and quite an aggressive kid at that. They've made significant inroads into creating a significant toolset and rendering API that holds well against any other engine. Their only problem is that they haven't been around for very long, and they don't have a top ten title in their trophy case. That will likely change.

- *API Style:* C++ API
- *Architecture*: Multipass rendering, subclassible scene graph hierarchy.
- *Renderer Features*: High level shaders, animation support, visibility culling, occlusion culling, simple collision, intersection processing, visibility pre-processing, multiresolution meshes, particle system

- *Exporters*: 3D Studio Max, Maya, Lightwave, and Softimage; remote viewers allow artists to view artwork directly on target platform
- *Special Tools*: Intrinsic Optimizer generates platform specific optimizations for exported geometry, performance analysis tools.
- *Platforms*: Playstation 2, Xbox, Gamecube, PC (Win32 and Linux)
- *Games You Might Have Played*: None yet but they've only been around since 2001.

NetImmerse by NDL

NetImmerse is another renderer that's been around the block a few times. While I've never used it myself, it would be something of a crime to exclude them from this survey. If you look at the games that used their technology, you'll be impressed with their technology. I don't know about you, but I thought Munch's Odyssey on the Xbox was pretty cool.

- *API Style*: C++ API.
- *Architecture*: Subclassible scene graph hierarchy that supports instancing
- *Renderer Features*: Classic culling via view frustrum, portals, multitexturing, bump mapping, particle systems, skinned characters, collision detection.
- *Exporters*: 3D Studio Max, Maya exporters will fully functional preview windows.
- *Special Tools*: Animation toolset helps blend and time multiple character animations as they'll be seen in the game, scene graph optimization.
- *Platforms*: Playstation 2, Xbox, Gamecube, PC (Win32 and Linux)
- *Games You Might Have Played*: Munch's Odyssey, Dark Age of Camelot.

Unreal Engine

The Unreal Engine by Epic is probably the grand dame of all the rendering engines available. There's no question that it provide some of the most compelling graphics outside of whatever John Carmack is working on right now. Unreal is far from a stagnant product, however. Every code build brings new changes that may affect your development and these code drops happen quickly—about every couple months. You can expect that Epic, being primarily a game company and not a game engine company, will direct the Unreal Engine however they see fit and if you want to tag along just pay your license fee and jump on.

- *API Style*: Mixed C and C++ API.

- *Architecture*: Subclassible scene list (not a graph) that supports instancing.
- *Renderer Features*: Classic culling via view frustrum, portals, multitexturing, bump mapping, particle systems, skinned characters, basic collision detection.
- *Exporters*: 3D Studio Max, Maya exporters will fully functional preview windows.
- *Special Tools*: Animation toolset helps blend and time multiple character animations as they'll be seen in the game.
- *Platforms*: Playstation 2, Xbox, PC.
- *Games You Might Have Played*: Unreal Tournament 2003, Deus Ex

Rolling Your Own 3D Engine

Hopefully you've surfed up to a few web sites for a deeper look at the tools and technologies you can pull off the shelf. If you're smart you've figured out that you could spend a cool half-million dollars and most of a year on half-baked technology, with tools that work on every alternate Thursday, and wonder why you can't get more than 12fps.

There's another drawback to rolling your own engine. Publishers generally won't touch you with a ten foot pole if you tell them you are about to write your own engine. That is, unless your name is John Carmack. They want to hear that you've got one that you own or you've already licensed one. Publishers see that kind of situation as a high risk scenario. They are much more likely to require you to use some crappy engine that they had in their basement rather than allow you to write one yourself.

If you haven't been scared out of your wits yet, and are convinced you are going to write your own engine I certainly hope you've written one before and shipped a game. If you've done that you won't be starting over from scratch, which is a real plus. One piece of advice is to evaluate some of the middleware anyway, it will give you a good idea on how your own tools measure up. If they fall short, you can either step up to the plate and fix your old code or perhaps you'll just bail and buy something off the shelf. Either way, never assume you have the hottest thing going. Go find out.

Physics Engines

Some relative newcomers to the middleware arena are physics engines. This software provides APIs to simulate the movements of 3D geometry under effects of gravity, friction, collision with other objects, and even soft body motions such as cloth. If your game needs to accurately simulate the motions of objects a physics engine might be just the ticket.

Before you read any further ask yourself if you really need a physics engine. If you only have a few simple objects that can move through your scene, such as a simple platform game, you can write this stuff yourself. Collision with simple shapes is a well published problem with relatively simple solutions. This is especially true if your objects move quickly enough to mask the effect of random rotations and they won't come to rest in piles. Perhaps having objects simply disappear after they've been hit is a good alternative to spending the annual salary of a good programmer on licensing fees.

Remember that most animations will come straight from your artists, especially character animation. Physics engines are never, ever used in the place of keyframed character animation. If you attempt to move characters around with physical forces, they'll walk around like those old CGI characters in that Dire Straits music video, *Money for Nothing*. Instead of simply telling a body joint to animate to a particular position and orientation over the next sequence of frames, you would have to accurately calculate the force vectors to apply to the 3D geometry making sure that any attached objects are also moved properly. Don't try it—it's a nightmare!

Instead, physics engines are used to take over after extreme forces come into play such as after a collision. A bike rider colliding into the front of a speeding bus will actually look much better under the control of a good physics system than having an artist try to keyframe it. Besides, when the rider gets crushed under the wheels of the bus the physics system will also be able to simulate the effects of the bus suspension.

Renderware has it's own physics engine—one that used to be called Mathengine, before Criterion bought them in 2002. It integrates fully with Renderware and is a natural choice if you're going to play with the Renderware solution. Another option is the Havok Game Dynamics SDK from Havok (**www.havok.com**). This physics and collision system is more advanced than Criterion's offering, and it includes interesting features such as vehicle SDK, where you can plug a few numbers into a little tool and create a data file for all kinds of cars and trucks. You can create a racing game with realistic steering, braking, and suspension movement in a single afternoon. Pretty impressive.

I was playing around with a collision system from UNC-Chapel Hill called ICOLLIDE. My task was to simulate the very cliché red rubber ball bouncing up and down on a black and white checkered floor. I installed the collision library, set up my scene graph, and watched the red ball fall right through the floor. After a few more attempts and a little debugging, I realized that the ball was moving too fast. At one moment it was on one side of the floor and the next simulation step moved the ball completely to the other side of the floor avoiding any actual collision detectable by the library. When I slowed the ball down, effectively increasing the sampling rate of the simulation, the problem disappeared and I had my bouncing ball.

I thought about this phenomenon a moment, and realized that this was very similar to quantum tunneling, where a particle seems to move right through a solid object. Interesting. Then it got scary. I began to wonder if quantum tunneling was a side effect of the universe's lack of accuracy, and that perhaps the reason the speed of light is a constant is due to the fact that that is the maximum sampling speed of the Universe. It kind of makes me want to find the debugger interrupt.

Still Hungry?

When this chapter was first outlined, I knew that I was going to leave plenty of questions completely unanswered. The chapter was going to end too soon, and I would leave all the readers with just enough vocabulary and ideas to play around in 3D without enough knowledge to make Quake VI. There's a lot to know, for one thing. The most recent advances in video hardware have replaced the fixed function graphics pipeline with the programmable pipeline. Now you can write little programs that draw pixels and move vertices, and some of these programs can be truly amazing.

At the 2003 Computer Game Developer's Conference I watched a simulation of fluid dynamics programmed completely with pixel shaders. Instead of manipulating texture values and red, green, and blue components of a texture, the values were things like pressure and velocity. The graphics card was performing partial differentials entirely in the GPU.

I don't know about you, but I haven't seen anything that cool since the first hardware accelerated 3D graphics card.

I hope you are still hungry—I certainly am.

Chapter 11

Special Considerations for Developing Windows Games

My first experience with Windows programming was Windows 3.1, a 16-bit cooperative multitasking operating system. Coming from DOS 5 programming, the weirdest thing for me by far was getting used to a message passing architecture instead of a process-based architecture. One annoying thing was having to learn the huge Win16 API. I had just become comfortable with ANSI C runtime, and new functions started falling out of the sky. Windows 3.1 had no fast way to draw bitmapped graphics—the curse for any game developer. Some operations, such as blitting with a color key, were nigh impossible. Actually, this wasn't impossible, but the calisthenics required to make a color keyed sprite under the GDI were insane.

The year was 1994, and Microsoft had just launched a serious initiative to court the computer game industry. Microsoft was bored with their total domination of the desktop business software industry and they wanted to enter our homes. They had the right idea: target games first and everything else will follow. Someone at Microsoft had a brilliant idea of gathering a collection of computer game programmers from the most successful companies of the day for an intensive workshop at the Microsoft campus in Redmond, Washington. The invited programmers lived in Redmond for a short while and helped the DirectX 1 team come up with the API for DirectDraw.

I wasn't one of the programmers to attend the workshop, but a few of my fellow collegues from Origin System were invited. They developed a little arcade game where you roamed the labyrinthine halls of Microsoft shooting Microsoft engineers as they popped out of their offices! I heard it was a lot of fun, and especially popular with the original DirectX engineers.

This technology was unleashed at the 1995 Game Developer's Conference in San Jose with a little demonstration of a simple Windows game called the Fox and the Bear. Sporting a gleaming white lab coat and grinning ear to ear, a jubilant Alex St. John demonstrated, for the very first time, a Windows game that could run full-screen at a blazing 60fps. To give you an idea of how cool this was, imagine taking a ride in my brand new car and the first thing I do is push a button, lift off the ground, and enter low earth orbit.

This event was a turning point in the computer game industry, much more so than the announcement of a new platform. Unlike Sony, Nintendo, and others launching their new hardware every few years to the oooos and ahhhhs of everyone, DirectX hit everyone square in the chest because developers could begin creating games for the new Windows platform immediately. The console groups had the same tight rein on developers that they do today. It takes a lot of work to become an approved developer for a console. At the same time, Windows 95 was just beginning its final approach. Most developers had beta copies of the new Windows operating system, codenamed Chicago, and were figuring out how cool it really was. First, it was a true 32-bit operating system, at least mostly it was. There were some 16-bit components here and there, but most programmers could ignore *thunking*—the process that describes the transition between 16-bit and 32-bit code.

The 32-bit memory space was really a leap, since the biggest single data element in a 16-bit system was 64Kb. That's not nearly big enough to hold a single 640x480 background sprite. For those of you now who are making the transition to 64-bit, it won't be nearly as cool. There aren't very many game data structures that are pressing on the 4Gb barrier. Back then we needed the extra space *now*, so much so that Ultima VII wrote a 32-bit memory manager for DOS 5.

The other real advantage was operating system supported multithreading. This was a convenient departure from our DOS-based solution: We trapped the timer interrupt and wrote a simple multitasker ourselves. Now we could have our threads without resorting to heavy metal programming, meaning that even I could do it. If you are getting the impression that Windows 95 solved all of our problems and we were saved from the messy burdens of DOS programming, you're somewhat correct. It did solve some sticky problems. It wasn't programming nirvana, however.

One source of this programming hell was the fact the operating system group at Microsoft never saw DirectX as a core component of the operating system. The DirectX group was managed under a completely different business unit, and was essentially treated no different than any other applications developer within Microsoft. This odd structure has led to DirectX being a bit of a rogue technology within the operating system, which is why DirectX itself is not Windows logo compliant in all aspects.

Win32 platforms are true multitasking, which means for the first time I can switch over to Excel or Word in the middle of my game, and convince my boss that I was a diligent and productive employee. Well, I could do this if the game was written right, which most are not. All Win32 applications have to handle a core set of messages properly to live and play nice with all the other Win32 programs. Games have an especially hard time with this because of what players can do to the machine while they hit the Alt-Tab key to select other tasks, or even worse they might change the desktop graphics format from 16-bit to 24-bit.

The innovation cycle for Microsoft is fast, much faster than the console world. It's a lot easier and cheaper to burn DVDs than etch silicon. This means that Microsoft can publish a new operating system version once every two years or so, whereas Sony gets to work hard for three or four years before the new PS{n+1} comes out. Console developers never have to worry about backwards compatibility for this reason. After all, who wants to play a game that's four years old? Desktop PCs have a long life, five to six years, and programs must be backwards compatible to some extent. This compatibility requirement with older operating system versions and old hardware makes desktop game coding a serious pain in the ass, and debugging and testing is certainly no easier as you'll learn in Chapters 12 and 15.

This entire book has a Win32 bias, but nowhere will you see this bias clearer than in this chapter. I've tried to concentrate the lion's share of Win32 witchcraft here, leaving the rest of the book to talk about more portable concerns. If you never program under Win32, don't stop reading. It might give you some good ideas anyway. If you are a Win32 game coder, this chapter may be the most important part of this book.

What About Microsoft Foundation Classes (MFC)?

If you are a die hard C++ programmer, one of the first things you want to do after you see the galaxy of Win32 functions is try to organize them into classes. This desire is especially strong when you consider all the Windows handles you have to remember to close after you are finished with a handled object like a device context. Once this homework is installed in C++ constructors and destructors, your resulting code looks cleaner and it certainly avoids resource leaks.

Being a wise programmer, you'll look carefully at MFC before rolling your own object-oriented Win32 system. As you look into Microsoft's implementation, you'll begin to wonder if rolling your own wasn't such a good idea in the first place. The decision is not an easy one: MFC has a lot to offer. The problem is that MFC has a little too much to offer, actually. It depends on what you really want to do with your game. I'll try to run through a few arguments for and against the use of MFC in your game. I've certainly been on both sides of the fence myself. I'll be completely honest with you, right now I'm on the "don't bother with MFC" side.

MFC—You Must Be Crazy!!?@!!

One argument against MFC is its size. Any EXE or DLL that is statically linked to MFC will be nearly one megabyte larger. That might not sound like too much when desktops are sporting many hundreds of megabytes of RAM and many tens of gigabytes of hard drive space, but consider the effect it will have on downloaded games.

I was working with the Microsoft Zone on a project submission and one of the first things they asked me was whether my game required MFC. At that time it did; our game was designed to run in a window, full-screen, or as an ActiveX control on a web page. The Zone folks loved that the game worked well in all those formats, but the added download size turned them off. Many of their customers still used dial-up and the added megabyte was simply too much.

The most compelling argument against using MFC in games is they don't need it. Games generally roll their own custom code for the user interface. The boring grey dialog boxes of standard Windows GDI fare are the antithesis of game interfaces, and, the last time I looked, I didn't see a special windows control for a 3D radar system anyway.

All the other MFC classes that deal with threads, windows, files, and other parts of the Win32 API are wrappers around Win32 objects. If you're curious about their implementation just load up the source code and find out how they did it; it's included with Visual Studio. If you don't want to use all of MFC but you like the implementation of one of their classes, by all means study their implementation and roll your own.

MFC—You Must Use It

Lately I've been feeling that the naked C Win32 API that I'm so used to is becoming buried under layers of MSDN. Every time I hunt for some documentation regarding a Win32 function I'm assaulted by MFC first. That's annoying. It's almost as if Microsoft doesn't believe that there are programmers out there who use the C functions. Probably the most compelling reason to use MFC are the pre-rolled controls and windows that you can use for rapid development. This is much more likely in code you'll write for internal tools and level editors than in your actual game. I don't know if you've ever tried to write a grid control—an object that sorts rows and columns of data—but it's not for the meek. It's much better to search for one on the Internet and plug your new toy into an MFC-based architecture.

This is especially true of the `CHtmlView` class. I'd argue against creating your own HTML renderer. The task is mind-numbing and time consuming. At the end of your hard work, you'll have something that might be HTML 1.0 compliant if you're lucky.

You are going to think I'm making this one up. The first Microsoft product I worked on was Microsoft Casino, and the year was 2000—a fact that will become important shortly. The casino game had tons of help text and our plan was to use MFC's `CHtmlView` class, which was a thin wrapper around the Internet Explorer's HTML renderer. We had it working, sort

of, when I got a phone call from the product manager at 'The Soft'. He told me we couldn't use `CHtmlView`, and that we were going to have to find our own HTML renderer. I was stunned beyond belief that Microsoft couldn't use technology they owned. He explained that the legal status of Microsoft products requiring Internet Explorer was under review from the United States Justice Department and various Attorney Generals at the state level. If I used `CHtmlView`, Microsoft Casino would require Internet Explorer, or a component of it anyway. I briefly considered using the then open source Netscape renderer, and figured that if I did I'd get a midnight visit from the Microsoft Secret Police. We ended up cobbling our own renderer together in the end. A few versions later, Microsoft engineers handed us an HTML-ish renderer that had nothing to do with Internet Explorer, and we used it. It's very odd to have a bunch of lawyers tell you how to write software.

Another compelling reason to use MFC is that it works. It is also extremely well tested, and is widely understood by many programmers. MFC has been unfairly panned in the game industry as bloated, irrelevant, and designed by crazy people. It turns out that the MFC engineers came up with a great solution strategy for implementing a C++ based windows object.

The problem the engineers had was message handling. They wanted the clarity of implementing member functions like `CWnd::OnPaint()` and `CWnd::OnMouseMove()` without the overhead of a truly staggering virtual function table—one VMT entry for each message would be way too big. Their solution implements a class specific jump table with `BEGIN_MESSAGE_MAP()` and `END_MESSAGE_MAP()` macros. It's interesting to dig into the MFC source to see how they did it. They essentially implemented a sparse virtual function table!

On the Ultima IX project at Origin Systems, we had the task of creating the Ultima IX editor. This world editor was a complicated tool that imported and organized game assets, built levels, scripted events, and did it all in a completely network aware environment so that multiple people could work on the same map simultaneously. It was a huge project, and we briefly thought about using MFC but decided against it, mostly because of fear. One of the programmers had started a C++ based Windows library called OFC—Origin's Foundation Classes. By the end of the project OFC's source code had many of the same elements and architecture as MFC. If I had to do it over again, I would have used MFC for Ultima IX's editor and spent the extra programming time doing other things.

The Final Verdict on MFC

A good reason to use MFC on your project is to avoid redeveloping something that already exists. There's nothing in MFC that can't be coded using naked Win32 calls and some elbow grease. All the native Windows components and controls like the edit control are available through C calls. You don't need MFC for creating a user interface, but you should be aware that MFC has already done most of the heavy lifting. If you really want to rewrite, re-debug, and retest a bunch of C++ that already exists in a stable and trusted form, by all means be my guest.

You also don't need MFC to fully support UNICODE either, especially now that MFC7 moved its `CString` class to the ATL string implementation. Your game can be fully UNICODE compliant without MFC. If you're going to be building tons of dialog boxes and other doodads in your resource editor or for an internal tool like a level editor, you might consider MFC. If you are building a game with one window and your home grown user interface there's no reason to feel compelled to use MFC.

Windowed Mode and Full-screen Mode

You should always ask yourself what your game buys by running in Windowed mode. (I'm talking about the release build of your game here.) It would be very normal to support a crippled form of windowed mode in a debug or test build, so that programmers and testers can develop on a single monitor system. A game that supports windowed and full-screen modes for the general public has a lot of work to do. I would humbly submit that unless your game is a mass market title like Microsoft Casino, you should resist the temptation to run in windowed mode and spend programming time doing other things.

The problem lies not in some deficiency in Microsoft engineers, rather it is one of design. Games, by their nature, are written to take the best advantage of the hardware to run as fast as they can. This means that games are device dependant, or at least device aware. They care if the video card supports hardware transforms and lighting. They care if the audio card supports surround sound. A normal Windows application, like Excel, couldn't care less.

To run fast on a wide variety of hardware, games tend to convert their graphics to a format that is closely aligned with the video cards' current configuration. This configuration is tweakable by the game, mostly in terms of the resolution and bit depth, but usually not in terms of the pixel format. This conversion, which usually takes place as assets are loaded to play the current level, makes switching hardware configuration on the fly expensive and fragile from the coder's viewpoint.

Here's an example of a game I worked on, Microsoft Casino, that was a mass market title and therefore had to run well in windowed and full-screen modes. The native resolution of the game was 800x600x16. Windowed mode would create a client window at 800x600 resolution and use the current bit depth and pixel format of the Window's desktop. The format and resolution of the player's desktop was not necessarily the same as the full-screen mode. Thus, when the player hit Alt-Enter to switch from one to the other, it was likely that all the graphics assets currently loaded had to be thrown out and reloaded to match the new format. Of course, the player could force the same event by changing the desktop settings while the game window was up. They could change from 16-bit to 32-bit, and the game would have to reinitialize the display surfaces and reload and reconvert all the graphics. DirectX surfaces cannot convert from one pixel format to another in a `Blt()` or `BltFast()` call, so if you change the display surface everything else in your game has to change to match it.

This doesn't apply to textures. The format of a texture is dependant on the capabilities of the video card and has little or nothing to do with the format of the display surface.

As you read the rest of this section, remember that you can consider the option of running your game in full-screen mode for the players. If you do this allow a functional windowed mode that doesn't support all of the compatibility concerns of regular Windows applications for development and debugging on a single monitor system. When these transitions take place, DirectX detects the change in pixel format, and marks all surfaces effected by this transition as a *lost surface*. It essentially means that the reference to a DirectX surface still exists, but the bits are invalid and need to be reconstructed to reflect the new format. Lost surfaces can also occur as a result of DirectX managing surface memory.

Under DirectX 9, most memory can be set to *managed* when you create it. This is true for textures, display surfaces, and even things like vertex buffers. If you allow DirectX to manage these resources, you won't have to worry about this memory becoming invalid, since DirectX will take control of doing the reallocations and conversions.

If you opt to manage the memory yourself, you'll have to write code to deal with lost or incompatible surfaces, lest your game suffer a nasty crash when the players do something wacky like change the screen display.

Lost or Incompatible Surfaces

Does this mean, exactly, that the surface is lost? It means that the operating system has taken away the bits that compose the surface and allocated it to something else, and there's not enough information for DirectX to recompose the bits without your help. The definition of the surface's structure is still intact, so DirectX can easily recreate it, assuming there's enough room. The actual bits on the surface, however, have been destroyed. If all that needs doing is reallocating the bits, you can simply call `Restore()`:

```
// assume m_pdds points to a DirectX surface
if (m_pdds->IsLost())
{
   m_pdds->Restore();
}
```

The code above might be all you need, in the case of a display surface that gets overwritten every frame, but what should you do about a surface whose bits were constructed by your tender loving care? Perhaps you created a nice fractal or simply drawn some text with a GDI font and placed the surface in video memory for super fast retrieval and screen composition. You'll need to recreate those bits if the surface is ever lost, which implies you have some way of reinitializing all your "losable" surfaces.

One way to do this is to define a C++ interface called `IRestorable`. The interface will have two methods that you can probably predict:

```
class IRestorable
{
public:
   virtual bool VIsLost() = 0;
   virtual bool VRestore() = 0;
};

class Surface : public IRestorable
{
   // Implement the IRestorable Surface

   LPDIRECTDRAWSURFACE7 m_pdds;
   virtual bool VIsLost() { return (!m_pdds || m_pdds->IsLost(); }
   virtual bool VRestore() { return (m_pdds && SUCCESS(m_pdds->Restore()) ); }

   // The remainder of the Surface class is yours to implement!
};
```

Of course, the `Surface` class would have more code in it that that—this is just an architecture lesson! The crazy surface I spoke of before would implement its own restore function, calling the base class first:

```
bool CrazyFractalTextSurface::VRestore()
{
   if (!Surface::VRestore())
      return false;

   DrawMyFractal();
   DrawMyText();
};
```

Assuming you have a list of these `Surface` classes around, it becomes a simple matter to iterate through the list and call `VRestore()` on every one of them.

When do you need to do this? Is it necessary to restore every surface in your whole game when you detect one that has gone to the dark side? Perhaps not; it depends on the return values from a failed DirectX call. There are two primary cases:

- **DDERR_SURFACELOST**: The surface's memory bits are gone, but the definition is still valid. Restoring the surface will make everything good again, and it doesn't mean you'll have to restore everything else.
- **DDERR_WRONGMODE**: The surface's bits are still intact, but the bits don't have a compatible pixel format. The surface can't be restored because it's isn't lost. It must be thrown out completely and reloaded with the correct pixel format. It's likely you'll have to do this for everything.

11

The player can only change the display settings by bringing up the desktop properties window, which should send a `WM_ACTIVE` message to your game—a good thing to catch. When your game goes active again, one of the first things you should do is check your backbuffer. If it is lost, you should try to restore it. If the restore fails, the most likely reason is a mode switch on the desktop. Here's what you can do about it:

```
// Note: This code is DirectX 7

inline HRESULT HandleModeChanges()
{
   HRESULT hr;
   hr = m_myDirectDrawObject->TestCooperativeLevel();

   do
```

```
    {
      if( SUCCEEDED( hr ) )
      {
        // This means that mode changes had taken place, surfaces
        // were lost but still we are in the original mode, so we
        // simply restore all surfaces and keep going.
        bool ok = RestoreEverything();

        // test the DisplayFrame one time to be sure....
        if( ok && SUCCEEDED( hr = yourcode::DisplayFrame() ) )
          return hr;
      }

      if( hr == DDERR_WRONGMODE )
      {
        // This means that the desktop mode has changed
        // we can destroy and recreate everything back again.

        return yourcode::InitDirectDrawMode( m_bWindowed );
      }

      // If we get here it means that some app took exclusive mode access
        // we need to sit in a loop till we get back to the right mode.

      Sleep(500);

    } while( DDERR_EXCLUSIVEMODEALREADYSET ==
                  (hr = m_myDirectDrawObject->TestCooperativeLevel()) );

  // Busted! Something has gone terribly wrong.
  return true;
}

bool RestoreEverything()
{
  for (SurfaceList::iterator i=m_surfaces.begin(); i!=m_surfaces.end(); i++)
    if (FAILED( (*i)->VRestore() ) )
                  return false;

  return true;
};
```

The call to `TestCooperativeLevel` tests the system to find out if the device is restorable. If the call returns anything other than `DD_OK` you get to tear down your display and reinitialize it from scratch. Since it is likely that the new display will have a different pixel format from the original, you'll likely throw out all your graphics resources as well.

Did you notice that the whole thing is in a while loop? The reason is that it is possible another application has exclusive control of the device. Our game has to wait until the other application is done, hence the while loop. The call to `RestoreEverything` simply iterates the list of surfaces and calls `VRestore()` for each surface.

Bad Windows

When you create a windowed mode game, it's a good idea to grab the pixel format of the desktop and set your DirectX surfaces to match it. Doing this will enhance the speed of your game significantly, since Windows won't have to perform a pixel-by-pixel conversion operation when you present the backbuffer. DirectX does this by default if you don't specify a pixel format—a nice convenience. This feature becomes significantly less convenient on those video cards that support 24-bit display formats. If the player's desktop is set to 24-bit, DirectX will happily create a 24-bit primary and backbuffer surface. Everything will work swimmingly until you attempt to attach that surface to a Direct3D device.

Most Direct3D devices don't support 24-bit video memory surfaces, and for good reason. They can be incredibly slow. The same problem exists with running Windows in 256-color mode, not that you could stand looking at it.

Another case that sneaks up on you is a desktop running in a very low resolution. If your game runs at 800x600, the smallest desktop that will support your game is 1024x768. Why? Because an 800x600 client area will completely cover your desktop, leaving you no room for a title bar or other non-client control areas. Players won't be able to drag the window around, with nothing to grab. You might as well run in full-screen.

Here's some code you can use to detect unsupported window modes:

```
bool ValidWindowedMode ( )
{
   CRect crDesktop;
   int iColorDepth;

   // Grab the new windows dimensions and color depth
   ::SystemParametersInfo( SPI_GETWORKAREA, 0, &crDesktop, 0 );
   HDC d = ::GetDC(NULL);
   iColorDepth = GetDeviceCaps(d, BITSPIXEL);
   ::ReleaseDC(NULL, d);

   if ( crDesktop.Width() <= yourcode::SCREEN_WIDTH ||
      crDesktop.Height() <= yourcode::SCREEN_HEIGHT ||
     ( iColorDepth == 24  ) ||
```

```
        ( iColorDepth < 16 ) )
    {
        return false;
    }
    else
    {
        return true;
    }
}
```

This function checks the current desktop dimensions with `SystemParametersInfo()`, and the color depth of the desktop with `GetDeviceCaps()`, both Win32 functions. This function sends back a negative result if the desktop is set to anything other than 16-bit or 32-bit, or is smaller than or equal to the expected client area of the game.

If you find that your player has their desktop in an unsupported mode, flip into full-screen mode and finish initializing your game. When your game is up and running, bring up a dialog box that tells them why they aren't in windowed mode any more.

GDI Dialog Boxes and Flipping

The GDI doesn't understand flipping surfaces, so if you ever try to call `MessageBox` and nothing happens, it's likely that the GDI just drew your message box to the backbuffer and is waiting for you to respond. If you are going to launch a GDI dialog box inside a DirectX application that uses flipping surfaces, you must call `FlipToGDISurface()` to make sure the GDI is drawing to the right place.

Many games create their own dialog boxes, and don't use the GDI at all. It stands to reason that if something goes wrong with your game's early stage initialization, you'll want to bring up a dialog of some kind. Thus, it seems that there is a dual purpose need for a smart message box system. In one of my games I created an `Ask()` method that accepted one parameter—a constant that defined the question. The function was smart enough to flip to GDI if necessary and use game dialogs and localized text strings if they were initialized. There were a few cases where a message box was needed to inform players of odd initialization errors, before the pretty game-specific dialog box assets or localized string table were loaded. In those cases I bailed and used English text and a GDI `MessageBox` to communicate the problem.

Messages You Have to Take

There are a few windows messages you shouldn't ignore. It might seem a lot of work to write all the code for these messages but in the end it's worth it. Your game will be a nicely behaved Windows application. I know what you're thinking, a nicely behaved

Windows application sounds a little like "cafeteria food" or "military intelligence" but in the end, you'd rather have a stable, predictable Windows application that something that broke every time a player hit Alt-Tab.

These messages happen during window creation:

- **WM_NCCREATE**: Handle this message if you must do something before your `WM_CREATE` message is sent. Other than that, there's nothing special about this message.
- **WM_CREATE**: This message is sent when you have a window ready to play with, but it hasn't been drawn yet.

While your window is alive, you should handle these messages:

- **WM_ACTIVATE**: This is the message that Windows sends to applications when they are going active or inactive, such as when a player hits Alt-Tab to cover the fact that they are playing games instead of working. This is a better message than `WM_SETFOCUS`.
- **WM_SYSCOMMAND**: This message is sent when the player hits a system command sequence such as Alt-F4 to close the game.
- **WM_MOVE**: This message is sent whenever your Window is dragged.
- **WM_NCLBUTTONDBCLK**: This is a message sent to the window when the player double clicks in the non-client area of the window. It's a common thing to switch to full-screen mode when users do this.
- **WM_DEVICECHANGE**: This is a good message to handle, because you can never tell when crazy players are going to remove their CDs or DVDs.
- **WM_POWERBROADCAST**: With so many people playing games on portables, you'd better deal with a low power condition if you can.
- **WM_DISPLAYCHANGE**: If you happen to catch it in the act, the display change message can give you a warning about display changes.
- **WM_ENTERSIZEMOVE, WM_EXITSIZEMOVE**: These messages are sent before and after the window is being moved or resized.
- **WM_GETMINMAXINFO**: Useful if you want the minimum or maximum size of your game window to be limited in scope.

When your window closes, you'll want to handle the following messages. There's nothing special at all about them, but it's useful to know that they arrive in your message pump in a specific order:

- **WM_CLOSE:** This message is sent to you when Windows wants your application to close, or you can send it to yourself when the player presses the exit controls. This is your last chance to abort closing, so don't forget to ask your player if he or she want to save his or her game!
- **WM_DESTROY:** Closing is not an option at this point. It's the future. It is one of the last messages your window will handle.
- **WM_NCDESTROY:** This is the last message your window will handle.

Let's look at some specific versions of some of these handlers to get a better idea of what some of the oddball messages are up to.

WM_ACTIVATE

This is the message that you handle to figure out any heinous trickery that some player has played on their computer while your game was sleeping:

```
case WM_ACTIVATE:
{
   bool active = wParam != WA_INACTIVE;
   HWND pWndOther = lParam;

   // Pause or resume audio
   if ( active )
   {
      yourcode::ResumeAudio();

      // Set the mode if it has changed
      if ( m_bWindowedMode && ! ValidWindowedMode() )
      {
         yourcode::ResetDisplay();
      }
   }
   else
   {
      yourcode::PauseAudio();
      yourcode::SavePausedBackground();
   }
   // This is a function that will do anything such as restart animations, etc.
```

```
    your::TogglePause(active);
}
```

The message parameters are sucked from `wParam` and `lParam` first. If the window has gone active there are two important tasks. First, you want to restart your audio, and second you want to call the function we discussed earlier to validate the current display. If it isn't compatible, you'll have to reinitialize to full-screen mode. If the application is going inactive you should also do two things. First, you should pause your audio. It can be really annoying to have the game audio squawking in the background while you're trying to talk to someone on the phone, especially if they thought you were doing something other than playing games.

It's also a good idea is to save your current backbuffer in a regular off-screen surface. Why bother? It turns out that when a player hits Ctrl-Alt-Del, video surfaces can be lost. This is an excellent way to force your game to suffer a surface loss condition. If you have a copy of your backbuffer in off-screen memory, you can use it to paint while your application is inactive. Just because your game is inactive doesn't mean that it doesn't get paint messages. You might drag another window over your game.

WM_SYSCOMMAND

This message covers a lot of ground, because like the `WM_COMMAND` message, it's lots of message rolled up into one. The `wParam` holds the message identifier. There are two that games should handle:

- SC_CLOSE: This is another message that is sent to close your game. Treat it exactly the same as you would if your player pressed the right controls to exit the game.
- SC_MAXIMIZE: This message can be a useful shortcut for putting your game in full-screen mode; it's completely up to you.

11

WM_MOVE

If your game holds local parameters about its screen whereabouts, you'll want to handle the `WM_MOVE` message. Here's an example:

```
case WM_MOVE:
{
    if( m_bWindowed )
    {
       GetClientRect( m_hWnd, &m_rcWindow );
       ClientToScreen( m_hWnd, &m_rcWindow );
```

```
      }
      else
      {
       SetRect( &m_rcWindow, 0, 0,
          GetSystemMetrics(SM_CXSCREEN),
          GetSystemMetrics(SM_CYSCREEN) );
      }

   yourcode::Present();     // this is a call to your draw function
}
```

This `WM_MOVE` handler shows the code you'll use to set your `RECT` and `m_rcWindow` to the correct coordinates whether your game is in windowed mode or full-screen mode. It's a good idea to call your draw function in the move handler as well, after the new screen coordinates have been set.

WM_DEVICECHANGE

You might feel as I do that if a player removes the CD from the drive while the game is running, they get what they deserve. But, hey everyone makes mistakes once in a while. If you handle this message, you can be reasonably sure that your game won't crash and burn. If the game is actively reading from the removable media and it is ripped from the drive, you can't really tell what will happen. This is especially true of memory mapped files. I'd avoid using them on any type of removable media such as a CD or DVD.

```
case WM_DEVICECHANGE:
{
   int eventType = wParam;

   if ( yourcode::IsMinimumInstall() )          // reads game data to find out
   {
      if ( (UINT) nEventType == DBT_DEVICEREMOVECOMPLETE )
      {
         TCHAR *searchFile = yourcode::CDCheckFile();
         while (!yourcode::FileExists(searchFile))
         {
            if (yourcode::Ask(QUESTION_WHERES_THE_CD)==IDCANCEL)
            {
               yourcode::AbortGame();
            }
         }
         return BROADCAST_QUERY_DENY;       // denied!
      }
```

```
    }

    return TRUE;
}
```

This code assumes you've written a few functions for your game. The first one, `yourcode::IsMinimumInstall()`, should return true if the player is running the game with a minimum install and therefore needs the CD in the drive. Presumably you'd read this from some install file or system registry key.

The next predicate, comparing the event type to `DBT_DEVICEREMOVECOMPLETE` is how Windows tells you the drive eject button has been pressed. The code then enters a loop, which checks for the existence of a marker file on the CD. A marker file is a file with either a unique name or unique contents, like a fingerprint. You could just as easily read the volume label but I've found that simulating removable media with a network drive is easier if you use a marker file. The IT staff gets nervous when programmers start requesting hourly volume name changes on network drives. I'd make it easy and look for a file that is guaranteed to be on the CD, uncompressed, and easy to find.

If the file isn't found you bring up a dialog box that asks the user to find the CD. It should have two buttons: OK and Cancel. If they press cancel, you should abort the game. If they press OK, you should check for the existence of the marker file just to be sure that everything is ok. The return value, `BROADCAST_QUERY_DENY`, tells Windows that you don't want the eject button to actually eject the CD.

You might wonder why the CD marker file is checked even though you are telling Windows to deny the eject command. Simple: Some removable media hardware doesn't give a damn about waiting for Windows to tell it what to do. A good example of this would be a mechanical eject system like you see on some floppy drives. It's a good idea to be safe and check for the marker file.

WM_POWERBROADCAST

There are plenty of people out there playing on portable computers, including me, I might add. Please handle this message, and do something with it!

```
case WM_POWERBROADCAST
{
    // Don't allow the game to go into sleep mode
    if ( wParam == PBT_APMQUERYSUSPEND )
        return BROADCAST_QUERY_DENY;
    else if ( wParam == PBT_APMBATTERYLOW )
    {
```

```
        yourcode::ForceGameToSaveAndExit();
    }

    return true;
}
```

One thing you can do is disable sleep mode while the game is running. We did this because on some machines DirectX drivers never recovered from sleep mode! You should definitely provide some mechanism for saving the game and exiting when the battery begins to run low on electrons.

WM_DISPLAYCHANGE

When the player resets the desktop settings, Windows sends this message to tell you what the new settings are. Save off the settings and you can use them to validate the new mode:

```
case WM_DISPLAYCHANGE:
{
    m_crDesktop = CRect( 0, 0, LOWORD(lParam), HIWORD(lParam) );
    m_iColorDepth = wParam;
    return 0;
}
```

WM_ENTERSIZEMOVE, WM_EXITSIZEMOVE

These messages are sent before and after you drag or resize your window. One useful thing to do is to deactivate your game when you begin the drag and reactivate it when you exit the drag. Why? If you've saved off the background buffer, the dragging or resizing will be much snappier, since your game isn't running in the background. This can be especially true for resizing.

WM_GETMINMAXINFO

This message is a great example of how Windows asks your application for a piece of information. In this case it is sent so Windows can figure out if your game has a minimum or maximum client area size:

```
case WM_GETMINMAXINFO:
{
    // effectively keeps the window at exactly it's current size!
    LPMINMAXINFO lpMMI = (LPMINMAXINFO)lParam;

    lpMMI->ptMinTrackSize.x = lpMMI->ptMaxTrackSize.x = m_crWindow.Width();
```

```
    lpMMI->ptMinTrackSize.y = lpMMI->ptMaxTrackSize.y = m_crWindow.Height();
    return 0;
}
```

We used this message to essentially disable resizing, but you could use it to keep your window from growing or shrinking beyond certain limits.

Operating System Specific Stuff

You might not have been aware of this, but the Win9x family and the WinNT family of operating systems are no closer related than humans are to chimps. Guess who the chimps are? The wise programmer would have chosen the Win9x family for the short and furry ones. In truth, the two operating systems were designed, written, and managed in two completely separate groups within Microsoft. I'm amazed beyond description that we have one API to deal with because, as you begin to look under the hood, the two families are very, very, *very* different.

The Win9x family includes Windows 95, Windows 98, and Windows ME. These operating systems were targeted primarily for the home, and were designed to have a maximum compatibility with legacy applications from the DOS world.

The WinNT family includes Windows NT, Windows 2000, and Windows XP. Unlike Win9x, these operating systems were written from the ground up with a serious internal architecture. These operating systems could leave legacy apps behind—perhaps where they belong—in favor of tightening the operating system in every aspect. For those of you who've spent any time at all on Win9x and WinNT, you'll recall that Win9x crashed quickly and easily. WinNT, on the other hand, is extremely robust. It recovers from application crashes extremely well.

API Compatibility and UNICODE

These operating systems, being extremely different, clearly don't support the Win32 APIs identically. Some functions are not supported at all on Win9x, such as the vast majority of wide character versions of the Win32 API. Let me say that last statement much more clearly: T*he Win9x family of operating systems does not support UNICODE, it is an entirely ANSI character based.*

Are you surprised that Win9x doesn't support UNICODE? Maybe, but not half as surprised as the Microsoft product manager I worked with when I told him. It was somewhat embarrassing at the time because I'd just spent an entire month porting our ANSI game engine to UNICODE.

Suddenly it didn't work on any Win9x box. When we dug around in MSDN a little we found the horrible truth—there was no UNICODE to be had on Win9x. Luckily my butt and the MS product manager's butt was saved by a little known extension called the Microsoft Layer for UNICODE. Basically it "fools" Win9x systems into believing they have all the wide character versions of the Win32 API. It doesn't really provide the wide character versions, it just converts the UNICODE text to ANSI, and calls the ANSI API instead.

So what? I'll tell you what: It means you can create a UNICODE app and run the executable on Win9x and WinNT without a problem. If you are going to create a UNICODE compliant game, you want to build one executable, and you want to support Win9x, your only hope is the Microsoft Layer for UNICODE. If you want to know how to set this up, search for it on MSDN, it's pretty easy.

If your game uses the Microsoft Layer for UNICODE and you don't set it up correctly, your game won't be able to create a window. This is an odd failure and very confusing to debug. You'll notice that any function that accepts a window handle like `LoadIcon()` will simply fail. If you see this, the Unicows.dll is most likely the culprit.

Every Win32 function has compatibility documentation in the help files or on MSDN. Get used to checking for the compatibility every time you use a new function. This is becoming a frequent occurrence for me to find a different solution to maintain compatibility with Win9x. Find it at the bottom of the documentation under the "Requirements" section.

Your Game's Registry Key

You should create a registry key for your game, not only for storing the odd registry data but the key designation is useful for finding a unique directory to store temporary files or application data on the hard drive. The key should contain the following information:

```
\Your Company Name\Your Product Name\Major Version.Minor Version
```

Here's an example of the registry key for the first version of Microsoft Casino:

```
\Microsoft\Microsoft Games\Microsoft Casino\1.0
```

Microsoft produces so many products it was convenient to add a product group description after the company name. This key will be used by the install program and your game in many different ways, many of which we'll discuss in the next section.

Windows 95

It was cool when it came out; there's no mistake there. At the time of this writing, Microsoft is no longer supporting Windows 95 in its own products. There are very few Win95 boxes out there any more anyway, so don't mourn its loss. Don't bother trying to support Windows 95 in your game. It's dead.

Windows 98 and Windows ME

There are plenty of Windows 98 and Windows ME boxes out there, mostly in the mass market. If you are making kids games or games for your parents, you'd be wise to support Windows 98 and ME in your game. You can count on Internet Explorer being installed, which is I imagine why Microsoft got in all that trouble. Still, it's nice to know you can format your game documentation and help files completely in HTML, put it on the CD-ROM and save a few trees. The biggest pain in the butt with supporting these remnants of the Win9x group is that you can't run Visual Studio.NET on a Win9x machine, so you'll have to do all your debugging remotely.

Since Microsoft dropped support for Windows 95 in mid-2002 and Windows ME was released in 2000 we can expect to have this monkey on our backs until at least 2006, perhaps 2007. One thing that might save us is that Windows ME didn't penetrate the market very well. Most home users were satisfied with Windows 98, and for good reason. It was actually much better than Windows ME. Other power users and office users moved from Windows 98 to Windows 2000 or Windows XP. Perhaps this will bode for an early retirement for Windows ME support. I hope so.

On Windows 98 and Windows ME machines you can lock your system up if you attempt to perform pixel-by-pixel operations on multiple video RAM surfaces. The classic example would be an alpha blit, where you have a source and destination surface and one more surface that holds the alpha values. If two or more of these surfaces are in video RAM, you can crash Windows 98 and Windows ME.

Windows NT

This was an extremely cool operating system mainly because it was Windows, and it didn't crash. Well, it didn't crash very often! When I was cussing up a storm rebooting my Windows 95 machine for the sixteenth time my buddy across the hall at Origin Systems would brag that he hadn't rebooted in a couple of weeks.

I thought he was kidding. He wasn't kidding.

Windows NT never really penetrated the home market or the computer game market at all, mostly because very few computer game companies wanted to support it and because it never supported DirectX after version 3.0. It was different enough from Win9x to require full test passes and hardware compatibility tests. Most of the multimedia hardware ran on Win9x anyway, so Windows NT never really caught on in the home.

The last survey we did on mass market usage of Windows NT was around 2% of our customers, and dropping every month. That survey was taken in mid-2002. I really liked Windows NT but there's no reason to keep it alive in your test lab.

Windows 2000

Windows 2000, on the other hand, is very much alive, and has good market penetration. The best thing about Windows 2000 is you can write applications for it as if it was Windows NT, for the most part. The only thing you have to do is check for the compatibility of the Win32 API functions you are using, and everything should be fine. You should make sure your games support Windows 2000, and likely do so until at least 2007.

Windows XP

Windows XP was not nearly so friendly. Since it is the first NT-based software to make it to the home market, it's no surprise there is will be a little hang wringing on the part of developers who've never supported NT.

One of the most significant differences involves security settings. For the first time in Windows history, security settings will prohibit any application from writing files to the Program Files directory. This is the default setting in Windows XP Home, and is a possible setting in Windows XP Pro. There are other issues as well, and it may be easiest to go over them one by one as you look at the next section.

"Designed for Windows" Logo Program

The logo program is an optional certification that allows you to affix the "Designed for Windows" logo on your box. This is much more important for kid's titles or other mass market games than hard core titles. The reason being that if my Mom were shopping for games and she had two essentially identical candidates in front of her, she'd probably choose the game that was designed for Windows.

There is an extensive feature checklist that your game must pass to be eligible for the logo program. While most of the list is a no-brainer, there are a few line items that will make you go "You're kidding, right?" The entire testing document with details of all the test cases is up on MSDN (**www.microsoft.com/winlogo/**). It's a whopping 105 pages long. I briefly thought about including it in this book in the hopes my editor wouldn't notice the extra pages, but in the end a summary of the checklist and a discussion of the tricky items seemed more appropriate.

The numbers designation "T#.#" is Microsoft's code for tests related to a general test requirement, and "TC#.#.#" denotes a specific test case.

There are tests for general compliancy as well as tests specific to games. We'll cover the tests for all Windows applications first:

T1.1 Perform primary functionality and maintain stability

TC1.1.1 Does the application perform its primary functions and maintain stability during functionality testing?

- Pass The application performed all its primary functions and did not crash, stop responding, or lose data.
- Fail The application failed to perform one or more primary functions, or it crashed, stopped responding, or lost data.

TC1.1.2 Does the application remain stable when a mouse with more than three buttons was used?

- Pass The application did not crash, stop responding, or lose data.
- Fail The application crashed, stopped responding, or lost data as a result of executing the test for at least one mouse button.

TC1.1.3 Does the application use the user's temporary folder for temporary files?

TC1.1.3.1 Does the application store its temporary files only in the user's temporary folder during installation?

- Pass No temporary folder was created and no temporary files were stored in the wrong places.
- Fail One or more new temporary folders were created or one or more temporary files were stored in the wrong places. Record the full paths for the folders and files.

TC1.1.3.2 Does the application store its temporary files only in the user's temporary folder during functionality testing?

- Pass No temporary folder was created and no temporary files were stored in the wrong places.

- **Fail** One or more new temporary folders were created or one or more temporary files were stored in the wrong places. Record the full paths for the folders and files.

TC1.1.4 Does the application not crash or lose data when presented with long path, file and printer names?

TC1.1.4.1 Does the application maintain stability when a file is saved by drilling down through the "User1 LFNPath1" path in User1's "My Documents" folder?

- **Pass** The application did not crash or lose the test document data.
- **Fail** The application crashed or lost the test document data.

TC1.1.4.2 Does the application maintain stability when a file is saved by entering the full "User1 LFNPath2" path?

- **Pass** The application did not crash or lose the test document data.
- **Fail** The application crashed or lost the test document data.

TC1.1.4.3 Does the application maintain stability when a file is saved using a long file name?

- **Pass** The application did not crash or lose the test document data.
- **Fail** The application crashed or lost the test document data.

TC1.1.4.4 Does the application maintain stability when a file is opened by drilling down through the "User1 LFNPath1" path in User1's "My Documents" folder?

- **Pass** The application did not crash or lose the test document data.
- **Fail** The application crashed or lost the test document data.

TC1.1.4.5 Does the application maintain stability when a file is opened by entering the full "User1 LFNPath2" path?

- **Pass** The application did not crash or lose the test document data.
- **Fail** The application crashed or lost the test document data.

TC1.1.4.6 Does the application maintain stability when a file is opened using a long file name?

- Pass The application did not crash or lose the test document data.
- Fail The application crashed or lost the test document data.

TC1.1.4.7 Does the application maintain stability when printing to a printer with a long name?

- Pass The application did not crash or lose the test document data.
- Fail The application crashed or lost the test document data.
- The application does not have a "print hard copy" feature. This is not a failure, but it is also very unusual. Make sure there is no printing functionality in any part of your application before you check this option.

TC1.1.5 Does the application perform primary functionality and maintain stability on a dual-processor computer?

TC1.1.6 Does the application not crash when devices it uses are not installed?

TC1.1.6.1 Does the application maintain stability when printing if no printer is installed?

- Pass The application did not crash or lose the test document data.
- Fail The application crashed or lost the test document data.
- The application does not have a "print hard copy" feature. This is not a failure, but it is also very unusual. Make sure there is no printing functionality in any part of your application before you check this option.

TC1.1.6.2 Does the application maintain stability when attempting to use devices that are not installed?

- Pass The application did not crash.
- Fail The application crashed upon attempting to use one or more devices that were not installed. Record the names of the devices.

TC1.1.7 Does the application switch the system's display mode back to the previous color mode, if application automatically changes to 256-color mode when it runs?

- **Pass The system color quality setting was the same after the application closed as it was before the application was started.**
- **Fail The system color quality setting was "256 colors" after the application was closed.**

One of the first tests to raise your eyebrows is TC1.1.3, where your game should locate temporary files. This is where your registry key, discussed a few pages back, comes in handy. Use the Win32 `GetTempPath()` API to get the root of the temporary directory, and add your registry key to create a unique space within the temporary directory to create your files.

Since your registry key is probably a few slashes deep, you'll need a function to parse through the path name and make sure the directory tree exists. Here's a function that starts at the temporary directory and creates the directory tree:

```
void MakeTempDirectory(CString &tempDirectory)
{
   TCHAR buffer[MAX_PATH];
   GetTempPath(MAX_PATH, buffer);

   CString tempDirectory = buffer;
   tempDirectory += "\\";
   tempDirectory += GAME_APP_DIRECTORY;

   if (0xffffffff == GetFileAttributes(tempDirectory))
   {
      // Ok - we have to go make a new directory to store temporary data.
      CString current = buffer;
      CString myAppData = GAME_APP_DIRECTORY;
      CString token;

      do {
         int left = myAppData.Find('\\');
         if (left==-1)
         {
            token = myAppData;
            myAppData = _T("");
         }
         else
```

```
        {
          assert(myAppData.GetLength()>=left);
          token = myAppData.Left(left);
          myAppData = myAppData.Right(myAppData.GetLength()-(left+1));
        }

        if (token.GetLength())
        {
          current += "\\";
          current += token;

          if (false == CreateDirectory(current, NULL))
          {
            int error = GetLastError();
            if (error != ERROR_ALREADY_EXISTS)
            {
                  return false;
            }
          }
        }

      } while (myAppData.GetLength());
    }

    tempDirectory += _T("\\");
}
```

The next set of tests, TC1.1.4 concern long file and printer names. Don't let this test fool you into thinking that you can get rid of 8.3 filenames in your application. It turns out that there are some older CD-ROM drivers that still cannot handle long files names on the CD. This is likely going to go away in 2003 or 2004 completely, and is probably already such a small percentage you don't have to be overly concerned. Still, it's a good thing to know.

11

If you're curious about long file name compatibility and you don't have a huge budget for doing hardware surveys, take a look at CD's coming out of Microsoft. When they start using long filenames on their CDs and DVDs it's probably safe for you to do so.

Test TC1.1.5 is a serious concern for games, since games are usually multithreaded applications. If you ever thought that debugging multithreaded apps on a single processor computer was tough, try it on a multi-processor box. Check the Debugging chapter for more tips on finding nasty bugs like that.

Test TC1.1.6 is also a concern for games. Your game must fail elegantly if it doesn't find the joystick, mouse, or sound card that it needs. Users can easily disable hardware with the device settings dialog box, which is effectively the same thing as physically removing the hardware.

TC1.1.7 is handled by DirectX if you use it. If you use another graphics API you should always restore the player's display to the setting your game detected when it started.

T1.2 Any kernel-mode drivers that the application installs must pass verification testing on Windows†XP

TC1.2.1 Do all related kernel-mode drivers pass testing as Windows†XP loaded them?

- Pass All kernel-mode drivers passed initial load tests.
- Fail At least one kernel-mode driver failed initial load tests.
- The application does not install kernel-mode drivers. This is not a failure.

TC1.2.2 Do all related kernel-mode drivers pass functionality testing with standard kernel testing enabled?

- Pass All kernel-mode drivers passed verifications during functionality testing.
- Fail At least one kernel-mode driver failed verifications during functionality testing.
- The application does not install kernel-mode drivers. This is not a failure.

TC1.2.3 Do all related kernel-mode drivers pass low-resources simulation testing?

- Pass All kernel-mode drivers passed verifications during low-resources testing.
- Fail At least one kernel-mode driver failed verifications during low-resources testing.
- The application does not install kernel mode drivers. This is not a failure.

T1.3 Any device or filter drivers included with the application must pass Windows HCT testing

TC1.3.1 Are proofs of WHQL testing attached to the submission for all required drivers?

- Pass All device and filter drivers have been tested by WHQL.
- Fail At least one device and filter driver has been tested by WHQL

- The application does not install drivers that require WHQL testing. This is not a failure.

TC1.3.2 Do no warnings appear about unsigned drivers during testing?

- Pass No unsigned driver warnings appeared during any testing.
- Fail At least one unsigned driver warning appeared during any testing. Record the name of the driver.

I don't know about you, but I've never written a kernel-mode driver or device driver and don't intend to. Most, if not all, games fall in this category so we don't have to worry about T1.2 and T1.3.

T1.4 Perform Windows version checking correctly

TC1.4.1 Does the application install correctly under current and future versions of Windows?

- Pass The application successfully installed on the future version of Windows, or it appropriately blocked the installation without hanging, crashing or losing data.
- Fail The application displayed an inappropriate version error message, hung, crashed or lost data during the installation.

TC1.4.2 Does the application perform all functionality tests correctly under current and future versions of Windows?

- Pass The application passed all functionality tests on the future version of Windows, or it appropriately blocked some or all tests without hanging, crashing or losing data.
- Fail The application displayed an inappropriate version error message, hung, crashed or lost data during functionality testing.
- The application blocks functionality for future versions as documented. This is not a failure.

Test T1.4 is absolutely hilarious. How in the name of Albert Einstein can I know if my game will properly install and function under all future versions of Windows? Actually, this is probably concerning any Windows operating system currently in beta test, and has little or nothing to do with Windows 3000.

T1.5 Support Fast User Switching

TC1.5.1 Does the application properly support Fast User Switching?

- Pass The application passed all CVTs as User2; or the application blocked User2 from starting the application; or the application blocked User2 from executing specific functionality.
- Fail The application failed some functionality testing, or incorrectly blocked User2 from starting the application.

TC1.5.2 Does the application properly support Remote Desktop?

- Pass The application passes all CVTs as the remote desktop user, or the application blocked the remote desktop user from starting the application; or the application blocked the remote desktop user from executing specific functionality
- Fail The application failed some functionality testing, or incorrectly blocked the remote desktop user from starting the application

TC1.5.3 If the application installs a replacement GINA, does the GINA propely support Remote Desktop?

- Pass The replacement GINA adheres to the current Winlogon APIs and functions properly.
- Fail The replacement GINA does not adhere to the current Winlogon APIs or does not function properly.

Fast user task switching is a serious concern for games. There are two things your game should be able to do to support fast user task switching: run minimized and run multiple copies of itself. The last one might seem weird, since most games detect their own window and simply bring themselves to the front. I'm talking about opening game files in a read-only sharable mode so that two users on the same box can open your game without a weird file sharing failure.

If your game stores user save game files in the users Application Data directory, required by test T3.1, you should be fine.

T1.6 Support new visual styles

TC1.6 Does the application pass all functionality tests with a Windows†XP theme applied?

- Pass The application did not lose functionality or usability when one of the new visual styles was selected.
- Fail The application lost some functionality or usability when one of the new visual styles was selected.

This is one place games get special dispensation from adhering with logo compliance: Games write their own interface that has nothing to do with Windows styles or themes. You can ignore this rule to the extent that you don't provide Windows-looking components that are deceiving, such as an "X" button in the upper right hand corner of your game that brings up a help window instead of closing your game.

T1.7 Support switching between tasks

TC1.7.1 Does the application display normally and not lose data when focus is switched among other applications with Alt+Tab?

- Pass No data was lost when switching among applications and all applications displayed normally.
- Fail Data was lost data switching among applications or some display irregularities appeared.

TC1.7.2 Does the application display normally and not lose data when Windows logo key and the taskbar are used to switch among applications?

- Pass No data was lost when switching among applications and all applications displayed normally.
- Fail Data was lost data switching among applications or some display irregularities appeared.

TC1.7.3 Does the Windows Security dialog box or the Task Manager display normally and can the application be cancelled or closed without losing data?

- Pass Everything displayed normally and the application did not lose data when canceling the Windows Security dialog box or closing the Task Manager.

- **Fail** Something displayed abnormally, or a dialog could not be closed, or the application could not be restored or lost data when canceling the Windows Security dialog box or closing the Task Manager.

This is where most games fall flat on their face, if they run in full-screen and windowed modes. It's critical to handle `WM_ACTIVATE` and check your DirectX surfaces for loss. If you do that correctly, your game will pass these tests.

T2.1 Do not attempt to replace files protected by Windows File Protection

TC2.1 Does the installation finish without any Windows File Protection messages appearing?

- **Pass** The installation completed and no WFP dialogs appeared.
- **Fail** At least one WFP dialog appeared during the installation. Write down the name of each file WFP had to replace. You may need to look in the System and Application logs using the Event Viewer to find the names of the files.

This install requirement is pretty easy to pass, just make sure that any special game DLLs don't collide with other DLLs in the Windows System32 directory.

T2.2 Migrate from earlier versions of Windows

TC2.2.1 Does the application successfully migrate from Windows†98 to Windows†XP Home Edition?

- **Pass** The application migrated successfully.
- **Fail** Migration was unsuccessful. Describe what went wrong.

TC2.2.2 Does the application successfully migrate from Windows†Me to Windows†XP Home Edition?

- **Pass** The application migrated successfully.
- **Fail** Migration was unsuccessful. Describe what went wrong.

TC2.2.3 Does the application successfully migrate from Windows†98 to Windows†XP Professional?

- **Pass** The application migrated successfully.

- Fail Migration was unsuccessful. Describe what went wrong.

TC2.2.4 Does the application successfully migrate from Windows†Me to Windows†XP Professional?

- Pass The application migrated successfully.
- Fail Migration was unsuccessful. Describe what went wrong.

TC2.2.5 Does the application successfully migrate from Windows†NT†4.0 Workstation to Windows†XP Professional?

- Pass The application migrated successfully.
- Fail Migration was unsuccessful. Describe what went wrong.

TC2.2.6 Does the application successfully migrate from Windows†2000 Professional to Windows†XP Professional?

- Pass The application migrated successfully.
- Fail Migration was unsuccessful. Describe what went wrong.

I don't know of any games that support migration. In fact there are plenty of legacy games that failed after Windows XP was installed due to the security measures on the Program Files directory.

T2.3 Do not overwrite non-proprietary files with older versions

TC2.3.1 Does the application not overwrite non-proprietary files with older versions?

- Pass The application did not overwrite any non-proprietary files with older versions.
- Fail At least one non-proprietary was overwritten with an older version. Record the file name and versions for each file.

TC2.3.2 Do all application executable files have file version, product name and company name information?

- Pass All executable files the application installs have version number, product name and company name information.

- **Fail** At least one executable file the application installs is missing version number, product name, or company name information. Record the names of the files that are missing information.

The take-away from this test is make sure all your game files have embedded version information. This is trivial for game EXEs and DLLs—just insert a version resource, and make sure your install program respects the old version by installing the new one in a parallel directory. It shouldn't just whack the old files. This is also handled if you use the registry key to locate your game in the Program Files directory. The two versions can safely coexist because they'll be installed in two different directories.

T2.4 Do not require a reboot inappropriately

TC2.4.1 Does the installation finish without requiring a reboot?

- **Pass** During installation, the application did not require or suggest a reboot, or it prompted for a reboot and one or more reasons detailed in the Specification requirement 2.4 are documented.

- **Fail** During installation, the application prompted for a reboot and no reasons are documented; or the reasons documented are not allowed by the Specification; or the application rebooted without giving the user the option to postpone the reboot (even if the documented reasons are allowed by the Specification).

TC2.4.2 Can all Test Framework testing be completed without application requiring a reboot?

- **Pass** During functionality testing, the application did not require or suggest a reboot, or it prompted for a reboot and one or more reasons detailed in the Specification requirement 2.4 are documented.

- **Fail** During functionality testing, the application prompted for a reboot and no reasons are documented; or the reasons documented are not allowed by the Specification; or the application rebooted without giving the user the option to postpone the reboot (even if the documented reasons are allowed by the Specification).

I know install programs love rebooting the machine, especially older install programs. If you use the most recent version of your installer, you should be fine.

T2.5 Install to Program Files by default

TC2.5 Does the application offer a default installation folder under "E:\Program Files?"

- **Pass** Both "E:" and "Program Files" appeared in the default installation path.
- **Fail** "E:" and/or "Program Files" was missing from the default installation path. Write down the actual default path the application used or offered you.

Duh. That's pretty easy.

T2.6 Install any shared files that are not side-by-side to the correct locations

TC2.6 Does the application install shared files only to correct locations?

- **Pass** Either all shared files are installed in the correct locations, or there are no shared files.
- **Fail** At least one shared file was not stored in the correct location. Record the full path and name of each incorrectly installed file.

That test seems a little cryptic. Here are more details from the logo compliancy document, describing the location of shared files:

- The file is located in "E:\Program Files\Common Files\<*company name*>"
- The file is located in "E:\Program Files\<*company name*>\Shared Files"
- The file is located in the system folder E:\Windows, or a subfolder of the system folder, and the file is documented as a service or driver. For example, a file with the extension SYS that is installed to the system32\drivers folder is clearly a driver and would need no other documentation.
- The file is located in the system folder E:\Windows, or a subfolder of the system folder, and the file is documented as a DLL or OCX required for legacy software support or documented as shared with applications from other vendors.
- The file is not a shared file.

The docs make it clear that shared files are files common to more than one application your company makes. This would be true for a common game engine DLL.

T2.7 Support Add or Remove Programs properly

TC2.7.1 Does installation add an uninstall to the Add or Remove Programs utility?

- Pass The application added all the required information to the registry.
- Fail Some required information is missing or appears to be incorrect.

TC2.7.2 Does uninstalling application as Owner remove and leave all the correct files and registry settings?

- Pass The application removed and left all the correct files and registry settings.
- Fail The application did not remove everything it should have (and there are no exemptions for the data), or the application removed user-created data without prompting the user for permission, or the application left user settings and preferences data without providing an option to completely remove them.

TC2.7.3 Does uninstalling application as User1 either degrade gracefully or both remove and leave all the correct files and registry settings?

- Pass Either the application degraded gracefully (and did not allow User1 to uninstall it), or it both removed and left all the correct files and registry settings.
- Fail The application failed to completely uninstall because User1 is a Limited User and the application did not degrade gracefully, or it did not remove everything it should have, or the application removed user-created data without prompting the user for permission, or the application left user settings and preferences data without providing an option to completely remove them.

TC2.7.4 Can the application be reinstalled after uninstalling it?

- Pass The application can be installed without problems.
- Fail The application could not be fully reinstalled, or Owner's preferences and settings were not fully retained.

T2.8 Support "All Users" installations

TC2.8.1 Does the application default to an "all users" installation or provide an "all users" installation as an option when installed by Owner?

- Pass The application successfully installed using one of the accepted "all users" installation options.
- Fail The application either could not be installed for all users, or it did not offer "all users" as the default option.

TC2.8.2 Does the application default to an "all users" installation or provide an "all users" installation as an option when installed by User1?

- Pass Either User1 installed the application successfully for "all users" or the installer degraded gracefully and did not install any files on the system.
- Fail Either User1 was able to install the application for User1 only, or the installation failed and did not degrade gracefully and/or installed some files on the system.

If you use the latest install programs you'll be automatically covered for T2.7 and T2.8.

T2.9 Support Autorun for CDs and DVDs

TC2.9.1 Does the application's installer start by way of Autorun?

- Pass The application's installation started using Autorun.
- Fail The application's installation did not start automatically.
- The application is not installed from CD/DVD.

TC2.9.2 Does the application's installer correctly detect that application is already installed and avoid restarting the installation?

- Pass The application's installer did not try to reinstall the application
- Fail The application's installer restarted the installation process as if the application was not already installed.
- The application is not installed from CD/DVD.

Autorun has been part of the operating system since Windows 95. If you're unsure about how to make this work, you can find it on MSDN. It's a relatively trivial matter to get autorun to work, but there is a nice trick you can employ: The Autorun should launch a program that detects if your game has already been installed. If it has, it should launch your game. Otherwise, it should launch your install program.

T3.1 Default to the correct location for storing user-created data

TC3.1.1 Does the application offer a correct location for opening User1's user-created data?

- Pass The application uses a correct default location.
- Fail The application used an incorrect default location. Record the full path the application used.

TC3.1.2 Does the application offer a correct location for saving User1's user-created data?

- q Pass The application uses a correct default location.
- q Fail The application used an incorrect default location. Record the full path the application used.

TC3.1.3 Does the application offer a correct location for opening User2's user-created data?

- Pass The application uses a correct default location.
- Fail The application used an incorrect default location. Record the full path the application used.

TC3.1.4 Does the application offer a correct location for saving User2's user-created data?

- Pass The application uses a correct default location.
- Fail The application used an incorrect default location. Record the full path the application used.

This is without a doubt the most significant change for Windows XP, because if your game ignores this requirement it will likely fail under Windows XP Home. There's a Win32 API that finds this directory for you:

```
// set the players data directory
TCHAR playerDataPath[MAX_PATH];
if (SHGetSpecialFolderPath(m_hWnd,playerDataPath,CSIDL_APPDATA, true)))
{
  // you've found the players data directory!
}
```

This call should be placed in your game initialization code after the main window has been created but before your first player data files are opened. These files aren't your game maps or sound files, rather they are your save game files or user options settings.

T3.2 Classify and store application data correctly

TC3.2.1 Does the application store less than 128K of application data in the registry for User1?

- Pass The application saved less than 128K of application data in the registry.
- Fail The application saved more than 128K of application data in the registry.

TC3.2.2 Does the application store configuration data for User1 only in acceptable folders?

- Pass The application stored configuration data for User1 in acceptable folders (or stored no configuration data in folders).
- Fail The application stored User1 configuration data in unacceptable locations. List the locations and file names.

That test seems pretty obvious. Clearly large save game files belong in the user's application data directory, not the registry.

T3.3 Deal gracefully with access-denied scenarios

TC3.3.1 Does the application prevent User1 from saving to the Windows system folder, E:\Windows?

- Pass The application prevented User1 from saving the file with a meaningful message and did not hang, crash or lose the test document.
- Fail The application allowed User1 to save the file, or it prevented the save but did not display meaningful message, or it hung, crashed or lost the test document.

TC3.3.2 Does the application prevent User1 from modifying documents owned by User2?

- Pass The application prevented User1 from saving the file with a meaningful message and did not hang, crash or lose the test document.
- Fail The application allowed User1 to save the file, or it prevented the save but did not display meaningful message, or it hung, crashed or lost the test document.

TC3.3.3 Does the application prevent User1 from modifying system-wide settings?

- Pass The application prevented User1 from making system-wide changes.
- Fail The application allowed User1 to system settings changes that User1 was blocked from making from outside the application.
- Does not apply. The application has no functionality that allows users to make system settings changes.

TC3.3.4 Does the application's installer either allow User1 to install application or degrade gracefully if the installation fails?

- Pass Either User1 was able to install the application, or the application gave User1 an appropriate dialog and degraded gracefully.
- Fail The application either failed to install so CVTs failed, or the application did not degrade gracefully.

T3.4 Support running as a Limited User

TC3.4 Does the application support running as User1, a Limited User?

- **Pass** All primary function tests succeeded with User1 running the application.
- **Fail** One or more primary functions failed with User1 running the application, and the failure was caused by insufficient privileges.

Tests T3.3 and T3.4 are all related to access-denied situations where your install program or your game is attempting to do something it shouldn't. An interesting "ahh-ha" in T3.4 is found when you recall that most programmers run their computers as an administrator or debugger user, which has much broader access rights as other users. When your game has one of those, "It crashes in QA but is completely "unreproducable" on the programmer's machine." For problems like this, you should look closely at the user access rights.

"Optimized for Games"

The tests for games cover additional install criteria as well as tests for audio, video and network support. If you look on MSDN, you'll find a vague reference to the tests that Microsoft will expect your game to pass, but absolutely no details. Since I worked with Microsoft, I had an early version of the test details, which I'll present here. Most of the tests are pretty self-explanatory, so if I have nothing to say about them I'll simply move on to something worth discussing. I hate it when books simply restate something to restate it. Again, I won't bother telling you something you already know.

S1.1 General Game Playing Experience

S1.1.1 The application should make sensible default choices for three-dimensional (3-D) device, resolution, and color depth without asking the user.

S1.1.2 The game should use LoadLibrary or CoCreateInstance to give itself the option of failing more gracefully instead of displaying the system "missing DLL" dialog box.

S1.1.3 If the game uses the LoadLibrary function to load any system components (that is, Microsoft Direct3DÆ, Microsoft DirectInputÆ, and so forth), do not hard-code paths.

S1.1.4 The game should perform its basic operational functions over at least four hours without any problems. The game must still function after crossing the date change barrier.

11

S1.1.5 **If any system components that the game relies upon change then another first-run analysis of the computer should be performed. For example, when a new input device or display adapter is installed another analysis should be executed.**

Test S1.1.1 deals with selecting the default game options based on the players computer and installed hardware. You would pass this test if you detected a multiple monitor setup and picked the best display for your game without asking the player. The last test, S1.1.5 is somewhat related: If the hardware configuration changes, your game should detect it, and fix the settings to make the best user experience possible. This means a player can go out and upgrade their box, maybe installing the latest video card from NVidia or something, and your game should notice the difference.

S1.1.2 and S1.1.3 are just common sense, really. I wonder why these tests are included in the games specific section and not included for the nominal logo tests ?

The test for stability over four hours, and over the date change is a good one, although I wonder if Sony and Nintendo have such lax requirements. Four hours isn't that long. I'd hate to buy a hard drive with a mean time between failure measured in the single digits, wouldn't you? If I were you, I'd take stability tests a lot longer than four hours.

S1.2 **Do Not Install or Depend on 16-bit Files: The application should not crash or fail to execute on 32-bit edition Windows XP because of a dependency on 16-bit code. The application must not read install or depend on 16-bit files.**

S1.3 **Do not write to Config,sys, Autoexec.bat, Win.ini, or System.ini files: The application must not read from or write to Win.ini, System.ini, Autoexec.bat, or Config.sys on any Windows operating system.**

Tests S1.2 and S1.3 make sure you've moved your game into the modern age. Back in the day game programmers had no problem putting crazy stuff into autoexec.bat, config.sys, and Windows INI files. If you are reading this and you have no idea what these files are, good for you. You're already ahead of the game. If your curious about them, find a computer museum and boot up a Windows 3.1 box.

S1.4 **Provide both manual and automatic install options: Near the start of installation (after any option license agreement), provide the user with the option of selecting either Automatic or Manual installation. The Automatic installation will make as many logical choices as possible for the user. The Manual installation may take the user to another dialog box where the user can choose any number of installation types: custom, typical, minimal, and so on.**

This is a really good idea, since many games have the possibility of installing different levels of game data on the player's hard drive, trading hard drive space for performance or level of detail in the game.

S1.5 Allow installation termination: The user should be able to cancel out of an installation at any time before the installation completes. For each dialog box of this install process, make sure that your application can stop the installation.

Again, another test that should probably be in the general tests for all applications, and not games. Still, this feature is a good common sense item to put in your install program.

S1.6 Running from CD or DVD

S1.6.1 If the game requires a CD or DVD for game play even with the game fully installed on the hard drive, launching the game from the Start menu\Games folder should display an "Insert CD or DVD" message if the CD or DVD is not in the drive. When the CD or DVD is inserted, then the game should continue to run without requiring the user to restart the game.

S1.6.2 The game must be able to be played on a different CD or DVD drive than the one from which it was installed.

S1.6.3 The game must work even in situations where Red Book audio is not available for a particular drive (for example, external drives).

Test S1.6.1 is satisfied by the code discussed in the `WM_DEVICECHANGE` section earlier in this chapter. S1.6.2 needs a little more work. Here's how to search the computer for the marker file:

```
enum CDPOLL_ENUM
{
   POLL_SUCCESSFUL,
   NO_CD_ROM_FOUND,
   NO_CD_DRIVE_FOUND
};

CDPOLL_ENUM PollForCD(const _TCHAR *markerFilePath)
{
   CDPOLL_ENUM       result = NO_CD_DRIVE_FOUND;   /* Assume failure. */
   unsigned int      drive_type = DRIVE_UNKNOWN;
   int               drive;
   _TCHAR            path[_MAX_PATH];
   _TCHAR            current_directory[_MAX_PATH];
   FILE              *test_file = NULL;
```

```
int                 Current_Drive_Index = 0;

/* Save current drive. */
GetCurrentDirectory( _MAX_PATH, current_directory );

Current_Drive_Index = _getdrive();

/* Set this to -1 for easy error checking. */
int iCDDriveIndex = -1;

/* If we can switch to the drive, it exists. */
for( drive = 3; drive <= 26; drive++ )
{
  if( 0 == _chdrive( drive ) )
  {
    GetCurrentDirectory( _MAX_PATH, path );
    drive_type = GetDriveType( path );

    if( (drive_type == DRIVE_CDROM)
    #ifdef _DEBUG
    || (drive_type == DRIVE_FIXED)
    || (drive_type == DRIVE_REMOVABLE)
    || (drive_type == DRIVE_REMOTE)
    #endif
    )
    {
      iCDDriveIndex = drive;

      /* Found the drive, now look for the CD-ROM. */
      result = NO_CD_ROM_FOUND;

      _TCHAR buffer[_MAX_PATH];
      _tcscpy(buffer, path);
      _tcscat(buffer, markerFilePath);

      if (0xFFFFFFFF == GetFileAttributes(buffer))
      {
        int a = GetLastError();
        result = NO_CD_ROM_FOUND;
      }
      else
      {
```

```
                result = POLL_SUCCESSFUL;
                break;
            }
        }
    }
  }

  /* Restore original drive.*/
  _chdrive( Current_Drive_Index );
  SetCurrentDirectory(current_directory);

  if (result == POLL_SUCCESSFUL)
  {
    m_CDPath.Format(_T("%c:\\"), iCDDriveIndex + 'A' - 1);
  }

#ifdef _DEBUG
  return POLL_SUCCESSFUL;
#else
  return result;
#endif
}
```

You would call this code in a while loop, with a message box or some other game dialog:

```
while (PollForCD(searchFile) != POLL_SUCCESSFUL)
{
  // Bring up a dialog box and ask the player to find their CD.
}
```

S1.7 Games must be rated: The game must be rated by and adhere to guidelines specified by the Entertainment Software Ratings Board (ESRB) if the game is to be distributed in North America and by the appropriate ratings for the country in which the game is distributed.

11

I often wonder what it would be like to play with a copy of Microsoft Word that had an ESRB rating for adults only. I would probably be less productive.

S1.8 3-D and Graphics Support

S1.8.1 If the game uses Direct3D, it should be the default method for displaying graphics.

S1.8.2 If the game employs 3-D graphics and runs in full-screen mode, all screen resolutions enabled in the game should be supported by the computer. If it runs in windowed mode, it should properly handle a range of resolutions. A friendly error dialog box must appear for any resolution that is not supported.

S1.8.3 The game must not rely on the presence of Microsoft DirectX/Æ color-keyed textures. Alpha channels and true-color textures are strongly preferred, and products must not crash simply because the hardware does not support the obsolete methods.

S1.8.4 The game must not rely on the presence of DirectX palette textures. Alpha channels and true-color textures are strongly preferred, and products must not crash simply because the hardware does not support the obsolete methods.

S1.8.5 The game must not use retained mode or the ramp-mode rasterizer.

S1.8.6 If the product employs 3-D graphics, it should support hardware acceleration.

S1.8.7 If the game supports 3-D graphics hardware acceleration then it must support cards from at least 2 chipset manufacturers.

S1.8.8 If the game uses Microsoft DirectDraw/Æ, it must not use device-independent bitmap (DIB) sections or other legacy methods.

S1.8.9 If the game changes the resolution or colors to play the game in full-screen mode, it must restore the original resolution and color depth when the game exits.

S1.8.10 The game must not rely on Hardware Cursor Support.

The first test in this and the next two test groups cracks me up. In order to get blessing from Microsoft you have to prefer Microsoft's technology. I'm not sure what I think about that exactly, but I'm not the one setting the rules.

Test S1.8.2 is directly related to the full-screen and windowed mode discussion at the beginning of this chapter.

Concerning S1.8.5, These old rasterizers refer to pre-DirectX 8 technologies. If the test was rewritten it would probably refer to the reference rasterizer, which is written to display accuracy instead of speed. This and the remaining tests fall into that "Duh, sure..." category.

S1.9 Audio Support

S1.9.1 If the game uses Microsoft DirectSound/Æ, it should be the default method for providing sound.

S1.9.2 The game should use the DirectSound API to handle all calls and not call the cards directly to use specific features of specific cards.

S1.9.3 On systems with more than two audio output channels, audio must emanate from appropriate speakers. For games that use 3-D audio, this means that sounds should pan around the listener using all available speakers. For games that do not use 3-D audio, audio may, but need not, emanate from the rear speakers.

S1.9.4 The game must not disturb volume settings. If the game can adjust its audio volume, settings must be unchanged on exiting the Windows Volume Control.

S1.9.5 If audio is not essential to the operation of the game, it must run on a computer without a sound card installed.

Again, tests S1.9.1 and S1.9.2 show a little chauvinism regarding other technologies, but that doesn't surprise anyone does it?

S1.10 Device Support

S1.10.1 If the game uses DirectInput, it should be the default method for input.

S1.10.2 The game must support game playing devices on more than ID1. Game playing devices on ID2 or higher must be supported.

S1.10.3 A method should be provided for the user to easily select which device he or she wants to use to play a game (that is, switching from one joystick to another or from a joystick to the keyboard and mouse).

S1.10.4 On platforms that support multiple keyboards, the game must work properly when there are two keyboards plugged into the system. Because the limitation on the number of keys pressed simultaneously is normally a hardware limitation, it can be overcome by using multiple keyboards. The game must not crash, stop responding, or lose data when multiple keyboards are used to cause more simultaneously pressed keys to be reported than would be possible with one keyboard.

S1.10.5 The game must not fail when used with mice with more than three-mouse buttons.

Test S1.10.4 implies that a platform with multiple keyboards exists. I haven't seen it, and even if I saw it I'm not sure I'd believe it. Perhaps I can have a different font setting for each keyboard? I guess it would be cool to have a machine with two different language keyboards; but alas I don't speak or read Japanese.

S1.11 Network Support

S1.11.1 If the game has an online component, it should recognize when it is in its offline state. For example, the game must not spend minutes trying to reach an unreachable master server.

S1.11.2 All non-working networking options should be detected and disabled from the list of choices presented to the user.

S1.11.3 During lengthy network transactions, the user should be able to cancel operations at any time.

Do you notice something missing from the network tests? DirectPlay! Again, that cracks me up. This is most likely due to the fact that there are a few networked-enabled Microsoft games that don't use DirectPlay. I won't point them out.

Conclusion

Something that always frustrates me when I'm learning new technology is the staggering amount of hidden knowledge. It's hidden because it can't be found in sample programs or API documentation. Instead, it's found after significant expenditure in your time pounding away at the keyboard. Nowhere is this more true than the subtle interactions between DirectX and Win32. DirectX has always been a kind of red-headed step-child at Microsoft, and I'll bet that the DirectX engineers would tell you that they could have used more support from the operating systems group. It may sound like I'm kissing their butts, and I may be, but the fact that Win32 is a viable gaming platform is a truly incredible achievement.

It's still not a trivial task to write a game under Win32, and it probably never will be trivial. If it were I wouldn't have to write a book like this. You'd better hope like hell Win32 remains tricky, or I might start writing novels. (Ed: Please Mike no novels; you've written enough fiction so far.)

Chapter 12

Debugging Your Game

By the end of any game development project, the programmers and others that they can recruit spend all of their time fixing bugs and tweaking performance. As important as debugging is (especially in game development), techniques in debugging are rarely taught. They tend to just come from experience, or are traded around the programming team. Since I'm communicating to you through a book, we can't trade much but since you bought the book I think we can call it even.

Games are complicated pieces of software and they push every piece of hardware in the system. Bugs are usually pilot error, but there are plenty of cases where bugs trace their roots to the compiler, operating system, drivers, and even specific pieces of hardware. Bugs also happen as a result of unexpected interactions between code written by different programmers; each module functions perfectly in a unit test but failures are seen after they are integrated. Programmers spend lots of time hunting down issues in code they didn't write.

If you are going to have a chance in hell of fixing broken code, whether you wrote it or not, you should have a few ideas and techniques in your toolbox. I've often considered myself a much better debugger than a programmer, which is lucky because I tend to find bugs caused by my own flawed code pretty fast. As I say be careful of harping on other people's mistakes because the next person to screw up could be you! This happened, I'm sure, because of how I learned to program. I programmed for years in BASIC on the old Apple][, which didn't have a debugger. When I went to college I programmed in PASCAL on the VAX mini computer at the University of Houston. After four years of college I noticed an odd looking screen in the computer lab. I asked the person sitting there what I was seeing. "A debugger," they replied. "What's a debugger?" I asked. I got this blank stare back as if I'd asked what electricity was.

I'd spent my entire college experience coding programs without using a symbolic debugger. Needless to say, programming got a lot easier after I was introduced to my first debugger, but the experience left me with some good programming practices and solution strategies that you can use whether you use debuggers or not.

I need to warn you up front that you're going to see some assembly code and other heavy metal in this chapter. ~~You simply can't perform the task of debugging without a basic working knowledge of assembly code and how the CPU really works.~~ This is not a gentle chapter, because we're not discussing a gentle problem. It's not brutally hard to learn assembly, and you have an excellent teacher: your debugger.

All debuggers, Visual Studio included, let you look at your source code at the same time as the assembly. Take some time to learn how each C++ statement is broken down into its assembly instructions and you'll end up being a much better programmer for it. Fear not: I'm with you in spirit, and I wasn't born with a full knowledge of assembly. You can learn it the same way I did, which was by playing with the debugger.

The Art of Handling Failure

If you are looking for some wisdom about handling personal failure, stop reading and call a shrink. My focus here is to discuss application failure, the situation where some defensive code has found an anomaly and needs to handle it. There's a great conversation you can start with a group of programmers about how to handle errors or failures in games. The subject has more grey area than you'd think, and therefore doesn't have a single best strategy. The debate starts when you ask if games should ignore failures or if they should stop execution immediately.

I'm talking about the release build, of course. The debug build should always report any oddity with an assert, so programmers can catch more bugs in the act. The release build strips asserts so there's a good question about what should happen if the assert condition would have been satisfied in the release build. Does the game continue, or should it halt? As with many things, there's no right answer. Here's an example of two functions that handle the same error in two different ways:

```
void DetectFixAndContinue(int variable)
{
   if (variable < VARIABLE_MINIMUM)
   {
      variable = VARIABLE_MINIMUM;
      assert(0 && "Parameter is invalid");
   }

   // More code follows...
}

void DetectAndBail(int variable)
{
   if (variable < VARIABLE_MINIMUM)
```

```
    {
        throw ("Parameter is invalid");
    }

    // More code follows...
}
```

The first function resets the errant variable and calls an assert to alert a programmer that something has gone wrong. The execution continues, since the variable now has a legal value. The second function throws an exception, clearly not allowing the execution to continue.

Notice the assert statement in this example. It's a conditional that includes a text string. Since the conditional is always false, the assert will always fire. The text string will appear in the assert dialog box, and can give testers a clue about reporting the problem, and even what to do about it. You might add, "You can always ignore this" to the text string so testers can continue playing.

The debate most programmers have goes something like this: If you ever reach code where an assert condition in debug mode evaluates to false, then something has gone horribly wrong. Since you can't predict the nature of the failure, you must assume a worst case scenario and exit the program as elegantly as possible. After all, the failure could be bad enough to corrupt data, save game files, or worse.

The other side of the argument takes a kinder, gentler approach. Failures can and will happen, even in the shipping product. If the program can fix a bogus parameter or ignore corrupt data and continue running, it is in the best interests of the player to do so. After all, they might get a chance to save their game and reload it later without a problem. Since we're working on computer games we have the freedom to fudge things a little; there are no human lives at stake and there is no property at risk due to a program failure. Both arguments are valid. I tend to favor the second argument because computer games are frequently pushed into testing before they are ready and released way before testing is completed. Bugs will remain in the software, and if the game can recover from them it should.

Never forget that your game's purpose is entertainment. You aren't keeping an airplane from getting lost and you aren't reporting someone's heartbeat. Remember that games can get away with lots of things that other software can't. If you are relatively sure that you can make a choice to allow the game to continue instead of crashing, I suggest you do it.

That's not to say that games can't find themselves in an unrecoverable situation. If a computer game runs out of memory, you're hosed. You have no choice but to bring up a dialog and say, "Sorry dude. You're hosed," and start throwing exceptions. If you're lucky, your exit code might be able to save the game into a temporary file, much like Microsoft

Word sometimes does when it crashes. When the game reloads it can read the temporary file and attempt to begin again just before everything went down the toilet. If this fails, you can exit again and lose the temporary file. All hope is lost. If it succeeds, your players will worship the ground you walk on. Trust me, as many times as Microsoft Word has recovered pieces of this book after my portable's batteries ran out of electrons, I can appreciate a little data recovery.

If a Win32 function fails, you must usually call `GetLastError()` to determine the exact nature of the error. Instead, simply put `@err,hr` in your debugger's watch window. This will show you a string formatted version of the error.

Debugging Basics

Before you learn some debugging tricks, you should know a little about how the debugger works and how to use it. Almost every computer has special assembly language instructions or CPU features that enable debugging. The Intel platform is no exception. A debugger works by stopping execution of a target program, and associating memory locations and values with variable names. This association is possible through symbolic information that is generated by the compiler. One human readable form of this information is a MAP file. Here's an example of a MAP file generated by the linker in Visual Studio.NET:

```
Sample

 Timestamp is 3c0020f3 (Sat Nov 24 16:36:35 2001)

 Preferred load address is 00400000

 Start         Length     Name                   Class
 0001:00000000 000ab634H .text                   CODE
 0001:000ab640 00008b5fH .text$AFX_AUX           CODE
 0001:000b41a0 0000eec3H .text$AFX_CMNCTL        CODE
 0002:00000000 000130caH .rdata                  DATA
 0002:000130d0 00006971H .rdata$r                DATA
 0002:000275d0 00000000H .edata                  DATA
 0003:00000000 00000104H .CRT$XCA                DATA
 0003:00000104 00000109H .CRT$XCC                DATA
 0003:00001120 00026e6aH .data                   DATA
 0003:00027f90 00011390H .bss                    DATA
 0004:00000000 00000168H .idata$2                DATA
 0004:00000168 00000014H .idata$3                DATA
 0005:00000000 00000370H .rsrc$01                DATA
 Address         Publics by Value              Rva+Base      Lib:Object
```

```
0001:00000b80       ??0GameApp@@QAE@XZ           00401b80 f   GameApp.obj
0001:00000ca0       ??_EGameApp@@UAEPAXI@Z       00401ca0 f i GameApp.obj
0001:00000ca0       ??_GGameApp@@UAEPAXI@Z       00401ca0 f i GameApp.obj
0001:00000d10       ??1GameApp@@UAE@XZ           00401d10 f   GameApp.obj
0001:00000e20       ?OnClose@GameApp@@UAEXXZ     00401e20 f   GameApp.obj
0001:00000ec0       ?OnRun@GameApp@@UAE_NXZ      00401ec0 f   GameApp.obj
0001:00001a10       ??0CFileStatus@@QAE@XZ       00402a10 f i GameApp.obj
0001:00001d00       ?OnIdle@GameApp@@UAEHJ@Z     00402d00 f   GameApp.obj
0001:00001e30       ?Update@GameApp@@UAEXK@Z     00402e30 f   GameApp.obj
```

The file maps the entire contents of the process as it is loaded into memory. The first section describes global data. The second section, which is much more interesting and useful, describes the memory addresses of methods and functions in your game.

Notice first that the symbol names are "munged." These are the actual name of the methods after the C++ symbol manager incorporates the class names and variable types into the names. The number that appears right after the name is the actual memory address of the entry point of the code. For example, the last function in the MAP file, `?Update@GameApp@@UAEXK@Z`, is loaded into memory addess 0x00402e30. You can use that information to track down crashes.

Have you ever seen a crash that reports the register contents? Usually you'll see the entire set of registers: EAX, EBX, and so on. You'll also see EIP, the extended instruction pointer. You many have thought that dialog box nothing more than an annoyance—a slap in the face that your program is flawed. Used with the MAP file, you can at least find the name of the function that caused the crash. Here's how:

1. Assume the crash dialog reported an EIP of 0x00402d20.
2. Look at the MAP file above, you'll see that `GameApp::OnIdle` has an entry point of 0x00402d00, and `GameApp::Update` has an entry point of 0x00402e30.
3. The crash thus happened somewhere inside `GameApp::OnIdle`, since it is located in between those two entry points.

A debugger uses a much more complete symbol table. For example, Visual Studio.NET stores these symbols in a PDB file, or program database file. That's one of the reasons it's so huge: It stores symbolic information of every identifier in your program. The debugger can use this information to figure out how to display the contents of local and global variables and figure out what source code to display as you step through the code. This doesn't explain how the debugger stops the debugged application cold in its tracks, however. That trick requires a little help from the CPU and a special interrupt instruction. If you use Visual Studio, you can try this little program:

```
void main()
{
    __asm int 3
}
```

You may have never seen a line of code that looks like this. It is a special line of code that allows inline assembly. The assembly statement evokes the breakpoint interrupt. Without dragging you through all the gory details of interrupt tables, suffice it to say that a program with sufficient privileges can "trap" interrupts, so that when they are evoked, a special function is called. This is almost exactly like registering a callback function, but it happens at a hardware level. DOS-based games used to grab interrupts all the time to redirect functions such as the mouse or display system to their own evil ends. Debuggers trap the breakpoint interrupt, and whenever you set a breakpoint the debugger overwrites the *opcodes,* or the machine level instructions, at the breakpoint location with those that correspond to `__asm int 3`. When the breakpoint is hit, control is passed to the debugger and it puts the original instructions back. If you hit the "Step into" or "Step over" commands, the debugger finds the right locations for a new breakpoint and simply puts it there without you ever being the wiser.

I've found it useful to add hardcoded breakpoints, like the one in the earlier code example, to functions in the game. It can be convenient to set one to make sure that if control ever passes through that section of code, the debugger will always trap it. If a debugger is not present, it has no effect whatsoever.

So now you have the most basic understanding of how a debugger does its work. It has a mechanism to stop a running program in its tracks and it uses a compiler and linker generated data file to present symbolic information to programmers.

Using the Debugger

When you debug your code, you usually set a few breakpoints and watch the contents of variables. You have a pretty good idea of what should happen and you'll find bugs when you figure out why the effect of your logic isn't what you planned. This assumes a few things. First, you know where to set the breakpoints, and second, you can interpret the effect the logic has on the state of your game. These two things are by no means trivial in all cases. This problem is made difficult by the size and complexity of the logic.

It's not necessarily true that a screwed up sound effect has anything at all to do with the sound system. It could be a problem with the code that loads the sound from the game data files or it could be a random memory "trasher" that changed the sound effect after it was loaded. The problem might also be a bad sound driver or it might even be a bogus sound effect file from the original recording. Knowing where to look first has more to do

> with gut feeling than anything else, but good debugger skills can certainly speed up the process of traversing the *fault tree*—a catch phrase NASA uses to describe all possible permutations of a possible systems failure.

Debuggers like the one in Visual Studio.NET can present an amazing amount of information as shown in Figure 12.1.

The debugger provides some important windows beyond the normal source code window you will use all of the time.

- *Call Stack*: From bottom to top, this window shows the functions and parameters that were used to call them. The function at the top of the list is the one you are currently running. It's extremely useful to double click on any row of the call stack window; the location of the function call will be reflected in the source code window. This helps you understand how control passes from the caller to the called.
- *Watch/Locals/etc*: These windows let you examine the contents of variables. Visual Studio.NET has some convenient windows like **Locals** and **This** that keep track of specific variables so you don't have to type them in yourself.
- *Breakpoints*: This window shows the list of breakpoints. Sometimes you want to enable/disable every breakpoint in your game at once or perform other bits of homework.

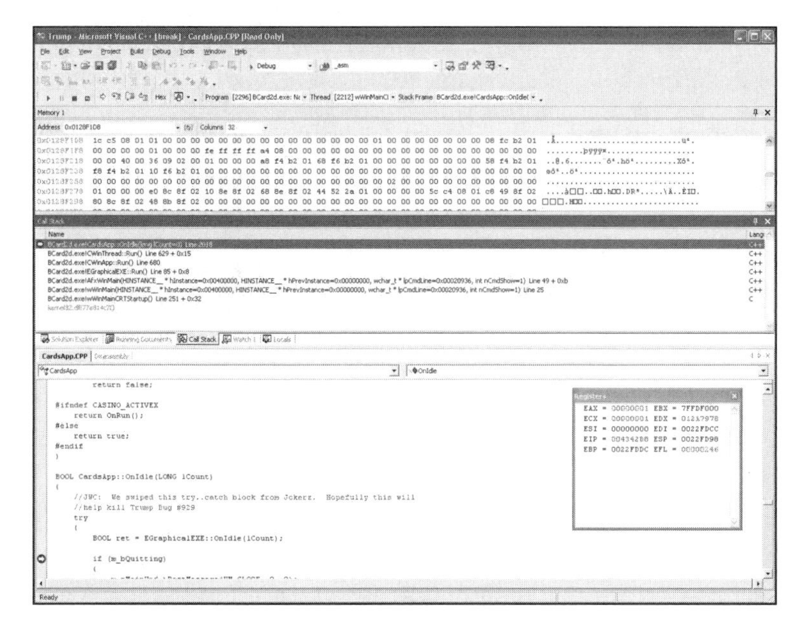

Figure 12.1
Using the Visual Studio.NET Debugger.

12

- *Threads*: This is probably the best addition to the debug window set in Visual Studio.NET. Most games run multiple threads to manage the sound system, resource caching, or perhaps the AI. If the debugger hits a breakpoint or is stopped, this window will show you what thread is running. This window is the only way to distinguish between different threads of execution and is critical to debugging multithreaded applications. If you double click on any line in this window, the source window will change to show the current execution position of that thread.
- *Disassembly*: This is a window that shows the assembly code for the current function. Sometimes you need to break a C++ statement down into its component parts to debug it, or perhaps skip over a portion of the statement. I'll have more to say about those techniques later.

Beyond the windows, there are some actions that you'll need to know how to perform.

- *Set/Clear Breakpoints*: A basic debugging skill.
- *Stepping the Instruction Pointer*: These are usually controlled by hotkeys because they are so frequently used. Debuggers will let you execute code one line at a time, and either trace into functions or skip over them (F11 and F10). There's also a really useful command that will let you step out of a current function (Shift-F11) without having to watch each line execute.
- *Setting the Instruction Pointer*: This takes a little care to use properly, since you can mess up the stack. I like to use it to skip over function calls or skip back to a previous line of code, so I can watch it execute again.

As we run through some debugging techniques I'll refer to these windows and actions. If you don't know how to do them in your debugger now is a good time to read the docs and figure it out.

Installing Windows Symbol Files

If you've ever had a program crash deep in some Windows API call, your call stack might look like this:

```
ntdll.dll!77f60b6f()
ntdll.dll!77fb4dbd()
ntdll.dll!77f79b78()
ntdll.dll!77fb4dbd()
```

Useless, right? Yes, that call stack is useless, but only because you didn't install the Windows symbol files. Even though I write letters to Bill Gates every day, Microsoft still hasn't published the source code for pretty much anything they ever wrote. They have, in their infinite wisdom, graciously supplied the next best thing.

You can install the debug symbols for your operating system, and that indecipherable call stack will turn into something you and I can read. Here's the same debug stack after the debug symbols have been installed:

```
ntdll.dll!_RtlDispatchException@8() + 0x6
ntdll.dll!_KiUserExceptionDispatcher@8() + 0xe
00031328()
ntdll.dll!ExecuteHandler@20() + 0x24
ntdll.dll!_KiUserExceptionDispatcher@8() + 0xe
000316f4()
ntdll.dll!ExecuteHandler@20() + 0x24
ntdll.dll!_KiUserExceptionDispatcher@8() + 0xe
00031ac0()
```

You might not know exactly what that call stack represents, but now you have a name of a function to help you. You can search the Web or MSDN for help, whereas before you installed the debug symbols you had nothing but a number.

There are a few ways to install debug symbols. You can install them from the Visual Studio .NET CD-ROM or you can download them from MSDN. Search for "System Debug Symbols" and you're sure to find them. The last time I downloaded them they were more than 170Mb, so make sure you have reasonable bandwidth. Once you have the right symbols installed for your OS, the debugger will happily report when it finds them when you begin a debug session:

```
'BCard2d.exe': Loaded 'C:\WINDOWS\system32\ntdll.dll', Symbols loaded.
'BCard2d.exe': Loaded 'C:\WINDOWS\system32\kernel32.dll', Symbols loaded.
'BCard2d.exe': Loaded 'C:\WINDOWS\system32\gdi32.dll', Symbols loaded.

Etc, etc,
```

The problem with this solution is that the symbols you install will eventually become stale since they won't reflect any changes in your operating system as you update it with service packs. You can find out why symbols aren't loading for any EXE or DLL with the help of DUMPBIN.EXE, a utility included with Visual Studio. Use the `/PDBPATH:VERBOSE` switch as shown here:

```
Microsoft (R) COFF/PE Dumper Version 7.00.9466
Copyright (C) Microsoft Corporation.  All rights reserved.

Dump of file c:\windows\system32\user32.dll

File Type: DLL
```

12

```
PDB file 'c:\windows\system32\user32.pdb' checked.  (File not found)
PDB file 'user32.pdb' checked.  (File not found)
PDB file 'C:\WINDOWS\symbols\dll\user32.pdb' checked.  (PDB signature mismatch)
PDB file 'C:\WINDOWS\dll\user32.pdb' checked.  (File not found)
PDB file 'C:\WINDOWS\user32.pdb' checked.  (File not found)

Summary

      2000 .data
      4000 .reloc
     2B000 .rsrc
     54000 .text
```

Do you see the `PDB signature mismatch` line about half way down this output? That's what happens when the user32.pdb file is out of synch with the `user32.dll` image on your computer. It turns out this is easy to fix, mainly because Microsoft engineers had this problem multiplied by about 100,000. They have thousands of applications out there with sometimes hundreds of different builds. How could they ever hope to get the debug symbols straight for all these things? They came up with a neat solution called the

Microsoft Symbol Server. It turns out you can use this server too; here's how:

First, install the Microsoft Debugging Tools which can be found at **www.microsoft.com/ddk/debugging**. Use the SYMCHK utility to pull the latest symbol information from Microsoft that matches a single EXE or DLL, or all of them in your Windows directory. Don't grab them all, though, if you can help it because you'll be checking and downloading hundreds of files. Here's how to grab an individual file:

```
C:\Program Files\Debugging Tools for Windows>symchk c:\windows\system32\user32.dll
/s SRV*c:\windows\symbols*http://msdl.microsoft.com/download/symbols

SYMCHK: FAILED files = 0
SYMCHK: PASSED + IGNORED files = 1
```

This crazy utility doesn't actually put the new USER32.DLL where you asked: It actually stuck it in `C:\WINDOWS\Symbols\user32.pdb\3DB6D4ED1`, which VS.NET will never find. The reason it does this is to keep all the USER32.PDB files from different operating systems or different service packs apart. If you installed the Windows symbols from MSDN into the default location, you'll want to copy it back into the directory C:\Windows\Symbols\dll where VS.NET will find it.

You can also set up your own symbol server, and even include symbols for your own applications. To find out how to do this, go up to **http://msdn.microsoft.com** and search for "Microsoft Symbol Server."

Debugging Full Screen Games

As much work as the Microsoft DirectX team has put into the effort of helping you debug full screen games, this still doesn't work very well if you have a single monitor setup. This has nothing to do with the folks on DirectX; it has more to do with Visual Studio.NET not overriding exclusive mode of the display. One manifestation of the problem occurs when your game hits a breakpoint while it's in full-screen mode. The game stops cold but the computer doesn't switch focus to the debugger. Basically, the only thing you can do at this point is tap the F5 button to resume execution of the game.

If your game runs exclusively in full-screen mode, your only solution is a multi-monitor setup. At least one programmer should have two monitors: one for displaying the game screen and the other for displaying the debugger. DirectX will use the primary display for full-screen mode by default. It is possible to write code that enumerates the display devices so your game can choose the best display. This is a good idea because you can't count on players setting their display properties up in the way that benefits your game. If your game runs in windowed mode as well as full-screen mode you have a few more options, even in a single monitor setup.

Most of the bugs in full-screen mode happen as a result of switching from full-screen to windowed mode or vice versa. This happens because DirectX surfaces are lost and need to be restored after the switch, something that is easily forgotten by coders. Another problem that happens as a result of the switch is that surfaces can have the wrong pixel format. There's no guarantee that the full-screen pixel depth and format is identical to that of windowed mode. When the switch happens, lost or invalid surfaces refuse to draw and return errors. Your program might handle these errors by exiting or attempting to restore all the surfaces again. Of course, since the surface in question won't get restored in the first place, your game might get caught in a weird obsessive and repetitive attempt to fix something that can't be fixed.

It would be nice if you could simulate this problem entirely in windowed mode. To a large extent, you can. If you've followed the advice of the DirectX SDK, you always check your display surfaces to see if they have been lost before you perform any action on them. It turns out that if you change your display settings while your game is running in windowed mode you will essentially simulate the event of switching between windowed mode and full-screen mode. There are a few windows messages your game should handle to make this a little easier. You'll need to handle the message that is sent when the display changes and the one that signifies gain and loss of focus.

About 90% of all full-screen display bugs can be found and solved with a single monitor setup using windowed mode. The other 10% can only be solved with a multi-monitor setup or via remote debugging. It's much easier to debug these problems on a multi-monitor rig, so make sure that at least one programmer has two monitors.

Remote Debugging

One solution for debugging full screen only games is remote debugging. The game runs on one computer and communicates to your development box via your network. One interesting thing about this setup is that it is as close to a pristine runtime environment as you can get—another way of saying it's very close to the environment people have when actually playing the game. I don't know about you, but people like my Mom don't have a copy of Visual Studio lying around. The presence of a debugger can subtly change the runtime environment, something that can make the hardest, nastiest bugs very difficult to find.

Remote debugging is a pain in the butt, not because it's hard to set up but because you have to make sure that the most recent version of your game executable is easily available for the remote machine. Most debuggers have a mechanism for remote debugging, and Visual Studio.NET is no exception. The dirty secret is that Visual Studio.NET doesn't run on Win9x architectures, which includes Windows 95, Windows 98, and Windows ME. Not that you'd want to run on these finicky operating systems, but it is a little surprising that remote debugging is your only choice if you want to find OS-specific bugs in a VS.NET compiled application.

If you have a fast network, 100 BaseT Ethernet or better, you can share a directory on your development machine and have the Win9x machine read your game's executable and data files right where you develop. If your network is slower, such as a 10 BaseT Ethernet, it's going to be faster to copy the entire image of your game over to the test machine and run it from there. The only problem with this solution is that you have to constantly copy files from your development box over to the text machine, and it's easy to get confused regarding which files have been copied where. On a fast network you can also eliminate file copying by sharing your development directory so the remote machine can directly access the most recent build.

On the remote system you will run a little utility that serves as a communications conduit for your debugger. This utility for VS.NET is called MSVCMON.EXE. Run a search for this file where you installed VS.NET, and copy the contents of the entire directory to a shared folder on your primary development machine. The utility runs on the remote machine, and a convenient way to get it there is to place it in a shared spot on your development machine. MSVCMON.EXE requires some of the DLLs in that directory and it's small enough to just copy the whole thing to the remote machine.

Once you have all the files in place, here's how you set up the remote debugger under VS.NET:

1. Go into your project's property pages by right clicking on your project in the solution window and select Properties.
2. Click on the Debugging selection under Configuration.
3. Under Remote Settings do the following:
   a. Set the Connection to Remote via TCP/IP.
   b. Set the Remote Machine to the IP address of the test machine. You can find the IP address of any machine by running "ipconfig" in a command line window.
   c. Set the Remote Command to the full path specification of the executable. For example, if you copied your game to a shared directory on the development machine this value might look something like this: **\\mrmike8000\shared\game\bin\game.exe.**
4. Under Action do the following:
   - Set the Working Directory to the full path specification of the game's executable. Following the example above, this would be set to: **\\mrmike8000\shared\game\bin**.
5. Enter a command window and run MSVCMON, with the -alluser switch as shown in Figure 12.2.

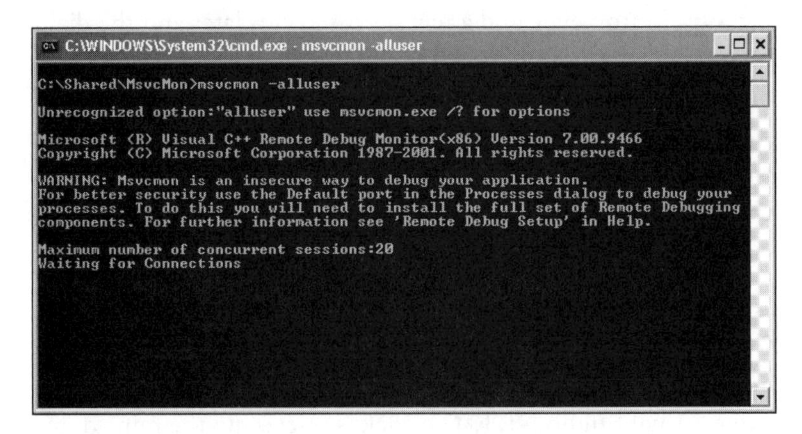

Figure 12.2
Running MSVCMON with the -alluser Switch.

12

The remote machine is ready to start your game. Start the debugging session on your development machine (F5 in VS.NET) and you'll see your game initialize on the remote machine. When you find a bug and rebuild your application, make sure that the remote machine has access to the most recent bits.

Debugging Mini-Dumps

Unix programmers have had a special advantage over Win32 programmers since the beginning of time. When a Unix program crashes, the operating system copies the entire memory image of the crashed program to disk. This is called a *core dump*.

Needless to say, it is usually quite large. Unix debuggers can read the core dump and allow a programmer to look at the state of the process at the moment the crash occurred. Assuming the symbol files for the executable in question are available, they can see the entire call stack and even find the contents of local variables. This doesn't always expose the bug entirely, as some crashes can happen as a result of a bug's misbehavior in a completely separate part of the program, but this information is much better than a tester just telling you the game crashed.

Win32 dump files have been debuggable by a little known Windows debugger called WinDBG since the Windows NT days. These dump files were just as huge as the Unix core dumps. It didn't matter very much, since most Windows developers didn't even know that WinDBG even existed: They always used the debugger in Visual Studio.

If you've been running Windows XP lately you've also noticed an odd behavior when applications crash: A little dialog box appears asking you if you want to send the crash information to Microsoft. One button click and a few short seconds later and the dialog thanks you for your cooperation. What in the heck is going on here? Windows XP is sending a mini-dump of the crashed application to Microsoft. A mini-dump, as the name implies, is a tiny version of the Unix style core dump. You can generate one yourself by going into the Debug menu under Visual Studio.NET and select "Save Dump As…" when your application is sitting at a breakpoint. This tiny file stores enough information to give you some clues about the crash.

For Windows geeks, it's time to let you in on a little secret: Visual Studio.NET can debug these very same mini-dump files. Here's how to reload it, because it isn't exactly obvious. Double click on the mini-dump file in the Windows Explorer, and it will launch a surprisingly blank looking Visual Studio.NET. The trick is to execute the mini-dump by hitting F5. VS.NET will prompt you to save a solution file. Go ahead and save it alongside the mini-dump. Once you do that the last state of your debugged process will appear before your very eyes.

The mini-dump is really convenient but there are a few gotchas to using mini-dumps. First, you must ensure that the mini-dump file matches exactly with the source code and symbol tables that were used to build the executable that crashed. This means that for any version of the executable that goes into your test department, you must save a complete build tree with source code and PDB files or the mini-dump will be useless. Second, the mini-dump's SLN file might need a hint about where to find the symbols. If the source window shows up with nothing but assembler, it's likely that your source code tree can't be located. Open the properties page and you'll see only one item under the Configuration tree: Debugging. Set the Symbol Path to the directory containing your PDB files and you'll see the source tree.

The only thing left out of this discussion is how to have your game generate mini-dump files when bad goes to worse. You'll need to call the `MiniDumpWriteDump` in your general exception handler, which is one of the functions exported from DBGHELP.DLL. This call will generate a DMP file. You can add more information to the DMP file if you define a callback function that can insert more information into the dump file, such as some specific game state information that might give a programmer a leg up on investigating the crash.

In 2001, Microsoft introduced our team to using mini-dumps. Microsoft's Dr. Watson team has established a huge database of mini-dumps for applications like Office and XP. At first we were skeptical about using them. We thought that these dump files wouldn't provide enough information to diagnose crashes. We were wrong. After the first week, we were able to diagnose and solve some of the most elusive crashes in our game. Every Windows game should make use of this technology.

Here's a simple class you can use to write your own mini-dumps:

```
#include "dbghelp.h"

class MiniDumper
{
protected:
   static MiniDumper *gpDumper;
   static LONG WINAPI Handler( struct _EXCEPTION_POINTERS *pExceptionInfo );

   _EXCEPTION_POINTERS *m_pExceptionInfo;
   TCHAR m_szDumpPath[_MAX_PATH];
   TCHAR m_szAppPath[_MAX_PATH];
   TCHAR m_szAppBaseName[_MAX_PATH];
   LONG WriteMiniDump(_EXCEPTION_POINTERS *pExceptionInfo );

   virtual void VSetDumpFileName(void);
```

```
    virtual MINIDUMP_USER_STREAM_INFORMATION *VGetUserStreamArray()
            { return NULL; }

public:
    MiniDumper(void);
};

// based on dbghelp.h
typedef BOOL (WINAPI *MINIDUMPWRITEDUMP)(HANDLE hProcess,
    DWORD dwPid, HANDLE hFile, MINIDUMP_TYPE DumpType,
    CONST PMINIDUMP_EXCEPTION_INFORMATION ExceptionParam,
    CONST PMINIDUMP_USER_STREAM_INFORMATION UserStreamParam,
    CONST PMINIDUMP_CALLBACK_INFORMATION CallbackParam);

MiniDumper *MiniDumper::gpDumper = NULL;

MiniDumper::MiniDumper( )
{
    // Detect if there is more than one MiniDumper.
    assert( !gpDumper );

    if (!gpDumper)
    {
        ::SetUnhandledExceptionFilter( Handler );
        gpDumper = this;
    }
}

LONG MiniDumper::Handler( _EXCEPTION_POINTERS *pExceptionInfo )
{
    LONG retval = EXCEPTION_CONTINUE_SEARCH;

    if (!gpDumper)
    {
        return retval;
    }

    return gpDumper->WriteMiniDump(pExceptionInfo);
}

LONG MiniDumper::WriteMiniDump(_EXCEPTION_POINTERS *pExceptionInfo )
{
    LONG retval = EXCEPTION_CONTINUE_SEARCH;
    m_pExceptionInfo = pExceptionInfo;

    // You have to find the right dbghelp.dll.
```

```
// Look next to the EXE first since the one in System32 might be old (Win2k)

HMODULE hDll = NULL;
TCHAR szDbgHelpPath[_MAX_PATH];

if (GetModuleFileName( NULL, m_szAppPath, _MAX_PATH ))
{
   TCHAR *pSlash = _tcsrchr( m_szAppPath, '\\' );
   if (pSlash)
   {
       _tcscpy( m_szAppBaseName, pSlash + 1);
       *(pSlash+1) = 0;
   }

   _tcscpy( szDbgHelpPath, m_szAppPath );
   _tcscat( szDbgHelpPath, _T("DBGHELP.DLL") );
   hDll = ::LoadLibrary( szDbgHelpPath );
}

if (hDll==NULL)
{
   // If we haven't found it yet - try one more time.
   hDll = ::LoadLibrary( _T("DBGHELP.DLL") );
}

LPCTSTR szResult = NULL;

if (hDll)
{
   MINIDUMPWRITEDUMP pMiniDumpWriteDump =
       (MINIDUMPWRITEDUMP)::GetProcAddress( hDll, "MiniDumpWriteDump" );

   if (pMiniDumpWriteDump)
   {
       TCHAR szScratch [_MAX_PATH];

       VSetDumpFileName();

       // ask the user if they want to save a dump file
       if (::MessageBox( NULL, _T("There was an unexpected error, would you
         like to save a diagnostic file?"), NULL, MB_YESNO )==IDYES)
       {
           // create the file
           HANDLE hFile =
               ::CreateFile( m_szDumpPath, GENERIC_WRITE,FILE_SHARE_WRITE,
              NULL, CREATE_ALWAYS,
```

```
                              FILE_ATTRIBUTE_NORMAL, NULL );

            if (hFile!=INVALID_HANDLE_VALUE)
            {
              _MINIDUMP_EXCEPTION_INFORMATION ExInfo;

              ExInfo.ThreadId = ::GetCurrentThreadId();
              ExInfo.ExceptionPointers = pExceptionInfo;
              ExInfo.ClientPointers = NULL;

              // write the dump
              BOOL bOK = pMiniDumpWriteDump(
                      GetCurrentProcess(), GetCurrentProcessId(),
                      hFile, MiniDumpNormal, &ExInfo,
                      VGetUserStreamArray(), NULL );

              if (bOK)
              {
              szResult = NULL;
              retval = EXCEPTION_EXECUTE_HANDLER;
              }
              else
              {
              sprintf( szScratch, _T("Failed to save dump file to '%s'
                      (error %d)"), m_szDumpPath, GetLastError() );
              szResult = szScratch;
              }
              ::CloseHandle(hFile);
            }
            else
            {
              sprintf( szScratch, _T("Failed to create dump file '%s'
                          (error %d)"), m_szDumpPath, GetLastError() );
              szResult = szScratch;
            }
          }
        }
        else
        {
          szResult = _T("DBGHELP.DLL too old");
        }
      }
      else
      {
        szResult = _T("DBGHELP.DLL not found");
      }
```

```
    if (szResult)
        ::MessageBox( NULL, szResult, NULL, MB_OK );

    TerminateProcess(GetCurrentProcess(), 0);
    return retval;
}
void MiniDumper::VSetDumpFileName(void)
{
    _tcscpy( m_szDumpPath, m_szAppPath );
    _tcscat( m_szDumpPath, m_szAppBaseName );
    _tcscat( m_szDumpPath, _T(".dmp") );
}
```

If you want to save the mini-dump file out with a different name, inherit from the `MiniDump` class and overload `VSetDumpFileName`. One thing you might consider doing is putting a time stamp in the dump file name, so that one mini-dump file doesn't overwrite another. If you'd like to include your own data stream, overload `VGetUserStreamArray()`. Here's an example of this class at work:

```
MiniDumper gMiniDumper;

int main()
{
    *(int *)0 = 12;          // CRASH!!!!!
    return 0;
}
```

Just declare a global singleton of the `MiniDumper`, and when an unhandled exception comes along your player will get asked if he or she wants to write out some diagnostic information. The mini-dump file will appear in the directory as your executable, ready for debugging.

Debugging Techniques

I think I could write an entire book about debugging. Certainly many people have, and for good reason. You can't be a good programmer unless you have at least passable debugging skills. Imagine for a moment that you are a programmer who never writes buggy code. Hey, stop laughing. I also want you to close your eyes and imagine that you have absolutely no skill at debugging. Why would you? Your code is always perfect! The moment you were assigned to a team of programmers your days are numbered. If you can't solve logic problems caused by other programmer's code, you are useless to a team.

If you have good debugging skills, you'll have much more fun programming. I've always looked at really tough bugs as a puzzle. Computers are deterministic and they execute instructions without interpretation. That truth paves your way to solve every bug if you devote enough patience and skill.

Debugging Is an Experiment

When you begin a bug hunt, one implication is that you know how to recognize a properly running program. For any piece of code you should be able to predict its behavior just by carefully reading each line. As an aggregate of modules, a large program should, in theory, accept user input and game data and act in a deterministic way.

Debugging a program requires that you figure out why the behavior of the program is different than what you expect. Certainly the computer's CPU isn't surprised. It executes exactly what you instructed. This delta is the cornerstone of debugging. As each instruction executes, the programmer tests the new state of the process against the predicted state by looking at memory and the contents of variables. The moment the prediction is different than the observed, the programmer has found the bug.

Clearly you have to be able to predict the behavior of the system, given certain stimulus such as user input or a set of game data files. You should be able to repeat the steps to watch the behavior on your machine or anyone else's machine. When the bug manifests itself as a divergence from nominal operation you should be able to use what you observed to locate the problem or at least narrow the source of the problem. Repeat these steps enough times and you'll find the bug. What I've just described is the method any scientist uses to perform experiments.

It might seem odd to perform experiments on software, certainly odd when you wrote the software in question. Scientists perform experiments on complicated phenomena that they don't understand in the hopes that they will achieve knowledge. Why then must programmers perform experiments on systems that spawned from their own minds? The problem is that even the simplest, most deterministic systems can behave unpredictably given particular initial states. If you've never read Stephen Wolfram's book, *A New Kind of Science*, take a few months off and try to get through it. This book makes some surprising observations about complex behavior of simple systems. I'll warn you that once you read it you may begin to wonder about the determinism of any system, no matter how simple!

Debugging is a serious scientific endeavor. If you approach each debugging task as an experiment, just like you were taught in high school, you'll find that debugging is more fun and less frustrating.

Complex and unpredicted behavior in computer programs requires setting up good debugging experiments. If you fell asleep during the lecture in high school on the scientific method, now's a good time to refresh your memory. The examples listed in Table 12.1 show you how to run a successful experiment, but there's a lot more to good debugging than blindly running through the experimental method.

Table 12. 1 How to Run a Successful Debugging Experiment.

Scientific Method as it Applies to Software Systems	Example #1	Example #2
Step 1: Observe the behavior of a computer game.	Observation: A call to OpenFile() always fails.	Observation: The game crashes on the low-end machine when it tries to initialize.
Step 2: Attempt to explain the behavior that is consistent with your observations and your knowledge of the system.	Hypothesis: The input parameters to OpenFile() are incorrect, specifically the filename.	Hypothesis: The game is crashing because it is running with out of video memory.
Step 3: Use your explanation to make predictions.	Predictions: If the proper filename is used, OpenFile() will execute successfully.	Predictions: If the amount of video memory were increased, the game will initialize properly. The game will crash when the original amount of video memory is restored.
Step 4: Test your predictions by performing experiments or making additional observations. Modify the hypothesis and predictions based on the results.	Experiment: Send the fully qualified path name of the file and try OpenFile() again.	Experiment: Switch the current video card with others that have more memory.
Step 5: Repeat steps three and four until there is no discrepancy between your explanations and the observations.	Results: OpenFile() executed successfully with a fully qualified path name.	Results: The game properly initializes with an 8Mb video card installed.
Step 6: Explain the results.	Explanation: The current working directory is different than the location of the file in question. The path name must be fully qualified.	Explanation: Video memory requirements have grown beyond expectations.

The first step seems easy: Observe the behavior of the system. Unfortunately, this is not so easy. The most experienced software testers I know do their very best to accurately observe the behavior of a game as it breaks. They record what keys they pressed, what options they turned off, and at best exactly what they did. In many cases, they leave out something innocuous. One of the first things I do when I don't observe the same problem a tester observed is I go down to the test lab myself and watch them reproduce the bug. Sometimes I'll notice a little wiggle of the mouse or the fact that they're running in full-screen mode and have a "Eureka" moment.

Unlike most software systems, games rely not only on random numbers but they change vast amounts of data extremely quickly in seemingly unpredictable ways. The difficulty in finding game bugs lies in the simple fact that games run so much code so quickly that it's easy for a bug to come from any of the many subsystems that manipulate the game state.

The second step, attempt to explain the behavior, can be pretty hard if you don't know the software like the back of your hand. It's probably safe to say that you should know the software, the operating system, the CPU, video hardware, and audio hardware pretty well too. Sound tough? It is. It also helps to have a few years of game programming under your belt, so that you've been exposed to the wacky behavior of broken games. This is probably one of the most frustrating aspects of programming in general—a lack of understanding and experience can leave you shaking your head in dismay when you see your game blow up in your face. Everybody gets through it, though, usually with the help of, dare I say, more experienced programmers.

Steps three through five represent the classic experiment-phase of debugging. Your explanation will usually inspire some sort of test, input modification, or code change that should have predictable results. There's an important trick to this rinse and repeat cycle: Take detailed notes of everything you do. Inevitably your notes will come in handy as you realize that you're chasing a dead-end hypothesis. They should send you back to the point where your predictions were accurate. This will put you back on track.

Another critical aspect to the experiment-driven debugging process is that you should try to limit your changes to one small thing at a time. If you change too much during one experiment cycle you won't be able to point to the exact change that fixed the problem. Change for change's sake is a horrible motivation to modify buggy code. Resist that temptation. Sometimes there is a desire to rip a subsystem out altogether and replace it without truly understanding the nature of the problem. This impulse is especially strong when the subsystem in question was written by a programmer that has less than, shall we say, stellar design and coding skills. The effect of this midnight remodeling is usually negative since it isn't guaranteed to fix the bug and you'll demoralize your teammate at the same time.

Assuming you follow Table 12.1 you'll eventually arrive at the source of the problem. If you're lucky the bug can be fixed with a simple tweak of the code—perhaps a loop exited too soon or a special case wasn't handled properly. You make your mod, rebuild the game, and perform your experiments one last time. Congratulations, your bug is fixed. Not every programmer is so lucky, certainly I haven't been. Some bugs, once exposed in their full glory, tell you things about your game that you don't want to hear. I've seen bugs that told us we had to completely redesign the graphics library we were using. Other bugs enjoy conveying the message that some version of Windows can't be supported without sweeping modifications. Others make you wonder how the game ever worked in the first place. If this ever happens to you, and I'm sure it will, I feel your pain. Grab some caffeine and your sleeping bag; it's going to be a long night.

Reproducing the Bug

A prerequisite of observing the behavior of a broken game is reproducing the bug. I've seen bug reports that say things like, "I was doing so-and-so and the game crashed. I couldn't get it to happen again." In light of an overwhelming number of reports of this kind, you might be able to figure out what's going on. Alone, these reports are nearly useless. *You cannot fix what you cannot observe.* After all, if you can't observe the broken system with certainty, how can you be sure you fixed the problem? You can't. Most bugs can be reproduced easily by following a specific set of steps, usually observed and recorded by a tester. It's important that each step, however minor, is recorded from the moment the game is initialized. Anything missing might be important. Also, the state of the machine, including installed hardware and software, might be crucial to reproducing the bug's behavior.

Bugs are sometimes tough to nail down. They can be intermittent or disappear altogether as you attempt to create a specific series of steps that will always result in a manifestation of the problem. This can be explained in two ways: Either an important step or initial state has been left out, or the bug cannot be reproduced because the system being tested is too complex to be deterministic. Even if the bug can be reproduced exactly, it might be difficult to create an explanation of the problem. In both of these cases, you must find a way to reduce the complexity of the system, only then can the problem domain become small enough to understand.

Eliminating Complexity

A bug can only manifest itself if the code that contains it is executed. Eliminate the buggy code, and the bug will disappear. By the process of elimination you can narrow your search over a series of steps to the exact line of code that is causing the problem. You can disable subsystems in your game, one by one. One of the first things to try is to disable the entire main loop and have your game initialize and exit without doing anything else. This is a good trick if the bug you're hunting is a memory leak. If the bug goes away you can be sure that it only exists in the main loop somewhere.

Sound systems are usually multi-threaded and can be a source of heinous problems. If you believe a bug is somewhere in the sound system, disable your sound system and rerun the game. If the bug disappears, turn the sound system back on but eliminate only sound effects. Leave the music system on. Divide and conquer as necessary to find the problem. If the bug is in the sound system somewhere you'll find it.

You should be able to creatively disable other systems as well, such as animation or AI. Once these systems are stubbed out, your game will probably act pretty strangely, and you don't want this strangeness to be interpreted as the bug you are looking for. You should have a pretty complete understanding of your game before you embark on excising large pieces of it from execution.

If you can't simply stub out the AI of your game, replace the AI routines with the most trivial AI code you can write, and make triply sure it is bug free and will have limited, predictable, side effects. You can then slowly add the complex AI systems back in, one at a time, and rerun your tests to see when the bug pops back in.

If your game has options for sound, animation, and other subsystems you can use these as debugging tools without having to resort to changing code. Turn everything off via your game options and try to reproduce the bug. Whether the bug continues to exist or disappears, the information you'll gain from the experiment is always valuable. As always, keep good records of what you try and try to change only one option at a time. You can take this tactic to extremes and perform a binary search of sorts to locate a bug. Stub out half of your subsystems and see if the bug manifests itself. If it does, stub out half of what remains and repeat the experiment. Even in a large code base, you'll quickly locate the bug.

If the bug eludes this process, it might depend on the memory map of the process. Change the memory contents of your process and the bug will change too. Because this might be true, it's a good idea to stub out subsystems via a simple boolean value, but leave their code and global data in place as much as possible. This is another example of making small changes rather than large ones.

Setting the next Statement

Most debuggers give you the power to set the next statement to be executed, which is equivalent to setting the instruction pointer directly. This can be useful if you know what you are doing, but it can be a source of mayhem applied indiscriminately. You might want to do this for a few reasons. You may want to skip some statements or rerun a section of code again with different parameters as a part of a debugging experiment. You might also be debugging through some assembler and you want to avoid calling into other pieces of code.

You can set the next statement in Visual C++ by right clicking on the target statement and selecting "Set Next Statement" from the popup menu. In other debuggers, you can bring up a register window and set the EIP register, also known as the instruction pointer, to the address of the target statement, which you can usually find by showing the disassembly window. You must be mindful of the code that you are skipping and the current state of your process. When you set the instruction pointer, it is equivalent to executing an assembly level JMP statement, which simply moves the execution path to a different statement.

In C++, objects can be declared inside local scopes such as for loops. In normal execution, these objects are destroyed when execution passes out of that scope. The C++ compiler inserts the appropriate code to do this, and you can't see it unless you look at a disassembly window. What do you suppose happens to C++ objects that go out of scope if you skip important lines of code? Let's look at an example:

```
class MyClass
{
public:
   int num;
   char *string;

   MyClass(int const n)
   {
      num = n;
      string = new char[128];
      sprintf(string, "%d  ", n);
   }

   ~MyClass() { delete string; }
};


void SetTheIP()
{
   char buffer[2048];
   buffer[0] = 0;

   for (int a=0; a<128; ++a)
   {
      MyClass m(a);
      strcat(buffer, m.string);     // START HERE...
   }
}                                   // JUMP TO HERE...
```

Normally the `MyClass` object is created and destroyed once for each run of the for loop. If you jump out of the loop using "Set Next Statement" the destructor for `MyClass` never runs, leaking memory. The same thing would happen if you jumped backwards, to the line that initializes the buffer variable. The `MyClass` object in scope won't be destroyed properly.

Luckily, you don't have to worry about the stack pointer as long as you do all your jumping around within one function. Local scopes are creations of the compiler; they don't actually have stack frames. That's a good thing, because setting the next statement to a completely different function is sure to cause havoc with the stack. If you want to skip the rest of the current function and keep it from executing, just right click on the last closing brace of the function and set the next statement to that point. The stack frame will be kept in tact.

Assembly Level Debugging

Inevitably you'll get to debug through some assembly code. You won't have source code or even symbols for every component of your application, so you should understand a little about the assembly window. Here's the assembly for the `SetTheIP` function we just talked about. Let's look at the Debug version of this code:

```
void SetTheIP()
{
00411A10 55                          push       ebp
00411A11 8B EC                       mov        ebp,esp
00411A13 81 EC E8 08 00 00           sub        esp,8E8h
00411A19 53                          push       ebx
00411A1A 56                          push       esi
00411A1B 57                          push       edi
00411A1C 8D BD 18 F7 FF FF           lea        edi,[ebp-8E8h]
00411A22 B9 3A 02 00 00              mov        ecx,23Ah
00411A27 B8 CC CC CC CC              mov        eax,0CCCCCCCCh
00411A2C F3 AB                       rep stos   dword ptr [edi]
   char buffer[2048];
   buffer[0] = 0;
00411A2E C6 85 F8 F7 FF FF 00        mov        byte ptr [buffer],0

   for (int a=0; a<128; ++a)
00411A35 C7 85 EC F7 FF FF 00 00 00 00 mov      dword ptr [a],0
00411A3F EB 0F                       jmp        SetTheIP+40h (411A50h)
00411A41 8B 85 EC F7 FF FF           mov        eax,dword ptr [a]
00411A47 83 C0 01                    add        eax,1
00411A4A 89 85 EC F7 FF FF           mov        dword ptr [a],eax
00411A50 81 BD EC F7 FF FF 80 00 00 00 cmp      dword ptr [a],80h
00411A5A 7D 35                       jge        SetTheIP+81h (411A91h)
   {
      MyClass m(a);
```

```
00411A5C 8B 85 EC F7 FF FF        mov       eax,dword ptr [a]
00411A62 50                       push      eax
00411A63 8D 8D DC F7 FF FF        lea       ecx,[m]
00411A69 E8 9C FA FF FF           call      MyClass::MyClass (41150Ah)
      strcat(buffer, m.string);
00411A6E 8B 85 E0 F7 FF FF        mov       eax,dword ptr [ebp-820h]
00411A74 50                       push      eax
00411A75 8D 8D F8 F7 FF FF        lea       ecx,[buffer]
00411A7B 51                       push      ecx
00411A7C E8 46 F7 FF FF           call      @ILT+450(_strcat) (4111C7h)
00411A81 83 C4 08                 add       esp,8
   }
00411A84 8D 8D DC F7 FF FF        lea       ecx,[m]
00411A8A E8 76 FA FF FF           call      MyClass::~MyClass (411505h)
00411A8F EB B0                    jmp       SetTheIP+31h (411A41h)
}
00411A91 52                       push      edx
00411A92 8B CD                    mov       ecx,ebp
00411A94 50                       push      eax
00411A95 8D 15 B6 1A 41 00        lea       edx,[ (411AB6h)]
00411A9B E8 FA F6 FF FF           call      @ILT+405(@_RTC_CheckStackVars@8)
(41119Ah)
00411AA0 58                       pop       eax
00411AA1 5A                       pop       edx
00411AA2 5F                       pop       edi
00411AA3 5E                       pop       esi
00411AA4 5B                       pop       ebx
00411AA5 81 C4 E8 08 00 00        add       esp,8E8h
00411AAB 3B EC                    cmp       ebp,esp
00411AAD E8 F0 F8 FF FF           call      @ILT+925(__RTC_CheckEsp) (4113A2h)
00411AB2 8B E5                    mov       esp,ebp
00411AB4 5D                       pop       ebp
00411AB5 C3                       ret
```


One thing you realize right off is that the disassembly window can be a big help in beginning to understand what assembly language is all about. I wish I had more time to go over each statement, addressing modes, and whatnot but there are better resources for that anyway.

Notice first the structure of the disassembly window. The column of numbers on the left hand side of the window is the memory address of each instruction. The list of one to ten hexadecimal codes that follows each address is the machine code bytes. Notice that the address of each line coincides with the number of machine code bytes. The more readable instruction on the far right is the assembler statement. Each group of assembler statements is preceded by the C++ statement that they execute, if the source is available. You can see that even a close brace can have assembly instructions, usually to return to the calling function or to destroy a C++ object.

The first lines of assembly, pushing various things onto the stack and messing with EBP and ESP, establish a local stack frame. The value 8E8h is the size of the stack frame, which is 2280 bytes.

Check out the assembly code for the `for` loop. The beginning of the loop has seven lines of assembly code. The first two initialize the loop variable and jump over the lines that increment the loop variable. Skip over the guts of the loop for now and check out the last three assembly lines. They call the destructor for the `MyClass` object and skip back to the beginning part of the loop that increments the loop variable and performs the exit comparison. If you've ever wondered why the debugger always skips back to the beginning of `for` loops when the exit condition is met, there's your answer. The exit comparison happens at the beginning.

The inside of the loop has two C++ statements: one to construct the `MyClass` object and another to call `strcat`. Notice the assembly code that makes these calls work. In both cases values are pushed onto the stack by the calling routine. The values are pushed from right to left, that is to say that the last variable in a function call is pushed first. What this means for you is that you should be mindful of setting the next statement. If you want to skip a call, make sure you skip any assembly statements that push values onto the stack, or your program will lose its mind.

One last thing: Look at all the code that follows the closing brace of `SetTheIP()`. There are two calls here to `CheckStackVars()` and `CheckESP()`. What the heck are those things? These are two functions inserted into the exit code of every function in Debug builds that perform sanity checks on the integrity of the stack. You can perform a little experiment to see how these things work. Put a breakpoint on the very first line of `SetTheIP()`, skip over all the stack frame homework and set the next statement to the one where the buffer gets initialized. The program will run fine until the sanity check code runs. You'll get a dialog box telling you your stack has been corrupted.

It's nice to know that this check will keep you from chasing ghosts. If you mess up a debug experiment where you set the next statement across statements important to maintaining a good stack frame, these sanity checks will catch the problem.

Peppering the Code

If you have an elusive bug that corrupts a data structure or even the memory system, you can hunt it down with a check routine. This assumes that the corruption is somewhat deterministic, and you can write a bit of code to see if it exists. Write this function and begin placing this code in strategic points throughout your game.

A good place to start this check is in your main loop, and at the top and bottom of major components like your resource cache, draw code, AI, or sound manager. Place the check at the top and bottom to ensure that you can pinpoint a body of code that caused the corruption. If a check succeeds before a body of code and fails after it, you can begin to drill down into the system, placing more checks, until you nailed the exact source of the problem. Here's an example:

```
void BigBuggySubsystem()
{
   BuggyObject crasher;

   CheckForTheBug("Enter BigBuggySubSystem.");

   DoSomething();

   CheckForTheBug("Calling DoSomethingElse");

   DoSomethingElse();

   CheckForTheBug("Calling CorruptEverything");

   CorruptEverything();

   CheckForTheBug("Leave BigBuggySubSystem");
}
```

In this example, `CheckForTheBug()` is a bit of code that will detect the corruption, and the other function calls are subsystems of the `BigBuggySubsystem`. It's a good idea to put a text string in your checking code, so that it's quick and easy to identify the corruption location, even if the stack is trashed.

Since there's plenty of C++ code that runs as a result of exiting a local scope, don't fret if your checking function finds a corruption on entry. You can target your search inside the destructors of any C++ objects used inside the previous scope. If the destructor for the `BuggyObject` code was wreaking some havoc it won't be caught by your last call to your checking function. You wouldn't notice it until some other function called your checking code.

Draw Debug Information

This might seem incredibly obvious, but since I forget it all the time myself I figure it deserves mentioning. If you are having trouble with graphics or physics related bugs it can help if you draw additional information on your screen such as wireframes, direction vectors, or coordinate axes. This is especially true for 3D games but any game can find draw helpers useful. Here's a few ideas:

- *Hot Areas*: If you are having trouble with user interface code, you can draw rectangles around your controls and change their color when they go active. You'll be able to see why one control is getting activation when you didn't expect it.
- *Memory/Framerate*: In debug versions of your game it can be very useful to draw current memory and framerate information every few seconds. Don't do it every frame because it will slow down your game too much.
- *Coordinate Axes*: A classic problem with 3D games is that the artist will create 3D models in the wrong coordinate system. Draw some additional debug geometry that shows the positive X axis in red, the positive Y axis in green, and the positive Z axis in blue. You'll always know which way is up!
- *Wireframe*: You can apply wireframe drawing to collision geometry to see if they match up properly. A classic problem in 3D games is when these geometries are out of sync, and drawing the collision geometry in wireframe can help you figure out what's going on.
- *Targets*: If you have AI routines that select targets or destinations, it can be useful to draw them explicitly by using lines. Whether you are a 3D game or a 2D game, line drawing can give you information about where the targets are. Use color information to convey additional information such as friend or foe.

In 3D games, it's a good idea to construct a special test object that is asymmetrical on all three coordinate axes. Your game renderer and physics system can easily display things like cubes in a completely wrong way, but they will look right because a cube looks the same from many different angles. A good example of an asymmetrical object is a shoe, since there's no way you can slice it and get a mirror image from one side to another. In your 3D game, build something with similar properties, but make sure the shape is so asymmetrical that it will be obvious if any errors pop up.

Lint and Other Code Analyzers

These tools can be incredibly useful. Their best application is one where code is being checked often, perhaps each night. Dangerous bits of code are fixed as they are found, and don't get the chance to exist in the system for any length of time. If you don't have

Lint, make sure you ramp up the warning level of the compiler as high as you can stand it. It will be able to make quite a few checks for you and catch problems as they happen.

A less useful approach involves using code analysis late in your project in the hopes it will pinpoint a bug. You'll probably be inundated with warnings and errors, any of which could be perfectly benign for your game. The reason this isn't as useful at the end of your project is that you may have to make sweeping changes to your code to address every issue. This is not wise. It is much more likely that sweeping changes will create a vast set of additional issues, the aggregate of which could be worse than the original problem. It's best to perform these checks often and throughout the life of your project.

BoundsChecker and Run Time Analyzers

BoundsChecker is a great program, and every team should have at least one copy. In some configurations it can run so slowly that your game will take three hours to display a single screen. Rather, use a targeted approach and filter out as many checks as you can and leave only the checks that will trap your problem.

Disappearing Bugs

The really nasty bugs seem to actually posses intelligence, awareness of itself and your attempts to destroy it. Just as you get close, the bug changes and it can't be reproduced using your previously observed steps. It's likely that recent changes such as adding checking code have altered the memory map of your process. The bug might be corrupting memory that is simply unused. This is where your notes will really come in handy. It's time to backtrack, remove your recent changes one at a time, and repeat until the bug reappears. Begin again, but try a different approach in the hopes you can get closer.

Another version of the disappearing bug is one where a known failure simply disappears without any programmer actually addressing it. The bug might have been related to another issue that someone fixed—you hope. The safest thing to do is to analyze recent changes and attempt to perform an autopsy of sorts. Given the recent fixes, you might even be able to recreate the original conditions and code that made the bug happen, apply the fix again, and prove beyond a shadow of a doubt that a particular fix addressed more than one bug.

What's more likely is that the number of changes to the code will preclude the possibility of this examination, especially on a large team. Then you have a decision to make: Is the bug severe enough to justify a targeted search through all the changes to prove the bug is truly fixed? It depends on the seriousness of the bug.

Tweaking Values

A classic problem in programming is getting a constant value "just right." This is usually the case for things like the placement of a user interface object like a button or perhaps the velocity value of a particle stream. While you are experimenting with the value, put it in a static variable in your code:

```
void MyWierdFountain::Update()
{
   static float __dbgVelocity = 2.74f;
   SetParticleVelocity(__dbgVelocity);

   // More code would follow…
}
```

It then becomes a trivial thing to set a breakpoint on the call to `SetParticleVelocity()` to let you play with the exact velocity value in real time. This is much faster than recompiling, and even faster than making the value data driven, since you won't even have to reload the game data. Once you find the values you're looking for, you can take the time to put them in a data file.

Caveman Debugging

If you can't use a debugger, or don't even know they exist as I did in college, you get to do something I call *caveman debugging*. You might be curious as to why you wouldn't be able to use a debugger, and it's not because you work for someone so cheap that they won't buy one. Sometimes you'll see problems only in the release build of the application. These problems usually result from uninitialized variables, unexpected or even incorrect code generation. The problem simply goes away in the debug version. You might also be debugging a server application that fails intermittently, perhaps after hours of running nominally. It's useless to attempt debugging in that case.

Make good use of `stderr` if you program in Unix or `OutputDebugString` if you program under Windows. These are your first and best tools for caveman debugging.

In both cases, you should resort to the caveman method: You'll write extra code to display variables or other important information on the screen, in the output window, or in a permanent log file. As the code runs, you'll watch the output for signs of misbehavior or you'll pour over the log file in the hopes you can discern the nature of the bug. This is a slow process and takes a great deal of patience, but if you can't use a debugger this method will work.

When I was on Ultima Online, one of my tasks was to write the UO login servers. These servers were the main point of connection for the Linux game servers and the SQL server, so login was only a small portion of what the software actually did. An array of statistical information flowed from the game servers, was collated in the login server, and was written to the SQL database. The EA executives liked pretty charts and graphs and we gave it to them. Anyway, the login process was a Win32 console application, and to help me understand what was going on I printed debug messages for logins, statistics data, and anything else that looked reasonable. When the login servers were running these messages were scrolling by so fast I certainly couldn't read them, but I could feel them. Imagine me sitting in the UO server room, staring blankly at three login server screens. I could tell just by the shape of the text flowing by whether or not a large number of logins were failing or a UO server was disconnected. It was very weird.

The best caveman debugging solution I ever saw was one that used the PC speaker. Herman was a programmer that worked on Ultima V through Ultima IX, and one of his talents was perfect pitch. He could tell you the difference between a B and a B flat and get it right every time. He used this to his advantage when he was searching for the nastiest crasher bugs of them all—they didn't even allow the debugger window to pop up. He wrote a special checker program that output specific tones through the PC speaker, and peppered the code with these checks. If you walked into his office while his spiced up version of the game was running, it sounded a little like raw modem noise, until the game crashed. Because the PC speaker wasn't dependant on the CPU it would remain emitting the tone of his last check. "Hrm....that's a D," he would say, and zero in on the line of code that caused the crash.

When all Else Fails

So you tried everything and hours later you are no closer to solving the problem than when you started. Your boss is probably making excuses to pass by your office and ask you cheerily, "How's it going?" You suppress the urge to jump up and make an example of his annoying behavior, but you still have no idea what to do. Here's a few last resort ideas.

First, go find another programmer and explain your problem. It doesn't really matter if you can find John Carmack or the greenest guy in your group, just find someone. Walk them through each step, explaining the behavior of the bug and each hypothesis you had however failed. Talk about your debugging experiments and step through the last one with them watching over your shoulder. For some odd reason, you'll find the solution to your problem without them ever even speaking a single word. It will just come as if it were handed to you by the Universe itself. I've never been able to explain that phenomenon, but it's real. This will solve half of the unsolvable bugs.

Another solution is static code analysis. You should have enough observations to guess at what is going on, you just can't figure out how the pieces of the puzzle fit together. Print out a suspect section of code on paper—the flat stuff you find in copy machines—and take it away from your desk. Study it and ask yourself how the code could fail. Getting away from your computer and the debugger helps to open your mind a bit, and removes your dependency on them.

If you get to this point and you still haven't solved the problem, you've probably been at it for a few solid hours if not all night. It's time to walk away—not from the problem, but from your computer. Just leave. Do something to get your mind off the problem. Drive home. Eat dinner. Introduce yourself to your family. Take a shower.

The last one is particularly useful for me—not that I need any of you to visualize me in the shower. The combination of me being away from the office and in a relaxing environment frees a portion of my mind to continue working on the problem without adding to my stress level. Sometimes, a new approach to the problem or an even better a solution will simply deposit itself in my consciousness. That odd event has never happened to me when I'm under pressure sitting at the computer. It's scary when you're at dinner and it dawns on you and you've solved a bug just by getting away from it.

Different Kinds of Bugs

Tactics and technique are great but they only describe debugging in the most generic sense. Everyone should build a taxonomy of bugs, a dictionary of bugs as it were, so that you can instantly recognize a type of bug and associate it with the beginning steps of a solution. One way to do this is constantly trade "bug" stories with other programmers—a conversation that will bore non-programmers completely to death.

Memory Leaks and Heap Corruption

A memory leak is caused when a dynamically allocated memory block is "lost." The pointer that holds the address of the block is reassigned without freeing the block, and it will remain allocated until the application exits. This kind of bug is especially problematic if this happens frequently. The program will chew up physical and virtual memory over time, and eventually fail. Here's a classic example of a memory leak. This class allocates a block of memory in a constructor, but fails to declare a virtual destructor:

```
class LeakyMemory : public SomeBaseClass
{
protected:
   int *leaked;

   LeakyMemory() { leaked = new int[128]; }
   ~LeakyMemory() { delete leaked; }
};
```

This code might look fine but there's a potential memory leak in there. If this class is instantiated, and is referenced by a pointer to `SomeBaseClass`, the destructor will never get called:

```
void main()
{
   LeakyMemory *ok = new LeakyMemory;
   SomeBaseClass *bad = new LeakyMemory;

   delete ok;
   delete bad;                        // MEMORY LEAK RIGHT HERE!
}
```

You fix this problem by declaring the destructor in the base class as virtual. Memory leaks are easy to fix if the leaky code is staring you in the face. This isn't always the case. A few bytes leaked here and there as game objects are created and destroyed can go unnoticed for a long time until it is obvious that your game is chewing up memory without any valid reason.

Memory bugs and leaks are amazingly easy to fix, but tricky to find, if you use a memory allocator that doesn't have special code to give you a hand. Under Win32, the C runtime library lends a hand under the debug builds with the debug heap. The debug heap sets the value of uninitialized memory and freed memory.

- Uninitialized memory allocated on the heap is set to 0xCDCDCDCD.
- Unintialized memory allocated on the stack is set to 0xCCCCCCCC. This is dependent on the /GX complier option in Microsoft Visual C++.
- Freed heap memory is set to 0xFEEEFEEE, before it has been reallocated. Sometimes this freed memory is set to OxDDDDDDDD, depending on how the memory was freed.
- The lead byte and trailing byte to any memory allocated on the heap is set to 0xFDFDFDFD.

Win32 programmers commit these values to memory. They'll come in handy when you are viewing memory windows in the debugger. You can tell what has happened to a block of memory.

The C-Runtime debug heap also provides many functions to help you examine the heap for problems. I'll tell you about three of them, and you can hunt for the rest in the Visual Studio help files or MSDN:

- **_CrtSetDbgFlag(int newFlag):** Sets the behavior of the debug heap.
- **_CrtCheckMemory(void):** Runs a check on the debug heap.
- **_CrtDumpMemoryLeaks(void):** Reports any leaks to stdout.

Here's an example of how to put these functions into practice:

```
#include <crtdbg.h>
#if defined _DEBUG
   #define new new(_NORMAL_BLOCK,__FILE__, __LINE__)
#endif

int main()
{
   // get the current flags
   int tmpDbgFlag = _CrtSetDbgFlag(_CRTDBG_REPORT_FLAG);

   // don't actually free the blocks
   tmpDbgFlag |= _CRTDBG_DELAY_FREE_MEM_DF;

   // perform memory check for each alloc/dealloc
   tmpDbgFlag |= _CRTDBG_CHECK_ALWAYS_DF;
   _CrtSetDbgFlag(tmpDbgFlag);


   char *gonnaTrash = new char[15];

   _CrtCheckMemory();                        // everything is fine....

   strcpy(gonnaTrash, "Trash my memory!"); // overwrite the buffer

   _CrtCheckMemory();                        // everything is NOT fine!

   delete gonnaTrash;                        // This brings up a dialog box too...
```

```
   char *gonnaLeak = new char[100];          // Prepare to leak!

   _CrtDumpMemoryLeaks();                    // Reports leaks to stderr

   return 0;
}
```

Notice that the new operator is redefined. A debug version of new is included in the debug heap that records the file and line number of each allocation. This can go a long way to help detecting the cause of a leak.

The first few lines set the behavior of the debug heap. The first flag tells the debug heap to keep deallocated blocks around in a special list instead of recycling them back into the useable memory pool. You might use this flag to help you track a memory corruption or simply alter your process's memory space in the hopes a tricky bug will be easier to catch. The second flag tells the debug heap that you want to run a complete check on the debug heap's integrity each time memory is allocated or freed. This can be incredibly slow, so turn it on and off only when you are sure it will do you some good. The output of the memory leak dump looks like this:

```
Detected memory leaks!
Dumping objects ->
c:\tricks\tricks.cpp(78) : {42} normal block at 0x00321100, 100 bytes long.
 Data: <                > CD CD CD CD CD CD CD CD CD CD CD CD CD CD CD CD
Object dump complete.
The program '[2940] Tricks.exe: Native' has exited with code 0 (0x0).
```

As you can see the leak dump pinpoints the exact file and line of the leaked bits. What happens if you have a core system that allocates memory like crazy, such as a custom string class? Every leaked block of memory will look like it's coming from the same line of code, because it is. It doesn't tell you anything about who called it, which is the real perpetrator of the leak. If this is happening to you, tweak the redeclaration of `new`, and store a self-incrementing counter instead of `__LINE__`:

```
#include <crtdbg.h>
#if defined _DEBUG
   static int counter = 0;
   #define new new(_NORMAL_BLOCK,__FILE__, counter++)
#endif
```

The memory dump report will tell you exactly when the leaky bits were allocated, and you can track it down easily.

12

You can't look at the Task Manager under Windows to determine if your game is leaking memory. The Task Manager is the process window you can show if you hit Ctrl-Alt-Del, and click the Task Manager button. This window lies. For one thing, memory might be reported wrong if you have set the `_CRTDBG_DELAY_FREE_MEM_DF` flag. Even if you are running a release build, freed memory isn't reflected in the process window until the window is minimized and restored. This one stymied even the Microsoft test lab. They wrote a bug telling us that our game was leaking memory like crazy, and we couldn't find it. It turned out that if you minimize the application window and restore it, the Task Manager will report the memory correctly, at least for a little while.

If you happen to write your own memory manager, make sure you take the time to write some analogs to the C runtime debug heap functions. If you don't, you'll find chasing memory leaks and corruptions a full time job.

Make sure your debug build detects and reports memory leaks, and convince every programmer that they should fix all memory leaks before they check in their code. It's a lot harder to fix someone else's memory leak than your own.

COM objects can leak memory too, and those leaks are also painful to find. If you fail to call `Release()` on a COM object when you're done with it, the object will remain allocated because it's reference count will never drop to zero. Here's a neat trick: first put the following function somewhere in your code:

```
int Refs(IUnknown *pUnk)
{
   pUnk->AddRef();
   return pUnk->Release();
}
```

You can then put `Refs(myLeakingResourcePtr)` in the watch window in your debugger. This will usually return the current reference count for a COM object. Be warned, however, that COM doesn't require that `Release()` return the current reference count, but it usually does.

Game Data Corruption

Most memory corruptions are easy to diagnose. Your game crashes and you find funky trash values where you were used to seeing valid data. The frustrating thing about memory corrupter bugs is that they can happen anywhere, anytime. Since the memory corruption is not trashing the heap, you can't use the debug heap functions, but you can use your own home grown version of them. You need to write your own version of `CrtCheckMemory()`, built especially for the data structures being vandalized. Hopefully, you'll have a reasonable set of steps you can use to reproduce the bug. Given those two things, the bug has only moments to live. If the trasher is intermittent, leave the data structure check code in the game. Perhaps someone will begin to notice a pattern of steps that can cause the corruption to occur.

I recall a truly excellent hack we encountered on Savage Empire, an Ultima VI spin-off that Origin shipped in late 1990. Origin was using Borland's 3.1 C Compiler, and the runtime module's exit code always checked memory location zero to see if a wayward piece of code accidentally overwrote that piece of memory, which was actually unused. If it detected the memory location was altered, it would print out "Error: (null) pointer assignment" at the top of the screen. Null pointer assignments were tough to find in those days since the CPU just happily assumed you knew what you were doing. Savage Empire programmers tried in vain to hunt down the null pointer assignment until the very last day of development. Origin's QA had signed off on the build, and Origin Execs wanted to ship the product, since Christmas was right around the corner. Steve, one of the programmers, "fixed" the problem with an amazing hack. He hex edited the executable, savage.exe, and changed the text string "Error: (null) pointer assignment." to another string exactly the same length: "Thanks for playing Savage Empire."

If the memory corruption seems random—writing to memory locations here and there without any pattern—here's a useful but brute force trick: Declare an enormous block of memory and initialize it with an unusual pattern of bytes. Write a check routine that runs through the memory block and finds any bytes that don't match the original pattern, and you've got something that can detect your bug. I've been using this trick since Ultima VII.

Ultima games classicly stored their game data in large blocks of memory, and the data was organized as a linked list. If the object lists became corrupted, all manner of mayhem would result. If you ever played Savage Empire, you might have been one of the lucky people to see a triceratops walking across the opening screen, in two pieces.

Another example of this object corruption was a bug I saw in Martian Dreams – as I was walking my character across the alien landscape, all the plants turned into pocket watches and my character turned into a pair of boots. If I hadn't seen it with my own eyes I wouldn't have believed it. The worst of these bugs became something of a legend at Origin Systems—"The Barge Bug." The Ultima VI team found that the linked object lists could be used to create barges, a generic term for a bunch of linked objects that could move about the map as a group. This led to neat stuff like flying carpets, boats, and the barges of Martian Dreams that navigated the canals.

QA was observing a bug that made barges explode. The objects and their passengers would suddenly shatter into pieces, and if you attempted to move them one step in any direction that game would crash. I was assigned the task of fixing this bug. I tried again and again, each time I was completely sure that barge bug was dead. QA didn't share my optimism, and for four versions of the game I would see the bug report come back—"Not fixed." The fourth time I saw the bug report my exhausted mind simply snapped. I don't need to tell you what happened, because an artist friend of mine, Denis, drew the picture of me shown in Figure 12.3.

Stack Corruption

Stack corruption is evil because it wipes evidence from the scene of the crime. Take a look at this lovely code:

Figure 12.3
Artist's Rendering of Earwax Blowing out of Mr.Mike's Ears.

```
void StackTrasher()
{
   char hello[10];
   memset(hello, 0, 1000);
}
```

The call to memset never returns, since it wipes the stack clean, including the return address. The most likely thing your computer will do is break into some crazy, codeless, area—the debugger equivalent of shrugging its shoulders and leaving you to figure it out for yourself. Stack corruptions almost always happen as a result of sending bad data into an otherwise trusted function, like memset. Again, you must have a reasonable set of steps you can follow to reproduce the error.

Begin your search by eliminating subsections of code, if you can. Set a breakpoint at the highest level of code in your main loop, and step over each function call. Eventually you should be able to find a case where stepping over a function call will cause the crash. Begin your experiment again, only this time step into the function and narrow the list of perpetrators. Repeat these steps until you've found the call that causes the crash.

Notice carefully with each step the call stack window. The moment it is trashed the debugger will be unable to display the call stack. It is unlikely that you'll be able to continue or even set the next statement to a previous line for retesting, so if you missed the cause of the problem you'll have to begin again. If the call that causes that stack to go south is something trusted like memset, study each input parameter carefully. Your answer is there: one of those parameters is bogus.

Cut and Paste Bugs

This kind of bug doesn't have a specific morphology, an SAT way of saying "pattern of behavior." It does have a common source, which is cutting and pasting code from one place to another. I know how it is; sometimes it's easier to cut and paste a little section of code rather than factor it out into a member of a class or utility function. I've done this myself many times to avoid a heinous recompile. I tell myself that I'll go back and factor the code later. Of course I never get around to it. The danger of cutting and pasting code is pretty severe.

First, the original code segment could have a bug that doesn't show up until much later. The programmer that finds the bug will likely perform a debugging experiment where a tentative fix is applied to the first block of code, but he misses the second one. The bug may still occur exactly as it did before, convincing our hero that he has failed to find the problem and begins a completely different approach. Second, the cut and pasted code might be perfectly fine in the original location, but cause a subtle bug in the destination. You might have local variables stomping on each other or some such thing.

If you're like me at all, you feel a pang of guilt every time you hit Ctrl-V and you see more than two or three line pop out of the clipboard. That guilt is there for a reason: Heed it and at least create a local free function while you get the logic straightened out. When you're done, you can refactor your work, make your change to game.h, and compile through the night.

Running out of Space

You should never run out of space. By space, I mean any consumable resource: memory, hard drive space, Windows handles, or memory blocks on a console's memory card. If you do run out of space, you're game is either leaking these resources, or never had them to begin with.

We've already talked about the leaking problem, so let's talk about the other case. If your game needs certain resources to run properly, like a certain amount of hard drive space or memory blocks for save game files, then by all means check for the appropriate headroom when your game initializes. If any consumable is in short supply, you should bail right there or at least warn the player that they won't be able to save games.

In the final days of Ultima VIII, it took nine floppy disks to hold all of the install files. Origin execs had a hard limit on eight floppy disks and we had to find some way of compressing what we had into one less disk. It made sense to concentrate on the largest file, SHAPES.FLX, which held all of the graphics for the game.

Zack, one of Origin's best programmers, came up with a great idea. The SHAPES.FLX file essentially held filmstrip animations for all the characters in Ultima VIII, and each frame was only slightly different from the previous frame. Before the install program compressed SHAPES.FLX, Zack wrote a program to delta compress all of the animations. Each frame stored only the pixels that changed from the previous frame, and the blank space left over was run length encoded. The whole shebang was compressed with a general compression algorithm for the install program. It didn't make installation any faster, that's for sure, but Zack saved Origin a few tens of thousands of dollars with a little less than a single night of hard core programming.

Release Mode Only Bugs

If you ever have a bug in the release build that doesn't happen in the debug build, most likely you have an uninitialized variable somewhere. The best way to find this type of bug is to use a run time analyzer like BoundsChecker.

Another source of this problem can be a compiler problem, in that certain optimization settings or other project settings are causing bugs. If you suspect this, one possibility is to start changing the project settings one by one to look more like the debug build, until the bug disappears. Once you have the exact setting that causes the bug, you may get some intuition about where to look next.

Multithreading Gone Bad

Multithreaded bugs are really nasty because they can be nigh impossible to reproduce accurately. The first clue you may have a multithreaded issue is by a bug's unpredictable behavior. If you think you have a multithreaded bug on your hands, the first thing you should do is disable multithreading and try to reproduce the bug.

A good example of a classic multithreaded bug is a sound system crash. The sound system in most games runs in a separate thread, grabbing sound bits from the game every now and again as it needs them. It's these communications points where two threads need to synch up and communicate that most multithreading bugs occur.

Sound systems like Miles from RAD Game Tools are extremely well tested. It's much more likely that a sound system crash is due to your game deallocating some sound memory before its time or perhaps simply trashing the sound buffer. In fact, this is so likely that my first course of action when I see a really strange, unreproducable bug is to turn off the sound system and see if I can get the problem to happen again.

The same is true for other multithreaded subsystems, such as AI or resource preloading. If your game uses multiple threads for these kinds of systems make sure you can turn it off easily for testing. Sure, the game will run in a jerky fashion since all the processing has to be performed in a linear fashion, but the added benefit is that you can eliminate the logic of those systems and focus on the communication and thread synchronization for the source of the problem.

Ultima VIII had an interrupt driven multi-tasking system, which was something of a feat in DOS 5. A random crash was occurring in QA, and no one could figure out how to reproduce it, which meant there was little hope of it getting fixed. It was finally occurring once every thirty minutes or so—way too often to be ignored. We set four or five programmers on the problem with each one attempting to reproduce the bug. Finally, the bug was reproduced by a convoluted path. We would walk the Avatar character around the map in a specific sequence, teleporting to one side of the map, then the other, and the crash would happen. We were getting close.

Herman, the guy with perfect pitch, turned on his pitch debugger. We followed the steps exactly, and when the crash happened Herman called it: a B-flat meant that the bug was somewhere in the memory manager. We eventually tracked it down to a lack of protection in the memory system. Two threads were accessing the memory management system at the same time, and the result was a trashed section of memory. Since the bug was related to multi-threading, it never corrupted the same piece of memory twice in a row.

Had we turned the multi-threading off, the bug would have disappeared, causing us to focus our effort on any shared data structure that could be corrupted by multiple thread access. In other words, we were extremely lucky to find this bug, and the only thing that saved us was a set of steps we could follow that made the bug happen.

Weird Ones

There are some bugs that are very strange, either by their behavior, intermittence, or the source of the problem. Driver related issues are pretty common, not necessarily because there's a bug in the driver. It's more likely that you are assuming the hardware or driver can do something that it cannot. Your first clue that an issue is driver related is that it only occurs on specific hardware, such as a particular brand of video card. Video cards are sources of constant headaches in Windows games because each manufacturer wants to have some feature stand out from the pack, and do so in a manner that keeps costs down. More often than not this will result in some odd limitations and behavior.

A great example of an unruly video card is found on an old video card that was once made by the now defunct 3Dfx company. This card had a limitation that no video memory surface could have a width to height ratio greater than 8:1. A 256x32 surface would work just fine, but a 512x32 surface would fail in a very strange way: It would create a graphic effect not unlike a scrambled TV channel. If you weren't aware of this limitation you would debug relentlessly through every line of code in your whole game and you'd never find the problem. It turns out that problems like this are usually found through a targeted search of the Internet. Google groups (groups.google.com) is my personal favorite.

Weird bugs can also crop up in specific operating system versions, for exactly the same reasons. Windows 9x based operating systems are very different than Windows 2000 and Windows XP, based on the much beefier NT kernel. These different operating systems make different assumptions about parameters, return values, and even logic for the same API calls. If you don't believe me just look at the bottom of the help files for any Win32 API like `GetPrivateProfileSection`. That one royally screwed me.

Again, you diagnose the problem by attempting to reproduce the bug on a different operating system. Save yourself some time and try a system that is vastly different. If the bug appears in Windows 98 try it again in Windows XP. If the bug appears in both operating systems it's extremely unlikely that your bug is OS specific.

Be especially aware of new things. One of the latest changes to MFC7 was a complete restructuring of how it handled strings. The old code was thrown out in favor of an ATL-based system. MFC7 was distributed with Visual Studio.NET, and we noticed immediately that our game was failing under Windows 98. After a painful remote debugging session it seemed that the tried and true `CFileFind` class was corrupting memory. Go figure! One of the reasons it took me so long to find it was that I wasn't looking inside `CFileFind` even though the source code was there right in front of me. I guess I'm just too trusting.

A much rarer form of the weird bug is a specific hardware bug, one that seems to manifest as a result of a combination of hardware and operating systems, or even a specific piece of defective or incompatible hardware. These problems can manifest themselves most often in portable computers, oddly enough. If you've isolated the bug to something this specific, the first thing you should try is to update all the relevant drivers. This is a good thing to do in any case, since most driver-related bugs will disappear when the fresh drivers are installed.

Finally, the duckbilled platypus of weird bugs are the ones generated by the compiler. It happens, more often that anyone would admit. The bug will manifest itself most often in a release build with full optimizations. This is the most fragile section of the compiler. You'll be able to reproduce the bug on any platform, but it may disappear when release mode settings are tweaked. The only way to find this problem is to stare at the assembly code and realize that the compiler generated code that is not semantically equal to the original source code. This is not that easy, especially in fully optimized assembly.

By the way, if you are wondering what you do if you don't know assembly, here's a clue: Go find a programmer that knows assembly. Watch them work, and learn something. Then convince yourself that maybe learning a little assembly is a good idea.

If you happen to be lucky (or unlucky) enough to find a weird compiler problem (especially one that could impact other game developers), do everyone a favor and write a tiny program that isolates the compiler bug, and post it to the internet so everyone can watch out for the problem. You'll be held in high regard if you find a workaround and post that too. Be really sure that you are right about what you see. The Internet lasts forever and it would be unfortunate if you blamed the compiler programmers for something they didn't do. In your posts, be gentle. Rather than say something like, "Those idiots who developed the xyz compiler really screwed up and put in this nasty bug...," try, "I think I found a tricky bug in the xyz compiler..."

Parting Thoughts

An important thing to keep in mind when debugging is that computers are at their core *deterministic entities*. They don't do things unless instructions are loaded into the CPU. This should give you hope, since the bug you seek is always findable.

You know that with enough time and effort you'll squash that bug. That thought alone can be a powerful motivating force.

Chapter 13

The Art of Scheduling

Some of you reading this chapter are probably wondering, I thought this was a non-fiction book. What's scheduling doing in here? Game developers really don't follow schedules do they? Many schedules for computer games are created by some producer with the ultimate goal of signing a deal, rather than creating a decent inventory and ordering of tasks assigned to people who can accomplish them. Schedules should be accurate and truthful estimates, not wishful thinking or even worse—guesses.

By the time you finish reading this chapter, you'll know how to create a schedule for a game development project, and one you can trust. This chapter covers milestones and how to define them, hidden things that effect every schedule that everyone always forgets, and how to break down your game project into reasonable chunks that any programmer worth his salt can handle and handle on time. Every project I've scheduled since 1997 has come in on time and on budget. As of this writing, that's five titles in five years with three different teams. The process works, and it doesn't involve crystal balls.

One of the best programmers I ever knew was famous for predicting how long he'd take to get something working. This made him one of the best guys to have around because he'd take the hardest and most complicated tasks and somehow always get them working on time. Once they were working he'd never have to touch them again. I think he was able to do this consistently because he could see the entire problem all the way down to its smallest components. This is, in essence, what scheduling is all about: discover all of the details of your problem and determine time estimates for *all of them*.

Good Schedules, Bad Schedules

Everyone I know uses milestones, but not everyone I know uses them correctly. Most of what I learned about defining and working with project milestones was from (can you believe it) Microsoft. For as much as Microsoft gets panned in the industry at large, I think they do many things right and one of those is planning around milestones. As a point of comparison, Origin used a more naïve approach when I was there, mostly because we thought we were pioneers in the development of games and we didn't have to look elsewhere for a better way. I attribute a lot of wasted weekends (or should I say entire summers) to this sophomoric approach.

You can tell if your scheduling process is a little off by looking for these warning signs:

- Your project has a critical "Alpha" and "Beta" stage, and these stages only define what the game is supposed to be like instead of defining *how* the team changes their work habits.
- Even worse, you can't get a consistent answer from anyone exactly what "Alpha" and "Beta" are supposed to be.
- There isn't any time specifically allocated ~~for fixing bugs during each milestone~~.
- The schedule doesn't take personal time, holidays, or other non-working time into account.
- The smallest defined task on a schedule is one week.
- You can't see if other assets from the art or sound department are going to be ready when the programmers need them.
- You can't break each major task down into specific programming, art, audio, design, testing, web, database, or other components.
- You can't verify that every team member knows exactly what is expected of them each and every milestone.
- The time estimates or task inventory were assembled by "outsiders."
- Your entire project schedule can be printed out in a smallish grid of boxes in Microsoft Excel.

I can already hear some of you screaming, "Somebody save me because every single one of those things is true about my game project!" Put your personal affairs in order and bring your sleeping bag to work because I can almost guarantee what's going to happen to your project—the dreaded crunch mode.

Why is it called crunch mode, anyway? I always thought a mode was by definition something that was a temporary transition destined to come to an end. I believe that every company's management makes a choice about allowing semi-permanent crunch modes, and I sincerely believe that crunch modes are the single most destructive practice in our industry today.

Don't get me wrong, I'm not some academic elitist pretending that Murphy is some fictional character. Murphy is alive and well in the gaming industry and bad things happen to the best planners and the most careful development teams. My point is why start the project off with a plan that isn't completely thought through? Murphy doesn't need a red carpet and someone to hold the door open.

Before you can learn how to create the bullet-proof schedule, you need to learn about milestones.

The Key to All Schedules: Milestones

Milestones are "pinch points" in your project where any outside observer can observe the progress of the development team and compare it with a list of milestone acceptance criteria. Depending on the nature of the milestone, certain development practices change to ensure the team is on track. Every milestone is defined in the following way:

- *A title*: Sometimes a keyword or short phrase describing the major accomplishment of the milestone.
- *A short description*: Usually a bullet list that exposes one level of detail about the tasks on the milestone.
- *A due date*: Usually on Wednesdays, to give the development and test teams a few days to tweak the build before the weekend, and spaced no less than five weeks apart and no more than nine weeks apart. They are never on holidays, either.
- *Production dates*: These are the dates the team focuses on production, as opposed to acceptance. Usually the production time is 80% of the acceptance time.
- *A non-subjective test for acceptance*: This is sometimes called the "Acceptance Criteria." Non-subjective means that the test is worded in such a manner that there is minimal room for opinion or interpretation regarding acceptance. This is the meat and potatoes of the definition of the milestone, and therefore your schedule. I'll have much more to say about this subject shortly.
- *A risk assessment*: A few words on the risk level of the milestone and what steps are being taken to mitigate that risk.
- *Deliverables*: What exactly is going to be delivered to the test team (documents only, documents and a working prototype, a release candidate, and so on).
- *Contributors*: A list of everyone expected to contribute to the milestone and a short description of their contribution (only one liners—a detailed individual milestone document will be created too).

The collection of all the milestones in one document is usually an integral part of any publishing contract, and is a serious commitment from the development team to the publisher.

Creating an internal milestone document for the team's eyes only and another document for external publication is a wise approach. Lies and deceit? Of course not! The internal milestone document will be 15% to 20% more aggressive than the external document, and may include things that the team wants in addition to the contractual deliverables, or simply has some tasks scheduled to complete sooner than they'll be expected by the publisher. This allows a development team a little wiggle room when unplanned events affect your game plan. And honestly, don't believe the publisher doesn't know you're doing this to begin with!

Writing a good milestone description is as difficult as writing an iron clad contract. The best way to prove this statement is to show an example of the same milestone description written poorly and written well.

Example A:
Physics System Integrated: The new physics library from Havok has been fully integrated into the game allowing objects to move and react under the effects of gravity, friction, collisions, and finally lie at rest.

Example B:
Physics System Integrated: The following can be demonstrated: The new physics library from Havok can be compiled and linked into the game with no warnings or errors. Havok's movement and orientation data are correctly translated to our custom renderer "SqueakMaster," our 3DStudio Max plugins work with Havok's exporter to provide a seamless export pipeline, a test script can "throw" all our dynamic objects into various map level areas with natural looking gravity, collisions, different coefficients of friction, and objects can lie at rest in a pile of other objects. All of this is done within the performance characteristics required in the technical specification and the object densities expected in the design specification.

The milestone description in Example A looked pretty good at first because it described what was supposed to be accomplished. The problem with it was that it was still vague. The phrase "fully integrated into the game pipeline" doesn't explicitly say anything about making the artists jobs easier by writing a 3DStudio Max plug-in, does it?

If you've ever heard anyone say, "I didn't know I was supposed to do that" or perhaps you've even said it yourself I'll bet my bottom dollar that the source of the communications problem was a bad milestone description. Two people read something that sounded a lot like the first example and read two completely different things. What usually follows is a clarification of the task very late in the milestone and the programmer is the one that gets nailed for weekend time.

After Martian Dreams shipped in March of 1991, I was asked to spend some time working on Ultima VII. I took a look at my assignment, which

was explained as "User Interface," and scheduled it for six weeks. The infamous "Gump" system, as it was called, had already been written by Zack Simpson so it wasn't unreasonable to think that I could knock out a series of dialog boxes for the game in six weeks. I didn't finish my work until nearly twelve months later. The problem was that much of the code that manipulated the data structures or actions controlled by the buttons and so on hadn't been written or even considered. In truth, the task was much larger than everyone expected.

Let's look at one more example:

Example A:
Special Rendering Effects—Sun Effect & Light Glare: The code for the sun is capable of showing a fake sun in the sky that looks real when the camera view is pointed towards the sun during the day. At night or twilight all lights have a glare that approximates camera lens effects.

Example B:
Special Rendering Effects—Sun Effect & Light Glare: The API for the sun effects must be able to recreate the actual sun location in the sky given a date, time, latitude and longitude, temperature of sun surface and relative size when compared to Sol. The setting sun must change color appropriately as specified in the design spec. The effects expected when the camera is pointed in the sun's direction is a general brightening of the view until pointed directly at the sun, which should wash everything out. If the sun is partially occluded, as when standing the shadow of a building, the light from the sun must appear to peek around the edges of the building. Light glares must be created by the artist using 3DStudio Max user data and exported along with models that have lights attached, such as street lamps or vehicles.

Once again you can see the difference between the two examples. The second example does a much better job explaining what the technology is supposed to accomplish, where the data comes from, and how it is created or interacts with production tools.

It's fun to be creative when designing technology. That creativity can lead you down the wrong path, though, if someone hands you a task description that looks more like the shorter examples that leave too much room for interpretation. One of the differences between good programmers and great programmers is that great programmers always clarify the nature of the work before they begin, and they always predict their expected effort with a high accuracy. Make sure that every milestone description on your project is as detailed as it can be, and leaves little room for error.

Stock Milestones

There are some milestones that are "stock," that is they happen for every game project whether you plan for them or not! Go ahead and admit they exist, plan for them properly, and you'll be better for it. Here they are:

- Project Kickoff
- Design and Functional Specification Draft
- First Production Milestone, Second Production Milestone, and so on
- Code Complete
- Content Complete
- Zero Bugs
- Release to Manufacturing (or Web)

Project Kickoff

The project kickoff represents the first day anyone is officially assigned to work on project tasks. Generally, an awful lot of planning and conference calls have already happened and everyone is confident enough to start spending real money on the project. The following things should be deliverables for the project kickoff:

- A summary of the functional specification and scope of the work.
- A list of primary contributors (team management, tech leads, and so on).
- A good faith estimate of the timeline and budget.
- A list of project constraints and priorities (time, budget, features, competition, and so on).
- For external developers, a first draft of the contract. (No one wants to see a deal breaker pop up in a contract after significant work has been accomplished.)

Don't do deals on a handshake. Don't give in because someone's legal department is backlogged. I've seen too many projects (one of my own, too) get two or three milestones under their belt before anyone realized there was a deal breaker clause in the contract. No one wins in that scenario; at least get an LOI (letter of intent) with reasonable termination language that protects you for any expenditures you'll incur while the contract is winding it's way through the legal department. In other words, "lawyer up" and cover your butt—there's simply too much money at stake.

During this milestone the team is getting its feet wet and getting their head around the plan. Any outstanding research projects (crazy rendering techniques or bleeding edge AI) should be underway and everyone should have high confidence in either the outcome of the research or the viability of the backup plan. Lots of specification writing is accomplished and the final milestones, schedule, and budget are finished.

"But wait a damn minute," you say. How can you finish the milestones, schedule, and budget before the final specifications are complete? More lies and deceit? Again, of course not. The general parameters of any project (time, money, and features) are known to some degree before the project begins. Producers are given budgets, manufacturing slots, and marketing deals that constrain the time window when a project can be released, and your feature set must compare well with your competition. The trick is to assemble the right team and the right solution strategy to succeed within these constraints. The project schedule and milestones are proof that this difficult task is actually possible.

Design and Functional Specification Draft

The main deliverable for this milestone is documentation. The entire product specification (user interface, features, level design, character design, missions, and so on) is described in all its glory. This documentation accomplishes a few important goals:

- The test team will use it to construct the test plan.
- The development and production groups use it as a bible to answer the question: Are we making the product we agreed to make?
- Since every detail of the final product is described, it can be cross referenced against the inventory of scheduled tasks and therefore increase everyone's confidence in the schedule.

Hold on though, how can you create a complete and detailed product specification for a game? Games are closer to art than science and you can't really insert a three week task assigned to Roofus McDoofus that says "Increase the *Fun* to 100%." That's very true: You can't specify fun as a task. So what do you do? Mostly, you make sure the development team is experienced enough to detect the fun factor in the design instead of attempting to retrofit it into the game late in the schedule.

The deliverables for this milestone include:

- The entire design and functional specification.
- Logistics document (coding practices, asset management plan, team meetings, disaster recovery plans, and so on).
- Buildable "Hello World" project with the Source Code Repository.

- An inventory of all external licensed materials: technology, fonts, sounds, and so on.

An important thing to note about the documents you create in this milestone is that they are *drafts*, to be further modified and corrected until the delivery of the first production milestone, usually six to eight weeks later. You should expect to change no more than 15% of the scope of the documents or your plan as the corrections are made. Mostly, you'll simply reduce the scope of the product since the timeline and budget will be difficult or impossible to change.

First Production Milestone, Second Production Milestone...

You and your team implement your entire development plan during these milestones. You'll want to be more aggressive in your planning at the beginning to kick-start the team into their best intensity. Don't forget that each of these milestones will take extra time—about one week for every four weeks of solid development—for the entire team to fix bugs and get the product to meet each and every item on the acceptance criteria. When you plan for these milestones, make sure that each team member has something to contribute. It's a risky thing to allow anyone on the team to go more than one milestone in between rigorous and public checks on their progress. Annoying middle manager types (sadly I consider myself exactly that) can push all they want, but nothing motivates someone like the prospect of letting their team down.

It's also a good idea to keep these milestones coming at a reasonable pace. Five weeks should be an absolute minimum. This leaves four weeks for development and one week for acceptance. Four weeks is a pretty short time for a development team to accomplish something truly worthy of spending the testing group's time on another acceptance pass. You shouldn't plan any milestone longer than nine weeks, either. Any longer and you run a significant risk of missing opportunities to make a course correction in your schedule.

You should expect acceptance on any milestone to take about 20% of the actual development time.

The second Microsoft Casino revision was planned with actual milestone dates only four weeks apart with no special time set aside for acceptance. This was a real mistake because by the third production milestone the team couldn't keep performing on both their task load and the steadily climbing bug count. Microsoft execs were getting reports of a project out of control and skyrocketing bug counts, and they were very worried about our ability to pull it off. We did make our ship date, but after way more overtime and lost weekends than I had planned on. Also, I believe

the quality of the product suffered because there were some low priority bugs that were postponed that would have made a noticeable difference in the product.

The deliverables for each production milestone should be:

- Two builds of the product: a release build and a debug build.
- Complete source code tree that can reproduce the build.
- Release notes and test data for the test team.
- The most recent product documentation, including the milestone acceptance criteria agreed upon by the test and development team.

Getting a release build working early in the project might seem onerous, especially since it takes valuable time away from implementing. Debugging release builds can be a real pain, further reducing any motivation that might exist. One thing is sure: The time and effort it takes to get a release build running again once it goes into limbo increases linearly with time. It's therefore a good idea to make every milestone dependant on a release build passing acceptance tests.

Whether or not you supply a complete "rebuildable" source code tree with your milestone submission is up to you, your publisher, and sometimes the lawyers. All the same, it's a good idea to create it and test it as a part of your milestone acceptance. Think of it as an insurance policy against a catastrophic failure of your network or some other similar disaster.

While I was at Compulsive Development we were working hard on two projects for Microsoft. For those of you who live in or around Austin, Texas you're already familiar with the violent springtime storms that have tornados, golf ball sized hail, and tons of rain. One afternoon a particularly large storm hit our area and dumped six to seven inches of rain in just a few hours, flooding a creekbed just down the street from our office. One of our employees, Ellen Hobbs, noticed a flowing stream of water entering her office and shortly thereafter the server room next door! We stopped everything to safeguard our computers, furniture, servers, and toys by moving them to other offices. By the end of the day water had seeped into almost every office, and we could float little boats in Ellen's swamp. Nothing had been damaged except for some waterlogged books (sorry about that Donavon!), but it could have been much worse. Well, the smell couldn't have been worse! Hot Texas weather and wet carpet don't make for the best software development environment.

If you include a rebuildable source code tree with each build, make sure that your network security limits access to the build machine. If anyone can take a blank CD and burn a copy of your entire build, game libraries and everything else it might walk right out of your door and you'll never be the wiser. I hate to think of the fact that people might be enticed to steal everything your team worked so hard to create, but face it, your game source code is a valuable thing and you should protect it.

Code Complete

The code complete milestone is the most important milestone beside the last one. Once this milestone passes the acceptance tests the programmers shift their effort from writing and engineering new code to fixing code. This might sound earth shattering but it is the first time in the projects life cycle that you can accurately predict the ship date of your product.

Microsoft has found that on average a programmer can reduce their bug debt between three and four bugs per day. That may not sound like a lot, but remember that while a programmer may fix eight to ten bugs per day, the test team is writing up new issues at a similar rate. After code complete the production staff will begin to postpone minor issues in favor of fixing more important ones.

The product should pass the hardware and performance tests as well. This might sound unreasonable at first but take a moment to consider carefully what "Code Complete" really means. If the product fails significant portions of the hardware or performance tests, it is quite likely that a significant body of code is missing.

The deliverables for the code complete milestone should be exactly the same as the production milestones, with the addition of the following:

- Proof that the product passes hardware and performance tests, especially on the minimum machine configuration.
- A permanent and complete archive of everything: source code repository, art and sound sources, and so on.
- A report of every change made to the source code since the last submitted build.
- The install program.

The permanent archive of code and media assets is a good idea at this point. That includes original sound WAV files, models and scenes from Max or Maya, and anything artists used to create anything in the game. The closer you get to the end of the project, it's a good idea to spend some time and effort on ensuring that even terrible events have a minimal effect on your ship date.

Regarding the detailed change report for every build, most source code repositories have command line mechanisms for creating the change report. Every Microsoft project I worked on required this report, and at first glance this requirement seems a little draconian. There's a good reason behind it, though. Late in the development cycle the development team is constantly tempted to make little last minute changes without involving the production or testing group. Hidden changes drastically increase the risk of introducing problems because they don't get tested properly. If the team commits to creating the change report for every submitted build, it will make sure that every change goes through the right channels: development, production, and test.

There's another reason the code complete milestone is important. It marks the first major change in not only what the programmers are doing, but how they should do it. The changes in their work habits are all geared to reducing risk in the schedule:

- Nothing changes in source code without an approved bug entered into the bug database.
- Every change is bracketed with comments that identify the bug number, the rationale for the change, and anything else that may be needed to answer questions about the change.
- Every change is code reviewed before it is checked in.

These additional work habits serve to double and triple check every change and solution strategy implemented by each member of the team. Doing this late in the project is important for everyone on the team because the work hours and stress have peaked. It's quite easy for someone to believe that a particular solution or change is the right way to go when it might actually set the project back.

The oddest thing about programmers working in a team is that the intelligence of any programmer is instantly tripled when a respected colleague is silently looking over their shoulder. The colleague in question is usually concentrating on their shopping list or some other inane thing while the person at the keyboard is explaining their problem in detail and at the same time solving it with a sudden unexplainable streak of brilliant thinking. I've been on both sides of this phenomenon. Countless times I've run up against some coding issue and I called a friend of mine into my office to have them help. As I explained the problem the solution presented itself. Laughing, they usually leave my office telling me how they are glad they could help.

The point of all this is to realize that the reviews and reports aren't some kind of Orwellian scheme to stifle the thinking and creativeness of programmers. This is a common misconception and is a normal first reaction to these ideas. Instead, consider the possibility that when individuals begin to rely on the strength of the team everyone benefits from reducing errors and in turn makes a better product.

Rely on the strength of the entire team by participating and encouraging code reviews, and by following rigorous development practices that somehow seem more at home at NASA. These development practices are useful for any kind of software, games included. If more teams relied on good habits, as well as raw talent, more games would ship on time and they'd be more fun.

Content Complete

Content complete is really a milestone that is pretty special to game development. This stage focuses on completing and installing all the other game data: sound effects, speech, music, map levels, help, and anything else that isn't a part of the executable. Content complete usually follows four to eight weeks after the code complete milestone, but it could take much longer depending on your project. Most projects I've worked on spent about 50% of the overall development effort on programming, 40% on art, and the rest on sound or other assets like help. Of course, your mileage will vary.

You can image a project like Myst spent their development time very differently. The technology effort might have been as little as 20% of the man-hours, meaning that their development team might have reached code complete very early. The artists were probably working on vast modeling, lighting, and rendering tasks long after the programmers finished the display and user interface systems. In that kind of project you would expect the code complete and content complete milestones to be separated by one or more implementation milestones.

The deliverables for the content complete milestone should be exactly the same as the code complete milestones, with the addition of the following:

- Proof that the full scope of the media fits onto the CD-ROM with enough room for extra material required by the publisher.
- Signed license agreements for any third-party materials such as fonts, sound effects libraries, licensed technologies such as renderers and physics engines.
- Proof that every piece of media (art, sounds, and speech) used in the product is either in the public domain, created from scratch, or is accompanied by the appropriate permissions from the owner.

One of the things that happen during content complete is a steady stream of media assets are installed on a daily basis. The size of the product will grow quickly during this phase, and should therefore be monitored closely. Your team shouldn't wait to find out about a bulky product from the test team, because solving it at that point is distracting task for a programmer.

Don't assume that you'll get 100% of the CD-ROM space for your product. Publishers will usually require 50Mb or more for the install program, the latest version of DirectX, and perhaps some marketing materials for other products. This is a good thing to clear up before you finalize the contract, and any costs you incur due to a change in this plan should be borne by the publisher.

Another big issue that's forgotten about regarding intellectual property in games these days is the proper use of fonts. Arguably, it is against the letter and spirit of copyright law to duplicate a font exactly into a bitmap form and use it in your game without licensing it. Some font companies will require you to pay huge license fees for using their fonts interactively, which would include the display of letters in an edit control, for example. Have someone check the terms of a font license to be sure.

Legally you also can't use a model of a Ferrari in a game without permission. This is especially true for company logos, as it may be seen by the company in question to be an illegal use of their intellectual property. Someone who knows the intricacies of the law should check the question of what falls into fair use of trademarked or copyrighted material. The last thing you need is to have your game pulled off the shelves because one of your more colorful characters wore a "Have a Coke and a Smile" t-shirt.

Programmers and artists are free spirits, unencumbered by little things like the law. It can be fun to put a picture of Mickey Mouse in your game somewhere, perhaps as a joke or even as a serious design idea. Different companies have different tolerances for this kind of thing, and Disney is well known for their relentless pursuit of anyone using their intellectual property without their permission. Bottom line: Be careful what goes into your game, and unless you work for Disney don't even think of using Mickey.

Zero Bugs

From the moment you have a code complete build, the programmers are working 100% on fixing approved bugs. After content complete the entire team is working towards this goal. The milestone is reached the moment the team submits a build to the test team with every active bug addressed. Depending on the size of your product, development team, and bug count, you can expect the timeline from content complete to zero bugs to be no less than four weeks. A good rule of thumb would be two weeks for every three months of development time.

It is technically possible that this build could pass every test that the test team has in its arsenal. This means that your zero bug build is actually the first release candidate. Clearly this means that as the team gets close, less than five bugs per developer, the development practices get extremely tight. Every change made to fix a bug risks breaking three other things. There's no escaping the fact that at least once during the march to zero bugs, someone on the team will make an innocent change that will have unexpected and serious results.

On Ultima VII I was asked to make a small change in a text string. I can't honestly remember the exact change but I'm pretty sure it had something to do with Sherry the Mouse. I made the change myself and submitted the code for the next build. Ultima VII didn't have a robust way for me to jump ahead to the point in the game where the change could be tested, so I had to hope for the best. The change overran a static buffer used to compose conversation strings, and the game crashed after QA had spent six hours playtesting the game. They weren't very happy about that. The next time I made the change it was witnessed by no fewer than five programmers and Richard "Lord British" Garriott himself. It worked the second time.

The deliverables for this milestone are the same as the content complete build, and remain the same until the final build.

Release to Manufacturing (or Web)

Every build from here on out has zero active bugs. A build is sent to test and a number of issues will show up, most of which will get postponed or the team will decide to leave it, since the risk of fixing it is much worse than letting the problem remain in the game. At some point, only one bug will pass muster and it will be the only change made before a new build is sent to test. You should plan on spending at least four weeks on this final milestone.

The test team will be hammered in this milestone, and it isn't unreasonable for the development team to help out. The team should have very little work to do and can even spend some time thinking about the next project. They could design changes to their game engine for the next version (surely you wouldn't consider actually making core changes to the engine code now), or work short hour days to catch up on some laundry or reintroduce themselves to their family.

Sometimes you might consider making a simple change without performing the entire build process. A good example of this might include a small text change to a help file or the credits. I'm steadfastly against this practice since it introduces a variable in the development process for what could be the final build. Every time I've seen this happen something important is forgotten.

Instead, go ahead and make the change as you would normally, perform the entire build process, and compare the results to the in situ change file by file. If they end up exactly the same, good for you. If they are different you should figure out why the difference exists and question the wisdom of creating a version outside of your normal build process.

When the last bug is fixed, get the whole team to look at it. Make an event out of it, even though you might make this event happen two or three times before your release candidate is accepted. In addition to the network archive of the source tree and all media assets, which you've been doing for every submitted build since content complete, you should also archive the hard drives of the build machine. This will record the exact build environment, operating system version, and service packs included for later use. It isn't uncommon for publishers to request all of the backup tapes when the final build is submitted. Of course, don't forget to keep a copy for yourself.

Compulsive Development, at the time a 12-person company, had just finished our Bicycle Casino project. We sent the backup tapes to Microsoft made on a brand new Dell multitape backup system. Microsoft has a central group responsible for testing and archiving every tape backup sent to them by a third party. It turned out they didn't have the exact make and model of backup tape drives and archive software we used at Compulsive.

We got a phone call from our main contact there that we had to make backup tapes that were compatible with their system before our last milestone would be accepted! Since we purchased our server hardware from Dell, we weren't entirely motivated to spend thousands of dollars on new backup hardware. We got in touch with the archival group at Microsoft and convinced them that Microsoft would probably benefit from buying the hardware and software themselves, especially since the systems we were talking about weren't exactly cobbled together from spare parts lying about. Just because you are a small developer doesn't mean you can't reason with a multibillion dollar company!

Things to Know Before Scheduling Begins

There are a number of miscellaneous subjects that are useful to anyone tasked with organizing the project schedule for a computer game. Let's explore them now.

Tip/Tricks Using Microsoft Project

I should call this section, "Death of a Programmer," because I remember a time when I was better at C++ than Microsoft Project. I'm pretty sure that's behind me now and I might as well suck it up and start becoming an Excel macro guru as clearly, that is my destiny. I've been using Microsoft Project since 1995 on Ultima VIII, and I'm sad to say there's nothing else on the market that performs the task of scheduling as well. Certainly nothing within the price range of a small computer game developer, anyway. The problem with Microsoft Project is that is was never designed to schedule software projects in general, and certainly not computer game projects. I heard some rumor that Microsoft Project hasn't changed significantly from an original software package that was used for building buildings, not software.

This heritage seems likely once you begin to dig into the project. The fluidity of computer game production isn't handled well in Microsoft Project, especially if you begin to set constraints such as begin/end dates or task predecessors. At first blush this seems like a good idea, but you'll quickly find that you won't be able to easily reassign tasks from one person to another or change which milestone a certain task should end. This is hard enough with little or no constraints, but it becomes nearly impossible when you assign dependencies.

Here are some things I generally do when working with Microsoft Project when building a schedule for a game:

- *Predecessors*: I never assign them, rather I generally attempt to make sure the tasks are set in the schedule in roughly the order in which they will be completed. If you want to assign predecessors, be frugal with them and delay as long as possible.
- *Resource Assignments*: I always assign resources to individual tasks, not summary tasks. Try to assign one person for each task, unless you can assign a task to a resource that represents a group of people, such as "Artists."
- *Custom Fields*: I use additional custom fields to help me store additional data about the tasks, specifically I use the *Text1* and *Text2* fields for describing which feature and subfeature to which the task is related. This helps me tally up all tasks that might have to do with, *Sound—Foreign Language Speech* for example. Don't make the mistake of thinking that the summary task descriptions are useful for this. They aren't.
- *Cost Field*: I always use the cost field, and put a special section in the schedule for things that need to be purchased specifically for the project such as technology licenses or the ship party.
- *Partial Time Assignments*: Sometimes a person on your team will have to spend some time managing, and the rest of their time performing task work. Put a line for them up in the management section and assign the resource like this: *Name [25%]*. On every other task assigned to them in the schedule, put *75%* in the brackets.
- *Linking Tasks:* I never link tasks, because it keeps me from being able to move tasks up and down in the schedule easily. I think of Microsoft Project as a tool to plan my project instead of one that helps me keep track of it after work begins.

- *Use Resource Pools*: If I'm planning multiple projects I use the resource pool to make sure that I'm not double scheduling someone.
- *Don't Bother with Email Task Updates*: This is another feature that simply doesn't work as well as you'd hope. The technology is fine and it's pretty easy to set up, but you simply don't get the information you want. To be honest, nothing beats walking around to see, hear, and play with things as they get done.

There's one point I should make clear: The features of Microsoft Project that I choose to ignore are not useless. In some large projects it might be impossible to understand the effect of moving or changing tasks that are on the critical path. If you choose to enter all the information to link tasks and set predecessors that's perfectly fine. My advice is do this as a last step since you'll find changes very difficult to make without seeing that "Can't level resource" message ten thousand times.

Key Programming Tasks in Computer Games

One of the best ways to transform a design specification, even a rough one, is to look at each component and figure out what key programming tasks are necessary to bring the feature online.

- *Graphics*: Every game has to paint pixels, whether you use an old sprite engine or the latest hardware accelerated 3D renderer. Your game will need a way to draw and manage the art assets for sprites, textures, models, in-game animations, and cinematics.
- *User Interface*: This task extends the graphics system and creates buttons, menus, fonts, dialogs, screen overlays, and so on. It also deals with translating user input from devices like joysticks, a mouse, game controllers, and even microphones into actions the game understands. Sometimes this translation is non-trivial, such as recognizing that the speed of a vehicle should affect the sensitivity of the steering input.
- *Sound*: This includes sound effects, speech, and music. Your game must find a way to blend these as smartly as a sound engineer would and somehow leave enough CPU speed to keep the graphics system happy. Sound systems are almost always running in a separate thread, so they tend to break easily.
- *Triggers/Events*: Your game needs to have an interactive environment and not just a pretty screen saver. Game code should be written for every object that isn't static scenery. This might be as simple as intercepting a collision event and playing a sound effect, or perhaps it might be a phantom object that spawns some evil zombies when your main character steps onto a platform.

- *Objects/Attributes*: Objects like weapons have attributes such as the size of magazine they carry or charge they hold. For every attribute you'll write some code to deal with it, hopefully in one place.
- *Character Interaction/AI*: You might spend a lot of time in this code. AI can be devilishly hard to write because it's one of those things that gets better the more time you spend on it, and until enough time is spent on it the game simply isn't challenging enough or doesn't "seem" right.
- *Physics*: A real physics system is incredibly complex, when you consider the problems of creating a general collision system and static dynamics solution that runs in real time. Even integrating some middleware can take a lot longer than you'd figure, since everyone stores coordinate systems differently, especially when you consider hierarchical objects.
- *Resource Caching/Data Streaming/Compression*: Your game doesn't just spring to system RAM fully grown; it has to be loaded from CD-ROM or a hard disk. You'll want to make some good trade-offs between taking a lot of time to decompress data when moving to a new level or storing much less, although uncompressed. You might even attempt to predict what needs to be streamed in constantly to create the illusion of a completely seamless world.
- *Network Communication/Prediction*: A multiplayer game is going to have some network communications code to exchange data over a LAN or the Internet, but also what to do when that communication isn't happening at nominal rates. This is the part of your code that will defy physics and send an arrow right around a corner. "I guess that guy needed killin'," as we sometimes say in Austin.
- *Tools*: The smallest game I ever worked on had a little tool we used to create simple animations. Tools can be as easy as that or as complicated as a multiuser networked level editor like we had on Ultima IX, which took longer to write than the game. Ask yourself where every piece of data is coming from as you design your system. Most likely you'll end up creating a tool to create it, package it, or optimize it.
- *Optimization*: This is a task that usually sneaks up all programmers because they don't think they'll have to do it. That's because they never knew that the rendering engine they are so proud of must run smoothly on computers that my grandmother thinks are pieces of junk.
- *Back End*: This little bullet item needs an entire book. If your game is a client/server game, you'll need some sort of back end to manage connections to your game. This will include the login system, account administration, server monitoring, and a whole galaxy of other tools.

Asset-Based Scheduling

Asset-based schedules approach the scheduling problem by creating the list of files or components that will be shipped with the game and enumerating tasks that will be required to create each one. This works best if you are creating a port, refreshing an existing title, or you've studied the data files and gameplay of an existing product. This method bases its success on the simple fact that a certain amount of work is needed to create each asset: code, textures, models, animations, sounds, help, and so on. If you made a comprehensive list of each asset in the product, and made some reasonable estimates of the work it would take to create or port each one you'd have a good start on an accurate schedule.

Don't think for a minute that this is some kind of silver bullet. It's impossible to look at the executable for a game and calculate the man-hours per megabyte. It might be an interesting way to do it but I doubt you'll achieve a high degree of accuracy. This method is a good place to start making lists of things you'll have to create.

One of the best ways to begin making connections with your game design and actual tasks is to break things down screen-by-screen. Sketch out each screen from the intro, character selection, midgame cinematic sequences, options screens, and every permutation of game screen and every dialog that will ever show itself. Figure out what actions will move the player from screen to screen: a button click, waiting a certain amount of time, or hitting a game trigger. If you hang all these screen designs up on a wall somewhere the team gets a really good idea what the game will become. It also helps the artists and designers keep a common look and feel throughout the game as they complete each component of each screen.

As each screen or game level reaches a content complete stage, take some screen shots and print them out. Create a huge storyboard of your game somewhere the team can see it, and watch as things begin to come together. The storyboard should start with pencil sketches and napkin drawings, and be slowly replaced with the screen shots. Over time the team will see the entire game come to life in blazing color. I like doing this because it's motivating to see members of the team post new screens and it has a secondary effect of keeping those annoying producers and executives away from the programmers and artists! They just stand in front of the wall and say, "Bonuses and raises for everybody on this team. Get the project leader in my office right now, I'm giving her my BMW."

Every screen up on your wall has active areas: buttons, objects, animations, overlays, and so on. Each one of these will likely have a sound component and a piece of code that runs when it is activated. Create an exhaustive inventory of every component and figure out what tasks need to be accomplished for each one. When you are done with that, consider all forms of user input: keyboard, mouse, joystick, and gamepad. Every permutation of button press or motion that will have some effect in the game must have some code, sounds, and art that you'll need to make work. Add all those tasks to your master inventory.

As you put all these tasks in the inventory, think about the derivative tasks that you'll need to make everything work. If you have a screen with a button on it, you'll need to write the code that executes when the button is activated. You'll also need code to detect and parse user input messages, animate the button, load the button art and sound effects from a media file, and much more. Repeat this process for every task until you're sure you've hit bedrock, so to speak, and you have everything you need to make everything work.

Write Your User Guide and Cluebook

Writing your user guide and cluebook before your game is done might seem nigh impossible, and I agree. You won't be able to know what wacky things every designer, programmer, artist, and sound engineer will create on the spur of the moment. There is, however, something to be said for using the user guides and cluebooks as design documents in miniature. You can take the critical information you find there and use it to create a task list.

Take a look at any user guide of any platform title and you'll see exactly what I mean. You'll see a description of every weapon, ally, opponent, and item you can use in the game. If your design document isn't two orders of magnitude better than a twenty page platform user guide you're already in big trouble.

Cluebooks are another story since they tend to be nearly as detailed as many design documents. I seem to remember some of the cluebooks at Origin were created nearly directly from original design documents or in some cases actual data tables in C code. This makes a lot of sense, when you figure that the best way to make sure the cluebook is right is to pull information like weapons tables, damage information, or item coordinates right from the horses mouth: the game.

I might as well come out and say it: if you know enough about your game design to write the cluebook ahead of time, you'll make a perfectly accurate task inventory, and a schedule that would make any producer weep tears of joy. Now if you can only get those time estimates right!

Know Your Team and Know Your Genre

If you've ever questioned the worth of experience versus simple enthusiasm I'd like you to perform the following experiment: The next time you undertake a programming task you've never attempted in the past, make a note of how much time you spent on it. Then, delete the code and do it again. You'll likely code a better system, and in about one-half the time. Please don't do this if someone is paying you. I don't want to get angry letters. The point of this experiment is that enthusiasm will help you stay awake longer but that's about it. I'll choose the experienced programmers over the enthusiasts every day because they'll know how to solve problems specific with the game genre. While it might be possible that a senior engineer at EA Sports could be an Ultima enthusiast (yeah, right), it would be a mistake to give the EA Sports programmers the task of creating a fantasy role playing game.

Still, sometimes you have to put food on the table and take that odd project. You and your programming buddies have never seen anything like it. Make sure you give yourself some extra time on the schedule to deal with the learning curve. After all, Barbie Fashion Designer 2004 might be a lot of fun; don't knock it until you've tried it!

Creating the Schedule

The milestones and milestone descriptions are the goal. You get there by creating a detailed task inventory, assign the tasks to the people on your team, and cutting the result into four to eight week chunks. The result is sent out to the team with instructions to write their own milestone descriptions. It might sound like a redundant task to get your team to write down a description of their work when you just handed them that very thing. After all, why should a programmer describe the details of how the user interface functions are used to select new weapons when the design specification contains an entire section about weapons selection?

The programmer writes down their milestone descriptions and passes them back upstream for three reasons. First, the user interface might not come online in totality in one milestone. The programmer should write his or her own milestone descriptions with the goal of explaining exactly how the user interface will look during each milestone while the task is a work in progress. It's a bad idea to accept a milestone description of "User interface is complete" three milestones after it was started. The second reason every team member composes their own milestone descriptions is to be 100% sure they know what tasks they are expected to complete during each stage of the project. Third, if there any dependent tasks that have been scheduled too late, they'll be identified. It doesn't make any sense for an artist to work on special effects four months after the programmer completes their coding tasks.

Computer game programming is an art. This scheduling stuff bores most people to tears, and to be honest I'm one of them. It's easy to get all glassy-eyed when you look at a schedule or a milestone document, and simply accept it as your lot in life. *Don't just accept it.* You are the only one in the universe that can stand up and say, "Uh, boss, the renderer can't be written in a week."

13

Collecting the Task Inventory

The task inventory is an exhaustive list of everything that needs to be done to complete the project. You must have a functional specification that's pretty complete before you can do this. There are two groups of people you should involve in this process: the development team to be, and anyone experienced in the game genre. With any luck these groups will be the same people. If you are missing either group, or even worse you don't have either one and you have to completely wing it to get a deal signed, you're already in a very risky situation.

Different games have vastly different task inventories. Only someone experienced in the genre will have the most accurate idea about what things need to be nailed together to make the game work. If you don't have someone experienced at least in an advisory capacity, you could be in a lot of trouble.

Depending on your game genre, you should have the following experts discuss each feature and subsystem:

- *Programmers*: If it doesn't run through a piece of code, it probably doesn't need to be talked about. Almost every task will have a programming component, even if it only involves a little programmer time to install a piece of media into the game.
- *Artists*: 80% of game features will have an art component. It's usually a bad idea to get programmers (or worse, producers) to create any art for a professional product.
- *Sound*: Many games and game designers forget sound and music, which is funny because sound and music bring an emotional quality to games that nothing else can. Even a simple button click will need a sound effect.
- *Design*: Design time should accompany each major task to keep the look and feel of the game consistent.
- *Database/Web*: If your game is an MMP (massively multiplayer game) you'll likely have backend database or web components for some subsystems.
- *Writing*: This component is often lumped into the design group, and includes things like character script, help, or even web content.

Grab copies of the functional specification and drag all these experts into a meeting room for an extended stay. Go over each subsystem of the game and break it down into tasks that are no longer than one week but no shorter than a single day. There may be occasions to lump some trivial tasks together in a day or two of work. Don't fall into the trap of detailing every minute of the day. The time you will spend creating and maintaining this level of detail will smother anyone tasked with that duty, and it will also annoy the team.

When Origin Systems started using Microsoft Project to perform scheduling tasks, the Project Manager for Ultima VII fell into this trap. It was hoped that listing every minute task in exhaustive detail was the solution to consistently late projects. When the schedule was complete the

printout of the task dependency chart covered a conference room wall floor to ceiling. For those of you who remember, Ultima VII shipped months later than expected. Clearly the detailed schedule wasn't the solution to our scheduling woes.

I suggest using a project scheduling tool to create the schedule instead of something like a word processor or spreadsheet program. Most spreadsheets are incredibly bad at handling calendars elegantly. The difference between calendars and simple date mathematics is that calendars can specify things like holidays, vacations, and the like. Word processors such as Microsoft Word are great at outlining but don't handle dates at all.

As the exhaustive interviews with your experts continue, remember to gather the following information about each task:

- Time estimates for each task component (programming, art, design, sound, and so on).
- Whether the time estimate is dependant on a particular individual's special skills.
- Whether the task depends on the completion of other tasks.
- Whether the completion of this task is critical to beginning work on other areas of the project.

This process is incredibly tedious and you'll find that most of the development team will become impatient after the first hour. These meetings will go on for multiple days, or at least they should. They'll be anxious to begin "real" work instead of just talking about it. Try to have breaks during the day or perhaps only meet in the mornings; do whatever it takes to get them through it.

Experienced teams are very careful about drastically over or underestimating the time each task will take. The problems of underestimating are easy to see; the team will end up working too hard to achieve an impossible goal. Star Trek's engineer, Montgomery Scott, would disagree, but arbitrarily doubling or tripling time estimates will put your team at risk of losing the project altogether. When someone tells everyone that it will take them two days to attach one button to one screen, the team should call them on the carpet.

If everyone drastically overestimates everything, a project's estimated schedule and budget will be horribly bloated. If more than one company is bidding on the same project, and you have to assume that that's true, you might get to watch another development team get the gig.

A Few Words about Estimating Time

A famous experiment conducted on a group of programmers rated their speed and quality of a particular assignment. It turned out that some programmers literally took 100 times as long to complete the assignment. That's a frightening ratio. If John Carmack takes one week to write a new 3D engine that means it might take me one hundred weeks! That sounds about right, actually.

This finding is depressing to anyone counting on getting a game finished in time for next Christmas season. How is it possible to estimate schedules when there's such an incredible delta of productivity from one programmer to another? One clear piece of insurance is to make sure your programmers are all qualified to be on your team by conducting brutal interviews. Another good practice is to make sure everyone has some measure of experience in their problem domain. Programmers love working on new things, I know I do. Try to balance the new and the old when everyone's grabbing tasks.

The most accurate time estimates always come from someone who's got experience in the problem domain. The experienced programmer remembers many details of a task, which can't be communicated: APIs for custom libraries, algorithms, gotchas, and dead ends. If you have a task that no one on your team has ever done before, go find someone who can lend some advice. Ask another programmer on another team or perhaps even at a different company.

I've mentioned this before but it's important enough to mention it again: The minimum time estimate for any task is one day. I know it doesn't take one day to perform some trivial task like hooking up a new "OK" button to a dialog box. Instead of estimating this task at ten minutes, lump this task with some other trivial user interface jobs and give it a day. The over estimate of a few hours here and there will come in handy as certain tasks slip.

Assigning Tasks and Balancing the Schedule

Before you go any further, determine if you have the time and resources to finish your task inventory, even if it were perfectly balanced. Add up all the time for programming, art, sound, design, and other disciplines and get a total for each in weeks. You've probably got some expectation of hitting a certain code and content completion date. Take those dates and find out how many linear weeks there are between that date and your project start date. Divide that number by the number of development team members in each area and you'll know how much (or little) slack time there is in your schedule for a given team size:

- **Formula:** (Actual weeks) * (Developers) = (Developer Weeks)
- **Example:** 10 weeks * 4 developers = 40 developer weeks
- Use that formula to calculate the number of developers you'll need to complete your tasks by a certain date, or perhaps the number of actual weeks it will take for a given number of developers.

Don't assume that you can add developers without limit. A working group of developers can only reach a certain size before you have to bring a higher order or hierarchy into play to manage it. A good rule of thumb is that no manager can be effective with any more than seven reports. Four to five reports is a good number.

Managers (like technical leads or art directors) can perform tasks from the schedule, but not at the same rate as the rest of the team. Don't assign a manager any more than 30 hours of task load per week.

With the entire task list in hand, take a look at each task and assign it to a particular team member or group. Group assignments work well if your art or audio department works as a service center and the tasks are easily communicated. Sometimes the assignments are done in a group, with the entire development team present. Getting everyone to volunteer for tasks is a good idea.

Try to keep the following things in mind while the task inventory is getting split up amongst the development team:

- *Type Casting*: Some people end up doing the same type of task on every project because they are good at it. Don't assume they want to continue this trend until they retire. Try to save something new for them while getting the best person to perform each job.
- *On the Job Training*: Never assign a critical piece of technology to someone who has no experience in the area. This induces a high degree of risk.

Ultima IX was supposed to be the first Ultima in 3D. The problem was that no one in Lord British Productions (our producer group within Origin Systems) had any 3D experience whatsoever. We thought, "How hard could it be—we're all pretty smart." What a horrible mistake! Back then we had to write our own software rasterizers, polygon sorting algorithms, mesh optimizers, and object culling. This was not a job for inexperienced programmers, even if we were somewhat brilliant. It certainly wasn't a job that had a specific ship date; and the project ran late. Ultimately, all the code we wrote was thrown out because DirectX and hardware acceleration finally caught up with our efforts.

- *Spread the Love*: The fun stuff and unpopular tasks shouldn't land anywhere in high concentrations.
- *Unfactorable Technology*: Some tasks are large and are difficult to break up.

13

On Ultima VII the combat system was broken up into two parts and handed off to two different programmers. One programmer was responsible for the "core" of the combat system while the other programmer was responsible for everything else. The two programmers had a difficult time working through all the combat related issues and especially who

was responsible for what. On Ultima VIII, one of the original Ultima VII combat programmers took the entire combat system under his wing. This solution worked much better from almost every angle, as the system was much better and everyone on the team knew who was responsible for combat.

The first problem you'll see with your first pass on task assignment is that one or more people will have drastically more work assigned to them than others. I tend to balance these loads by moving the task to another person, usually the person who has the smallest task load. If you find that the tasks cannot be moved because of special skills, you'd better start combing the websites for a good contractor, which is another good solution if you have a little budget to spare. If neither of these is a workable solution you should consider moving the date or cutting features.

If someone has a long vacation or even a sabbatical you'd be wise to put that in your schedule! Microsoft Project allows you to use individual calendars where you can mark days, weeks, or even months as non-working time. Don't forget to include company holidays too, or any time your team will spend away from the project (is your company going to move offices?)

Similar to cooking a huge dinner with multiple courses, you'll have to make sure every team member finishes their tasks close to the appropriate date. This date for programmers will become your code complete milestone, and the dates for art, audio, and everything else will become the content complete milestone. You don't want to schedule some programmer to finish anything after code complete, and you may have to jump through some hoops to get that to happen.

On the Microsoft Card project I worked on the folks in Redmond wanted us to hit a particular code complete date. Their test department had a heavy schedule that summer and if the product was late it wouldn't have enough test time. We were five programmer months over the date, and we negotiated with Microsoft to add a few contractors, at their expense, to hit our code complete date on time. We did this before the contract was signed, of course, and there were no surprises in the middle of the project. If you need to hit a specific date with a particular feature set, the only thing you can do is add developers; and in our case we hired a contractor for five months.

When you're done assigning tasks and balancing the schedule, double check that you didn't screw up some task dependencies. Look for anything that expects the code to be written before the design work is complete, for example. Some of these dependencies will be too subtle to catch on your own, and you'll have to depend on your development team to identify them when they are writing their own milestone descriptions.

When you're done you'll have an exhaustive task inventory with time estimates and perhaps they'll even be assigned to development team members. Some teams make the mistake of stopping here, handing out this huge task list, and begin working. Some teams will even draw some lines in arbitrary points in the schedule and call them milestones. That's still not enough.

For one thing there isn't any time set aside for milestone acceptance. If your schedule omits this, your development team will have a harder and harder time making their milestone dates and the bug count will skyrocket out of control. Plan on spending about one week per production milestone on nothing but fixing bugs and getting the milestone accepted. Code complete is the last milestone that should need this week of acceptance, since programmers get 90% of the bugs. Solve this problem ahead of time—put real milestones in your schedule and set aside time for them.

Production Black Holes

While were thinking about inserting time in the schedule for milestone acceptance, it's a good idea to recognize that other events during the year bring production on your project to a complete halt. I've listed these in ascending order of disruption. You'd be wise to consider them:

- Annual performance reviews
- Moving to new offices
- Religious holidays
- Trade shows (E3, ECTS, GDC, and so on)

Companies like Electronic Arts schedule annual performance reviews for everyone at the same time. This is a serious distraction from production and deserves a few days of non-working time on the part of the staff and perhaps a week for each middle manager.

If your group or your entire company is moving to new digs, you should definitely schedule three to four days of downtime. Every time I've moved, the plan was to have everyone shut down work after lunch on the day of the move and pack. The move would happen and everything would magically appear in the new office. Unpacking was a short affair that would put everyone back into high gear with only a few hours of lost time. Crazy talk! Count on two or three days of lost time from the staff and one additional day or two from each manager.

All religious holidays of any faith can and should take a backseat to work. This can be particularly difficult with members of the game industry who tend to worship at the altar of EA Sports and Sony rather than more traditional venues. Still, it's wise to study your development team and determine, as I usually do, that the entire month of December is an off month (if you haven't shipped by now you're not making Christmas!). Don't get me wrong, I almost always plan for a milestone due one week before the company holidays kick in, but it's not overly aggressive.

All of the production black holes I mentioned so far are nothing compared to the burden placed on the team by trade shows. This is especially true of E3 (Electronic Entertainment Expo), when teams are invariably asked at the very last minute if they can throw a demo together.

It won't matter that many promises were made early on that the game won't be shown at E3 this year and that the team won't have to make a demo. Never believe it for a minute. Always assume that your game will need a demo, even if you only show it internally. You may be asked to go to E3 and show the game on the floor of the convention center, which will take a week out of your schedule. Other industry trade shows like GDC (Game Developer's Conference), SIGGRAPH, and ECTS (European Computer Trade Show) can also suck some development bandwidth from your team.

Each of these distractions isn't a schedule killer on its own. Well, maybe an exception should be made for the E3 demo. Still, if you attempt to make reasonable allowances for these "black holes" you'll end up with a more realistic schedule.

Breaking the Schedule into Milestones

Production milestones should be scheduled for every four to eight weeks of production time. Adding one week for milestone acceptance will put your actual milestones five to nine weeks apart. There are a few things in addition to this you should keep in mind when inserting milestones into your schedule:

- Try to put milestone due dates at a convenient time during the week. If you'd rather get some feedback from the test team quickly, don't schedule your milestones on Fridays. Mondays are bad too, because your development team will usually crunch on the weekend to make their date. I prefer Wednesdays as a good compromise.
- Don't schedule a milestone on the last day of work before an extended holiday like Christmas; try to make it at least a week before.

I usually like to schedule short milestones (four weeks of development and one week of acceptance) over longer ones, but sometimes a longer milestone is better if a significant body of work is going to complete during that time. For example, lets assume that one of your programmers is working on a new tool designed to compute visible objects, but isn't scheduled to complete it until November 1st. Your original cut placed a milestone date one week earlier. You could expect a nice increase in the framerate and smoother gameplay if you could push back the milestone to November 5th or so. Since the work will demonstrate a huge improvement to the production staff and the test department, it's a good idea to change the milestone date.

If your game signs off on December 24th, I'm sorry but you didn't make Christmas. Your game needs time to be manufactured and shipped to all the retail outlets. This can take four to six weeks and in some cases it could take a lot longer. The Microsoft Casino project had to be finished by October 5th to make its schedule slot in the manufacturing pipeline. If we missed that, that game would not have shipped before Christmas.

When the dates for your milestones are set, put the acceptance time in your schedule and find out what tasks should be counted in that milestone. If a task completes very close to the due date, I usually put the task in that milestone. It's an aggressive practice but I never compress the actual task time any more than 10% or so. If the compression is too much to take, it will wash out when the individual milestones get written. You should always expect some push back from the development team; if they don't push back at all they probably aren't carefully considering their task load.

Everything else being equal, you can't compress the actual time it takes to perform a task more than 20%. This compression usually comes in the form of simply working overtime.

It turns out that most people can accomplish tasks in aggregate more efficiently than if they tackle each task one at a time. Because the time estimates were done in a team setting, they should be relatively accurate if weighted perhaps a bit on the conservative side. That means the task will likely take a little less time to accomplish than the team estimates. When you add all of the component tasks of a particular subsystem together, you'll probably think that there's a little too much pork in the estimate. That's normal. Bring the estimate back a bit by scheduling the milestone dates aggressively and get the team to sign up for it. If you're being an ogre, they'll come at you with torches and pitchforks. Instead of being an ogre, consider being a football coach and push your team 10% harder than they think they can be pushed.

Writing the Project Milestones Document

You should have your milestone dates and a complete task inventory that gets completed during each milestone. Summarize each person's contribution to the milestone and summarize it in paragraph form. This might seem smarmy, but don't include the original time estimates in this document. You are doing this to double check the team's estimates of task groups instead of each task as a discrete unit. This might seem like a lot of extra work for whoever has control over the schedule; in truth it is an amazing amount of work.

Instead of going through this exercise some decide to stop here and simply hand out the entire task inventory to the team. One look at it and you'll watch their eyes glaze right over lost in the magnitude of the next eighteen to thirty six months of their professional lives. When these tasks are converted into summaries that describe the goal of their work, things begin to take on a clear focus.

The milestone descriptions should focus on the functional goal of the work instead of the details of a particular implementation. If the timeline for a milestone begins to run tight one of the best strategies is to cut to a simpler solution rather than force a difficult solution into a smaller timeframe. Never forget that programmers really enjoy solving difficult problems and will sometimes choose them over stock solutions that have been written by everyone else.

The result of all this work is a milestone document that describes the following things:

- The major accomplishments expected of the team during the production dates and a risk assessment.
- A due date that takes into account enough time for milestone acceptance.
- A list of deliverables.
- Non-subjective tests that the deliverables must pass to gain acceptance.
- A list of contributors to the production work and a paragraph or bullet list summary of what they need to finish before the milestone due date.

Writing the Individual Milestones Document

Now comes the hardest part. You've just finished what has seemed like interminable hours of meetings where the entire team has questioned and re-questioned each microscopic task of the project. If there was ever a time they wanted to get away from Microsoft Word and start typing curly braces and semicolons this is it. Enthusiasm for more planning is going to be at an all time low, because your team wants to be let loose on the first milestone. Whatever you do, don't let them. Not yet!

The last and by far the most critical part of the planning phase is still coming: The team must write their detailed milestone descriptions using the project milestone document as a guide. Their job is to provide one or perhaps two more levels of detail to what they see in the project milestone document.

Yours truly included, programmers are some of the worst writers and communicators on the planet. I couldn't have written this book without my editors and you certainly couldn't have read it. Be prepared to push on them to give you the detailed milestone descriptions. It is the last chance the team has to catch huge mistakes in the schedule and hopefully save some of those potential lost weekends. As they write about each goal, everyone should keep some things in mind:

- Does the amount of work in the milestone seem too light or too onerous? If a milestone seems light they should double check what's expected in the following milestone.
- What about dependent tasks? Everyone should double check that anything that must be complete before they begin is described in the milestone document.
- Does the task match the skills of the person? Sometimes as a schedule is balanced to end work on or about a particular date, a person might be mistakenly assigned something they shouldn't.
- Does the order of work seem right? It is sometimes possible that ordering the work differently is more efficient.
- Do the detailed descriptions explain a development goal? Goals say nothing of a particular implementation, and this gives the team more freedom.
- Are the detailed descriptions actually detailed enough? They shouldn't gloss over features with a simple sentence. Even button clicks should be mentioned or at least referenced by citing a particular section of the functional specification.

You'll find that some team members will want to review the original task inventory as they double check their milestone assignments. That's fine, of course. You don't want to hide anything or attempt to fool the development team into believing they can do the impossible. They'll hang you for pulling tricks like that, and you'll deserve it.

There's a subtle thing going on here as you might begin to suspect. Trust me. As the team writes verbal descriptions of what they hope to accomplish on each milestone, they realize that they are making a commitment to themselves and their team. They'll study their promises carefully before submitting it to the team at large for final approval. So far I haven't seen anyone take this process lightly. I believe that you never achieve this level of seriousness until you get everyone on the team to write his or her own milestones.

There's another benefit: When someone explains in their own words what they will accomplish for each milestone you can be sure that everyone is on the same page. How many post mortems have you read that put "team communications" at the top of the big problems? I'm not telling you that this process will remove any and all communications problems, but it will make a huge dent in them.

One More Thing Before You Release the Hounds

As painful as this sounds, you have one more planning meeting to attend. Luckily it's a short one. Drag the experts back into the conference room to review the entire milestones document as a group, including the individual milestone descriptions. Hold the plan up to the light and see if anything shines though. Everyone should make sure that someone didn't gloss over something that deserves more attention. Make sure that everyone understands that once everyone signs off on the milestones document it is considered a team commitment. It usually helps if everyone understands that company milestones are serious business and missed milestones should shake everyone down to their foundations.

A dear friend of mine, Ellen Guon Beeman, had a hard line policy at her company, Illusion Machines, an independent third-party development studio in Austin, Texas. Anyone who caused the company to miss any two project milestones was sent packing. This might seem cruel and unusual, but in truth it was put in place because missing a milestone usually meant missing payroll. Most game company employees I know live paycheck to paycheck and a delayed paycheck meant no food on the table. When that happens it further hurts productivity which means longer hours to make up for that which is a vicious cycle. If more employees treated project schedules and milestones with that level of seriousness, our industry would be an amazing place to work. Oh, Ellen's company never missed a milestone.

You'll finally cover the tasks in content complete, the last milestone with new tasks, and everyone will look around the conference table and wonder if all that planning was worth it. They'll find out when they hit that content complete date with a reasonable bug count and an easy glide all the way to release.

So what are you waiting for? Release the hounds. Wait, I mean release the programmers!

Getting It Right

Back when I worked at Origin I realized that handing out a huge task list to the team was counter productive. Looking at my task list, I couldn't judge the scope of the work because it was too big to look at all at once. For anyone who saw the task list of Ultima VII or Ultima VIII they needn't bother traveling to the Grand Canyon. Cross that, I'll bet the Grand Canyon is much prettier, unless it was your job to fill it in with a hand shovel.

It's not enough to discover the tasks and put time estimates on them, after all. You have to be sure your team is up to the challenge. The only way everyone can be sure is to have everyone take those nasty task lists and specification documents and put their assignments down in their own words.

After all, who'd be crazy enough to write a milestone description that describes something as impossible as filling the Grand Canyon with pea gravel using nothing more than a hand shovel?

Oh, and please get it done before Christmas!

Chapter 14

Everything (You Hate) to Know About Testing

When you've finished reading this chapter you'll have some great tools to create or improve your testing process. You'll learn about creating and using test plans, automated testing, and when to perform certain kinds of tests. You'll also learn who does the testing and what makes them tick, how to keep the development team and the test team from brawling, and most importantly, how to predict your ship date from statistical analysis of your bug database.

Why Are Games Buggy?

Most avid game players complain about the quality of software in the games industry. Even the very best games have bugs you can find easily for a laugh. Some bugs are so catastrophic, and yet simple to reproduce that it makes you wonder how in the hell they made it through the testing lab. Are the programmers and testers just a bunch of losers that have no idea what they are doing? The answer is absolutely not.

Every programmer and tester I've worked with were passionate about the quality of their products, and worked extremely hard to make the very best games they could. So what gives? If everyone is so excited about quality why do our games crash?

Reason 1: The Team Never Saw the Bug Reproduce

This has nothing to do with bugs getting it on with cheesy saxophone music in the background. Reproducing a bug involves identifying the *exact* procedure a tester uses to get the bug to raise its head in your game. If the team never saw a bug reproduce in their test lab, the bug will become an undocumented feature, much to the happiness of the competition. With significant application of time, money, and legions of testers it is possible to get rid of this problem and create a completely bug free game. In some industries such as health care, aerospace, and finance, this approach had better work because lives or money can be at stake.

I know a programmer who worked at a company that develops software for real time financial transactions, who I will call Scott—not his real name of course. He was a new guy and he'd just finished upgrading one of the older modules and it went online at 9:00 a.m. the next day. After a few hours, one of the auditing subsystems caught an enormous error and shut the offending module down, alerting everyone and their dog that something heinous was afoot. After the dust settled, Scott was called into conference with all the honchos. Scott was notified that in the three hours the module was live, the company lost enough money to pay his annual salary. Needless to say, Scott wasn't the only person called into conference that day with the expected string of management hierarchy, because any number of people should have caught this bug. Scott may have typed in the proper sequence of characters that created this horrible flaw in the code, but it was the lack of process that lost the company Scott's annual salary. The upside is that both the company and Scott learned a valuable lesson and everyone was motivated to change the process and give a higher priority to testing.

When it comes to games, no one will likely lose money, their life, or their property playing a game. Well, with the possible exception of all those folks paying out reams of cash for time on EverQuest—they're a special case. However, more and more gamers are expecting their games to be error free. A few years ago Disney had a horrible time with huge complaints from parents who had purchased one of its Lion King games. This decidedly non-technical audience reminds us that not every purchaser of a game is going to tolerate patches, and other configuration troubleshooting sessions to make things work.

Game testing procedures can be extremely tight or extremely loose, depending on the company and the people. It goes without saying that loose testing procedures will cause bugs, sometimes really embarrassing ones, to fall through the cracks.

Reason 2: The Team Decided to Leave the Bug in Its Natural Habitat

Sacrilege, you say! Why would any self-respecting team actually leave a known flaw in any application? Believe it or not, there are good reasons. There are also some excuses. The reason almost always involves time. I would argue that almost any bug can be addressed with enough time and effort applied to it, but time doesn't come free of charge. Time tends to drain the company coffers, adds shelf life to your competitors' products, or worse, moves your manufacturing slot to January!

Teams decide to leave bugs where they lie because they compared the time and costs required to fix them with the costs or risks associated with leaving the bugs. Here's an example of a bug like this:

"Screen was in 1280x1024 resolution, started the game and Alt-Tabbed back to desktop, desktop was in 1024x768. Machine: 833 Mhz IBM Thinkpad 384 MB RAM DX 8.1 onboard S3 graphics chipset attached to external monitor Sony G500. The true bug is that game doesn't launch in this resolution on my Dell."

This problem isn't exactly catastrophic, and it only affected machines using the S3 graphics chipset. Sometimes bugs fall into the *corner case* category, which means that they are highly unlikely for someone using the software to experience the bug because of the odd nature of the reproducible steps. Here's an example:

1. Open the game in full screen mode and start your last saved mission.
2. Open game options dialog.
3. Click the OK button of the game options dialog, and immediately afterward press Alt-Tab to minimize the game.
4. Restore the game window back to full screen mode.
5. Notice that most of the game textures have severe artwork corruption.

It turns out that the user had to press Alt-Tab in an extremely short amount of time after hitting the OK button—something like 150ms. Anyone who saw this bug was specifically looking for it, because it didn't fit into the common interface usage profile of people playing the game normally. The team decided that there were plenty of other bugs that deserved attention. In a perfect world there would be enough time to fix everything, but in truth time simply does not exist in sufficient quantity to accomplish that task.

Any modern piece of software is extremely complicated and has hundreds of closely interacting parts. This easily creates the possibility that an observed flaw in the application is actually hiding a truly nasty bug. The team made a choice between the lesser of two evils.

Now that you've seen some unfortunate but reasonable conditions under which known flaws can remain in computer software, compare them to their lesser cousins: *the excuses*. A classic excuse is not testing the application on the most recent operating system release. The opposite end of that spectrum is failure to bench test the game on the minimum machine configuration or common hardware configurations. Perhaps the saddest of all is a lack of communication between the designers and the testers. If the designers don't tell the testers about every feature of the game, how can they test it? If you create a rigorous testing process and consistently strive to improve it you will minimize the existence of these problems.

Testing is typically the bastard stepchild for many developers. It's like the paper you don't write until the last second and then you decide to wing it. This of course turns the end process into an organization and scheduling nightmare. So if there is any lesson to this chapter it's teaching all game developers how to integrate the testing process into every aspect of your development process. You will *hate* having to do this, but you will *love* the professionalism, headache savings, and time you gain by doing things the way I learned to from my experiences with Microsoft, Mattel, and at Origin. Testing is among a handful of processes that separate successful developers from the ones who never make it.

Test Plans

The test plan is an exhaustive restatement of the design document. It goes without saying that if you don't have a design document you simply can't create a reasonable test plan. I can already hear people out there tapping away nasty emails to me saying, "Design documents? "We don't need no steenkin design documents!" They probably never had to write one, and they are writing fantastic games from the seat of their pants and are quite happy about it. More power to you. I wish I were that good, or perhaps I should say I wish I was that lucky. Perhaps those same people sending me smug emails are also the people who've worked every weekend for the last year on a project that is "Still in Beta, but tracking well toward the ship date." I can truthfully say that any project I've worked on that had detailed design documents and its associated test plan shipped on time and on budget. As of this writing, that is five projects over the last five years, creating a consecutive on time ship record. I'm not bragging. I'm trying to save you from interminable crunch mode, lost weekends, and buggy games.

I should also mention that my product development teams worked little overtime, too. I attribute that success to the talent of the team, surely, but also to their hard line organization. Test plans are a big part of that organization. We use six different kinds of formal testing in our projects:

- *Functional Tests*: These are checklists that touch each feature of the game as it was intended by the designers to be touched.
- *Stress Tests*: These tests are written by truly the most evil and imaginative testers on the team and include crazy things like setting Ethernet cables on fire to see how the application will react.
- *Playability Tests*: These tests focus on the attitude of the player about game features (sound, graphics, design, and so on) and how they compare to other games.

- *Usability Tests*: These tests focus primarily on the user interface and the accessibility of the features and controls of the game by the intended audience.
- *Configuration Tests*: These tests focus on running the games under all possible hardware and operating system configurations.

Functional Tests

If the design document is a blueprint for the developers to create a game, the functional test is a series of checklists to determine how close the resulting application comes to the construction ideal. If you ever build a house you'll be presented with a set of blueprints and perhaps some architectural sketches to give you an idea of what the real house will look like and how its subsystems will function when it is complete. As the house is built, the builder will ask you to perform a "walk-through" from time to time so you catch any misinterpretations as they happen. As you check each part of the house, you perform a functional test against the blueprints. If the blueprints specified a three-car garage, you'll probably object to finding a two-car garage during your inspection. The same process works for evaluating the various construction phases of software.

Functional tests are customized heavily for each game, but they do have a common format. You should remember that functional tests are going to be handed out to testers that have never seen the game. The test document should include exhaustive details on what is being tested, how to begin the test, exactly what steps to follow to complete the test, and how to record the results. If you want to see the entire functional test for a game we need to focus on a really simple game such as Roulette. You may not know every detail but you know that you bet on a number, and if the ball lands on the number you get paid. Sounds simple, right? It's more complicated than you'd thing, so let's look at an example of the functional test for a game of roulette.

Description:

Wagers are made by placing your chips on the table in positions correlating with where you expect the ball to land on the wheel. You can bet on color, odd/even, single numbers (including zero/double zero), combinations of numbers, or groups of numbers.

The Roulette operator known as the banker, croupier, or dealer spins the wheel after wagers have been placed and releases an ivory marble into the bowl in the opposite direction of the spinning wheel. When the spinning wheel slows, the marble will come to rest in one of the compartments that will be the winning bet. The marker is placed on the Roulette Table's corresponding number to where the ball landed and wagers are paid appropriately before removing the marker and moving on to the next game.

Gameflow/Interface:

- *SPIN* Spins the roulette wheel (see payoff table below)
- Notice that the maximum pause between pushing the spin button and the release of the ball is less than 1.5 seconds.
- Notice that the ball always makes at least 4 orbits before beginning to bounce around.
- All animations are synced properly with each other, there is no jumping or skipping.
- Notice that the ball lands in the correct pocket.
- Speech plays and informs player of spin result.
- *REPEAT BET*: After a spin and bets are resolved, pressing this button will duplicate the bets made in the previous round
- *EXIT*: Returns player to appropriate casino floor.
- Roulette Wheel Close up
- Displays the cup where the ball eventually lands.
- Displays the total of all bets on the table.
- Displays winnings after a spin.
- The close up image matches the wheel shown on the table.
- Number Tracking (chart located on the top right corner) keeps track of number and color of past spins.

Betting :

- Bet placed before spin.
- Bankroll is decreased by the appropriate amount of the bet.
- Maximum total of all bets on the table is $1,000.00.
- Able to bet by left-clicking on chip denomination and left-clicking betting spot.
- Able to remove bet by right-clicking on chip.
- Tool tip displays bet amount and payout odds for ANY chip placed on the betting table.
- The table clearing animation happens in the following way:
- The losing bets are drawn translucently and begin to disappear from left to right.
- The winning bets are paid off individually, with a sound effect.
- Each players winning chips are slid over the felt towards them.
- At each stage of the animation, the OK button can be hit and the animation will abort; clearing the table instantly.

Bet	Type	Return	
1 to 18	Win: number is 1 through 18	Payoff is 1-1 (e.g., $1 bet = $2 return)	Bankroll is adjusted correctly
19 to 36	Win: number is 19 through 36	Payoff is 1-1 (e.g., $1 bet = $2 return)	Bankroll is adjusted correctly
Even	Win: number is EVEN	Payoff is 1-1 (e.g., $1 bet = $2 return)	Bankroll is adjusted correctly
Odd	Win: number is ODD	Payoff is 1-1 (e.g., $1 bet = $2 return)	Bankroll is adjusted correctly
RED	Win: number is RED	Payoff is 1-1 (e.g., $1 bet = $2 return)	Bankroll is adjusted correctly
BLACK	Win: number is BLACK	Payoff is 1-1 (e.g.,` $1 bet = $2 return)	Bankroll is adjusted correctly
1st 12	Win: number is 1-12	Payoff is 2-1 (e.g., $1 bet = $3 return)	Bankroll is adjusted correctly
2nd 12	Win: number is 13-24	Payoff is 2-1 (e.g., $1 bet = $3 return)	Bankroll is adjusted correctly
3rd 12	Win: number is 25-36	Payoff is 2-1 (e.g., $1 bet = $3 return)	Bankroll is adjusted correctly
Column Bet 1 (1-34)	Win: number is in column beginning with 1 ending with 34	Payoff is 2-1 (e.g., $1 bet = $3 return)	Bankroll is adjusted correctly
Column Bet 2 (2-35)	Win: number is in column beginning with 2 ending with 35	Payoff is 2-1 (e.g., $1 bet = $3 return)	Bankroll is adjusted correctly
Column Bet 3 (3-36)	Win: number is in column beginning with 3 ending with 36	Payoff is 2-1 (e.g., $1 bet = $3 return)	Bankroll is adjusted correctly
Line Bet Placed on the top edge of betting table between 2 numbers (e.g., corner of 21 24 line bet covers #19-24)	Win: number is in either row touching chip (e.g., corner of 21 and 24 line bet wins on #19-24)	Payoff is 5-1 (e.g., $1 bet = $6 return)	Bankroll is adjusted correctly
Five Number Bet (only 1 spot that is a 5 number bet on the table) Placed on the top edge of betting table at the corner of 3 and 00	Win: number is 1,2,3,0,00	Payoff is 6-1 (e.g., $1 bet = $7 return)	Bankroll is adjusted correctly

(Continued)

Bet	Type	Return	
Corner Bets Placed at the corner of 4	Win: number is one of the 4 numbers the chip touches	Payoff is 8-1 (e.g., $1 bet = $9 return) numbers	Bankroll is adjusted correctly
Street Bet (Trio Bet) Placed on the top edge of betting table along the side of a single number (e.g., edge of 15 covers numbers 13,14,15)	Win: number is in the same row as chip (e.g., edge of 15 covers 13,14,15)	Payoff is 11-1 (e.g., $ 1 bet = $12 return)	Bankroll is adjusted correctly
Split bet Bet is placed on the edge	Win : number is one of the 2 numbers that the chip	Payoff is 17-1 (e.g., $1 bet =touches $18 return)	Bankroll is adjusted correctly
Straight Bet Bet is placed on a single number	Win: Exact number	Payoff is 35 to 1 (e.g., $1 bet = $36 return)	Bankroll is adjust correctly

Shortcut Keys :

- Testing Keys
- 'H' brings up a dialog that will set the next winning number. NOTE: Activate this dialog only *after* all bets have been placed on the table.
- 'W' tests the wheel balance. See the results in **Roulette Test.txt**.
- 'B' places $1 on each betting location on the table. This is useful for checking correct payouts. NOTE: There is a significant pause (6-7 seconds) while waiting for all the bets to be placed.
- Enter - Clear Table
- S - Spin Wheel
- Up Arrow - Same Bet
- Down Arrow- retract last bet

The functional test starts with some user education, again making no assumptions regarding the background of the tester. The person performing the test has perhaps heard of roulette, but has never played it. Even if they are a roulette expert, they've never before played your implementation of it and will need some basic instruction to get the game started.

The gameflow/interface section goes into detail about how the game is played and what to expect. The checklist describes animations, sound effects, and speech the tester should experience. Many functional tests are like this one and are order dependant, which means that the tester must complete each test in a specific order. It would be a good idea to specify that fact for the tester somewhere in the document; if a subsystem is broken the tester might be able to continue the functional test on a different subsystem. It is extremely important that this is made absolutely clear in the document, since bad test results on one subsystem may invalidate any later tests. The tester will usually have a good idea that something is wrong when all the tests fail one after the other and will likely abort the remaining checklists.

Take a look at the next section containing tests for bets and win results. This is a good example of a complete test of all the betting and winning combinations possible on a roulette table. There are 18 sections corresponding to the different payouts on a roulette table. If you are a roulette expert you'll remember that there are over 200 places to bet on a roulette table. Should each betting location be exposed in the functional test? I'm pretty sure that if a tester was forced to place a bet on each betting location in turn and wait the 15 seconds or so for the roulette ball to land in a pocket over 200 times, there would certainly be a killing spree. The tester's time is extremely valuable, and functional tests should always strive to be constructed to save them time while maximizing the testing coverage.

The goal of a functional test is to verify the development plan against the bits created by the development team. This kind of verification takes a human mind since it is frequently subjective. If the development plan calls for "realistic animations of spinning roulette wheel," a human being must make that judgement. I'd expect when automated testing gets good enough to make those calls we'll probably have automated software development as well and both automated systems could argue at 10Ghz over whether the animation is realistic enough. You and I will be sitting on the beach somewhere either collecting royalties or hunting for food.

Stress Testing

Stress tests try to push the application to run at or past the edge of reasonable operating limits. Many issues found after running all the stress tests are fixed, but some are relegated to the "readme" file or a troubleshooting FAQ on a web site somewhere. You can assume that if your game sells a few million copies (lucky you) that the one crazy bug that happens after a million hours of gameplay will happen to some poor sod every few hours. Hopefully, not to the same person! If it's going to happen, you should certainly understand how bad it can be and whether a workaround will exist.

Stress tests should test the application under limited system memory. Low memory is trickier on Windows applications, since the virtual memory manager swaps under used memory pages out to the hard disk. Many games wisely pre-allocate all memory requirements when the game initializes, or perhaps at the beginning of a mission or level. A role playing game uses memory in a much more dynamic fashion. Continuous worlds and freedom of character movement require sophisticated resource caching, which can result in unpredictable memory usage. Any memory leaks quickly become a problem in this type of game. Cracking the computer case and removing memory is the very best test of any low memory configuration. Developers have a little more trouble debugging memory issues, since the development environment takes significantly more memory than the standalone application. For them, the best alternative is to find or write a little application that simply "eats" a specified block of memory, and then runs the application.

Similar to the low system RAM tests, you can also run stress tests in low VRAM situations. That is, of course, except for all you Xbox developers out there because the Xbox has a unified memory architecture (you lucky bastards).

The Windows Task manager might not be telling you the truth about how much memory you are using. Under some memory management schemes, MFC included, freed memory is not reflected in the task manager immediately. If you want to see how much memory your game is really using, minimize it. Any freed memory will be reflected in the task manager.

Stress tests should include any use of secondary storage, whether it is PC disk space or console memory units. Tests should include initializing the game with little or no extra secondary storage space. You should also test to see what happens if secondary storage space is extinguished while the game is running. PC game developers should also include tests of other applications sucking up the hard drive space while your game is running.

Most games expect certain hardware, such as input devices and sound cards. Stress tests should always include a suite where expected hardware requirements are not available when the game initializes. Some programmers forget that fact when writing code, and simply assume that everyone is going to have a sound card installed in their PC. While it may be rare to find a PC without a sound card, it is probably a lot less rare to find that someone simply disabled his or her sound card in the current hardware configuration. Doing that is equivalent to removing the hardware, and any game should at least make an effort to detect missing hardware during initialization.

Properly handing the case where the user changes the hardware configuration while the game is running is, I believe, a little too much to ask for any developer, and would certainly fall under the "Doctor, doctor, it hurts when I disable my video card while the game is running." No kidding, you doofus.

One caveat to this for PC developers is properly handling someone changing the video resolution or bit depth during game play. This can be a real pain in the ass, but it's important to support because what's happening in the background is a lost surface (or texture) is detected during the render loop. If a surface is lost, you must write code to restore it, because there are tons of possibilities where this can occur. A screen saver that uses Direct3D to display psychedelic pictures will cause any other DirectX based game to lose surfaces if it ever takes control. If the programmers didn't properly detect and restore those lost surfaces the game will crash. It's the kind of thing that makes PC programmers flock to console development. Tests to cover this should include running DirectX based screen savers in the background, minimizing the game and changing the desktop bit depth or resolution, and flipping back and forth from windowed mode (if you attempt to support running in windowed mode, which can make your life much harder), to full screen mode.

Video bit depth is serious business for Windows games that run in windowed mode. DirectX applications will not run in 8-bit or 24-bit windowed modes on some video cards. Most games simply default to full screen when they detect they can't run in a window. This also goes for game windows that use a full 800x600 window. Customers running in 640x480 or 800x600 do not have the screen real estate to run in windowed mode, requiring your application to detect it and default to full screen.

The last topic in stressing limited resource availability could clearly fill an entire book all by itself—network connectivity. I spoke earlier of setting the Ethernet cable on fire, and while that is a valid test it would perhaps be easier for your IT group if you simply unplugged it before and during game play. Other tests should include anything you can do to force limits on the size and quality of the bandwidth.

All applications should detect limited resources when they initialize. Every stress test should establish the application's ability to detect a lack of any kind of resource: secondary storage, CPU speed, or other hardware. If a needed resource is lacking when the game initializes, the application should notify the user and perhaps even give them a solution. "The system is low on memory—close some applications and try again." This is the bare minimum and every game should do this—no excuses.

Detecting and handling dwindling resources while the game is running is much, much harder. It is much rarer for a game to elegantly handle all out of memory conditions or file I/O errors. Stress tests can and should test these scenarios, especially since it is important to understand how your game will fail. Most likely the user will have to go back to a saved game, resulting in some lost time. Certainly if the programming team is going to write code to handle these issues properly, specific stress tests should be added to the test plan to ensure that they actually succeed.

Stress testing can also push the game interface. Going bananas on the keyboard, mouse, or joystick buttons can expose weaknesses in the code or game design. Imagine a game that can support only a few simultaneous sound effects, but also plays a short sound effect when a key is pressed. Mashing tons of keys at the same time may expose a weakness if the programmer wasn't thoughtful enough to check how many sound effects are currently playing before launching a new one. This is a case where stress testing will expose a weakness that is important to fix.

Playability Testing

A game that is playable is one that captures and keeps the attention of the target audience and gives them great entertainment. One way to perform this test is to find people who are hard core players and knowledgeable about the game genre and have them play the game for an hour and answer questions about it and themselves. By the way, there is such as thing as a hard core solitaire player—I've met them.

A typical questionnaire will ask the person about their profession, how many games they play, which games in particular they've played lately, and their hardware. The results of the questionnaire allow the proctors of the test to tabulate the results based on similarities of player profile. Imagine you are working on a game with a wide audience such as a trivia game. If your playability tests measured the age brackets of your players you may very well find that older players enjoyed the game but gave the user interface low marks. You might use this information to increase your font size to make your user interface easier to read.

After the personal demographics, a playability test will ask users what they thought about the game design: the graphics, sound, tutorials, online help, in short, about every major subsystem. It is common to have playability tests performed not only on your game in production, but published versions of your competitor's games. It can give you excellent ideas about how to improve upon your design.

Playability testing is a deep exploration of the game. Each person playing the game may spend a few hours with it and some extra time filling out the questionnaire. It is pretty common for the developers to help people find the features and by giving hints and making themselves available for questions. Remember that the idea is to expose the testers to as much of the game as possible, so they can compare it to other games they've played.

Console companies will also do playability testing on your product as well. Since most console companies fear an overall weak library of games will destroy their product, they are careful to evaluate all games for their systems. They will rigorously test your game for quality and playability ideas.

Usability Testing

Usability testing specifically tests the discoverability of the user interface and the mechanics of the game. The people taking part in the test are given a list of tasks to perform in the game and absolutely no instructions on how to go about completing those tasks. It may sound odd, but it accurately recreates the exact conditions of someone playing the game for the first time. Absolutely no interaction between the developers and testers is allowed, since that would invalidate the test. Watching someone attempt to perform a task in the game, and failing to do so, is extremely educational for developers.

The first leisure title I ever worked on was Microsoft Casino. I thought this would be a piece of cake after working on the Ultima series at Origin Systems; boy was I ever wrong. Creating a discoverable game interface for my target audience, which turned out to be people my parent's age, was much more challenging than I thought it was. Microsoft has fantastic usability labs and working with them was my first experience with this kind of testing. When the first usability tests came back negative, I thought surely something had gone wrong in the test. I simply couldn't believe that people couldn't figure out how to place bets in Blackjack, our first working game. All you had to do was click on the table! Frustrated, I took the weekend off and went to see my parents in North Texas. I was so proud to show my Mom the game I made, because she loves casino games. Sure enough I watched her struggle to figure out how to place the initial bet. I had to tell her how to do it, and I never doubted the usability labs again.

You can learn a lot by quietly watching people play your game. Even if you don't have formal usability testing in your company you can perform some simple experiments yourself by grabbing some passerby on their way back from the bathroom. Invite them into your office and tell them to perform some task in your game, and watch them do it. Their first choice of how they think it is supposed to work will usually surprise you, but there is almost always a subconscious reason they make that choice. It may be impossible for them to tell you why they thought it should work, but after sampling five or six people it may very well become clear that you've either designed something brilliant or you've gone down the wrong track.

Configuration Testing

Configuration testing is critical in PC products because of the wide range of processors, BIOSs, video cards, sound cards, and every other kind of wacky peripherals people choose to install in their systems. Some of these peripherals can be quite widespread and yet have odd failure cases that you'll only find in configuration testing. Before you console developers skip to the next section, remember that there are many after market peripheral companies making all kinds of interesting things for consoles: fishing poles, gloves, dance pads, and even stationary bicycles. You'd be wise to take some of these peripherals into account when you test your game.

Generally the configuration tests will expose particular weaknesses in compatibility between your application and drivers that were shipped stock with video and sound cards. That's why it's important to test with drivers that shipped with the original equipment and the most recent drivers, so that certain problems can be identified and solved by upgrading the drivers. This information is valuable for customer service and for FAQs on your company Web site.

Occasionally, you'll find a real incompatibility that needs to be addressed. One of the games I worked on was having odd display problems on 3DFx cards (may they rest in peace). You'd look at an animating sprite and see it appear as if the vertical sync had gone out of a TV set. After consulting with the 3DFx engineers we discovered that there was a limitation on VRAM surface dimensions; they couldn't have a height to width ratio higher than 8:1. Go figure. We reworked the organization of our animating sprites and all was good. The scary part of this story is that none of the developers on the team had a VooDoo card installed because (to put it mildly) they preferred other video cards. VooDoo cards were installed in 20% to 30% of our user base, which would have resulted in crushing return rates had the flaw escaped the configuration testing.

Another part of configuration testing is measuring performance, which can be extremely difficult to solve if it's a problem, so early detection is very important. When our development team was working on Bicycle Casino and Bicycle Card, performance was a huge issue on our minimum specification machine, mostly due to the size of the animations we were cramming through only 2Mb of VRAM. The CPU target was a 166MHz Pentium, a machine that was 5 to 6 years old at that point in time. Our competition, Sierra's Hoyle games ran fine on 133MHz machines because they had lighter 8-bit animations. Throughout the entire development cycle we made incremental improvements to the performance. Had we delayed performance testing to the end of the development cycle we would not have had time to make as many improvements, and our game would have been unplayable on many machines for our projected target audience.

Take great pains to measure performance carefully, and measure it exactly the same way following an exact checklist. This is especially true on the PC platform where many things can adversely affect performance, which have nothing to do with your game. In our performance testing we create big spreadsheets of exact timing information for each section of the game. As programmers make modifications to fix performance problems, we make sure to re-run these tests in exactly the same way so the programmers will know if their efforts were successful. Keep a running record of the changes and the resulting changes in performance. They may be able to give the programmers additional clues as to what they can do to enhance performance. It's not enough to just figure you'll optimize this or that. One can actually over-optimize, by pursuing optimizations where, while welcomed, don't add anything to the overall performance of the product.

Testing your game against Beta versions of operating systems is also a really good idea. While a game is in development it is common for programmers (and pretty much everyone else) to forgo installing the latest Beta operating system release because it takes time and might cause weird system behavior. Since most developers will work on an established operating system release. it is unlikely that they will find incompatibilities during development. Make sure you have one machine in your test lab that has the latest pre-release OS from Microsoft.

When Microsoft released Beta versions of Windows XP Home it was quickly discovered that when the OS was installed with the default configuration it was illegal for an application to write to the hard drive under the Program Files directory. Applications developers had to store their saved game data under the Documents and Settings/userid/Application Data directory tree. Anyone who was developing an application for Christmas 2001 release, and who didn't test against Windows XP Home would have crashed under that operating system.

Scheduling Testing

Scheduling the testing effort can be tricky. If you schedule testing too late, the development team won't have enough time to react to critical issues found by the test team. If you schedule it too early, the test team will flood the team with bugs that are related to incomplete features. How do you decide? The truth is that testing is always present in some form throughout the life of the development cycle. At the very beginning, a senior tester should be involved in giving feedback about the game design, machine requirements, and development schedule. Most of the testers I know are quite sensitive to game design issues and can be invaluable in creating a brand new game or refreshing an existing title. Many of the luminaries of the industry started their careers in testing, so take advantage of their expertise. In fact, the guy that started the company I work for used to be a tester for Origin Systems.

When the game design document is in final draft, a few testers should be assigned to the product for a month to create the test plan. You'll be surprised how many potential issues they'll find having nothing more than some PDF files and notebook paper. Usually their feedback will be used to tweak the design document before it gets laminated.

The first usability test can actually occur before the first build. The sketches of the user interface design can be presented to usability testers in the place of an actual build. This is especially important when the development team is curious about different design directions of a user interface or tutorial. Of course, someone will have to be in the testing room interacting with the tester since there is nothing more than sketches on the table! The other rules still apply, of course. Don't give the subject any clues about how something is supposed to work.

At some point the development team will begin submitting builds to a small test team whose main focus will be to check the build against the milestone acceptance criteria. The initial builds will have tons of broken code and missing features, which is why you want a small test team until a critical mass of working code begins to emerge. The small test team is working on functional tests at this stage. The test team grows in step with the development effort, reaching a maximum size as the team reaches the milestone before code complete. This is an excellent time to submit a good build for a full test suite: playability, usability, stress, and configuration. In the best of all possible worlds, you'll want to run each of these tests once just before code complete, and once just before content complete. This will give the development team some assurance that they've made some improvements to the game based on the first full test pass. It will also ensure they haven't broken something important.

Automated Testing

When I described functional test checklists I mentioned that it was unreasonable to expect a tester to be physically and mentally capable of a 100% test of every game feature and permutations of those features in combination. Most games are extremely complicated and tend to be peppered with random events to make the game experience interesting. Wise developers and test teams create their game with special instrumentation, test tools, and event playback and recording systems to help the test team run through an immense test suite in a fraction of the time.

An excellent example of this is the problem of verifying the payout and animations of a video poker machine. One card combination in particular has about a 1:40,000 chance of appearing (the royal flush in five-card draw). This isn't even an extreme case—some slot machines have a very small chance, 1:500,000, of hitting the jackpot. This situation is far from unique because almost every game is based on the outcome of combinations of random events and the input of a player, which is essentially random.

The first set of test tools we created to help the Microsoft test team were simple dialog boxes to preset the outcome of any roll of the dice or shuffle of the deck. The testers would use the tools (or *cheats*, as they are called if they aren't removed from the release build), to be able to run through their functional tests without relying on random events. To be honest this made testing these games possible, not just convenient. The test team wanted more in the next version, and after talking with them we understood that what they were asking for was an interface to our game systems that basically ran the functional tests automatically.

We created a playback/record system in our game based on user input events, and the testers at Microsoft wrote a Visual Basic tool to run the recorded scripts in batches and compare the output to known good builds. Take a look at a small piece of the test script for blackjack:

```
//
// Automation RECORD file
//
// This script file was generated via
// the automated record/playback feature
//
// Product:        Casino 2.0
// Build:          02.02.07.0052
// Filename:       d:\automation tool\scripts\bj.dbg.txt
// Date:           04/11/2003
// Time:           10:25:22
//
// All comments are proceeded by '//'
// Commands end with ';'
//

0000 : RANDOM_SEED("1018545922");
0000 : SET_START_BALANCE("999900.00");
0000 : LEAN("1");
0000 : ADD_SCREEN("SCREEN_BLACKJACK");
0000 : RANDOM_SEED("1018545930");
[TCBegin] Verify changing table limits working correctly
[ExRes] [GAME] Table Limits Set: min=100.00 max=5000.00
0023 : MOUSE_MOVE("0","368","278");
0036 : MOUSE_MOVE("0","106","73");
0009 : MOUSE_LBUTTON_DOWN("1","106","73");
0002 : MOUSE_LBUTTON_UP("0","106","73");
0000 : MOUSE_MOVE("0","106","73");
0039 : MOUSE_MOVE("0","170","142");
0015 : KEYBOARD_KEY_DOWN("88","1","45","X");
0004 : KEYBOARD_KEY_UP("88","1","49197","X");
0023 : KEYBOARD_KEY_DOWN("88","1","45","X");
0006 : KEYBOARD_KEY_UP("88","1","49197","X");
[TCEnd]
0023 : KEYBOARD_SYSKEY_DOWN("18","1","8248");
0005 : MOUSE_MOVE("0","170","142");
```

```
0005 : KEYBOARD_SYSKEY_UP("9","1","40975");
0006 : KEYBOARD_KEY_UP("18","1","49208","VK_MENU");
0000 : MOUSE_MOVE("0","482","312");
0000 : KEYBOARD_KEY_UP("9","1","49167","VK_TAB");
0003 : MOUSE_MOVE("0","482","312");
0018 : KEYBOARD_KEY_DOWN("38","1","328","VK_UP");
0002 : KEYBOARD_KEY_UP("38","1","49480","VK_UP");
0014 : MOUSE_MOVE("0","482","313");
0002 : MOUSE_MOVE("0","482","313");
0006 : KEYBOARD_KEY_DOWN("69","1","18","E");
0000 : SET_CARDS("11","1","0","1","0","4","2","1","1","11","0","1","0",
                 "1","0","13","3","1","0","8","0","10","1");
0001 : MOUSE_MOVE("0","590","413");
0006 : MOUSE_MOVE("0","590","413");
0016 : KEYBOARD_KEY_DOWN("90","1","44","Z");
0006 : KEYBOARD_KEY_UP("90","1","49196","Z");
0010 : KEYBOARD_KEY_DOWN("90","1","44","Z");
0007 : KEYBOARD_KEY_UP("90","1","49196","Z");
[TCBegin] Verify payout on loss (dealer has blackjack)
[ExRes] [GAME_STATUS] Player 2 (1) Won=0.00
0010 : KEYBOARD_KEY_DOWN("68","1","32","D");
0004 : KEYBOARD_KEY_UP("68","1","49184","D");
0019 : ADD_SCREEN("COMMON_DIALOG");
0000 : MOUSE_MOVE("0","580","417");
0036 : KEYBOARD_KEY_DOWN("27","1","1","VK_ESCAPE");
0001 : REMOVE_SCREEN("COMMON_DIALOG");
0001 : MOUSE_MOVE("0","580","417");
0001 : KEYBOARD_KEY_UP("27","1","49153","VK_ESCAPE");
0001 : MOUSE_MOVE("0","580","417");
0044 : KEYBOARD_KEY_DOWN("13","1","284","VK_RETURN");
0002 : KEYBOARD_KEY_UP("13","1","49436","VK_RETURN");
0036 : KEYBOARD_KEY_DOWN("88","1","45","X");
0005 : KEYBOARD_KEY_UP("88","1","49197","X");
0006 : KEYBOARD_KEY_DOWN("88","1","45","X");
0006 : KEYBOARD_KEY_UP("88","1","49197","X");
[TCEnd]
0014 : KEYBOARD_SYSKEY_DOWN("18","1","8248");
0013 : KEYBOARD_SYSKEY_DOWN("115","1","8254");
0000 : SYSCOMMAND("61536","0");
0000 : ADD_SCREEN("COMMON_DIALOG");
0000 : MOUSE_MOVE("0","580","417");
0002 : KEYBOARD_SYSKEY_UP("115","1","57406");
0001 : KEYBOARD_KEY_UP("18","1","49208","VK_MENU");
0009 : KEYBOARD_KEY_DOWN("13","1","284","VK_RETURN");
0001 : REMOVE_SCREEN("COMMON_DIALOG");
0000 : MOUSE_MOVE("0","580","417");
```

```
0000 : REMOVE_SCREEN("SCREEN_BLACKJACK");
0000 : ADD_SCREEN("SCREEN_DEMOEXIT");
0000 : KEYBOARD_KEY_UP("13","1","49436","VK_RETURN");
0000 : MOUSE_MOVE("0","580","417");
0002 : MOUSE_MOVE("0","580","417");
0009 : KEYBOARD_KEY_DOWN("13","1","284","VK_RETURN");
0001 : REMOVE_SCREEN("SCREEN_DEMOEXIT");

// Date:            04/11/2003
// Time:            10:26:49
// End of file
```

Our game could be run with a command switch that told it to ignore mouse and keyboard input and grab events through the test script instead. Needless to say, we had to modify our core game engine significantly to make this possible.

When the script was executed, the output of the game was logged into a text file that would be compared with similar output from a known good run. If the two outputs were different, it identified a change in the system that could be a bug. Take a look at the output for the above blackjack script:

```
//
// Automation OUTPUT file
//
// Generated from script 'd:\automationtool\scripts\bj.dbg.txt'
//
// This script file was generated via
// the automated record/playback feature
//
// Product:         Casino 2.0
// Build:           02.00.00.0056
// Filename:        d:\automationtool\results\batchrun\results[apr_16_2003].txt
// Date:            04/16/2003
// Time:            17:21:00
//
// All comments are proceeded by '//'
// Commands end with ';'
//

//
// Automation RECORD file
//
// This script file was generated via
// the automated record/playback feature
//
```

```
// Product:        Casino 2.0
// Build:          .00.00.0056
// Filename:       d:\automation tool\scripts\bj.dbg.txt
// Date:           04/11/2003
// Time:           10:25:22
//
// All comments are proceeded by '//'
// Commands end with ';'
//
0000 : RANDOM_SEED("1018545922");

[ENVIRONMENT] Player 'Wanda Jean' balance set: 526.00

0000 : SET_START_BALANCE("999900.00");
0000 : LEAN("1");

[UI] Activating control 'Blackjack'

0001 : REMOVE_SCREEN("SCREEN_LOBBY");
0000 : ADD_SCREEN("SCREEN_BLACKJACK");
0000 : RANDOM_SEED("1018545930");
0000 : MOUSE_MOVE("0","374","342");
0000 : KEYBOARD_KEY_UP("74","1","49188","J");
0000 : RANDOM_SEED("1018545930");

[GAME] Table Limits Set: min=25.00 max=1000.00

0000 : MOUSE_MOVE("0","374","342");
0000 : RANDOM_SEED("89009");

[GAME_STATUS] Beginning of Round
[GAME_STATUS] Checking Player Balance (w): 5,000.00

[GAME_STATE] Current state is now BLACKJACK_STATE_TAKE_BETS.

0047 : KEYBOARD_SYSKEY_DOWN("18","1","8248");
0008 : KEYBOARD_SYSKEY_UP("9","1","40975");
0020 : KEYBOARD_KEY_UP("18","1","49208","VK_MENU");
0000 : MOUSE_MOVE("0","371","278");
0000 : KEYBOARD_KEY_UP("9","1","49167","VK_TAB");
0003 : MOUSE_MOVE("0","371","278");
0016 : KEYBOARD_KEY_DOWN("90","1","44","Z");

[UI] Activating control 'Cycle Avatars'

0006 : KEYBOARD_KEY_UP("90","1","49196","Z");
```

```
0048 : KEYBOARD_KEY_DOWN("90","1","44","Z");

[UI] Activating control 'Cycle Avatars'

0005 : KEYBOARD_KEY_UP("90","1","49196","Z");
[TCBegin] Verify changing table limits working correctly
[ExRes] [GAME] Table Limits Set: min=100.00 max=5000.00
0023 : MOUSE_MOVE("0","368","278");

[UI] Mouse over control 'Raise Limit'

0036 : MOUSE_MOVE("0","106","73");
0009 : MOUSE_LBUTTON_DOWN("1","106","73");
0002 : MOUSE_LBUTTON_UP("0","106","73");
0000 : MOUSE_MOVE("0","106","73");

[UI] Activating control 'Raise Limit'

[GAME] Table Limits Set: min=100.00 max=5000.00

[GAME_STATUS] Checking Player Balance (w): 5,000.00

[GAME_STATE] Current state is now BLACKJACK_STATE_GAME_OVER.

[GAME_STATUS] Beginning of Round
[GAME_STATUS] Checking Player Balance (w): 5,000.00

[GAME_STATE] Current state is now BLACKJACK_STATE_TAKE_BETS.

0039 : MOUSE_MOVE("0","170","142");
0015 : KEYBOARD_KEY_DOWN("88","1","45","X");
0004 : KEYBOARD_KEY_UP("88","1","49197","X");
0023 : KEYBOARD_KEY_DOWN("88","1","45","X");
0006 : KEYBOARD_KEY_UP("88","1","49197","X");
[TCEnd]
0023 : KEYBOARD_SYSKEY_DOWN("18","1","8248");
0005 : MOUSE_MOVE("0","170","142");
0005 : KEYBOARD_SYSKEY_UP("9","1","40975");
0006 : KEYBOARD_KEY_UP("18","1","49208","VK_MENU");
0000 : MOUSE_MOVE("0","482","312");
0000 : KEYBOARD_KEY_UP("9","1","49167","VK_TAB");
0003 : MOUSE_MOVE("0","482","312");
0018 : KEYBOARD_KEY_DOWN("38","1","328","VK_UP");

[UI] Activating control 'Bet Area'
```

```
[GAME_STATUS] Player 2 (w) placed bet: 100.00

0002 : KEYBOARD_KEY_UP("38","1","49480","VK_UP");
0014 : MOUSE_MOVE("0","482","313");
0002 : MOUSE_MOVE("0","482","313");
0006 : KEYBOARD_KEY_DOWN("69","1","18","E");

[UI] Activating control 'Cheat Field'

0000 : SET_CARDS("11","1","0","1","0","4","2","1","1","11","0","1",
                 "0","1","0","13","3","1","0","8","0","10","1");

[GAME] Deck stacked with 1h 1h 4c 1d 11h 1h 1h 13s 1h 8h 10d

0001 : MOUSE_MOVE("0","590","413");
0006 : MOUSE_MOVE("0","590","413");
0016 : KEYBOARD_KEY_DOWN("90","1","44","Z");

[UI] Activating control 'Deal Cards'

[GAME_STATE] Current state is now BLACKJACK_STATE_DEAL.

0003 : KEYBOARD_KEY_UP("68","1","49184","D");

[GAME_STATUS] Player 2 (w) (hand 0) got card: 4 of CLUBS
[GAME_STATUS] Player 2 (w) (hand 0) has evaluated to: 4
[GAME_STATUS] Dealer  got card: JACK of HEARTS
[GAME_STATUS] Dealer  has evaluated to: 10
[GAME_STATUS] Player 2 (w) (hand 0) got card: KING of SPADES
[GAME_STATUS] Player 2 (w) (hand 0) has evaluated to: 14
[GAME_STATUS] Dealer  got card: 8 of HEARTS

[GAME_STATE] Current state is now BLACKJACK_STATE_OFFER_INSURANCE.
[GAME_STATE] Current state is now BLACKJACK_STATE_CHECK_10_FOR_BLACKJACK.
[GAME_STATE] Current state is now BLACKJACK_STATE_PLAYER_HAND.

[GAME_STATUS] Player 2 (w) chose to stand

0033 : KEYBOARD_KEY_DOWN("83","1","31","S");

[UI] Activating control 'Stand'

[GAME_STATE] Current state is now BLACKJACK_STATE_DEALER_HAND.

[GAME_STATUS] Dealer  has evaluated to: 18
```

```
[GAME_STATE] Current state is now BLACKJACK_STATE_PAY_WINNERS.

0004 : KEYBOARD_KEY_UP("83","1","49183","S");

[GAME_STATUS] Player 2 (w) LOST
[GAME_STATUS] Player 2 (w) Bet=100.00
[GAME_STATUS] Player 2 (w) Won=0.00
[GAME_STATUS] Player 2 (w) Net=-100.00

[GAME_STATE] Current state is now BLACKJACK_STATE_ACKNOWLEDGE_RESULTS.

[GAME_STATUS] End of Round

0031 : KEYBOARD_KEY_DOWN("13","1","284","VK_RETURN");

[UI] Activating control 'Clear Table'

[GAME_STATE] Current state is now BLACKJACK_STATE_CLEAR_TABLE.

0002 : KEYBOARD_KEY_UP("13","1","49436","VK_RETURN");

[GAME_STATE] Current state is now BLACKJACK_STATE_CLEAR_DEALER.
[GAME_STATE] Current state is now BLACKJACK_STATE_GAME_OVER.

0037 : KEYBOARD_KEY_DOWN("13","1","284","VK_RETURN");

[UI] Activating control 'Clear Table'

[GAME_STATE] Current state is now BLACKJACK_STATE_CLEAR_TABLE.

0002 : KEYBOARD_KEY_UP("13","1","49436","VK_RETURN");

[GAME_STATE] Current state is now BLACKJACK_STATE_CLEAR_DEALER.
[GAME_STATE] Current state is now BLACKJACK_STATE_GAME_OVER.
[GAME_STATUS] Beginning of Round
[GAME_STATUS] Checking Player Balance (w): 4,900.00

[GAME_STATE] Current state is now BLACKJACK_STATE_TAKE_BETS.

0036 : KEYBOARD_KEY_DOWN("88","1","45","X");
0005 : KEYBOARD_KEY_UP("88","1","49197","X");
0006 : KEYBOARD_KEY_DOWN("88","1","45","X");
0006 : KEYBOARD_KEY_UP("88","1","49197","X");
[TCEnd]
0014 : KEYBOARD_SYSKEY_DOWN("18","1","8248");
0013 : KEYBOARD_SYSKEY_DOWN("115","1","8254");
```

```
0000 : SYSCOMMAND("61536","0");
0000 : ADD_SCREEN("COMMON_DIALOG");
0000 : MOUSE_MOVE("0","580","417");
0002 : KEYBOARD_SYSKEY_UP("115","1","57406");
0001 : KEYBOARD_KEY_UP("18","1","49208","VK_MENU");
0009 : KEYBOARD_KEY_DOWN("13","1","284","VK_RETURN");

[UI] Activating control 'Yes'

0001 : REMOVE_SCREEN("COMMON_DIALOG");
0000 : MOUSE_MOVE("0","580","417");
0000 : REMOVE_SCREEN("SCREEN_BLACKJACK");
0000 : ADD_SCREEN("SCREEN_DEMOEXIT");
0000 : KEYBOARD_KEY_UP("13","1","49436","VK_RETURN");

[UI] Mouse over control '25'

0000 : MOUSE_MOVE("0","580","417");
0002 : MOUSE_MOVE("0","580","417");
0009 : KEYBOARD_KEY_DOWN("13","1","284","VK_RETURN");

[UI] Activating control '23'

0001 : REMOVE_SCREEN("SCREEN_DEMOEXIT");
// Date:           04/11/2003
// Time:           10:26:49
// End of file

// Date:           04/16/2003
// Time:           17:21:50
// End of file
```

It turned out that test scripts were fairly sensitive to changes in the code. Anytime a button moved around on the screen the events would fail to press it, and the test script would report an error. A better design for automation would have insulated the test scripts from simple changes in the interface such as a button moving around, but they'll still break if a button is removed. Still, this kind of automation is excellent when it is used to quickly verify stable parts of a game as other development continues. It is also fairly inexpensive to implement in any game that uses a message pump to deliver user input to the game's user interface code.

Any user interface system that uses polling instead of a message pump is extremely difficult, if not impossible to automate.

Our Microsoft Card product used a much better solution for automation, knowing full well the shortcomings of the design on the Casino product. Instead of relying on low level user input, it recorded high level game events, such as moving a card from one position to another. This design was much more robust and worked well in the automation tool.

If possible, you should design your game so that it can play itself. Our card game was written by describing rules in C++ code written to a particular interface. One of the methods in the interface calculated the set of legal moves for that game state, and another method evaluated a move for its desirability. It was then completely trivial to write a piece of code that allowed the game to play itself. Programmers would run their games all night long and find 75% of the bugs before the test team even saw the game.

All of these test tools could be run from the command line, which enabled significant functional testing as a part of the build process. Our development team had a turnkey build process that automatically ran on a build machine, leaving the programmers doing the build plenty of time for some rousing games of Robotron and Joust in our lounge. After a successful build, the automation tool developed by the Microsoft test team would run a few of the most stable test scripts. As a result we never sent the Microsoft team a bad build, saving everyone's weekends.

For those skeptics out there who say that their game is too complicated for automatic testing tools I'll say you aren't thinking hard enough. We had automatic record / playback scripts in Ultima VIII, a multithreaded real time RPG. If Ultima VIII can have it, *any* project can have it.

Automated testing can also be invaluable in ad-hoc testing. Imagine a tester that is having a hard time coming up with the exact steps to reproduce a bug. If she is recording each and every play session and somehow gets the bug to reproduce, all she has to do is attach the recorded events to the bug report. A programmer will most likely be able to play back her session, see the bug, and fix it.

The bottom line is that every application can and should have as much automation built into it as a part of the overall design. It may be impossible to retrofit an existing title for serious automation, as we found in the Casino project. The results are worth the effort. The team works more efficiently and eliminates monkey work. The best part is you'll only have to make the investment once, because you can install the automation tools in your core libraries and every game you make will have automation.

The Bug Database

I've worked with a few different bug databases. Good ones can actually help you predict when you'll ship your game (more on that later). Bad ones can make everyone's life a living hell. Don't think for a moment that you can do without one. Even better, convince yourself that writing your own database in MySQL is a horrible idea; go out there and find something that works today. Your job, after all, is to write a fantastic game for your players. Don't waste time writing, fixing, and tweaking a home-grown bug database.

When I was at Origin Systems the bug database was not much more than a simple system built on FoxPro, an off the shelf database system. The bug database was difficult to use, extremely slow, and didn't provide useful information beyond simple bug counts. This *system,* and I use that term loosely, motivated me to make a horrible decision when I was the project director on Ultima VIII. I decided not to use the database at all. Instead, I decided it would be better for the team to use paper bugs, one bug per piece of paper clipped on a clipboard. What a tragic error! A few months before the ship date the test team called me into a meeting where they were concerned about the high bug count. I didn't show a high bug count (maybe 2 to 3 inches of paper) in my "records." The reality was that somehow an enormous stack of bugs, many hundreds of them, had never been assigned to the team. A few others and I spent hours sorting through the mess, assigning bugs, and coming to a serious understanding about the magnitude of my error in judgment. Since then, I've been very serious about bug databases.

Perhaps the best bug database I've ever used is RAID. Don't go searching for it on the Internet because you won't find it for sale. It is the internal application Microsoft uses to track bugs. It's a proprietary client application to a Microsoft SQL back end, and it has a number of important features that every good bug database must have. There are some excellent bug databases out there, and I'm sure some will run circles around RAID. The particular database product you choose should at least provide a few basic features. On non-Microsoft projects, I use PVCS Tracker for our bug database. It's not quite as good as RAID, but it gets the job done. It has all of the features a good bug database needs.

It goes without saying that the database should have flexible searching criteria. Almost any game will have hundreds, if not thousands, of issues. Finding all the bugs assigned to a particular person is pretty simple, but searching through the thousands of bugs that have been closed for a particular text string in the bug history might be a lot tougher. Inevitably you'll remember something about a previous bug that has relevance to today's project stopping problem. If the bug database puts every byte of information at your fingertips you'll be able to make good use of solutions in the can.

Essentially, you want a database that exposes an ad-hoc query mechanism that lets you construct your own queries. Stay away from a database that uses a simple menu system or dialog box. Those might be nice for some executives out there but programmers and other folks in the trenches want to construct very specific searches. If your database lets you construct SQL queries or something similar, you're way ahead of the game.

Here are some examples of common queries to a bug database:

- *Find all my active bugs for this milestone sorted by priority*: Individual developers on a team will use this query most every day.
- *Find all active bugs, sorted by team member*: Team leads will use this query to get a bird's eye view of the bug fixing effort.
- *Find all active bugs, sorted by severity*: Team leads can use this query to see how serious the bug problems are getting.
- *Find all resolved bugs that we've fixed in the previous build*: This is a good one to gauge the efforts of the testing team. They shouldn't be letting resolved bugs pile up.
- *Find all resolved bugs fixed in the next build*: If your resolved bug count is getting higher than 20 bugs per tester, you should consider firing a new build to the test team.

Storing and categorizing information in a database is just the starting point. You need to be able to make use of that information to increase the quality of your game. Take a look at the fields that are commonly used in most every bug database, and how they can be used.

- *Title or Short Description*: A one line description of the bug. A good title is really useful for scanning enormous lists of bugs when you are assigning them to team members or just estimating whether or not you'll see the sun the following weekend.
- *Who Found the Bug*: The name of the tester, preferably in the form of their email address. Sometimes developers must talk directly to a tester. Never keep your testers and developers blind to each other in the bug database.
- *When*: The date and time the bug was found. This information will be extremely useful in finding out how long bugs stay active in the database.
- *Revision Number*: The version number of your game. It's not enough to use the date and time of the build. Make things easy on yourself and put a version number easily accessible in the application.
- *Machine Configuration*: This is nice if it is automatically recorded when testers write bugs. It should contain everything and then some: CPU speed, system RAM, VRAM, hard disk, OS, additional hardware, or anything that might be important.

- *Severity*: A subjective field at best, but it's still important to rate the bug by its severity to give the programmers a chance to sort their bugs. After all if a bug nukes a hard drive it's a good idea to get it fixed fast.
- *Issue Type*: This field is a general classification. Good examples of issue types include code defect, documentation, localization, specification issue, suggestion, or work item. Use this field to direct the bug to the right group before it is assigned.

The bug description should be incredibly detailed. If it is done properly a programmer should be able to diagnose the problem quickly. It should include instructions to reproduce the bug, what the bug did, and what was expected. Take a look at the following example:

===== Opened by a-joekit on 01/29/2002 10:44AM =====

Description:

Selecting Undo at the end of a game after several games have been played (two or more) and then playing to end again results in an inaccurate number of games played in scorecard. There is one less than there should be.

Repro:

1. Open Trump.

2. Open Gin Rummy.

3. Play a game to completion (i.e., past 100 points, not just one hand unless you lose that badly). You may use "A" to have it auto play but this will not repro if you select AI vs. AI at the beginning because you do not have the Undo button.

4. Play another game to completion.

5. Press Undo after viewing the scorecard from your second game.

6. Play the game to completion again.

7. Look at the scorecard.

Results:

The number of games is one less than it should be. If your scorecard previously showed 2 games played, it will now show only one. If you play 3 games and then undo and complete, it will show 2 games, etc.

Expected Results:

Scorecard should accurately reflect the number of games played.

The description is a short summary of the bug. When the programmer follows the repro steps exactly, they should be guaranteed to see the same results in the debugger, hopefully catching the bug in the act. The results are what the tester observed after the repro steps were followed, and the expected results were what the tester expected to observe.

Some bugs cannot be reproduced 100%. As hard as the testers try, they might not be able to find a clear set of steps that will always result in the bug appearing. All good testers check each questionable bug before writing it up. If they can't reproduce the bug every single time with the steps they suggest, they *must* also include the percentage chance that it will occur. Every developer should insist on this from their test team, because if a bug only happened once and was never seen again it shouldn't have a high priority. The percentage chance might also be a valuable clue to a programmer, so always get it in the bug report.

You might wonder why we bother writing the expected results—shouldn't it be obvious? The answer is decidedly not. Testers make use of the design document heavily when they create their test plans, and where the design document leaves off their imaginations and creativity picks up. Their expectations of your game's response to their wacky input might be completely justified either by the design document or their intuition.

The most commonly searched field in a database is the status field. Most databases I've worked with have a status field with three states:

- *Active*: The bug belongs to the development team and is in the process of being resolved.
- *Resolved*: The bug belongs to the test team where they will check the game to see if the programmer actually managed to fix the bug without breaking five other things.
- *Closed*: The bug has been addressed and belongs only to the database.

An important feature of many databases that I've worked with is that some database fields, especially the status field, are secure and can't be edited directly. It wouldn't be appropriate (as much as some programmers would want to) for a development team member to simply 'close' a bug without having it run though the test team. Even if all fields are editable, a record of each change to the bug should be kept in a running log of the bug's history. This is extremely useful for mining information out of the database. You'll get to see a great example of this when we see the next bug report.

When the test team works like crazy they'll write hundreds of bug reports and dump them onto the development team, usually on a Friday afternoon! Usually the lead programmer and the project director will sit in front of the bug database and try to make reasonable decisions about assigning bugs to others on the development team. The bug database must make this process fast and painless or it will be deemed useless by people that need it most. Make sure your bug database can do the following things:

- Edit many bugs at the same time (such as assigning all selected bugs to one person).
- Page to the next bug or the previous bug with a hotkey or toolbar button. You'll be doing this a lot.
- Add a team member.
- Minimize keystrokes, such as having field value prediction like Quicken!

Now that the bugs are all assigned, your team members will want to be able to look through the bug on their list. There are a couple of good fields that the team can use to prioritize bugs and bug fixing:

- *Priority*: Bugs with a higher priority get worked on first. The production team usually sets priority so the team leads can direct effort in the right place. The test team might weigh in on priority also, so keep them in the loop.
- *Milestone*: If a bug doesn't need to be fixed until a certain milestone is reached, make sure you reflect that in the bug. This is a great way of focusing development effort on the problems that will help the team make the next milestone.

When you have tons of bugs on your plate you tend to mechanically work on each one as it is sorted, without really even looking at the bug. Sometimes you'll even wonder "why in the hell is this bug assigned to me? That code isn't mine!" or "Hey, I thought the game was supposed to work that way." Always approach a bug with 10% skepticism. The bug might not even be a real bug. This is especially true when everyone is tired and overworked. Try to keep just enough neurons firing to make your own judgment calls about each bug before you start to fix it.

When the bug is finally resolved the following fields should get filled in:

- *Resolved By*: This should be the email address of the person who resolved the bug. If the bug needs to bounce back for additional work, this is the person who will get it first.
- *Resolved Date*: By subtracting the opened date from the resolved date, you can create a report that analyzes how long it takes for your development team to fix bugs on average. This can be invaluable for predicting your ship date.
- *Resolved Revision*: This field is critical, because it tells the testers when they can expect a build that has the fix. If the developer gets this wrong when he resolves the bug, the tester might test it too early and find the bug still exists. They'll send it back to the developer, who will emphatically deny that the bug exists and that the entire test team is smoking crack. You get the idea: Get this field right and avoid a brawl.

- *Cause*: This field allows the developer to record why the bug occurred. This is a great candidate for a drop down box, and here are some suggested values:
  - *Dev Error*: The bug was a development error; most bugs fall into this category.
  - *Dev Missing Code*: The bug was caused by code that didn't exist when the developer thought it was supposed to be there.
  - *Not Yet Implemented*: The testers saw something that didn't exist yet and it wasn't supposed to exist.
  - *Specification Change/Flaw*: The bug was actually in the design document and not a code problem.
  - *Content Change*: A change in any asset other than code fixed this bug: art, sound, help files, or whatever.
  - *External Change*: The bug was fixed by updating a licensed library, hardware driver, or something like that.
- *Resolution*: This field tells the test team how the developer fixed the bug. Some values that are good for this are:
  - *Fixed*: The bug was fixed by the developer.
  - *Not Reproducible*: The bug could not be reproduced by the developer using the steps given by the tester.
  - *Won't Fix*: It is agreed by the development team and the test team that the issue is a problem, but it won't be fixed.
  - *By Design*: This bug is actually a feature of the game.
  - *External*: The bug was fixed by something external to the development and test teams.
  - *Postponed*: The bug will be fixed in the next version of the game, assuming there is a next version of the game.
  - *Duplicate*: This happens when two or more bug reports actually refer to the same issue. It is important that when a bug is marked as a duplicate, that the bug database retain a record of the original bug.

Beyond those fields it's also a great idea to make use of the bug history to record some details about the exact nature of the fix. It's not uncommon to see snippets of code in our bug history showing the change and why the code was broken in the first place.

A Sample Bug Report

I promised you a good bug with some decent bug history, and here it is. This is a bug report written up by one of the senior testers at Microsoft on a version of Freecell that I wrote for one of their card game products. It turns out that I didn't quite understand the nuances of Freecell. It also turns out that the original programmer of Microsoft Freecell, Jim Horne, chimed in to set me straight.

===== Opened by jkburns on 05/17/2002 05:02PM =====

DESCRIPTION:

The automatic movement of cards to the foundation piles by the engine is inconsistent—sometimes cards are moved, other times cards can be moved and are not.

REPRO:

1) Open Trump.

2) Go to Freecell.

3) Move a card to one of the 4 free cells such that the next card up in the tableau pile can be moved to the foundation pile.

4) Move a card from one tableau column to another such that a card that can be moved to the foundation pile is exposed.

ACTUAL:

The first case (#3) results in an automatic move of the card to the foundation pile. The second case (#4) results in nothing happening.

EXPECTED:

Anytime a card can be automatically moved to the foundation piles, it should be.

NOTES:

===== Edited by jkburns on 05/17/2002 05:16PM =====

Cards in the free cells are not automatically moved to the foundation piles either...

===== Assigned by joye.mcburnett on 05/28/2002 02:54PM =====

—> AssignedTo: Active -> mike.mcshaffry

===== Assigned by robjera on 05/28/2002 02:55PM =====

—> AssignedTo: mike.mcshaffry -> joye.mcburnett

Please check for consistency with Windows Freecell.

===== Assigned by robjera on 05/28/2002 02:56PM =====

—> AssignedTo: joye.mcburnett -> jkburns

===== Edited by jkburns on 05/31/2002 09:05AM =====

—> AssignedTo: jkburns -> Active

I have extensively played the PC version of Freecell, and my conclusion is that it is really buggy... It seems to automatically move cards to the foundations if the rank is less than or equal to 3, but then it will suddenly remove all cards and report that you won. One game I played I had 4's as the top cards of my diamonds and hearts foundation piles, and 5's as the top cards of my clubs and spades foundation piles; I made a move and the game ended saying I won through a dialog! But I had to manually move the 4's and 5's to the foundation piles when they were exposed. Sometimes the cards in the free cells are not moved to the foundation piles, but I think this has to do with the fact that it avoids automatic movements of 4's and up...

Here's what I think should happen if we are to have automatic movements implemented for freecell, since the actual freecell game seems inconsistent as well:

- anytime a move is made (any move), all fully exposed cards, including those cards in the free cells, are scanned to see if they can be placed on a foundation pile top.

- if this scan results in card(s) moving to the foundation pile, then the card(s) exposed from this move should be checked to see if they can be moved to the foundation pile—a recursive check until the newly exposed cards are determined not to be a legal move to the foundation piles...

I don't know if there is a spec out there that more clearly outlines the logic behind automatic movements in freecell, perhaps it is doing the right thing after all, I just can't figure out why some cards when exposed are not moved to the foundation piles. I'll see if I can get in touch with the windows freecell devs for clarification.

I think if we are to have the automatic movement of cards to the foundation piles implemented, it should be consistent and fully implemented.

===== Assigned by matt.lamari on 06/04/2002 02:09PM =====

—> AssignedTo: Active -> mike.mcshaffry

===== Resolved as By Design by mike.mcshaffry in 02.00.06.0016 on 06/05/2002

09:30AM =====

—> AssignedTo: mike.mcshaffry -> jkburns

Hi John - Freecell isn't buggy as far as I can tell, but the rules of when a card can go onto the foundation automatically are a little weird. The automatic move is only made if the card in question isn't needed. The card is deemed "needed" if there exists anywhere in the tableau columns another card that can legally sit on top of the card that move automatically to the foundation.

In Freecell, it is illegal to move a card away from a foundation pile once it is placed there. This means that if cards were automatically moved as soon as they could, the game could easily end up in an "unwinnable" state.

Do you think you're observing what I describe above?

===== Activated by jkburns on 06/17/2002 03:12PM =====

—> AssignedTo: jkburns -> Active

Mike, you are correct that the cards 1 less than the card in question are considered before automatically moving it to the foundation piles, but cards of rank 2 are an exception. I spoke with Jim Horne, the creator of Freecell, and he explained the logic of automatic movements from the original windows FreeCell. He was pretty cool about telling me about FreeCell! Here is the email that he sent me:

Ok, here it is. Note that this is not the most aggressive logic, which is by design. It is, however, very clear why each card can be moved to the home cells.

I go through each card in the free cells, and the cards on the bottom of each column looking for cards that are useless (defined below), and repeat that until no more are found or until no cards are left.

A card is useless if:

1. If it's an ace, it's useless with no further checks.
2. If it's a deuce, all that needs to be checked is if the corresponding ace is already up in a home cell. If so, it's useless.
3. Any other card is marked useless if both cards which are one number smaller and of the opposite color are already up in a home cell.

I verified this in Windows FreeCell: there can be an ace of the opposite color on the tableau and a deuce will still automatically move up to the foundation pile if its ace is placed there. This did not happen in Trump's FreeCell. I think this is the only discrepancy between Windows FreeCell and Trump FreeCell automatic movement logic...

===== Edited by jkburns on 06/17/2002 03:59PM =====

In addition to the above, I just noticed the following: An ace that is fully exposed when the game begins, if moved to the free cells, is automatically moved to the foundation piles in Windows FreeCell, but not in Trump FreeCell. In Trump, the ace stays in the free cell...

===== Edited by jkburns on 06/17/2002 05:04PM =====

I have also noticed that the cards in the free cells are not checked for automatic movement to the foundations, either in Windows FreeCell, if a card is in a free cell that, upon a user move, should be automatically moved to the foundation piles (given rules described above), it is. In Trump this is not the case for cards in the free cells.

===== Assigned by joye.mcburnett on 06/18/2002 08:30AM =====

—> AssignedTo: Active -> mike.mcshaffry

===== Resolved as Fixed by mike.mcshaffry in 02.00.06.0019 on 06/18/2002 01:54PM

=====

—> AssignedTo: mike.mcshaffry -> ben.roberts

Man, you're good. No fair getting to talk to the original programmer, either, I think that's cheating!

Anyway, the result of my labor should be an exact as possible replica of Windows Freecell, using the rules he describes. Really the only thing I did was:

1. Implemented Rule #3 by looking at what exists in the home cells, versus what didn't exist in the tableau columns. A subtle, but meaningful, difference.
2. Implemented Rule #1 and Rule #2 specifically, as special cases of Rule #3.
3. Run the first check right after the deal, instead of right after the first move.
4. Made sure that all rules check top cards in the tableau as well as the free cells—that wasn't being done.

That should do it. Enjoy!

===== Assigned by marshall.andrews on 06/20/2002 11:23AM =====

—> AssignedTo: ben.roberts -> jkburns

===== Closed by jkburns on 07/01/2002 10:18AM =====

—> AssignedTo: jkburns -> Closed

Verified as fixed in 02.00.06.0019—rules as stated above are implemented correctly.

The bug history contains a lot of information, not the least of which is a conversation between the tester and me. It also shows each change that was made to the bug during its lifetime as it was being assigned to various developers, managers, and testers.

Other Nice Features

There were some extremely nice features in some of the bug databases in my past. These features made life much easier. If you can find a bug database with all these features don't ask how much it is, just go get it. You'll be glad you did.

Customizable fields let the test and production teams add very game specific information to the database, and make searching on these fields much more robust. An excellent example would be the addition of a "Mission" field to an action adventure game, or a "Map Coordinates" field to an RPG or MMP game. Driving games might have a field for the kind of car or the weather conditions. This information helps the team figure out who is the best person to fix the bug, and where the majority of problems collect.

The bug database should be remotely accessible via the web or proprietary client. The team leads can log in from wherever they are (airport, home, trade show) and deal with any problems or issues. It goes without saying that third-party developers are far flung from their testing team, and sending the bug database via FTP just won't cut it. The bug database is constantly changing and should always be available to every team member wherever they are.

The database should be able to include file attachments as a part of the bug. This can be invaluable for getting a test script, screen shot, saved game file, or other piece of information from the test team to the developers. A web based bug database makes this trivial, since you can simply put a link in the bug history.

Which Bugs Get Fixed?

I've been in tons of arguments about which bugs get fixed and which get left behind. After a few years of this I've noticed a few trends that will perhaps save you from the same arguments. It may also save you and some of your programming buddies some time at the desk. Mind you, I'm not going to talk here about design issues, just bugs.

Crashes can be a nightmare, especially the ones that don't seem to have any reproducible steps. When your game crashes a lot your customers will wonder why they paid hard earned money for something that doesn't work right or even worse erases their hard drive. Here's a good rule of thumb: If your game crashes more than once every two to three hours of solid play, you should fix it. Beyond 5 to 6 hours of continuous play, things get pretty fuzzy. If it takes that long to find the bug it will be extremely difficult for programmers and testers to verify the fix. Give that one a low priority. If the crash destroys anything more than the last saved game, you should fix it regardless of how often it happens. Do everything you can to find those reproducible steps to nail that bug. Have every tester and programmer spend an entire day on it and try to find by brute force if that's all you have left.

Memory leaks can be the hardest or easiest bugs to find, depending on how you've engineered your memory management. The one certain thing is that you simply cannot tolerate any memory leaks in your game, period. This is especially true for console games, but PC games should set just as high a quality bar as far as leaking resources is concerned.

The reason memory leaks are insidious has a lot to do with how people really play your games. Casual players sometimes leave them up and running for long periods of time even when they aren't playing. Hardcore players will invest themselves in 36-hour marathon sessions without stopping. Either way your game will eventually run out of resources and melt down, even if there is a small leak somewhere.

Bugs that point to hardware incompatibility or unsupported operating systems can cut your sales and increase your returns. Sometimes it can be hard to tell if a certain video card, sound card, or particular flavor of Windows is important to your game's market. Do whatever you can to find out and try to make it work. Don't assume anything about these bugs; they can be trivial to fix or impossible depending on your architecture and some unwise choices you may have made in the past. When you get this kind of bug the first thing you should do is reproduce the bug on a different machine. Eliminate the possibility that the problem is driver related by installing the latest driver. Eliminate the chance that the card is a bad one by using a different card of the exact same make and model. Don't use a different operating system, though. Sometimes drivers differ from OS to OS. Once you've done all these things you can be sure you have a bona fide hardware issue on your hands.

Don't go about solving hardware problems alone. You can get help from the manufacturer. Call up the developer relations group (every hardware company has one) and tell them about your trouble. They'll usually ask you to ship a CD of your application to them, or they may have you run your application against a special set of hardware drivers that are used to find problems. Hardware companies are very motivated to help developers find problems, so get their help as soon as you've figured out you have a real problem.

DirectX developers can actually use the DirectX samples to identify operating system incompatibilities. DirectX is not 100% reliable under every possible operating system configuration (such as running under terminal services with a dual monitor setup on the remote machine). If the test team has found some strange issue with your game, try running a DirectX sample under the same configuration. Odds are the DirectX sample will fail in the same way. You can be pretty sure that whatever the issue is, it's not something you did and it will probably be impossible for you to fix.

The irony about hardware related bugs is that it takes you and your team forever to find out that the bug isn't your problem after all. Try your best to stay out of a never-ending bug hunt with these kinds of issues by eliminating your code as a culprit early on.

Bad performance can turn a fun game into an annoying nightmare. I'd almost rather have the game crash outright than suffer though a slideshow. At least the pain and suffering is time-limited! Performance issues are probably the hardest issues to fix, especially if you wait until every last piece of code has been written. Look at it this way—you won't speed your game up by adding features. Performance issues are difficult to fix because generally you are turning some naïve algorithm (just load all the data into memory, and everything will be fine!) into a solution. I've never seen a performance enhancement that made the code simpler, unless you call cutting an entire subsystem a performance enhancement.

Establish your CPU budget early and keep your code to that budget. If you've implemented 60% of the subsystems and you are already at your target framerate, you've got a serious problem. Perhaps most people get into this kind of trouble because they don't have a CPU budget in place, or no one was watching the shop. The bottom line is to catch a performance problem early, they always take forever to fix.

The last kind of bugs that need to get fixed at all costs are the embarrassing ones. Everyone on the team should be amenable to fixing these issues, usually because they have a low risk and they usually mean a lot to the team.

If anyone out there remembers Ultima VIII, you'll recall that it was the first Ultima to include jumping puzzles. I hate jumping puzzles, especially when you can't control where you land. Oh, and I should mention that the penalty for missing any jump was *death*! What a horrible design flaw (for which we were crucified by more than a few reviewers). By the time Ultima VIII was finishing up, everyone on the team had gotten pretty good at jumping, especially because you died when you missed, and almost no one was aware how hard it was for new players. It turned out the fixing the jumping bug took only a few hours—the fix was released in a patch a few months later.

Never Fix these Bugs

There is definitely a class of bugs you shouldn't spend any more time on them than it takes to get a good laugh out of it and mark it "Won't Fix" or "By Design." You have to be careful, though, and you should remember that some tester wrote it up because they thought it was important enough to write. Still, there are some funny ones to be had in every bug database, and others that just belong on the trash heap. Sometimes testers are really game designers in disguise—and good ones at that. Some of them just think they are game designers. On the first Casino game I did, one of the testers wrote up a bug saying that the game needed a "Luck Slider" in the game options. That might be the action/adventure equivalent of unlimited ammo, but I wasn't buying it.

Test tools are fantastic for getting a lot of testing done in a hurry, but they can be used for evil purposes. Make sure that testers know that when they use test tools or cheats they can break the game, and it is a dumb idea to write up bugs caused in this manner.

Archaic hardware and operating systems are a great source for impossible bugs. Granted it's good to know how things will fail on these older systems but you shouldn't be responsible for this stuff unless somehow your target market sill has this old garbage installed in their computers. If an old video or sound card driver is causing problems with your game, check the latest version. Clearly if the most recent driver works, put something in the

README file and move on. Don't waste any time trying to find a workaround for an outdated driver.

Hallucinations are my favorite. Sometimes I wonder if the test team really is smoking better stuff than any human deserves. Anyway, take a look at this one:

> Description: CTRL Z is not sensitive enough.
>
> Steps to Repro:
>
> 1. Open any game.
>
> 2. Make one move.
>
> 3. Use CTRL Z to undo (quickly once, slowly once).
>
> 4. Compare that to using a very quick ALT ENTER to reduce screen size.
>
> Results: CTRL Z takes a very deliberate keystroke to perform whereas ALT ENTER and the like can be a very quick keystroke combo.
>
> Expected Results: Should be more sensitive along the vein of ALT ENTER and other such hotkeys.

I think it is just as likely that this tester spilled a little Dr. Pepper in his keyboard, and the Z key was a little sticky. Any engineer knows that it isn't the application that controls the sensitivity of the keyboard. What you want to watch out for here assigning this bug to a junior programmer without reading it fully and having the poor sod spend a few days writing new keyboard drivers to "solve" the problem. I get nightmares just thinking about it. Watch out for strange bugs like these, and don't forget to point these out to junior team members. They won't know to throw these bugs back to the testers; it is more likely they'll want to fix everything that comes their way and try to make everyone happy. It's a shame that testers sometimes write these issues up, but hey there is such a thing as junior testers, right? Senior testers would never write this stuff into the bug database.

That's another good reason to take a close look at the name of the tester who wrote the bug. Sometimes you'll catch things a little earlier if you know what, and who, you are looking for.

Bugs Are Expensive

There's an interesting exercise that illustrates the cost of writing a single bug in terms of time and money. This example shows the shortest possible lifecycle of a bug, something that is fixable in a short time by a programmer. We'll put the economics under the spotlight and set the average cost of a developer or tester at $100,000 per year ($0.84/minute). I can already hear the laughing, so stop and do your own math. I like mine easy.

- Tester sees the bug, checks the reproducible steps, and writes it up in the bug database: 2 minutes.
- Team lead assigns the bug to a team member: 10 seconds.
- Developer reads the bug and decides to fix it: 60 seconds.
- Developer finds the code to make the fix, and happens to find it in an isolated section of code that can be changed without recompiling the entire application: 60 seconds.
- Developer compiles, links, and tests the fix: 60 seconds.
- Developer records the change in the bug database and checks in the source code: 60 seconds.
- Team tester checks the bug fix before it is sent to the publisher: 60 seconds.
- Publishers tester checks the bug fix and closes the bug: 60 seconds.

```
Total time: 4 minutes for testing, 4 minutes 10 seconds for development.
```

```
Total cost: $6.79
```

That may not seems like a lot of time, but it adds up. For every 100 issues that are this trivial, the team spends about 13 hours and $679. I could have a nice trip to a sandy beach for less than that.

Let's look at something more typical, and throw a little human error in to boot:

- Tester sees the bug, forgets to check the reproducible steps, and writes it up in the bug database: 1 minute.
- Team lead assigns the bug to a team member: 10 seconds.
- Developer realizes that the bug got assigned to the wrong place. She reassigns it back to the team lead: 25 seconds.
- Team lead talks to a few developers and finds the right person to fix it: 15 minutes.
- Developer reads the bug and decides to fix it: 60 seconds.
- Developer finds that the bug can't be reproduced as the tester suggested, and tries a few other things to get the bug to happen, and fails: 5 minutes.
- Developer assigns the bug to internal test to try to find repro steps: 10 seconds.

- Internal test tries to reproduce the bug, and fails: 15 minutes.
- Internal test reassigns the bug back to original tester, marked "Not Repro": 10 seconds.
- Publishers tester reproduces the bug instantly and bounces the bug back to the developer: 1 minute.
- Developer gets the latest code, does a complete rebuild: 45 minutes.
- Developer again attempts to reproduce the bug and fails: 30 minutes.
- Developer calls the tester at the publisher and they try to find the problem: 45 minutes.
- Developer FTPs entire image of testers machine for on site analysis: 20 minutes. (I'm assuming the developer doesn't just wait for the FTP.)
- Developer reproduces the bug and finds that the save game file is corrupted: 15 minutes.
- Developer records the findings in the bug database: 60 seconds.

```
Total time: 2 minutes 25 seconds for testing, 177 minutes 35 seconds
for development.
```

```
Total cost: $151.20
```

Clearly this is a more extreme case and it does pick on the testing group. I could have just as easily come up with a case where development submitted a bad build causing all kinds of lost time, but that's a different subject.

What's so tragic about this case is it caused nearly 3 hours of development time to be lost to a non-issue. If you have 100 issues like this on your project, you've just burned fifteen thousand dollars and change. That's enough money to take your whole team to a sandy beach. Mistakes like this can and will happen on every project. It is up to the entire team, development and test, to try their best to minimize these problems.

Statistical Analysis of Your Bug Database

Another good title for this section should be "Looking into Your Crystal Ball." Once the team can consistently fix more bugs than the test team writes, you can use your bug database to predict your ship date. If that seems impossible or farfetched, I completely understand. I once felt the same way. It comes down to simple mathematics, really.

First there is a cold hard fact to consider. There is a maximum sustainable rate of bug debt your team can retire each working day. Every project is different, but after looking at the outcome of many different computer game projects Microsoft pegs this rate is somewhere between 3 and 5 bugs per team member per day.

Programmers can fix only 3 to 5 bugs per day, huh? I can already hear you jeering and calling me a fool. I understand. I did the same thing to the test manager at Microsoft, and it turned out he was completely right. I know how many bugs I can fix per day, and it's more than five, especially if I'm really cranking. I thought this number was closer to 10 or 15 bugs per day. I got into a huge disagreement over this fact on a conference call with one of the test managers at Microsoft. I told him that my developers were the best and they'd blow his socks off, yadda, yadda. Six weeks later I was eating crow, on a conference call, with the same people in attendance. Sure, my developers were fixing 10 bugs per day and more, but the test team was still writing bugs. At the end of the day, the analysis clearly showed that our development team was right on the expected average at 3.75 bugs per day per team member over the life of the project.

It turns out that you don't even want to fix too many more than that, assuming they are real bugs that require some planning, checking, and whatnot. Serious problems require more than an hour to fix correctly, and if you fix them too fast, you're likely not paying due care and attention to your bugs.

Believe it or not, your team can retire bugs no faster than five bugs per team member per day. Period. It doesn't matter how good they are, they are still human.

Let's assume you've topped the bug curve, and the number of active bugs is consistently dropping. It's time to predict your ship date:

```
active bug count / ( number of developers n bug fix rate ) = days until zero bugs.
```

Here's a real life example. Our last project had 5 programmers, and 1 producer/designer. On June 15, the project had just shy of 300 active bugs. Using the formula above, we show:

```
300 / ( 6 * 3.5 ) = 14.285 days until we hit zero bugs.
```

It turns out we hit our ZBR date in around 16 working days. Our average fix rate was a little slower than we projected, but we didn't work weekends either.

Certainly one of the worrying times on a project is when the bug count is climbing, and perhaps climbing rapidly. This will occur naturally as the programming team is concentrating all of its effort on finishing new features rather than working on bugs. Take a look at the graph shown in Figure 14.1.

You can see a few humps early on where the development team attempted to keep the bug count in check. The amount of time they could devote to fixing bugs wasn't enough to keep the active bug count from growing. This wasn't a problem because we always calculated the maximum allowable active bug count. This maximum count is the number of bugs that can be fixed from the code complete milestone (where programmers are doing nothing but fixing bugs) to the ZBR date (the scheduled date for reaching zero active bugs for the first time). Use the same formula to solve for the active bug count given a certain number of workdays and developers:

```
number of developers * bug fix rate n number of working days = maximum active bugs
```

In our case this formula worked out to be:

```
6 developers * 3.5 bugs fixed per day n 40 days = 840 bugs
```

There is a small problem with that formula, however subtle. It assumes that every developer on the team has an equal share of bugs. That is never the case. One of the programmers is usually stuck with a higher than average count. Remove the "developers" part of the formula to determine the maximum number of bugs allowable for each person:

```
3.5 bugs fixed per day * 40 days = 140 bugs.
```

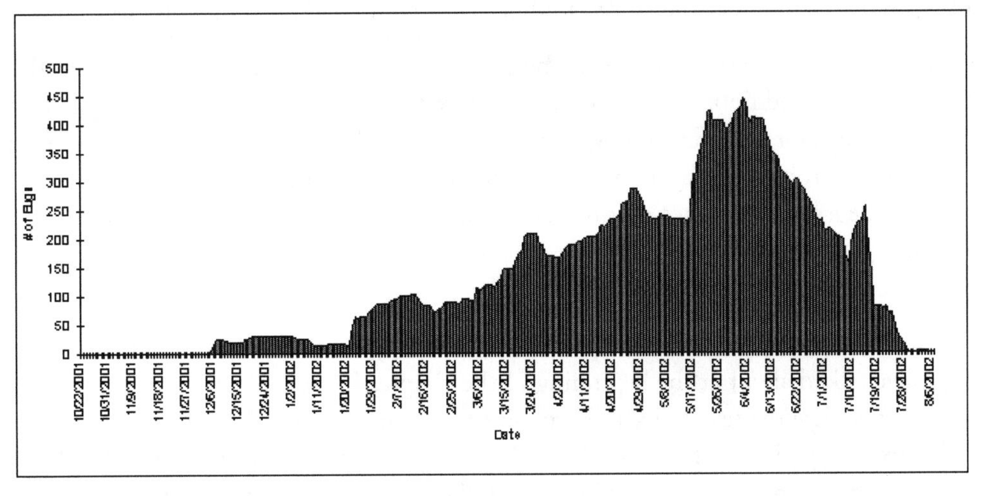

Figure 14.1
Daily Active Bug Count Graph.

If you run these numbers yourself and find your counts are too high, what can be done? You already know you have a few options just by looking at the formula. You can clearly increase the number of days you are working by putting in some weekend time. You can also increase the number of bugs the team fixes per day by working longer hours or "punting" low priority bugs. To some extent you can add some extra development help, although they don't ever match the expected bug fix rate. The formula is pretty clear, and there are no other inputs.

This kind of analysis helps a team figure out how much effort to put into bug fixing all along the development of the project. Use these numbers to set the throttle. If you burn too hot your team will be dead tired before the final bugs are fixed, which are usually the hardest ones. Burn too lean and you'll find the active bug count spiraling out of control. Most importantly, use these numbers to justify giving your team a weekend off every now and then. If they're under their expected bug count they deserve it.

The Testing Team

There are a few different kinds of testing organizations, and you can expect different kinds of feedback from each of them. Many projects will use two or more of these testing styles or groups on the same project. The first two are the most common: internal testing, and publisher testing.

If you happen to work at a big development house like Microsoft or Electronic Arts you'll find both your internal testing and publisher testing under the same roof. Internal testing groups are assigned close to the development team. Their job is to help the programmers save time. They support the programming staff in many different ways, from checking their bug fixes to looking at the latest build before it is shipped off to the publisher.

Internal testers can be part time or full time game enthusiasts that want to break into the industry at the ground floor. They tend to get abused by the programmers, finding better reproducible steps for a confusing bug or swapping out video cards to help a programmer find a hardware problem. They are important to keep the programmers working efficiently on code issues instead of getting caught up in busy work. A good internal tester can root out good repro steps for a bug just as fast as a programmer can, and they tend to work for a lot less money.

The testing groups that work for the publisher have the job of pouring through all those test plans we talked about at the beginning of the chapter. They look at the design document and write the test plans and organize the entire testing effort. They'll usually be a fair mix of experienced testers and freshly picked temporary staff without a single clue about testing games. Watch out for these folks—they tend to think of themselves as game designers! The senior testers will do their best to train and guide them but they can't watch them every second.

It's probably a good idea to mention here that there tends to be a fair bit of animosity between developers and testers. I think that has much more to do with the stress of the work and the pressured timelines than anything else. Everybody is working hard for the same goal, a great game. Whenever I write comments in bugs I always try to make a joke when possible or perhaps make light of a situation to brighten the mood, which can all too easily get dark in real hurry. Try to do the same thing, ok? Testers are the only thing that stand between your customers and the nasty buggy code you wrote at 3:00am. Give them a break and they'll likely save your ass.

The publisher's testing group will also have a test lead for your project and a test manager for the entire group. Get to know these people and get a good relationship with them as soon as you can. Communication with the test group starts with the test lead. The test lead is the only one that will call you and tell you ahead of time some juicy intelligence; like the press is going to take a sneak peek at the next build. I get more information consistently from the test group than any other group in any publisher I've ever worked with. So can you, if you play your cards right. Forget the executives—your best friends are the testers.

The same kind of testing most publishers do in house can also be had for a price in special out of house testing companies. These companies are a great resource for smaller developers that can't quite justify a dedicated testing department of their own. Out of house testing companies are capable of any kind of testing you can imagine, but be prepared to get out your checkbook if you want everything.

For those of you working on console titles there is a special testing group that will pour over your title: the console manufacturer. Sony, Nintendo, and Microsoft won't allow your product into the manufacturing pipe until they are satisfied that it meets their requirements for product features and quality.

The Public Beta

A public beta test is conducted by sending your game to a large audience sometime before it is released to the market. A public beta test is critical for massively multiplayer games because an internal test team simply cannot duplicate the loads and actions of tens of thousands of players distributed on the internet. Any game can benefit from a public beta, especially if your game targets a mass market audience with a wide range of players. Microsoft consistently uses its thousands of employees to beta test all manner of software, from games to applications software.

Selecting the right beta testers is important to getting good results from the test. These people must be hard core players who are willing to put in some serious time into testing. The last thing you need is a bunch of players that try your game for a few hours and spend the rest of the time on the beta test flaming your development team on Google groups.

Make sure you give your beta testers something in return for their effort and they'll be motivated to give you great feedback on each version they download. You might send them a free copy of the game or waive subscription fees for a few months. Another great idea is to give away prizes to your beta testers. Do whatever it takes to keep them working for you.

If you have thousands of people playing your game it stands to reason you'll have hundreds of people sending you feedback. The signal to noise ratio on this feedback is really low and you have to find clever ways of filtering out the vast majority of issues that your internal test team has already found. One way of doing this is by setting up a newsgroup and let the beta testers sort it out for themselves. Related issues will tend to collect in individual threads, and beta testers will check out the threads before creating a new one.

Another good way to get good test feedback from your beta testers is to take a survey approach. Have them fill out a web based questionnaire after every version. Track the answers in a database so you see how changes your dev team makes are affecting the opinion of the public. This method is great for detecting improvements in the game or how the game compares to the competition.

I was involved in the Ultima Online Public Beta, which many folks believe was still continuing well after the product shipped. That wasn't very far from the truth. Massively multiplayer games were in their infancy and no one at Origin had experience with the size and scope of the game we were creating. After a few weeks of testing, the executive staff of the project was called in to a meeting where the question of going live was posed. The game was experiencing rapid improvements and rapid change, but it seemed clear that the audience was ready to start playing for real. Electronic Arts was ready to have Ultima Online ship months before Christmas, ahead of Everquest. After the meeting the IT staff was instructed to wipe the game data back to its pristine state and open the ports for the public. The code still had bugs and was undergoing rapid change, even when the public was paying for the game. There was an outcry from the players and even a frivolous lawsuit, but people kept logging on and sending in subscription fees. Who's to say when the public beta really ended?

A Final Word

While I was employed at Origin Systems it was very common to send games into test way before they were ready. The games were broken, had few features, and testing was nothing more than a waste of time. Through sheer force of will, Origin's product development and testing teams pulled some amazing product to completion in spite of this mistake. It's equally bad to send a game into test at the last minute, or without a reasonable plan.

By the time a game is content complete, you can't really add significant development resources to shorten the testing cycle. You can add testers like crazy, but the development team won't be able to keep up. Face it, if a programmer wrote some buggy code it might take ten times as long for another programmer to jump in and figure things out.

Every game has inertia to it, and before the game is shipped the team will have fixed a finite number of bugs, which equates to a very definable amount of work. When you hit the sweet spot, and your game goes into test at the right time, you'll have more fun at the end. More importantly, you'll make a better game.

Chapter 15

Driving to the Finish

At some point in your schedule, you begin to realize that you're a lot closer to the end than the beginning. While the calendar might imply this harsh fact, your workload seems to increase exponentially. For every task that goes final, two or three seem to take its place. What's more, the team is likely working overtime, already exhausted, and somehow everyone has to pull together for another long weekend.

Sound familiar?

If you've ever worked on a game, it should. This phenomenon is pretty common in many project oriented businesses, but games are especially susceptible because there's something games are required to deliver that doesn't exist anywhere else. Games have to be fun.

I've said it a few times in this book already but it deserves another mention: You can't schedule fun and you can't predict fun. Fun is the direct result of a few things: a great vision, a mountain of effort, and a flexible plan. Any one of these three things in abundance can make up something lacking in the other two. Most game companies simply rely on the effort component—a valiant but somewhat naïve mistake.

If you've ever been in a sustained endurance sport like biking, you know that you start any event with lots of excitement and energy. Towards the end of the ride you've probably suffered a few setbacks, like a flat tire or running out of water, making it hard to keep your rhythm. Your tired body begins to act robotically, almost as if your brain has checked out and the highest thinking you are doing is working a few muscle groups. You refuse food and water, believing you don't need it. Then things really start to go wrong. You'll be lucky to cross the finish line.

The same thing happens to game development teams after a long stretch of overtime. Tired minds can't think, and not only do they make mistakes they don't even recognize them when they happen, and they attempt to solve the entire mess with even more mandatory overtime. This is not only tragic, it is a choice doomed to fail.

Getting a project over the finish line is tough, and you'll be called upon to solve some sticky problems along the way. Some of these problems will happen fast, too fast for you to have a solution in your back pocket. You'll have to think on your feet—not unlike someone who happens upon an emergency situation. When you learn first aid, you are taught that you must be able to recognize a problem when you see it, have the skills to do something about it, and most importantly, you must decide to act.

I can give you the first two. The final one is up to you.

Finishing Issues

If your project is going well, you'll likely only need a few tweaks here and there to make sure you "stick the landing," so to speak. You can recognize this on your project by looking for a few telltale signs:

- *Your bug count is under control.* Your developers have less than 4 active bugs to fix per day until the "zero bugs" date.
- *Everyone is in good spirits.*
- *The game is fun to play, performs well, and has only polishing issues remaining.*

If this describes your project, congratulations! Don't get too cocky, because there are some easy missteps you can make, even at this late stage.

Quality

Perhaps the two biggest questions you and everyone else on the team asks at this point are likely to be, "Is the game good enough? Is it fun?" If a bug comes out of the testing group, it's because they want something changed to make the game better. Anyone on the development team can motivate a change as well, and they should if they think the game will become better because of it.

The closer the project gets to the scheduled zero bugs milestone, the less likely a bug will actually get fixed. This rule of thumb is directly related to the fact that any change in content or code induces some risk. I've seen a single bug fix create multiple new bugs. This implies that any high-risk change should either happen much earlier in the schedule, or there has to be some incredibly compelling reason, like there's no other choice, and the project is in jeopardy if the change isn't made.

Everyone on a project has his or her pet feature, something he or she really wants to see in the game. The best time to install these features is before the code complete milestone. There are a few good reasons for this. First, it gives the team a huge burst of energy. Everyone is working on their top tier wish lists, and tons of important features make it into the game at a time where the risk of these changes is pretty tolerable. Second, it gives the team a message: either put your change in now or forever hold your peace. After code complete, nothing new code-wise should be installed into the game. For artists and other content folks, this rule is the same, just the milestone is different. They use the content complete milestone as their drop-dead date for pet features.

One more note about programmers and artists adding anything: If the game isn't reaching target performance goals, it's a bad idea to add anything. More code and more art is unlikely to add any speed to the game. Make sure the performance issues are completely taken care of before code complete, and monitor it closely until the project ships.

It's a common practice to put inside jokes or "Easter Eggs" into a game. On Ultima VII, the team installed a special way to kill Lord British, especially since Richard Garriott wanted Lord British to be completely invincible. You need a little background first:

Origin was in an office building in the west Austin hill country, and the building had those glass front doors secured with powerful magnets at the top of the door. One day, Richard and some other folks were headed out to lunch, and when Richard opened the door the large block of metal that formed a part of the magnetic lock somehow became detached from the glass and fell right on Richard's head. Lord British must truly be unkillable, because that metal block weighed something like 10 pounds and had sharp edges....

The team decided to use that event as an inside way to kill the monarch or Britannia. At noon, the Lord British character's schedule took him into the courtyard of the castle. He would pause briefly under the doorway, right under a brass plaque that read, "Lord British's Throne Room." If you double-clicked the sign, it would fall on his head, and kill him straightaway.

Perhaps the weirdest thing about this story is that a few weeks later the same metal block on the same door fell on Richard a second time, again with no permanent damage. The guy is truly protected by some supernatural force, but he did buy a hard-shell construction helmet, and he wasn't so speedy to be the first person to open the door anymore.

By the time the team is working solidly to zero bugs, all the code and content is installed and there is nothing to do but fix bugs. It's a good idea to add a few steps to the bug fixing protocol. Here's the usual way bugs get assigned and fixed:

1. A bug is written up in test, and assigned to a team member to fix.
2. The bug is fixed, and is sent back to test for verification.
3. The bug is closed when someone in test gets a new version and observes the game behaving properly.

Close to the zero bug date, a bit of sanity checking is in order. This sanity checking puts some safety valves on the scope of any change. By this time in the project it usually takes two overworked human brains to equal the thinking power of a normal brain:

4. A bug is written up in test, and discussed in a small group—usually the team leads.
5. If the bug is serious enough, it is assigned to someone on the team to investigate a solution.
6. Someone investigates a potential solution. If a solution seems too risky they pull the plug then and there and report back that the bug should remain in its natural habitat.
7. The solution is coded, and checked on the programmer's machine by a colleague.
8. The solution is presented to the leads, and a final decision to check in the code or abandon the change is made.
9. The bug is sent back to test for verification.
10. The bug is closed when someone in test gets a new version and observes the game behaving properly.

If you think that the bureaucracy is a little out of control I'd understand. It does seem out of control, but it's out of control for a reason. Most bugs, about 70% to 80%, never make it out of step #1. Of those that remain, one-half to three-quarters of those are deemed too risky to fix, and never make it out of step #4.

My first experience with bugs in games was on Martian Dreams at Origin Systems. The whole team would gather in the conference room and each new bug from test was read aloud to the whole team. Sometimes the bugs would be so funny the whole room was paralyzed with laughter, and while it wasn't the most efficient way to run a meeting it sure took the edge off the day.

On Ultima VII, Ultima VIII, and Ultima Online, the teams were simply too big, and the bugs too numerous to read aloud in a team meeting. Between the inevitable laughter and complaining about fixing the object lists again we'd probably still be working on those games.

Even on smaller projects, like Bicycle Casino and even Magnadoodle we held bug meetings with the team leads. It turned out that the rest of the developers would rather spend their time making the game better and fixing as many bugs as they could, rather than sitting in meetings. Outside of that, time away from the computer and sleep was a great diversion.

Of course, everything hinges on your active bug count. If you are two months away from your scheduled zero bug date, and you are already sitting at zero bugs (yeah, right!) then you have more options than a team skidding into their zero bug date with a high bug count. I hope you find yourself in that situation someday. I've never seen it myself.

The only hard and fast rule is how many bugs your team can fix per day—somewhere between three and four bugs per person. Of course, your mileage may vary, but probably not by much. If your team is over this limit, or even a single person is over this limit, start getting conservative on approving bug fixes. If things are looking good, loosen the screws a little and make your game better while you can.

Code

At the end of every game project, the programmers are the ones who are hammered the most. Artists, level builders, and audio are hit especially hard during the content complete milestone, but after that their work levels off, mostly because it is usually more predictable. If you don't believe me, just ask an artist how long it will take him to tweak the lighting on a model. Or ask a level designer how long it will take to place a few more power-ups in a level, and he will not only give you a solid answer, he will be right about it.

Ask a programmer how long it will take to find the random memory trasher bug and he will shrug and say something like, "I don't, know—a few hours maybe?" You may find that same programmer, 48 hours later, bashing his head against the same bug, no closer to fixing it than when he started.

These setbacks happen all the time, and there's not much to do about it but get as much caffeine into their bloodstream as they can stand, get the other programmers to take up the slack in the bug debt, and maybe lend a few more neurons to the problem. Don't forget about the advice earlier in the book: Any two programmers looking at the same problem are at least three times as smart as a lone programmer.

When the bug is eventually found, there is sometimes a decision that has to be made about the nature of the solution. Sometimes a simple hack will suffice, but a "real" solution exists that will touch a lot of code and perhaps induce more risk. At the very late stages of a project, I suggest hacking. Wonton, unabashed, hacking.

Some of you may be reeling at this sacrilege, but I'm sure as many of you are cheering. The fact is that a well thought out hack can be the best choice, especially if you can guarantee the safety and correctness of the change. "Hack" is probably a bad word to use to fully describe what I'm talking about, because is has somewhat negative connotations. Let me try to be specific in my definition:

> **Hack – n.** A piece of code written to solve a specific corner case of a specific problem, as opposed to code written to solve a problem in the general case.

Let me put this in a different light: Everyone should be familiar with searching algorithms, where the choice of a particular search can achieve a "first solution" or a "best solution" criteria. At the beginning of a project, coding almost always follows the "best solution" path, because there is sufficient time to code a more complicated, albeit more general algorithm. At the end of the project, it is frequently the case that the best solution would lead a programmer down a complete reorganization of an entire subsystem, if not the entire code base.

Instead, games have a "get out of jail free" card, because the players don't generate the game data. Since the game inputs are predictable, or even static, the problem domain is reduced to a manageable level. A programmer can be relatively sure that a specific bit of code can be written to solve a specific problem, on a specific map level, with specific character attributes. It seems ugly, and to be honest it *is* ugly. As a friend of mine at Microsoft taught me, shipping your game is its most important feature.

The hack doesn't have to live in the code base forever, although it frequently does. If your game is even mildly successful, and you get the chance to do a sequel, you might have time to rip out the hacks and install an upgraded algorithm. You'll then be able to sleep at night.

At Origin it was common practice for programmers to add an appropriate comment if they had to install a hack to fix a bug. A couple of programmers were discussing which game had the most hacks—Ultima VII or Strike Commander. There was a certain pride in hacking in those days, since we

were all young, somewhat arrogant, and enjoyed a good hack from time to time. The issue was settled with *grep*—a text file search utility. The Strike Commander team was the clear winner, with well over 500 hacks in their code.

Ultima VII wasn't without some great comments, though. My favorite one was something like, "This hack must be removed before the game ships." It never was. What's more I think the same hack made it into Ultima VIII.

Commenting your code changes is a fantastic idea, especially late in the project. After the code complete milestone the changes come so fast and furious that it's easy to lose track of what code changed, who changed it, and why. It's not uncommon for two programmers to make mutually exclusive changes to a piece of code, each change causing a bug in the other's code. You'll recognize this pretty fast, usually because you'll go into piece of code and fix a bug, only to have the same bug reappear a few versions later. When you pop back into the code you fixed, you'll see the code has mysteriously reverted to the buggy version. This might not be a case of source code control gone haywire, as you would first suspect. It could be another programmer reverting your change because it caused another bug.

That situation is not nearly as rare as you think, but there is a more common scenario. Sometimes I'll attempt a bug fix, only to have the testers throw it back to me saying that the bug still lives. By the time it comes back I may have forgotten why I chose the solution, or what the original code looked like. Even better, I may look at the same block of code months later, and not have a clue what the fix is attempting to fix, or what test case exposed the bug.

The solution to the problem of short term programmer memories is comments, as always, but comments in the late stages of development need some extra information to be especially useful. Here's an example of a late stage comment structure we used on the Microsoft projects:

```
if (CDisplay::m_iNumModals == 0)
{
      // ET - 04/10/02 - Begin
      // Jokerz #2107 - Close() here causes some errors,
      // instead use Quit() as it allows the app to shutdown
      // gracefully
      Quit(); // Close();
      // ET - 04/10/02 - End
}
```

The comment starts with the initials of the programmer, and the date of the change. The entire change is bracketed with the same thing, the only difference between the two being a "begin" and "end" keyword. If the change is a trivial one-liner with an ultra short explanation, the comment can sit on the previous line or out to the right.

The explanation of the change is preceded with the code name for the project, and the bug number that motivated the change. Codenames are important because the bug might exist in code shared between multiple projects, which might be in parallel development or as a sequel. The explanation of the change follows, and where it makes sense the old code is left in, commented out.

Most programmers will instantly observe that the source code repository should be the designated keeper of all this trivia, and the code should be left clean. I respectfully disagree. I think it belongs in both places. Code reads like a story, and if you are constantly flipping from one application to another to find out what is going on, it is quite likely you'll miss the meaning of the change.

At the end of the project, it's a good idea, although somewhat draconian, to convince the team to attach an approved bug number with every change made to the code. This measure might seem extreme but I've seen changes "snuck" into the code base at the last minute without any involvement from the rest of the team. The decision to do that shouldn't be made by a programmer at 3 a.m. on Sunday morning. If every change is required to have a bug number, it becomes a trivial matter to hunt down and revert any midnight changes made by well meaning but errant programmers.

There are plenty of software companies that employ some form of code review in their process. The terms "code review" and "game software" don't seem to belong in the same universe let alone the same book. This false impression comes from programmers that don't understand how a good code review process can turn a loose collection of individual programmers into a well oiled team of coding machines.

When most programmers think of code reviews they picture themselves standing in front of a bunch of people who laugh at every line of code they present. They think it will cramp their special programming style. Worst of all, they fear that a bad code review will kill their chances at a lead position or a raise.

I've been working with code reviews in a very informal sense for years, and while it probably won't stand up to NASA standards I think it performs well in creative software, especially games. It turns out there are two primary points of process that make code reviews for games work well: who initiates the review, and who performs the review.

The person who writes the code that needs review should actually initiate the review. This has a few beneficial side effects. First, the code will definitely be ready to review, since the person needing it won't ask otherwise. Programmers hate surprises of the "someone just walked in my office and wants to see my code" kind. Because the code is ready, the programmer will be in a great state of mind to explain it. After all, they should take a little pride in their work, right? Even programmers are capable of craftsmanship, and there's not nearly enough opportunity to show it off. A code review should be one of those opportunities.

The person performing the review isn't the person you think it should be. Most of you reading this would probably say, "the lead programmer." This is especially true if you *are* the lead programmer. Well, you're wrong. Any programmer on the team should be able to perform a code review. Something that is a lot of fun is to have a junior programmer perform code reviews on the lead programmer's code. It's a great chance for everyone to share his or her tricks, experience, and double check things that are critical to your project.

This implies that the programmers all trust each other, respect each other, and seek to learn more about their craft. I've had the privilege of working on a programming team that is exactly like that, and the hell of being on the other side as well. I'll choose the former, thank you very much. Find me a team that enjoys code reviews, and performs them often, and I'll show you a programming team that will ship their games on time.

When I worked on the Microsoft casual games, the programmers performed code reviews for serious issues all throughout the project, but they were done constantly after content complete, for each change, no matter how minor. Most of the time a programmer would work all day on five or six bugs, and call someone who happened to be on their way back from the bathroom to do a quick code review before they checked everything in. This was pretty efficient, since the programmer doing the review was already away from their computer. Studies have shown that a programmer doesn't get back into the "zone" until 30 minutes after an interruption. I believe it, too.

Bottom line: The closer you get to zero bugs the more checking and double checking you do, on every semicolon. You even double check the need to type a semicolon. This checking installs a governor on the number, the scope, and quality of every code change, and the governor is slowly throttled down to zero until the last bug is fixed. After that, the game is ready to ship.

Content

Programmers aren't immune to the inevitable discussions, usually late at night, about adding some extra content into the game at the eleventh hour. It could be something as innocuous as a few extra names in the credits, or it could be a completely new terrain system. You think I'm kidding, don't you?

Whether it is code, art, sounds, models, map levels, weapons, or whatever makes your game fun you've got to be serious about finishing your game. You can't finish it if you keep screwing with it! If you are really lucky, you'll wind up at a company like Bungie or id, who can pretty much release games when they're damn good and ready. The rest of us have to ship games when we get hungry, and sometimes the desire to make the best game can actually supercede basic survival. At some point, no matter how much you tweak it, your game is what it is, and even superhuman effort will only achieve a tiny amount of quality improvement. If you've ever heard of something called the "theory of diminishing returns" you know what I'm talking about. When this happens, you've already gone too far. Pack your game up and ship it, and hope it sells well enough for you to get a second try.

The problem most people have is recognizing when this happens—it's brutally difficult. If you're like me you get pretty passionate about games, and sometimes you get so close to a project you can't tell when it's time to throw in the towel.

Microsoft employs late stage beta testers. These people work in other parts of Microsoft but play their latest games. Beta testers are different from play testers because they don't play the game every day. They are always just distant enough and dispassionate enough to make a good judgment about when the game is fun, or when it's not. If you don't have Microsoft footing your development bills, find ad-hoc testers from just about anywhere. You don't need professional testing feedback. You just need to know if people would be willing to plunk down $60 for your game, and keep it forever.

As you've seen many times in this book, there are balancing issues. When I worked on the Ultima series, it wasn't uncommon for truly interesting things to be possible, code-wise, at a very late stage of development. On Ultima VIII, a particular magic spell had a bug that caused a huge wall of fire that destroyed everything in its path. It was so cool we decided to leave it in the game, and replace one of the lamer spells. It wasn't exactly a low risk move, completely replacing a known spell with a bug turned feature, but it was an awesome effect and we all felt the game was better for it.

I'm trying my very best to give you some solid advice instead of some wishy-washy pabulum. The truth is there's no right answer regarding last minute changes to your game. The only thing you can count on is 20-20 hindsight, and the only people that write the history books are the winners. In other words, when you are faced with a decision to make a big change late in the game, trust your experience, try to be at least a little bit conservative and responsible in your choices, and hope like hell that you are right.

Dealing with Big Trouble

Murphy is alive and well in the computer game industry, and I'm sure he's been an invisible team member on most of my projects—some more than others, but most especially at Origin Systems, where Murphy had a corner office. I think his office was nicer than mine!

Big trouble on game projects comes in a few flavors: too much work and too little time, human beings under too much pressure, competing products in the target market, and dead-ends. There aren't necessarily standard solutions for these problems, but I can tell you what has been tried and how well it worked, or didn't work, as the case may be.

Projects Seriously Behind Schedule

Microsoft has a great way of describing a project behind schedule. They say it's "coming in hot and steep." I know because the first Microsoft Casino project was exactly like that. We had too much work to do but too little time to do it in. There are a few solutions to this problem such as working more overtime or throwing bodies at the problem. Each solution can work, but it can also have a dark side.

The Dreaded Crunch Mode—Working More Hours

It amazes me how much project managers choose to work their teams to death when the project falls behind schedule.

On my very first day at Origin Systems, October 22, 1990, I walked by a whiteboard with an ominous message written in block letters: " 84 Hour Workweeks – MANDATORY." With a simple division I realized that 84 divided by 7 is 12. Twelve hours per day, seven days per week, was Origin's solution for shipping Savage Empire for the Christmas, 1990 season. To the Savage Empire team's credit, they shipped the game a few tortured weeks later, and this "success" translated into more mandatory overtime to solve problems.

We were all young, mostly in our late 20s, and the amount of overtime that was worked was bragged about. There was a company award called the "100 Club," which was awarded to anyone who worked more than 100 hours in a single workweek. At Origin, this club wasn't very exclusive.

Humans are resilient creatures, and under extraordinary circumstances can go long stretches with very little sleep or a break from work. Winston Churchill, during World

War II, was famous for taking little cat naps in the Cabinet War Rooms lasting just a cumulative few hours per day, and he did this for years. Mr. Churchill had good reason to do this. He was trying to lead England in a war against Nazi Germany, and the cost of failure would have been catastrophic for his country and the entire world.

Game companies consistently ask for a similar commitment on the part of their employees—to work long hours for months, even years on end. What a crime! It's one thing to save a people from real tyranny, it's quite another to make a computer game. This is especially true when the culprit is bad planning, blindness to the reality of a situation, and a lack of skill in project management.

It is a known fact that under a normal working environment, projects can be artificially time compressed up to 20% by working more hours. This is the equivalent of asking the entire team to work eight extra hours on Saturday. I define a normal working environment as one where people don't have their lives, liberty, or family at stake, and all they expect from their effort is a paycheck. This schedule can be kept up for months, if the team is well motivated.

It was this schedule that compressed Ultima VIII after a last minute feature addition: Origin asked the team to ship the game in two extra languages: German and French. The team bloated to nearly three times it's original size, adding native German and French speakers to write the tens of thousands of lines of conversation and test the results. We worked overtime for 5 weeks—60 hours per week, and we took the sixth week and worked a normal workweek, which averaged 50 hours. This schedule went on from August to March, or eight months. Youth and energy went a long way, and in the end we did ship the game when the team thought we were going to ship the game, but everyone was exhausted beyond their limits.

For short periods of time, perhaps a week or two weeks, truly extraordinary efforts are possible. Twelve hour days for a short burst can make a huge difference in your game. Well managed and planned, it can even boost team morale. It feels a little like summer camp. A critical piece of this strategy is a well-formed goal such as:

- Fix 50 bugs per developer in one week.
- Finish integrating the major subsystems of the game.
- Achieve a playthrough of the entire game without cheating

The goal should be something the team can see on the horizon, well within sprinting distance. They also have to be able to see their progress on a daily basis. It can be quite demoralizing to sprint to a goal you can't see, because you have no idea how to gauge your level of effort.

On Ultima VII, Richard Garriott was always doing crazy things to support the development team. One night he brought in steaks to grill on Origin's BBQ pit. Another night, very late, he brought in his monster cappuccino machine from home and made everyone on the team some latte. One Saturday he surprised the team and declared a day off, taking everyone sky diving. Richard was long past the time where he could jump into C++ and write some code, but his support of the team and simply being there during the wee hours made a huge difference.

There's a dark side to overtime in the extreme that many managers and producers can't see until it's too late. It happened at Origin, and it happens all the time in other companies. When people work enough hours to push their actual pay scale below minimum wage, they begin to expect something extraordinary in return, perhaps in the form of end of project bonuses, raises, promotions, and so on.

The evil truth is that the company usually cannot pay anything that will equal their level of effort. The crushing overtime is a result of a project in trouble, and that usually equates to a company in trouble. If it wasn't so, company managers wouldn't push staggering overtime onto the shoulders of the team. At the end of the day, the project will ship, probably vastly over budget and most likely at a lower quality than was hoped. These two things do not translate into huge amounts of money flowing into company coffers, and subsequently into the pockets of the team.

A few months after these nightmare projects ship, the team begins to realize that all those hours amounted to nothing more than lost time away from home. Perhaps their firstborn took a few wobbling steps or spoke their first words, "Hey where in the hell is Daddy, anyway?" This frustration works into anger, and finally into people leaving the company for what they think is greener pastures. High turnover right after a project ships is pretty common in companies that require tons of overtime.

Someone once told me that you'll never find a tombstone with the following epitaph: "I wish I worked more weekends." As team member, you can translate that into a desire to predict your own schedule as best you can, and send up red flags when things begin to get off track. If you ever get to be a project lead, I hope you realize that there's a place for overtime, but it can't replace someone's life.

Pixel Fodder—Throw Warm Bodies at the Problem

Perhaps the second most common solution to projects seriously behind schedule is to throw more developers on the project. Well managed, this can have a positive effect, but it's never very cost effective, and there's a higher risk of mistakes. It turns out there's a sweet spot in the number of people that can work on any single project.

Ultima Online was the poster child of a bloated team. In December of 1996, the entire Ultima IX team was moved to Ultima Online, in the hopes that throwing bodies at the problem would speed the project to completion. This ended up being something of a disaster, for a few reasons. First, the Ultima IX team really wanted to work on Ultima IX. Their motivation to work on another project was pretty low. Second, the Ultima Online team had a completely different culture and experience level, and there were clashes of philosophy and control. Third, Ultima Online didn't have a detailed project plan, somewhat due to the fact that no one had ever made a massive multiplayer game before. This made it difficult to deploy everyone in their area of expertise. I happened to find myself working with SQL servers, for example, and I didn't have a shred of experience!

Through a staggering amount of work—an Origin hallmark—on the part of the original Ultima Online team and the Ultima IX newcomers the project went live less than nine months after the team was integrated. The cost was overwhelming, however, especially in terms of employee turnover in the old Ultima IX team. Virtually none of the programmers, managers, or designers of Ultima IX remained at Origin to see it completed.

One effect of overstaffing is an increased need to communicate and coordinate amongst the team members. It's a generally accepted fact that a manager's effectiveness falls sharply if they have any more than seven reports, and it is maximized at five reports. If you have a project team of 12 programmers, 14 artists, and 10 designers, you'll have two programming leads reporting to a technical director, and a similar structure for artists and designers. You'll likely have a project director as well, creating a project management staff of ten people.

If your management staff is anything less than that, you'll probably run into issues like two artists working on the same model, or perhaps a programming task that falls completely through the cracks. To be honest, even with an experienced management team you'll never be completely free of these issues.

Sometimes you get lucky, and you can add people to a project simply because a project is planned and organized in the right way. A good example of this is the Bicycle Cards project, basically a bunch of little

games packaged up in one product. When some of the games began to run behind schedule, we hired two contractors to take on a few games apiece. The development went completely smoothly with seven programmers in parallel. Their work was compartmentalized, communication of their tasks were covered nearly 100% by the design document, and this helped ease any problems.

They say that nine women can't make a baby in one month. That's true. There is also a documented case of a huge group of people who built an entire house from the ground up in three days, due to an intricately coordinated plan, extremely skilled people, and very specialized building techniques. Your project could exist on either side of these extremes.

Slipping the Schedule

This solution seems de rigor in the games industry, even with a coordinated application of crunch mode and bloating the team. There's a great poster of Ultima VII and Strike Commander that Origin published in 1992, in the style of movie posters that bragged "Coming this Christmas." It turns out that those posters got the season right, they just had the wrong year.

There's a long list of games that shipped before their time, perhaps the worst offender in my personal history was Ultima Online. There was even a lawsuit to that effect, where some subscribers filed a class action lawsuit against Electronic Arts for shipping a game that wasn't ready. Thankfully it was thrown out of court. A case like that could have had drastic effects on the industry!

The pressure to ship on schedule is enormous. You might think that companies want to ship on time because of the additional costs of the development team, and while the weekly burn rate of a gigantic team can be many hundreds of thousands of dollars, it's not the main motivation. While I worked with Microsoft, I learned that the manufacturing schedule of our game was set in stone. We had to have master disks ready by such and such a date, or we would lose our slot in the manufacturing facility. Considering that the other Microsoft project coming out that particular year was Windows XP, I realized that losing my place in line meant a huge delay in getting the game out.

While things like manufacturing can usually be worked out, there's another, even bigger, motivation for shipping on time. Months before the game is done, most companies begin spending huge money on marketing. Ads are bought in magazines or sometimes television, costing hundreds of thousands of dollars. You might not know this, but those special kiosks at the end of the shelves in retail stores, called *endcaps*, are bought and paid for like prime rental real estate, usually on a month by month basis. If your game isn't ready for the moment those ads are published or those kiosks are ready to show off your game, you lose the money. No refunds here!

This is one of the reasons you see the executives poking around your project six to eight months before you are scheduled to ship. It's because they are about to start writing big checks to media companies and game retail chains in the hopes that all this cash will drive up the sales of your game. The irony is, if the execs don't believe you can finish on time, they won't spend the big bucks on marketing, and your game will be buried somewhere on a bottom shelf in a dark corner of the store. Oh, and no ads either. You're best advertising will be by personal email to all your friends, and that just won't cut it. In other words, your game won't sell.

The difference between getting your marketing pressure at maximum and nothing at all may only be a matter of slipping a few weeks, or even a few days. What's worse, this judgment call is made months before you are at code complete—a time when your game might not be much more than a pretty face. Crazy, huh?

Probably the best advice I can give you is make sure you establish a track record of hitting each and every milestone on time, throughout the life of your project. Keep your bug count under control, too. These two things will convince the suits that you'll ship on time, with all the features you promised. Whatever you do, don't choose schedule slippage at the last minute. If you must slip, slip it once and make sure you give the suits enough time to react to all the promises they made on your behalf. This is probably at least six months prior to your release date, but it could be more.

Cutting Features and Postponing Bugs

Perhaps the most effective method of pulling a project out of the fire is reducing the scope of work. You can do it in two ways: nuke some features of the game and choose to leave some bugs in their natural habitat, perhaps to be fixed on the sequel. Unless you've been a bit arrogant in your project, the players and the media won't know about everything you wanted to install in the game. You might be able to shorten or remove a level from your game, reduce the number of characters or equipment, or live with a less accurate physics system.

Clearly, if you are going to cut something big you have to do it as early in the project as you can. Game features tend to work themselves in to every corner of the project, and removing them wholesale can be tricky at best, impossible at worst. Also, you can't have already represented to the outside world that your game has 10,000 hours of game play when you're only going to have time for a fraction of that. It makes your team look young and a little stupid.

Always give yourself some elbow room when making promises to anyone, but especially the game industry media. They love catching project teams in arrogant promises. It's great to tell them things about your game, but try to give them specifics in those features you are 100% sure are going be finished.

After code complete, and the programmers are doing virtually nothing but fixing bugs like crazy, an obvious solution for reducing the workload is to spirit away some of the less important bugs. As the ship date approaches, management's desire to "fix" bugs in this manner becomes somewhat ravenous, even to the point of leaving truly embarrassing bugs in the game, such as misspelled names in the credits or nasty crashes.

Anything can be bad in great quantities, and reducing your game's scope or quality is no exception. One thing is certainly true—your players won't miss what they never knew about in the first place. I can tell you that the book you now hold in your hands had three chapters that got cut. Perhaps you can guess what they might have contained. Just like any game project, my publisher and I decided to cut some chapters to get the book out on time, because that was more important than some of the other solutions, which included slipping the due date.

Only time will tell if we made the right decision, and the same will be true of your game project. It is incredibly difficult to step away from the guts of your project and look at it, objectively, from the outside. I've tried to do this many times, and it is one of the most difficult things to do, especially in those final days. Anyone who cares about their game won't want to leave a bug unfixed or cut a feature.

Ask yourself two serious questions when faced with this kind of decision: will my decision sell more copies? Will it keep someone from returning the game? If your answer is yes, do what it takes. Otherwise, move on and get your game shipped.

Personnel Related Problems

At the end of a project, everyone on the team is usually stretched to the limit. Good natured and even keeled people aren't immune to the stresses of overtime and the pressure of a mountain of tasks. Some game developers are far from good natured and even keeled! Remember always that whatever happens at the end of a project, it should be taken in the context of the stresses of the day, not necessarily as someone's habitual behavior. After all, if someone loses their cool at 3 a.m. after having worked 36 hours straight, I think a little slack is in order. If this same person loses his cool on a normal workday after a calm weekend, perhaps some professional adjustments are a good idea.

Exhaustion

The first and most obvious problem faced by teams is simple exhaustion. Long hours and missed weekends create pressure at home and a robotic sense of purpose at work. The team begins to make mistakes, and for every hour they work the project slips back three hours. The only solution for this is a few days away from the project. Hopefully you and your team won't let the problem get this bad. Sometimes all it takes is for someone to stand up and point to the last three days of non-progress and notice that the wheels are spinning but the car isn't going anywhere. Everyone should go home for 48 hours, even if it's Tuesday. You'd be surprised how much energy people will bring back to the office.

One other thing: They may be away from their desks for 48 hours but their minds will still have some background processes mulling over what they'll do when they get back to work. Oddly enough these background thoughts can be amazingly productive, since they tend to concentrate on planning and the big picture rather than every curly brace. When they get back, the additional thought works to create an amazing burst of productivity.

Late in the Magnadoodle project for Mattel Media, I was working hard on a graphic bug. I had been programming nearly 18 hours per day for the last week, and I was completely spent. At 3 a.m., I finally left the office, unsuccessful after four hours working on the same problem, and went to sleep. I specifically didn't set my alarm, and I unplugged all the telephones. I slept. The next morning, I awoke at a disgusting 11 a.m. and walked into the office with a fresh cup of Starbuck's in hand. I sat down in front of the code I was struggling with the night before and instantly solved the problem. The bug that had eluded me for four hours the day before was solved in less than fifteen seconds. If that isn't a great advertisement for sleep gaining efficiency in a developer, I don't know what is.

Morale

Team morale is directly proportional to their progress towards their goal, and isn't related to their workload. This may seem somewhat counter intuitive, but it's true. One theory that has been proposed regarding the people that built the great pyramids of Egypt is that teams of movers actually competed with each other to see how many blocks they could move up the ramps in a single day. Their workload and effort was backbreaking and their project schedule spanned decades. The constant competition, as the theory suggests, created high productivity and increased morale at the same time.

Morale can slide under a few circumstances, all of which are completely controllable. As the previous paragraph suggests, the team must be convinced they are on track to achieving their goal. This implies that the goal shouldn't be a constantly moving target. If a project continually changes underneath the developers, they'll lose faith that it will ever be completed. The opposite is also true—a well designed project that is built to spec as if it had blueprints is a joy to work on, and developers will work amazingly hard to get to a finish line they can see.

There's also a lot to be said for installing a few creature comforts for the development team. If they are working long hours, you'll be surprised what a little effort towards team appreciation will accomplish.

Get out the company credit card and make sure people on the project are well cared for. Stock the refrigerator with drinks and snacks, buy decent dinners every night, and bring in donuts in the morning. Bring in good coffee and get rid of the cheap stuff. Every now and then, make sure the evening meal is a nice one, and send them home afterwards instead of burning the midnight oil for the tenth night in a row.

Something I've seen in the past that affects morale is the relationship between the development team and the testing team. I've seen the entire range, from teams that wanted to beat each other with pipes to others that didn't even communicate verbally—they simply read each other's minds and made the game better. Someone needs to take this pulse every now and then, and apply a little rudder pressure when needed to keep things nice and friendly. Some warning signs to watch for include unfriendly japes in the bug commentary, discussion about the usefulness of an individual on either team or their apparent lack of skill, or the beginnings of disrespect for their leadership.

Perhaps the best insurance against this problem is forging personal relationships among the development leadership and testing leadership, and if possible with individuals on the team. Make sure they get a chance to meet each other in person if at all possible, which can be difficult since most game developers are a few time zones away from their test team. Personal email, telephone conversations, conference calls, and face to face meetings can help forge these professional friendships, and keep them going when discussions about bugs get heated.

This leads into something that may have the most serious affect on morale, both positive and negative. The developers need to feel like they are doing something worthwhile, and that they have the support of everyone. The moment they feel that their project isn't worth anything, due to something said in the media or perhaps an unfortunate comment by an executive, you can see the energy drain away to nothing. The opposite of this can be used to boost morale. Bring in a member of the press to see some kick-ass previews, or have a suit from the publisher shower the team with praise, and they'll redouble their effort. If you happen to work in a company with multiple projects, perhaps the best thing I've seen is one project team telling another that they have a great game. Praise from one's closest colleagues is far better than any other.

Other Stuff

Perhaps the darkest side of trouble on teams is when one person crosses the line and begins to behave in an unprofessional manner. I've seen everything from career blackmail to arrogant insubordination, and the project team has to keep this butthead on the team or risk losing their "genius." My suggestion here is to remember that the team is more important than any single individual. If someone leaves the team, even figuratively, during the project you should invite them to please leave in a more concrete manner.

Your Competition Beats You to the Punch

There's nothing that bursts your bubble quite as much as having someone walk into your office with a game in their hand, just released, that not only kicks butt but is exactly like your game in every way. You might think I'm crazy, but I'll tell you that you have nothing to worry about. The fact is that you can learn a lot from someone else's game simply by playing it, studying their graphics system, testing their user interface, and finding other chinks in their armor. After all, you can still compile your game, whereas they've burned theirs on optical media.

True, you won't be the first to market. Yes, you'd better be no later than second to market, and certainly you'd better make sure you don't repeat their mistakes. At least you have the benefit of having a choice, and you also have the benefit of dissecting another competitor's product before you put your game on the shelf.

They say that loose lips sink ships, right? This is certainly true in the game industry. Strike Commander, Origin's first 3D game, was due out in Christmas of 1992. In the summer of 1992, Origin took Strike Commander to the big industry trade show at the time, the Consumer Electronics Show, and made a big deal of Strike Commander's advanced 3D technology. They went so far as to give away technical details of the 3D engine, to which the competition immediately researched and installed in their own games. Origin's competitive advantage was trumped by their own marketing department, and since the team had to slip the schedule past Christmas, the competition had more time to react. What a disaster!

The game industry tends to follow trends until they bleed out. That's because there's a surprisingly strong aversion to unique content on the part of game executives. If a particular game is doing well, every company in the industry puts out a clone until there are fifty games out there that all look alike. Only the top two or three will sell worth a damn, so make sure you are in that top two or three.

There's No Way Out—Or Is There?

Sometimes you have to admit there's a grim reality—your game has coded itself into a corner. The testers say the game just isn't any fun. You might have gone down a dead-end technology track, such as coding your game for a dying platform.

What in the hell do you do now?

Mostly, you find a way to start over. If you're lucky, you might be able to recycle some code, art, map levels, or sounds. If you're really lucky, you might be able to replace a minor component and save the project. Either way, you have to find the courage to see the situation for what it is and act. Putting your head in the sand won't do any good.

After Ultima IX was put on ice, and I was working hard on the Ultima Online project, I secretly continued work on Ultima IX at my house in the evenings and on weekends. My goal wasn't so much to resurrect Ultima IX or try to finish it single-handedly. I just wanted to learn more about 3D hardware accelerated polygon rasterization, which was pretty new at the time. I was playing around with Glide, a 3D API from 3DFx that worked on the VooDoo series of video cards. In a surprisingly little amount of work, I installed a Glide compliant rasterizer into Ultima IX, complete with a basic, ultra stupid, texture cache.

What I saw was really amazing—Ultima IX running at over 40fps. The best framerate I'd seen so far was barely 10fps using our best software rasterizer. I took my work into Origin to show it off a bit, and the old Ultima IX team just went wild. A few months later, the project was back in development, with a new direction. Ultima IX would be the first Origin game that was solely written for hardware accelerated video cards. A bold statement, but not out of character with the Ultima series. Each Ultima game pushed the limits of bleeding edge technology every time a new one was published, and Ultima IX was no exception.

One Last Word—Don't Panic

There are other things that can go terribly wrong on projects, such as when someone deletes the entire project from the network or when the entire development team walks out of the door to start their own company. Yes, I've seen both of these things happen, and no, the projects in question didn't instantly evaporate. Every problem can be fixed, but it does take something of a cool head. Panic and overreaction—some might say these are hallmarks of your humble author—rarely lead to good decisions.

Try to stay calm, and try to gather as much information about whatever tragedy is befalling you. Don't go on a witchhunt. You'll need every able-bodied programmer and artist to get you out of trouble. Whatever it is, your problem is only a finite string of 1s and 0s in the right order. Try to remember that you'll probably sleep better.

The Light—It's Not a Train After All

It's a day you'll remember for every project. At some point, there will be a single approved bug in your bug database. It will be assigned to someone on the team, and likely it will be fixed in a crowded office with every team member watching. Someone will start the build machine, and after a short while the new game will be sent to the testing folks. Then the wait begins for the final word the game has been signed off, and sent to manufacturing. You may have to go through this process two or three times—something I find unnerving but inevitable. Eventually though, the phone will ring and the lead tester will give you the good news.

Your game is done. There will likely be a free flow of appropriate beverages. I keep a bottle of nice tequila or maybe a good single malt scotch in my office for just such an occasion. You have a few weeks to wait for the channel to push your game into every store and online site, so what do you do in the meantime?

Test the Archive

The first thing you do is take a snapshot of the build machine and the media files on your network. Your job is to rebuild the game from scratch, using all your build scripts, to make sure that if you ever need to you can restore a backup of the game source and rebuild your game. Start with a completely clean machine, and install the build machine backup. It should include all the build tools such as your compiler, and special tools that you used to create your game.

Restore a backup of the network files to a clean spot on your network. This may take some doing, since your network might be pretty full. It's a good idea to buy some extra hard drives to perform this task, since it is the only way you can be 100% sure your project backup will work.

Once you have a duplicate of your build machine and a second copy of the network files, build your game again and compare it to the image that is signed off. If they compare bit for bit, make some copies of the backups and store them in a cool dark place, safe for all eternity. It is quite likely that your publisher will want a copy of the backup too, so don't forget to make enough copies. If the files don't match, do your best to figure out why. It wouldn't be completely unusual for a few bits to be mysteriously different on the first attempt. The existence of a completely automated build process usually makes the archive perfectly accurate, which is a great reason to have it in the first place.

As a last resort, if your files don't match the best thing you can do is document the delta and have your testers run the rebuilt archive through the testing process once more. This will ensure that at least the game is still in a shippable state, even though some of the bits are different.

Don't forget to backup the bug database in some readable format, such as an Excel spreadsheet or even a CSV file. Store it along with your project archive and if you ever want to start a sequel, the first thing you'll do is figure out which postponed bugs you'll fix.

The Patch Build or the Product Demo

It's not crazy to start working on a patch build or downloadable demo immediately after the project signs off. The patch build is something PC developers are somewhat well known for, and if you know you need to build one there's no reason to wait. A downloadable demo is always a good idea, and many game industry magazines can also place a demo in an included CD.

I suggest you leave the patch build in your main line of development in your source code repository. The patch build should simply be the next minor version of your game, and is exactly what you've been doing since your zero bug date. You can release the thumbscrews a little, and consider some slightly more radical solutions to problems that you wouldn't have considered just a few days ago—it all depends on your schedule for the patch.

It wouldn't be uncommon to wait for initial customer feedback for finalizing the features and fixes that you'll include in your patch. Your customer base can be tens of thousands if not hundreds of thousands of people. They will likely find something your testers missed, or you may discover that a known problem is a much bigger deal than anyone expected.

The downloadable demo should exist in a separate branch in your source code repository. This is especially true if you code the demo with #ifdef _DEMO blocks or some such mechanism to cut your game down to a tiny version of itself. It wouldn't be crazy for some programmers to work on the demo and the patch simultaneously, and a separate code branch will help keep everything organized.

The Post Mortem

A good post-mortem should be held a few weeks after you sign off your game. There are tons of ways to handle it, but there are a few common goals. Every project is a chance to learn about game development, and the post mortem is a mechanism that formalizes those lessons, which will ultimately change the way you work. It isn't a forum to complain about things that went wrong and leave it at that. Instead, your post mortem should identify opportunities to improve your craft. It is a forum to recognize a job well done, whether on the part of individuals or as a group.

In post-mortems, it's really easy to get off track because everyone on the team wants to say their piece about nearly everything. That's good but it can degenerate into a chaotic meeting. It's also not a crazy idea to split the team into their areas of expertise, and have them conduct mini-post mortems in detail. For example, the programmers might get together to talk about aspects of the technology or their methodologies, surely stuff that will bore the artists to the point of chewing their own limbs off to escape the meeting. Each group: programmers, artists, designers, producers, and whomever can submit their detailed report for any other similar group who wants to learn their lessons.

The team post-mortem should focus on the game design, the project schedule, lines of communication, and team process. If someone believes they have a good idea of how to improve things, they should speak up and if the group thinks the idea has merit, then they should act on the idea.

One thing that isn't immediately obvious is the fact that you won't learn everything in a public meeting. Some of the most important information might be better discussed in private, in the hopes that someone's feelings won't be bruised. If you get the chance to run a post-mortem, don't forget to follow the public meeting with private interviews with the team. It will take a long time, but it's a good idea.

What to Do with Your Time

When I reached the end of my longest project to date, Ultima VIII, my first act was to walk outside Origin's offices, sit down at a picnic table, and enjoy the light, smells, and sounds of a springtime Texas afternoon. I had been in a dark office working overtime for two years, and I'd forgotten what daytime was like. I went home and found a person there. After introductions, and reviewing surprising evidence in the form of a photo album, I realized that the person in my apartment was actually my wife of over three years. I asked her out on a date, and she accepted. Then I asked her to accompany me on a diving trip to Cozumel. She accepted that too.

I suggest you follow my lead. If you don't have a spouse go somewhere fun with a friend. See the world. Get away from your computer at all costs. It will do you some good, and may give you some fun ideas.

You won't be able to stay away from work forever. The paycheck is nice but the desire to make another great game will soon overwhelm you. You may embark on a sequel to the game you just shipped or you might get to do something entirely new. Either way, you'll be surprised at the energy level. People on the team who looked like the living dead just a few weeks ago will be ready to go around again.

There's nothing quite like starting a new project. You feel renewed, smarter, and if you're really lucky you'll get to work with the same team. After what you've just been through, it's likely you'll have a good portion of mental telepathy worked out, and you won't need quite so many meetings.

One thing everyone will quietly do is make excuses to walk into computer game stores looking for the box. Eventually you'll see it for the first time. There's nothing like it, holding a shrink-wrapped version of your game in your own hands. I sincerely hope you get the chance to do that someday. Everybody deserves that kind of reward for such mammoth effort.

The game industry is a wacky place. The hours are long and the money sucks. I know because I've been in it up to my neck since games ran on floppy disks. Somehow I find the energy to stay in the game. Am I just a glutton for punishment?

I guess there's a lot to be said for a profession that has one goal—fun. I learned in scouting that you should always leave a campsite better than you found it. I guess that working on computer games is a way to do that for much more than a campsite. My work in the computer game industry has hopefully had an effect on the people that enjoyed the games with my name somewhere in the credits. My work on this book has hopefully made working on the games themselves more fun and more enjoyable.

Only time will tell, eh?

Index

C

H

N

O

P

Q

R

S

T